Pro jQuery

Adam Freeman

Apress®

Pro jQuery

ISBN-13 (pbk): 978-1-4302-4095-2

ISBN-13 (electronic): 978-1-4302-4096-9

President and Publisher: Paul Manning
Lead Editor: Ewan Buckingham
Technical Reviewer: Fabio Claudio Ferracchiati
Editorial Board: Steve Anglin, Mark Beckner, Ewan Buckingham, Gary Cornell, Morgan Ertel, Jonathan Gennick, Jonathan Hassell, Robert Hutchinson, Michelle Lowman, James Markham, Matthew Moodie, Jeff Olson, Jeffrey Pepper, Douglas Pundick, Ben Renow-Clarke, Dominic Shakeshaft, Gwenan Spearing, Matt Wade, Tom Welsh
Coordinating Editor: Jennifer L. Blackwell
Copy Editors: Kim Wimpsett and Roger LeBlanc
Compositor: Bytheway Publishing Services
Indexer: SPI Global
Artist: SPI Global
Cover Designer: Anna Ishchenko

Distributed to the book trade worldwide by Springer Science+Business Media New York, 233 Spring Street, 6th Floor, New York, NY 10013. Phone 1-800-SPRINGER, fax (201) 348-4505, e-mail `orders-ny@springer-sbm.com`, or visit `www.springeronline.com`.

For information on translations, please e-mail rights@apress.com, or visit www.apress.com.

Apress and friends of ED books may be purchased in bulk for academic, corporate, or promotional use. eBook versions and licenses are also available for most titles. For more information, reference our Special Bulk Sales–eBook Licensing web page at `www.apress.com/bulk-sales`.

Any source code or other supplementary materials referenced by the author in this text is available to readers at www.apress.com. For detailed information about how to locate your book's source code, go to www.apress.com/9781430240952

This book is dedicated to the memory of my father, Anthony Freeman.
6th September 1941 – 16th December 2011.
We love you and miss you.

(And also dedicated to my wife, Jacqui Griffyth. She is very much alive.
I have dedicated all of my books to her over the years, and I didn't want to break with tradition.)

Contents at a Glance

Contents

About the Author

Adam Freeman is an experienced IT professional who has held senior positions in a range of companies, most recently serving as chief technology officer and chief operating officer of a global bank. Now retired, he spends his time writing and running. This is his 14th technology book.

About the Technical Reviewer

■ Fabio Claudio Ferracchiati is a senior consultant and a senior analyst/developer using Microsoft technologies. He works for Brain Force (`www.brainforce.com`) in its Italian branch (`www.brainforce.it`). Fabio is a Microsoft Certified Solution Developer for .NET, a Microsoft Certified Application Developer for .NET, a Microsoft Certified Professional, and a prolific author and technical reviewer. Over the past 10 years, he has written articles for Italian and international magazines and has coauthored more than 10 books on a variety of computer topics.

Acknowledgments

I would like to thank everyone at Apress for working so hard to bring this book to print. In particular, I would like to thank Jennifer Blackwell for keeping me on track (and for putting up with my refusal to use SharePoint) and Ewan Buckingham for commissioning and editing this book. I would also like to thank Fabio, Kim, and Roger for their reviews and copyediting.

Adam Freeman

PART 1

Getting Ready

CHAPTER 1

Putting jQuery in Context

At its heart, jQuery does something that sounds pretty dull: it lets you modify the contents of HTML documents by manipulating the model that the browser creates when it processes the HTML (known as *DOM manipulation*, as I'll explain later). If you are reading this, you have probably already done some DOM manipulation, either using another JavaScript library or even using the built-in API that most modern web browsers support, and you have picked up this book because you want to do it in a better way.

jQuery goes beyond *better*. It makes DOM manipulation a pleasure and, on occasion, an actual joy. There is something so elegant and graceful about the way that jQuery works that transforms a task that can be pure drudgery into something that is simple and easy, and once you start using jQuery, there is no going back. Here are the top reasons that I use jQuery in my projects:

- jQuery is expressive. I can do more work with much less code than when using the browser DOM API.
- jQuery methods apply to multiple elements. The DOM API approach of select-iterate-modify is gone, meaning fewer `for` loops to iterate through elements and fewer mistakes.
- jQuery deals with implementation differences between browsers. I don't have to worry about whether IE supports a feature in an odd way, for example; I just tell jQuery what I want, and it works around the implementation differences.
- jQuery is open source. When I don't understand how something works or I don't quite get the result I was expecting, I can read through the JavaScript code and, if needed, make changes.

Not everything is perfect, of course, and there are one or two rough edges, which I'll explain as I get into the details. But even with the occasional flaw, I love working with jQuery, and I hope you will find it equally compelling and enjoyable to use. To me, the genius of jQuery is that it takes something that is a major grind in web development and makes it simple, quicker, and easier. I can't ask for more than that.

Understanding jQuery UI and jQuery Mobile

In addition to the core jQuery library, I also cover *jQuery UI* and *jQuery Mobile*, which are user interface libraries built on top of the jQuery. jQuery UI is a general-purpose UI toolkit intended to be used on any device, and jQuery Mobile is designed for use with touch-enabled devices such as smartphones and tablets.

Understanding jQuery Plugins

jQuery plugins extend the functionality of the basic library. There are some plugins that are so good and so widely used that I have covered them in this book. There are a lot of plugins available (although the quality can vary), so if you don't like the plugins I describe in this book, you can be confident that an alternative approach is available.

What Do I Need to Know?

Before reading this book, you should be familiar with the basics of web development, have an understanding of how HTML and CSS work, and, ideally, have a working knowledge of JavaScript. If you are a little hazy on some of these details, I provide refreshers for HTML, CSS, and JavaScript in Chapters 2, 3, and 4. You won't find a comprehensive reference for HTML elements and CSS properties, though. There just isn't the space in a book about jQuery to cover HTML in its entirety. If you want a complete reference for HTML and CSS, then I suggest another of my books: *The Definitive Guide to HTML5*, also published by Apress.

What Is the Structure of This Book?

This book is split into six parts, each of which covers a set of related topics.

Part 1: Getting Ready

Part 1 of this book provides the information you need to get ready for the rest of the book. It includes this chapter and primers/refreshers for HTML, CSS, and JavaScript. Later in this chapter, I'll describe the software that you will need in order to follow along.

Part 2: Working with jQuery

Part 2 of this book introduces you to the jQuery library, starting with a basic example and building up to include each of the core features: element selection, DOM manipulation, events, and effects.

Part 3: Working with Data and Ajax

Part 3 of this book shows how jQuery makes it possible to work with inline or remote data. I show you how you can generate HTML content from data, how you can validate data entered into web forms, and how you can use jQuery to perform asynchronous operations, including Ajax.

Part 4: Using jQuery UI

jQuery UI is one of the two user interface libraries that I describe in this book. Built on, and integrated with, the core jQuery library, jQuery UI allows you to create rich and responsive interfaces for your web applications.

Part 5: Using jQuery Mobile

jQuery Mobile is the other user interface library that I cover in this book. jQuery Mobile is built on top of jQuery and incorporates some basic feature from jQuery UI but has been optimized for creating smartphone and tablet interfaces. Fewer user interface widgets are available in jQuery Mobile, but those that are supported are optimized for touch interaction and for use presentation on smaller displays.

Part 6: Advanced Features

The final part of this book describes some jQuery and jQuery UI features that are not commonly used but that can be helpful in complex projects. These are advanced features that require a better understanding of HTML, CSS, and jQuery itself. In the case of Chapter 35, a basic knowledge of asynchronous programming is very helpful.

Are There Lots of Examples?

There are *loads* of examples. One of the nice aspects of jQuery is that almost any task can be performed in several different ways, allowing you to develop a personal jQuery style. To show the different approaches you can take, I have included a lot of different examples—so many, in fact, that I include the complete HTML document you are working with only once in each chapter in order to fit everything in. The first example in every chapter will be a complete HTML document, as shown in Listing 1-1, for example.

Listing 1-1. A Complete Example Document

```
<!DOCTYPE html>
<html>
<head>
    <title>Example</title>
    <script src="jquery-1.7.js" type="text/javascript"></script>
    <link rel="stylesheet" type="text/css" href="styles.css"/>
    <script type="text/javascript">
        $(document).ready(function() {

            var labelElems = document.getElementsByTagName("label");
            var jq = $('img[src*=daffodil]');

            $('img:even').add('img[src*=primula]').add(jq)
                .add(labelElems).css("border", "thick double red");

        });
    </script>
</head>
<body>
    <h1>Jacqui's Flower Shop</h1>
    <form method="post">
        <div id="oblock">
            <div class="dtable">
                <div id="row1" class="drow">
                    <div class="dcell">
```

```
                        <img src="astor.png"/><label for="astor">Astor:</label>
                        <input name="astor" value="0" required>
                    </div>
                    <div class="dcell">
                        <img src="daffodil.png"/><label for="daffodil">Daffodil:</label>
                        <input name="daffodil" value="0" required >
                    </div>
                    <div class="dcell">
                        <img src="rose.png"/><label for="rose">Rose:</label>
                        <input name="rose" value="0" required>
                    </div>
                </div>
                <div id="row2"class="drow">
                    <div class="dcell">
                        <img src="peony.png"/><label for="peony">Peony:</label>
                        <input name="peony" value="0" required>
                    </div>
                    <div class="dcell">
                        <img src="primula.png"/><label for="primula">Primula:</label>
                        <input name="primula" value="0" required>
                    </div>
                    <div class="dcell">
                        <img src="snowdrop.png"/><label for="snowdrop">Snowdrop:</label>
                        <input name="snowdrop" value="0" required>
                    </div>
                </div>
            </div>
        </div>
        <div id="buttonDiv"><button type="submit">Place Order</button></div>
    </form>
</body>
</html>
```

This listing is taken from Chapter 5. Don't worry about what it does; just be aware that the first example in each chapter will be a complete HTML document, similar to the one shown in the listing. Almost all of the examples are based around the same basic HTML document, which displays a simple flower shop. It isn't the most exciting example, but it is self-contained and includes all of the things we are interested in when working with jQuery.

For the second and subsequent examples, I just show you the elements that change. This is generally just the `script` element, which is where your jQuery code lives. You can spot a partial the listing because it starts and ends with ellipsis (`...`), as shown in Listing 1-2.

Listing 1-2. A Partial Listing

```
...
<script type="text/javascript">
    $(document).ready(function() {

        var jq = $('label');

        // select and operate on the first element
        jq.first().css("border", "thick double red");

        // select and operate on the last element
        jq.last().css("border", "thick double green");

        // select and operate on an element by index
        jq.eq(2).css("border", "thick double black");
        jq.eq(-2).css("border", "thick double black");

    });
</script>
...
```

This is the second listing from Chapter 5. You can see that just the `script` element appears, and I have highlighted a number of statements. This is how I draw your attention to the part of the example that shows the jQuery feature I am using. In a partial listing like this, only the element that is shown has changed from the complete document shown at the start of the chapter.

I have kept the examples in this book very focused on individual features. This is to give you the best coverage of how jQuery operates. But in doing this, you can lose sight of how different features fit together, so at the end of each part of the book, there is a short chapter in which I refactor the example document to incorporate all of the topics in the previous chapters and present a joined-up view of what's possible.

Where Can I Get the Example Code?

You can download all of the examples for all of the chapters in this book from Apress.com. The download is available without charge and includes all of the supporting resources that are required to re-create the examples without having to type them in (including images, JavaScript libraries, and CSS style sheets). You don't have to download the code, but it is the easiest way of experimenting with the examples and cutting and pasting techniques into your own projects.

■ **Tip** Even though I list just the changes in a lot of the code listings in the chapters, each example in the source code download is a complete HTML document that you can load directly into your browser.

What Software Do I Need for This Book?

To follow the examples in this book, you will need various pieces of software, as described in the following sections.

Getting jQuery

The very first thing you need is the jQuery library, which is available from `http://jquery.com`. There is a download button right on the front page of the web site and an option to choose either the production or development release, as shown in Figure 1-1.

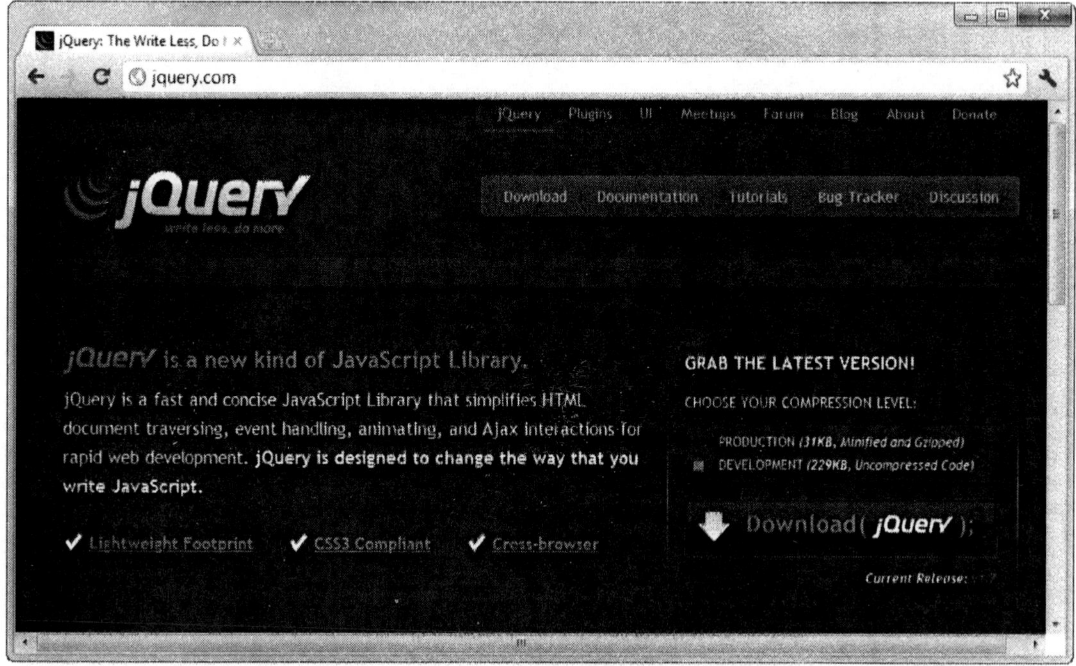

Figure 1-1. Downloading the jQuery library

You'll be using the development version for this book. I explain the difference between these versions and show you how to use the jQuery library in Chapter 5.

■ **Tip** I tell you how to obtain and install the jQuery UI and jQuery Mobile libraries in Chapters 17 and 26, respectively.

Getting an HTML Editor

One of the most important tools for web development is an editor with which you can create HTML documents. HTML is just text, so you can use a very basic editor, but there are some dedicated packages available that make the development smoother and simpler, and many of them are available without charge.

I tend to use Komodo Edit from Active State. It is free, it is simple, and it has pretty good support for HTML, JavaScript, and jQuery. I have no affiliation with Active State, other than I use its software. You can get Komodo Edit from `http://activestate.com`, and there are versions for Windows, Mac, and Linux.

As an alternative, JsFiddle is a popular online editor that provides support for working with jQuery. I don't get on with it (it is structured in a way that conflicts with my development habits), but it does seem pretty flexible and powerful. It is free to use and is available at `http://jsfiddle.net`.

Getting a Web Browser

You need a web browser to view your HTML documents and test your jQuery and JavaScript code. I like Google Chrome: I find it quick, I like the simple UI, and the developer tools are pretty good. Whenever you see a screenshot in this book (which is often), it will be Google Chrome that you see.

That said, you don't have to use the same browser I do, but I do recommend you pick one with good developer tools. Mozilla Firefox has some excellent JavaScript tools available through the Firebug extension, which you can get at `http://getfirebug.com`.

If you don't like Chrome or Firefox, then your next best bet is Internet Explorer. A lot of web programmers have issues with IE, but version 9 is pretty good in my experience, and IE10 (which is in beta as I write this) looks very promising. The developer tools are not as comprehensive as with Chrome or Firefox, but they are entirely adequate for the purposes of this book.

Getting a Web Server

If you want to re-create the examples in this book, you will need a web server so that the browser has somewhere from which to load the example HTML document and related resources (such as images and JavaScript files). A lot of web servers are available, and most of them are open source and free of charge. It doesn't matter which web server you use. I have used Microsoft's IIS 7.5 in this book, but that's just because I have a Windows Server machine already set up and ready to go.

Getting Node.js

Starting in Part 3, you'll start using `Node.js` in addition to a regular web server. `Node.js` is very popular at the moment, but I have used it for the simple reason that it is based on JavaScript, so you don't have to deal with a separate web application framework. You won't be digging into any detail at all about `Node.js`, and I'll be treating it as a black box (although I do show you the server scripts so you can see what's happening on the server if you are interested).

You can download `Node.js` from `http://nodejs.org`. There is a precompiled binary for Windows and source code that you can build for other platforms. In this book, I am using version 0.5.9, which is likely to be superseded by the time you read this, but the server scripts should still work without any problems.

Setting Up and Testing Node.js

The simplest way to test Node.js is with a simple script. Save the contents of Listing 1-3 to a file called NodeTest.js. I have done this in the same directory as my Node.js binary.

Listing 1-3. A Node.js Test Script

```
var http = require('http');
var url = require('url');


http.createServer(function (req, res) {
    console.log("Request: " + req.method + " to " + req.url);

    res.writeHead(200, "OK");
    res.write("<h1>Hello</h1>Node.js is working");
    res.end();

}).listen(80);
console.log("Ready on port 80");
```

This is a simple test script that returns a fragment of HTML when it receives an HTTP GET request.

■ **Tip** Don't worry if that last sentence didn't make complete sense. You don't need to know how HTTP and web servers work to use jQuery, and I provide a crash course in HTML in Chapter 2.

To test Node.js, run the binary specifying the file you just created as an argument. For my Windows installation, I typed the following at the console prompt:

```
node NodeTest.js
```

To make sure everything is working, navigate to port 80 on the machine that is running Node.js. You should see something very similar to Figure 1-2, indicating that everything is as expected.

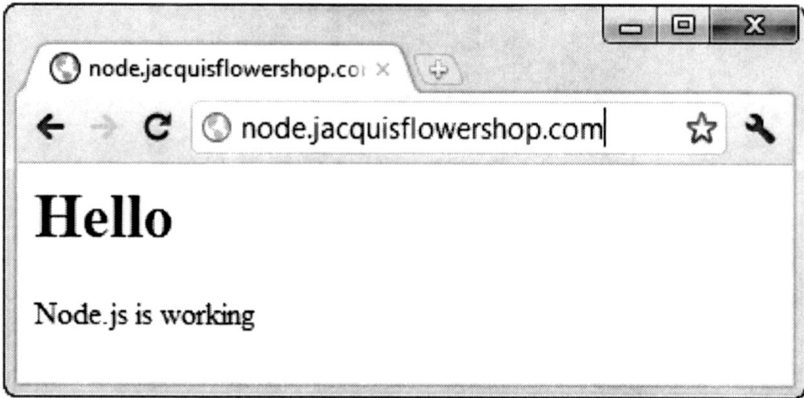

Figure 1-2. Testing Node.js

I run `Node.js` on a different machine to the regular web server, which means that using port 80 doesn't cause me any problems. If you have only one machine available, run the web server on port 80 and change the `Node.js` script to use another port. I have highlighted the part of the test script in Listing 1-3 that specifies which port is used.

Image Attribution

Throughout this book, I use a set of images in the examples. Thanks to the following people for kind permission to use their photographs: Horia Varlan, David Short, *Geishaboy500*, Tanaka Juuyoh, Mervi Eskelinen, *Fancy Speed Queen*, Alan "*craigie3000*" Craigie, and *melalouise*.

Summary

In this chapter, I outlined the content and structure of this book and set out the software that is required for jQuery web development, all of which can be obtained free of charge. The next three chapters refresh your basic skills in HTML, CSS, and JavaScript. If you are familiar with these topics, then skip to Chapter 5 where I introduce jQuery.

CHAPTER 2

HTML Primer

We are going to spend a lot of time in this book working on HTML documents. In this chapter, I set out the information you'll need to understand what we are doing later in the book. This isn't an HTML tutorial but rather a summary of the key characteristics of HTML that I'll rely on in later chapters.

The latest version of HTML, which is known as *HTML5*, is a topic in its own right. HTML5 has more than 100 elements, and each of them has its own purpose and functionality. That said, you need only a basic knowledge of HTML to understand how jQuery works, but if you want to learn about the details of HTML, then I suggest another of my books: *The Definitive Guide to HTML5*, also published by Apress.

Introducing a Basic HTML Document

The best place to start is to look at an HTML document. From this, you can see the basic structure and hierarchy that all HTML documents follow. Listing 2-1 shows a simple HTML document. I'll use this document throughout this chapter to introduce the core concepts of HTML.

Listing 2-1. A Simple HTML Document

```
<!DOCTYPE html>
<html>
<head>
    <title>Example</title>
    <script src="jquery-1.7.js" type="text/javascript"></script>
    <style>
        h1 {
            width: 700px; border: thick double black; margin-left: auto;
            margin-right: auto; text-align: center; font-size: x-large; padding: .5em;
            color: darkgreen; background-image: url("border.png");
            background-size: contain; margin-top: 0;
        }
        .dtable {display: table;}
        .drow {display: table-row;}
        .dcell {display: table-cell; padding: 10px;}
        .dcell > * {vertical-align: middle}
        input {width: 2em; text-align: right; border: thin solid black; padding: 2px;}
        label {width: 5em;  padding-left: .5em;display: inline-block;}
        #buttonDiv {text-align: center;}
```

```
            #oblock {display: block; margin-left: auto; margin-right: auto; width: 700px;}
        </style>
    </head>
    <body>
        <h1>Jacqui's Flower Shop</h1>
        <form method="post">
            <div id="oblock">
                <div class="dtable">
                    <div class="drow">
                        <div class="dcell">
                            <img src="astor.png"/><label for="astor">Astor:</label>
                            <input name="astor" value="0" required>
                        </div>
                        <div class="dcell">
                            <img src="daffodil.png"/><label for="daffodil">Daffodil:</label>
                            <input name="daffodil" value="0" required >
                        </div>
                        <div class="dcell">
                            <img src="rose.png"/><label for="rose">Rose:</label>
                            <input name="rose" value="0" required>
                        </div>
                    </div>
                    <div class="drow">
                        <div class="dcell">
                            <img src="peony.png"/><label for="peony">Peony:</label>
                            <input name="peony" value="0" required>
                        </div>
                        <div class="dcell">
                            <img src="primula.png"/><label for="primula">Primula:</label>
                            <input name="primula" value="0" required>
                        </div>
                        <div class="dcell">
                            <img src="snowdrop.png"/><label for="snowdrop">Snowdrop:</label>
                            <input name="snowdrop" value="0" required>
                        </div>
                    </div>
                </div>
            </div>
            <div id="buttonDiv"><button type="submit">Place Order</button></div>
        </form>
    </body>
</html>
```

This is a short and basic HTML document, but it contains some of the most important characteristics associated with HTML. You can see how this document appears in a browser in Figure 2-1.

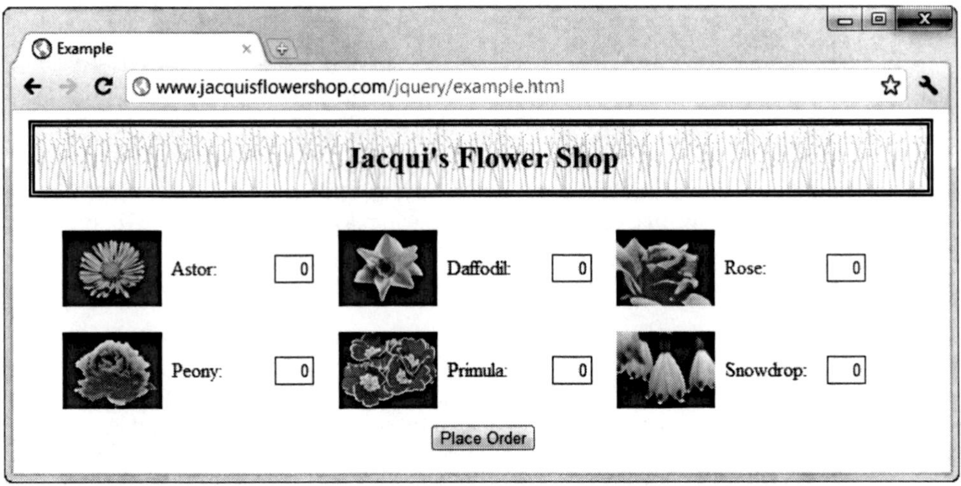

Figure 2-1. Displaying the example HTML document in the browser

Understanding the Anatomy of an HTML Element

At the heart of HTML is the notion of an *element.* This tells the browser what kind of content each part of an HTML document contains. Here is an element from the example:

```
<h1>Jacqui's Flower Shop</h1>
```

This element has three parts: the start tag, the end tag, and the content, as illustrated by Figure 2-2.

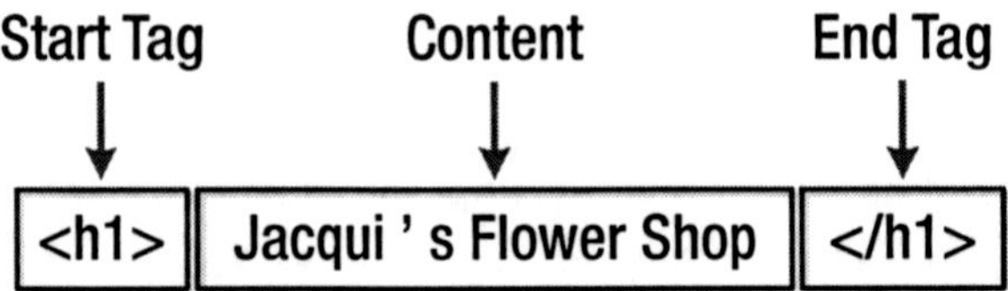

Figure 2-2. The anatomy of a simple HTML element

The *name* of this element (also referred to as the *tag name*) is `h1`, and it indicates to the browser that the content between the tags should be treated as a top-level header. You create the start tag by placing the tag name in angle brackets, the < and > characters. You create the end tag in a similar way, except that you also add a / character after the left-angle bracket (`<`).

Understanding Attributes

You can provide additional information to the browser by adding *attributes* to your elements. Listing 2-2 shows an element from the example document that has an attribute.

Listing 2-2. Defining an Attribute

```
<label for="astor">Astor:</label>
```

This is a label element, and it defines an attribute called for. I have emphasized the attribute to make it easier to see. Attributes are always defined as part of the start tag. This attribute has a *name* and a *value*. The name is for, and the value is astor. Not all attributes require a value; just defining them sends a signal to the browser that you want a certain kind of behavior associated with the element. Listing 2-3 shows an example of an element with such an attribute.

Listing 2-3. Defining an Attribute That Requires No Value

```
<input name="snowdrop" value="0" required>
```

This element has three attributes. The first two, name and value, are assigned a value like with the previous example. (This can get a little confusing. The names of these attributes are name and value. The value of the name attribute is snowdrop, and the value of the value attribute is 0.) The third attribute is just the word required. This is an example of an attribute that doesn't need a value, although you can define one by setting the attribute value to its name (required="required") or by using the empty string (required="").

The id and class Attributes

Two attributes are particularly important in this book: the id and class attributes. One of the most common tasks you need to perform with jQuery is to locate one or more elements in the document so that you can perform some kind of operation on them. The id and class attributes are very useful for performing the location stage.

Using the id Attribute

You use the id attribute to define a unique identifier for an element in a document. No two elements are allowed to have the same value for the id attribute. Listing 2-4 shows a very simple document that uses the id attribute.

Listing 2-4. Using the id Attribute

```
<!DOCTYPE html>
<html>
<head>
    <title>Example</title>
</head>
<body>
    <h1 id="mainheader">Welcome to Jacqui's Flower Shop</h1>
    <h2 id="openinghours">We are open 10am-6pm, 7 days a week</h2>
    <h3 id="holidays">(closed on national holidays)</h3>
</body>
</html>
```

I have defined the id attribute on three of the elements in the document. The h1 element has an id value of mainheader, the h2 element has an id value of openinghours, and the h3 element has an id value of holidays. Using the id value lets you find a specific element in the document.

Using the class Attribute

You use the class attribute to arbitrarily associate elements together. Many elements can be assigned to the same class, and elements can belong to more than one class, as shown in Listing 2-5.

Listing 2-5. Using the class Attribute

```
<!DOCTYPE html>
<html>
<head>
    <title>Example</title>
</head>
<body>
    <h1 id="mainheader" class="header">Welcome to Jacqui's Flower Shop</h1>
    <h2 class="header info">We are open 10am-6pm, 7 days a week</h2>
    <h3 class="info">(closed on national holidays)</h3>
</body>
</html>
```

In this example, the h1 element belongs to the header class, the h2 element belongs to the header and info classes, and the h3 element belongs just to the info class. As you can see, you can add an element to multiple classes just by separating the class names with spaces.

Understanding Element Content

Elements can contain text, but they can also contain other elements. Here is an example of an element that contains other elements:

```
<div class="dcell">
    <img src="rose.png"/>
    <label for="rose">Rose:</label>
    <input name="rose" value="0" required>
</div>
```

The div element contains three others: an img, a label, and an input element. You can define multiple levels of *nested* elements, not just the one level shown here. Nesting elements like this is a key concept in HTML because it imparts the significance of the outer element to those contained within (this is a theme I will return to later). You can mix text content and other elements, like this:

```
<div class="dcell">
    Here is some text content
    <img src="rose.png"/>
    Here is some more text!
    <input name="rose" value="0" required>
</div>
```

Understanding Void Elements

Not all elements can contain content. Those that can't are called *void elements*, and they are written without a separate end tag. Here is an example of a void element:

```
<img src="rose.png"/>
```

A void element is defined in a single tag, and you add a / character before the last angle bracket (the > character). Strictly speaking, there should be a space between the last character of the last attribute and the / character, like this:

```
<img src="rose.png" />
```

However, browsers are very tolerant toward interpreting HTML, and you can happily omit the space character. Void elements are often used when the element refers to an external resource. In this case, the img element is used to link to an external image file called rose.png.

Understanding the Document Structure

In any HTML document, some key elements define the basic structure. These are DOCTYPE, html, head, and body. Listing 2-6 shows the relationship between these elements with the rest of the content removed.

Listing 2-6. The Basic Structure of an HTML Document

```
<!DOCTYPE html>
<html>
<head>
    ...head content...
</head>
<body>
    ...body content...
</body>
</html>
```

Each of these elements has a very specific role to play in an HTML document. The first, the DOCTYPE element, tells the browser that this is an HTML document and, more specifically, that this is an *HTML5* document. Earlier versions of HTML required additional information. For example, here is the DOCTYPE element for an HTML4 document:

```
<!DOCTYPE HTML PUBLIC "-//W3C//DTD HTML 4.01//EN"
    "http://www.w3.org/TR/html4/strict.dtd">
```

The html element denotes the region of the document that contains the HTML content. This element always contains the other two key structural elements, head and body. As I said at the start of this chapter, I am not going to cover the individual HTML elements. There are too many of them, and describing HTML5 completely took me more than 1,000 pages in my HTML5 book. That said, I will provide brief descriptions of the elements I use so that you have a good idea of what a document does. Table 2-1 summarizes the elements used in the example document, some of which I describe in a little more detail later in this chapter.

Table 2-1. HTML Elements Used in the Example Document

Element	Description
DOCTYPE	Indicates the type of content in the document
body	Denotes the region of the document that contains content elements (described in a moment)
button	Denotes a button; often used to submit a form to the server
div	A generic element; often used to add structure to a document for presentation purposes
form	Denotes an HTML form, which allows you to gather data from the user and send it to a server for processing
h1	Denotes a header
head	Denotes the region of the document that contains metadata (described in a moment)
html	Denotes the region of the document that contains HTML (which is usually the entire document)
img	Denotes an image
input	Denotes an input field used to gather a single data item from the user, usually as part of an HTML form
script	Denotes a script, typically JavaScript, which should be executed as part of the document
style	Denotes a region of Cascading Style Sheet settings; see Chapter 3
title	Denotes the title of the document; used by the browser to set the title of the window or tab used to display the document's content

Understanding the Metadata Elements

The head element contains the metadata for the document, in other words, one or more elements that describe or operate on the content of the document but that are not directly displayed by the browser. The example document contains three metadata elements in the head section: `title`, `script`, and `style`. The `title` element is the most basic. The contents of this element are used by browser to set the title of the window or tab, and all HTML documents are required to have a `title` element. The other two elements are more important for this book, as I explain in the sections that follow.

Understanding the script Element

The script element lets you include JavaScript in your code. This is an element that you will be spending a lot of time with once I start covering jQuery in depth. The example document contains one script element, which is shown in Listing 2-7.

Listing 2-7. The script Element from the Example Document

```
<script src="jquery-1.7.js" type="text/javascript"></script>
```

When you define the src attribute for the script element, you are telling the browser that you want to load the JavaScript contained in another file. In this case, this is the main jQuery library, which the browser will find in the file jquery-1.7.js. A single HTML document can contain more than one script element, and you can include the JavaScript code between the start and end tags if you prefer, as shown in Listing 2-8.

Listing 2-8. Using the script Element to Define Inline JavaScript Code

```
<!DOCTYPE html>
<html>
<head>
    <title>Example</title>
    <script src="jquery-1.7.js" type="text/javascript"></script>
    <script type="text/javascript">
        $(document).ready(function() {
            $('#mainheader').css("color", "red");
        });
    </script>
</head>
<body>
    <h1 id="mainheader" class="header">Welcome to Jacqui's Flower Shop</h1>
    <h2 class="header info">We are open 10am-6pm, 7 days a week</h2>
    <h3 class="info">(closed on national holidays)</h3>
</body>
</html>
```

This example has two script elements. The first imports the jQuery library to the document, and the second is a simple script that uses some basic jQuery functionality. Don't worry about what the second script does for the moment. We'll get into jQuery properly starting in Chapter 5. The script element can appear in the head or body element in an HTML document. In this book, I tend to put scripts only in the head element, but this is just a matter of personal preference.

■ **Tip** The order of script elements is important. You have to import the jQuery library before you can make use of its features.

Understanding the style Element

The style element is one of the ways you can introduce Cascading Style Sheets (CSS) properties into your documents. In short, you can use CSS to manage the way your document is presented when displayed to the user in the browser. Listing 2-9 shows the style element and its contents from the example document.

Listing 2-9. Using the style Element

```
<style>
    h1 {
        width: 700px; border: thick double black; margin-left: auto;
        margin-right: auto; text-align: center; font-size: x-large; padding: .5em;
        color: darkgreen; background-image: url("border.png");
        background-size: contain; margin-top: 0;
    }
    .dtable {display: table;}
    .drow {display: table-row;}
    .dcell {display: table-cell; padding: 10px;}
    .dcell > * {vertical-align: middle}
    input {width: 2em; text-align: right; border: thin solid black; padding: 2px;}
    label {width: 5em;  padding-left: .5em;display: inline-block;}
    #buttonDiv {text-align: center;}
    #oblock {display: block; margin-left: auto; margin-right: auto; width: 700px;}
</style>
```

The browser maintains a set of properties, the values of which are used to control the appearance of each element. The style element allows you to select elements and change the value of one or more of those properties. I'll get into this in more detail in Chapter 3.

The style element, like the script element, can appear in the head and body elements, but in this book you will find that I place them only in the head section, as in the example document. This is another matter of personal preference; I like to separate my styles from my content.

Understanding the Content Elements

The body element contains the *content* in an HTML document. These are the elements that the browser will display to the user and that the metadata elements, such as script and style, operate on.

Understanding the Semantic/Presentation Divide

One of the major changes in HTML5 is a philosophical one: the separation between the semantic significance of an element and the effect an element has on the presentation of content. This is a sensible idea. You use HTML elements to give structure and meaning to your content and then control the presentation of that content by applying CSS styles to the elements. Not every consumer of HTML documents needs to display them (because some consumers of HTML are automated programs rather than browsers, for example), and by keeping presentation separate, you make HTML easier to process and draw meaning from automatically.

Each HTML element has a specific meaning. For example, you use the article element to denote a self-contained piece of content that is suitable for syndication, and you use the h1 element to denote a heading for a content section.

This concept is at the heart of HTML. You apply elements to denote what kind of content you are dealing with. People are very good at inferring significance by context. You immediately understood that the header for this section on the page is subordinate to the previous header because it is printed in a smaller typeface (and because this is a pattern that you have seen in most nonfiction books you have read). Computers can't infer context anywhere near as well, so you apply elements to sections of your content to denote how they relate to one another. Listing 2-10 shows an example document that uses elements to confer structure and significance.

Listing 2-10. Using HTML Elements to Add Structure and Meaning to Content

```
<!DOCTYPE html>
<html>
<head>
    <title>Example</title>
</head>
<body>
    <article>
        <header>
            <hgroup>
                <h1>New Delivery Service</h1>
                <h2>Color and Beauty to Your Door</h2>
            </hgroup>
        </header>
        <section>
            We are pleased to announce that we are starting a home delivery service for
            your flower needs. We will deliver within a 20 mile radius of the store
            for free and $1/mile thereafter. All flowers are satisfaction-guaranteed and
            we offer free phone-based consultation.
        </section>
        <section>
            Our new service starts on <b>Wednesaday</b> and there is a $10 discount
            for the first 50 customers.
        </section>
        <footer>
            <nav>
                More Information:
                <a href="http://jacquisflowershop.com">Learn More About Fruit</a>
            </nav>
        </footer>
    </article>
</body>
</html>
```

There are no hard-and-fast rules about when to apply a section or article element, but I recommend you apply them consistently in your content. Elements like section and article don't provide any information to the browser about how the content they contain should be displayed. This is the very heart of the semantic/presentation divide. The browser has a *style convention* for most HTML elements, which determines how they will be displayed if the presentation is not changed using CSS, but the idea is that you will make liberal use of CSS to create the presentation you require for your document. This is something you can do with the style element and that jQuery makes very easy to do in a script element.

Some of the elements that existed in HTML4 were created when there was no notion of separating presentation from meaning, and that puts us in an odd situation. A great example is the b element. Until HTML5, the b element instructed the browser to show the content contained by the start and end tags as bold text. In HTML5, you don't want elements to be just presentational, so you have a new definition. Here it is:

> *The b element represents a span of text offset from its surrounding content without conveying any extra emphasis or importance, and for which the conventional typographic presentation is bold text; for example, keywords in a document abstract, or product names in a review.*
>
> —HTML: The Markup Language, w3c.org

This is a long-winded way of telling us that the b element tells the browser to make text bold. There is no semantic significance to the b element; it is all about presentation. And this weasel-worded definition tells us something important about HTML5: we are in a period of transition. We would *like* there to be a complete separation between elements and their presentation, but the reality is that we also want to maintain compatibility with the countless documents that have been written using earlier versions of HTML, and so we have to compromise.

Understanding Forms and Inputs

One of the most interesting elements in the body of the example document is the form element. This is a mechanism you can use to gather data from the user so that you can send it to the server. As you'll see in Chapter 13, jQuery has some excellent support for working with forms, both directly in the core library and in some commonly used plugins. Listing 2-11 shows the body element from the example document and its contents, with the form element emphasized.

Listing 2-11. The content Elements of the Example Document

```
<body>
    <h1>Jacqui's Flower Shop</h1>
    <form method="post">
        <div id="oblock">
            <div class="dtable">
                <div class="drow">
                    <div class="dcell">
                        <img src="astor.png"/><label for="astor">Astor:</label>
                        <input name="astor" value="0" required>
                    </div>
                    <div class="dcell">
                        <img src="daffodil.png"/><label for="daffodil">Daffodil:</label>
                        <input name="daffodil" value="0" required >
                    </div>
                    <div class="dcell">
                        <img src="rose.png"/><label for="rose">Rose:</label>
                        <input name="rose" value="0" required>
                    </div>
                </div>
```

```
                <div class="drow">
                    <div class="dcell">
                        <img src="peony.png"/><label for="peony">Peony:</label>
                        <input name="peony" value="0" required>
                    </div>
                    <div class="dcell">
                        <img src="primula.png"/><label for="primula">Primula:</label>
                        <input name="primula" value="0" required>
                    </div>
                    <div class="dcell">
                        <img src="snowdrop.png"/><label for="snowdrop">Snowdrop:</label>
                        <input name="snowdrop" value="0" required>
                    </div>
                </div>
            </div>
        </div>
        <div id="buttonDiv"><button type="submit">Place Order</button></div>
    </form>
</body>
```

When there is a form element, the input element can usually be found nearby. This is the element you use to get a particular piece of information from the user. Listing 2-12 shows an example input element from the document.

Listing 2-12. Using the input Element

```
<input name="snowdrop" value="0" required>
```

This input element gathers a value from the user for a data item called snowdrop, which has an initial value of zero. The required attribute tells the browser that the user should not be able to send the form to the server unless they have supplied a value for this data item. This is a new feature in HTML5 called *form validation*, but frankly you can achieve much better validation using jQuery, as I demonstrate in Chapter 13.

Closely related to forms is the button element, which is often used to submit the form to the server (and can also be used to reset the form to its initial state). Listing 2-13 shows the button element I defined in the example document.

Listing 2-13. Using the button Element

```
<button type="submit">Place Order</button>
```

Setting the type attribute to submit tells the browser I want the form submitted when the button is pressed. The contents of the button element are displayed within the button control in the browser, as you can see in Figure 2-3.

Figure 2-3. Using the content of the button element

Understanding Structural Elements

You will notice that there are a lot of `div` elements in the body of the `example` document. This is an element that has no specific semantic significance and that is often used to control the layout of content. In the case of the example document, I use the `div` element to create a *table layout*, such that the elements that the `div` elements contain are presented to the user in a grid. The layout is applied to the `div` elements by some of CSS contained in the `style` element. I'll be using CSS throughout this book, and I give a quick primer in Chapter 3.

Understanding Elements with External Resources

Some elements allow you to bring external resources into your document. A great example of this is the `img` element, which you can use to add images to documents. In the example document, I used the `img` element to display pictures of the different flowers on sale, as shown in Listing 2-14.

Listing 2-14. Using the img Element to Refer to an External Image

```
<img src="snowdrop.png"/>
```

The `src` attribute is used to specify the image. I have used the image `snowdrop.png`. This is an example of a *relative URL*, which means the browser will use the URL of the document that contains the element to work out the URL of the image I want.

The alternative to a relative URL is an *absolute URL* (also known as a *fully qualified URL*). This is a URL that has all of the basic components defined, as shown in Figure 2-4. (I have included the port in the figure, but if this is omitted, then the browser will use the default port associated with the scheme. For the `http` scheme, this is port `80`.)

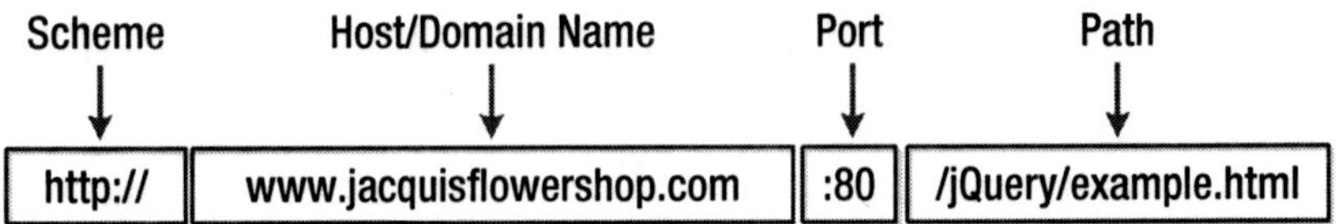

Figure 2-4. The basic structure of a URL

It can be tiresome to have to type out fully qualified URLs for every resource you want, which is why relative URLs are so useful. When I specified a value of `snowdrop.png` for the `src` attribute of the `img` element, I was telling the browser that it could find the image at the same location that it obtained the document that contains the `img` element. Table 2-2 shows the different kinds of relative URL you can use and the absolute URLs that are created from them. These all assume that the document has been loaded from `http://www.jacquisflowershop.com/jquery/example.html`.

Table 2-2. *Relative URL Formats*

Relative URL	Equivalent To
`snowdrop.png`	**`http://www.jacquisflowershop.com/jquery/snowdrop.png`**
`/snowdrop.png`	**`http://www.jacquisflowershop.com/snowdrop.png`**
`/`	**`http://www.jacquisflowershop.com/jquery/`**
`//www.mydomain.com/index.html`	`http://www.mydomain.com/index.html`

The last example in the table is rarely used because it doesn't save much typing, but it can be useful to ensure that resources are requested using the same scheme as was used to retrieve the main document. This avoids a problem where some content is requested over an encrypted connection (using the `https` scheme) and other content is requested over an unencrypted connection (using the `http` scheme). Some browsers, especially Internet Explorer, don't like mixing secure and unsecure content and will warn the user when it occurs.

■ **Caution** You can use the two periods (`..`) to navigate relative to the directory on the web server that contains the main HTML document. I recommend avoiding this technique, not least because many web servers will reject requests that contain these characters as a security precaution.

Understanding the Element Hierarchy

The elements in an HTML document form a natural hierarchy. The `html` element contains the `body` element, which contains content elements, each of which can contain other elements, *ad infinitum*.

Understanding this hierarchy is important when you want to navigate the document, either to apply styles using CSS (which I describe in Chapter 3) or to use jQuery to find elements in the document (which I explain in Chapters 5 and 6).

The most important part of the hierarchy is the relationships that exist between elements. To help me describe these relationships, I have represented the hierarchy for some of the elements from the flower shop example document in Figure 2-5.

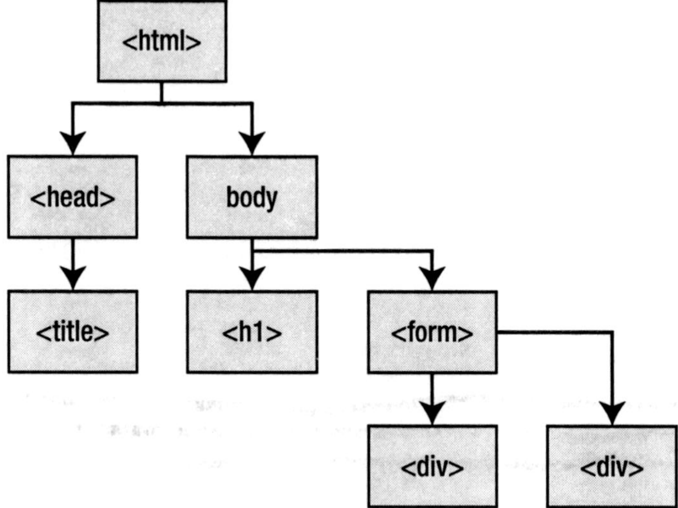

Figure 2-5. Part of the document hierarchy

The figure shows just part of the hierarchy of elements from the document, just enough so you can see that the relationships correspond directly to the way that one element can contain another. There are various kinds of relationship, as described in the following sections.

Understanding Parent-Child Relationships

A parent-child relationship exists when one element contains another, for example. The `form` element is a *child* of the `body` element in the figure. Conversely, the `body` element is the *parent* of the `form` element. An element can have more than one child but only one parent. In the example, the `body` element has two children (the `form` and `h1` elements) and is the parent to both of them.

The parent-child relationship exists only between an element and elements that are directly contained within it. So, for example, the `div` elements are children of the `form` element, but they are not children of the `body` element.

There are some variations on the child relationship. The *first child* is the child element that is defined first in the document. For example, the `h1` element is the first child of the `body` element. The *last child* is the last child element defined in the document. The `form` element is the last child of the `body` element. You can also refer to the `nth-child`, where you start with the first child element and start counting children until you get to `n` (you start counting at `1`).

Understanding Ancestor-Descendant Relationships

An element's descendants are its children, its children's children, and so on. In fact, any element contained directly or indirectly is a descendant. For example, the descendants of the body element are the `h1`, `form`, and both `div` elements, and all of the elements shown in the figure are descendants of the `html` element.

The opposite relationship is *ancestors*, which are an element's parent, the parent's parent, and so on. For the `form` element, for example, the descendants are the body and `html` elements. Both `div` elements have the same set of ancestors: the `form`, body, and `html` elements.

Understanding Sibling Relationships

Siblings are elements that share a common parent. In the example, the `h1` and `form` elements are siblings because they share the body element as their parent. When working with siblings, we tend to refer to the *next siblings* and the *previous siblings*. These are the siblings defined before and after the current element. Not all elements have both previous and next siblings; the first and last child elements will have only one or the other.

Understanding the Document Object Model

When the browser loads and processes an HTML document, it creates the *Document Object Model* (DOM). The DOM is a model where JavaScript objects are used to represent each element in the document, and the DOM is the mechanism by which you can programmatically engage with the content of an HTML document.

■ **Note** In principle, the DOM can be used with any programming language that the browser cares to implement. In practice, JavaScript dominates the mainstream browsers, so I am not going to differentiate between the DOM as an abstract idea and the DOM as a collection of related JavaScript objects.

One of the reasons that you should care about the relationship between elements that I described in the previous section is that they are preserved in the DOM. As a consequence, you can use JavaScript to traverse the network of objects to learn about the nature and structure of the document that has been represented.

■ **Tip** Using the DOM means using JavaScript. If you require a refresher in the basics of the JavaScript language, then see Chapter 4.

In this part of the chapter, I will demonstrate some of the basic features of the DOM. For the rest of the book, I will focus on using jQuery to access the DOM, but in this section I will show you some of the built-in support, in part, to demonstrate how much more elegant the jQuery approach can be.

Using the DOM

The JavaScript object that defines the basic functionality that is available in the DOM for all types of elements is called `HTMLElement`. The `HTMLElement` object defines properties and methods that are common to all HTML element types, including the properties shown in Table 2-3.

Table 2-3. *Basic HTMLElement Properties*

Property	Description	Returns
`className`	Gets or sets the list of classes to which the element belongs	`string`
`id`	Gets or sets the value of the `id` attribute	`string`
`lang`	Gets or sets the value of the `lang` attribute	`string`
`tagName`	Returns the tag name (indicating the element type)	`string`

Many more properties are available. The exact set depends on which version of HTML you are working with. But these four are sufficient for me to demonstrate the basic workings of the DOM.

The DOM uses objects that are derived from `HTMLElement` to represent the unique characteristics of each element type. For example, the `HTMLImageElement` object is used to represent `img` elements in the DOM, and this object defines the `src` property, which corresponds to the `src` attribute of the `img` element. I am not going to go into any detail about the element-specific objects, but as a rule, you can rely on properties being available that correspond to the element's attributes.

You access the DOM through the global `document` variable, which returns a `Document` object. The `Document` object represents the HTML document that is being displayed by the browser and defines some methods that allow you to locate objects in the DOM, as described by Table 2-4.

Table 2-4. *Document Methods to Find Elements*

Property	Description	Returns
`getElementById(<id>)`	Returns the element with the specified `id` value	`HTMLElement`
`getElementsByClassName(<class>)`	Returns the elements with the specified `class` value	`HTMLElement[]`
`getElementsByTagName(<tag>)`	Returns the elements of the specified type	`HTMLElement[]`
`querySelector(<selector>)`	Returns the first element that matches the specified CSS selector	`HTMLElement`
`querySelectorAll(<selector>)`	Returns all of the elements that match the specified CSS selector	`HTMLElement[]`

Once again, I am just picking the methods that are useful for this book. The last two methods described in the table use *CSS selectors*, which I describe in Chapter 3. Listing 2-15 shows how you can use the Document object to search for elements of a specific type in the document.

Listing 2-15. Searching for Elements *in the DOM*

```
<!DOCTYPE html>
<html>
<head>
    <title>Example</title>
    <style>
        h1 {
            width: 700px; border: thick double black; margin-left: auto;
            margin-right: auto; text-align: center; font-size: x-large; padding: .5em;
            color: darkgreen; background-image: url("border.png");
            background-size: contain; margin-top: 0;
        }
        .dtable {display: table;}
        .drow {display: table-row;}
        .dcell {display: table-cell; padding: 10px;}
        .dcell > * {vertical-align: middle}
        input {width: 2em; text-align: right; border: thin solid black; padding: 2px;}
        label {width: 5em;  padding-left: .5em;display: inline-block;}
        #buttonDiv {text-align: center;}
        #oblock {display: block; margin-left: auto; margin-right: auto; width: 700px;}
    </style>
</head>
<body>
    <h1>Jacqui's Flower Shop</h1>
    <form method="post">
        <div id="oblock">
            <div class="dtable">
                <div class="drow">
                    <div class="dcell">
                        <img src="astor.png"/><label for="astor">Astor:</label>
                        <input name="astor" value="0" required>
                    </div>
                    <div class="dcell">
                        <img src="daffodil.png"/><label for="daffodil">Daffodil:</label>
                        <input name="daffodil" value="0" required >
                    </div>
                    <div class="dcell">
                        <img src="rose.png"/><label for="rose">Rose:</label>
                        <input name="rose" value="0" required>
                    </div>
                </div>
                <div class="drow">
                    <div class="dcell">
                        <img src="peony.png"/><label for="peony">Peony:</label>
                        <input name="peony" value="0" required>
                    </div>
                    <div class="dcell">
```

```
                    <img src="primula.png"/><label for="primula">Primula:</label>
                    <input name="primula" value="0" required>
                </div>
                <div class="dcell">
                    <img src="snowdrop.png"/><label for="snowdrop">Snowdrop:</label>
                    <input name="snowdrop" value="0" required>
                </div>
            </div>
        </div>
    </div>
    <div id="buttonDiv"><button type="submit">Place Order</button></div>
</form>
<script>
    var elements = document.getElementsByTagName("img");
    for (var i = 0; i < elements.length; i++) {
        console.log("Element: " + elements[i].tagName + " " + elements[i].src);
    }
</script>
</body>
</html>
```

In this example, I have added a script element at the end of the body element. When browsers find a script element in a document, they execute the JavaScript statements right away, before the rest of the document has been loaded and processed. This presents a problem when you are working with the DOM because it means your searches for elements via the Document object are performed before the objects you are interested in have been created in the model. To avoid this, I have placed the script element at the end of the document. jQuery provides a nice way of dealing with this issue, as I explain in Chapter 5.

In the script, I use the getElementsByTagName method to find all of the img elements in the document. This method returns an array of objects, which I then enumerate to print out the value of the tagName and src properties for each object to the console. The output written to the console is as follows:

```
Element: IMG http://www.jacquisflowershop.com/jquery/astor.png
Element: IMG http://www.jacquisflowershop.com/jquery/daffodil.png
Element: IMG http://www.jacquisflowershop.com/jquery/rose.png
Element: IMG http://www.jacquisflowershop.com/jquery/peony.png
Element: IMG http://www.jacquisflowershop.com/jquery/primula.png
Element: IMG http://www.jacquisflowershop.com/jquery/snowdrop.png
```

Modifying the DOM

The objects in the DOM are *live*, meaning that changing the value of a DOM object property affects the document that the browser is displaying. Listing 2-16 shows a script that has this effect. (I am just showing the script element here to reduce duplication. The rest of the document is the same as for the last example.)

Listing 2-16. Modifying a DOM Object Property

```
...
<script>
    var elements = document.getElementsByTagName("img");
    for (var i = 0; i < elements.length; i++) {
        elements[i].src = "snowdrop.png";
    }
</script>
...
```

In this script, I set the value of the `src` attribute to be `snowdrop.png` for all of the `img` elements. You can see the effect in Figure 2-6.

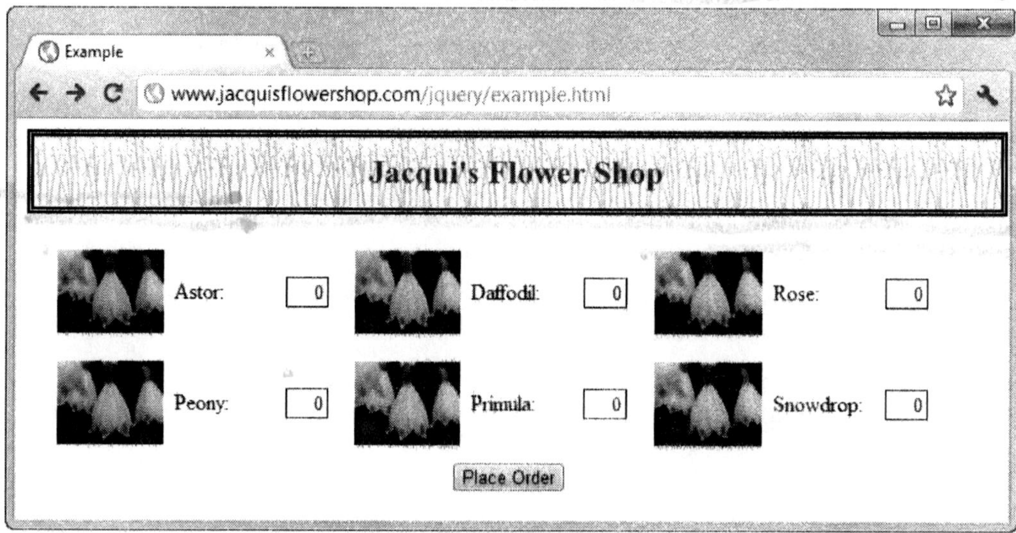

Figure 2-6. Using the DOM to modify the HTML document

Modifying Styles

You can use the DOM to change the values for CSS properties. (Chapter 3 provides a primer in CSS if you need it.) The DOM API support for CSS is pretty comprehensive, but the simplest way of doing this is to use the `style` property, which is defined by the `HTMLElement` object. The object returned by the `style` property defines properties that correspond to CSS properties (I realize that there are a lot of *properties* in this sentence, for which I apologize).

The naming scheme of properties as defined by CSS and by the object that `style` returns is slightly different. For example, the `background-color` CSS property becomes the `style.backgroundColor` object property. Listing 2-17 gives a demonstration of using the DOM to manage styles.

Listing 2-17. Using the DOM to Modify Element Styles

```
...
<script>
    var elements = document.getElementsByTagName("img");
    for (var i = 0; i < elements.length; i++) {
        if (i > 0) {
            elements[i].style.opacity = 0.5;
        }
    }
</script>
...
```

In this script, I change the value of the opacity property for all but the first of the img elements in the document. I left one element unaltered so you can see the difference in Figure 2-7.

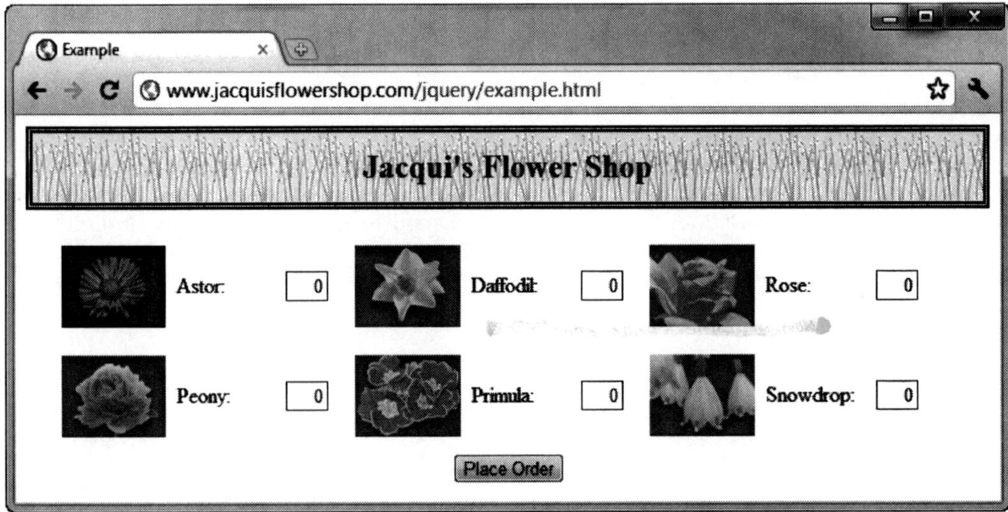

Figure 2-7. Using JavaScript to change CSS property values

Handling Events

Events are a signal sent by the browser to indicate a change in status of one or more elements in the DOM. There are different events defined for different kinds of state change. For example, the click event is triggered when the user clicks an element in the document, and the submit element is triggered when the user submits a form. Many events are related. For example, the mouseover event is triggered when the user moves the mouse over an element, and the mouseout event is triggered when the user moves the mouse out again.

You can respond to an event by associating a JavaScript function with an event for a DOM element. Listing 2-18 gives an example.

Listing 2-18. Handling an Event

```
...
<script>
    var elements = document.getElementsByTagName("img");
    for (var i = 0; i < elements.length; i++) {
        elements[i].onmouseover = handleMouseOver;
        elements[i].onmouseout = handleMouseOut;
    }

    function handleMouseOver(e) {
        e.target.style.opacity = 0.5;
    }

    function handleMouseOut(e) {
        e.target.style.opacity = 1;
    }
</script>
...
```

This script defines two handler functions, which I assign as the values for the onmouseover and onmouseout properties on the img DOM objects. The effect of this script is that the images become partially transparent when the mouse is over them and return to normal when the mouse exits. I don't intend to get too deeply into the DOM API event handling mechanism, because the jQuery support for events is the topic of Chapter 9. I do, however, want to look at the object that is passed to the event handling functions: the Event object. Table 2-5 shows the most important members of the Event object.

***Table 2-5.** Functions and Properties of the Event Object*

Name	Description	Returns
type	The name of the event, i.e., mouseover.	string
target	The element at which the event is targeted.	HTMLElement
currentTarget	The element whose event listeners are currently being invoked.	HTMLElement
eventPhase	The phase in the event life cycle.	number
bubbles	Returns true if the event will bubble through the document; returns false otherwise.	boolean
cancelable	Returns true if the event has a default action that can be canceled; returns false otherwise.	boolean
stopPropagation()	Halts the flow of the event through the element tree after the event listeners for the current element have been triggered.	void

`stopImmediatePropagation()`	Immediately halts the flow of the event through the element tree. Untriggered event listeners for the current element will be ignored.	`void`
`preventDefault()`	Prevents the browser from performing the default action associated with the event.	`void`
`defaultPrevented`	Returns `true` if `preventDefault()` has been called.	`boolean`

In the previous example, I used the `target` property to get hold of the element for which the event was triggered. Some of the other members relate to *event flow* and to *default actions*, which I explain (very briefly) in the next section. I just want to lay the groundwork in this chapter.

Understanding Event Flow

An event has three phases to its life cycle: *capture*, *target*, and *bubbling*. When an event is triggered, the browser identifies the element that the event relates to, which is referred to as the *target* for the event. The browser identifies all of the elements between the body element and the target and checks each of them to see whether they have any event handlers that have asked to be notified of events of their descendants. The browser triggers any such handler before triggering the handlers on the target itself. (I'll show you how to ask for notification of descendant events in Chapter 9.)

Once the capture phase is complete, you move to the *target phase*, which is the simplest of the three. When the capture phase has finished, the browser triggers any listeners for the event type that have been added to the target element.

Once the target phase has been completed, the browser starts working its way up the chain of ancestor elements back toward the body element. At each element, the browser checks to see whether there are listeners for the event type that are not capture-enabled (which I'll explain how to do in Chapter 9). Not all events support bubbling. You can check to see whether an event will bubble using the `bubbles` property. A value of `true` indicates that the event will bubble, and `false` means that it won't.

Understanding Default Actions

Some events define a default action that will be performed when an event is triggered. As an example, the default action for the `click` event on the a element is that the browser will load the content at the URL specified in the `href` attribute. When an event has a default action, the value of its `cancelable` property will be `true`. You can stop the default action from being performed by calling the `preventDefault` method. Note that calling the `preventDefault` function doesn't stop the event flowing through the capture, target, and bubble phases. These phases will still be performed, but the browser won't perform the default action at the end of the bubble phase. You can test to see whether the `preventDefault` function has been called on an event by an earlier event handler by reading the `defaultPrevented` property. If it returns `true`, then the `preventDefault` function has been called.

Summary

In this chapter, I took you on a tour of how HTML functions, albeit without describing any of the 100+ elements in detail. I showed you how to create and structure a basic HTML document, how elements can contain a mix of text content and other elements, and how this leads to a hierarchy of elements with specific types of relationship.

CHAPTER 3

CSS Primer

Cascading Style Sheets (CSS) are closely associated with HTML and are the means by which you control the presentation of HTML elements. CSS has a special significance for jQuery for two reasons. The first is that you can use *CSS selectors* (which I describe in this chapter) to tell jQuery how to find elements in an HTML document. The second reason is that one of the most common tasks that jQuery is used for is to change the CSS styles that are applied to elements.

There are more than 130 *CSS properties*, each of which controls an aspect of an element's presentation. As with the HTML elements, there are too many CSS properties for me to be able to describe them in this book. Instead, I have focused on how CSS works and how you apply styles to elements. If you want detailed coverage of CSS, then I suggest another of my books: *The Definitive Guide to HTML5*, which is also published by Apress.

Getting Started with CSS

When the browser displays an element on the screen, it uses a set of properties, known as *CSS properties*, to work out how the element should be presented. Listing 3-1 shows a simple HTML document.

Listing 3-1. A Simple HTML Document

```
<!DOCTYPE html>
<html>
<head>
    <title>Example</title>
</head>
<body>
    <h1>New Delivery Service</h1>
    <h2>Color and Beauty to Your Door</h2>
    <h2>(with special introductory offer)</h2>
    <p>We are pleased to announce that you are starting a home delivery service for
    your flower needs. You will deliver within a 20 mile radius of the store
    for free and $1/mile thereafter.</p>
</body>
</html>
```

You can see how a browser displays the document in Figure 3-1.

Figure 3-1. Displaying a simple document in the browser

There are a *lot* of CSS properties—too many to cover in detail in this book—but you can learn a lot about how CSS works by looking at just a small number of properties, as described in Table 3-1.

***Table 3-1.** Some CSS Properties*

Property	Description
`color`	Sets the foreground color of the element (which typically sets the color of text)
`background-color`	Sets the background color of the element
`font-size`	Sets the size of the font used for text contained in the element
`border`	Sets the border for the element

I haven't defined any values for these properties, but the browser has still managed to display the content, and, as the figure shows, each of the content elements has been presented in a slightly different way. The browser has to work with something if you haven't provided values for the properties, so each element has a *style convention.* That is, the browser has a set of default values that it uses for CSS properties when you don't supply a value. Although the HTML specification defines the style conventions for elements, browsers are free to vary them, and there are minor differences in how elements are displayed by default. Table 3-2 shows the default values that are used by Google Chrome.

Table 3-2. Some CSS Properties and Their Style Convention Values

Property	h1	h2	p
color	black	black	black
background-color	transparent	transparent	transparent
font-size	2em	1.5em	16px
border	none	none	none

You can see from the table that all three types of element have the same values for the color, background-color, and border properties and that it is only the font-size property that changes. Later in the chapter, I'll describe the units that are used for these property values and explain why the font-size property is expressed in em units for the h1 and h2 elements but in px units for the p element. For the moment, though, we are going to focus on setting values for properties without worrying about the units in which those values are expressed.

Setting an Inline Value

The most direct way to set values for CSS properties is to apply the style attribute to the element whose presentation you want to change. Listing 3-2 shows how this is done.

Listing 3-2. Using the style Attribute to Set a CSS Property on an Element

```
<!DOCTYPE html>
<html>
<head>
    <title>Example</title>
</head>
<body>
    <h1>New Delivery Service</h1>
    <h2 style="background-color: grey; color: white">Color and Beauty to Your Door</h2>
    <h2>(with special introductory offer)</h2>
    <p>We are pleased to announce that we are starting a home delivery service for
    your flower needs. We will deliver within a 20 mile radius of the store
    for free and $1/mile thereafter.</p>
</body>
</html>
```

In this example, I have used *style declarations* to specify values for two of the CSS properties. You can see the anatomy of the attribute value in Figure 3-2.

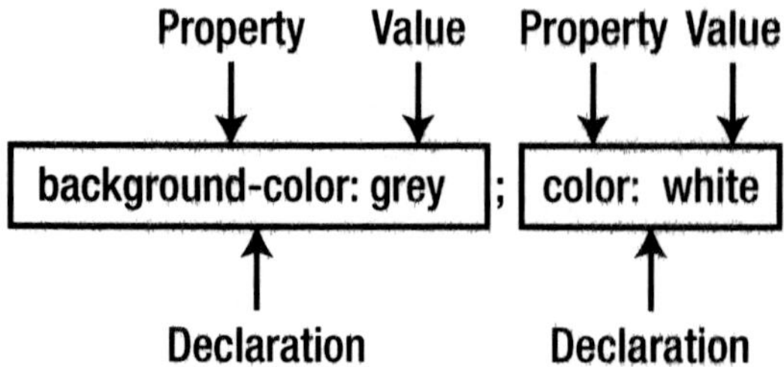

Figure 3-2. The anatomy of a style attribute value

Each style declaration specifies the name of a property you want to change and the value that you want to use, separated by a colon (`:`). You can put multiple declarations together using a semicolon character (`;`). In this example, I set the value of the `background-color` to `grey` and the value of the `color` property to `white`. These values are specified in the `style` attribute of the `h2` element and will affect only that element (other elements in the document remain unaffected, even if they are also `h2` elements). You can see the effect that these new property values have in the presentation of the first `h2` element in Figure 3-3.

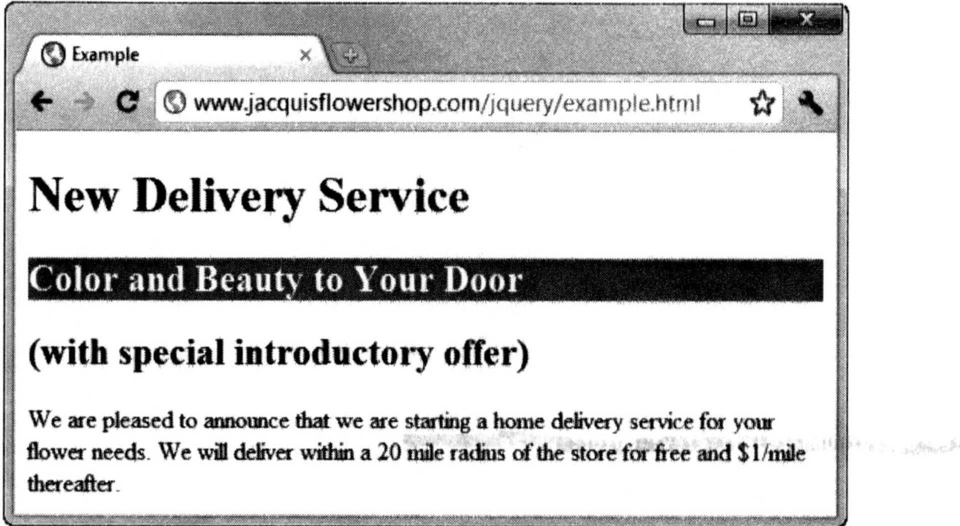

Figure 3-3. The effect of changing CSS values in the style attribute of the h2 element

Defining an Embedded Style

Using the `style` attribute is easy, but it applies to only a single element. You could use simple style declarations for every element that you wanted to change, but it becomes difficult to manage and error-prone very quickly, especially if you need to make revisions later. A more powerful technique is to use the `style` *element* (rather than the `style` *attribute*) to define an *embedded style* and direct the browser to apply it with a *selector*. Listing 3-3 shows an embedded style.

Listing 3-3. Defining an Embedded Style

```
<!DOCTYPE html>
<html>
<head>
    <title>Example</title>
    <style>
        h2 { background-color: grey; color: white;}
    </style>
</head>
<body>
    <h1>New Delivery Service</h1>
    <h2>Color and Beauty to Your Door</h2>
    <h2>(with special introductory offer)</h2>
    <p>We are pleased to announce that we are starting a home delivery service for
    your flower needs. We will deliver within a 20 mile radius of the store
    for free and $1/mile thereafter.</p>
</body>
</html>
```

We still use declarations in an embedded style, but they are enclosed in braces (the { and } characters) and are preceded by a *selector*. You can see the anatomy of an embedded style in Figure 3-4.

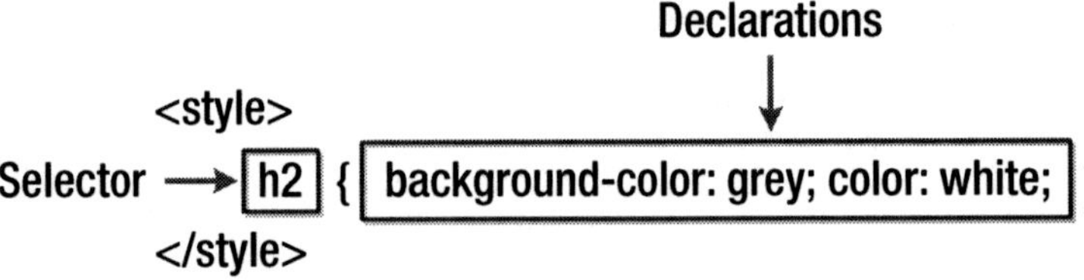

Figure 3-4. The anatomy of an embedded style

■ **Tip** I have placed the `style` element within the `head` element, but I could have equally put it inside the `body` element. I prefer using the `head` element for styles because I like the idea of separating the content from the metadata.

CSS selectors are very important in jQuery, since they are the basis by which you select elements in the DOM in order to perform operations on them. The selector I used in the example is `h2`, which means that the style declarations contained in the braces should be applied to every `h2` element in the document. You can see the effect this has on the `h2` elements in Figure 3-5.

Figure 3-5. The effect of an embedded style

You can use a style element to contain more than one embedded style. Listing 3-4 shows the flower shop document that you first saw in Chapter 2, which has a more complex set of styles.

Listing 3-4. A More Complex Set of Styles in an HTML Document

```
<!DOCTYPE html>
<html>
<head>
    <title>Example</title>
    <script src="jquery-1.7.js" type="text/javascript"></script>
    <style>
        h1 {
            min-width: 700px; border: thick double black; margin-left: auto;
            margin-right: auto; text-align: center; font-size: x-large; padding: .5em;
            color: darkgreen; background-image: url("border.png");
            background-size: contain; margin-top: 0;
        }
        .dtable {display: table;}
        .drow {display: table-row;}
        .dcell {display: table-cell; padding: 10px;}
        .dcell > * {vertical-align: middle}
        input {width: 2em; text-align: right; border: thin solid black; padding: 2px;}
        label {width: 5em;  padding-left: .5em;display: inline-block;}
        #buttonDiv {text-align: center;}
        #oblock {display: block; margin-left: auto;
            margin-right: auto; min-width: 700px;}
    </style>
</head>
<body>
```

```
    <h1>Jacqui's Flower Shop</h1>
    <form method="post">
        <div id="oblock">
            <div class="dtable">
                <div class="drow">
                    <div class="dcell">
                        <img src="astor.png"/><label for="astor">Astor:</label>
                        <input name="astor" value="0" required>
                    </div>
                    <div class="dcell">
                        <img src="daffodil.png"/><label for="daffodil">Daffodil:</label>
                        <input name="daffodil" value="0" required >
                    </div>
                    <div class="dcell">
                        <img src="rose.png"/><label for="rose">Rose:</label>
                        <input name="rose" value="0" required>
                    </div>
                </div>
                <div class="drow">
                    <div class="dcell">
                        <img src="peony.png"/><label for="peony">Peony:</label>
                        <input name="peony" value="0" required>
                    </div>
                    <div class="dcell">
                        <img src="primula.png"/><label for="primula">Primula:</label>
                        <input name="primula" value="0" required>
                    </div>
                    <div class="dcell">
                        <img src="snowdrop.png"/><label for="snowdrop">Snowdrop:</label>
                        <input name="snowdrop" value="0" required>
                    </div>
                </div>
            </div>
        </div>
        <div id="buttonDiv"><button type="submit">Place Order</button></div>
    </form>
</body>
</html>
```

The `style` element in this example contains several embedded styles, and some of them, especially the one with the `h1` selector, define values for many properties.

Defining an External Style Sheet

Rather than define the same set of styles in each of your HTML documents, you can create a separate *style sheet*. This is an independent file, conventionally with the `.css` file extension, into which you put your styles. Listing 3-5 shows the contents of the file `styles.css`, into which I have placed the styles from the flower shop document.

Listing 3-5. The styles.css File

```
h1 {
    min-width: 700px; border: thick double black; margin-left: auto;
    margin-right: auto; text-align: center; font-size: x-large; padding: .5em;
    color: darkgreen; background-image: url("border.png");
    background-size: contain; margin-top: 0;
}
.dtable {display: table;}
.drow {display: table-row;}
.dcell {display: table-cell; padding: 10px;}
.dcell > * {vertical-align: middle}
input {width: 2em; text-align: right; border: thin solid black; padding: 2px;}
label {width: 5em;  padding-left: .5em;display: inline-block;}
#buttonDiv {text-align: center;}
#oblock {display: block; margin-left: auto; margin-right: auto; min-width: 700px;}
```

You don't need to use a style element in a style sheet. You just define the selector and declarations directly. You can then use the link element to bring the styles into your document, as shown in Listing 3-6.

Listing 3-6. Importing an External Style Sheet

```
<!DOCTYPE html>
<html>
<head>
    <title>Example</title>
    <script src="jquery-1.7.js" type="text/javascript"></script>
    <link rel="stylesheet" type="text/css" href="styles.css"/>
</head>
<body>
    <h1>Jacqui's Flower Shop</h1>
    <form method="post">
        <div id="oblock">
            <div class="dtable">
                <div class="drow">
                    <div class="dcell">
                        <img src="astor.png"/><label for="astor">Astor:</label>
                        <input name="astor" value="0" required>
                    </div>
                    <div class="dcell">
                        <img src="daffodil.png"/><label for="daffodil">Daffodil:</label>
                        <input name="daffodil" value="0" required >
                    </div>
                    <div class="dcell">
                        <img src="rose.png"/><label for="rose">Rose:</label>
                        <input name="rose" value="0" required>
                    </div>
                </div>
                <div class="drow">
                    <div class="dcell">
```

```
                    <img src="peony.png"/><label for="peony">Peony:</label>
                    <input name="peony" value="0" required>
                </div>
                <div class="dcell">
                    <img src="primula.png"/><label for="primula">Primula:</label>
                    <input name="primula" value="0" required>
                </div>
                <div class="dcell">
                    <img src="snowdrop.png"/><label for="snowdrop">Snowdrop:</label>
                    <input name="snowdrop" value="0" required>
                </div>
            </div>
        </div>
    </div>
    <div id="buttonDiv"><button type="submit">Place Order</button></div>
</form>
</body>
</html>
```

You can link to as many style sheets as you need, one per link element. The order in which you import style sheets is important if you define two styles with the same selector. The one that is loaded last will be the one that is applied.

Understanding CSS Selectors

Notice that the selectors in the flower shop style sheet have differing natures. Some are element names (such as h1 and input), others start with a period (such as .dtable and .row), and yet others start with a pound (#butonDiv and #oblock). If you are particularly observant, you will notice that one of the selectors has multiple components: .dcell > *. Each CSS selector selects elements in the document, and the different kinds of selector tell the browser to look for elements in different ways. In this section, I'll describe the different kinds of selector that are defined by CSS. You start with the *core selectors,* which are summarized in Table 3-3.

Table 3-3. *The Core Selectors*

Selector	Description
*	Selects all elements
<type>	Selects elements of the specified type
.<class>	Selects elements of the specific class (irrespective of element type)
<type>.<class>	Selects elements of the specified type that are members of the specified class
#<id>	Selects elements with the specified value for the id attribute

These selectors are the most widely used (they cover almost all of the styles I defined in the example document, for instance).

Selecting by Attribute

Although the basic selectors work on the id and class attributes (which I described in Chapter 2), there are also selectors available that let you work with any attribute. These are described in Table 3-4.

***Table 3-4.** The Attribute Selectors*

Selector	Description
[attr]	Selects elements that define the attribute attr, irrespective of the value assigned to the attribute
[attr="val"]	Selects elements that define attr and whose value for this attribute is val
[attr^="val"]	Selects elements that define attr and whose value for this attribute starts with the string val
[attr$="val"]	Selects elements that define attr and whose value for this attribute ends with the string val
[attr*="val"]	Selects elements that define attr and whose value for this attribute contains the string val
[attr~="val"]	Selects elements that define attr and whose value for this attribute contains multiple values, one of which is val
[attr|="val"]	Selects elements that define attr and whose value is a hyphen-separated list of values, the first of which is val

Listing 3-7 shows a simple document with an embedded style whose selector is based on attributes.

Listing 3-7. Using the Attribute Selectors

```
<!DOCTYPE html>
<html>
<head>
    <title>Example</title>
    <style>
        [lang] { background-color: grey; color: white;}
        [lang="es"] {font-size: 14px;}
    </style>
</head>
<body>
    <h1 lang="en">New Delivery Service</h1>
    <h2 lang="en">Color and Beauty to Your Door</h2>
    <h2 lang="es">(Color y belleza a tu puerta)</h2>
    <p>We are pleased to announce that we are starting a home delivery service for
    your flower needs. We will deliver within a 20 mile radius of the store
    for free and $1/mile thereafter.</p>
```

```
</body>
</html>
```

The first selector matches any element that has the lang attribute, and the second selector matches any element whose lang attribute value is es. You can see the effect of these styles in Figure 3-6.

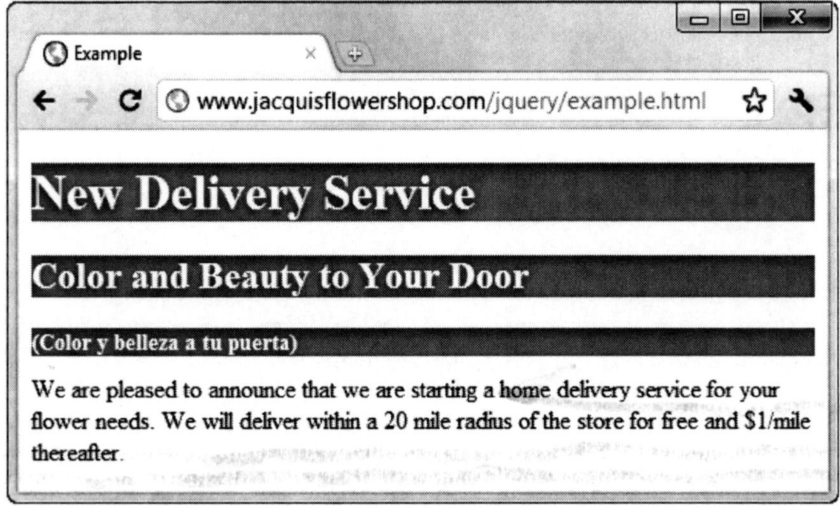

Figure 3-6. Applying styles using attribute selectors

■ **Note** There is something important to note in this figure. Look at how the h2 element has been affected by *both* of the embedded styles. The first style is applied to all elements with a lang attribute. The second style is applied to all elements that have a lang attribute whose value is es. The second h2 element in the document meets both of those criteria, and so the values for the background-color, color, and font-size properties are all changed. I'll explain more about how this works in the "Understanding Style Cascading" section later in this chapter.

Selecting by Relationship

In Chapter 2, I explained that elements (and the object that represents them in the DOM) have a hierarchy that gives rise to different kinds of relationship. There are CSS selectors that allow you to select elements based on those relationships, as described in Table 3-5.

Table 3-5. The Relationship Selectors

Selector	Description
`<selector> <selector>`	Selects elements that match the second selector and that are descendants of the elements matched by the first selector
`<selector> > <selector>`	Selects elements that match the second selector and that are children of the elements matched by the first selector
`<selector> + <selector>`	Selects elements that match the second selector and are the next sibling to an element that matches the first selector
`<selector> ~ <selector>`	Selects elements that match the second selector and that are siblings to (and that appear after) an element that matches the first selector

I used one of these selectors in the flower shop example document, like this:

```
.dcell > * {vertical-align: middle}
```

This selector matches all of the elements that are children of elements that belong to the `dcell` class, and the declaration sets the `vertical-align` property to the value `middle`. Listing 3-8 shows some of the other relationship selectors being used.

Listing 3-8. Using the Relationship Selectors

```
<!DOCTYPE html>
<html>
<head>
    <title>Example</title>
    <style>
        h1 ~ [lang] { background-color: grey; color: white;}
        h1 + [lang] {font-size: 12px;}
    </style>
</head>
<body>
    <h1 lang="en">New Delivery Service</h1>
    <h2 lang="en">Color and Beauty to Your Door</h2>
    <h2 lang="es">(Color y belleza a tu puerta)</h2>
    <p>We are pleased to announce that we are starting a home delivery service for
    your flower needs. We will deliver within a 20 mile radius of the store
    for free and $1/mile thereafter.</p>
</body>
</html>
```

I have used both of the sibling selectors in this example. The first selector, the one that uses the tilde (~) character, matches any element that has a `lang` attribute and that is defined after and is a sibling to an `h1` element. In the example document, this means that both the `h2` elements are selected (since they have the attribute and are siblings to and are defined after the `h1` element). The second selector, the one that uses the plus character, is similar but matches only the immediate sibling of an h1 element. This means that only the first of the h2 element is selected. You can see the effect in Figure 3-7.

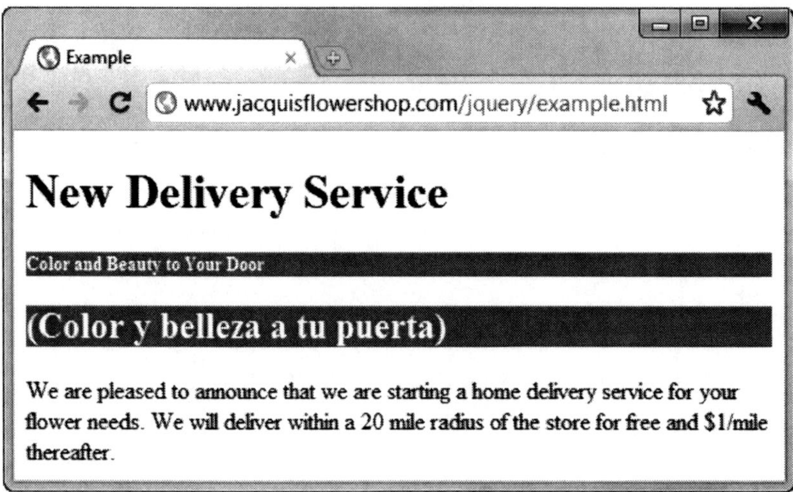

Figure 3-7. Using the sibling relationship selectors

Selecting Using the Pseudo-element and Pseudo-class Selectors

CSS supports a set of *pseudo-element and pseudo-class selectors.* These provide convenient functionality that doesn't correspond directly to elements or class membership in the document. These selectors are described in Table 3-6.

Table 3-6. *The Pseudo-selectors*

Selector	Description
:active	Selects elements that are presently activated by the user. This usually means those elements that are under the pointer when the mouse button is pressed.
:checked	Selects elements that are in a checked state.
:default	Selects default elements.
:disabled	Selects elements that are in their disabled state.
:empty	Selects elements that contain no child elements.
:enabled	Selects elements that are in their enabled state.
:first-child	Selects elements that are the first children of their parent.

:first-letter	Selects the first letter of a block of text.
:first-line	Selects the first line of a block of text.
:focus	Selects the element that has the focus.
:hover	Selects elements that occupy the position on-screen under the mouse pointer.
:in-range :out-of-range	Selects constrained input elements that are within or outside the specified range.
:lang(<language>)	Selects elements based on the value of the lang attribute.
:last-child	Selects elements that are the last children of their parent.
:link	Selects link elements.
:nth-child(n)	Selects elements that are the nth child of their parent.
:nth-last-child(n)	Selects elements that are the nth from last child of their parent.
:nth-last-of-type(n)	Selects elements that are the nth from last child of their type defined by their parent.
:nth-of-type(n)	Selects elements that are the nth child of their type defined by their parent.
:only-child	Selects elements that are the sole element defined by their parent.
:only-of-type	Selects elements that are the sole element of their type defined by their parent.
:required :optional	Selects input elements based on the presence of the required attribute.
:root	Selects the root element in the document.
:target	Selects the element referred to by the URL fragment identifier.
:valid :invalid	Selects input elements that are valid or invalid based on input validation in forms.
:visited	Selects link elements that the user has visited.

Listing 3-9 shows the use of some pseudo-selectors.

Listing 3-9. Using Pseudo-selectors

```
<!DOCTYPE html>
<html>
<head>
    <title>Example</title>
    <style>
        :nth-of-type(2) { background-color: grey; color: white;}
        p:first-letter {font-size: 40px;}
    </style>
</head>
<body>
    <h1 lang="en">New Delivery Service</h1>
    <h2 lang="en">Color and Beauty to Your Door</h2>
    <h2 lang="es">(Color y belleza a tu puerta)</h2>
    <p>We are pleased to announce that we are starting a home delivery service for
    your flower needs. We will deliver within a 20 mile radius of the store
    for free and $1/mile thereafter.</p>
</body>
</html>
```

You can use the pseudo-selectors on their own or as a modifier to another selector. I have shown both approaches in the example. The first selector matches any element that is the second element of its type defined by its parent. The second selector matches the first letter of any p elements. You can see the application of these styles in Figure 3-8.

Figure 3-8. Using pseudo-selectors to apply styles

Unions and the Negation Selectors

You can get a lot of additional flexibility by arranging selectors together. Specifically, you can create unions by combining selections and inverting a selection through negation. Both of these approaches are described in Table 3-7.

Table 3-7. *Flexibly Arranging Selectors*

Selector	Description
`<seclector>, <selector>`	Selects the union of elements matched by the first selector and the elements matched by the second selector
`:not(<selector>)`	Selects the elements that are not matched by the specified selector

Listing 3-10 shows how you can create unions and negations.

Listing 3-10. Using Selector Unions and Negation

```
<!DOCTYPE html>
<html>
<head>
    <title>Example</title>
    <style>
        h1, h2 { background-color: grey; color: white;}
        :not(html):not(body):not(:first-child) {border: medium double black;}
    </style>
</head>
<body>
    <h1 lang="en">New Delivery Service</h1>
    <h2 lang="en">Color and Beauty to Your Door</h2>
    <p>We are pleased to announce that we are starting a home delivery service for
    your flower needs. We will deliver within a 20 mile radius of the store
    for free and $1/mile thereafter.</p>
</body>
</html>
```

The first selector in this example is the union of the `h1` and `h2` selectors. As you might imagine, this matches all `h1` and `h2` elements in the document. The second selector is a little more esoteric. I wanted to demonstrate how you could use pseudo-selectors as modifiers to other pseudo-selectors, including negation:

```
:not(html):not(body):not(:first-child) {border: medium double black;}
```

This selector matches any element that is not an `html` element, that is not a body element, and that is not the first child of its parent. You can see how the styles in this example are applied in Figure 3-9.

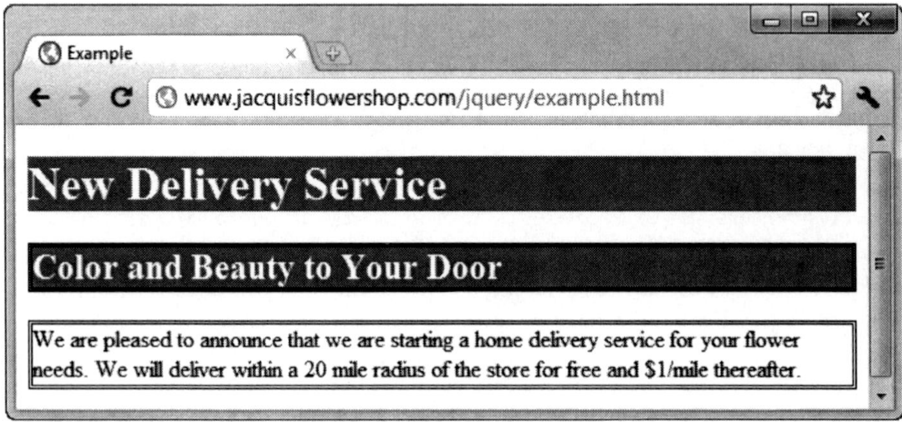

Figure 3-9. Creating selector unions and negations

Understanding Style Cascading

The key to understanding style sheets is to understand how they *cascade* and *inherit*. There can be multiple sources for CSS properties, and cascading and inheritance are the means by which the browser determines which values should be used when it displays an element. You have seen three different ways you can define styles (inline, embedded, and from an external style sheet), but you need to know about two other sources of styles: *browser styles* and *user styles*.

The *browser styles* (more properly known as the *user agent styles*) are the style conventions that a browser applies to an element if no other style has been specified. You saw an example of style conventions being used at the start of this chapter.

In addition, most browsers allow users to define their own style sheets. The styles that these style sheets contain are called *user styles*. This isn't a widely used feature, but those users who do define their own style sheets often attach great importance in being able to do so, not least because it provides a way of making pages more accessible.

Each browser has its own mechanism for user styles. Google Chrome on Windows, for example, creates a file in the user's profile directory called `Default\User StyleSheets\Custom.css`. Any styles added to this file are applied to *any* site that the user visits, subject to the cascading rules that I describe in the following section.

Understanding How Styles Cascade

Now that you have seen all of the sources of styles that a browser has to consider, you can look at the order in which the browser will look for a property value when it comes to display an element. The order is very specific:

1. Inline styles (styles that are defined using the `style` attribute on an element)
2. Embedded styles (styles that are defined in a `style` element)
3. External styles (styles that are imported using the `link` element)
4. User styles (styles that have been defined by the user)

5. Browser styles (the style conventions applied by the browser)

Imagine that the browser needs to display a p element. One of the things it needs to know is what color the text should be displayed in. To answer this question, it will need to find a value for the CSS color property. First, it will check to see whether the element it is trying to display has an inline style that defines a value for color, like this:

```
<p style="color: red">We are pleased to announce that we are starting a home delivery
    service for your flower needs. We will deliver within a 20 mile radius of the store
    for free and $1/mile thereafter.</p>
```

If there is no inline style, then the browser will look for a style element that contains a style that applies to the element, like this:

```
<style>
    p {color: red};
</style>
```

If there is no such style element, the browser looks at the style sheets that have been loaded via the link element, and so on, until either the browser finds a value for the color property, and that means using the value defined in the default browser styles if no other value is available.

■ **Tip** The first three sources of properties (inline styles, embedded styles, and style sheets) are collectively referred to as the *author styles*. The styles defined in the user style sheet are known as the *user styles*, and the styles defined by the browser are known as the *browser styles*.

Tweaking the Order with Important Styles

You can override the normal cascade order by marking your property values as *important*, as shown in Listing 3-11.

Listing 3-11. Marking Style Properties as Important

```
<!DOCTYPE html>
<html>
<head>
    <title>Example</title>
<style>
    p {color: black !important};
</style>
</head>
<body>
    <h1 lang="en">New Delivery Service</h1>
    <h2 lang="en">Color and Beauty to Your Door</h2>
    <p style="color: red">We are pleased to announce that we are starting a home delivery
    service for your flower needs. We will deliver within a 20 mile radius of the store
    for free and $1/mile thereafter.</p>
```

```
</body>
</html>
```

You mark individual values as important by appending `!important` to the declaration. The browser gives preference to important styles, irrespective of where they are defined. You can see the effect of property importance in Figure 3-10, where the embedded value for the `color` property overrides the inline value (this may be a little hard to make out on the printed page, but all of the text is black).

Figure 3-10. Important property values overriding inline property values

---

■ **Tip** The only thing that will take precedence over an important value that you define is an important value defined in the user style sheet. For regular values, the author styles are used before the user styles, but this is reversed when dealing with important values.

Tie-Breaking with Specificity and Order Assessments

You enter a tie-break situation if there are two styles that can applied to an element defined at the same cascade level and they both contain values for the CSS property that the browser is looking for. To decide which value to use, the browser assesses the *specificity* of each style and selects the one that is most specific. The browser determines the specificity of a style by counting three different characteristics:

- The number of `id` values in the style's selector
- The number of other attributes and pseudo-classes in the selector
- The number of element names and pseudo-elements in the selector

The browser combines the values from each assessment and applies the property value from the style that is most specific. You can see a very simple example of specificity in Listing 3-12.

Listing 3-12. Specificity in Styles

```
<!DOCTYPE html>
<html>
<head>
    <title>Example</title>
    <style>
        p {background-color: grey; color: white;}
        p.details {color:red;}
    </style>
</head>
<body>
    <h1 lang="en">New Delivery Service</h1>
    <h2 lang="en">Color and Beauty to Your Door</h2>
    <p class="details">We are pleased to announce that we are starting a home delivery
    service for your flower needs. We will deliver within a 20 mile radius of the store
    for free and $1/mile thereafter.</p>
</body>
</html>
```

When assessing specificity, you create a number in the form a-b-c, where each letter is the total from one of the three characteristics that are counted. This is not a three-digit number. A style is more specific if it's a value is the greatest. Only if the a values are equal does the browser compare b values. The style with the greater b value is more specific in this case. Only if both a and b values are the same does the browser consider the c value. This means that a specificity score of 1-0-0 is more specific than 0-5-5.

In this case, the selector p.details includes a class attribute, which means that the specificity of the style is 0-1-1 (0 id values + 1 other attributes + 1 element names). The other selector has a specificity of 0-0-1 (it contains no id values or other attributes and one element name).

When rendering a p element, the browser will look for a value for the color property. If the p element is a member of the details class, then the style with the p.details selector will be the most specific, and the value of red will be used. For all other p elements, the value white will be used. You can see how the browser selects and applies values for this example in Figure 3-11.

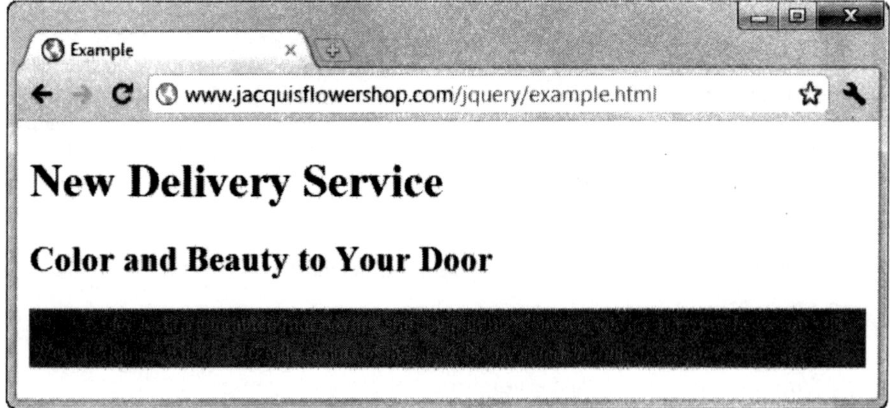

Figure 3-11. Applying values from styles based on specificity

When there are values defined in styles with the same specificity, then the browser selects the value it uses based on the order in which the values are defined. The one that is defined last is the one that will be used. Listing 3-13 shows a document that contains two equally specific styles.

Listing 3-13. Styles That Are Equally Specific

```
<!DOCTYPE html>
<html>
<head>
    <title>Example</title>
    <style>
        p.details {color:red;}
        p.information {color: blue;}
    </style>
</head>
<body>
    <h1 lang="en">New Delivery Service</h1>
    <h2 lang="en">Color and Beauty to Your Door</h2>
    <p class="details information">We are pleased to announce that we are starting a home
    Delivery service for your flower needs. We will deliver within a 20 mile radius of
    the store for free and $1/mile thereafter.</p>
</body>
</html>
```

Both styles defined in the `style` element have the same specificity score, and both apply to the `p` element. When the browser displays the `p` element in the page, it will select the `blue` property for the `color` property since that is the value defined in the latter style. You can see this in Figure 3-12.

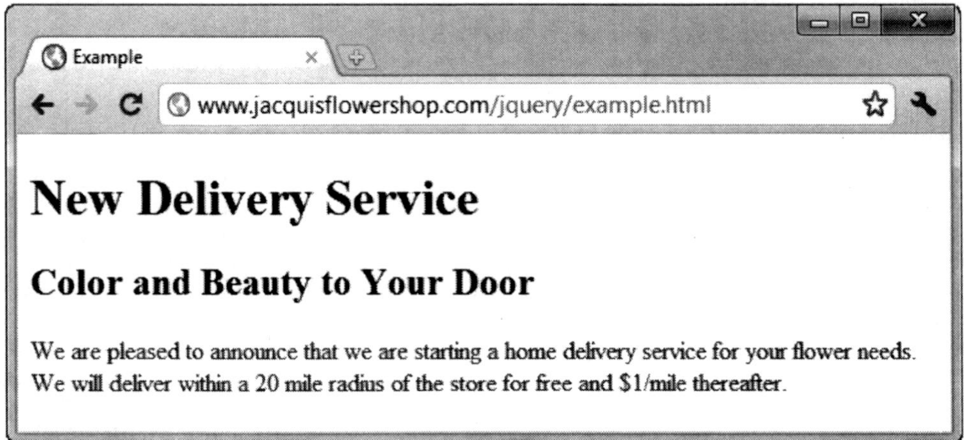

Figure 3-12. Selecting property values based on the order in which styles are defined

---

■ **Tip** These specificity rules are applied only to styles that are defined at the same cascade level. This means that a property defined in a `style` attribute will always take precedence over a style defined in a `style` element, for example.

Understanding CSS Units

Earlier in the chapter, I showed you the values that the browser uses by default for some CSS properties. These are the style convention for some of the elements in the examples, and I have duplicated this information in Table 3-8.

***Table 3-8.** Some CSS Properties and Their Values*

Property	h1	h2	p
`color`	`black`	`black`	`black`
`background-color`	`transparent`	`transparent`	`transparent`
`font-size`	`2em`	`1.5em`	`16px`
`border`	none	none	none

CSS defines a broad range of different unit types, and in the sections that follow I'll show you some of the more commonly used ones, including those that I will use in this book.

Working with CSS Colors

Colors used by a lot of the CSS properties, including the `color` and `background-color` properties I have been using in the examples in this chapter. The simplest way to specify a color is to use a predefined color name or to use a decimal or hexadecimal value for each of the red, green, and blue components. Decimal values are separated by a comma, and hex values are usually prefixed with `#`, such as `#ffffff`, which represents white. You can see some of the predefined names for colors and their decimal and hex equivalents in Table 3-9.

***Table 3-9.** Selected CSS Colors*

Color Name	Hex	Decimal	Color Name	Hex	Decimal
`black`	#000000	`0,0,0`	`green`	#008000	`0,128,0`
`silver`	#C0C0C0	`192,192,192`	`lime`	#00FF00	`0,255,0`
`grey`	#808080	`128,128,128`	`olive`	#808000	`128,128,0`

white	#FFFFFF	255,255,255	yellow	#FFFF00	255,255,0
maroon	#800000	128,0,0	navy	#000080	0,0,128
red	#FF0000	255,0,0	blue	#0000FF	0,0,255
purple	#800080	128,0,128	teal	#008080	0,128,128
fushia	#FF00FF	255,0,255	aqua	#00FFFF	0,255,255

These are known as the *basic* color names. CSS also defines the *extended colors*. There are too many to detail here, but you can find a complete list at `www.w3.org/TR/css3-color`. In addition to the basic colors, a lot of slight variations are available. As an example, Table 3-10 shows the extended set of gray shades that can be used.

Table 3-10. *Selected CSS Colors*

Color Name	Hex	Decimal
darkgrey	#a9a9a9	169,169,169
darkslategrey	#2f4f4f	47,79,79
dimgrey	#696969	105,105,105
grey	#808080	128,128,128
lightgrey	#d3d3d3	211,211,211
lightslategrey	#778899	119,136,153
slategrey	#708090	112,128,144

Specifying More Complex Colors

Color names and simple hex values aren't the only way you can specify colors. A number of functions allow you to select a color. Table 3-11 describes each of the functions available.

Table 3-11. *CSS Color Functions*

Function	Description	Example
`rgb(r, g, b)`	Specifies a color using the RGB model.	`color: rgb(112, 128, 144)`
`rgba(r, g, b, a)`	Specifies a color using the RGB model, with the addition of an alpha value to	`color: rgba(112, 128, 144, 0.4)`

	specify opacity. (A value of 0 is fully transparent; a value of 1 is fully opaque.)	
`hsl(h, s, l)`	Specifies a color using the hue, saturation, and lightness (HSL) model.	`color: hsl(120, 100%, 22%)`
`hsla(h, s, l, a)`	Like HSL, but with the addition of an alpha value to specify opacity.	`color: hsla(120, 100%, 22%, 0.4)`

You can use the `rgba` function to specify a color with transparency, but if you want a completely transparent element, then you can use the special color value `transparent`.

Understanding CSS Lengths

Many CSS properties require you to specify a *length*, such as the `font-size` property, which is used to specify the size of font used to render an element's content. When you specify a length, you concatenate the number of units and the unit identifier together, without any spaces or other characters between them. For example, a value of `20pt` for the `font-size` property means 20 of the units represented by the `pt` identifier (which are *points*, explained in a moment). CSS defines two kinds of length unit: those that are absolute and those that are relative to another property. I'll explain both in the sections that follow.

Working with Absolute Lengths

Absolute units are real-world measurements. CSS supports five types of absolute unit, which are described in Table 3-12.

Table 3-12. *CSS Absolute Units of Measurement*

Unit Identifier	Description
`in`	Inches
`cm`	Centimeters
`mm`	Millimeters
`pt`	Points (1 point is 1/72 of an inch)
`pc`	Picas (1 pica is 12 points)

You can mix and match units in a style and also mix absolute and relative units. Absolute units can be useful if you have some prior knowledge of how the content will be rendered, such as when designing for print. I find that I don't use the absolute units that much in my CSS styles. I find the relative units more flexible and easier to maintain, and I rarely create content that has to correspond to real-world measurements.

■ **Tip** You might be wondering where pixels are in the table of absolute units. In fact, CSS tries to make pixels a relative unit of measurement, although, sadly, the specification makes a very botched attempt at doing so. You can learn more in the "Working with Pixels" section.

Working with Relative Lengths

Relative lengths are more complex to specify and implement than absolute units and require tight and concise language to define their meaning unambiguously. A relative unit is measured in terms of some other unit. Unfortunately, the language in the CSS specifications isn't precise enough (a problem that has plagued CSS for years). This means CSS defines a wide range of interesting and useful relative measurements, but you can't use some of them because they don't have widespread or consistent browser support. Table 3-13 shows the relative units that CSS defines and that can be relied on in mainstream browsers.

***Table 3-13.** CSS Relativeunits of Measurement*

Unit Identifier	Description
`em`	Relative to the font size of the element
`ex`	Relative to `x-height` of the element's font
`rem`	Relative to the font size of the root element
`px`	A number of CSS pixels (assumed to be on a 96dpi display)
`%`	A percentage of the value of another property

When you use a relative unit, you are effectively specifying a multiple of another measurement. Listing 3-14 gives an example that sets a property relative to the `font-size`.

Listing 3-14. Using a Relative Unit

```
<!DOCTYPE html>
<html>
<head>
    <title>Example</title>
    <style>
        p.details {
            font-size: 15pt;
            height: 3em;
            border: thin solid black;
        }
    </style>
</head>
```

```
<body>
    <h1 lang="en">New Delivery Service</h1>
    <h2 lang="en">Color and Beauty to Your Door</h2>
    <p class="details information">We are pleased to announce that we are starting a home
    delivery service for your flower needs. We will deliver within a 20 mile radius of
    the store for free and $1/mile thereafter.</p>
</body>
</html>
```

In this example, I have specified the value of the `height` property (which sets the height of an element) to be `3em`, which means that `p` elements should be rendered so that the height of the element on the screen is three times the `font-size`. You can see how the browser displays these elements in Figure 3-13. I added a border (using the `border` property) so you can see the size of the element more readily.

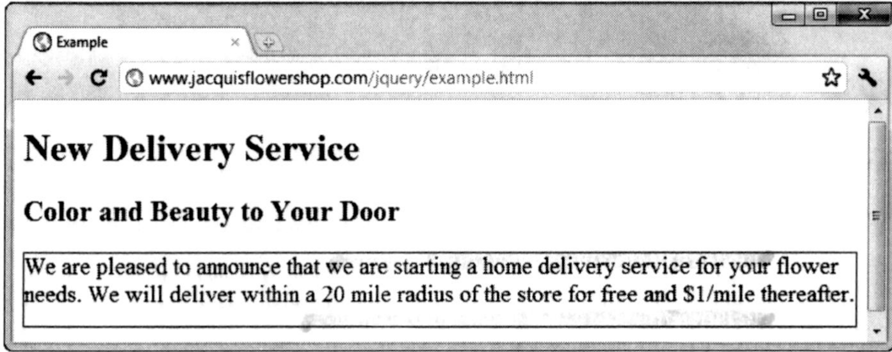

Figure 3-13. The effect of using relative measurements

Working with Pixels

Pixels in CSS are not what you might expect. The usual meaning of the term *pixel* refers to the smallest addressable unit on a display: one picture element. CSS tries to do something different and defines a pixel as follows:

The reference pixel is the visual angle of one pixel on a device with a pixel density of 96dpi and a distance from the reader of an arm's length.

This is the kind of vague definition that plagues CSS. I don't want to rant, but specifications that are dependent on the length of a user's arm are problematic. Fortunately, the mainstream browsers ignore the difference between pixels as defined by CSS and pixels in the display and treat 1 pixel to be 1/96th of an inch. (This is the standard Windows pixel density; browsers on platforms with displays that have a different pixel density usually implement a translation so that 1 pixel is still roughly 1/96th of an inch.)

■ **Tip** Although it isn't much use, you can read the full definition of a CSS pixel at `www.w3.org/TR/CSS21/syndata.html#length-units`.

The net effect of this is that although CSS pixels are intended to be a relative unit of measure, they are treated as an absolute unit by browsers. Listing 3-15 demonstrates specifying pixels in a CSS style.

Listing 3-15. Using Pixel Units in a Style

```
<!DOCTYPE html>
<html>
<head>
    <title>Example</title>
    <style>
        p.details {
            font-size: 20px;
            width: 400px;
            border: thin solid black;
        }
    </style>
</head>
<body>
    <h1 lang="en">New Delivery Service</h1>
    <h2 lang="en">Color and Beauty to Your Door</h2>
    <p class="details information">We are pleased to announce that we are starting a home
    delivery service for your flower needs. We will deliver within a 20 mile radius of
    the store for free and $1/mile thereafter.</p>
</body>
</html>
```

In this example, I have expressed both the `font-size` and `width` properties in pixels (the `width` property is the complement to the `height` property and sets the width of an element). You can see how the browser applies this style in Figure 3-14.

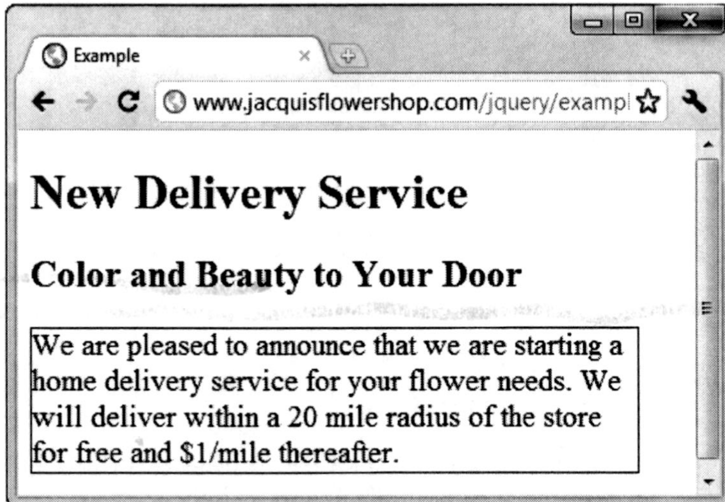

Figure 3-14. Specifying units in pixels

■ **Tip** Although I often use pixels as units in CSS, it tends to be a matter of habit. I find em units more flexible. This is because I have to alter the size of the font only when I need to make a change, and the rest of the style works seamlessly. It is important to remember that while CSS pixels were intended to be relative units, they are absolute units in practice and can be inflexible as a consequence.

Working with Percentages

You can express a unit of measurement as a percentage of another property value. You do this using the % (percent) unit, as demonstrated in Listing 3-16.

Listing 3-16. Expressing Units as a Percentage of Another Property Value

```
<!DOCTYPE html>
<html>
<head>
    <title>Example</title>
    <style>
        p.details {
            font-size: 200%;
            width: 50%;
            border: thin solid black;
        }
    </style>
</head>
<body>
    <h1 lang="en">New Delivery Service</h1>
    <h2 lang="en">Color and Beauty to Your Door</h2>
    <p class="details information">We are pleased to announce that we are starting a home
    delivery service for your flower needs. We will deliver within a 20 mile radius of
    the store for free and $1/mile thereafter.</p>
</body>
</html>
```

There are two complications in using percentages as units. The first is that not all properties can be expressed in this way, and the second is that each property that *can* be expressed as a percentage individually defines which *other* property the percentage refers to. For example, the font-size property uses the inherited font-size value from the parent element, and the width property uses the width of the containing element.

Using Shorthand Properties and Custom Values

Not all properties are set using units and colors. Some have special values that are unique to the kind of behavior they control. A good example of this is the border property, which I used in some of the examples to draw a border around elements. You set the border property using three values, like this:

```
border: thin solid black;
```

The first value is the thickness of the border, the second value is the style of the border, and the final value is the color of the border. Table 3-14 shows the values you can use to specify the thickness of the border.

Table 3-14. *Values for the Border Width*

Value	Description
<length>	A length expressed in CSS measurement units such as `em`, `px`, or `cm`
<perc>%	Percent of the *width* of the area around which the border will be drawn

`thin`
`medium`
`thick`
	Preset widths, the meanings of which are defined by each browser, but which are progressively thicker

Table 3-15 shows the values you can use for the style of the border.

Table 3-15. *Values for the Border Style*

Value	Description
`none`	No border will be drawn.
`dashed`	The border will be a series of rectangular dashes.
`dotted`	The border will be a series of circular dots.
`double`	The border will be two parallel lines with a gap between them.
`groove`	The border will appear to have been sunken into the page.
`inset`	The border will be such that the content looks sunken into the page.
`outset`	The border will be such that the content looks raised from the page.
`ridge`	The border will appear raised from the page.
`solid`	The border will be a single, unbroken line.

By combining values from these tables with a color, you can achieve a wide range of border effects. You can see the range of styles displayed in the browser in Figure 3-15.

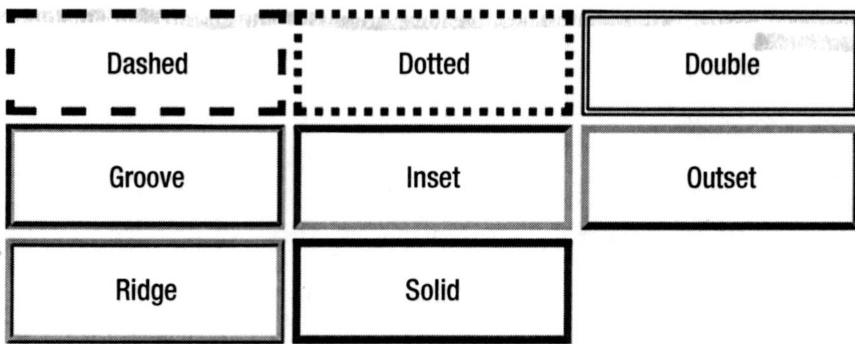

Figure 3-15. The border styles

The border property is also a good example of a *shorthand property*. These properties allow you to set the value of several related properties in a single declaration. This means a border such as the one shown earlier is equivalent to the 12 declarations shown in Listing 3-17.

Listing 3-17. The Individual Border Properties

```
border-top-color: black;
border-top-style: solid;
border-top-width: thin;
border-bottom-color: black;
border-bottom-style: solid;
border-bottom-width: thin;
border-left-color: black;
border-left-style: solid;
border-left-width: thin;
border-right-color: black;
border-right-style: solid;
border-right-width: thin;
```

CSS allows you to dig into the details and set individual properties for fine control or to use the shorthand properties when all of the related values are the same.

Summary

In this chapter, I gave you a brief overview of CSS, showing you how to set properties using the style attribute, how to use the style element (including the wide range of selectors that are available), and how the browsers use cascading and specificity to work out which property values should be applied to elements when they are displayed. I finished with a tour of the CSS units, custom values, and shorthand properties. You can express values for properties in a number of different ways, which adds flexibility (and a little confusion) to CSS styles.

CHAPTER 4

JavaScript Primer

jQuery is a JavaScript library that you add to your HTML documents. On its own, the jQuery library doesn't do anything. You take advantage of the jQuery functionality from your own scripts that you add alongside the jQuery library. In this chapter, I provide a primer for the JavaScript language, focusing on the features that are most pertinent when working with jQuery.

JavaScript has had a difficult life and was rushed through standardization before it had a chance to mature properly. This has resulted in a language that can be very pleasant to work with but that has some odd behavioral and syntactical quirks.

Tip To get the best from this book, you will need some experience of programming and an understanding of concepts such as variables, functions, and objects. If you are new to programming, a good starting point is a series of articles posted on the popular Lifehacker.com. No programming knowledge is assumed, and all of the examples are conveniently in JavaScript. The guide is available here: `http://lifehacker.com/5744113/learn-to-code-the-full-beginners-guide`.

Getting Ready to Use JavaScript

You can define scripts in an HTML document in a couple of different ways. You can define an *inline script,* where the content of the script is part of the HTML document. You can also define an *external script,* where the JavaScript is contained in a separate file and referenced via a URL (which is how you access the jQuery library, as you'll see in Chapter 5). Both of these approaches rely on the `script` element. In this chapter, I will be using inline scripts. You can see a simple example in Listing 4-1.

Listing 4-1. A Simple Inline Script

```
<!DOCTYPE HTML>
<html>
<head>
    <title>Example</title>
    <script type="text/javascript">
        console.log("Hello");
    </script>
```

```
</head>
<body>
    This is a simple example
</body>
</html>
```

This is a trivially simple script that writes a message to the *console*. The console is a basic (but useful) tool that the browser provides that lets you display debugging information as your script is executed. Each browser has a different way of showing the console. For Google Chrome, you must select the "JavaScript console" item from the Tools menu. You can see how the console is displayed in Chrome in Figure 4-1; the other browsers have very similar features.

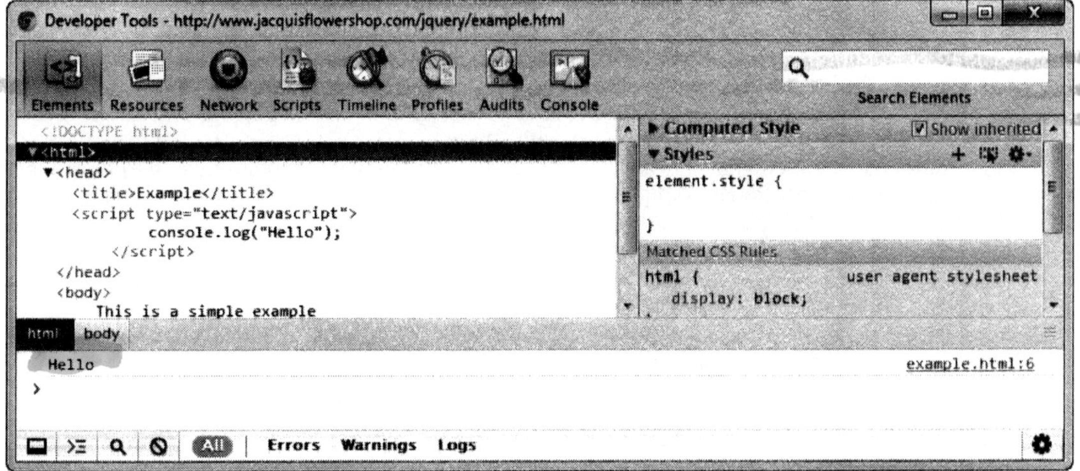

Figure 4-1. The Google Chrome JavaScript console

You can see that the output from calling the `console.log` method is displayed in the console window, along with the details of where the message originated (in this case on line 7 of the `example.html` file). In this chapter, I won't show screenshots; I'll show just the results from some of the examples. So, for example, for Listing 4-1, the output is as follows:

```
Hello
```

I have formatted some of the results to make them easier to read. In the sections that follow, I'll show you the core features of the JavaScript language. If you have had any experience programming in any other modern language, you will find the JavaScript syntax and style familiar.

Using Statements

The basic JavaScript building block is the *statement*. Each statement represents a single command, and statements are usually terminated by a semicolon (`;`). In fact, the semicolon is optional, but using them makes your code easier to read and allows for multiple statements on a single line. Listing 4-2 shows a couple of statements in a script, which is defined in the document using a `script` element.

Listing 4-2. Using JavaScript Statements

```
<!DOCTYPE HTML>
<html>
    <head>
        <title>Example</title>
    </head>
    <body>
        <script type="text/javascript">
            console.log("This is a statement");
            console.log("This is also a statement");
        </script>
    </body>
</html>
```

The browser executes each statement in turn. In this example, I simply write out a pair of messages to the console. The results are as follows:

```
This is a statement

This is also a statement
```

Defining and Using Functions

If you define statements directly in the script element, as I did in Listing 4-2, then the browser will execute those statements as soon as it reaches them as the document is loaded. As an alternative, you can package multiple statements into a *function*, which won't be executed until the browser encounters a statement that invokes the function, as shown in Listing 4-3.

Listing 4-3. Defining a JavaScript Function

```
<!DOCTYPE HTML>
<html>
<head>
    <title>Example</title>
    <script type="text/javascript">
        function myFunc() {
            console.log("This is a statement");
        };

        myFunc();
    </script>
</head>
<body>
    This is a simple example
</body>
</html>
```

The statements contained by a function are encompassed by braces ({ and }) and are referred to as the *code block*. This listing defines a function called myFunc, which contains a single statement in the code block. JavaScript is a case-sensitive language, which means that the keyword function must be lowercase. The statement in the function won't be executed until the browser reaches another statement that calls the myFunc function, like this:

```
myFunc();
```

This example isn't especially useful because the function is invoked immediately after it has been defined. You will see some examples where functions are much more useful when you look at events in Chapter 9.

Defining Functions with Parameters

In common with most programming languages, JavaScript allows you to define parameters for functions, as shown in Listing 4-4.

Listing 4-4. Defining Functions with Parameters

```
<!DOCTYPE HTML>
<html>
<head>
    <title>Example</title>
    <script type="text/javascript">
        function myFunc(name, weather) {
            console.log("Hello " + name + ".");
            console.log("It is " + weather + " today");
        };

        myFunc("Adam", "sunny");
    </script>
</head>
<body>
    This is a simple example
</body>
</html>
```

In this listing, I have added two parameters to the myFunc function. They are called name and weather. JavaScript is a loosely typed language, which means you don't have to declare the data type of the parameters when you define the function. I'll come back to loose typing later in the chapter when I cover JavaScript variables. To invoke a function with parameters, you provide values as argument when you invoke the function, like this:

```
myFunc("Adam", "sunny");
```

The results from this listing are as follows:

```
Hello Adam.

It is sunny today
```

The number of arguments when you invoke a function doesn't need to match the number of parameters in the function. If you call the function with fewer arguments than it has parameters, then the value of any parameters you have not supplied values for is undefined. If you call the function with more arguments than there are parameters, then the additional arguments are simply ignored.

The consequence of this is that you can't create two functions with the same name and different parameters and expect JavaScript to differentiate between them based on the arguments you provide when invoking the function. This is called *polymorphism*, and although it is supported in languages such as Java and C#, it isn't available in JavaScript. Instead, if you define two functions with the same name, then the second definition replaces the first.

Defining Functions That Return Results

You can return results from functions using the `return` keyword. Listing 4-5 shows a function that returns a result.

Listing 4-5. Returning a Result from a Function

```
<!DOCTYPE HTML>
<html>
<head>
    <title>Example</title>
    <script type="text/javascript">
        function myFunc(name) {
            return ("Hello " + name + ".");
        };

        console.log(myFunc("Adam"));
    </script>
</head>
<body>
    This is a simple example
</body>
</html>
```

This function defines one parameter and uses it to generate a simple result. I invoke the function and pass the result as the argument to the `console.log` function, like this:

```
console.log(myFunc("Adam"));
```

Notice that you don't have to declare that the function will return a result or denote the data type of the result. The result from this listing is as follows:

```
Hello Adam.
```

Using Variables and Types

You define variables using the `var` keyword and can optionally assign a value to the variable in a single statement. Variables that are defined in a function are *local variables* and are available for use only within that function. Variables that are defined directly in the `script` element are *global variables* and can be accessed anywhere, including other scripts. Listing 4-6 demonstrates the use of local and global variables.

Listing 4-6. Using Local and Global Variables

```
<!DOCTYPE HTML>
<html>
    <head>
        <title>Example</title>
    </head>
    <body>
        <script type="text/javascript">
            var myGlobalVar = "apples";

            function myFunc(name) {
                var myLocalVar = "sunny";
                return ("Hello " + name + ". Today is " + myLocalVar + ".");
            };
            document.writeln(myFunc("Adam"));
        </script>
        <script type="text/javascript">
            document.writeln("I like " + myGlobalVar);
        </script>
    </body>
</html>
```

Again, JavaScript is a loosely typed language. This doesn't mean JavaScript doesn't have types. It just means you don't have to explicitly declare the type of a variable and that you can assign different types to the same variable without any difficulty. JavaScript will determine the type based on the value you assign to a variable and will freely convert between types based on the context in which they are used. The result from Listing 4-6 is as follows:

```
Hello Adam. Today is sunny.

I like apples
```

Using the Primitive Types

JavaScript defines a small set of primitive types. These are `string`, `number`, and `boolean`. This may seem like a short list, but JavaScript manages to fit a lot of flexibility into these three types.

Working with Strings

You define `string` values using either the double quote or single quote characters, as shown in Listing 4-7.

Listing 4-7. Defining String Variables

```
<!DOCTYPE HTML>
<html>
<head>
    <title>Example</title>
    <script type="text/javascript">
        var firstString = "This is a string";
        var secondString = 'And so is this';
    </script>
</head>
<body>
    This is a simple example
</body>
</html>
```

The quote characters that you use must match. You can't start a string with a single quote and finish with a double quote, for example.

Working with Booleans

The boolean type has two values: `true` and `false`. Listing 4-8 shows both values being used, but this type is most useful when used in conditional statements, such as an `if` statement.

Listing 4-8. Defining boolean Values

```
<!DOCTYPE HTML>
<html>
<head>
    <title>Example</title>
    <script type="text/javascript">
        var firstBool = true;
        var secondBool = false;
    </script>
</head>
<body>
    This is a simple example
</body>
</html>
```

Working with Numbers

The `number` type is used to represent both *integer* and *Floating-point* numbers (also known as *real numbers*). Listing 4-9 provides a demonstration.

Listing 4-9. Defining number Values

```
<!DOCTYPE HTML>
<html>
<head>
    <title>Example</title>
    <script type="text/javascript">
        var daysInWeek = 7;
        var pi = 3.14;
        var hexValue = 0xFFFF;
    </script>
</head>
<body>
    This is a simple example
</body>
</html>
```

You don't have to specify which kind of number you are using. You just express the value you require, and JavaScript will act accordingly. In the listing, I have defined an integer value, defined a floating-point value, and prefixed a value with `0x` to denote a hexadecimal value.

Creating Objects

JavaScript supports the notion of objects, and there are different ways in which you can create them. Listing 4-10 gives a simple example.

Listing 4-10. Creating an Object

```
<!DOCTYPE HTML>
<html>
<head>
    <title>Example</title>
    <script type="text/javascript">
        var myData = new Object();
        myData.name = "Adam";
        myData.weather = "sunny";

        console.log("Hello " + myData.name + ". ");
        console.log("Today is " + myData.weather + ".");
    </script>
</head>
<body>
    This is a simple example
</body>
</html>
```

I create an object by calling `new Object()`, and I assign the result (the newly created object) to a variable called `myData`. Once the object is created, I can define properties on the object just by assigning values, like this:

```
myData.name = "Adam";
```

Prior to this statement, my object doesn't have a property called name. After the statement has executed, the property does exist, and it has been assigned the value Adam. You can read the value of a property by combining the variable name and the property name with a period, like this:

```
console.log("Hello " + myData.name + ". ");
```

Using Object Literals

You can define an object and its properties in one step using the *object literal* format. Listing 4-11 shows how this is done.

Listing 4-11. Using the Object Literal Format

```
<!DOCTYPE HTML>
<html>
<head>
    <title>Example</title>
    <script type="text/javascript">
        var myData = {
            name: "Adam",
            weather: "sunny"
        };

        console.log("Hello " + myData.name + ". ");
        console.log("Today is " + myData.weather + ".");
    </script>
</head>
<body>
    This is a simple example
</body>
</html>
```

Each property that you want to define is separated from its value using a colon (:), and properties are separated using a comma (,).

Using Functions as Methods

One of the features that I like most about JavaScript is the way that you can add functions to your objects. A function defined on an object is called a *method*. I don't know why, but I find this elegant and endlessly pleasing. Listing 4-12 shows how you can add methods in this manner.

Listing 4-12. Adding Methods to an Object

```
<!DOCTYPE HTML>
<html>
<head>
    <title>Example</title>
    <script type="text/javascript">
        var myData = {
            name: "Adam",
```

```
            weather: "sunny",
            printMessages: function() {
                console.log("Hello " + this.name + ". ");
                console.log("Today is " + this.weather + ".");
            }
        };
        myData.printMessages();
    </script>
</head>
<body>
    This is a simple example
</body>
</html>
```

In this example, I have used a function to create a method called `printMessages`. Notice that to refer to the properties defined by the object, I have to use the `this` keyword. When a function is used as a method, the function is implicitly passed the object on which the method has been called as an argument through the special variable `this`. The output from the listing is as follows:

```
Hello Adam.

Today is sunny.
```

Working with Objects

Once you have created objects, you can do a number of things with them. In the following sections, I'll describe the activities that will be useful later in this book.

Read and Modify the Property Values

The most obvious thing to do with an object is to read or modify the values assigned to the properties that the object defines. There are two different syntax styles you can use, both of which are shown in Listing 4-13.

Listing 4-13. Reading and Modifying Object Properties

```
<!DOCTYPE HTML>
<html>
<head>
    <title>Example</title>
    <script type="text/javascript">
        var myData = {
            name: "Adam",
            weather: "sunny",
        };

        myData.name = "Joe";
        myData["weather"] = "raining";
```

```
        console.log("Hello " + myData.name + ".");
        console.log("It is " + myData["weather"]);
    </script>
</head>
<body>
    This is a simple example
</body>
</html>
```

The first style is the one that most programmers with be familiar with and that I used in earlier examples. You concatenate the object name and the property name together with a period, like this:

```
myData.name = "Joe";
```

You can assign a new value to the property by using the equals sign (=) or read the current value by omitting it. The second style is an array-style index, like this:

```
myData["weather"] = "raining";
```

In this style, you specify the name of the property you want between square braces ([and]). This can be a very convenient way to access a property because you can pass the property you are interested in using a variable, like this:

```
var myData = {
    name: "Adam",
    weather: "sunny",
};

var propName = "weather";
myData[propName] = "raining";
```

This is the basis for how you enumerate the properties of an object, which I describe next.

Enumerating an Object's Properties

You enumerate the properties that an object has using the for...in statement. Listing 4-14 shows how you can use this statement.

Listing 4-14. Enumerating an Object's Properties

```
<!DOCTYPE HTML>
<html>
<head>
    <title>Example</title>
    <script type="text/javascript">
        var myData = {
            name: "Adam",
            weather: "sunny",
            printMessages: function() {
                console.log("Hello " + this.name + ". ");
                console.log("Today is " + this.weather + ".");
            }
        };
```

```
        for (var prop in myData) {
            console.log("Name: " + prop + " Value: " + myData[prop]);
        }

    </script>
</head>
<body>
    This is a simple example
</body>
</html>
```

The `for...in` loop performs the statement in the code block for each property in the `myData` object. The `prop` variable is assigned the name of the property being processed in each iteration. I use the array-index style to retrieve the value of the property from the object. The output from this listing is as follows (I have formatted the results to make them easier to read):

```
Name: name Value: Adam
Name: weather Value: sunny
Name: printMessages Value: function () {
    console.log("Hello " + this.name + ". ");
    console.log("Today is " + this.weather + ".");
}
```

From the result, you can see that the function I defined as a method is also enumerated. This is as a result of the flexible way that JavaScript handles functions.

Adding and Deleting Properties and Methods

You are still able to define new properties for an object, even when you have used the object literal style. Listing 4-15 gives a demonstration.

Listing 4-15. Adding a New Property to an Object

```
<!DOCTYPE HTML>
<html>
<head>
    <title>Example</title>
    <script type="text/javascript">
        var myData = {
            name: "Adam",
            weather: "sunny",
        };

        myData.dayOfWeek = "Monday";
    </script>
</head>
<body>
```

```
    This is a simple example
</body>
</html>
```

In this listing, I have added a new property to the object called dayOfWeek. I have used the dot notation (concatenating the object and property names with a period), but I could as readily used the index-style notation.

As you might expect by now, you can also add new methods to an object by setting the value of a property to be a function, as shown in Listing 4-16.

Listing 4-16. Adding a New Method to an Object

```
<!DOCTYPE HTML>
<html>
<head>
    <title>Example</title>
    <script type="text/javascript">
        var myData = {
            name: "Adam",
            weather: "sunny",
        };

        myData.SayHello = function() {
          console.write("Hello");
        };
    </script>
</head>
<body>
    This is a simple example
</body>
</html>
```

You can delete a property or method from an object using the delete keyword, as shown in Listing 4-17.

Listing 4-17. Deleting a Property from an Object

```
<!DOCTYPE HTML>
<html>
<head>
    <title>Example</title>
    <script type="text/javascript">
        var myData = {
            name: "Adam",
            weather: "sunny",
        };

        delete myData.name;
        delete myData["weather"];
        delete myData.SayHello;
    </script>
</head>
```

```
<body>
    This is a simple example
</body>
</html>
```

Determine Whether an Object Has a Property

You can check to see whether an object has a property using the in expression, as shown in Listing 4-18.

Listing 4-18. Checking to See Whether an Object Has a Property

```
<!DOCTYPE HTML>
<html>
<head>
    <title>Example</title>
    <script type="text/javascript">
        var myData = {
            name: "Adam",
            weather: "sunny",
        };

        var hasName = "name" in myData;
        var hasDate = "date" in myData;

        console.log("HasName: " + hasName);
        console.log("HasDate: " + hasDate);
    </script>
</head>
<body>
    This is a simple example
</body>
</html>
```

In this example, I test for a property that exists and one that doesn't. The value of the hasName variable will be true, and the value of the hasDate property will be false.

Using JavaScript Operators

JavaScript defines a largely standard set of operators. I've summarized the most useful in Table 4-1.

Table 4-1. *Useful JavaScript Operators*

Operator	Description
++, --	Pre- or post-increment and decrement
+, -, *, /, %	Addition, subtraction, multiplication, division, remainder
<, <=, >, >=	Less than, less than or equal to, more than, more than or equal to

==, !=	Equality and inequality tests
===, !==	Identity and nonidentity tests
&&, ||	Logical AND and OR
=	Assignment
+	String concatenation
?:	Three operand conditional statement

Using Conditional Statements

Many of the JavaScript operators are used in conjunction with conditional statements. In this book, I tend to use the if/else and switch statements. Listing 4-19 shows the use of both (which will be familiar if you have worked with pretty much any programming language).

Listing 4-19. Using the if/else and switch Conditional Statements

```
<!DOCTYPE HTML>
<html>
<head>
    <title>Example</title>
    <script type="text/javascript">

        var name = "Adam";

        if (name == "Adam") {
            console.log("Name is Adam");
        } else if (name == "Jacqui") {
            console.log("Name is Jacqui");
        } else {
            console.log("Name is neither Adam or Jacqui");
        }

        switch (name) {
            case "Adam":
                console.log("Name is Adam");
                break;
            case "Jacqui":
                console.log("Name is Jacqui");
                break;
            default:
                console.log("Name is neither Adam or Jacqui");
                break;
        }
    </script>
```

```
</head>
<body>
    This is a simple example
</body>
</html>
```

The Equality Operator vs. the Identity Operator

The equality and identity operators are of particular note. The equality operator will attempt to coerce operands to the same type in order to assess equality. This is a handy feature, as long as you are aware it is happening. Listing 4-20 shows the equality operator in action.

Listing 4-20. Using the Equality Operator

```
<!DOCTYPE HTML>
<html>
<head>
    <title>Example</title>
    <script type="text/javascript">

        var firstVal = 5;
        var secondVal = "5";

        if (firstVal == secondVal) {
            console.log("They are the same");
        } else {
            console.log("They are NOT the same");
        }
    </script>
</head>
<body>
    This is a simple example
</body>
</html>
```

The output from this script is as follows:

```
They are the same
```

JavaScript is converting the two operands into the same type and comparing them. In essence, the equality operator tests that values are the same irrespective of their type. If you want to test to ensure that the values *and* the types are the same, then you need to use the identity operator (===, three equals signs, rather than the two of the equality operator), as shown in Listing 4-21.

Listing 4-21. Using the Identity Operator

```
<!DOCTYPE HTML>
<html>
<head>
    <title>Example</title>
    <script type="text/javascript">

        var firstVal = 5;
        var secondVal = "5";

        if (firstVal === secondVal) {
            console.log("They are the same");
        } else {
            console.log("They are NOT the same");
        }
    </script>
</head>
<body>
    This is a simple example
</body>
</html>
```

In this example, the identity operator will consider the two variables to be different. This operator doesn't coerce types. The result from this script is as follows:

```
They are NOT the same
```

JavaScript primitives are compared by value, but JavaScript objects are compared by reference. Listing 4-22 shows how JavaScript handles equality and identity tests for objects.

Listing 4-22. Performing Equality and Identity Tests on Objects

```
<!DOCTYPE HTML>
<html>
<head>
    <title>Example</title>
    <script type="text/javascript">

        var myData1 = {
            name: "Adam",
            weather: "sunny",
        };

        var myData2 = {
            name: "Adam",
            weather: "sunny",
        };
```

```
        var myData3 = myData2;

        var test1 = myData1 == myData2;
        var test2 = myData2 == myData3;
        var test3 = myData1 === myData2;
        var test4 = myData2 === myData3;

        console.log("Test 1: " + test1 + " Test 2: " + test2);
        console.log("Test 3: " + test3 + " Test 4: " + test4);
    </script>

</head>
<body>
    This is a simple example
</body>
</html>
```

The results from this script are as follows:

```
Test 1: false Test 2: true
Test 3: false Test 4: true
```

Listing 4-23 shows the same tests performed on primitives.

Listing 4-23. Performing Equality and Identity Tests on Objects

```
<!DOCTYPE HTML>
<html>
<head>
    <title>Example</title>
    <script type="text/javascript">

        var myData1 = 5;
        var myData2 = "5";
        var myData3 = myData2;

        var test1 = myData1 == myData2;
        var test2 = myData2 == myData3;
        var test3 = myData1 === myData2;
        var test4 = myData2 === myData3;

        console.log("Test 1: " + test1 + " Test 2: " + test2);
        console.log("Test 3: " + test3 + " Test 4: " + test4);
    </script>

</head>
<body>
    This is a simple example
</body>
</html>
```

The results from this script are as follows:

```
Test 1: true Test 2: true
Test 3: false Test 4: true
```

Explicitly Converting Types

The string concatenation operator (+) has a higher precedence than the addition operator (also +), which means that when it can, JavaScript will concatenate variables in preference to adding them. This can cause confusion because JavaScript will also convert types freely to produce a result and isn't always the result that is expected, as shown in Listing 4-24.

Listing 4-24. String Concatentation Operator Precedence

```
<!DOCTYPE HTML>
<html>
<head>
    <title>Example</title>
    <script type="text/javascript">

        var myData1 = 5 + 5;
        var myData2 = 5 + "5";

        console.log("Result 1: " + myData1);
        console.log("Result 2: " + myData2);

    </script>
</head>
<body>
    This is a simple example
</body>
</html>
```

The result from this script is as follows:

```
Result 1: 10
Result 2: 55
```

The second result is the kind that causes confusion. What might be intended to be an addition operation is interpreted as string concatenation through a combination of operator precedence and over-eager type conversion. To avoid this, you can explicitly convert the types of values to ensure you perform the right kind of operation.

Converting Numbers to Strings

If you are working with multiple number variables and want to concatenate them as strings, then you can convert the numbers to strings with the `toString` method, as shown in Listing 4-25.

Listing 4-25. Using the number.toString Method

```
<!DOCTYPE HTML>
<html>
<head>
    <title>Example</title>
    <script type="text/javascript">
        var myData1 = (5).toString() + String(5);
        console.log("Result: " + myData1);
    </script>
</head>
<body>
    This is a simple example
</body>
</html>
```

Notice that I have placed the numeric value in parentheses, and then I called the toString method. This is because you have to allow JavaScript to convert the literal value into a number before you can call the methods that the number type defines. I have also shown an alternative approach to achieve the same effect, which is to call the String function and pass in the numeric value as an argument. Both of these techniques have the same effect, which is to convert a number to a string, meaning that the + operator is used for string concatenation and not addition. The output from this script is as follows:

```
Result: 55
```

There are some other methods that allow you to exert more control over how a number is represented as a string. I have briefly described these in Table 4-2. All of the methods shown in the table are defined by the number type.

***Table 4-2.** Useful Number to String Methods*

Method	Description	Returns
toString()	Represents a number in base 10	string
toString(2) toString(8) toString(16)	Represent a number in binary, octal, or hexadecimal notation	string
toFixed(n)	Represents a real number with the n digits after the decimal point	string
toExponential(n)	Represents a number using exponential notation with one digit before the decimal point and n digits after	string
toPrecision(n)	Represents a number with n significant digits, using exponential notation if required	string

Converting Strings to Numbers

The opposite problem is to convert strings to numbers so that you can perform addition rather than concatenation. You can do this with the `Number` function, as shown in Listing 4-26.

Listing 4-26. Converting Strings to Numbers

```
<!DOCTYPE HTML>
<html>
<head>
    <title>Example</title>
    <script type="text/javascript">

        var firstVal = "5";
        var secondVal = "5";

        var result = Number(firstVal) + Number(secondVal);

        console.log("Result: " + result);
    </script>
</head>
<body>
    This is a simple example
</body>
</html>
```

The output from this script is as follows:

```
Result: 10
```

The `Number` method is quite strict in the way that is parses string values, but there are two other functions you can use that are more flexible and will ignore trailing non-number characters. These functions are `parseInt` and `parseFloat`. I have described all three methods in Table 4-3.

***Table 4-3.** Useful String to Number Methods*

Method	Description
`Number(str)`	Parses the specified string to create an integer or real value
`parseInt(str)`	Parses the specified string to create an integer value
`parseFloat(str)`	Parses the specified string to create an integer or real value

Working with Arrays

JavaScript arrays work pretty much like arrays in most other programming languages. Listing 4-27 shows how you can create and populate an array.

Listing 4-27. Creating and Populating an Array

```
<!DOCTYPE HTML>
<html>
<head>
    <title>Example</title>
    <script type="text/javascript">

        var myArray = new Array();
        myArray[0] = 100;
        myArray[1] = "Adam";
        myArray[2] = true;

    </script>
</head>
<body>
    This is a simple example
</body>
</html>
```

I have created a new array by calling `new Array()`. This creates an empty array, which I assign to the variable `myArray`. In the subsequent statements, I assign values to various index positions in the array.

There are a couple of things to note in this example. First, I didn't need to declare the number of items in the array when I created it. JavaScript arrays will resize themselves to hold any number of items. The second point of note is that I didn't have to declare the data types that the array will hold. Any JavaScript array can hold any mix of data types. In the example, I have assigned three items to the array: a `number`, a `string`, and a `boolean`.

Using an Array Literal

The array literal style lets you create and populate an array in a single statement, as shown in Listing 4-28.

Listing 4-28. Using the Array Literal Style

```
<!DOCTYPE HTML>
<html>
<head>
    <title>Example</title>
    <script type="text/javascript">

        var myArray = [100, "Adam", true];

    </script>
</head>
<body>
    This is a simple example
</body>
</html>
```

In this example, I specified that the myArray variable should be assigned a new array by specifying the items I wanted in the array between square brackets ([and]).

Reading and Modifying the Contents of an Array

You read the value at a given index using square braces ([and]), placing the index you require between the braces, as shown in Listing 4-29.

Listing 4-29. Reading the Data from an Array Index

```
<!DOCTYPE HTML>
<html>
<head>
    <title>Example</title>
    <script type="text/javascript">
        var myArray = [100, "Adam", true];
        console.log("Index 0: " + myArray[0]);
    </script>
</head>
<body>
    This is a simple example
</body>
</html>
```

You can modify the data held in any position in a JavaScript array simply by assigning a new value to the index. Just as with regular variables, you can switch the data type at an index without any problems. Listing 4-30 demonstrates modifying the contents of an array.

Listing 4-30. Modifying the Contents of an Array

```
<!DOCTYPE HTML>
<html>
<head>
    <title>Example</title>
    <script type="text/javascript">
        var myArray = [100, "Adam", true];
        myArray[0] = "Tuesday";
        console.log("Index 0: " + myArray[0]);
    </script>
</head>
<body>
    This is a simple example
</body>
</html>
```

In this example, I have assigned a string to position 0 in the array, a position that was previously held by a number.

Enumerating the Contents of an Array

You enumerate the content of an array using a `for` loop. Listing 4-31 shows how to apply the loop to display the contents of a simple array.

Listing 4-31. Enumerating the Contents of an Array

```
<!DOCTYPE HTML>
<html>
<head>
    <title>Example</title>
    <script type="text/javascript">
        var myArray = [100, "Adam", true];
        for (var i = 0; i < myArray.length; i++) {
            console.log("Index " + i + ": " + myArray[i]);
        }
    </script>
</head>
<body>
    This is a simple example
</body>
</html>
```

The JavaScript loop works just the same way as loops in many other languages. You determine how many elements there are in the array by using the `length` property. The output from the listing is as follows:

```
Index 0: 100 Index 1: Adam Index 2: true
```

Using the Built-in Array Methods

The JavaScript `Array` object defines a number of methods that you can use to work with arrays. Table 4-4 describes the most useful of these methods.

***Table 4-4.** Useful Array Methods*

Method	Description	Returns
`concat(otherArray)`	Concatenates the contents of the array with the array specified by the argument. Multiple arrays can be specified.	`Array`
`join(separator)`	Joins all of the elements in the array to form a string. The argument specifies the character used to delimit the items.	`string`
`pop()`	Treats an array like a stack and removes and returns the last item in the array.	`object`

push(item)	Treats an array like a stack and appends the specified item to the array.	void
reverse()	Reverses the order of the items in the array.	Array
shift()	Like pop, but operates on the first element in the array.	object
slice(start,end)	Returns a subarray.	Array
sort()	Sorts the items in the array.	Array
unshift(item)	Like push, but inserts the new element at the start of the array.	void

Handling Errors

JavaScript uses the try...catch statement to deal with errors. For the most part, you won't be worrying about errors in this book because my focus is on explaining the features of jQuery and not general programming technique. Listing 4-32 shows how to use this kind of statement.

Listing 4-32. Handling an Exception

```
<!DOCTYPE HTML>
<html>
<head>
    <title>Example</title>
    <script type="text/javascript">
        try {
            var myArray;
            for (var i = 0; i < myArray.length; i++) {
                console.log("Index " + i + ": " + myArray[i]);
            }
        } catch (e) {
            console.log("Error: " + e);
        }
    </script>
</head>
<body>
    This is a simple example
</body>
</html>
```

The problem in this script is a common one. I am trying to use a variable that has not been initialized properly. I have wrapped the code that I suspect will cause an error in the try clause of the statement. If no problems arise, then the statements execute normally, and the catch clause is ignored.

However, if there is an error, then execution of the statements in the try clause stops immediately, and control passes to the catch clause. The error that you have encountered is described by an Error object, which is passed to the catch clause. Table 4-5 shows the properties defined by the Error object.

Table 4-5. The Error Object

Property	Description	Returns
message	A description of the error condition.	string
name	The name of the error. This is Error, by default.	string
number	The error number, if any, for this kind of error.	number

The catch clause is your opportunity to recover from or clear up after the error. If there are statements that need to be executed whether or not there has been an error, you can place them in the optional finally clause, as shown in Listing 4-33.

Listing 4-33. Using a finally Clause

```
<!DOCTYPE HTML>
<html>
<head>
    <title>Example</title>
    <script type="text/javascript">
        try {
            var myArray;
            for (var i = 0; i < myArray.length; i++) {
                console.log("Index " + i + ": " + myArray[i]);
            }
        } catch (e) {
            Console.log("Error: " + e);
        } finally {
            console.log("Statements here are always executed");
        }
    </script>
</head>
<body>
    This is a simple example
</body>
</html>
```

Comparing undefined and null Values

JavaScript defines a couple of special values that you need to be careful with when you compare them: undefined and null. The undefined value is returned when you read a variable that hasn't had a value assigned to it or try to read an object property that doesn't exist. Listing 4-34 shows how undefined is used in JavaScript.

Listing 4-34. The undefined Special Value

```
<!DOCTYPE HTML>
<html>
<head>
    <title>Example</title>
    <script type="text/javascript">
        var myData = {
            name: "Adam",
            weather: "sunny",
        };
        console.log("Prop: " + myData.doesntexist);
    </script>
</head>
<body>
    This is a simple example
</body>
</html>
```

The output from this listing is as follows:

```
Prop: undefined
```

JavaScript is odd in that is also defined null, another special value. The null value is slightly different from undefined. The undefined value is returned when no value is defined, and null is used when you want to indicate that you have assigned a value but that value is not a valid object, string, number, or boolean; that is, you have defined a value of *no value*. To help clarify this, Listing 4-35 shows the transition from undefined to null.

Listing 4-35. Using undefined and null

```
<!DOCTYPE HTML>
<html>
<head>
    <title>Example</title>
    <script type="text/javascript">

        var myData = {
            name: "Adam",
        };

        console.log("Var: " + myData.weather);
        console.log("Prop: " + ("weather" in myData));

        myData.weather = "sunny";
        console.log("Var: " + myData.weather);
        console.log("Prop: " + ("weather" in myData));

        myData.weather = null;
```

```
        console.log("Var: " + myData.weather);
        console.log("Prop: " + ("weather" in myData));

    </script>
</head>
<body>
    This is a simple example
</body>
</html>
```

I create an object and then try to read the value of the weather property, which is not defined:

```
console.log("Var: " + myData.weather);
console.log("Prop: " + ("weather" in myData));
```

There is no weather property, so the value returned by calling myData.weather is undefined, and using the in keyword to determine whether the object contains the property returns false. The output from these two statements is as follows:

```
Var: undefined

Prop: false
```

I then assign a value to the weather property, which has the effect of adding the property to the object:

```
myData.weather = "sunny";
console.log("Var: " + myData.weather);
console.log("Prop: " + ("weather" in myData));
```

I read the value of the property and check to see whether the property exists in the object again. As you might expect, you learn that the object *does* define the property and that its value is sunny:

```
Var: sunny
Prop: true
```

Now I set the value of the property to null, like this:

```
myData.weather = null;
```

This has a very specific effect. The property is still defined by the object, but I have indicated it doesn't contain a value. When I perform my checks again, I get the following results:

```
Var: null
Prop: true
```

This distinction is important when it comes to comparing undefined and null values because null is an object and undefined is a type in its own right.

Checking to See Whether a Variable or Property Is null or undefined

If you want to check to see whether a property is null or undefined (and you don't care which), then you can simply use an if statement and the negation operator (!), as shown in Listing 4-36.

Listing 4-36. Checking to See Whether a Property is null or undefined

```
<!DOCTYPE HTML>
<html>
<head>
    <title>Example</title>
    <script type="text/javascript">

        var myData = {
            name: "Adam",
            city: null
        };

        if (!myData.name) {
            console.log("name IS null or undefined");
        } else {
            console.log("name is NOT null or undefined");
        }

        if (!myData.city) {
            console.log("city IS null or undefined");
        } else {
            console.log("city is NOT null or undefined");
        }

    </script>
</head>
<body>
    This is a simple example
</body>
</html>
```

This technique relies on the type coercion that JavaScript performs such that the values you are checking are treated as boolean values. If a variable or property is null or undefined, then the coerced boolean value is false.

Differentiating Between null and undefined

If you want to compare two values, then you have a choice. If you want to treat an undefined value as being the same as a null value, then you can use the equality operator (==) and rely on JavaScript to convert the types. An undefined variable will be regarded as being equal to a null variable, for example. If you want to differentiate between null and undefined, then you need to use the identity operator (===). Listing 4-37 shows both comparisons.

Listing 4-37. Equality and Identity Comparisons for null and undefined Values

```
<!DOCTYPE HTML>
<html>
<head>
    <title>Example</title>
    <script type="text/javascript">

        var firstVal = null;
        var secondVal;

        var equality = firstVal == secondVal;
        var identity = firstVal === secondVal;

        console.log("Equality: " + equality);
        console.log("Identity: " + identity);

    </script>
</head>
<body>
    This is a simple example
</body>
</html>
```

The output from this script is as follows:

```
Equality: true
Identity: false
```

Summary

In this chapter, I showed you the core JavaScript features that you will use throughout this book. Understanding basic JavaScript is essential to using jQuery, as you'll see in the chapters ahead.

PART 2

Working with jQuery

CHAPTER 5

jQuery Basics

In this chapter, I will introduce you to your first jQuery script. The script is simple, but it demonstrates many of the most important characteristics of jQuery, including how you select elements in the document, how such selections are presented to you, and the nature of the relationship between jQuery and the built-in DOM API that is part of the HTML specification. Table 5-1 provides the summary for this chapter.

Table 5-1. *Chapter Summary*

Problem	Solution	Listing
Add jQuery to an HTML document.	Use the `link` element to import the jQuery element, linking either to your web server or to a CDN. Add a `script` element to define your jQuery script.	1, 2
Select elements in the document.	Pass a CSS selector to the $ or `jQuery` function.	3, 10
Rename the $ function.	Use the `noConflict` method.	4, 5
Defer execution of your jQuery script until the document has been loaded.	Register a handler for the `ready` event on the global `document` variable or pass a function to the $ function.	6–8
Take control of when the ready event is triggered.	Use the `holdReady` event.	9
Restrict element selection to part of the document.	Pass a context to the $ function.	11, 12
Determine the selector used to create a `jQuery` object.	Read the `selector` property.	13
Determine the context used to create a `jQuery` object.	Read the `context` property.	14
Create a `jQuery` object from `HTMLElement` objects.	Pass the objects as the argument to the $ function.	15

Enumerate the contents of a jQuery object.	Treat the jQuery object as an array or use the each method.	16, 17
Find a specific element in a jQuery element.	Use the index or get methods.	18–20
Apply an operation to multiple elements in the document.	Use a jQuery method on a jQuery object.	21
Apply multiple operations to a jQuery object.	Chain methods calls together.	22, 23
Handle an event.	Use one of the jQuery event handler methods.	24

Setting Up jQuery

The very first thing you need to do with jQuery is add it to the document you want to work with. Listing 5-1 shows the flower shop example document you first saw in Chapter 2.

Listing 5-1. The Flower Shop Example Document

```
<!DOCTYPE html>
<html>
<head>
    <title>Example</title>
    <script src="jquery-1.7.js" type="text/javascript"></script>
    <link rel="stylesheet" type="text/css" href="styles.css"/>
</head>
<body>
    <h1>Jacqui's Flower Shop</h1>
    <form method="post">
        <div id="oblock">
            <div class="dtable">
                <div id="row1" class="drow">
                    <div class="dcell">
                        <img src="astor.png"/><label for="astor">Astor:</label>
                        <input name="astor" value="0" required>
                    </div>
                    <div class="dcell">
                        <img src="daffodil.png"/><label for="daffodil">Daffodil:</label>
                        <input name="daffodil" value="0" required >
                    </div>
                    <div class="dcell">
                        <img src="rose.png"/><label for="rose">Rose:</label>
                        <input name="rose" value="0" required>
                    </div>
                </div>
                <div id="row2" class="drow">
                    <div class="dcell">
```

```
                    <img src="peony.png"/><label for="peony">Peony:</label>
                    <input name="peony" value="0" required>
                </div>
                <div class="dcell">
                    <img src="primula.png"/><label for="primula">Primula:</label>
                    <input name="primula" value="0" required>
                </div>
                <div class="dcell">
                    <img src="snowdrop.png"/><label for="snowdrop">Snowdrop:</label>
                    <input name="snowdrop" value="0" required>
                </div>
            </div>
        </div>
    </div>
    <div id="buttonDiv"><button type="submit">Place Order</button></div>
  </form>
</body>
</html>
```

To help maintain focus on the content, I have moved the CSS styles to a separate style sheet called `styles.css`, as demonstrated in Chapter 3. You can see how I have added the jQuery library to the document, as follows:

```
<script src="jquery-1.7.js" type="text/javascript"></script>
```

Two files are available for download from the `jquery.com` web site. The first is `jQuery-1.7.js`, which is the version that is generally used during the development of a web site or application. This file is around 230KB and contains the uncompressed JavaScript code. You can simply open and read the file to learn about how jQuery implements its features and easily unwind a stack trace if you encounter problems in your code.

■ **Tip** As I write this book, the latest version of jQuery is 1.7. jQuery is very actively developed, so by the time you read this, a later version will almost certainly have been released, although the techniques I show you in this book should still all work.

The other file is `jquery.1.7.min.js` and is intended for use when you deploy your site or web application to users. It contains the same JavaScript code but has been *minimized*, meaning that all of the whitespace characters have been removed, and the meaningful variable names have been replaced with single-character names to save space. The minimized script is almost impossible to read for the purposes of debugging, but it is much smaller. The minimized file is only 31KB. If you are serving up a lot of pages that rely on jQuery, then this difference can save you significant amounts of bandwidth (and therefore money).

USING A CDN FOR JQUERY

An alternative to storing the jQuery library on your own web servers is to use one of the public content distribution networks (CDNs) that host jQuery. A CDN is a distributed network of servers that deliver files to the user using the server that is closest to them. There are a couple of benefits to using a CDN. The first is a faster experience to the user, because the jQuery library file is downloaded from the server closest to them, rather than from your servers. Often the file won't be required at all. jQuery is so popular that the user's browser may have already cached the library from another application that also uses jQuery. The second benefit is that none of your precious and expensive bandwidth is spent delivering jQuery to the user. For high-traffic sites, this can be a significant cost savings.

When using a CDN, you must have confidence in the CDN operator. You want to be sure that the user receives the file they are supposed to and that service will always be available. Google and Microsoft both provide CDN services for jQuery (and other popular JavaScript libraries) free of charge. Both companies have good experience running highly available services and are unlikely to deliberately tamper with the jQuery library. You can learn about the Microsoft service at `www.asp.net/ajaxlibrary/cdn.ashx` and about the Google service at `http://code.google.com/apis/libraries/devguide.html`.

The CDN approach isn't suitable for applications that are delivered to users within an intranet because it causes all the browsers to go to the Internet to get the jQuery library, rather than access the local server, which is generally closer and faster and has lower bandwidth costs.

A First jQuery Script

Now that you have added the jQuery library to the document, you can write a script that uses jQuery functionality. Listing 5-2 contains a simple script that shows off some of the basic jQuery features.

Listing 5-2. A First jQuery Script

```
<!DOCTYPE html>
<html>
<head>
    <title>Example</title>
    <script src="jquery-1.7.js" type="text/javascript"></script>
    <link rel="stylesheet" type="text/css" href="styles.css"/>
    <script type="text/javascript">
        $(document).ready(function () {
            $("img:odd").mouseenter(function(e) {
                $(this).css("opacity", 0.5);
            }).mouseout(function(e) {
                $(this).css("opacity", 1.0);
            });
        });
    </script>
</head>
<body>
```

```
    <h1>Jacqui's Flower Shop</h1>
    <form method="post">
        <div id="oblock">
            <div class="dtable">
                <div id="row1" class="drow">
                    <div class="dcell">
                        <img src="astor.png"/><label for="astor">Astor:</label>
                        <input name="astor" value="0" required>
                    </div>
                    <div class="dcell">
                        <img src="daffodil.png"/><label for="daffodil">Daffodil:</label>
                        <input name="daffodil" value="0" required >
                    </div>
                    <div class="dcell">
                        <img src="rose.png"/><label for="rose">Rose:</label>
                        <input name="rose" value="0" required>
                    </div>
                </div>
                <div id="row2" class="drow">
                    <div class="dcell">
                        <img src="peony.png"/><label for="peony">Peony:</label>
                        <input name="peony" value="0" required>
                    </div>
                    <div class="dcell">
                        <img src="primula.png"/><label for="primula">Primula:</label>
                        <input name="primula" value="0" required>
                    </div>
                    <div class="dcell">
                        <img src="snowdrop.png"/><label for="snowdrop">Snowdrop:</label>
                        <input name="snowdrop" value="0" required>
                    </div>
                </div>
            </div>
        </div>
        <div id="buttonDiv"><button type="submit">Place Order</button></div>
    </form>
</body>
</html>
```

This is a short script, but it demonstrates some of the most important features and characteristics of jQuery. I'll break down the script line by line in this chapter, but it will take you the rest of the part of this book to fully understand all of the functional areas that this script touches upon. To start with, Figure 5-1 shows the effect that this script creates.

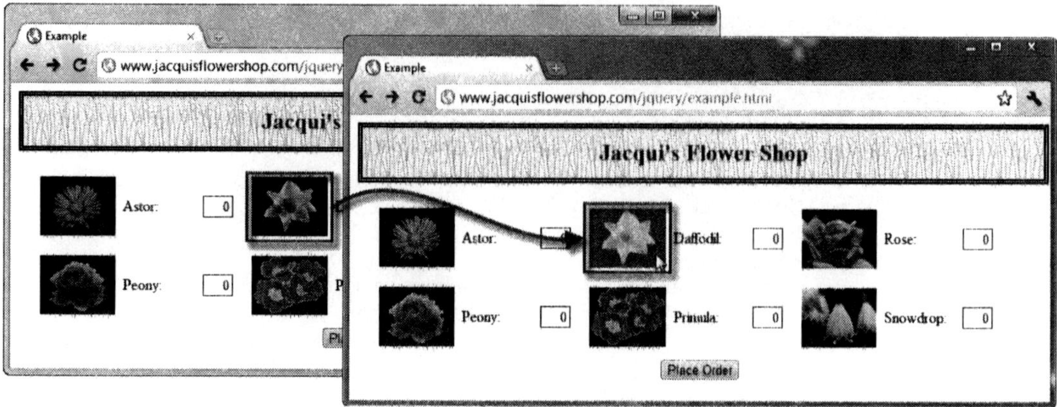

Figure 5-1. Increasing image opacity

The script changes the opacity of the daffodil, peony, and snowdrop images when the mouse is moved over them. This has the effect of making the image look a little brighter and washed out. When the mouse is moved away from the image, the opacity returns to its previous value. The images for the aster, rose, and primula are unaffected.

Understanding the jQuery $ Function

You access jQuery by using the `$(...)` function, which I will refer to as the *$ function* for simplicity. The $ function is the entry point to the wonderful world of jQuery and is a shorthand for the `jQuery` function. You can rewrite the script to use the full function name if you prefer, as shown in Listing 5-3.

Listing 5-3. Using the jQuery Function in Place of the Shorthand

```
...
<script type="text/javascript">
    jQuery(document).ready(function () {
        jQuery("img:odd").mouseenter(function(e) {
           jQuery(this).css("opacity", 0.5);
        }).mouseout(function(e) {
           jQuery(this).css("opacity", 1.0);
        });
    });
</script>
...
```

This script provides the same functionality as the previous example. It requires slightly more typing but has the advantage of making the use of jQuery explicit.

jQuery is not the only JavaScript library that uses the $ notation, which can cause problems if you are trying to use multiple libraries in the same document. You can make jQuery relinquish control of the $ by calling the `jQuery.noConflict` method, as shown in Listing 5-4.

Listing 5-4. Releasing jQuery's Control of $

```
<script type="text/javascript">
    jQuery.noConflict();
    jQuery(document).ready(function () {
        jQuery("img:odd").mouseenter(function(e) {
           jQuery(this).css("opacity", 0.5);
        }).mouseout(function(e) {
           jQuery(this).css("opacity", 1.0);
        });
    });
</script>
```

You can also define your own shorthand notation. You do this by assigning the result of the noConflict method to a variable, as shown in Listing 5-5.

Listing 5-5. Using an Alternative Shorthand

```
<script type="text/javascript">
    var jq = jQuery.noConflict();
    jq(document).ready(function () {
        jq("img:odd").mouseenter(function(e) {
           jq(this).css("opacity", 0.5);
        }).mouseout(function(e) {
           jq(this).css("opacity", 1.0);
        });
    });
</script>
```

In this example, I created my own shorthand, jq, and then used this shorthand throughout the rest of my script.

■ **Tip** I will be using the $ notation throughout this book, since it is the normal convention for jQuery (and because I won't be using any other library that wants control of $).

Irrespective of how you refer to the main jQuery function, you can pass the same set of arguments. These are described in Table 5-2. All of these types of argument are described later in this chapter except the last one, which is described in Chapter 7.

***Table 5-2.** Arguments to the Main jQuery Function*

Argument	Description
$(function)	Specifies a function to be executed when the DOM is ready
$(selector)	Selects elements from the document

$(selector, context)	
$(HTMLElement) $(HTMLElement[])	Creates a jQuery object from an HTMLElement or an array of HTMLElement objects
$()	Creates an empty selection
$(HTML)	Creates new elements from a fragment of HTML

Waiting for the Document Object Model

In Chapter 2, I placed the script element at the end of the document so that the browser would create all of the objects in the DOM before executing my JavaScript code. You can neatly avoid this issue by using jQuery. Listing 5-6 shows the relevant code.

Listing 5-6. Waiting for the DOM

```
<script type="text/javascript">
    $(document).ready(function () {
        // ...code to execute...
    });
</script>
```

You pass the document variable (which I introduced in Chapter 1) to the $ function and call the ready method, passing in a function that you want executing when the DOM is loaded and ready to be used. You can then place the script element wherever you prefer in the document, safe in the knowledge that jQuery will prevent the function from being executed prematurely.

■ **Note** Passing a function to the ready method creates a handler for the jQuery ready event. I cover jQuery events fully in Chapter 9. For the moment, please just accept that the function you pass to the ready method will be invoked when the document is loaded and the DOM is ready for use.

Forgetting the Function

A common error is to omit the function part of this incantation and just pass a series of JavaScript statements to the ready method. This doesn't work. The statements are executed by the browser immediately and not when the DOM is ready. Listing 5-7 provides a demonstration.

Listing 5-7. Omitting the Function from the ready Event Handler

```
...
<script type="text/javascript">

    function countImgElements() {
        return $('img').length;
    }

    $(document).ready(function() {
      console.log("Ready function invoked. IMG count: " + countImgElements());
    });

    $(document).ready(
      console.log("Ready statement invoked. IMG count: " + countImgElements())
    );
</script>
...
```

In this example, I call the ready method twice, once with a `function` and once just passing in a regular JavaScript statement. In both cases, I call the `countImgElements` function, which returns the number of `img` elements that are present in the DOM. (Don't worry about how this method works for the moment. I explain the call to the `length` property later in this chapter.) When I load the document, the script is executed, and the following output is written to the console:

```
Ready statement invoked. IMG count: 0
Ready function invoked. IMG count: 6
```

As you can see, the statement without the function is executed as the document is loaded and before the browser has discovered the `img` elements in the document and created the corresponding DOM objects.

Using the Alternative Notation

You can pass your function as the parameter to the jQuery `$` function if you prefer. This has the same effect as using the `$(document).ready` approach. Listing 5-8 provides a demonstration.

Listing 5-8. Deferring Execution of a Function Until the DOM Is Ready

```
...
<script type="text/javascript">
    $(function() {
        $("img:odd").mouseenter(function(e) {
           $(this).css("opacity", 0.5);
        }).mouseout(function(e) {
           $(this).css("opacity", 1.0);
        })
```

```
    });
</script>
...
```

Deferring the ready Event

You can control when the ready event is triggered by using the holdReady method. This can be useful if you need to load external resources dynamically (an unusual and advanced technique). The holdReady method must be called before the ready event is triggered and can then be called again when you are ready. Listing 5-9 gives an example of using this method.

Listing 5-9. Using the holdReady Method

```
...
<script type="text/javascript">

    $.holdReady(true);

    $(document).ready(function() {
        console.log("Ready event triggered");
        $("img:odd").mouseenter(function(e) {
            $(this).css("opacity", 0.5);
        }).mouseout(function(e) {
            $(this).css("opacity", 1.0);
        })
    });

    setTimeout(function() {
        console.log("Releasing hold");
        $.holdReady(false);
    }, 5000);

</script>
...
```

In this example, I call the holdReady method at the start of the script element. I have passed a value of true as the argument, indicating that I want the ready event to be held. I then define the function I want to be called when the ready event is fired (this is the same set of statements that I opened the chapter with, which alter the opacity of some of the images).

Finally, I use the setTimeout method to invoke a function after 5,000 milliseconds. This function calls the holdReady method with an argument of false, which tells jQuery to trigger the ready event. The net effect is that I delay the ready event for five seconds. I have added some debug messages that write the following output to the console when the document is loaded into the browser:

```
Releasing hold
Ready event triggered
```

■ **Tip** You can call the `holdReady` method multiple times, but the number of calls to the `holdReady` method with the `true` argument must be balanced by the same number of calls with the `false` argument before the `ready` event will be triggered.

Selecting Elements

One of the most important areas of jQuery functionality is how you select elements from the DOM. In the example script, I located all of the *odd* `img` elements, as shown in Listing 5-10.

Listing 5-10. Selecting Elements from the DOM

```
...
<script type="text/javascript">
    $(document).ready(function() {
        $("img:odd").mouseenter(function(e) {
           $(this).css("opacity", 0.5);
        }).mouseout(function(e) {
           $(this).css("opacity", 1.0);
        })
    });
</script>
...
```

To select elements, you simply pass a selector to the `$` function. jQuery supports all of the CSS selectors I described in Chapter 3, plus some additional ones that give you some very handy fine-grained control. In the example I used the `:odd` pseudo-selector, which selects the odd-numbered elements matched by the main part of the selector (`img` in this case, which selects all of the `img` elements, as described in Chapter 2). The `:odd` selector is zero-based, meaning that the first element is considered to be even. This can be a little confusing at first. Table 5-3 lists the most useful jQuery selectors.

■ **Tip** You can create an empty selection by calling the `$` function without any arguments (`$()`). I mention this for completeness, but it is not a feature that I have ever had cause to use.

Table 5-3. *jQuery Extension Selectors*

Selector	Description
`:animated`	Selects all elements that are being animated
`:contains(text)`	Selects elements that contain the specified text

`:eq(n)`	Selects the element at the `n`th index (zero-based)
`:even`	Selects all the event-numbered elements (one-based)
`:first`	Selects the first matched element
`:gt(n)`	Selects all of the elements with an index greater than `n` (zero-based)
`:has(selector)`	Selects elements that contain at least one element that matches the specified selector
`:last`	Selects the last matched element
`:lt(n)`	Selects all of the elements with an index smaller than `n` (zero-based)
`:odd`	Selects all the odd-numbered elements (one-based)
`:text`	Selects all text elements

I have called these the most useful because they define functionality that would be difficult to re-create using CSS selectors. These selectors are used just like the CSS pseudo-selectors. They can be used on their own, in which case they are applied to all of the elements in the DOM, like this:

```
$(':even')
```

or combined with other selectors to restrict their effect, like this:

```
$('img:even')
```

In addition, jQuery defines some selectors that select elements based on type, as described in Table 5-4.

***Table 5-4.** jQuery Type Extension Selectors*

Selector	Description
`:button`	Selects all buttons
`:checkbox`	Selects all check boxes
`:file`	Selects all file elements
`:header`	Selects all header elements (`h1`, `h2`, and so on)
`:hidden`	Selects all hidden elements
`:image`	Selects all image elements

`:input`	Selects all input elements
`:last`	Selects the last matched element
`:parent`	Selects all of the elements that are parents to other elements
`:password`	Selects all password elements
`:radio`	Selects all radio elements
`:reset`	Selects all elements that reset a form
`:selected`	Selects all elements that are selected
`:submit`	Selects all form submission elements
`:visible`	Selects all visible elements

Narrowing the Selection with a Context

By default, jQuery searches the entire DOM for elements. You can narrow the scope of a search by providing an additional argument to the $ function. This gives the search a *context*, which is used as the starting point for matching elements. Listing 5-11 provides a demonstration.

Listing 5-11. Narrowing a Search with a Context

```
<script type="text/javascript">
    $(document).ready(function() {

        $("img:odd", $('.drow')).mouseenter(function(e) {
           $(this).css("opacity", 0.5);
        }).mouseout(function(e) {
           $(this).css("opacity", 1.0);
        })
    });
</script>
```

In this example, I use one jQuery selection as the context for another. The context is evaluated first, and it matches all of the elements that are members of the `drow` class. This set of elements is then used as the context for the `img:odd` selector.

When you supply a context that contains multiple elements, then each element is used as a starting point in the search. There is an interesting subtlety in this approach. The elements that match the context are gathered together, and then the main selection is performed. In the example, this means the `img:odd` selector is applied to the results of the `drow` selector, which means that the odd-numbered elements are not the same as when you search the entire document. The net result is that the opacity effect is applied to the odd-numbered `img` elements in each `div` element in the `drow` class. This is the daffodil and primula images. When you omitted the context, the effect was applied to the daffodil, peony, and snowdrop images.

If you just want to match elements starting at a given point in the document, then you can use an HTMLElement object as the context. Listing 5-12 contains an example. I show you how to easily switch between the jQuery world and HTMLElement objects in the next section.

Listing 5-12. Using an HTMLElement as the Context

```
<script type="text/javascript">
    $(document).ready(function() {
        var elem = document.getElementById("oblock");

        $("img:odd", elem).mouseenter(function(e) {
           $(this).css("opacity", 0.5);
        }).mouseout(function(e) {
           $(this).css("opacity", 1.0);
        })
    });
</script>
```

The script in this example searches for odd-numbered img elements, limiting the search to those elements that are descended from the element whose id is oblock. Of course, you could achieve the same effect using the descendant CSS selector. The benefit of this approach arises when you want to narrow a search programmatically, without having to construct a selector string. A good example of such a situation is when handling an event. You can learn more about events (and see how HTMLElement objects arise in this situation) in Chapter 9.

Understanding the Selection Result

When you use jQuery to select elements from the DOM, the result from the $ function is a confusingly named jQuery object, which represents zero or more DOM elements. In fact, when you perform a jQuery operation that modifies one or more elements, the result is likely to be a jQuery object, which is an important characteristic that I'll return to shortly.

The methods and properties that are defined by the jQuery object are essentially the contents for the rest of the book, but there are some basic members that I can cover in this chapter, as described in Table 5-5.

Table 5-5. *Basic jQuery Object Members*

Selector	Description	Returns
context	Returns the set of elements used as the search context	HTMLElement
each(function)	Performs the function on each of the selected elements	jQuery
get(index)	Gets the HTMLElement object at the specified index	HTMLElement
index(HTMLElement)	Returns the index of the specified HTMLElement	number
index(jQuery)	Returns the index of the first element in the jQuery object	number

index(selector)	Returns the index of the first element in the jQuery object in the set of elements matched by the selector	number
length	Returns the number of elements contained by the jQuery object	number
selector	Returns the selector	string
size()	Returns the number of elements in the jQuery object	number
toArray()	Returns the HTMLElement objects contained by the jQuery object as an array	HTMLElement[]

Determining the Selector

The selector property returns a selector that describes the elements in the jQuery object. When you narrow or widen the selection (which I describe in Chapter 6), the selector property returns a selector that describes the combined set of operations. Listing 5-13 shows the selector property in use.

Listing 5-13. Using the selector Property

```
<script type="text/javascript">
    $(document).ready(function() {
        var selector =  $("img:odd").selector
        console.log("Selector: " + selector);
    });
</script>
```

This script produces the following output to the console:

```
Selector: img:odd
```

Determining the Context

The context property provides you with details of the context used when the jQuery was created. If a single HTMLElement object was used as the context, then the context property will return that HTMLElement. If no context was used or if multiple elements were used (as in the example I used earlier in the chapter), then the context property returns undefined instead. Listing 5-14 shows this property in use.

Listing 5-14. Determining the Context for a jQuery Object

```
...
<script type="text/javascript">
    $(document).ready(function() {
        var jq1 = $("img:odd");
        console.log("No context: " + jq1.context.tagName);

        var jq2 = $("img:odd", $('.drow'));
        console.log("Multiple context elements: " + jq2.context.tagName);

        var jq3 = $("img:odd", document.getElementById("oblock"));
        console.log("Single context element: " + jq3.context.tagName);
    });
</script>
...
```

This script selects elements using no context, multiple context objects, and a single context object. The output is as follows:

```
No context: undefined
Multiple context elements: undefined
Single context element: DIV
```

Dealing with DOM Objects

jQuery doesn't replace the DOM; it just makes it a lot easier to work with. The HTMLElement objects (which I introduced in Chapter 2) are still used, and the jQuery library makes it easy to switch between jQuery objects and DOM objects. To my mind, the ease with which you can move from the traditional DOM to jQuery and back is part of the elegance of jQuery and helps you maintain compatibility with non-jQuery scripts and libraries.

Creating jQuery Objects from DOM Objects

You can create jQuery objects by passing an HTMLElement object or an array of HTMLElement objects as the argument to the $ function. This can be useful when dealing with JavaScript code that isn't written in jQuery or in situations where jQuery exposes the underlying DOM objects, such as event processing. Listing 5-15 contains an example.

Listing 5-15. Creating jQuery Objects from DOM Objects

```
...
<script type="text/javascript">
    $(document).ready(function() {

        var elems = document.getElementsByTagName("img");

        $(elems).mouseenter(function(e) {
```

```
            $(this).css("opacity", 0.5);
        }).mouseout(function(e) {
            $(this).css("opacity", 1.0);
        })
    });
</script>
...
```

In this example, I select the img elements in the document using the document.getElementsByTagName method, rather than using jQuery directly with a selector. I pass the results of this method (which is a collection of HTMLElement objects) to the $ function, which returns a regular jQuery object that I can use just as in the previous examples.

This script also demonstrates how you can create a jQuery object from a single HTMLElement object:

```
$(this).css("opacity", 1.0);
```

When you are handling events, jQuery sets the value of the this variable to the HTMLElement that is processing the event. I describe the jQuery event support in Chapter 9, so I don't want to get into the subject in this chapter (although I do mention the functions that contain these statements again a little later in this chapter).

Treating a jQuery Object As An Array

You can treat the jQuery object as an array of HTMLElement objects. This means you get to use the advanced features that jQuery provides but still get to the DOM directly. You can use the length property or the size method to determine how many elements are collected in the jQuery object and access individual DOM objects by using an array-style index (using the [and] brackets).

■ **Tip** You can use the toArray method to extract the HTMLElement objects from the jQuery object as an array. I like to use the jQuery object itself, but sometimes it is useful to work with the DOM objects, such as when dealing with legacy code that wasn't written using jQuery.

Listing 5-16 shows how you can enumerate the contents of a jQuery object to access the HTMLElement objects contained within.

Listing 5-16. Treating a jQuery Object As an Array

```
...
<script type="text/javascript">
    $(document).ready(function() {
        var elems = $('img:odd');
        for (var i = 0; i < elems.length; i++) {
            console.log("Element: " + elems[i].tagName + " " + elems[i].src);
        }
    });
```

```
</script>
...
```

In the listing, I use the $ function to select the odd-numbered img elements and enumerate the selected elements to print out the value of the tagName and src properties to the console. The results are as follows:

```
Element: IMG http://www.jacquisflowershop.com/jquery/daffodil.png
Element: IMG http://www.jacquisflowershop.com/jquery/peony.png
Element: IMG http://www.jacquisflowershop.com/jquery/snowdrop.png
```

Iterate a Function Over DOM Objects

The each method lets you define a function that is performed for each DOM object in the jQuery object. Listing 5-17 gives a demonstration.

Listing 5-17. Using the each Method

```
...
<script type="text/javascript">
    $(document).ready(function() {
        $('img:odd').each(function(index, elem) {
            console.log("Element: " + elem.tagName + " " + elem.src);
        });
    });
</script>
...
```

jQuery passes two arguments to the specified function. The first is the index of the element in the collection, and the second is the element object itself. In this example, I write the tag name and the value of the src property to the console, producing the same results as the previous script.

Finding Indices and Specific Elements

The index method lets you find the index of an HTMLElement in a jQuery object. You can pass the index that you want using either an HTMLElement or jQuery object as the argument. When you use a jQuery object, the first matched element is the one whose index is returned. Listing 5-18 gives a demonstration.

Listing 5-18. Locating the Index of an HTMLElement

```
...
<script type="text/javascript">
    $(document).ready(function() {

        var elems = $('body *');

        // find an index using the basic DOM API
        var index = elems.index(document.getElementById("oblock"));
```

```
        console.log("Index using DOM element is: " + index);

        // find an index using another jQuery object
        index = elems.index($('#oblock'));
        console.log("Index using jQuery object is: " + index);
    });
</script>
...
```

In this example, I locate a method using the DOM API's `getElementById` method to find a `div` element by the `id` attribute value. This returns an `HTMLElement` object. I then use the `index` method on a jQuery object to find the index of the object that represents the `div` element. I repeat the process using a jQuery object, which I obtain through the `$` function. I write the results from both approaches to the console, which produces the following results:

```
Index using DOM element is: 2
Index using jQuery object is: 2
```

You can also pass a `string` to the `index` method. When you do this, the `string` is interpreted as a selector. However, this approach causes the `index` method to behave in a different way than the previous example. Listing 5-19 provides a demonstration.

Listing 5-19. Using the Selector Version of the index Method

```
<script type="text/javascript">
    $(document).ready(function() {

        var imgElems = $('img:odd');
        // find an index using a selector
        index = imgElems.index("body *");
        console.log("Index using selector is: " + index);

        // perform the same task using a jQuery object
        index = $("body *").index(imgElems);
        console.log("Index using jQuery object is: " + index);

    });
</script>
```

When you pass a `string` to the `index` method, the order in which the collection of elements is used changes. jQuery matches elements using the selector and then returns the index in the matched elements of the first element in the jQuery object on which you called the `index` method. This means that this statement:

```
index = imgElems.index("body *");
```

is equivalent to this statement:

```
index = $("body *").index(imgElems);
```

In essence, passing a string argument reverses the way in which the two sets of elements are considered.

■ **Tip** We can use the `index` method without an argument to get the position of an element relative to its siblings. This can be useful when using jQuery to explore the DOM, which is the topic of Chapter 7.

The get method is the complement to the index method, such that you specify an index and receive the HTMLElement object at that position in the jQuery object. This has the same effect as using the array-style index I described earlier in this chapter. Listing 5-20 provides a demonstration.

Listing 5-20. Getting the HTMLElement Object at a Given Index

```
...
<script type="text/javascript">
    $(document).ready(function() {
        var elem = $('img:odd').get(1);
        console.log("Element: " + elem.tagName + " " + elem.src);
    });
</script>
...
```

In this script, I select the odd-numbered img elements, use the get method to retrieve the HTMLElement object at index 1, and write the value of the tagName and src properties to the console. The output from this script is as follows:

```
Element: IMG http://www.jacquisflowershop.com/jquery/peony.png
```

Modifying Multiple Elements and Chaining Method Calls

One of the features that make jQuery so concise and expressive is that calling a method on a jQuery object usually modifies all of the elements that the object contains. I say usually, because some methods perform operations that just don't make sense for multiple elements, and you'll see examples of this in later chapters. Listing 5-21 shows how jQuery makes life a lot easier than the basic DOM API.

Listing 5-21. Operating on Multiple Elements

```
...
<script type="text/javascript">
    $(document).ready(function() {

        $('label').css("color", "blue");

        var labelElems = document.getElementsByTagName("label");
        for (var i = 0; i < labelElems.length; i++) {
            labelElems[i].style.color = "blue";
        }
    });
</script>
...
```

In this example, I select all of the label elements in the document and change the value of the CSS color property to blue. I do this in a single statement in jQuery, but it takes a bit more effort using the basic DOM API—not a lot more effort, I must admit, but it mounts up in a complex web application. I also find the meaning of the jQuery statement is immediately apparent, but that's just a personal thing.

One of the other nice features of the jQuery object is that it implements a *fluent API*. This means that whenever you call a method that modifies the contents of the object, the result of the method is another jQuery object. This may seem simple, but it allows you to perform method chaining, as shown in Listing 5-22.

Listing 5-22. Method Chaining Method Calls on a jQuery Object

```
...
<script type="text/javascript">
    $(document).ready(function() {

        $('label').css("color", "blue").css("font-size", ".75em");

        var labelElems = document.getElementsByTagName("label");
        for (var i = 0; i < labelElems.length; i++) {
            labelElems[i].style.color = "blue";
            labelElems[i].style.fontSize = ".75em";
        }
    });
</script>
...
```

In this example, I create a jQuery object using the $ function, call the css method to set a value for the color property, and then call the css method again, this time to set the font-size property. I have also shown the equivalent addition using the basic DOM API. You can see that it doesn't require much work to achieve the same effect, because you already have a for loop that is enumerating the selected elements.

You start to get some real benefits when you start chaining methods that make more substantial changes to the set of elements contained in the jQuery object. Listing 5-23 provides a demonstration.

Listing 5-23. A More Sophisticated Chaining Example

```
<script type="text/javascript">
    $(document).ready(function() {

        $('label').css("color", "blue").add("input[name!='rose']")
                    .filter("[for!='snowdrop']").css("font-size", ".75em");

        var elems = document.getElementsByTagName("label");
        for (var i = 0; i < elems.length; i++) {
            elems[i].style.color = "blue";
            if (elems[i].getAttribute("for") != "snowdrop") {
                elems[i].style.fontSize= ".75em";
            }
        }
        elems = document.getElementsByTagName("input");
        for (var i = 0; i < elems.length; i++) {
            if (elems[i].getAttribute("name") != "rose") {
```

```
                elems[i].style.fontSize= ".75em";
            }
        }
    });
</script>
```

This is a slightly over-the-top example, but it nicely demonstrates the flexibility that jQuery offers. Let's break down the chained methods to make sense of what is happening. You start with this:

```
$('label').css("color", "blue")
```

This is a nice and simple start. I have selected all of the `label` elements in the document and set the value of the CSS `color` property to be `blue` for all of them. The next step is as follows:

```
$('label').css("color", "blue").add("input[name!='rose']")
```

The `add` method adds the elements that match the specified selector to the jQuery object. In this case, I have selected all `input` elements that don't have a `name` attribute whose value is `rose`. These are combined with the previously matched elements to give me a mix of `label` and `input` elements. You'll see more of the add method in Chapter 6. Here is the next addition:

```
$('label').css("color", "blue").add("input[name!='rose']").filter("[for!='snowdrop']")
```

The `filter` method removes all of the elements in a jQuery object that don't meet a specified condition. I explain this method in more depth in Chapter 6, but for the moment it is enough to know that this allows me to remove any element from the jQuery object that has a `for` attribute whose value is `snowdrop`.

```
$('label').css("color", "blue").add("input[name!='rose']")
    .filter("[for!='snowdrop']").css("font-size", ".75em");
```

The final step is to call the `css` method again, this time setting the `font-size` property to `.75em`. The net result of this is as follows:

1. All `label` elements are assigned the value `blue` for the `color` CSS property.
2. All label elements except the one that has the `for` attribute value of `snowdrop` are assigned the value `.75em` for the CSS `font-size` property.
3. All `input` elements that don't have a `name` attribute value of `rose` are assigned the value of `.75em` for the CSS `font-size` property.

Achieving the same effect using the basic DOM API is a lot more complex, and I ran into some difficulties while writing this script. For example, I thought I could use the `document.querySelectorAll` method, described in Chapter 2, to select input elements using the selector `input[name!='rose']`, but it turns out that this kind of attribute filter doesn't work with that method. I then tried to avoid duplicating the call to set the `font-size` value by concatenating the results of two `getElementsByTagName` calls together, but that turns out to be a painful experience in its own right. I don't want to belabor the point, especially since you must already have a certain commitment to jQuery to be reading this book, but jQuery provides a level of fluidity and expressiveness that is impossible to achieve using the basic DOM API.

Handling Events

Returning to the script you started the chapter with, you can see that I chained together two method calls, as highlighted in Listing 5-24.

Listing 5-24. Chained Method Calls in the Example Script

```
...
<script type="text/javascript">
    $(document).ready(function() {
        $("img:odd").mouseenter(function(e) {
           $(this).css("opacity", 0.5);
        }).mouseout(function(e) {
           $(this).css("opacity", 1.0);
        })
    });
</script>
...
```

The methods I chained were mouseenter and mouseout. These methods let me define handler functions for the mouseenter and mouseout events that I described in Chapter 2. I cover the jQuery support for events in Chapter 9, but I just wanted to show how you can use the behavior of the jQuery object to specify a single handler method for all of the elements that you have selected.

Summary

In this chapter, I introduced you to your first jQuery script and used it to demonstrate some of the key characteristics of the jQuery library: the $ function, the ready event, the jQuery result object, and how jQuery complements, rather than replaces, the built-in DOM API that is part of the HTML specification.

CHAPTER 6

Managing the Element Selection

Most of the time, you use jQuery in a pretty distinct two-step pattern. The first step is to select some elements, and the second step is to perform one or more operations on those elements. In this chapter, I focus on the first step, showing you how to take control of the jQuery selection and tailor it to your exact needs. I'll also show you how to use jQuery to navigate the DOM. In both cases, you start with one selection and perform operations on it until it contains just the elements you require. As you'll see, the correlation between the elements you start with and those you finish with can be as simple or as sophisticated as you like. Table 6-1 provides the summary for this chapter.

***Table 6-1.** Chapter Summary*

Problem	Solution	Listing
Expand the selection.	Use the `add` method.	1
Reduce the selection to a single element.	Use the `first`, `last`, or `eq` method.	2
Reduce the selection to a range of elements.	Use the `slice` method.	3
Reduce the selection by applying a filter.	Use the `filter` or `not` method.	4, 5
Reduce the selection based on the descendants of the selected elements.	Use the `has` method.	6
Project a new selection from the existing selection.	Use the `map` method.	7
Check to see that at least one selected element meets a specific condition.	Use the `is` method.	8
Revert to the previous selection.	Use the `end` method.	9
Add the previous selection to the current selection.	Use the `andSelf` method.	10
Navigate to the children and descendants of selected elements.	Use the `children` and `find` methods.	11–13

Navigate to the parents of selected elements.	Use the `parent` method.	14
Navigate to the ancestors or selected elements.	Use the `parents` method.	15
Navigate to the ancestors of element until a specific element is encountered.	Use the `parentsUntil` method.	16, 17
Navigate to the nearest ancestor that matches a selector or that is a specific element.	Use the `closest` method.	18, 19
Navigate to the nearest positioned ancestor.	Use the `offsetParent` method.	20
Navigate to the siblings of the selected elements.	Use the `siblings` method.	21, 22
Navigate to the previous or next siblings for the selected elements.	Use the next, `prev`, `nextAll`, `prevAll`, `nextUntil`, or `prevUntil` method.	23

Expanding the Selection

The add method allows you to expand the contents of a `jQuery` object by adding additional elements. Table 6-2 shows the different arguments you can use.

***Table 6-2.** add Method Argument Types*

Arguments	Description
`add(selector)` `add(selector, context)`	Adds all of the elements that are matched by the selector, with or without a context
`add(HTMLElement)` `add(HTMLElement[])`	Adds a single `HTMLElement` or an array of `HTMLElements`
`add(jQuery)`	Adds the contents of the specified `jQuery` object

Like many jQuery methods, the add method returns a `jQuery` object on which you can call other methods, including further calls to the add method. Listing 6-1 demonstrates the use of the add method to broaden a set of elements.

■ **Caution** A common mistake is to assume that the `remove` method is the counterpart to the `add` method and will narrow the selection. In fact, the `remove` method changes the structure of the DOM, as I explain in Chapter 7. Use one of the methods I describe in the "Narrowing the Selection" section instead.

Listing 6-1. Using the add Method

```
<!DOCTYPE html>
<html>
<head>
    <title>Example</title>
    <script src="jquery-1.7.js" type="text/javascript"></script>
    <link rel="stylesheet" type="text/css" href="styles.css"/>
    <script type="text/javascript">
        $(document).ready(function() {

            var labelElems = document.getElementsByTagName("label");
            var jq = $('img[src*=daffodil]');

            $('img:even').add('img[src*=primula]').add(jq)
                .add(labelElems).css("border", "thick double red");

        });
    </script>
</head>
<body>
    <h1>Jacqui's Flower Shop</h1>
    <form method="post">
        <div id="oblock">
            <div class="dtable">
                <div id="row1" class="drow">
                    <div class="dcell">
                        <img src="astor.png"/><label for="astor">Astor:</label>
                        <input name="astor" value="0" required>
                    </div>
                    <div class="dcell">
                        <img src="daffodil.png"/><label for="daffodil">Daffodil:</label>
                        <input name="daffodil" value="0" required >
                    </div>
                    <div class="dcell">
                        <img src="rose.png"/><label for="rose">Rose:</label>
                        <input name="rose" value="0" required>
                    </div>
                </div>
                <div id="row2"class="drow">
                    <div class="dcell">
                        <img src="peony.png"/><label for="peony">Peony:</label>
                        <input name="peony" value="0" required>
```

```
                    </div>
                    <div class="dcell">
                        <img src="primula.png"/><label for="primula">Primula:</label>
                        <input name="primula" value="0" required>
                    </div>
                    <div class="dcell">
                        <img src="snowdrop.png"/><label for="snowdrop">Snowdrop:</label>
                        <input name="snowdrop" value="0" required>
                    </div>
                </div>
            </div>
        </div>
        <div id="buttonDiv"><button type="submit">Place Order</button></div>
    </form>
</body>
</html>
```

The script in this example uses all three approaches to add elements to the initial selection: with another selector, with some HTMLElement objects, and with another jQuery object. Once I have built up my set of objects, I call the css method to set a value for the border property, which has the effect of drawing a thick red border, as shown in Figure 6-1.

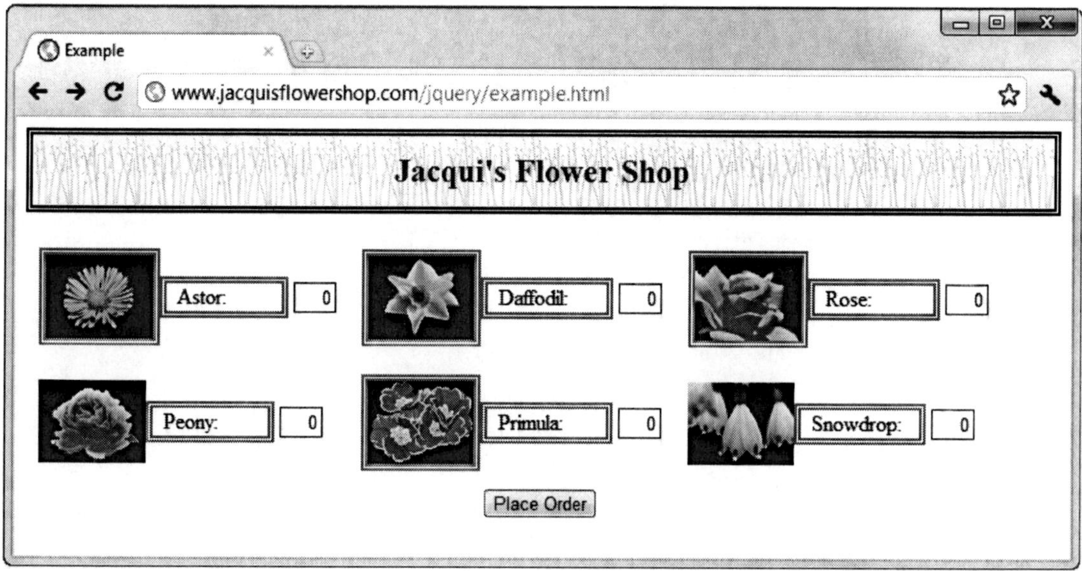

Figure 6-1. Expanding the selection with the add method

Narrowing the Selection

A number of methods allow you to remove elements from the selection. They are described in Table 6-3. In every case, the methods return a new jQuery object that contains the reduced element selection. The jQuery object on which the method was called remains unchanged.

Table 6-3. Methods to Filter Elements

Method	Description
`eq(index)`	Removes all of the elements except the one at the specified index.
`filter(condition)`	Removes elements that don't match the specified condition. See the later discussion for details of the arguments you can use with this method.
`first()`	Removes all of the elements except the first.

`has(selector)`
`has(jQuery)`
`has(HTMLElement)`
`has(HTMLElement[])`
	Removes elements that don't have a descendant matched by the specified selector or `jQuery` object or whose descendants don't include the specified `HTMLElement` objects.

`last()`	Removes all but the last element.
`not(condition)`	Removes all elements that match the condition. See the later discussion for details of how the condition can be specified.
`slice(start, end)`	Removes all elements outside the specified range of index values.

Reducing the Selection to a Specific Element

The three most basic reduction methods are `first`, `last`, and `eq`. These three methods allow you to select a specific element based on its position in the `jQuery` object. Listing 6-2 provides a demonstration.

Listing 6-2. Reducing the Selection Based on Element Position

```
...
<script type="text/javascript">
    $(document).ready(function() {

        var jq = $('label');

        // select and operate on the first element
        jq.first().css("border", "thick double red");

        // select and operate on the last element
        jq.last().css("border", "thick double green");

        // select and operate on an element by index
        jq.eq(2).css("border", "thick double black");
        jq.eq(-2).css("border", "thick double black");

    });
</script>
...
```

Notice that I call the eq method twice. When the argument to this method is positive, the index is counted from the first element in the jQuery object. When the argument is negative, the counting is done backward, starting from the last element. You can see the effect of this script in Figure 6-2.

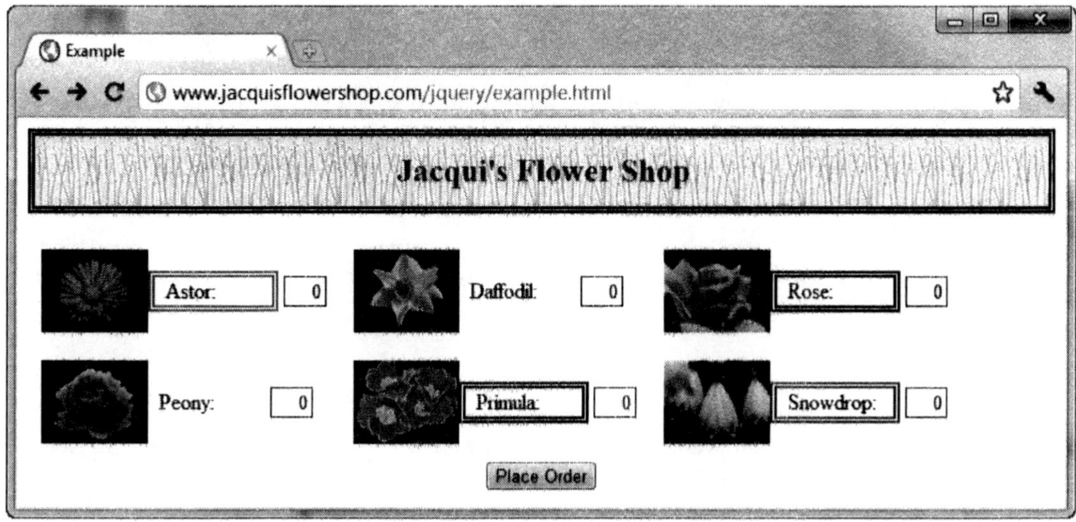

Figure 6-2. Reducing the selection to a specific element

Reducing the Selection by Range

The slice method lets you reduce the selection to a range of elements, specified by index. Listing 6-3 provides a demonstration.

Listing 6-3. Using the slice Method

```
...
<script type="text/javascript">
    $(document).ready(function() {

        var jq = $('label');

        jq.slice(0, 2).css("border", "thick double black");
        jq.slice(4).css("border", "thick solid red");

    });
</script>
...
```

The arguments to the slice method are the index to begin selection and the index to end selection. Indexes are zero-based, so the arguments I used in the example (0 and 2) have the effect of selecting the first two elements. If you omit the second argument, then the selection continues to the end of the set of elements. By specifying a single argument of 4 for a set of six elements, I selected the last two elements (which have the index values of 4 and 5). You can see the result of this script in Figure 6-3.

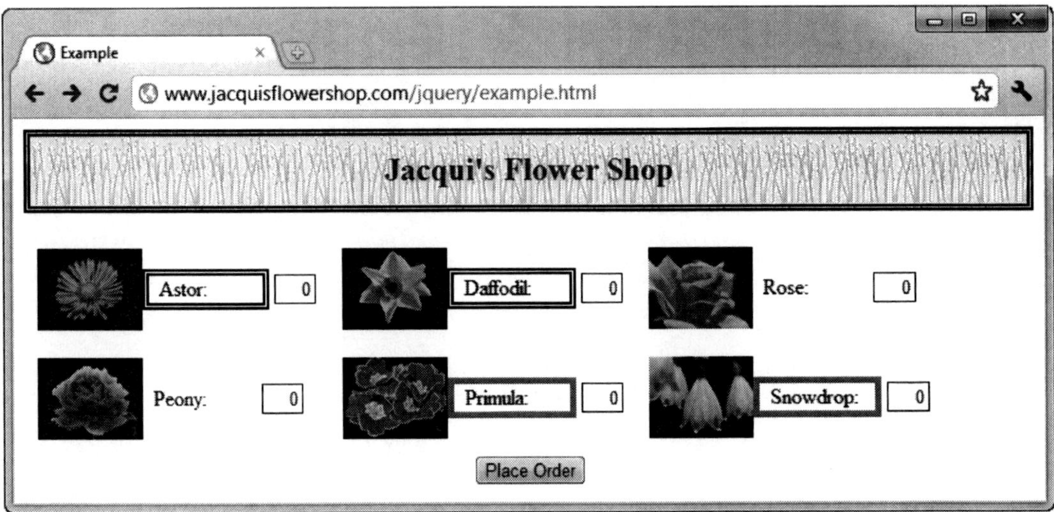

Figure 6-3. Reducing the selection by range

Filtering Elements

The `filter` method lets you specify a condition. Any elements that don't meet the condition are removed from the selection. Table 6-4 shows the different arguments you can use to express the filtering condition.

***Table 6-4.** filter Method Argument Types*

Arguments	Description
`filter(selector)`	Removes elements that don't match the selector.
`filter(HTMLElement)`	Removes all but the specified element.
`filter(jQuery)`	Removes elements that are not contained in the specified `jQuery` object.
`filter(function(index))`	The function is called for each element; those for which the function returns `false` are removed.

Listing 6-4 shows all four ways of specifying a filter.

Listing 6-4. Specifying a Filter

```
...
<script type="text/javascript">
    $(document).ready(function() {
        // remove elements whose src attribute contains the letter 's'
        $('img').filter('[src*=s]').css("border", "thick double red");

        // remove elements that don't contain the letter p
        var jq = $('[for*=p]');
        $('label').filter(jq).css("color", "blue");

        // remove elements that are not the specified element
        var elem = document.getElementsByTagName("label")[1];
        $('label').filter(elem).css("font-size", "1.5em");

        // remove elements using a function
        $('img').filter(function(index) {
            return this.getAttribute("src") == "peony.png" || index == 4;
        }).css("border", "thick solid red")
    });
</script>
...
```

The first three techniques are self-evident. You can filter based a selector, another `jQuery` object, or an `HTMLElement` object. The fourth technique, which relies on a `function`, requires a little more explanation. This is the technique that I have highlighted in the listing.

jQuery calls your function once for every element contained by the `jQuery` object. If you return `true` from the method, the element for which the function has been called is retained. If you return `false`, then the element is removed. There is one argument passed to the function, which is the index of the element for which the function is being called. In addition, the `this` variable is set to the `HTMLElement` object that you need to process. In the listing, I return `true` if the element has a particular value for the `src` attribute and for a specific index value.

■ **Tip** You might be wondering why I have used the `getAttribute` method on the `HTMLElement` in the filter function, as opposed to calling the `src` property. The reason is that the `getAttribute` method will return the value that I set for the `src` *attribute* in the document (which is a relative URL), but the `src` *property* will return a fully qualified URL. For this example, the relative URL was simpler to work with.

The complement to the `filter` method is `not`, which works in much the same way but inverts the filtering process. Table 6-5 shows the different ways in which you can apply a condition using the `not` method.

Table 6-5. not Method Argument Types

Arguments	Description
`not(selector)`	Removes elements that match the selector.
`not(HTMLElement[])` `not(HTMLElement)`	Removes the specified element or elements.
`not(jQuery)`	Removes elements that are contained in the specified `jQuery` object.
`not(function(index))`	The function is called for each element; those for which the function returns `true` are removed.

Listing 6-5 shows the use of the `not` method, based on the previous example.

Listing 6-5. Using the not Function

```
...
<script type="text/javascript">
    $(document).ready(function() {

        $('img').not('[src*=s]').css("border", "thick double red");

        var jq = $('[for*=p]');
        $('label').not(jq).css("color", "blue");

        var elem = document.getElementsByTagName("label")[1];
        $('label').not(elem).css("font-size", "1.5em");

        $('img').not(function(index) {
            return this.getAttribute("src") == "peony.png" || index == 4;
        }).css("border", "thick solid red")
    });
</script>
...
```

You can see the effect of this script in Figure 6-4. It is, of course, the inverse of the effect of the previous example.

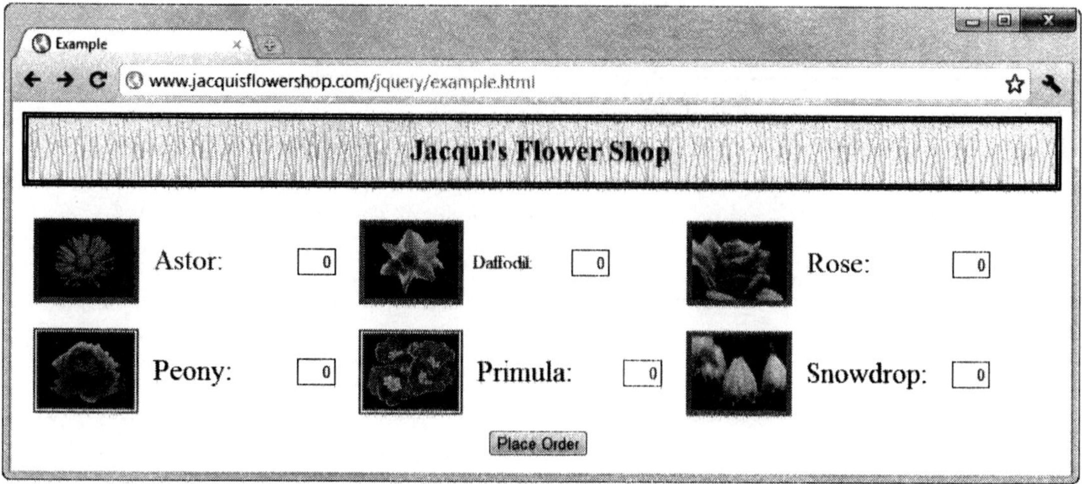

Figure 6-4. Filtering elements using the not method

Reducing the Selection Based on Descendants

You can use the has method to reduce the selection to elements that have particular descendants, by specifying either a selector or one or more HTMLElement objects. Listing 6-6 shows the use of the has method.

Listing 6-6. Using the has Method

```
<script type="text/javascript">
    $(document).ready(function() {

        $('div.dcell').has('img[src*=astor]').css("border", "thick solid red");

        var jq = $('[for*=p]');
        $('div.dcell').has(jq).css("border", "thick solid blue");

    });
</script>
```

In this script, I reduce the selection by removing elements that don't have specific descendants. In the first case, where I use a selector, I remove elements that don't have at least one descendant img element with a src attribute value that contains astor. In the second case, where I use a jQuery object, I remove elements that don't have at least one descendant that has a for attribute with a value that contains the letter p. You can see the effect of this script in Figure 6-5.

Figure 6-5. Using the has method to reduce the selection

Mapping the Selection

The map method provides a flexible way to use one jQuery object as a means to create another. You pass a function to the map method. This function is called for every element in the source jQuery object, and the HTMLElement objects that you return from the function are included in the result jQuery object. Listing 6-7 shows the map method in use.

Listing 6-7. Using the map Method

```
...
<script type="text/javascript">
    $(document).ready(function() {

        $('div.dcell').map(function(index, elem) {
            return elem.getElementsByTagName("img")[0];
        }).css("border", "thick solid red");

        $('div.dcell').map(function(index, elem) {
            return $(elem).children()[1];
        }).css("border", "thick solid blue");

    });
</script>
...
```

In this script, I perform two mapping operations. The first uses the DOM API to return the first img element contained in each element, and the second uses jQuery to return the first item in the jQuery object returned by the children method (I'll explain this method fully later in this chapter, but as its name suggests, it returns the child nodes of each element in a jQuery object).

■ **Tip** You can return only one element each time the function is called. If you want to project multiple result elements for each source element, you can combine the each and add methods, which I described in Chapter 8.

Testing the Selection

You can use the is method to determine whether one of more elements in a jQuery object meets a specified condition. Table 6-6 shows the arguments you can pass to the is method.

Table 6-6. *is Method Argument Types*

Arguments	Description
is(selector)	Returns true if the jQuery object contains at least one of the elements matched by the selector
is(HTMLElement[]) is(HTMLElement)	Returns true if the jQuery object contains the specified element, or at least one of the elements in the specified array
is(jQuery)	Returns true if the jQuery object contains at least one of the elements in the argument object
is(function(index))	Returns true if the function returns true at least once

When you specify a function, jQuery will invoke that function once for each element in the jQuery object, passing the index of the element as the function argument and setting the this variable to the element itself. Listing 6-8 shows the is method in use.

■ **Note** This method returns a boolean value. As I mentioned in Chapter 5, not all jQuery methods return a jQuery object.

Listing 6-8. Using the is Method

```
...
<script type="text/javascript">
    $(document).ready(function() {

        var isResult = $('img').is(function(index) {
```

```
            return this.getAttribute("src") == "rose.png";
        });
        console.log("Result: " + isResult);

    });
</script>
...
```

This script tests to see whether the jQuery object contains an element whose src attribute value is rose.png and writes out the result to the console, as follows:

```
Result: true
```

Changing and Then Unwinding the Selection

jQuery preserves a history stack when you modify the selection by chaining methods together, and you can use a couple of methods to take advantage of this, as described in Table 6-7.

Table 6-7. Methods to Unwind the Selection Stack

Method	Description
end()	Pops the current selection off the stack and returns to the previous selection
andSelf()	Adds the previous selection to the current selection

You can use the end method to return to the previous selection, which allows you to select some elements, expand or reduce the selection, perform some operations, and then return to the original selection, as demonstrated by Listing 6-9.

Listing 6-9. Using the end Method

```
...
<script type="text/javascript">
    $(document).ready(function() {

        $('label').first().css("border", "thick solid blue")
            .end().css("font-size", "1.5em");

    });
</script>
...
```

In this script, I start by selecting all of the label elements in the document. I then reduce the selection by calling the first method (to get the first matched element) and then set a value for the CSS border property using the css method.

I then call the end method to return to the previous selection (which moves you from the first label element back to *all* of the label elements) and then call the css method again, this time to set a value for the font-size property. You can see the effect of this script in Figure 6-6.

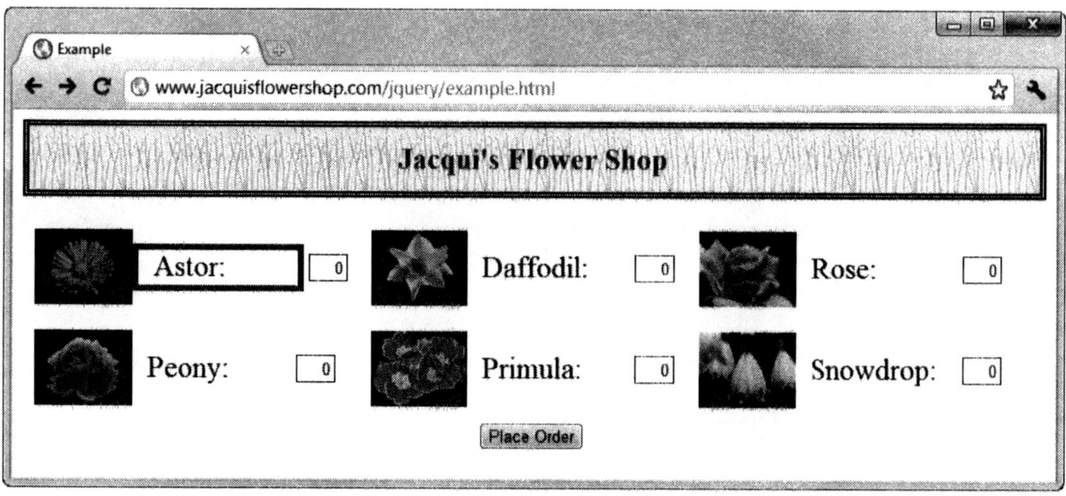

Figure 6-6. Using the end method

The andSelf method adds the contents of the previous selection on the stack to the current selection. Listing 6-10 shows the addSelf method in use.

Listing 6-10. Using the andSelf Method

```
...
<script type="text/javascript">
    $(document).ready(function() {
        $('div.dcell').children('img').andSelf().css("border", "thick solid blue");
    });
</script>
...
```

In this example, I select all of the div elements that are members of the dcell class and then use the children method to select all of the img elements that are their children (I explain the children method fully in the "Navigating the DOM" section later in this chapter). I then call the andSelf method, which combines the previous selection (the div element) with the current selection (the img elements) in a single jQuery object. Finally, I call use the css method to set a border for the selected elements. You can see the effect of this script in Figure 6-7.

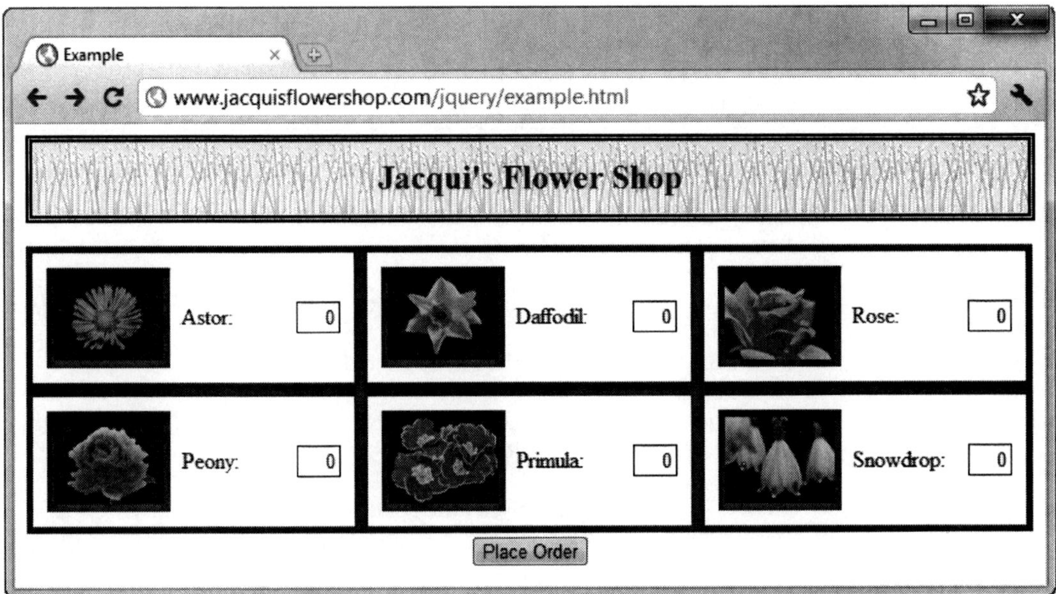

Figure 6-7. Using the andSelf method

Navigating the DOM

You can use a selection as the start point for navigating elsewhere in the DOM, in essence using one selection as the start point for creating another. In the following sections, I'll describe and demonstrate the jQuery navigation methods. I explained the different kinds of relationships that can exist between elements in a document in Chapter 2.

■ **Tip** All of the methods that are described in the following sections return a `jQuery` object. This object will contain the matched elements if there are any and will be empty (i.e., the `length` property will be zero) if there are not.

Navigating Down the Hierarchy

When you navigate down the DOM hierarchy, you are selecting children and descendants of the elements contained in a `jQuery` object. Table 6-8 describes the relevant jQuery methods.

Table 6-8. Methods to Navigate Down the DOM Hierarchy

Method	Description
children()	Selects the children of all of the elements in the jQuery object
children(selector)	Selects all of the elements that match the selector and that are children of the elements in the jQuery object
contents()	Returns the children and text content of all the elements in the jQuery object
find()	Selects the descendants of the elements in the jQuery object
find(selector)	Selects the elements that match the selector and that are descendants of the elements in the jQuery object
find(jQuery) find(HTMLElement) find(HTMLElement[])	Selects the intersection between the children of the elements in the jQuery object and the argument object

The children method will select only those elements that are immediate descendants of each element in the jQuery object, optionally filtered by a selector. The find method will select all descendant elements, not just the immediate ones. The contents method will return the children elements, plus any text content. Listing 6-11 shows the children and find methods in use.

Listing 6-11. Using the children and find Methods

```
...
<script type="text/javascript">
    $(document).ready(function() {

        var childCount = $('div.drow').children().each(function(index, elem) {
            console.log("Child: " + elem.tagName + " " + elem.className);
        }).length;
        console.log("There are " + childCount + " children");

        var descCount = $('div.drow').find('img').each(function(index, elem) {
            console.log("Descendant: " + elem.tagName + " " + elem.src);
        }).length;
        console.log("There are " + descCount + " img descendants");

    });
</script>
...
```

In this example, I use the children method without a selector and the find method with one. I write the details of the selected elements to the console along with how many were selected. The console output from this script is as follows:

```
Child: DIV dcell
Child: DIV dcell
Child: DIV dcell
Child: DIV dcell
Child: DIV dcell
Child: DIV dcell
There are 6 children

Descendant: IMG http://www.jacquisflowershop.com/jquery/astor.png
Descendant: IMG http://www.jacquisflowershop.com/jquery/daffodil.png
Descendant: IMG http://www.jacquisflowershop.com/jquery/rose.png
Descendant: IMG http://www.jacquisflowershop.com/jquery/peony.png
Descendant: IMG http://www.jacquisflowershop.com/jquery/primula.png
Descendant: IMG http://www.jacquisflowershop.com/jquery/snowdrop.png
There are 6 img descendants
```

One of the nice features of the children and find methods is that you don't receive duplicate elements in the selection. Listing 6-12 provides a demonstration.

Listing 6-12. Generating a Selection with Overlapping Descendants

```
...
<script type="text/javascript">
    $(document).ready(function() {

        $('div.drow').add('div.dcell').find('img').each(function(index, elem) {
            console.log("Element: " + elem.tagName + " " + elem.src);
        });

    });
</script>
...
```

In this example, I start by creating a jQuery object that contains all of the div elements that are members of the drow class and all of the div elements that are members of the dcell class. The key point to note is that all of the members of the dcell class are contained within members of the drow class, meaning that you have overlapping sets of descendants and the potential for duplication when I use the find method with the img selector, since the img elements are descendants of both classes of div elements. But jQuery comes to the rescue and ensures that there are no duplicates in the elements returned, as demonstrated in the output from this script:

```
Element: IMG http://www.jacquisflowershop.com/jquery/astor.png
Element: IMG http://www.jacquisflowershop.com/jquery/daffodil.png
Element: IMG http://www.jacquisflowershop.com/jquery/rose.png
Element: IMG http://www.jacquisflowershop.com/jquery/peony.png
Element: IMG http://www.jacquisflowershop.com/jquery/primula.png
Element: IMG http://www.jacquisflowershop.com/jquery/snowdrop.png
```

Using the find Method to Create an Intersection

You can pass a jQuery object, an HTMLElement object, or an array of HTMLElement objects as the argument to the find method. When you do this, you select the intersection between the descendants in the source jQuery object and the elements in the argument object. Listing 6-13 provides a demonstration.

Listing 6-13. Using the find Method to Create an Intersection

```
<script type="text/javascript">
    $(document).ready(function() {

        var jq = $('label').filter('[for*=p]').not('[for=peony]');
        $('div.drow').find(jq).css("border", "thick solid blue");

    });
</script>
```

As this script demonstrates, the advantage of this approach is that you can be very specific about the elements that intersect with the descendants. I create a jQuery object that I then reduce using the filter and not methods. This object then becomes the argument to the find method on another jQuery object that contains all of the div elements in the drow class. The final selection is the intersection between the descendants of the div.drow elements and my reduced set of label elements. You can see the effect of the script in Figure 6-8.

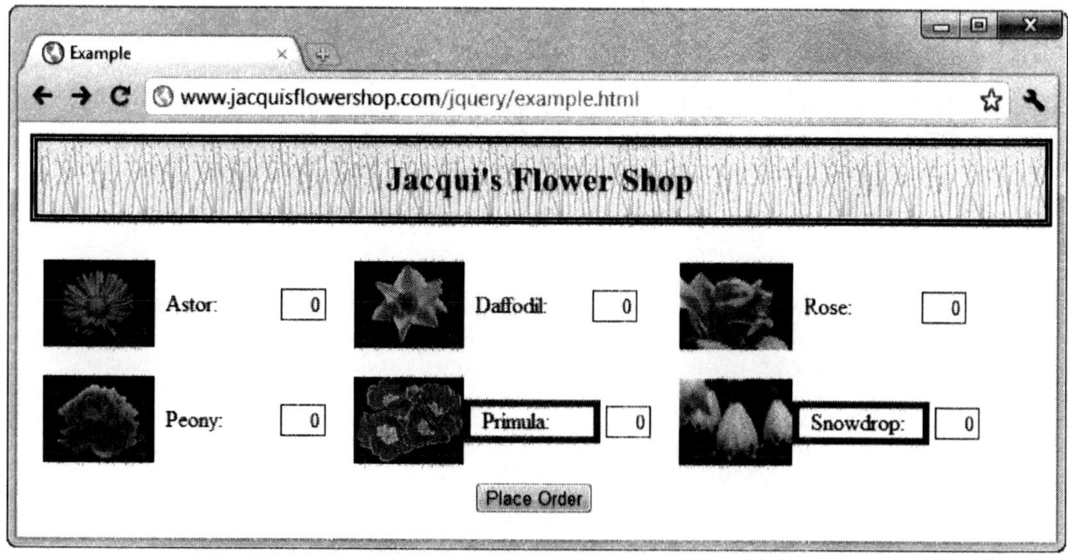

Figure 6-8. Using the find method to create an intersection

Navigating Up the Hierarchy

When you navigate up the DOM hierarchy, you are interested in parents and ancestors of the elements contained in a jQuery object. Table 6-9 shows the methods you can use to navigate upward.

Table 6-9. Methods to Navigate Up the DOM Hierarchy

Method	Description
closest(selector) closest(selector, context)	Selects the nearest ancestor for each element in the jQuery object that intersects with the specified selector.
closest(jQuery) closest(HTMLElement)	Selects the nearest ancestor for each element in the jQuery object that intersects with the elements contained in the argument object.
offsetParent()	Finds the nearest ancestor that has a value for the CSS position property of fixed, absolute, or relative.
parent() parent(selector)	Selects the parent for each element in the jQuery object, optionally filtered by a selector.
parents() parents(selector)	Selects the ancestors for each element in the jQuery object, optionally filtered by a selector.
parentsUntil(selector) parentsUntil(selector, selector)	Selects the ancestors for each element in the jQuery object until a match for the selector is encountered. The results can be filtered using a second selector.
parentsUntil(HTMLElement) parentsUntil(HTMLElement, selector) parentsUntil(HTMLElement[]) parentsUntil(HTMLElement[], selector)	Selects the ancestors for each element in the jQuery object until one of the specified elements is encountered. The results can be filtered using a selector.

Selecting Parent Elements

The parent method lets you select the parent element for each of the elements in a jQuery object. If you provide a selector, then only parent elements that match the selector will be included in the result. Listing 6-14 shows the parent element in use.

Listing 6-14. Using the Parent Element

```
...
<script type="text/javascript">
    $(document).ready(function() {

        $('div.dcell').parent().each(function(index, elem) {
            console.log("Element: " + elem.tagName + " " + elem.id);
        });
```

```
        $('div.dcell').parent('#row1').each(function(index, elem) {
            console.log("Filtered Element: " + elem.tagName + " " + elem.id);
        });

    });
</script>
...
```

In this script, I select all of the div elements who are members of the dcell class and then call the parent method to select the parent elements. I have also demonstrated using the parent method with a selector. I use the each method to write information about the selected parent elements to the console, which produces the following output:

```
Element: DIV row1
Element: DIV row2
Filtered Element: DIV row1
```

Selecting Ancestors

The parents method (note the final letter s) lets you select all of the ancestors of elements in a jQuery object, not just the immediate parents. Once again, you can pass a selector as a method to the argument to filter the results. Listing 6-15 demonstrates the parents method.

Listing 6-15. Using the parents Method

```
...
<script type="text/javascript">
    $(document).ready(function() {

        $('img[src*=peony], img[src*=rose]').parents().each(function(index, elem) {
            console.log("Element: " + elem.tagName + " " + elem.className + " "
                                + elem.id);
        });

    });
</script>
...
```

In this example, I have selected two of the img elements and used the parents method to select their ancestors. I then write information about each ancestor to the console, to produce the following output:

```
Element: DIV dcell
Element: DIV drow row2
Element: DIV dcell
Element: DIV drow row1
Element: DIV dtable
Element: DIV  oblock
```

```
Element: FORM
Element: BODY
Element: HTML
```

A variation on selecting ancestors is presented by the `parentsUntil` method. For each element in the jQuery object, the `parentsUntil` method works its way up the DOM hierarchy, selecting ancestor elements until an element that matches the selector is encountered. Listing 6-16 provides a demonstration.

Listing 6-16. Using the parentsUntil Method

```
...
<script>
    $(document).ready(function() {

        $('img[src*=peony], img[src*=rose]').parentsUntil('form')
            .each(function(index, elem) {
                console.log("Element: " + elem.tagName + " " + elem.className
                        + " " + elem.id);
        });

    });
</script>
...
```

In this example, the ancestors for each element are selected until a `form` element is encountered. The output from the script is as follows:

```
Element: DIV dcell
Element: DIV drow row2
Element: DIV dcell
Element: DIV drow row1
Element: DIV dtable
Element: DIV  oblock
```

Notice that elements that match the selector are excluded from the selected ancestors. In this example, this means that the form element is excluded. You can filter the set of ancestors by providing a second selector argument, as shown in Listing 6-17.

Listing 6-17. Filtering the Set of Elements Selected by the parentsUntil Method

```
...
<script type="text/javascript">
    $(document).ready(function() {

        $('img[src*=peony], img[src*=rose]').parentsUntil('form', ':not(.dcell)')
            .each(function(index, elem) {
            console.log("Element: " + elem.tagName + " " + elem.className
                        + " " + elem.id);
```

```
        });

    });
</script>
...
```

In this example, I have added a selector that will filter out elements that belong to the dcell class. The output from this script is as follows:

```
Element: DIV drow row2
Element: DIV drow row1
Element: DIV dtable
Element: DIV  oblock
```

Selecting the First Matching Ancestor

The closest method lets you select the first ancestor that is matched by a selector for each element in a jQuery object. Listing 6-18 provides a demonstration.

Listing 6-18. Using the closest Method

```
...
<script type="text/javascript">
    $(document).ready(function() {

        $('img').closest('.drow').each(function(index, elem) {
            console.log("Element: " + elem.tagName + " " + elem.className
                        + " " + elem.id);
        });

        var contextElem = document.getElementById("row1");
        $('img').closest('.drow', contextElem).each(function(index, elem) {
            console.log("Context Element: " + elem.tagName + " " + elem.className
                        + " " + elem.id);
        });

    });
</script>
...
```

In this example, I select the img elements in the document and then use the closest method to find the nearest ancestor that belongs to the drow class.

You can narrow the scope for selecting ancestors by specifying an HTMLElement object as the second argument to the method. Ancestors that are not the context object or are not descendants of the context object are excluded from the selection. The output from the script is as follows:

```
Element: DIV drow row1
Element: DIV drow row2
Context Element: DIV drow row2
```

When you specify a jQuery object or one or more HTMLElement objects as the argument to the closest method, jQuery works its way up the hierarchy for each element in the source jQuery object, matching the first argument object it finds. This is demonstrated by Listing 6-19.

Listing 6-19. Using the Closest Method with a Set of Reference Objects

```
...
<script type="text/javascript">
    $(document).ready(function() {

        var jq = $('#row1, #row2, form');

        $('img[src*=rose]').closest(jq).each(function(index, elem) {
            console.log("Context Element: " + elem.tagName + " " + elem.className
                        + " " + elem.id);
        });

    });
</script>
...
```

In this example, I select one of the img elements in the document and then use the closest method to select the ancestor elements. I have supplied a jQuery object containing the form element and the elements with the row1 and row2 ID as the argument to the closest method. jQuery will select whichever of the elements is the nearest ancestor to the img element. In other words, it will start to work its way up the hierarchy until it encounters one of the elements in the argument object. The output for this script is as follows:

```
Context Element: DIV drow row1
```

The offsetParent is a variation on the closest theme and funds the first ancestor that has a value for the position CSS property of relative, absolute, or fixed. Such an element is known as a *positioned ancestor*, and finding one can be useful when working with animation (see Chapter10 for details of jQuery support for animation). Listing 6-20 contains a demonstration of this method.

Listing 6-20. Using the offsetParent Method

```
<!DOCTYPE html>
<html>
<head>
    <title>Example</title>
    <script src="jquery-1.7.js" type="text/javascript"></script>
    <link rel="stylesheet" type="text/css" href="styles.css"/>
    <style type="text/css">
```

```
            #oblock {position: fixed; top: 120px; left: 50px}
        </style>
        <script type="text/javascript">
            $(document).ready(function() {
                $('img[src*=astor]').offsetParent().css("background-color", "lightgrey");
            });
        </script>
</head>
<body>
    <h1>Jacqui's Flower Shop</h1>
    <form method="post">
        <div id="oblock">
            <div class="dtable">
                <div id="row1" class="drow">
                    <div class="dcell">
                        <img src="astor.png"/><label for="astor">Astor:</label>
                        <input name="astor" value="0" required>
                    </div>
                    <div class="dcell">
                        <img src="daffodil.png"/><label for="daffodil">Daffodil:</label>
                        <input name="daffodil" value="0" required >
                    </div>
                    <div class="dcell">
                        <img src="rose.png"/><label for="rose">Rose:</label>
                        <input name="rose" value="0" required>
                    </div>
                </div>
            </div>
        </div>
        <div id="buttonDiv"><button type="submit">Place Order</button></div>
    </form>
</body>
</html>
```

In this cut-down version of the example document, I have used CSS to set a value for the position property for the element with the id of oblock. In the script, I use jQuery to select one of the img elements and then call the offsetParent method to find the closest positioned element. This method works its way up the hierarchy until it reaches an element with one of the required values. I use the css property to set a value for the background-color property for the selected element, as you can see in Figure 6-9.

Figure 6-9. Finding the closest positioned ancestor

Navigating Across the Hierarchy

The final form of DOM navigation deals with siblings. The methods that jQuery provides for this are described in Table 6-10.

Table 6-10. *Methods to Navigate Across the DOM Hierarchy*

Method	Description
`next()` `next(selector)`	Selects the immediate next sibling for each element in the `jQuery` object, optionally filtered by a selector.
`nextAll()` `nextAll(selector)`	Selects all of the next siblings for each element in the `jQuery` object, optionally filtered by a selector.

`nextUntil((selector)`
`nextUntil(selector, selector)`
`nextUntil(jQuery)`
`nextUntil(jQuery, selector)`
`nextUntil(HTMLElement[])`
`nextUntil(HTMLElement[], selector)`
	Selects the next siblings for each element up to (and excluding) an element that matches the selector or an element in the `jQuery` object or the `HTMLElement` array. The results can optionally be filtered by a selector as the second argument to the method.

`prev()` `prev(selector)`	Selects the immediate previous sibling for each element in the `jQuery` object, optionally filtered by a selector.
`prevAll()` `prevAll(selector)`	Selects all of the previous siblings for each element in the `jQuery` object, optionally filtered by a selector.

`prevUntil(selector)`
`prevUntil(selector, selector)`
`prevUntil(jQuery)`
	Selects the previous siblings for each element up to (and excluding) an element that matches the selector or an element in the `jQuery` object or the `HTMLElement` array. The

`prevUntil(jQuery, selector)`
`prevUntil(HTMLElement[])`
`prevUntil(HTMLElement[], selector)`
	results can optionally be filtered by a selector as the second argument to the method.

`siblings()` `siblings(selector)`	Selects all of the siblings for each of the elements in the jQuery object, optionally filtered by a selector.

Selecting All Siblings

The siblings method selects all of the siblings for all of the elements in a jQuery object. Listing 6-21 shows this method in use. (For this listing, I have returned to the full flower shop document shown in Listing 6-1).

Listing 6-21. Using the siblings Method

```
...
<script type="text/javascript">
    $(document).ready(function() {

        $('img[src*=astor], img[src*=primula]')
            .parent().siblings().css("border", "thick solid blue");

    });
</script>
...
```

In this example, I select two of the img elements, call the parent method to select their parent elements, and then call the siblings method to select their sibling elements. Both the previous and next siblings will be selected, and I use the css method to set a value for the border property. You can see the effect in Figure 6-10. (I used the parent method to make the effect of the CSS property clearer.)

Figure 6-10. Selecting sibling elements

Notice that only the siblings are selected, not the elements themselves. Of course, this changes if one element in the jQuery object is a sibling of another, as shown in Listing 6-22.

Listing 6-22. Overlapping Sets of Siblings

```
...
<script type="text/javascript">
    $(document).ready(function() {
        $('#row1 div.dcell').siblings().css("border", "thick solid blue");
    });
</script>
...
```

In this script, I start by selecting all of the div elements that are children of the row1 element and then call the siblings method. Each of the elements in the selection is the sibling to at least one of the other elements, as you can see in Figure 6-11.

Figure 6-11. Overlapping sibling elements

Selecting Next and Previous Siblings

I am not going to demonstrate all of the methods for selecting next and previous siblings, because they work in the same way as the other navigation methods. Listing 6-23 shows the `nextAll` and `prevAll` methods in use.

Listing 6-23. Using the nextAll and prevAll Methods

```
<script type="text/javascript">
    $(document).ready(function() {
        $('img[src*=astor]').parent().nextAll().css("border", "thick solid blue");
        $('img[src*=primula]').parent().prevAll().css("border", "thick double red");
    });
</script>
```

This script selects the next siblings for the parent of the astor image and the previous siblings for the primula image. You can see the effect of this script in Figure 6-12.

Figure 6-12. Selecting next and previous siblings

Summary

In this chapter, I showed you how to take control of the jQuery selection and tailor it to your exact needs, including adding elements, filtering elements, using mapping, and testing the selection to assess a condition. I also showed you how you can use a jQuery selection as the starting point to navigate the DOM, using one selection as the starting point for traversing the document in order to create another.

CHAPTER 7

Manipulating the DOM

In the previous chapter, I showed you how to select elements. One of the most powerful things you can do with the selection is to change the structure of the HTML document itself, known as *manipulating the DOM*. In this chapter, I'll show you the different ways in which you can alter the structure, including inserting elements as children, parents, or siblings of other elements. I'll also show you how to create new elements, how to move elements from one part of the document to another, and how to remove elements entirely. Table 7-1 provides the summary for this chapter.

***Table 7-1.** Chapter Summary*

Problem	Solution	Listing
Create new elements.	Pass an HTML fragment to the $ function, by using the `clone` method or by using the DOM API.	1–3
Insert elements as last children.	Use the `append` method.	4
Insert elements as first children.	Use the `prepend` method.	5, 6
Insert the same elements in different positions.	Clone the elements before inserting them.	7–8
Insert the contents of a `jQuery` object as children of other elements.	Use the `appendTo` or `prependTo` methods.	9
Insert child elements dynamically.	Pass a function to the `append` or `prepend` methods.	10
Insert parent elements.	Use the `wrap` method.	11
Insert a common parent to several elements.	Use the `wrapAll` method.	12, 13
Wrap the contents of elements.	Use the `wrapInner` method.	14

Wrap elements dynamically.	Pass a function to the `wrap` or `wrapInner` method.	15
Insert sibling elements.	Use the `after`, `before`, `insertAfter`, or `insertBefore` method.	16, 17
Insert sibling elements dynamically.	Pass a function to the `before` or `after` method.	18
Replace elements with other elements.	Use the `replaceWith` or `replaceAll` method.	19
Replace elements dynamically.	Pass a function to the `replaceWith` method.	20
Remove elements from the DOM.	Use the `remove` or `detach` method.	21–23
Remove the contents of an element.	Use the `empty` method.	24
Remove the parents of elements.	Use the `unwrap` method.	25

Creating New Elements

You often need to create new elements before you can insert them into the DOM (although you can insert existing elements, as I'll explain later in the chapter). In the sections that follow, I'll show you some different ways that you can create content.

■ **Tip** It is important to understand that creating new elements doesn't automatically add them to the DOM. You need to explicitly tell jQuery where the new elements should be placed in the document, which I explain later in this chapter.

Creating Elements Using the $ Function

You can create new elements by passing an HTML fragment string to the $ function. jQuery parses the string and creates the corresponding DOM objects. Listing 7-1 contains an example.

Listing 7-1. Creating New Elements Using the $ Function

```
<!DOCTYPE html>
<html>
<head>
    <title>Example</title>
    <script src="jquery-1.7.js" type="text/javascript"></script>
```

```
    <link rel="stylesheet" type="text/css" href="styles.css"/>
    <script type="text/javascript">
        $(document).ready(function() {

            var newElems = $('<div class="dcell"><img src="lily.png"/></div>');

            newElems.each(function (index, elem) {
                console.log("New element: " + elem.tagName + " " + elem.className);
            });

            newElems.children().each(function(index, elem) {
                console.log("Child: " + elem.tagName + " " + elem.src);
            });
        });
    </script>
</head>
<body>
    <h1>Jacqui's Flower Shop</h1>
    <form method="post">
        <div id="oblock">
            <div class="dtable">
                <div id="row1" class="drow">
                    <div class="dcell">
                        <img src="astor.png"/><label for="astor">Astor:</label>
                        <input name="astor" value="0" required>
                    </div>
                    <div class="dcell">
                        <img src="daffodil.png"/><label for="daffodil">Daffodil:</label>
                        <input name="daffodil" value="0" required >
                    </div>
                    <div class="dcell">
                        <img src="rose.png"/><label for="rose">Rose:</label>
                        <input name="rose" value="0" required>
                    </div>
                </div>
                <div id="row2"class="drow">
                    <div class="dcell">
                        <img src="peony.png"/><label for="peony">Peony:</label>
                        <input name="peony" value="0" required>
                    </div>
                    <div class="dcell">
                        <img src="primula.png"/><label for="primula">Primula:</label>
                        <input name="primula" value="0" required>
                    </div>
                    <div class="dcell">
                        <img src="snowdrop.png"/><label for="snowdrop">Snowdrop:</label>
                        <input name="snowdrop" value="0" required>
                    </div>
                </div>
            </div>
        </div>
```

```
        <div id="buttonDiv"><button type="submit">Place Order</button></div>
    </form>
</body>
</html>
```

In this example, I have created two new elements from an HTML fragment: a div element and an img element. Since you are dealing with HTML, you can use fragments that contain structure. In this case, the img element is a child of the div element.

The jQuery object that is returned by the $ function contains only the top-level elements from the HTML fragment. To demonstrate this, I have used the each function to write information about each element in the jQuery object to the console. jQuery doesn't discard the child elements. They are accessible via the usual navigation methods (which I described in Chapter 6). To demonstrate this, I have called the children method on the jQuery object and printed information about each child element to the console as well. The output from this script is as follows:

```
New element: DIV dcell
Child: IMG http://www.jacquisflowershop.com/jquery/lily.png
```

Creating New Elements by Cloning Existing Elements

You can create new elements from existing elements by using the clone method. This duplicates all of the elements in a jQuery object, along with all of their descendant elements. Listing 7-2 gives an example.

Listing 7-2. Cloning Elements

```
...
<script type="text/javascript">
    $(document).ready(function() {

        var newElems = $('div.dcell').clone();

        newElems.each(function (index, elem) {
            console.log("New element: " + elem.tagName + " " + elem.className);
        });

        newElems.children('img').each(function(index, elem) {
            console.log("Child: " + elem.tagName + " " + elem.src);
        });

    });
</script>
...
```

In this script I have selected and cloned all of the div elements that are members of the dcell class. To demonstrate that the descendant elements are cloned as well, I have used the children method with a selector to obtain the cloned img elements. I have written details of the div and img elements to the console, producing the following output:

```
New element: DIV dcell
New element: DIV dcell
New element: DIV dcell
New element: DIV dcell
New element: DIV dcell
New element: DIV dcell
Child: IMG http://www.jacquisflowershop.com/jquery/astor.png
Child: IMG http://www.jacquisflowershop.com/jquery/daffodil.png
Child: IMG http://www.jacquisflowershop.com/jquery/rose.png
Child: IMG http://www.jacquisflowershop.com/jquery/peony.png
Child: IMG http://www.jacquisflowershop.com/jquery/primula.png
Child: IMG http://www.jacquisflowershop.com/jquery/snowdrop.png
```

■ **Tip** You can pass the value `true` as an argument to the `clone` method to include the event handlers and data associated with the elements in the copying process. Omitting this argument or specifying a value of `false` omits the event handlers and data. I explain the jQuery support for events in Chapter 9 and explain how to associate data with elements in Chapter 8.

Creating Elements Using the DOM API

You can use the DOM API directly to create new `HTMLElement` objects, which is essentially what jQuery is doing for you when you use the other techniques. I am not going to explain the details of the DOM API, but Listing 7-3 contains a simple example to give you a sense of how you can approach this technique.

Listing 7-3. Using the DOM API to Create New Elements

```
...
<script type="text/javascript">
    $(document).ready(function() {

        var divElem = document.createElement("div");
        divElem.classList.add("dcell");

        var imgElem = document.createElement("img");
        imgElem.src = "lily.png";

        divElem.appendChild(imgElem);

        var newElems = $(divElem);

        newElems.each(function (index, elem) {
            console.log("New element: " + elem.tagName + " " + elem.className);
        });

        newElems.children('img').each(function(index, elem) {
```

```
            console.log("Child: " + elem.tagName + " " + elem.src);
        });

    });
</script>
...
```

In this example, I create and configure a div HTMLElement and an img HTMLElement and assign the img as the child of the div, just as I did in the first example. There is nothing wrong with creating elements this way, but since this is a book about jQuery, I don't want to go off-topic by straying too far into the DOM API.

I pass the div HTMLElement as an argument to the jQuery $ function so I can use the same each functions as for the other examples. The console output is as follows:

```
New element: DIV dcell
Child: IMG http://www.jacquisflowershop.com/jquery/lily.png
```

Inserting Child and Descendant Elements

Now that you have seen how to create elements, you can start to insert them into the document. You will start by looking at the methods that allow you to insert one element inside another in order to create child and descendant elements. Table 7-2 describes these methods.

Table 7-2. *Methods for Inserting Child and Descendant Elements*

Method	Description
append(HTML) append(jQuery) append(HTMLElement[])	Inserts the specified elements as the last children of all of the elements in the DOM
prepend(HTML) prepend(jQuery) prepend(HTMLElement[])	Inserts the specified elements as the first children of all of the elements in the DOM
appendTo(jQuery) appendTo(HTMLElement[])	Inserts the elements in the jQuery object as the last children of the elements specified by the argument
prependTo(HTML) prependTo(jQuery) prependTo(HTMLElement[])	Inserts the elements in the jQuery object as the first children of the elements specified by the argument
append(function) prepend(function)	Appends or prepends the result of a function to the elements in the jQuery object

---

■ **Tip** You can also insert child elements using the `wrapInner` method, which I describe in the "Wrapping the Contents of Elements" section. This method inserts a new child between an element and its existing children. Another technique is to use the `html` method, which I describe in Chapter 8.

The elements that you pass as arguments are inserted as children to *every* element in the `jQuery` object, which makes it especially important to use the techniques I showed you in Chapter 6 to manage the selection so that it contains only the elements you want to work with. Listing 7-4 gives a demonstration of using the append method.

Listing 7-4. Using the append Method

```
...
<script type="text/javascript">
    $(document).ready(function() {
        var newElems = $("<div class='dcell'></div>")
            .append("<img src='lily.png'/>")
            .append("<label for='lily'>Lily:</label>")
            .append("<input name='lily' value='0' required />");

        newElems.css("border", "thick solid red");

        $('#row1').append(newElems);
    });
</script>
...
```

I use the append method in this script in two different ways: first to build up my set of new elements and then to insert those elements into the HTML document. Since this is the first DOM manipulation method that you have encountered, I am going to spend a moment demonstrating some behaviors that will help you avoid the most common DOM-related jQuery errors. But first, let's look at the effect of the script. You can see the result of adding the new elements in Figure 7-1.

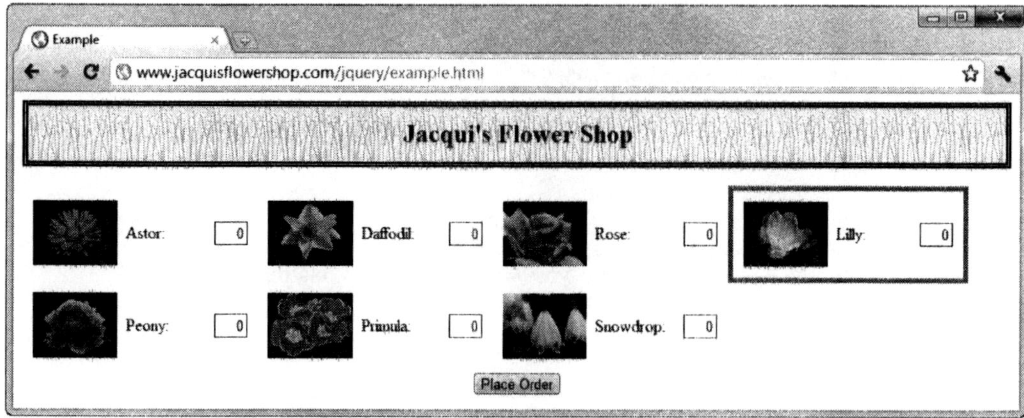

Figure 7-1. Inserting new elements into the document

The first thing you need to look at is the way I built up my new elements using the append method:

```
var newElems = $("<div class='dcell'/>").append("<img src='lily.png'/>")
    .append("<label for='lily'>Lily:</label>")
    .append("<input name='lily' value='0' required />");
```

I could have just created a single, bigger block of HTML that contained all of the elements, but I wanted to show a key facet of the DOM manipulation methods, which is that the jQuery objects returned by these methods contain the same elements as the object on which the methods were called. For example, I started with a jQuery object that contained a div element, and the result of each append method was a jQuery object that contained the same div element and not the element that I added. This means that chaining append calls together creates multiple new child elements for the originally selected elements.

The next behavior I wanted to point out was that newly created elements may not be attached to the document, but you can still use jQuery to navigate and modify them. I wanted to highlight the new elements with a border, so I made the following call:

```
newElems.css("border", "thick solid red");
```

This is a nice feature that allows you to create and manage complex sets of elements and prepare them fully before adding them to the document.

Finally, I add the new elements to the document, like this:

```
$('#row1').append(newElems);
```

The new elements are added to each element in the selection. There is only one element in this selection (the one with the row1 id), and so you have the new lily product on your flower shop page.

Prepending Elements

The complement to the append method is prepend, which inserts the new elements as the first children of the elements in the jQuery object. Listing 7-5 contains an example.

Listing 7-5. Using the prepend Method

```
...
<script type="text/javascript">
    $(document).ready(function() {

        var orchidElems = $("<div class='dcell'/>")
            .append("<img src='orchid.png'/>")
            .append("<label for='orchid'>Orchid:</label>")
            .append("<input name='orchid' value='0' required />");

        var newElems = $("<div class='dcell'/>")
            .append("<img src='lily.png'/>")
            .append("<label for='lily'>Lily:</label>")
            .append("<input name='lily' value='0' required />").add(orchidElems);

        newElems.css("border", "thick solid red");

        $('#row1, #row2').prepend(newElems);
    });
</script>
...
```

In addition to the prepend method, this script demonstrates another jQuery DOM manipulation characteristic: *all* of the elements passed as an argument to one of these methods are added as children to *all* of the elements in the jQuery object. In this example, I create two div elements, one for lilies and one for orchids. I use the add method (highlighted in the listing) to bring both sets of elements together in a single jQuery.

■ **Tip** The add method will also accept a string containing an HTML fragment. You can use this feature as an alternative to building up new elements using jQuery objects.

I then create another jQuery object that contains the elements with the row1 and row2 id values and use the prepend method to insert the orchid and lily elements into the document. You can see the effect in Figure 7-2.

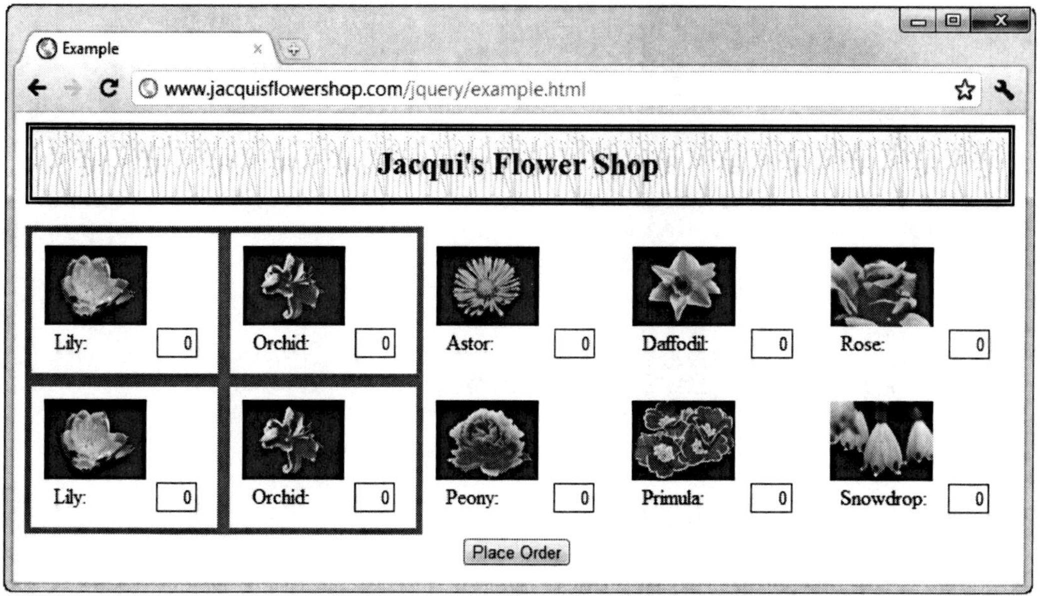

Figure 7-2. Adding multiple new elements to multiple selected elements

The new elements are highlighted with a red border again. As the figure shows, the lily and orchid elements have both been added to both row elements. As an alternative to using the add method, you can pass multiple elements to the DOM modification methods, as shown in Listing 7-6.

Listing 7-6. Passing Multiple Arguments to the prepend Method

```
...
<script type="text/javascript">
    $(document).ready(function() {

        var orchidElems = $("<div class='dcell'/>")
            .append("<img src='orchid.png'/>")
            .append("<label for='orchid'>Orchid:</label>")
            .append("<input name='orchid' value='0' required />");

        var lilyElems = $("<div class='dcell'/>")
            .append("<img src='lily.png'/>")
            .append("<label for='lily'>Lily:</label>")
            .append("<input name='lily' value='0' required />");

        lilyElems.css("border", "thick solid red");

        $('#row1, #row2').prepend(lilyElems, orchidElems);
    });
</script>
...
```

Inserting the Same Elements in Different Positions

You can add new elements to the document only once. At this point, using them as arguments to a DOM insertion method moves the elements, rather than duplicates them. Listing 7-7 shows the problem.

Listing 7-7. Adding New Elements to the Document Twice

```
...
<script type="text/javascript">
    $(document).ready(function() {

        var orchidElems = $("<div class='dcell'/>")
            .append("<img src='orchid.png'/>")
            .append("<label for='orchid'>Orchid:</label>")
            .append("<input name='orchid' value='0' required />");

        var newElems = $("<div class='dcell'/>")
            .append("<img src='lily.png'/>")
            .append("<label for='lily'>Lily:</label>")
            .append("<input name='lily' value='0' required />").add(orchidElems);

        newElems.css("border", "thick solid red");

        $('#row1').append(newElems);
        $('#row2').prepend(newElems);
    });
</script>
...
```

The intent in this script is clear: to append the new elements to `row1` and prepend them to `row2`. Of course, this isn't what happens, as Figure 7-3 demonstrates.

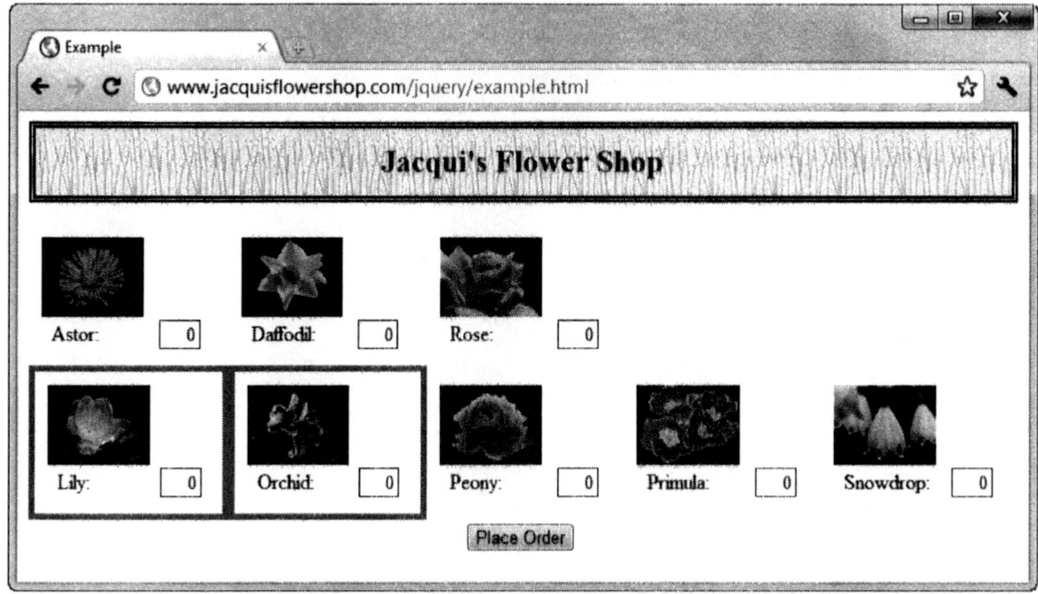

Figure 7-3. Trying (and failing) to add new elements to the document twice

The elements *were* appended to row1, but the call to prepend has the effect of moving the elements rather than adding them twice. To address this issue, you need to create copies of the elements you want to insert by using the clone method. Listing 7-8 shows the revised script.

Listing 7-8. Cloning Elements So They Can Be Added to the Document More Than Once

```
<script type="text/javascript">
    $(document).ready(function() {

        var orchidElems = $("<div class='dcell'/>")
            .append("<img src='orchid.png'/>")
            .append("<label for='orchid'>Orchid:</label>")
            .append("<input name='orchid' value='0' required />");

        var newElems = $("<div class='dcell'/>")
            .append("<img src='lily.png'/>")
            .append("<label for='lily'>Lily:</label>")
            .append("<input name='lily' value='0' required />").add(orchidElems);

        newElems.css("border", "thick solid red");

        $('#row1').append(newElems);
        $('#row2').prepend(newElems.clone());
    });
</script>
```

The elements are now copied and inserted in both locations, as shown in Figure 7-4.

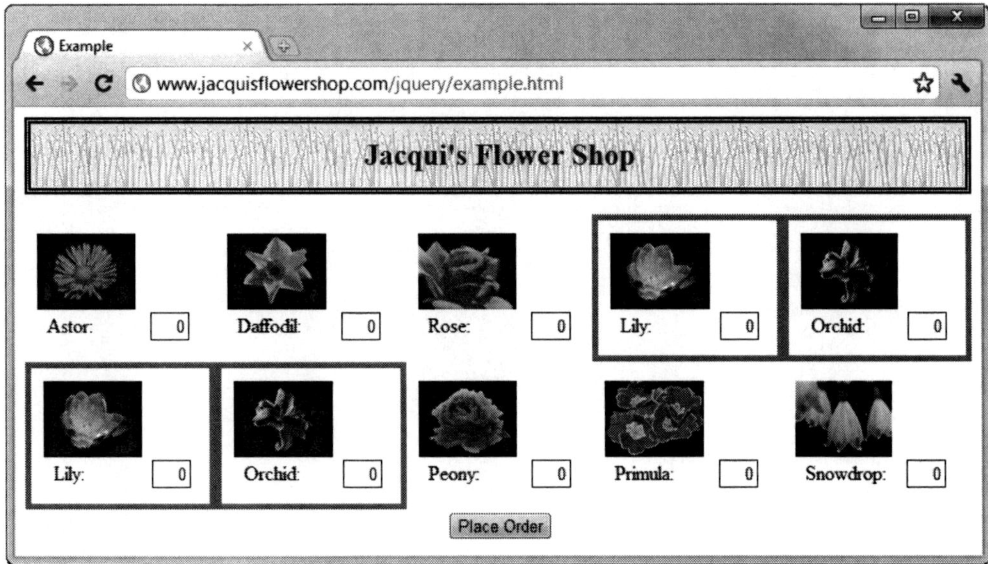

Figure 7-4. Cloning and inserting elements

Inserting from a jQuery Object

You can use the appendTo and prependTo methods to change the relationship around. The elements are in the jQuery object are inserted as the children of the elements specified by the argument. Listing 7-9 provides an example.

Listing 7-9. Using the appendTo Method

```
...
<script type="text/javascript">
    $(document).ready(function() {

        var newElems = $("<div class='dcell'/>");

        $('img').appendTo(newElems);

        $('#row1').append(newElems);
    });
</script>
...
```

In this script, I create jQuery objects to contain a new div element and the img elements in the document. I then use the appendTo method to append the img elements as the children of the div element. You can see the result in Figure 7-5. As you can see, the effect of the script is to move the img elements to the new div element, which I appended to the row1 element.

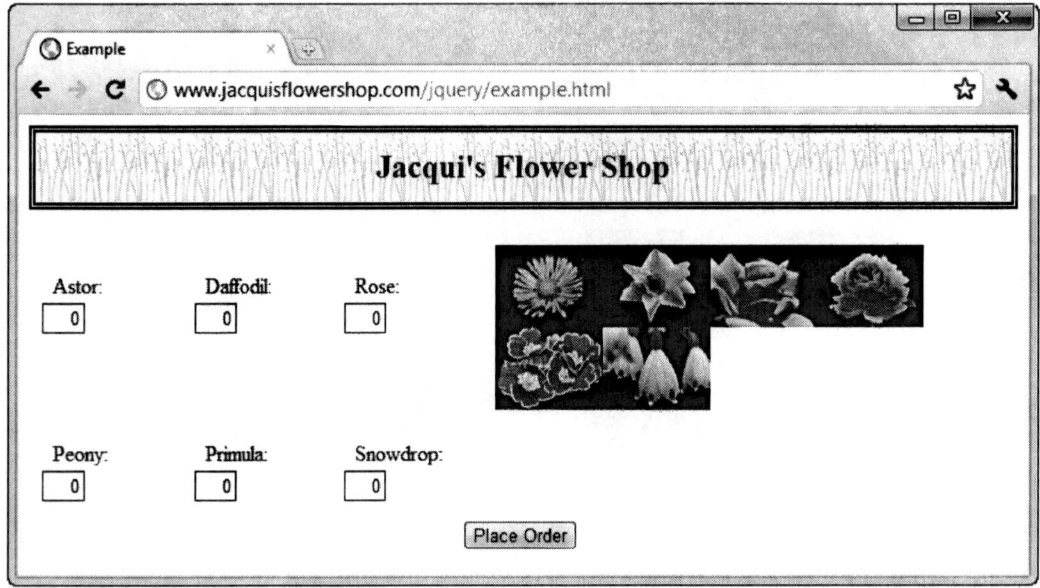

Figure 7-5. Using the appendTo method

Inserting Elements Using a Function

You can pass a function to the append and prepend methods. This allows you to dynamically insert children for the elements selected by the jQuery object, as shown by Listing 7-10.

Listing 7-10. Adding Child Elements Dynamically with a Function

```
<script type="text/javascript">
    $(document).ready(function() {

        var orchidElems = $("<div class='dcell'/>")
            .append("<img src='orchid.png'/>")
            .append("<label for='orchid'>Orchid:</label>")
            .append("<input name='orchid' value='0' required />");

        var lilyElems = $("<div class='dcell'/>")
            .append("<img src='lily.png'/>")
            .append("<label for='lily'>Lily:</label>")
            .append("<input name='lily' value='0' required />");

        $(orchidElems).add(lilyElems).css("border", "thick solid red");

        $('div.drow').append(function(index, html) {
            if (this.id == "row1") {
                return orchidElems;
            } else {
```

```
                return lilyElems;
            }
        });
    });
</script>
```

The function is invoked once for each element in the jQuery object. The arguments passed to the function are the index of the element in the selection and the HTML of the element that is being processed; the HTML is a string. In addition, the value of the this variable is set to the appropriate HTMLElement. The result from the function will be appended or prepended to the element being processed. You can return an HTML fragment, one or more HTMLElement objects, or a jQuery object.

In this example, I prepare by creating sets of elements for the lily and orchid products and then return them from the append function based on the value of the id property. You can see the result in Figure 7-6.

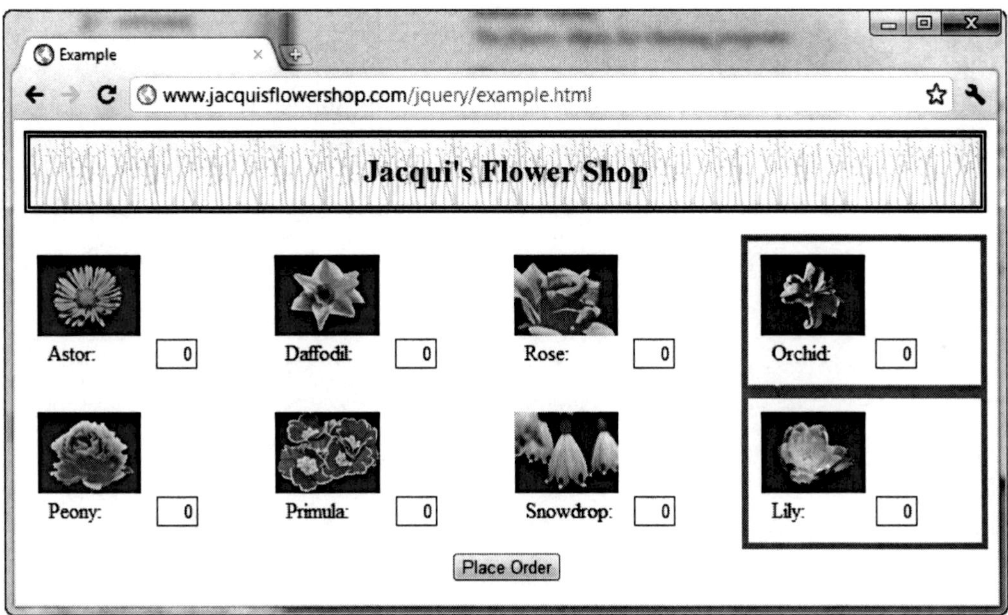

Figure 7-6. Inserting elements dynamically based on a function

Inserting Parent and Ancestor Elements

jQuery provides you with a set of methods for inserting elements as parents or ancestors of other elements. This is known as *wrapping* (because one element is wrapped by another). Table 7-3 describes these methods.

Table 7-3. Methods for Wrapping Elements

Method	Description
wrap(HTML) wrap(jQuery) wrap(HTMLElement[])	Wraps the specified elements around each of the elements in the jQuery object
wrapAll(HTML) wrapAll(jQuery) wrapAll(HTMLElement[])	Wraps the specified elements around the set of elements in the jQuery object (as a single group)
wrapInner(HTML) wrapInner(jQuery) wrapInner(HTMLElement[])	Wraps the specified elements around the content of the elements in the jQuery object
wrap(function) wrapInner(function)	Wraps elements dynamically using a function

■ **Tip** The complement to the wrapping methods is `unwrap`, which I describe in the "Removing Elements" section later in this chapter.

When you perform wrapping, you can pass multiple elements as the argument, but you must make sure that there is only one inner element. Otherwise, jQuery can't figure out what to do. This means that each element in the method argument must have at most one parent and at most one child. Listing 7-11 demonstrates the use of the `wrap` method.

Listing 7-11. Using the wrap Method

```
...
<script type="text/javascript">
    $(document).ready(function() {

        var newElem = $("<div/>").css("border", "thick solid red");
        $('div.drow').wrap(newElem);

    });
</script>
...
```

In this script, I create a new `div` element and use the `css` method to set a value for the CSS `border` property. I then use the `wrap` method to insert the `div` element as the parent to all of the `label` elements in the document. You can see the effect in Figure 7-7.

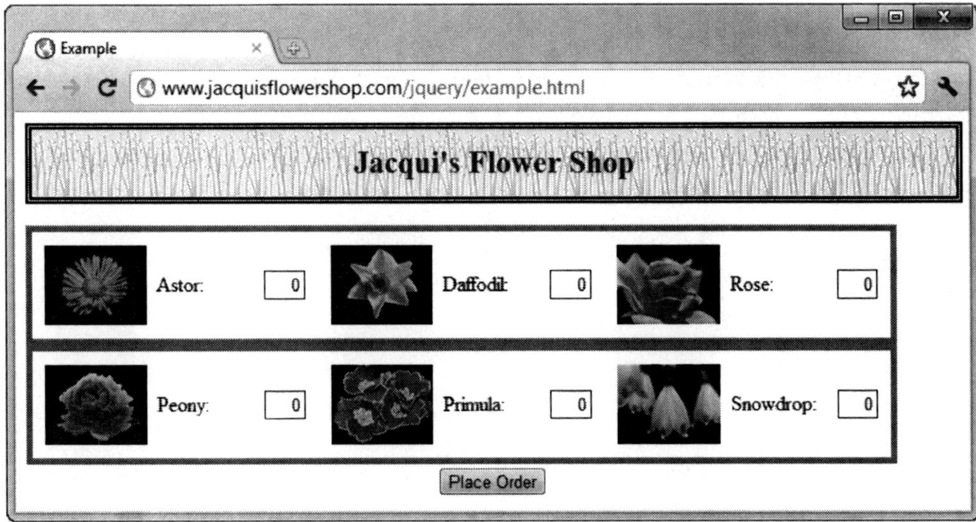

Figure 7-7. Using the wrap method to add a parent to elements

The elements that you pass as arguments to the `wrap` method are inserted between each element in the `jQuery` object and their current parents. So, for example, this fragment of HTML:

```
...
<div class="dtable">
    <div id="row1" class="drow">
        ...
    </div>
    <div id="row2" class="drow">
        ...
    </div>
</div>
...
```

is transformed like this:

```
...
<div class="dtable">
    <div style="...style properties...">
        <div id="row1" class="drow">
            ...
        </div>
    </div>
    <div style="...style properties...">
        <div id="row2" class="drow">
            ...
        </div>
    </div>
</div>
...
```

Wrapping Elements Together

When you use the wrap method, the new elements are cloned, and each element in the jQuery object gets its own new parent element. You can insert a single parent for several elements by using the wrapAll method, as shown in Listing 7-12.

Listing 7-12. Using the wrapAll Method

```
...
<script type="text/javascript">
    $(document).ready(function() {

        var newElem = $("<div/>").css("border", "thick solid red");
        $('div.drow').wrapAll(newElem);

    });
</script>
...
```

The only change in this script is the use of the wrapAll method. You can see the effect in Figure 7-8.

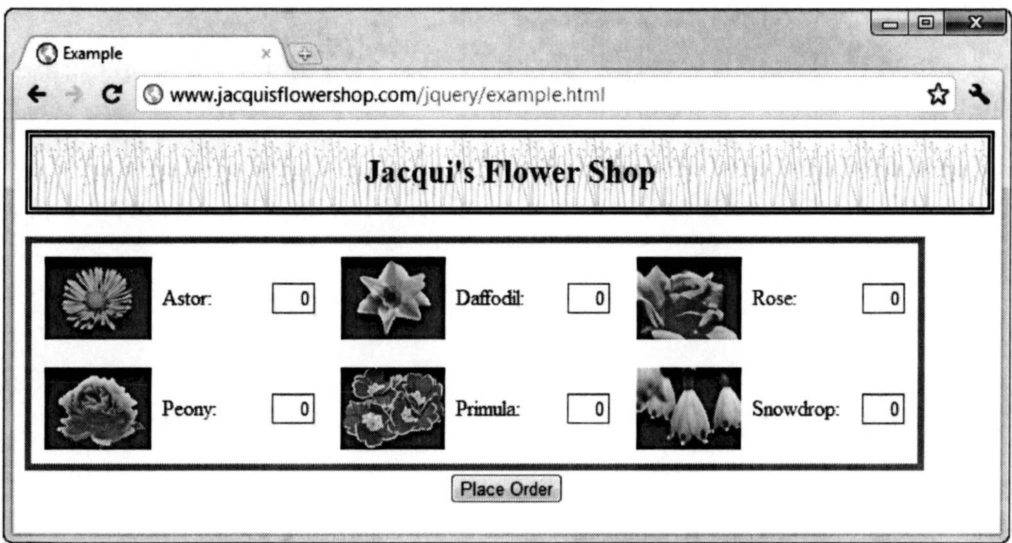

Figure 7-8. Using the wrapAll method

The new element is used to insert a common parent to the selected elements, such that the HTML is transformed like this:

```
...
<div class="dtable">
    <div style="...style properties...">
        <div id="row1" class="drow">
            ...
```

```
        </div>
        <div id="row2" class="drow">
        </div>
    </div>
</div>
...
```

Be careful when using this method. If the selected elements don't already share a common parent, then the new element is inserted as the parent to the first selected element. Then jQuery moves all of the other selected elements to be siblings of the first one. Listing 7-13 contains a script that shows this use of the method.

Listing 7-13. Using the wrapAll on Elements Without a Common Parent

```
...
<script type="text/javascript">
    $(document).ready(function() {

        var newElem = $("<div/>").css("border", "thick solid red");
        $('img').wrapAll(newElem);

    });
</script>
...
```

I have selected the img elements in the document, none of which share a common parent. You can see the effect of this script in Figure 7-9. The new div element has been inserted into the document as the parent to the astor image, and all of the other images have been inserted as siblings.

Figure 7-9. Using wrapAll on elements that don't share a common parent

Wrapping the Content of Elements

The wrapInner method wraps elements around the contents of the elements in a jQuery (as opposed to the elements themselves). Listing 7-14 provides a demonstration.

Listing 7-14. Using the wrapInner Method

```
<script type="text/javascript">
    $(document).ready(function() {

        var newElem = $("<div/>").css("border", "thick solid red");
        $('.dcell').wrapInner(newElem);

    });
</script>
```

The wrapInner method inserts new elements between the elements in the jQuery object and their immediate children. In the script, I select the elements that belong to the dcell class and wrap their contents with a new div element. You can see the effect in Figure 7-10.

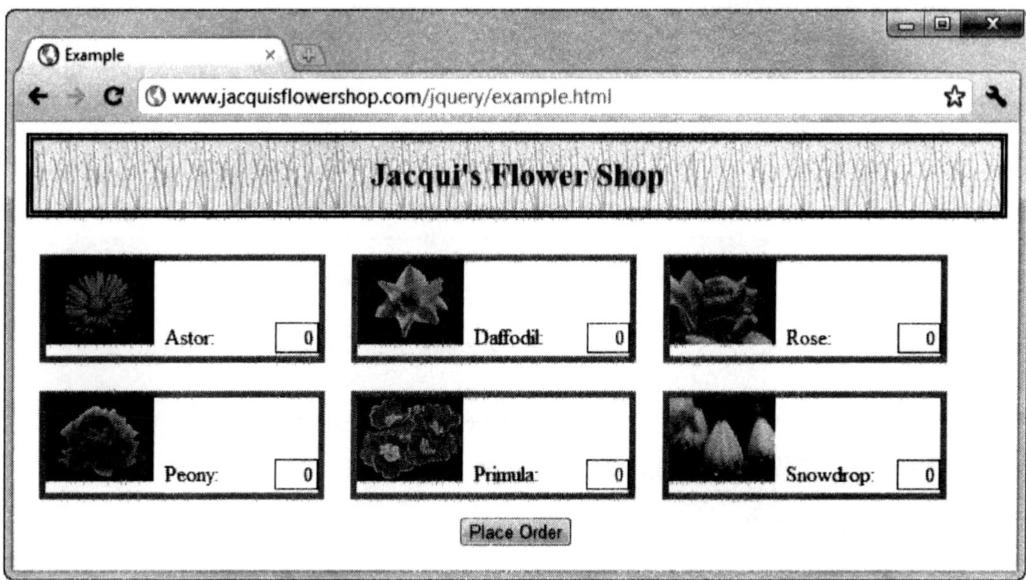

Figure 7-10. Using the wrapInner method

As an aside, you can achieve the effect of the wrapInner method using append. Just for reference, here is the equivalent script:

```
<script type="text/javascript">
    $(document).ready(function() {

        var newElem = $("<div/>").css("border", "thick solid red");
        $('.dcell').each(function(index, elem) {
```

```
            $(elem).append(newElem.clone().append($(elem).children()));
        });

    });
</script>
```

I am not suggesting you use this approach (the wrapInner method is easier to read and more convenient), but I think this is a good example of how you can use jQuery to approach the same problem in a number of different ways.

Wrapping Elements Using a Function

You can pass a function to the wrap and wrapInner methods to generate elements dynamically. The sole argument for this function is the index of the element in the selected elements. The special variable this is set to the element to be processed. The script in Listing 7-15 shows how you can wrap dynamically.

Listing 7-15. Wrapping Elements Dynamically

```
...
<script type="text/javascript">
    $(document).ready(function() {

        $('.drow').wrap(function(index) {
            if ($(this).has('img[src*=rose]').length > 0) {
                return $("<div/>").css("border", "thick solid blue");;
            } else {
                return $("<div/>").css("border", "thick solid red");;
            }
        });

    });
</script>
...
```

In this example, I use a function with the wrap method to tailor the new parent element based on the descendants of each of the selected elements. You can see the effect of this script in Figure 7-11.

Figure 7-11. Using the wrap method with a function to generate parent elements dynamically

Inserting Sibling Elements

As you might imagine, jQuery also provides you with a set of methods to insert elements into the document as siblings of existing elements. Table 7-4 describes these methods.

***Table 7-4.** Methods for Inserting Sibling Elements*

Method	Description

`after(HTML)`
`after(jQuery)`
`after(HTMLElement[])`
	Inserts the specified elements as next siblings to each element in the jQuery object

`before(HTML)`
`before(jQuery)`
`before(HTMLElement[])`
	Inserts the specified elements as previous siblings to each element in the `jQuery` object

`insertAfter(HTML)`
`insertAfter(jQuery)`
`insertAfter(HTMLElement[])`
	Inserts the elements in the `jQuery` object as the next siblings for each element specified in the argument

`insertBefore(HTML)`
`insertBefore(jQuery)`
`insertBefore(HTMLElement[])`
	Inserts the elements in the `jQuery` object as the previous siblings for each element specified in the argument

`after(function)` `before(function)`	Inserts siblings dynamically using a function

The before and after methods follow the same pattern you saw when inserting other kinds of element in the document. Listing 7-16 contains a demonstration of both methods.

Listing 7-16. Using the before and after Methods

```
...
<script type="text/javascript">
    $(document).ready(function() {

        var orchidElems = $("<div class='dcell'/>")
            .append("<img src='orchid.png'/>")
            .append("<label for='orchid'>Orchid:</label>")
            .append("<input name='orchid' value='0' required />");

        var lilyElems = $("<div class='dcell'/>")
            .append("<img src='lily.png'/>")
            .append("<label for='lily'>Lily:</label>")
            .append("<input name='lily' value='0' required />");

        $(orchidElems).add(lilyElems).css("border", "thick solid red");

        $('#row1 div.dcell').after(orchidElems);
        $('#row2 div.dcell').before(lilyElems);

    });
</script>
...
```

In this script, I create new sets of elements for orchids and lilies and use them with the before and after methods to insert them as siblings for each of the elements in the dcell class. The orchid elements are inserted as next siblings for all the elements in row1, and the lily elements are inserted as previous siblings for all of the elements in row2. You can see the effect of this script in Figure 7-12.

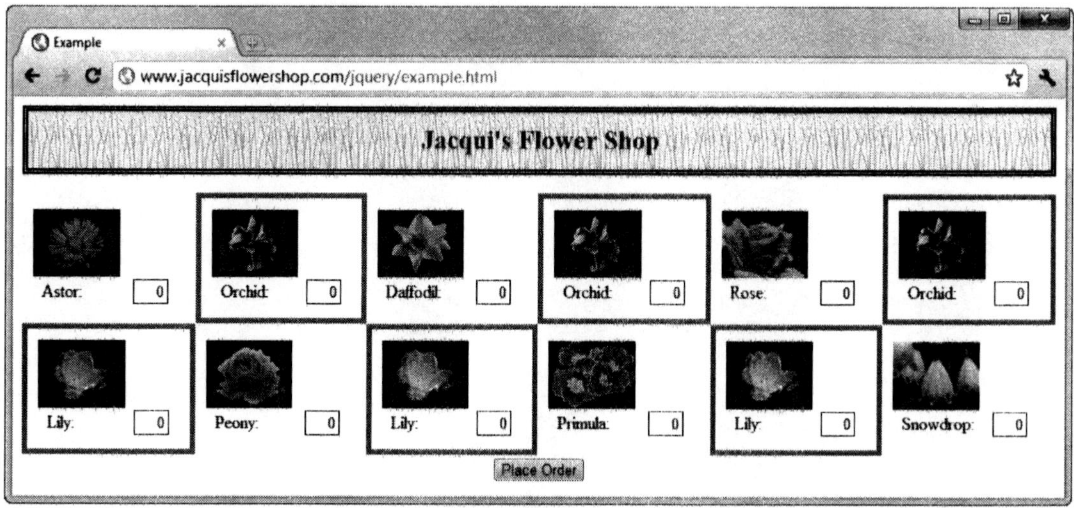

Figure 7-12. Using the before and after elements to create siblings

Inserting Siblings from a jQuery Object

The `insertAfter` and `insertBefore` methods insert the elements in the `jQuery` object as the next or previous siblings to the elements in the method argument. This is the same functionality as in the `after` and `before` methods, but the relationship between the `jQuery` object and the argument is reversed. Listing 7-17 shows the use of these methods. This script creates the same effect, as shown in Figure 7-12.

Listing 7-17. Using the insertAfter and InsertBefore Methods

```
<script type="text/javascript">
    $(document).ready(function() {

        var orchidElems = $("<div class='dcell'/>")
            .append("<img src='orchid.png'/>")
            .append("<label for='orchid'>Orchid:</label>")
            .append("<input name='orchid' value='0' required />");

        var lilyElems = $("<div class='dcell'/>")
            .append("<img src='lily.png'/>")
            .append("<label for='lily'>Lily:</label>")
            .append("<input name='lily' value='0' required />");

        $(orchidElems).add(lilyElems).css("border", "thick solid red");

        orchidElems.insertAfter('#row1 div.dcell');
        lilyElems.insertBefore('#row2 div.dcell');
    });
</script>
```

Inserting Siblings Using a Function

You can insert sibling elements dynamically using a function with the after and before methods, just as you did for parent and child elements. Listing 7-18 contains an example of dynamically generating sibling elements.

Listing 7-18. Generating Sibling Elements Dynamically with a Function

```
...
<script type="text/javascript">
    $(document).ready(function() {

        $('#row1 div.dcell').after(function(index, html) {
            if (index == 0) {
                return $("<div class='dcell'/>")
                    .append("<img src='orchid.png'/>")
                    .append("<label for='orchid'>Orchid:</label>")
                    .append("<input name='orchid' value='0' required />")
                    .css("border", "thick solid red");
            } else if (index == 1) {
                return $("<div class='dcell'/>")
                    .append("<img src='lily.png'/>")
                    .append("<label for='lily'>Lily:</label>")
                    .append("<input name='lily' value='0' required />")
                    .css("border", "thick solid red");
            }
        });

    });
</script>
...
```

In this script, I use the index argument to generate siblings when the index of the element being processed is 0 or 1. You can see the effect of this script in Figure 7-13.

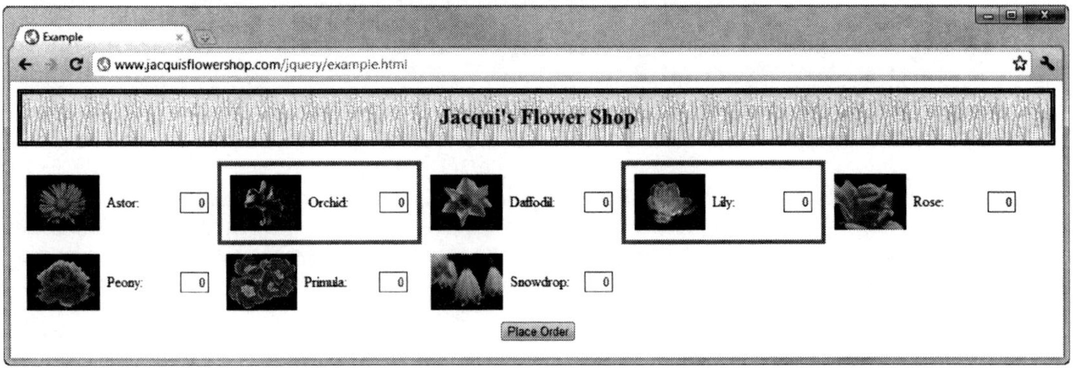

Figure 7-13. Adding sibling elements using a function

Replacing Elements

You can replace one set of elements with another using the methods described in Table 7-5.

***Table** 7-5. Methods for Wrapping Elements*

Method	Description
replaceWith(HTML) replaceWith(jQuery) replaceWith(HTMLElement[])	Replace the elements in the jQuery object with the specified content
replaceAll(jQuery) replaceAll(HTMLElement[])	Replace the elements specified by the argument with the elements in the jQuery object
replaceWith(function)	Replaces the elements in the jQuery object dynamically using a function

The replaceWith and the replaceAll methods work in the same way, with the exception that the role of the jQuery object and the argument are reversed. Listing 7-19 demonstrates both methods.

Listing 7-19. Using the replaceWith and replaceAll Methods

```
<script type="text/javascript">
    $(document).ready(function() {

        var newElems = $("<div class='dcell'/>")
                    .append("<img src='orchid.png'/>")
                    .append("<label for='orchid'>Orchid:</label>")
                    .append("<input name='orchid' value='0' required />")
                    .css("border", "thick solid red");

        $('#row1').children().first().replaceWith(newElems);

        $("<img src='carnation.png'/>").replaceAll('#row2 img')
            .css("border", "thick solid red");

    });
</script>
```

In this script, I use the replaceWith method to replace the first child of the row1 div element with new content (this has the effect of replacing the astor with the orchid). I also use the replaceAll method to replace all of the img elements that are descendants of row2 with the image of a carnation. You can see the effect of this script in Figure 7-14.

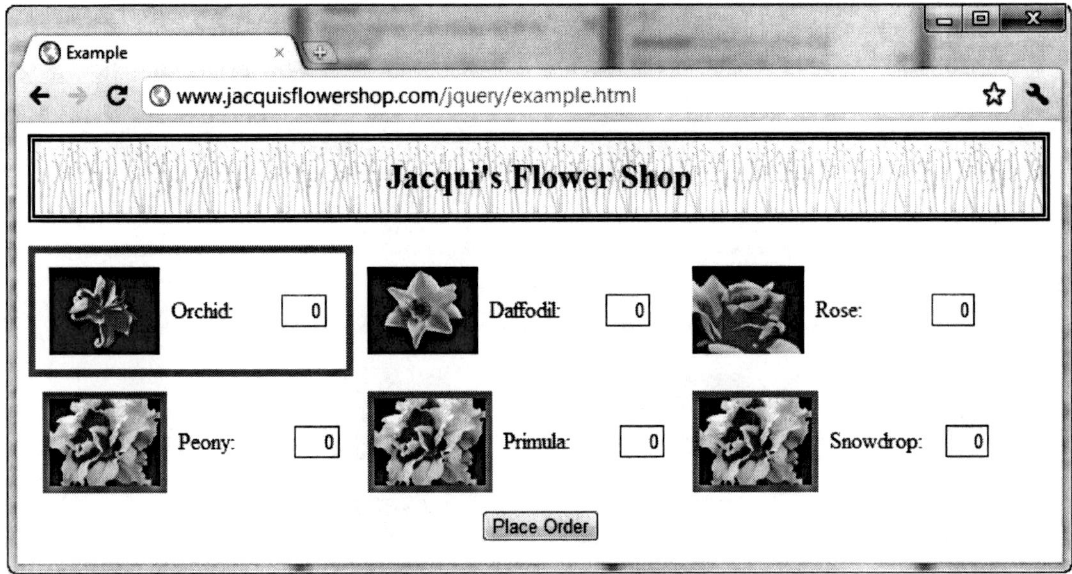

Figure 7-14. Replacing content with the replaceWith and replaceAll methods

Replacing Elements Using a Function

You can replace elements dynamically by passing a function to the `replaceWith` method. This function is not passed any arguments, but the `this` variable is set to the element being processed. Listing 7-20 provides a demonstration.

Listing 7-20. Replacing Elements Using a Function

```
...
<script type="text/javascript">
    $(document).ready(function() {
        $('div.drow img').replaceWith(function() {
            if (this.src.indexOf("rose") > -1) {
                return $("<img src='carnation.png'/>").css("border", "thick solid red");
            } else if (this.src.indexOf("peony") > -1) {
                return $("<img src='lily.png'/>").css("border", "thick solid red");
            } else {
                return $(this).clone();
            }
        });
    });
</script>
...
```

In this script, I replace `img` elements based on their `src` attribute. If the `src` attribute contains `rose`, then I replace the `img` element with one displaying `carnation.png`. If the `src` attribute contains `peony`, then I replace the element with one displaying `lily.png`. Both of the replacement elements have a red border to make their position in the document evident.

Otherwise, I return a clone of the element being processed, which has the effect of replacing the element with a copy of itself. You can see the effect in Figure 7-15.

Figure 7-15. Replacing elements using a function

■ **Tip** If you don't want to replace an element, then you can simply return a clone. If you don't clone the element, then jQuery ends up removing the element entirely. Of course, you could avoid this issue by narrowing your selection, but that isn't always an option.

Removing Elements

To complement your ability to insert and replace elements, jQuery provides a set of methods that you can use to remove elements from the DOM. Table 7-6 describes these methods.

Table 7-6. *Methods for Removing Elements*

Method	Description
`detach()` `detach(selector)`	Removes elements from the DOM. The data associated with the elements is preserved.
`empty()`	Removes all of the child nodes from each element in the `jQuery` object.

`remove()` `remove(selector)`	Removes elements from the DOM. As the elements are removed, the data associated with the elements is destroyed.
`unwrap()`	Removes the parent of each of the elements in the `jQuery` object.

Listing 7-21 shows how you can use the `remove` elements to remove elements from the DOM.

Listing 7-21. Removing Elements from the DOM with the remove Method

```
<script type="text/javascript">
    $(document).ready(function() {
        $('img[src*=daffodil], img[src*=snow]').parent().remove();
    });
</script>
```

This script selects the `img` elements whose `src` attributes contain `daffodil` and `snow`, gets their parent elements, and then removes them. You can filter the elements that you remove if you pass a selector to the `remove` method, as shown in Listing 7-22.

Listing 7-22. Filtering Elements to Remove Using a Selector

```
<script type="text/javascript">
    $(document).ready(function() {

        $('div.dcell').remove(':has(img[src*=snow], img[src*=daffodil])');

    });
</script>
```

Both of these scripts have the same effect, as shown in Figure 7-16.

■ **Tip** My experience with the `remove` method is that not all selectors will work as a filter. I recommend thorough testing and relying on the initial selection where possible.

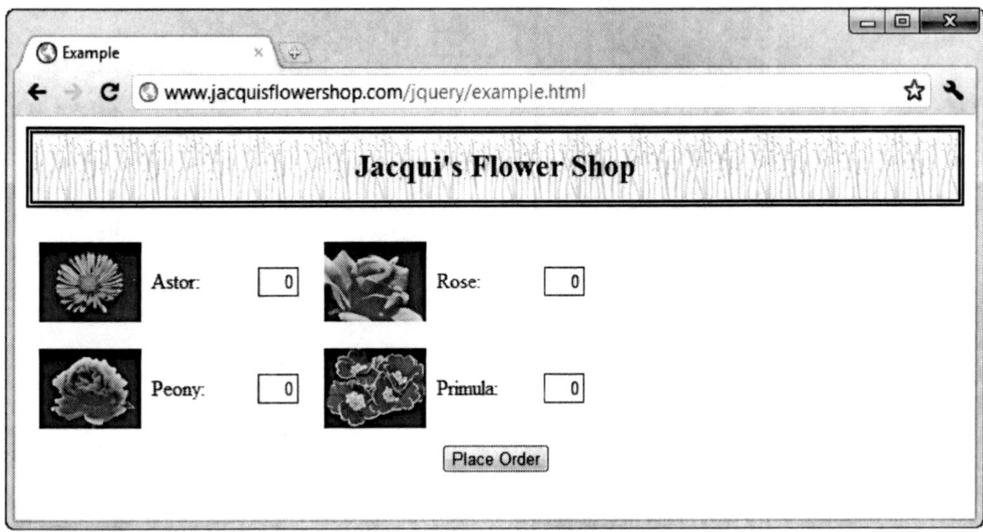

Figure 7-16. Removing elements from the DOM

■ **Tip** The `jQuery` object returned from the `remove` method contains the original set of selected elements. In other words, the removal of elements is not reflected in the method result.

Detaching Elements

The `detach` method works in the same as the `remove` method, with the exception that data associated with the elements is preserved. I explain associating data with elements in Chapter 8, but for this chapter it is enough to know that this is usually the best method to use if you intend to insert the elements elsewhere in the document. Listing 7-23 shows the detach method in use.

Listing 7-23. Using the detach Method to Remove Elements While Preserving the Associated Data

```
<script type="text/javascript">
    $(document).ready(function() {
        $('#row2').append($('img[src*=astor]').parent().detach());
    });
</script>
```

This script detaches the parent element of the `img` element whose `src` attribute contains `astor`. The elements are then inserted back into the document using the append method, which I described earlier in the chapter. I tend not to use this method, because using append without `detach` has the same effect. You can rewrite the key statement in the listing as follows:

```
$('#row2').append($('img[src*=astor]').parent());
```

You can see the effect of the script in Figure 7-17.

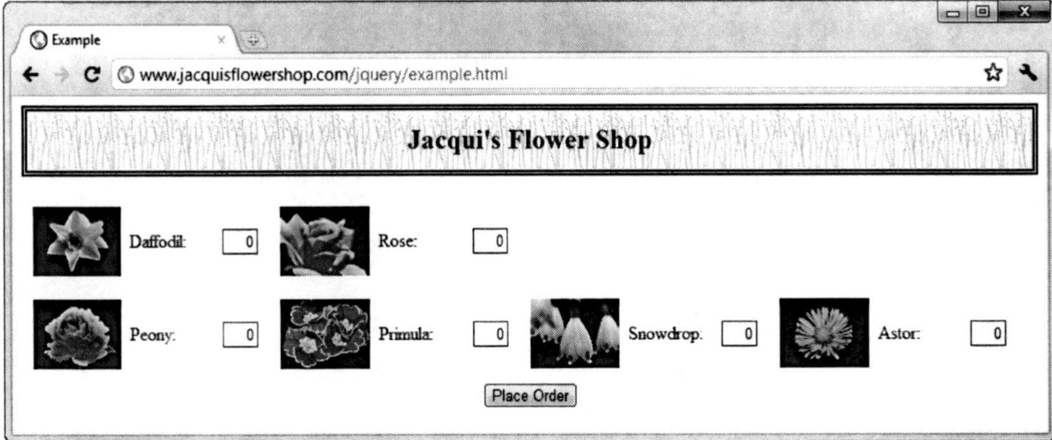

Figure 7-17. Using the detach element

Empting Elements

The empty method removes any descendants and text from the elements in a jQuery object. The elements themselves are left in the document, as demonstrated by Listing 7-24.

Listing 7-24. Using the empty Method

```
<script type="text/javascript">
    $(document).ready(function() {
        $('#row1').children().eq(1).empty().css("border", "thick solid red");
    });
</script>
```

In this script, I select the child of the row1 element at index 1 and call the empty method. To make the change more evident, I added a border using the css method. You can see the effect in Figure 7-18.

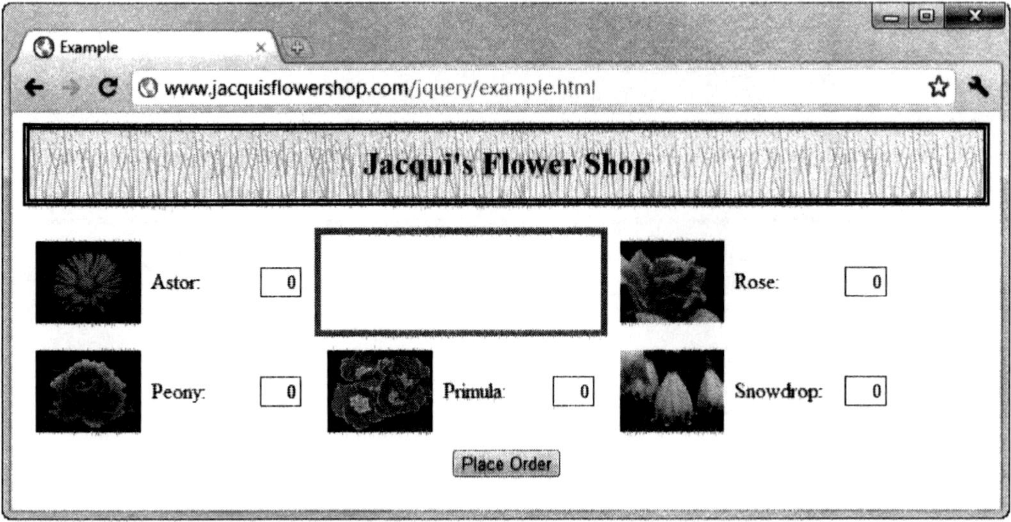

Figure 7-18. Using the empty method

Unwrapping Elements

The `unwrap` method removes the parents of the elements in the `jQuery` object. The selected elements become children of their grandparent elements. Listing 7-25 shows the unwrap method in use.

Listing 7-25. Using the unwrap Method

```
<script type="text/javascript">
    $(document).ready(function() {
        $('#row1 div').unwrap();
    });
</script>
```

In this script, I select the `div` elements that are descendants of the element whose `id` is `row1` and call the `unwrap` method. This has the effect of removing the `row1` element, as shown in Figure 7-19. The change in alignment of the unwrapped elements arises because the CSS styles I defined in the CSS style sheet rely on the `row1` elements to maintain the grid layout in the page.

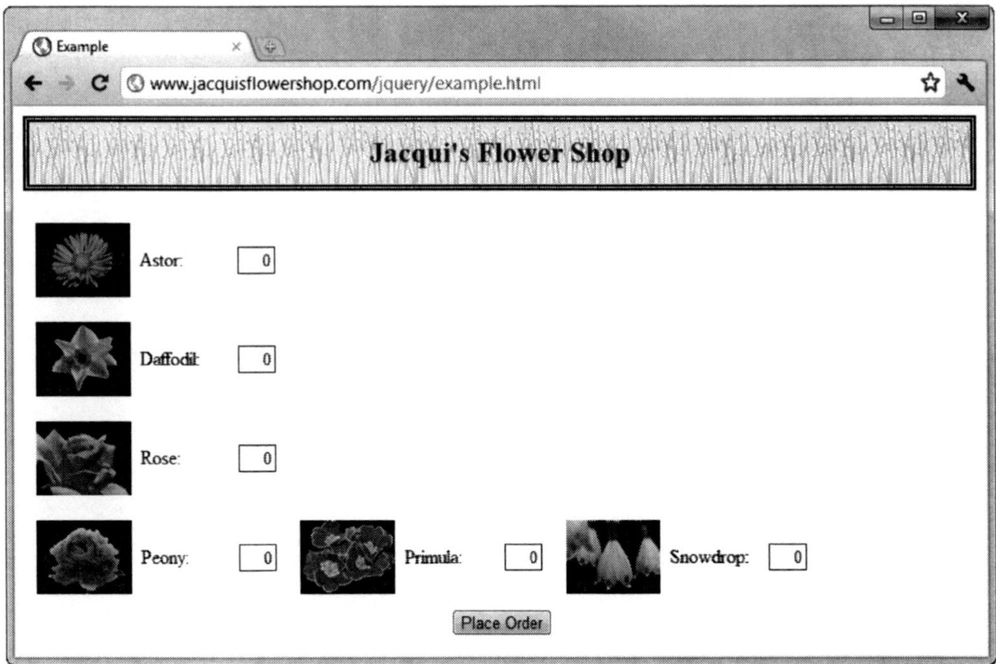

Figure 7-19. Using the unwrap method

Summary

In this chapter, I showed you how to use jQuery in order to manipulate the DOM. I showed you how to create new elements and the many different ways in which elements (new or existing) can be inserted into the DOM as children, parents, and siblings. I also showed you how to move elements within the DOM and how to remove elements entirely.

CHAPTER 8

Manipulating Elements

In this chapter, I'll show you how to use jQuery to work with elements, including how to get and set attributes, how to use the jQuery convenience methods for working with classes and CSS properties, and how to get and set HTML and text content. I'll also show you a nice feature that allows you to associate data with elements. jQuery has its own internal mechanism for storing this data but also supports the new HTML5 data attributes. Table 8-1 provides the summary for this chapter.

***Table 8-1.** Chapter Summary*

Problem	Solution	Listing
Get the value of an attribute from the first element in a `jQuery` object.	Use the `attr` method.	1
Get the value of an attribute from every element in a `jQuery` object.	Use the `each` and `attr` methods together.	2
Set an attribute for all of the elements in a `jQuery` object.	Use the `attr` method, optionally with a function.	3
Set multiple attributes in a single operation.	Use the `attr` method with a map object.	4, 5
Unset an attribute.	Use the `removeAttr` method.	6
Get or set a property defined by the `HTMLElement` object.	Use the `prop` counterparts to the `attr` methods.	7
Control the classes that elements belong to.	Use the `addClass`, `hasClass`, and `removeClass` methods, optionally with a function.	8–10
Toggle the classes that elements belong to.	Use the `toggleClass` method.	11–16
Set the contents of the `style` attribute.	Use the `css` method.	17–21

Get details of the position of elements.	Use the CSS property-specific methods.	22–23
Get or set the text or HTML content of elements.	Use the `text` or `html` method.	24–26
Get or set the value of form elements.	Use the `val` method.	27–29
Associate data with elements.	Use the `data` method.	30, 31

Working with Attributes and Properties

You can get and set the values of attributes for the elements in a `jQuery` object. Table 8-2 shows the methods that relate to attributes.

Table 8-2. *Methods for Working with Attributes*

Method	Description
`attr(name)`	Gets the value of the attribute with the specified name for the first element in the `jQuery` object
`attr(name, value)`	Sets the value of the attribute with the specified name to the specified value for all of the elements in the `jQuery` object
`attr(map)`	Sets the attributes specified in the map object for all of the elements in the `jQuery` object
`attr(name, function)`	Sets the specified attribute for all of the elements in the `jQuery` object using a function
`removeAttr(name)` `removeAttr(name[])`	Remove the attribute from all of the elements in the `jQuery` object
`prop(name)`	Returns the value of the specified property for the first element in the `jQuery` object
`prop(name, value)` `prop(map)`	Sets the value for one or more properties for all of the elements in the `jQuery` object
`prop(name, function)`	Sets the value of the specified property for all of the elements in the `jQuery` object using a function
`removeProp(name)`	Removes the specified property from all of the elements in the `jQuery` object

When you call the attr method with a single argument, jQuery returns the value of the specified attribute from the first element in the selection. Listing 8-1 contains a demonstration.

Listing 8-1. Reading the Value of an Attribute

```
<!DOCTYPE html>
<html>
<head>
    <title>Example</title>
    <script src="jquery-1.7.js" type="text/javascript"></script>
    <link rel="stylesheet" type="text/css" href="styles.css"/>
    <script type="text/javascript">
        $(document).ready(function() {
            var srcValue = $('img').attr('src');
            console.log("Attribute value: " + srcValue);
        });
    </script>
</head>
<body>
    <h1>Jacqui's Flower Shop</h1>
    <form method="post">
        <div id="oblock">
            <div class="dtable">
                <div id="row1" class="drow">
                    <div class="dcell">
                        <img src="astor.png"/><label for="astor">Astor:</label>
                        <input name="astor" value="0" required />
                    </div>
                    <div class="dcell">
                        <img src="daffodil.png"/><label for="daffodil">Daffodil:</label>
                        <input name="daffodil" value="0" required />
                    </div>
                    <div class="dcell">
                        <img src="rose.png"/><label for="rose">Rose:</label>
                        <input name="rose" value="0" required />
                    </div>
                </div>
                <div id="row2"class="drow">
                    <div class="dcell">
                        <img src="peony.png"/><label for="peony">Peony:</label>
                        <input name="peony" value="0" required />
                    </div>
                    <div class="dcell">
                        <img src="primula.png"/><label for="primula">Primula:</label>
                        <input name="primula" value="0" required />
                    </div>
                    <div class="dcell">
                        <img src="snowdrop.png"/><label for="snowdrop">Snowdrop:</label>
                        <input name="snowdrop" value="0" required />
                    </div>
                </div>
```

```
            </div>
        </div>
        <div id="buttonDiv"><button type="submit">Place Order</button></div>
    </form>
</body>
</html>
```

In this script, I select all of the img elements in the document and then use the attr method to get the value for the src attribute. The result from the attr method when you read an attribute value is a string, which I write out to the console. The output from this script is as follows:

```
Attribute value: astor.png
```

You can combine the each method with attr to read the value of an attribute for all of the elements in a jQuery object. I described the each method in Chapter 5, and Listing 8-2 shows how you can use it in this situation.

Listing 8-2. Using the each and attr Methods to Read Attribute Values from Multiple Objects

```
...
<script type="text/javascript">
    $(document).ready(function() {
        $('img').each(function(index, elem) {
            var srcValue = $(elem).attr('src');
            console.log("Attribute value: " + srcValue);
        });
    });
</script>
...
```

In this script, I pass the HTMLElement object passed as the argument to the function to create a new jQuery object via the $ function. This object contains only one element, which is ideally suited to the attr method. The output from this script is as follows:

```
Attribute value: astor.png
Attribute value: daffodil.png
Attribute value: rose.png
Attribute value: peony.png
Attribute value: primula.png
Attribute value: snowdrop.png
```

Setting an Attribute Value

When you use the attr method to set an attribute value, the change is applied to all of the elements in the jQuery object. This is in contract to the read version of this method, which returns a value from only a single element. When setting a value, the attr method returns a jQuery object, which means that you can perform method chaining. Listing 8-3 demonstrates how to set an attribute.

Listing 8-3. Setting an Attribute

```
...
<script type="text/javascript">
    $(document).ready(function() {
        $('img').attr("src", "lily.png");
    });
</script>
...
```

In this script, I select all of the `img` elements and set the value of the `src` attribute to `lily.png`. This value is applied to the `src` attribute of all the selected elements, and you can see the effect in Figure 8-1.

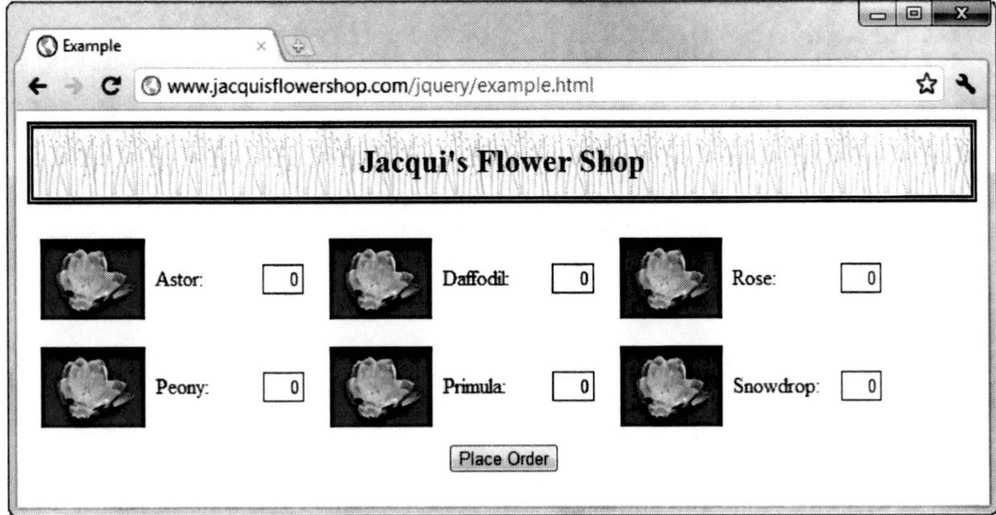

Figure 8-1. Setting an attribute to the same value for multiple elements

Setting Multiple Attributes

You can set multiple attributes in a single method call by passing an object to the `attr` method. The properties of this object are interpreted as the attribute names, and the property values will be used as the attribute values. This is known as a *map object*. Listing 8-4 provides a demonstration.

Listing 8-4. Setting Multiple Elements Using a Map Object

```
...
<script type="text/javascript">
    $(document).ready(function() {
        var attrValues = {
            src: 'lily.png',
            style: 'border: thick solid red'
        };

        $('img').attr(attrValues);
    });
</script>
...
```

In this script I create a map object that has properties called `src` and `style`. I select the `img` elements in the document and pass the map object to the `attr` value. You can see the effect in Figure 8-2.

■ **Tip** Although I have set the `style` property explicitly in this example, jQuery provides some methods that simplify working with CSS. See the "Working with CSS" section in this chapter for details.

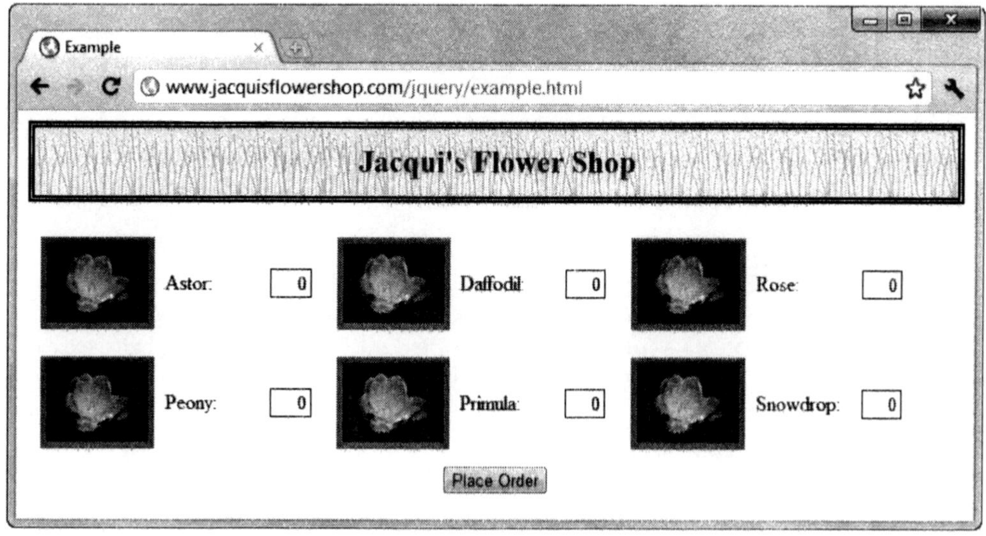

Figure 8-2. Setting multiple attributes with the attr method

Setting Attribute Values Dynamically

You can tailor the values that you assign to an attribute by passing a function to the attr method. Listing 8-5 provides a demonstration.

Listing 8-5. Setting Attribute Values with a Function

```
...
<script type="text/javascript">
    $(document).ready(function() {
        $('img').attr("src", function(index, oldVal) {
            if (oldVal.indexOf("rose") > -1) {
                return "lily.png";
            } else if ($(this).closest('#row2').length > 0) {
                return "carnation.png";
            }
        });
    });
</script>
...
```

The arguments passed to the function are the index of the element being processed and the old attribute value. The this variable is set to the HTMLElement being processed. If you want to change the attribute, then your function must return a string containing the new value. If you don't return a result, then the existing value is used. In the example, I use the function to selectively change the images shown by the img elements. You can see the effect in Figure 8-3.

Figure 8-3. Changing attribute values with a function

Removing an Attribute

You can remove (unset) attributes by using the removeAttr method, as shown in Listing 8-6.

Listing 8-6. Removing Attribute Values

```
...
<script type="text/javascript">
    $(document).ready(function() {

        $('img').attr("style", "border: thick solid red");
        $('img:odd').removeAttr("style");

    });
</script>
...
```

In this example, I use the attr method to set the style attribute and then use the removeAttr method to remove the same attribute from the odd-numbered elements. You can see the effect in Figure 8-4.

Figure 8-4. Removing attributes from elements

Working with Properties

For each form of the attr method, there is a corresponding prop method. The difference is that the prop methods deal with properties defined by the HTMLElement object, rather than attribute values. Often, the attributes and properties are the same, but this isn't always the case. A simple example is the class attribute, which is represented in the HTMLElement object using the className property. Listing 8-7 shows the use of the prop method to read this property.

Listing 8-7. Using the prop Method to Read a Property Value

```
...
<script type="text/javascript">
    $(document).ready(function() {
        $('*[class]').each(function(index, elem) {
            console.log("Element:" + elem.tagName + " " + $(elem).prop("className"));
        });
    });
</script>
...
```

In this example, I select all of the elements that have a class attribute and use the each method to enumerate them. For each element, I print out the type and the value of the className property.

Working with Classes

Although you can use the general attribute methods to manage classes, jQuery provides a set of much more convenient methods. These methods are described in Table 8-3. The most common use for classes in an HTML document is to cause the browser to apply a set of CSS properties defined in a style element. See Chapter 8 for details.

Table 8-3. *Methods for Working with Classes*

Method	Description
addClass(name name)	Adds all of the elements in a jQuery object to the specified class
addClass(function)	Assigns the elements in a jQuery object to classes dynamically
hasClass(name)	Returns true if at least one of the elements in the jQuery object is a member of the specified class
removeClass(name name)	Removes the elements in the jQuery object from the specified class
removeClass(function)	Removes the elements in a jQuery object from classes dynamically
toggleClass()	Toggles all of the classes that the elements in the jQuery object belong to
toggleClass(boolean)	Toggles all of the classes that the elements in the jQuery object belong to in one direction
toggleClass(name) toggleClass(name name)	Toggles one or more named classes for all of the elements in the jQuery object

toggleClass(name, boolean)	Toggles a named class for all of the elements in the jQuery object in one direction
toggleClass(function, boolean)	Toggles classes dynamically for all of the elements in a jQuery object

You can assign elements to a class with the addClass method, remove elements from classes using the removeClass method, and determine whether an element belongs to a class using the hasClass method. Listing 8-8 demonstrates all three methods in use.

Listing 8-8. Adding, Removing, and Testing for Class Membership

```
...
<style type="text/css">
    img.redBorder {border: thick solid red}
    img.blueBorder {border: thick solid blue}
</style>
<script type="text/javascript">
    $(document).ready(function() {

        $('img').addClass("redBorder");
        $('img:even').removeClass("redBorder").addClass("blueBorder");

        console.log("All elements: " + $('img').hasClass('redBorder'));
        $('img').each(function(index, elem) {
            console.log("Element: " + $(elem).hasClass('redBorder') + " " + elem.src);
        });

    });
</script>
...
```

To begin, I have used a style element to define two styles that will be applied based on class membership. Classes don't have to be used to manage CSS, but they make demonstrating the effect of changes easier in this chapter.

To begin with, I select all of the img elements in the document and assign them to the redBorder class using the addClass method. I then select the even-numbered img elements, remove them from the redBorder class, and assign them to the blueBorder class using the removeClass method.

■ **Tip** The addClass method does not remove any existing classes from the elements; it just adds the new class in addition to those classes that have already been applied.

Finally, I use the hasClass method to test for the redBorder class on the set of all img elements (which returns true if at least one of the elements is a member of the class) and each element individually. You can see the effect of the class membership in Figure 8-5.

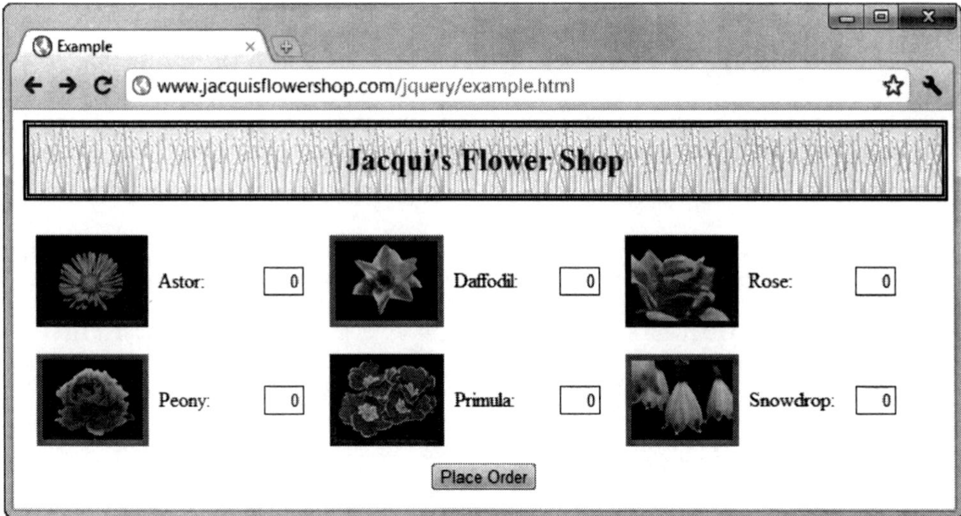

Figure 8-5. Applying styles through class membership

The output from the script, where I test for class membership, is as follows:

```
All elements: true
Element: false http://www.jacquisflowershop.com/jquery/astor.png
Element: true http://www.jacquisflowershop.com/jquery/daffodil.png
Element: false http://www.jacquisflowershop.com/jquery/rose.png
Element: true http://www.jacquisflowershop.com/jquery/peony.png
Element: false http://www.jacquisflowershop.com/jquery/primula.png
Element: true http://www.jacquisflowershop.com/jquery/snowdrop.png
```

Adding and Removing Classes Using a Function

You can decide dynamically which classes should be added or removed from a set of elements by passing a function to the addClass or removeClass method. Listing 8-9 shows the use of a function with the addClass method.

Listing 8-9. Using the addClass Method with a Function

```
...
<style type="text/css">
    img.redBorder {border: thick solid red}
    img.blueBorder {border: thick solid blue}
</style>
<script type="text/javascript">
    $(document).ready(function() {
        $('img').addClass(function(index, currentClasses) {
            if (index % 2 == 0) {
```

```
                return "blueBorder";
            } else {
                return "redBorder";
            }
        });
    });
</script>
...
```

The arguments to the function are the index of the element and the current set of classes for which the element is a member. As with similar functions, the this variable is set to the HTMLElement object of the element being processed. You return the class that you want the element to join. In this example, I use the index argument to assign alternate elements to either the blueBorder or redBorder class. The effect is the same as the one shown in Figure 8-5.

You take a similar approach to removing elements from classes. You pass a function to the removeClass method, as shown in Listing 8-10.

Listing 8-10. Removing Elements from Classes Using a Function

```
...
<style type="text/css">
    img.redBorder {border: thick solid red}
    img.blueBorder {border: thick solid blue}
</style>
<script type="text/javascript">
    $(document).ready(function() {

        $('img').filter(':odd').addClass("redBorder").end()
            .filter(':even').addClass("blueBorder");

        $('img').removeClass(function(index, currentClasses) {
            if ($(this).closest('#row2').length > 0
                && currentClasses.indexOf('redBorder') > -1) {
                    return "redBorder";
            } else {
                return "";
            }
        });
    });
</script>
...
```

In this script, the function I pass to the removeClass method uses the HTMLElement object and the current set of classes to remove the redBorder class from any img element that is a member and that is a descendant of the element with the ID of row2. You can see the effect of this script in Figure 8-6.

■ **Tip** Notice that I return the empty string when I don't want to remove any classes. If you don't return a value, then jQuery removes *all* of the classes from the element.

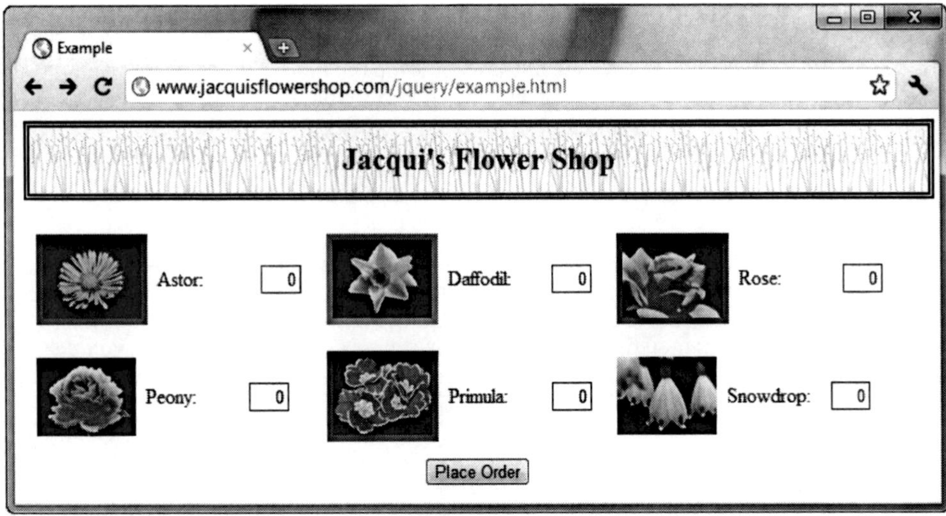

Figure 8-6. Removing classes with a function

Toggling Classes

In its most basic form, toggling a class means adding it to any element that is not a member and removing it from any element that it. You can achieve this effect by passing the name of the class you want to toggle to the `toggleClass` method, as shown in Listing 8-11.

Listing 8-11. Using the toggleClass Method

```
...
<style type="text/css">
    img.redBorder {border: thick solid red}
    img.blueBorder {border: thick solid blue}
</style>
<script type="text/javascript">
    $(document).ready(function() {

        $('img').filter(':odd').addClass("redBorder").end()
            .filter(':even').addClass("blueBorder");

        $("<button>Toggle</button>").appendTo("#buttonDiv").click(doToggle);

        function doToggle(e) {
            $('img').toggleClass("redBorder");
            e.preventDefault();
        };

    });
</script>
...
```

I start this script by applying the redBorder class to the odd-numbered img elements and the blueBorder class to the even-numbered ones. I then create a new button element and append it to the element whose id is buttonDiv. This places my new button alongside the Place Order button that is already on the page. I have used the click method to specify a function that jQuery will invoke when the user clicks the button. This is part of the jQuery support for events, which I describe fully in Chapter 9.

The function that is executed when the button is clicked is called doToggle, and the key statement is this one:

```
$('img').toggleClass("redBorder");
```

This statement selects all of the img elements in the document and toggles the redBorder class. The argument to the function and the call to the preventDefault method are not important in this chapter. I'll explain these in Chapter 9. You can see the effect of this script in Figure 8-7, although this kind of example makes most sense when you load the document into a browser and click the button yourself.

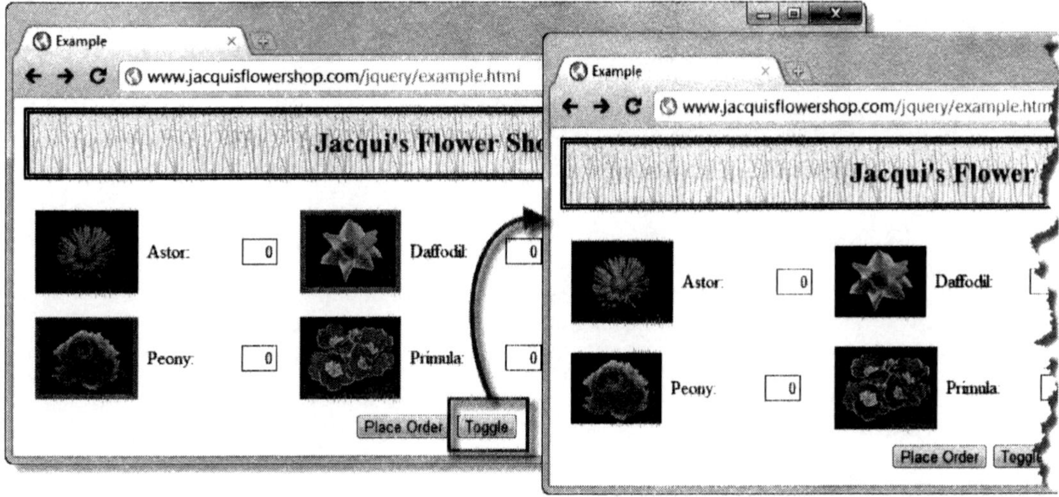

Figure 8-7. Toggling class membership with the toggleClass method

If you are observant, you will notice something a little odd in the figure. Those elements with red borders no longer have them, but the elements that started with blue borders still have blue borders. What happened was that jQuery removed the redBorder class from the odd-numbered img elements and added it to the even-numbered element, just as expected, but the element to which the redBorder class was added is also a member of blueBorder. The blueBorder style is defined after redBorder in the style element, which means that its property values have higher precedence, as I explained in Chapter 3. So, the class toggling is working, but you have to take into account the subtleties of CSS as well. If you want the red borders to show through, then you can reverse the declaration order of the styles, as shown in Listing 8-12.

Listing 8-12. Matching Style Declaration to Suit Class Toggling

```
...
<style type="text/css">
    img.blueBorder {border: thick solid blue}
    img.redBorder {border: thick solid red}
</style>
<script type="text/javascript">
    $(document).ready(function() {
        $('img').filter(':odd').addClass("redBorder").end()
            .filter(':even').addClass("blueBorder");

        $("<button>Toggle</button>").appendTo("#buttonDiv").click(doToggle);

        function doToggle(e) {
            $('img').toggleClass("redBorder");
            e.preventDefault();
        };
    });
</script>
...
```

Now when an element belongs to both the blueBorder and redBorder classes, the redBorder setting for the border property will be used by the browser. You can see the effect of this change in Figure 8-8.

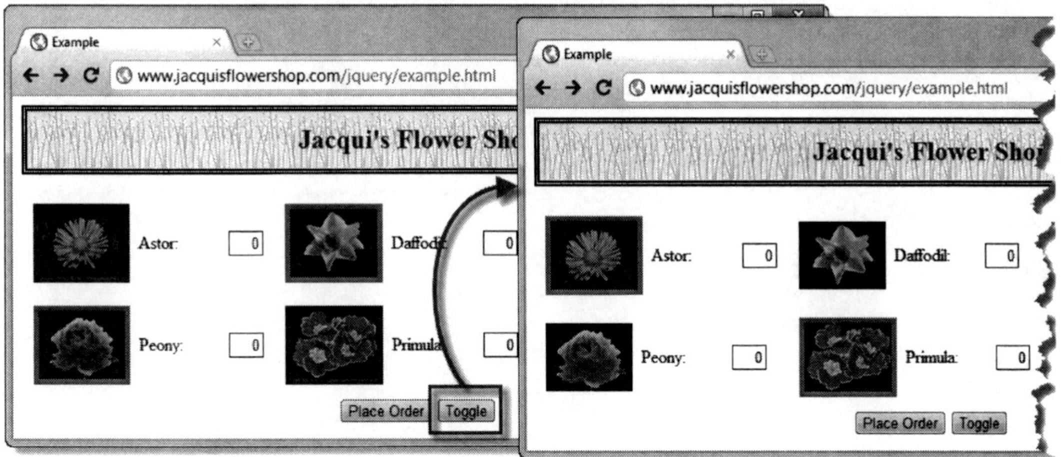

Figure 8-8. The effect of coordinating the CSS declaration order with class toggling

Toggling Multiple Classes

You can supply multiple class names, separated by a space, to the toggleClass method, and each will be toggled for the selected elements. Listing 8-13 shows a single example.

Listing 8-13. Toggling Multiple Classes

```
...
<style type="text/css">
    img.blueBorder {border: thick solid blue}
    img.redBorder {border: thick solid red}
</style>
<script type="text/javascript">
    $(document).ready(function() {

        $('img').filter(':odd').addClass("redBorder").end()
            .filter(':even').addClass("blueBorder");

        $("<button>Toggle</button>").appendTo("#buttonDiv").click(doToggle);

        function doToggle(e) {
            $('img').toggleClass("redBorder blueBorder");
            e.preventDefault();
        };

    });
</script>
...
```

In this example, I toggle the redBorder and blueBorder classes on all of the img elements. You can see the effect in Figure 8-9.

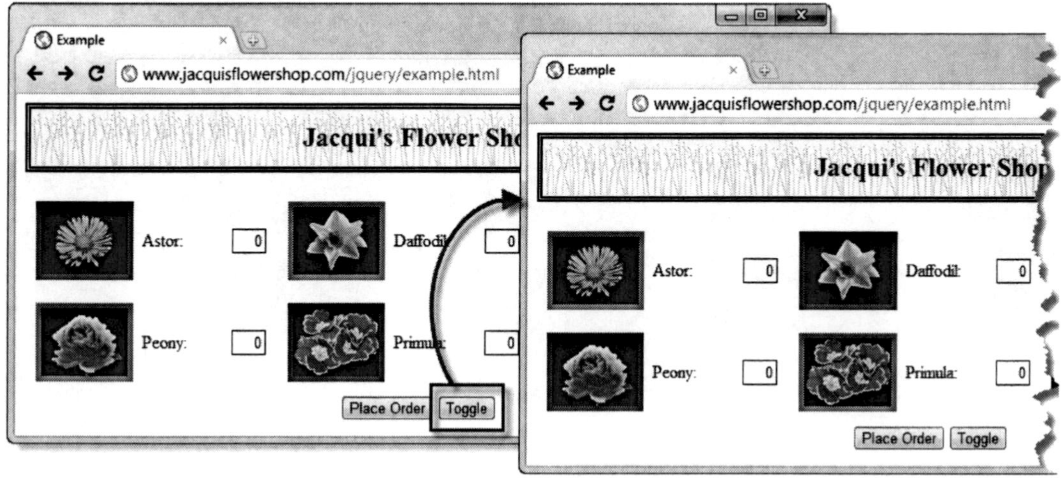

Figure 8-9. Toggling multiple elements

Toggling All Classes

You can toggle all of the classes that a set of elements belong to by calling the `toggleClass` method with no arguments. This is a clever technique because jQuery stores the classes that have been toggled so they are applied and removed correctly. Listing 8-14 contains an example of this use of the method.

Listing 8-14. Toggling All of the Classes for Selected Elements

```
...
<style type="text/css">
    img.blueBorder {border: thick solid blue}
    img.redBorder {border: thick solid red}
    label.bigFont {font-size: 1.5em}
</style>
<script type="text/javascript">
    $(document).ready(function() {

        $('img').filter(':odd').addClass("redBorder").end()
            .filter(':even').addClass("blueBorder");
        $('label').addClass("bigFont");

        $("<button>Toggle</button>").appendTo("#buttonDiv").click(doToggle);

        function doToggle(e) {
            $('img, label').toggleClass();
            e.preventDefault();
        };

    });
</script>
...
```

In this example, I used the `addClass` method to add classes to the `img` and `label` elements. When the `Toggle` button is clicked, I select those same elements and call the `toggleClass` method without any arguments. You get a very specific effect, which is shown in Figure 8-10.

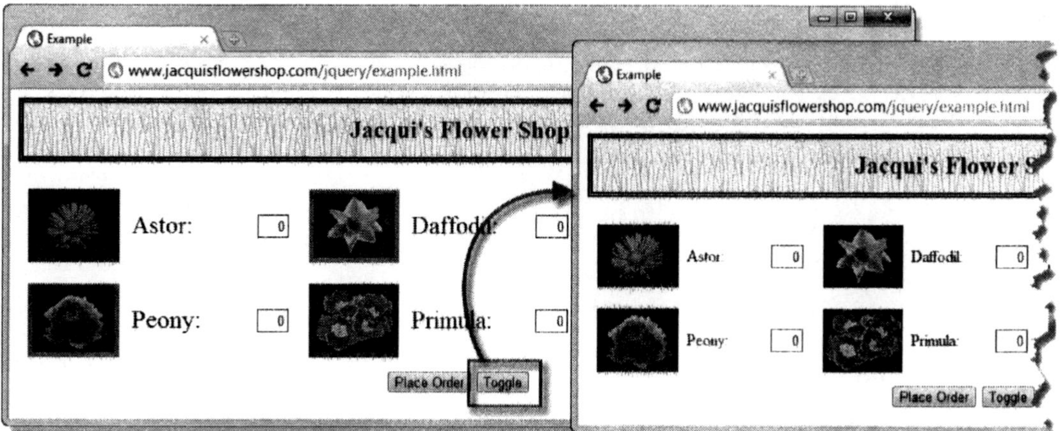

Figure 8-10. Toggling all of the classes for an element

When you first click the button, all of the classes are toggled off for the selected elements. jQuery makes a note of which classes were removed so that they can be reapplied when you click the button again.

Toggling Classes in One Direction

You can limit the way that toggling is performed by passing a boolean argument to the toggleClass method. If you pass false, the classes will only be removed, and if you pass true, the classes will only be added. This is the same effect you achieved using the addClass and removeClass methods, so I tend not to use this feature. Listing 8-15 gives an example.

Listing 8-15. Restricting the Toggle Direction

```
...
<style type="text/css">
    img.blueBorder {border: thick solid blue}
    img.redBorder {border: thick solid red}
</style>
<script type="text/javascript">
    $(document).ready(function() {

        $('img').filter(':odd').addClass("redBorder").end()
            .filter(':even').addClass("blueBorder");

        $("<button>Toggle On</button>").appendTo("#buttonDiv").click(doToggleOn);
        $("<button>Toggle Off</button>").appendTo("#buttonDiv").click(doToggleOff);

        function doToggleOff(e) {
            $('img, label').toggleClass("redBorder", false);
            e.preventDefault();
        };
```

```
        function doToggleOn(e) {
            $('img, label').toggleClass("redBorder", true);
            e.preventDefault();
        };
    });
</script>
...
```

I have added two buttons to the document, each of which will toggle the `redBorder` class in only one direction. Once one of the buttons has been clicked, it will have no further effect until the other button is clicked too (because each button can toggle in only one direction).

Toggling Classes Dynamically

You can decide which classes should be toggled for elements dynamically by passing a function to the `toggleClass` method. Listing 8-16 provides a simple demonstration.

Listing 8-16. Toggling Classes with a Function

```
...
<style type="text/css">
    img.blueBorder {border: thick solid blue}
    img.redBorder {border: thick solid red}
</style>
<script type="text/javascript">
    $(document).ready(function() {

        $('img').addClass("blueBorder");
        $('img:even').addClass("redBorder");

        $("<button>Toggle</button>").appendTo("#buttonDiv").click(doToggle);

        function doToggle(e) {
            $('img').toggleClass(function(index, currentClasses) {
                if (index % 2 == 0) {
                    return "redBorder";
                } else {
                    return "";
                }
            });
            e.preventDefault();
        };
    });
</script>
...
```

I apply the `blueBorder` class to all of the `img` elements and the `redBorder` class to the even-numbered `img` elements. The arguments to the function are the index of the element you are processing and the current set of classes it belongs to. In addition, the `this` variable is set to the `HTMLElement` object for the current element. The result from the function is the name of the classes that should be toggled. If you don't want to toggle any classes for the elements, then you return the empty string (not returning a result for an element toggles all of its classes).

Working with CSS

In an earlier example, I used the basic attribute methods to set the value of the style attribute, thereby defining values for a CSS property for a set of elements. jQuery provides a set of convenience elements that make dealing with CSS much easier. The most broadly useful of these methods is css, which is described in Table 8-4.

■ **Tip** These methods operate on the style attribute of individual elements. If you want to work with styles defined in a style element, then you should use the class-related methods described earlier in this chapter.

Table 8-4. *The css Method*

Method	Description
css(name)	Gets the value of the specified property from the first element in the jQuery object
css(name, value)	Sets the value of the specific property for all elements in the jQuery object
css(map)	Sets multiple properties for all of the elements in a jQuery object using a map object
css(name, function)	Sets values for the specified property for all of the elements in a jQuery object using a function

When you read the value of a property using the css method, you receive the value only from the first element in the jQuery object. However, when you set a property, the change is applied to all of the elements. Listing 8-17 shows the basic use of the css property.

Listing 8-17. Using the css Method to Get and Set CSS Property Values

```
...
<script type="text/javascript">
    $(document).ready(function() {
        var sizeVal = $('label').css("font-size");
        console.log("Size: " + sizeVal);
        $('label').css("font-size", "1.5em");
    });
</script>
...
```

In this script, I select all of the label elements and use the css method to get the value of the font-size property and write it to the console. I then select all of the label elements again and apply a new value for the same property to all of them.

■ **Tip** Although I used the actual property name (`font-size`) and not the camel-case property name defined by the `HTMLElement` object (`fontSize`), jQuery happily supports both.

The output of the script is as follows:

```
Size: 16px
```

■ **Tip** Setting a property to the empty string ("") has the effect of removing the property from the element's `style` attribute.

Setting Multiple CSS Properties

You can set multiple properties in two different ways. The first is simply by chaining calls to the `css` method, as shown in Listing 8-18.

Listing 8-18. Chaining Calls to the css Method

```
...
<script type="text/javascript">
    $(document).ready(function() {
        $('label').css("font-size", "1.5em").css("color", "blue");
    });
</script>
...
```

In this script, I set values for the `font-size` and `color` properties. You can achieve the same effect using a map object, as shown in Listing 8-19.

Listing 8-19. Setting Multiple Value Using a Map Object

```
...
<script type="text/javascript">
    $(document).ready(function() {
        var cssVals = {
            "font-size": "1.5em",
            "color": "blue"
        };

        $('label').css(cssVals);
    });
</script>
...
```

Both of these scripts create the effect shown in Figure 8-11.

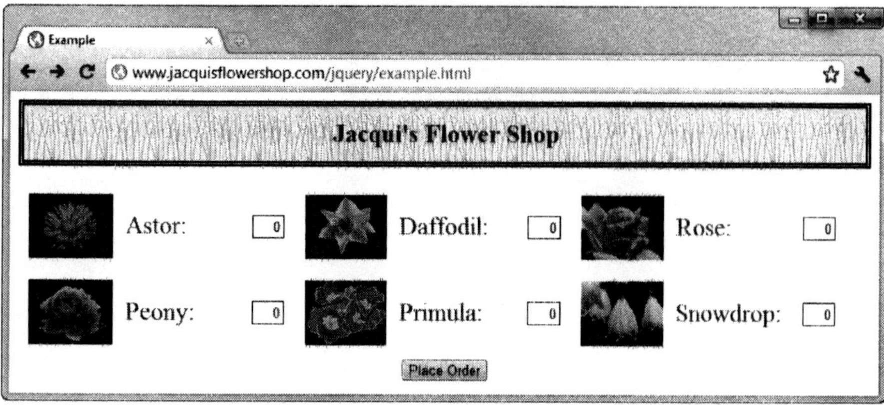

Figure 8-11. Setting multiple properties

Setting Relative Values

The css method can accept relative values. These are numeric values that are preceded by += or -= and that are added to or subtracted from the current value. This technique can be used only with numeric units. Listing 8-20 gives a demonstration.

Listing 8-20. Using Relative Values with the css Method

```
...
<script type="text/javascript">
    $(document).ready(function() {

        $('label:odd').css("font-size", "+=5")
        $('label:even').css("font-size", "-=5")

    });
</script>
...
```

These values are read as being in the same units as are returned when you read the property value. In this case, I have increased the font size of the odd-numbered label elements by 5 pixels and decreased it for the even-numbered label elements by the same amount. You can see the effect in Figure 8-12.

Figure 8-12. Using relative values

Setting Properties Using a Function

You can set property values dynamically by passing a function to the css method. Listing 8-21 provides a demonstration. The arguments passed to the function are the index of the element and the current value of the property. The this variable is set to the HTMLElement object for the element, and you return the value you want to set.

Listing 8-21. Setting CSS Values with a Function

```
...
<script type="text/javascript">
    $(document).ready(function() {
        $('label').css("border", function(index, currentValue) {
            if ($(this).closest("#row1").length > 0) {
                return "thick solid red";
            } else if (index % 2 == 1) {
                return "thick double blue";
            }
        });
    });
</script>
...
```

You can see the effect of this script in Figure 8-13.

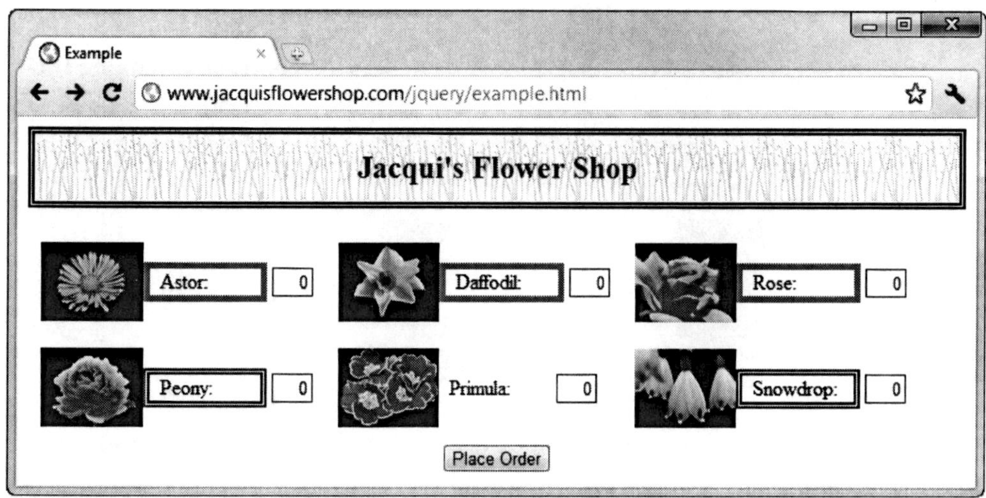

Figure 8-13. Setting CSS property values with a function

Using the Property-Specific CSS Convenience Methods

In addition to the css method, jQuery defines a number of methods that can be used to get or set specific properties. These methods are described in Table 8-5.

Table 8-5. *Methods for Working ith Specific CSS Properties*

Method	Description
`height()`	Gets the height in pixels for the first element in the `jQuery` object.
`height(value)`	Sets the height for all of the elements in the `jQuery` object.
`innerHeight()`	Gets the inner height of the first element in the `jQuery` object (this is the height including padding but excluding the border and margin).
`innerWidth()`	Gets the inner width of the first element in the `jQuery` object (this is the width including padding but excluding the border and margin).
`offset()`	Returns the coordinates of the first element in the `jQuery` object relative to the document.
`outerHeight(boolean)`	Gets the height of the first element in the `jQuery` object, including padding and border. The argument determines if the margin is included.
`outerWidth(boolean)`	Gets the width of the first element in the `jQuery` object, including padding and border. The argument determines whether the margin is included.

position()	Returns the coordinates of the first element in the jQuery object relative to the offset.
scrollLeft() scrollTop()	Get the horizontal or vertical position of the first element in the jQuery object.
scrollLeft(value) scrollTop(value)	Set the horizontal or vertical position of all the elements in a jQuery object.
width()	Gets the width of the first element in a jQuery object.
width(value)	Sets the width of all of the elements in a jQuery object.
height(function) width(function)	Set the width or height for all of the elements in the jQuery object using a function.

Most of these methods are self-evident, but a couple warrant explanation. The results from the offset and position methods is an object that has top and left properties, indicating the location of the element. Listing 8-22 provides a demonstration using the position method.

Listing 8-22. Using the position Method

```
...
<script type="text/javascript">
    $(document).ready(function() {

        var pos = $('img').position();
        console.log("Position top: " + pos.top + " left: " + pos.left);

    });
</script>
...
```

This script writes out the value of the top and left properties of the object returned by the method. The result is as follows:

```
Position top: 108 left: 18
```

Setting the Width and Height Using a Function

You can set the width and height for a set of elements dynamically by passing a function to the width or height method. The arguments to this method are the index of the element and the current property value. As you might expect by now, the this variable is set to the HTMLElement of the current element, and you return the value you want assigned. Listing 8-23 provides an example.

Listing 8-23. Setting the Height of Elements Using a Function

```
...
<script type="text/javascript">
    $(document).ready(function() {

        $('#row1 img').css("border", "thick solid red")
            .height(function(index, currentValue) {
                return (index + 1) * 25;
            });
    });
</script>
...
```

In this script, I use the index value as a multiplier for the height. You can see the effect in Figure 8-14.

Figure 8-14. Using a function to set the height for elements

Working with Element Content

You have been looking at the attributes of elements so far in this chapter, but jQuery also provides you with the means to work with the content of elements as well. Table 8-6 describes the methods available for this purpose.

Table 8-6. Methods for Working with Element Content

Method	Description
text()	Gets the combined text contents of all the element in the jQuery object and their descendants
text(value)	Sets the content of each element in the jQuery object
html()	Gets the HTML contents of the first element in the jQuery object
html(value)	Sets the HTML content of each element in the jQuery object
text(function) html(function)	Sets the text or HTML content using a function

Unusually for jQuery, when you use the text method without arguments, the result that you receive is generated from all of the selected elements. The html method is more consistent with the rest of jQuery and returns just the content from the first element, as Listing 8-24 shows.

Listing 8-24. Using the html Method to Read Element Content

```
...
<script type="text/javascript">
    $(document).ready(function() {
        var html = $('div.dcell').html();
        console.log(html);
    });
</script>
...
```

This script uses the html method to read the HTML contents of the first element matched by the div.dcell selector. This is written to the console, producing the following results. Notice that the HTML of the element itself is not included.

```
<img src="astor.png">
<label for="astor">Astor:</label>
<input name="astor" value="0" required="">
```

Setting Element Content

You can set the content of elements using either the html or text method. My flower shop example document doesn't have any text content to speak of, so Listing 8-25 shows how to use the html method.

Listing 8-25. Using the html Method to Set Element Content

```
...
<script type="text/javascript">
    $(document).ready(function() {
        $('#row2 div.dcell').html($('div.dcell').html());
    });
</script>
...
```

This script sets the HTML contents of the div elements in the dcell class that are descendants of the row2 element. For the content I have used the html method to read the HTML from the first div.dcell element. This has the effect of setting the lower row of cells in the layout to have the astor content, as shown in Figure 8-15.

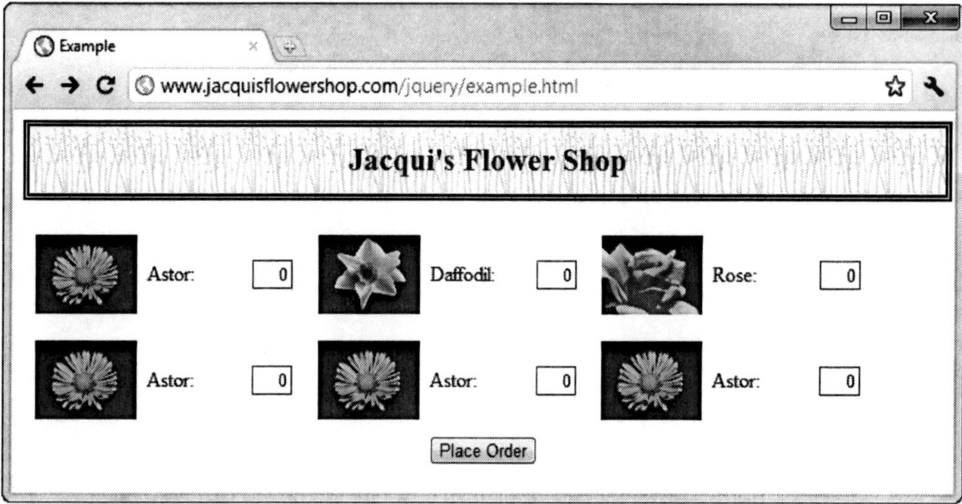

Figure 8-15. Setting the content of elements with the html method

Setting Element Content Using a Function

As with many of the other methods in this chapter, you can use the html and text methods with a function to set content dynamically. In both cases, the arguments are the index of the element in the jQuery object and the current text or HTML content. The this variable is set to the element's HTMLElement object, and you return the value you want to set as the result from the function. Listing 8-26 shows how you can use a function with the text method.

Listing 8-26. Setting Text Content Using a Function

```
...
<script type="text/javascript">
    $(document).ready(function() {
        $('label').css("border", "thick solid red").text(function(index, currentValue) {
            return "Index " + index;
        });
    });
</script>
...
```

In this script I set the text content of the label elements using the index value (I also use the css method to add a border to the elements I change). You can see the result in Figure 8-16.

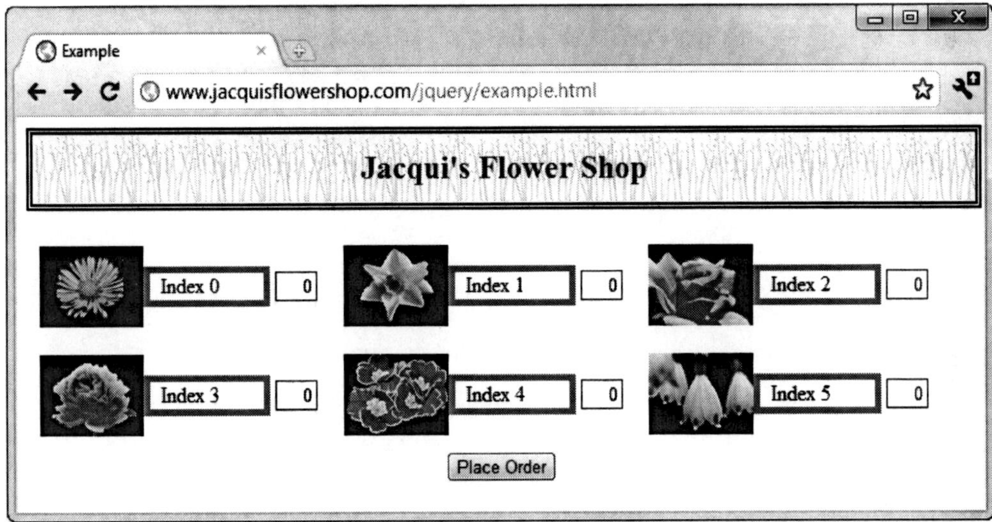

Figure 8-16. Setting text content using a function

Working with Form Elements

You can get and set the value of form elements (such as input) using the val method, which is described in Table 8-7.

Table 8-7. The val method

Method	Description
val()	Returns the value of the first element in the jQuery object
val(value)	Sets the value of all of the elements in the jQuery object
val(function)	Sets the values for the elements in the jQuery object using a function

Listing 8-27 shows how you can use the val method to get the value from the first element in the jQuery object. In this script, I have used the each method so that I can enumerate the values of the set of input elements in the document.

Listing 8-27. Using the val Method to Get the Value from an input Element

```
...
<script type="text/javascript">
    $(document).ready(function() {
       $('input').each(function(index, elem) {
            console.log("Name: " + elem.name + " Val: " + $(elem).val());
       });
    });
</script>
...
```

I write the values to the console, which produces the following output:

```
Name: astor Val: 0
Name: daffodil Val: 0
Name: rose Val: 0
Name: peony Val: 0
Name: primula Val: 0
Name: snowdrop Val: 0
```

Setting Form Element Values

You can use the val method to set the value of all of the elements in a jQuery object by simply passing the value you want as an argument to the method. Listing 8-28 provides a demonstration.

Listing 8-28. Setting Element Values with the val Method

```
...
<script type="text/javascript">
    $(document).ready(function() {

        $("<button>Set Values</button>").appendTo("#buttonDiv").click(setValues);
```

```
        function setValues(e) {
            $('input').val(100);
            e.preventDefault();
        }
    });
</script>
...
```

In this script I have added a button element to the document and specified that the setValues function should be called when it is clicked. The function selects all of the input elements in the document and uses the val method to set their value to 100. You can see the effect in Figure 8-17.

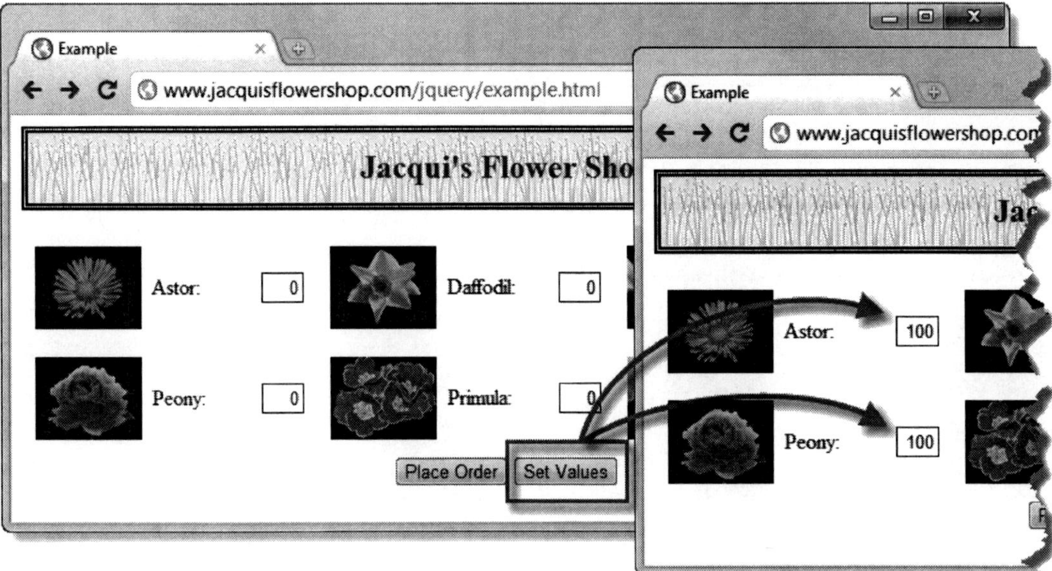

Figure 8-17. Using the val method to set input element values

Setting Form Element Values Using a Function

As you might expect by now, you can also use a function to set values with the val method. The arguments to the method are the index of the element and the present values. The this variable is set to the HTMLElement object representing the element being processed. By using the val method in this way, you can set new values dynamically, as demonstrated in Listing 8-29.

Listing 8-29. Using the val Method with a Function

```
...
<script type="text/javascript">
    $(document).ready(function() {
        $('input').val(function(index, currentVal) {
            return (index + 1) * 100;
        });
    });
</script>
...
```

In this example, I set the value based on the index argument. You can see the effect in Figure 8-18.

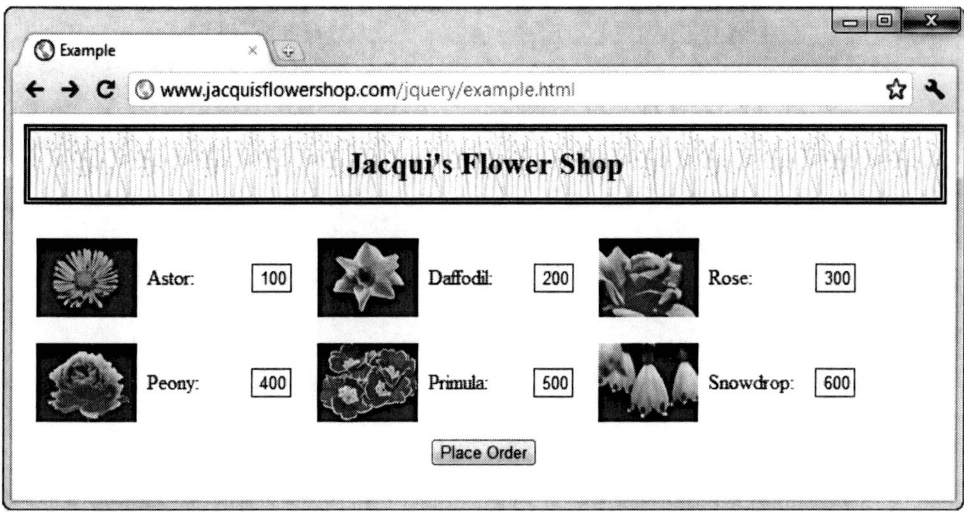

Figure 8-18. Setting the values dynamically using the val method with a function

Associating Data with Elements

jQuery allows you to associate arbitrary data with an element, which you can then test for and retrieve later. Table 8-8 describes the methods associated with this feature.

Table 8-8. *Methods for Working with Arbitrary Element Data*

Method	Description
`data(key, value)` `data(map)`	Associate one or more key/value pairs with the elements in a jQuery object
`data(key)`	Retrieves the value associated with the specified key from the first element in the jQuery object

data()	Retrieves the key/value pairs from the first element in the jQuery object
removeData(key)	Removes the data associated with the specified key from all of the elements in the jQuery object
removeData()	Removes all of the data items from all of the elements in the jQuery object

Listing 8-30 demonstrates setting, testing for, reading, and deleting data values.

■ **Note** When you use the clone method, the data you have associated with elements is removed from the newly copied elements unless you explicitly tell jQuery that you want to keep it. See Chapter 7 for details of the `clone` method and how to preserve the data.

Listing 8-30. Working with Element Data

```
...
<script type="text/javascript">
    $(document).ready(function() {

        // set the data
        $('img').each(function () {
            $(this).data("product", $(this). siblings("input[name]").attr("name"));
        });

        // find elements with the data and read the values
        $('*').filter(function() {
            return $(this).data("product") != null;
        }).each(function() {
            console.log("Elem: " + this.tagName + " " + $(this).data("product"));
        });

        // remove all data
        $('img').removeData();

    });
</script>
...
```

There are three stages to this script. In the first, I use the data method to associate an item of data with the product key. I get the data by navigating from each img element to the input sibling that has a name attribute.

In the second state, I select all of the elements in the document and then use the filter method to find those that have a value associated with the product key. I then use the each method to enumerate those elements and write the data values to the console. This is duplicative, but I wanted to demonstrate the best technique for selecting elements that have data. There is no dedicated selector or method, so you must make do with the filter method and a function.

Finally, I use the removeData to remove all data from all of the img elements. This script produces the following output on the console:

```
Elem: IMG astor
Elem: IMG daffodil
Elem: IMG rose
Elem: IMG peony
Elem: IMG primula
Elem: IMG snowdrop
```

Working with HTML5 Data Attributes

The HTML5 specification defines *data attributes*, which also allow you to associate data with elements. Data attributes, also known as *expand attributes*, have names that are prefixed with data, and they are useful for adding extra meaning to your element above and beyond what you can achieve with classes. The data method gets and sets data attributes values automatically, as demonstrated in Listing 8-31.

Listing 8-31. Using the data Method with HTML5 Data Attributes

```
<!DOCTYPE html>
<html>
<head>
    <title>Example</title>
    <script src="jquery-1.7.js" type="text/javascript"></script>
    <link rel="stylesheet" type="text/css" href="styles.css"/>
    <script type="text/javascript">
        $(document).ready(function() {
            $('div.dcell').each(function () {
               var productVal = $(this).data("product");
               console.log("Product: " + productVal);
            });
        });
    </script>
</head>
<body>
    <h1>Jacqui's Flower Shop</h1>
    <form method="post">
        <div id="oblock">
            <div class="dtable">
                <div id="row1" class="drow">
                    <div class="dcell" data-product="astor">
                        <img src="astor.png"/><label for="astor">Astor:</label>
                        <input name="astor" value="0" required />
                    </div>
                    <div class="dcell" data-product="daffodil">
                        <img src="daffodil.png"/><label for="daffodil">Daffodil:</label>
                        <input name="daffodil" value="0" required />
```

```
                </div>
                <div class="dcell" data-product="rose">
                    <img src="rose.png"/><label for="rose">Rose:</label>
                    <input name="rose" value="0" required />
                </div>
            </div>
        </div>
    </div>
    <div id="buttonDiv"><button type="submit">Place Order</button></div>
  </form>
</body>
</html>
```

In this example, I have added HTML5 data attributes to a cut-down version of the example document. The script selects the elements with the data attributes and uses the data method to retrieve the associated values and print them to the console. Notice that I omit the data- part of the attribute name; for example, I refer to data-product simply as product. Here is the output from the script:

```
Product: astor
Product: daffodil
Product: rose
```

■ **Tip** The data method takes the data attributes into account when setting values as well. When you specify a key, such a product, the data method checks to see whether there is a corresponding HTML5 data attribute, such as data-product. If there is, then the value you specified is assigned to the attribute. If not, then the data is stored internally by jQuery.

Summary

In this chapter, I showed you the different ways that you can manipulate elements in the DOM. I showed you how to get and set attributes, including the jQuery convenience methods for working with classes and CSS properties. I also showed you how to get and set the text or HTML content of elements and how jQuery supports associated arbitrary data with elements, both through the HTML5 data attributes and through its own internal mechanism.

CHAPTER 9

Working with Events

In this chapter, I describe the jQuery support for events. If you are unfamiliar with events, then I provided a very brief overview of how they work and how they are propagated through the DOM in Chapter 2. jQuery provides some very nice event-related features, of which my favorite is the ability to automatically associate event handler functions with elements as they are added to the DOM. Table 9-1 provides the summary for this chapter.

***Table 9-1.** Chapter Summary*

Problem	Solution	Listing
Register a function to handle one or more event.	Use the `bind` method or one of the shorthand methods.	1–4, 18, 19, 22
Suppress the default action for an event.	Use the `Event.preventDefault` method or use the `bind` method without specifying a handler function.	5–6
Remove an event handler function from an element.	Use the `unbind` method.	7–9
Create a handler function that is executed only once for each element it is associated with.	Use the `one` method.	10
Automatically apply an event handler function to elements as they are added to the document.	Use the `live` method.	11, 12
Remove a handler created using the `live` method.	Use the `die` method.	13
Apply an automatically added handler to a specific element in the DOM.	Use the `delegate` and `undelegate` methods.	14
Manually invoke the event handler functions for an element.	Use the `trigger` or `triggerHandler` method or one of the shorthand methods.	15–17, 20, 21

Handling Events

jQuery provides a set of methods that let you register functions that are called when specified events are triggered on elements you are interested in. These methods are described in Table 9-2.

Table 9-2. *Methods for Handling Events*

Method	Description
`bind(eventType, function)` `bind(eventType, data, function)`	Add an event handler to the elements in a `jQuery` object with an optional data item.
`bind(eventType, boolean)`	Creates a default handler that always returns false, preventing the default action. The `boolean` argument controls event bubbling.
`bind(map)`	Adds a set of event handlers based on a map object to all elements in the `jQuery` object.
`one(eventType, function)` `one(eventType, data, function)`	Add an event handler to each element in a `jQuery` object with an optional data item. The handler will be unregistered from an element once it has been executed.
`unbind()`	Removes all event handlers on all elements in the `jQuery` object.
`unbind(eventType)`	Removes a previously registered event handler from all elements in the `jQuery` object.
`unbind(eventType, boolean)`	Removes a previously registered always-false handler from all elements in the `jQuery` object.
`unbind(Event)`	Removes an event handler using an `Event` object.

The various flavors of the `bind` method let you specify a function that will be invoked when an event is triggered, and since this is jQuery, the function is used for all of the elements in the `jQuery` object on which you use the `bind` method. Listing 9-1 shows a simple example.

Listing 9-1. Using the bind Method to Register an Event Handler Function

```
<!DOCTYPE html>
<html>
<head>
    <title>Example</title>
    <script src="jquery-1.7.js" type="text/javascript"></script>
    <link rel="stylesheet" type="text/css" href="styles.css"/>
    <script type="text/javascript">
        $(document).ready(function() {
```

```
            $('img').bind("mouseenter", handleMouseEnter)
                .bind("mouseout", handleMouseOut);

            function handleMouseEnter(e) {
                $(this).css({
                    "border": "thick solid red",
                    "opacity": "0.5"
                });
            };

            function handleMouseOut(e) {
                $(this).css({
                    "border": "",
                    "opacity": ""
                });
            }
        });
    </script>
</head>
<body>
    <h1>Jacqui's Flower Shop</h1>
    <form method="post">
        <div id="oblock">
            <div class="dtable">
                <div id="row1" class="drow">
                    <div class="dcell">
                        <img src="astor.png"/><label for="astor">Astor:</label>
                        <input name="astor" value="0" required />
                    </div>
                    <div class="dcell">
                        <img src="daffodil.png"/><label for="daffodil">Daffodil:</label>
                        <input name="daffodil" value="0" required />
                    </div>
                    <div class="dcell">
                        <img src="rose.png"/><label for="rose">Rose:</label>
                        <input name="rose" value="0" required />
                    </div>
                </div>
                <div id="row2"class="drow">
                    <div class="dcell">
                        <img src="peony.png"/><label for="peony">Peony:</label>
                        <input name="peony" value="0" required />
                    </div>
                    <div class="dcell">
                        <img src="primula.png"/><label for="primula">Primula:</label>
                        <input name="primula" value="0" required />
                    </div>
                    <div class="dcell">
```

```
                        <img src="snowdrop.png"/><label for="snowdrop">Snowdrop:</label>
                        <input name="snowdrop" value="0" required />
                    </div>
                </div>
            </div>
        </div>
        <div id="buttonDiv"><button type="submit">Place Order</button></div>
    </form>
</body>
</html>
```

In this example, I select all of the img elements in the document and use the bind method to register handler functions for the mouseenter and mouseout events. These handlers use the css method to set values for the border and opacity properties. When the user moves the mouse pointer over one of the img elements, the border is drawn, and the image is made more transparent, returning to its previous state when the pointer is moved away.

When jQuery calls the handler function, the this variable is set to the element to which the handler is attached. The object passed to the handler function is jQuery's own Event object, which is different from the Event object defined by the DOM specification. Table 9-3 describes the properties and methods of the jQuery Event object.

Table 9-3. *Members of the jQuery Event Object*

Name	Description	Returns
currentTarget	Gets the element whose listeners are currently being invoked.	HTMLElement
data	Gets the optional data passed to the bind method when the handler was registered. See the following section for details.	Object
isDefaultPrevented()	Returns true if the preventDefault method has been called.	Boolean
isImmediatePropagationStopped()	Returns true if the stopImmediatePropagation method has been called.	Boolean
isPropagationStopped()	Returns true if the stopPropagation method has been called.	Boolean
originalEvent	Returns the original DOM Event object.	Event
pageX pageY	Return the mouse position relative to the left edge of the document.	number
preventDefault()	Prevents the default action associated with the event from being performed.	void

relatedTarget	For mouse events, returns the related element. This varies depending on which event has been triggered.	HTMLElement
result	Returns the result from the last event handler that processed this event.	Object
stopImmediatePropagation()	Prevents any other event handlers being called for this event.	void
stopPropagation()	Prevents the event from bubbling but allows handlers attached to the current target element to receive the event.	void
target	Gets the element that triggered the event.	HTMLElement
timeStamp	Gets the time at which the event was triggered.	number
type	Gets the type of the event.	string
which	Returns the button or key that was pressed for mouse and keyboard events.	number

The jQuery Event object also defines most of the properties from the standard DOM Event object. So, for almost all situations, you can treat the jQuery Event object as having a superset of the functionality defined by the DOM standard.

Registering a Function to Handle Multiple Event Types

A common technique is to use a single function to handle two or more kinds of event. These events are usually related in some way, such as the mouseenter and mouseout events. When using the bind method, you can specify multiple event types in the first argument, separated by a space. This is demonstrated in Listing 9-2.

Listing 9-2. Registering a Function to Handle Multiple Event Types

```
...
<script type="text/javascript">
    $(document).ready(function() {

        $('img').bind("mouseenter mouseout", handleMouse);

        function handleMouse(e) {
            var cssData = {
                "border": "thick solid red",
                "opacity": "0.5"
            }
            if (event.type == "mouseout") {
                cssData.border = "";
                cssData.opacity = "";
            }
            $(this).css(cssData);
        }
    });
</script>
...
```

In this script, I have used a single call to the bind method to specify that the mouseenter and mouseout events should be handled by the handleMouse function for all of the img elements in the document. Of course, you can also use a single function and chain the bind calls, like this:

```
$('img').bind("mouseenter", handleMouse).bind("mouseout", handleMouse);
```

You can also register handlers using a map object. The properties of the object are the names of the events, and their values are the functions that will be invoked when the events are triggered. Listing 9-3 shows the use of a map object with the bind method.

Listing 9-3. Using a Map Object to Register Event Handlers

```
...
<script type="text/javascript">
    $(document).ready(function() {

        $('img').bind({
            mouseenter: function() {
                $(this).css("border", "thick solid red");
            },
            mouseout: function() {
                $(this).css("border", "");
            }
        });

    });
</script>
...
```

In this example, I have defined the handler functions inline, as part of the map object. The bind method gets the details of the events I am interested in and my functions and creates the associations I have specified.

Providing Data to the Event Handler Function

You can pass an object to the `bind` method, which jQuery will then make available to the handler function through the `Event.data` property. This can be useful when using a single function to handle events from different sets of elements. The `data` value can help determine what kind of response is required. Listing 9-4 shows how to define and use the data value.

Listing 9-4. Passing Data to the Event Handler Function via the bind Method

```
...
<script type="text/javascript">
    $(document).ready(function() {

        $('img:odd').bind("mouseenter mouseout", "red", handleMouse);
        $('img:even').bind("mouseenter mouseout", "blue", handleMouse);

        function handleMouse(e) {
            var cssData = {
                "border": "thick solid " + e.data,
            }
            if (event.type == "mouseout") {
                cssData.border = "";
            }
            $(this).css(cssData);

        }
    });
</script>
...
```

In this script, I use the optional argument to the `bind` method to specify which color border should be displayed when the `mouseenter` event is triggered. For the odd-numbered `img` elements, the border will be `red`, and for the even-numbered it will be `blue`. In the event handler function I use the `Event.data` property to read the data and use it to create the value for the CSS `border` property. You can see the effect in Figure 9-1.

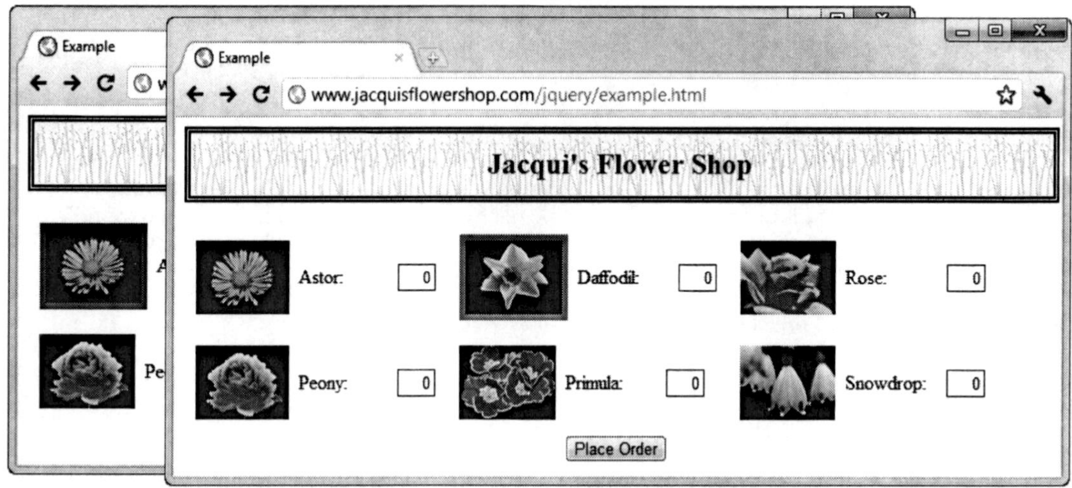

Figure 9-1. Passing data to the handler function via the bind method

Suppressing the Default Action

As I mentioned in Chapter 2, some events have a default action when they are triggered on certain elements. A good example occurs when the user clicks a button whose type attribute is submit. If the button is contained in a form element, the default action is for the browser to submit the form. To prevent the default action from being performed, you can call the preventDefault method on the Event object, as shown in Listing 9-5.

Listing 9-5. Preventing the Default Action on an Event

```
<script type="text/javascript">
    $(document).ready(function() {

        $('button:submit').bind("click", function(e) {
            e.preventDefault();
        });

    });
</script>
```

Now, usually you want to suppress the default action so you can perform some other activity instead. For example, you stop the browser from submitting the form because you want to do it with Ajax (which is the topic of Chapters 14 and 15). Instead of writing a one-line function, you can use the bind method, as shown in Listing 9-6.

Listing 9-6. Using the bind Method to Create a Handler That Prevents the Default Action

```
...
<script type="text/javascript">
    $(document).ready(function() {
        $('button:submit').bind("click", false);
    });
</script>
...
```

The first argument is the event or events whose default action you want to suppress, and the second argument allows you to specify whether the event should be prevented from bubbling up the DOM (I explain event bubbling in Chapter 2).

Removing Event Handler Functions

The `unbind` method removes a handler function from an element. You can unbind all of the handlers associated with all events for all elements in a `jQuery` object by calling the `unbind` method with no arguments, as shown in Listing 9-7.

Listing 9-7. Unbinding All Event Handlers

```
...
<script type="text/javascript">
    $(document).ready(function() {

        $('img').bind("mouseenter mouseout", handleMouse);

        $('img[src*=rose]').unbind();

        function handleMouse(e) {
            var cssData = {
                "border": "thick solid red",
                "opacity": "0.5"
            }
            if (event.type == "mouseout") {
                cssData.border = "";
                cssData.opacity = "";
            }
            $(this).css(cssData);
        }
    });
</script>
...
```

In this example, I `bind` a handler for the `mouseenter` and `mouseout` events for all of the `img` elements and then use the `unbind` method to remove all of the handlers for the `img` element whose `src` attribute contains `rose`. You can be more selective by passing the events you want to unbind as an argument to the `unbind` method, as shown in Listing 9-8.

Listing 9-8. Selectively Unbinding Events

```
...
<script type="text/javascript">
    $(document).ready(function() {

        $('img').bind("mouseenter mouseout", handleMouse);

        $('img[src*=rose]').unbind("mouseout");

        function handleMouse(e) {
            var cssData = {
                "border": "thick solid red",
                "opacity": "0.5"
            }
            if (event.type == "mouseout") {
                cssData.border = "";
                cssData.opacity = "";
            }
            $(this).css(cssData);
        }
    });
</script>
...
```

In this script I unbind only the `mouseout` event, leaving the handler for the `mouseenter` event untouched.

Unbinding from Within the Event Handler Function

The final option for unbinding is to do so from within the event handler function. This can be useful only if you want to handle an event a certain number of times, for example. Listing 9-9 contains a simple demonstration.

Listing 9-9. Unbinding from an Event Inside the Event Handler

```
...
<script type="text/javascript">
    $(document).ready(function() {

        $('img').bind("mouseenter", handleMouseEnter).bind("mouseout", handleMouseExit)

        var handledCount = 0;

        function handleMouseEnter(e) {
            $(this).css("border", "thick solid red");
        }
        function handleMouseExit(e) {
            $(this).css("border", "");
            handledCount ++;
```

```
            if (handledCount == 2) {
                $(this).unbind(e);
            }
        }
    });
</script>
...
```

In the handleMouseEvent function, I increment a counter each time that I handle the mouseout event. After I have handled the event twice, I pass the Event object to the unbind method to unregister the function as a handler. jQuery figures out the details it requires from the object itself.

Executing a Handler Once

The one method lets you register an event handler that will be executed only once for an element and then removed. Listing 9-10 provides an example.

Listing 9-10. Using the one Method to Register a Single-Shot Event Handler Function

```
...
<script type="text/javascript">
    $(document).ready(function() {

        $('img').one("mouseenter", handleMouseEnter).one("mouseout", handleMouseOut);

        function handleMouseEnter(e) {
            $(this).css("border", "thick solid red");
        };

        function handleMouseOut(e) {
            $(this).css("border", "");
        };
    });
</script>
...
```

I have used the one method to register handlers for the mouseenter and mouseout events. The handler functions will be called when the user moves the mouse in and out of one of the img elements, and then the function will be unbound (but just for that element; the others will still have the handlers until the mouse is moved over them).

Performing Live Event Binding

One limitation of the bind method is that your event handler functions are not associated with any new element that you add to the DOM. Listing 9-11 contains an example.

Listing 9-11. Adding Elements After Setting Up the Event Handlers

```
...
<script type="text/javascript">
    $(document).ready(function() {
        $('img').bind({
            mouseenter: function() {
                $(this).css("border", "thick solid red");
            },
            mouseout: function() {
                $(this).css("border", "");
            }
        });

        $('#row1').append($("<div class='dcell'/>")
            .append("<img src='lily.png'/>")
            .append("<label for='lily'>Lily:</label>")
            .append("<input name='lily' value='0' required />"));
    });
</script>
...
```

In this script, I use the bind method to set up handlers for the mouseenter and mouseout events for all of the img elements. I then use the append methods to insert some new elements in the document, including another img element. This new img element didn't exist when I used the bind method, and my handler functions are not associated with it. The result of this is that I have six img elements that display a border when the mouse hovers over them and one that doesn't.

In an example as simple as this, the easy answer is to call the bind method again, but it can be difficult to keep track of which handlers are required for different types of elements. Fortunately, jQuery makes this easy for you with a set of methods that automatically register event handlers when new elements that match a selector are added to the DOM. These methods are described in Table 9-4.

***Table 9-4.** Methods for Automatically Registering Event Handlers*

Method	Description
live(eventType, function) live(eventType, data, function) live(map)	Add an event handler to the elements that match the selector of a jQuery, now or in the future
die()	Removes all of the event handlers created with the live method
die(eventType)	Removes event handlers created with the live method for the specified event types
delegate(selector, eventType, function) delegate(selector, eventType, data, function)	Add an event handler to the elements that match the selector (now or in the future) attached to the elements in the jQuery object.

`delegate(selector, map)`	
`undelegate()` `undelegate(selector, eventType)`	Remove event handlers created with the `delegate` method for the specified event types

Listing 9-12 shows the previous example updated to use the `live` method. The change is minor, but the effect is significant. Any elements that I add to the DOM that match the selector `img` will have the specified event handler functions added automatically.

■ **Tip** The `live` method doesn't actually need to add the handler functions directly to the element. In fact, it just creates an event handler on the `document` object and looks for events that were triggered by elements that match the selector. When it sees such an event, it triggers the event handler. However, for all practical purposes, it is just easier to imagine the `live` method diligently adding handles to new elements.

Listing 9-12. Using the live Method

```
...
<script type="text/javascript">
    $(document).ready(function() {

        $('img').live({
            mouseenter: function() {
                $(this).css("border", "thick solid red");
            },
            mouseout: function() {
                $(this).css("border", "");
            }
        });

        $('#row1').append($("<div class='dcell'/>")
            .append("<img src='lily.png'/>")
            .append("<label for='lily'>Lily:</label>")
            .append("<input name='lily' value='0' required />"));
    });

</script>
...
```

In this example, the newly added `img` element matches the selector of the jQuery object that I used with the `live` method and is associated with the handlers for the `mouseenter` and `mouseout` events.

The complement to the `live` method is `die`, which you can use to remove the handlers and prevent them from being assigned to any new elements that match the selector. Listing 9-13 shows the use of the `die` method.

Listing 9-13. Using the die Method

```
...
<script type="text/javascript">
    $(document).ready(function() {

        $('img').live({
            mouseenter: function() {
                $(this).css("border", "thick solid red");
            },
            mouseout: function() {
                $(this).css("border", "");
            }
        });

        $('img').die();
    });

</script>
...
```

■ **Caution** It is important to use the same selector with the `live` and `die` methods; otherwise, the `die` method won't undo the effect of `live`.

Limiting DOM Traversal for Live Event Handlers

One problem with the `live` method is that the events have to propagate all the way up to the `document` element before your handler functions are executed. You can take a more direct approach by using the `delegate` method, which allows you to specify where the event listener will be located in the document. Listing 9-14 provides an example.

Listing 9-14. Using the delegate Method

```
...
<script type="text/javascript">
    $(document).ready(function() {

        $('#row1').delegate("img", {
            mouseenter: function() {
                $(this).css("border", "thick solid red");
            },
            mouseout: function() {
                $(this).css("border", "");
            }
        });
```

```
        $('#row1').append($("<div class='dcell'/>")
            .append("<img src='carnation.png'/>")
            .append("<label for='carnation'>Carnation:</label>")
            .append("<input name='carnation' value='0' required />"));

        $('#row2').append($("<div class='dcell'/>")
            .append("<img src='lily.png'/>")
            .append("<label for='lily'>Lily:</label>")
            .append("<input name='lily' value='0' required />"));
    });
</script>
...
```

In this example, I use the `delegate` method to add the listener to the element whose ID is `#row1`, and the selector I specified matches the `img` element. The effect of this is that my handler functions will be executed when a `mouseenter` or `mouseout` event that originated from an `img` element propagates to the `row1` element. When I add another `img` element to `row1`, it is automatically covered by my call to the `delegate` method, which is not the case when I add elements to `row2`.

The main benefit of using the `delegate` method is speed, which can become an issue if you have a particularly large and complex document and a lot of event handlers. By pushing the point where the events are intercepted down into the documents, you reduce the distance that events have to travel in the DOM before they lead to the handler functions being invoked.

■ **Tip** To remove handlers added with the `delegate` method, you have to use `undelegate`. The `die` method works only with the `live` method.

Manually Invoking Event Handlers

You can manually invoke the event handling functions on elements using the methods described in Table 9-5.

Table 9-5. *Methods for Manually Invoking Event Handlers*

Method	Description
`trigger(eventType)`	Triggers the handler functions for the specified event types on all of the elements in a `jQuery` object
`trigger(Event)`	Triggers the handler functions for the specified event on all of the elements in a `jQuery` object
`triggerHandler(eventType)`	Triggers the handler function on the first element in the `jQuery` object, without performing the default action or bubbling the event

Listing 9-15 shows how you can trigger the event handlers manually.

Listing 9-15. Triggering Event Handlers Manually

```
...
<script type="text/javascript">
    $(document).ready(function() {

        $('img').bind({mouseenter: function() {
                $(this).css("border", "thick solid red");
            },
            mouseout: function() {
                $(this).css("border", "");
            }
        });

        $("<button>Trigger</button>").appendTo("#buttonDiv").bind("click", function (e) {
            $('#row1 img').trigger("mouseenter");
            e.preventDefault();
        });

    });

</script>
...
```

In this script, I use the `bind` method to set up a pair of event handler functions on the `img` elements in the document. I then use the `appendTo` method to insert a `button` element into the document method and the `bind` method to register a handler function for the `click` event.

When the button is pressed, the event handler function selects the `img` elements that are descendants of `row1` and uses the `trigger` method to invoke their handlers for the `mouseenter` button. The effect, which is shown in Figure 9-2, is as though the mouse were simultaneously moved over all three `img` elements.

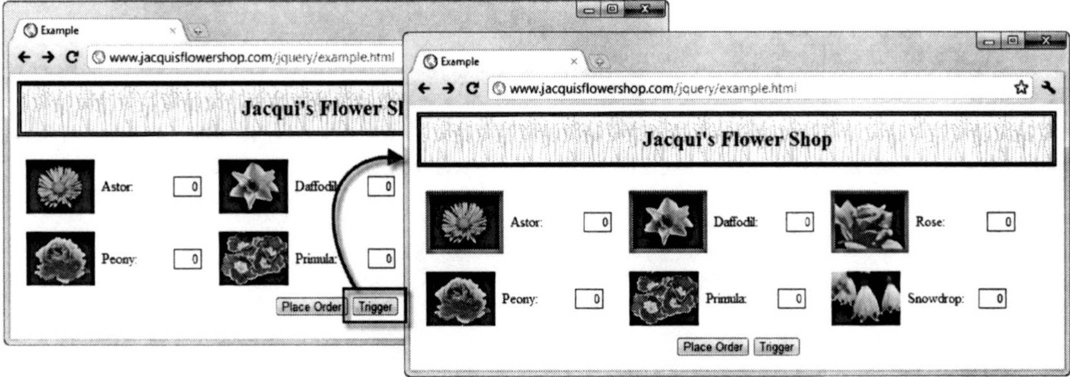

Figure 9-2. Manually triggering event handler functions

Using an Event Object

You can also use an Event object to trigger other elements' event handlers. This can be a convenient technique to use inside a handler, as demonstrated in Listing 9-16.

Listing 9-16. Manually Triggering Event Handles with an Event Object

```
...
<script type="text/javascript">
    $(document).ready(function() {

        $('#row1 img').bind("mouseenter", function() {
            $(this).css("border", "thick solid red");
        });

        $('#row2 img').bind("mouseenter", function(e) {
            $(this).css("border", "thick solid blue");
            $('#row1 img').trigger(e);
        });

    });

</script>
...
```

In this example, I use the bind method to add a red border to the img descendants of the row1 element in response to the mouseenter event. I do the same with a blue border to the row2 img elements, but in the handler, I have added the following statement:

```
$('#row1 img').trigger(e);
```

The effect of this addition is that when the mouse enters one of the row2 img elements, the handler for the same event type is triggered on the row1 img elements as well. You can see the effect in Figure 9-3.

Figure 9-3. Triggering event handlers using an event

This approach is convenient when you want to trigger the handlers for the event type currently being processed, but you could as easily get the same effect by specifying the event type.

Using the triggerHandler Method

The `triggerHandler` method invokes the handler functions without performing the event's default action or allowing the event to bubble up through the DOM. And, unlike the `trigger` method, `triggerHandler` invokes the handler function only on the first element in a jQuery object. Listing 9-17 shows the use of this method. Another difference is that the result from the `triggerHandler` method is the result returned by the handler function. This means you cannot chain the `triggerHandler` method.

Listing 9-17. Using the triggerHandler Method

```
...
<script type="text/javascript">
    $(document).ready(function() {
        $('#row1 img').bind("mouseenter", function() {
            $(this).css("border", "thick solid red");
        });

        $('#row2 img').bind("mouseenter", function(e) {
            $(this).css("border", "thick solid blue");
            $('#row1 img').triggerHandler("mouseenter");
        });
    });
</script>
...
```

You can see the effect of this script in Figure 9-4.

Figure 9-4. Using the triggerHandler method

Using the Event Shorthand Methods

jQuery defines some convenience methods that you can use as a shorthand to register an event handler for commonly used events. In the tables that follow, I have shown these shorthand methods with a `function` argument. This is the most common use and is equivalent to calling the `bind` method, but they require less typing and (at least to my mind) make it more obvious which events you are binding to. Listing 9-18 shows how you can use a shorthand method in this way.

Listing 9-18. Using an Event Shorthand Method to Bind a Handler Function

```
...
<script type="text/javascript">
    $(document).ready(function() {

        $('img').mouseenter(function() {
           $(this).css("border", "thick solid red");
        });

    });
</script>
...
```

This is equivalent to using the `bind` event for the `mouseenter` event, which I have shown in Listing 9-19.

Listing 9-19. Using the bind Method for the mouseenter Event

```
...
<script type="text/javascript">
    $(document).ready(function() {

        $('img').bind("mouseenter", function() {
            $(this).css("border", "thick solid red");
        });

    });
</script>
...
```

That's all well and good, and by this point, you should be comfortable with how this example works. However, you can also use the shorthand methods as an analog to the `trigger` method. You do this by calling the method without arguments. Listing 9-20 shows how you can do this.

Listing 9-20. Using the Event Shorthand Methods to Trigger Event Handlers

```
...
<script type="text/javascript">
    $(document).ready(function() {

        $('img').bind("mouseenter", function() {
            $(this).css("border", "thick solid red");
        });

        $("<button>Trigger</button>").appendTo("#buttonDiv").click(function (e) {
            $('img').mouseenter();
            e.preventDefault();
        });
    });
</script>
...
```

I add a `button` to the document that, when clicked, selects the `img` elements and invokes their handlers for the `mouseenter` event. For completeness, Listing 9-21 shows the equivalent functionality written using the `trigger` method.

Listing 9-21. Using the trigger Method

```
...
<script type="text/javascript">
    $(document).ready(function() {

        $('img').bind("mouseenter", function() {
            $(this).css("border", "thick solid red");
        });

        $("<button>Trigger</button>").appendTo("#buttonDiv").click(function (e) {
```

```
            $('img').trigger("mouseenter");
            e.preventDefault();
        });
    });
</script>
...
```

In the sections that follow, I list the different categories of shorthand methods and the events they correspond to.

Using the Document Event Shorthand Methods

Table 9-6 describes the jQuery shorthand methods that apply to the document object.

Table 9-6. *Document Event Shorthand Methods*

Method	Description
load(function)	Corresponds to the load event, triggered when the subelements and resources in the document have been loaded
ready(function)	Triggered when the elements in the document have been processed and the DOM is ready to use
unload(function)	Corresponds to the unload event, triggered when the user navigates away from the page

The ready method deserves special mention. It doesn't correspond directly to a DOM event but is incredibly useful when using jQuery. You can see the different ways you can use the ready method in Chapter 5, when I explain how to defer execution of a script until the DOM is ready and how you can control the execution of the ready event.

Using the Browser Event Shorthand Methods

Table 9-7 describes the browser events, which are usually targeted at the window object (although the error and scroll events are also used with elements as well).

Table 9-7. *Browser Event Shorthand Methods*

Method	Description
error(function)	Corresponds to the error event, triggered when there is a problem loading an external resource, such as an image
resize(function)	Corresponds to the resize event, triggered when the browser window is resized
scroll(function)	Corresponds to the scroll event, triggered when the scrollbars are used

Using the Mouse Event Shorthand Methods

Table 9-8 describes the set of shorthand methods that jQuery provides for dealing with mouse events.

Table 9-8. *Mouse Event Shorthand Methods*

Method	Description
`click(function)`	Corresponds to the `click` event, triggered when the user presses and releases the mouse.
`dblclick(function)`	Corresponds to the `dblclick` event, triggered when the user presses and releases the mouse twice in quick succession.
`focusin(function)`	Corresponds to the `focusin` event, triggered when the element gains the focus.
`focusout(function)`	Corresponds to the `focusout` event, triggered when the element loses the focus.
`hover(function)` `hover(function, function)`	Triggered when the mouse enters or leaves an element. When one function is specified, it is used for both enter and exit events.
`mousedown(function)`	Corresponds to the `mousedown` event, triggered when the mouse button is pressed over an element.
`mouseenter(function)`	Corresponds to the `mouseenter` event, triggered when the mouse enters the region of screen occupied by an element.
`mouseleave(function)`	Corresponds to the `mouseleave` event, triggered when the mouse leaves the region of screen occupied by an element.
`mousemove(function)`	Corresponds to the `mousemouse` event, triggered when the mouse is moved within the region of screen occupied by an element.
`mouseout(function)`	Corresponds to the `mouseout` event, triggered when the mouse leaves the region of screen occupied by an element.
`mouseover(function)`	Corresponds to the `mouseover` event, triggered when the mouse enters the region of screen occupied by an element.
`mouseup(function)`	Corresponds to the `mouseup` event, triggered when the mouse button is pressed over an element.

The `hover` method is a convenient way of binding a handler function to the `mouseenter` and `mouseleave` events. If you provide two functions as arguments, then the first is invoked in response to the `mouseenter` event and the second in response to `mouseleave`. If you specify only one function, it will be invoked for both events. Listing 9-22 shows the use of the `hover` method.

Listing 9-22. Using the hover Method

```
...
<script type="text/javascript">
    $(document).ready(function() {

        $('img').hover(handleMouseEnter, handleMouseLeave);

        function handleMouseEnter(e) {
            $(this).css("border", "thick solid red");
        };

        function handleMouseLeave(e) {
            $(this).css("border", "");
        }
    });
</script>
...
```

Using the Form Event Shorthand Methods

Table 9-9 describes the shorthand methods that jQuery provides for dealing with events that are usually associated with forms.

Table 9-9. *Form Event Shorthand Methods*

Method	Description
`blur(function)`	Corresponds to the `blur` event, triggered when an element loses the focus
`change(function)`	Corresponds to the `change` event, triggered when the value of an element changes
`focus(function)`	Corresponds to the `focus` event, triggered when an element gains the focus
`select(function)`	Corresponds to the `select` event, triggered when the user selects the element value
`submit(function)`	Corresponds to the `submit` event, triggered when the user submits a `form`

Using the Keyboard Event Shorthand Methods

Table 9-10 describes the shorthand methods that jQuery provides for dealing with keyboard events.

Table 9-10. Keyboard Event Shorthand Methods

Method	Description
`keydown(function)`	Corresponds to the `keydown` event, triggered when the user presses a key
`keypress(function)`	Corresponds to the `keypress` event, triggered when the user presses and releases a key
`keyup(function)`	Corresponds to the `keyup` event, triggered when the user releases a key

Summary

In this chapter, I showed you the jQuery support for events. As with much of jQuery, the benefit of the event functionality is simplicity and elegance. You can create and manage event handlers with little effort. I particularly like the support for creating live event handlers, such that elements that are added to the DOM that match a particular selector are automatically associated with event handlers. It significantly reduces the amount of time that I spend tracking down problems with event handling in my web applications.

CHAPTER 10

Using jQuery Effects

For the most part, jQuery UI contains the user-interface functionality associated with jQuery, but some basic effects and animations are included in the core library, and these are the topic of this chapter. Although I describe them as basic, they can be used to achieve some pretty sophisticated effects. The main focus is on animating the visibility of elements, but you can use these features to animate a range of CSS properties in a number of ways. Table 10-1 provides the summary for this chapter.

***Table 10-1.** Chapter Summary*

Problem	Solution	Listing
Show or hide elements.	Use the `show` or `hide` method.	1
Toggle the visibility of elements.	Use the `toggle` method.	2, 3
Animate the visibility of elements.	Provide a timespan argument to the `show`, `hide`, or `toggle` method.	4
Call a function at the end of an animation.	Provide a callback argument to the `show`, `hide`, or `toggle` method.	5–7
Animate visibility along the vertically.	Use the `slideDown`, `slideUp`, or `slideToggle` method.	8
Animate visibility using opacity.	Use the `fadeIn`, `fadeOut`, `fadeToggle`, or `fadeTo` method.	9–11
Create a custom effect.	Use the `animate` method.	12–14
Inspect the queue of effects.	Use the `queue` method.	15, 16
Stop and clear the effect queue.	Use the `stop` method.	17
Insert a delay into the effect queue.	Use the `delay` method.	18

Insert custom functions into the queue.	Use the queue method with a function argument and ensure that the next function in the queue is executed.	19, 20
Disable the animation of effects.	Set the `$.fx.off` property to `true`.	21

Using the Basic Effects

The most basic effects are simply to show or hide elements. The methods that you can use for this are described in Table 10-2.

Table 10-2. *Basic Effects Methods*

Method	Description
`hide()`	Hides all of the elements in a `jQuery` object
`hide(time)` `hide(time, easing)`	Hide the elements in a `jQuery` object over the specified period of time with an optional easing style
`hide(time, function)` `hide(time, easing, function)`	Hide the elements in a `jQuery` object over the specified period of time with an optional easing style and a function that is called when the effect is complete
`show()`	Shows all of the elements in a `jQuery` object
`show(time)` `show(time, easing)`	Show the elements in a `jQuery` object over the specified period of time with an optional easing style
`show(time, function)` `show(time, easing, function)`	Show the elements in a `jQuery` object over the specified period of time with an optional easing style and a function that is called when the effect is complete
`toggle()`	Toggles the visibility of the elements in a `jQuery` object
`toggle(time)` `toggle(time, easing)`	Toggle the visibility of the elements in a `jQuery` object over the specified period of time with an optional easing style
`toggle(time, function)` `toggle(time, easing, function)`	Toggle the visibility of the elements in a `jQuery` object over the specified period of time with an optional easing style and a function that is called when the effect is complete
`toggle(boolean)`	Toggles the elements in a `jQuery` object in one direction

Listing 10-1 shows the simplest of these effects, which is to use the show and hide methods without any arguments.

Listing 10-1. Using the Show and Hide Methods Without Arguments

```
<!DOCTYPE html>
<html>
<head>
    <title>Example</title>
    <script src="jquery-1.7.js" type="text/javascript"></script>
    <link rel="stylesheet" type="text/css" href="styles.css"/>
    <script type="text/javascript">
        $(document).ready(function() {
            $("<button>Hide</button><button>Show</button>").appendTo("#buttonDiv")
                .click(function(e) {
                   if ($(e.target).text() == "Hide") {
                        $('#row1 div.dcell').hide();
                   } else {
                        $('#row1 div.dcell').show();
                   }
                   e.preventDefault();
                });
        });
    </script>
</head>
<body>
    <h1>Jacqui's Flower Shop</h1>
    <form method="post">
        <div id="oblock">
            <div class="dtable">
                <div id="row1" class="drow">
                    <div class="dcell">
                        <img src="astor.png"/><label for="astor">Astor:</label>
                        <input name="astor" value="0" required />
                    </div>
                    <div class="dcell">
                        <img src="daffodil.png"/><label for="daffodil">Daffodil:</label>
                        <input name="daffodil" value="0" required />
                    </div>
                    <div class="dcell">
                        <img src="rose.png"/><label for="rose">Rose:</label>
                        <input name="rose" value="0" required />
                    </div>
                </div>
                <div id="row2"class="drow">
                    <div class="dcell">
                        <img src="peony.png"/><label for="peony">Peony:</label>
                        <input name="peony" value="0" required />
                    </div>
                    <div class="dcell">
                        <img src="primula.png"/><label for="primula">Primula:</label>
                        <input name="primula" value="0" required />
```

```
                    </div>
                    <div class="dcell">
                        <img src="snowdrop.png"/><label for="snowdrop">Snowdrop:</label>
                        <input name="snowdrop" value="0" required />
                    </div>
                </div>
            </div>
        </div>
        <div id="buttonDiv"><button type="submit">Place Order</button></div>
    </form>
</body>
</html>
```

In the script in this example, I manipulate the DOM to add two button elements and provide a function to be called when either of them is clicked. This function uses the text method to figure out which button has been used and calls either the hide or show method. In both cases, I call this method on a jQuery object with the selector #row1 div.dcell, meaning that those div elements in the dcell class that are descendants of the element with the row1 id will be made invisible or visible. Figure 10-1 illustrates what happens when I click the Hide button.

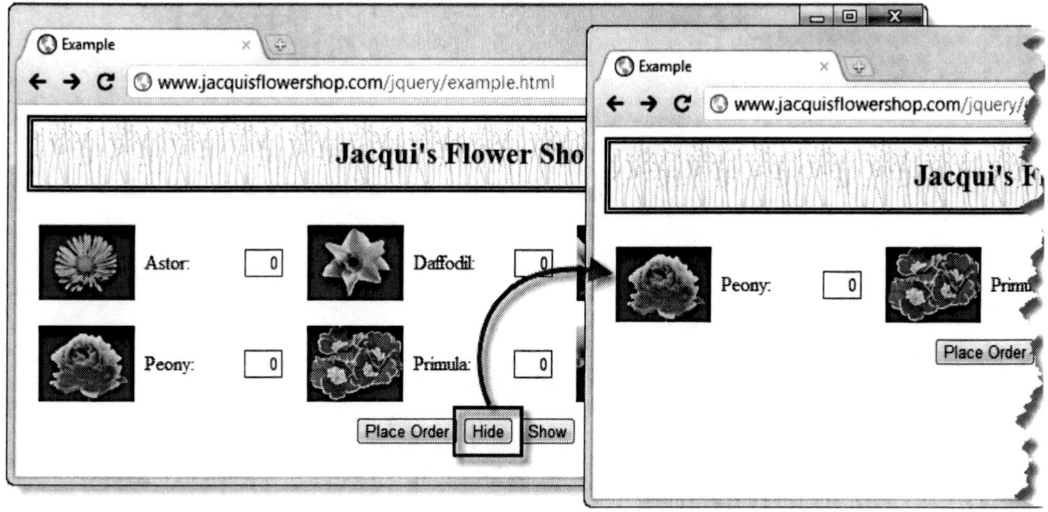

Figure 10-1. Hiding elements with the hide element

Clicking the Show button calls the show method, restoring the hidden elements, as Figure 10-2 shows.

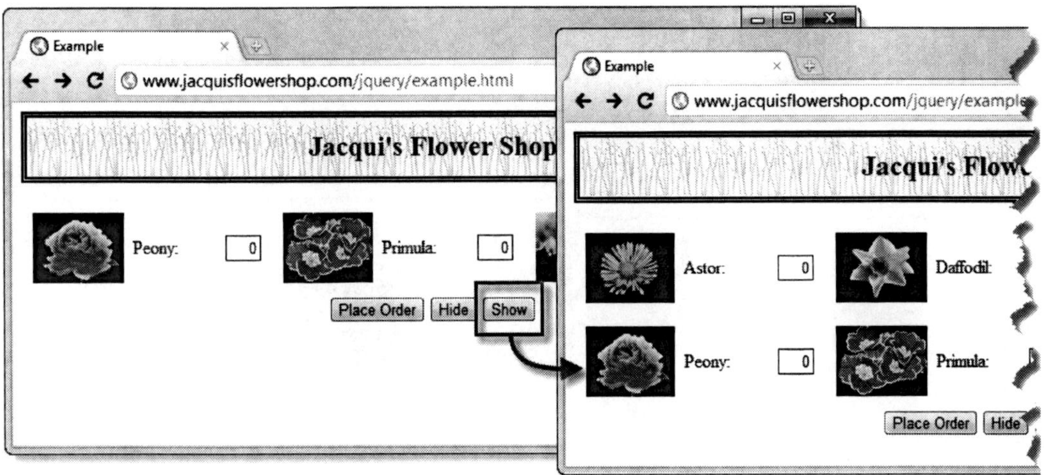

Figure 10-2. Showing elements with the show method

It is hard to show transitions using figures, but there are a few of points to note. The first is that the transition is immediate. There is no delay or effect, and the elements just appear and disappear. Second, calling `hide` on elements that are already hidden has no effect and nor does calling `show` on elements that are visible. Finally, when you hide or show an element, you also show or hide all of its descendants.

■ **Tip** You can select elements using the `:visible` and `:hidden` selectors. See Chapter 5 for details of the jQuery extension CSS selectors.

Toggling Elements

You can flip elements from being visible or hidden and back using the `toggle` method. Listing 10-2 gives an example.

Listing 10-2. Using the toggle Method to Switch Element Visibility

```
...
<script type="text/javascript">
    $(document).ready(function() {
        $("<button>Toggle</button>").appendTo("#buttonDiv")
            .click(function(e) {
                $('div.dcell:first-child').toggle();
                e.preventDefault();
            });
    });
</script>
...
```

In this example I add a single button to the document, and when it is clicked, I use the toggle element to change the visibility of the div.dcell elements that are the first children of their parents. You can see the effect in Figure 10-3.

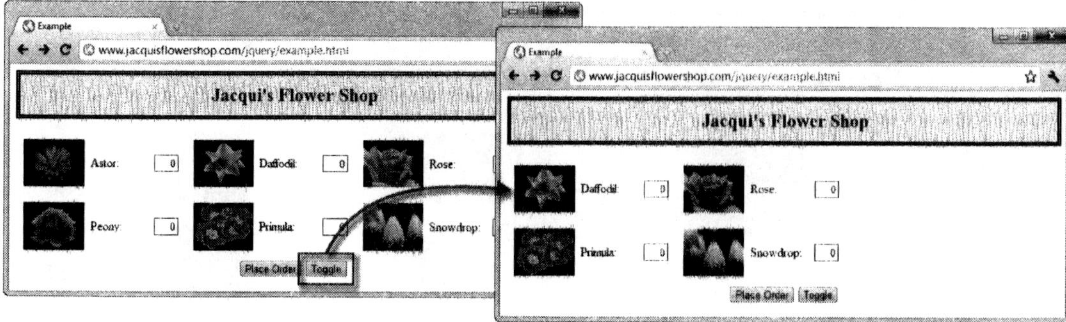

Figure 10-3. Toggling the visibility of elements

■ **Tip** Notice that the structure of the document collapses around the hidden elements. If you want to hide the elements and leave space on the screen, then you can set the CSS visibility property to hidden.

Toggling in One Direction

You can pass a boolean argument to the toggle method to restrict the way that visibility is toggled. If you pass true as the argument, then only hidden elements will be shown (visible elements will not be hidden). If you pass false as the argument, then you get the opposite effect. Visible elements will be hidden, but hidden elements will not be made visible. Listing 10-3 shows the use of this flavor of the toggle method. I must confess that I have never found this feature useful, but I include it for completeness.

Listing 10-3. Using the toggle Method in One Direction

```
...
<script type="text/javascript">
    $(document).ready(function() {
        $("<button>Toggle</button>").appendTo("#buttonDiv")
            .click(function(e) {
                $('div.dcell:first-child').toggle(false);
                e.preventDefault();
            });
    });
</script>
...
```

Animating the Visibility of Elements

You can animate the process of showing and hiding elements by passing a time span to the `show`, `hide`, or `toggle` methods. The process of showing and hiding elements is then performed gradually, over the specified period. Table 10-3 shows the different time span arguments you can use.

***Table 10-3.** Time Span Arguments*

Method	Description
`milliseconds`	Specifies a duration in milliseconds
`slow`	A shorthand equivalent to 600 milliseconds
`fast`	A shorthand equivalent to 200 milliseconds

Listing 10-4 shows how you can animate showing and hiding elements.

Listing 10-4. Animating the Visibility of Elements

```
...
<script type="text/javascript">
    $(document).ready(function() {

        $("<button>Toggle</button>").appendTo("#buttonDiv")
            .click(function(e) {
                $('img').toggle("fast", "linear");
                e.preventDefault();
            });

    });
</script>
...
```

In this example, I have used the `fast` value to specify that toggling the visibility of the `img` elements in the document should be done over a period of 600 milliseconds.

■ **Tip** When specifying a duration in milliseconds, be sure that the value is not quoted. That is, use `$('img').toggle(500)` and not `$('img').toggle("500")`. If you do use quotes, then the value will be ignored, and the default internal will be used.

I have also provided an additional argument, which specifies the style of the animation, known as the *easing style* or *easing function*. Two easing styles are available, `swing` and `linear`. When animating with the `swing` style, the animation starts slowly, speeds up, and then slows down again as the animation reaches conclusion. The `linear` style maintains a constant pace throughout the animation. If you omit the argument, `swing` is used.

You can see the effect of the animation as it hides elements in Figure 10-4. It is difficult to show animation in this way, but you'll get a sense of what happens.

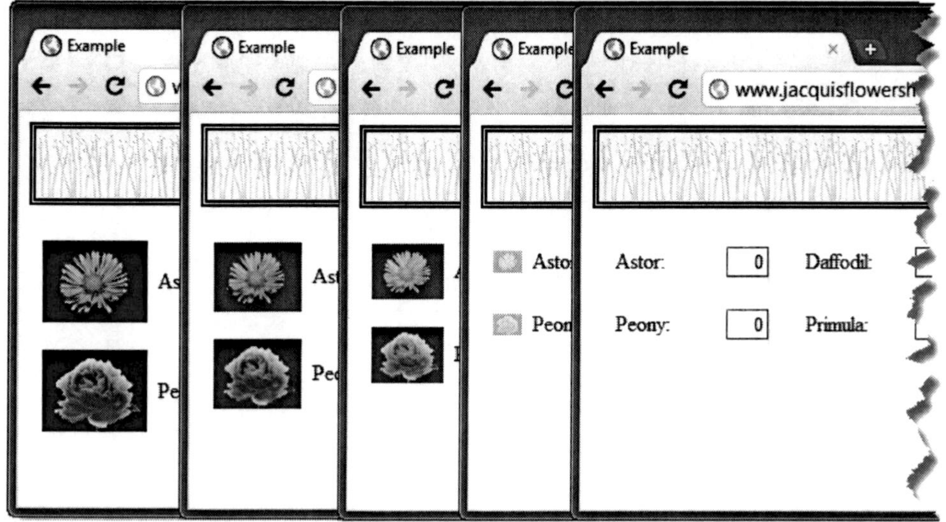

Figure 10-4. Animating hiding elements

As you can see, the animation effect reduces the size of the image in both dimensions and decreases the opacity. At the end of the animation, the `img` elements are invisible. The images disappear smoothly and elegantly, but this doesn't always happen. Figure 10-5 shows what happens if you click the Toggle button again to make the `img` elements visible.

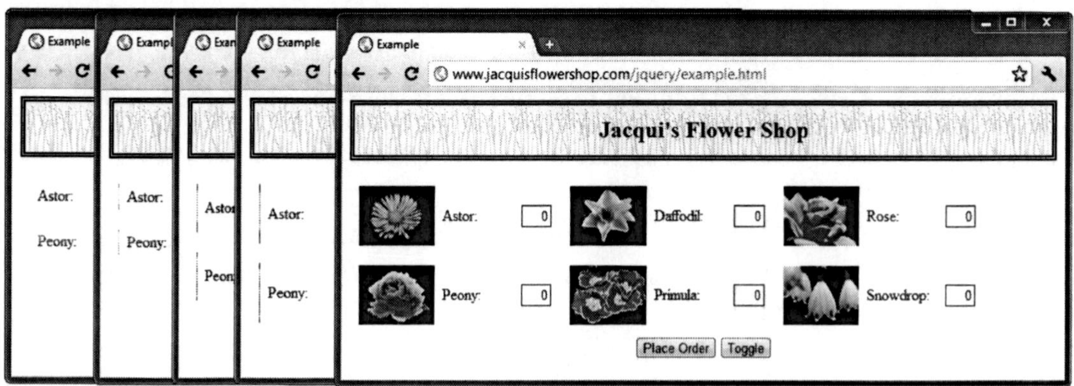

Figure 10-5. Animating showing elements

The `img` elements grow only vertically until right at the end of the sequence when they snap back horizontally. This is an unfortunate interaction between the way that jQuery animates visibility and the

CSS table-style layout that I am using in the document. This isn't a critical issue. You can use one of the other animation styles that animates in one dimension only, but it does make the point that animations need to be tested carefully.

Using Effect Callbacks

You can supply a function as an argument to the show, hide, and toggle methods, and the function will be called when these methods finish performing their effect. This can be useful for updating other elements to reflect the change in status, as shown in Listing 10-5.

■ **Tip** If you want to perform multiple sequential effects on a single element, then you can use regular jQuery method chaining. See the "Creating and Managing the Effect Queue" section later in this chapter for details.

Listing 10-5. Using an Event Callback

```
...
<script type="text/javascript">
    $(document).ready(function() {

        var hiddenRow = "#row2";
        var visibleRow = "#row1";

        $(hiddenRow).hide();

        $("<button>Switch</button>").insertAfter("#buttonDiv button")
            .click(function(e) {
                hideVisibleElement();
                e.preventDefault();
            });

        function hideVisibleElement() {
            $(visibleRow).hide("fast", showHiddenElement);
        }

        function showHiddenElement() {
            $(hiddenRow).show("fast", switchRowVariables);
        }

        function switchRowVariables() {
            var temp = hiddenRow;
            hiddenRow = visibleRow;
            visibleRow = temp;
        }
    });
</script>
...
```

To make this example clearer, I have broken down the effect activities into separate functions. To get set up, I hide one of the div elements that acts as a row in my CSS table layout and define two variables that I use to track which row is visible and which row is not. I add a button element to the document, and when this is clicked, I call the hideVisibleElement function, which uses the hide method to animate hiding the visible row:

```
$(visibleRow).hide("fast", showHiddenElement);
```

I specify the name of the function I want performed when the effect has completed, in this case showHiddenElement.

■ **Tip** The callback function is not passed any arguments, but the this variable is set to the DOM element being animated. If multiple elements are being animated, then the callback function will be called once for each of them.

This function uses the show method to animate revealing the element, as follows:

```
$(hiddenRow).show("fast", switchRowVariables);
```

Once again, I specify a function to perform at the end of the effect. In this case, it is the switchRowVariables function, which shuffles the variables that track visibility so that you perform the effects on the right elements the next time the button is clicked. The result is that when the button is clicked, the current row is replaced by the hidden row, with a quick animation to make the transition less jarring to the user. Figure 10-6 shows the effect (although, once again, the true effect becomes apparent only when you load the example in the browser).

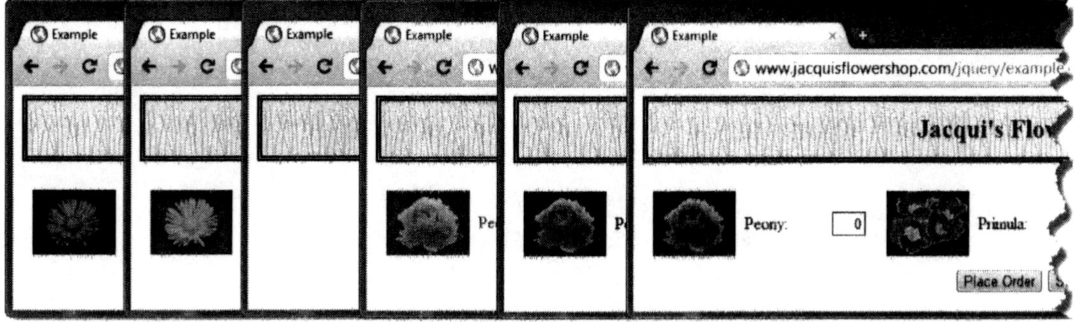

Figure 10-6. Using callback functions to chain effects

The transition between the rows is smooth, and there is no interaction with the CSS table layout because you are dealing with the rows and not the cells of the table. You wouldn't usually need to break out the individual functions as I did, so Listing 10-6 shows the same example rewritten using a more terse set of inline functions.

Listing 10-6. Using Inline Callback Functions

```
...
<script type="text/javascript">
    $(document).ready(function() {

        var hiddenRow = "#row2";
        var visibleRow = "#row1";

        $(hiddenRow).hide();

        $("<button>Switch</button>").insertAfter("#buttonDiv button")
            .click(function(e) {
                $(visibleRow).hide("fast", function() {
                    $(hiddenRow).show("fast", function() {
                        var temp = hiddenRow;
                        hiddenRow = visibleRow;
                        visibleRow = temp;
                    });
                });

                e.preventDefault();
            });
    });
</script>
...
```

Creating Looping Effects

You can use the callback functions to produce effects that are performed in a loop. Listing 10-7 provides a demonstration.

Listing 10-7. Using Callback Functions to Create a Looping Effect

```
...
<script type="text/javascript">
    $(document).ready(function() {

        $("<button>Toggle</button>").insertAfter("#buttonDiv button")
            .click(function(e) {
                performEffect();
                e.preventDefault();
            });

        function performEffect() {
            $('h1').toggle("slow", performEffect)
        }
    });
</script>
...
```

In this example, clicking the button leads to the `performEffect` function being executed. This function uses the `toggle` method to change the visibility of the `h1` element in the document and passes itself as the callback argument. The result is that the `h1` element loops between being visible and hidden.

■ **Tip** Some caution is required when using the current function as the callback function. Eventually you will exhaust the JavaScript call stack, and your script will stop working. The easiest way to solve this problem is with the `setTimeout` function, which will schedule a callback to your target function without nesting the function calls, like this: `$('h1').toggle("slow", setTimeout( performEffect, 1))`. It is actually pretty hard to exhaust the call stack, and it usually means leaving a page with animations running for a very long time, but it is worth taking this into account.

USING EFFECTS RESPONSIBLY

To my mind, loops like this should be used sparingly and only when they serve a purpose (and by that, I mean a purpose for the user and not to show off your excellent jQuery effect skills). In general, the impact of any kind of effect should be carefully considered. It may look great during development, but injudicious use of effects destroys the user's enjoyment of your web application, especially if it is an application they use every day.

As a simple example, I am a keen runner (keen but not any good). I have a runner's wristwatch that collects data about my heart rate, speed, distance, calories burned, and 100 other data points. At the end of a run, I upload to the data to the manufacturer's web site for storage and analysis.

Here's where the pain starts. Every time I click a button on the page, the content I want is revealed through a long effect. I know the browser has received the data I want because I can see it being gradually revealed, but it is a couple of seconds before I can read it. A couple of seconds may not sound a lot, but it is, especially when I want to look at between five and ten different data items at any time.

I am sure that the designer of the application thought the effects were nice and that they enhanced the experience. But they don't. They suck so much that it makes using the application a teeth-grinding experience. This web application has some useful data analysis tools, but I have gotten to the point where it annoys me so much that I can't be bothered to use them and my data goes unanalyzed. I could be a champion marathon runner by now if not for those effects (and maybe the beer and pizza I find myself consuming with shocking frequency).

If you think I am exaggerating (about the effects...just take my word about the pizza), then take one of the examples in this chapter and set the time span to two seconds. Then get a feel for how long that is when you are waiting for the effect to complete.

My advice is that *all* effects should be used sparingly. I tend to use them only when making a change to the DOM that would be jarring otherwise (elements suddenly disappearing from the page). When I do use them, I keep the time spans short, typically 200 milliseconds. I *never* employ endless loops. That's just a recipe for giving the user a headache. I urge you to take the time to think about how your users engage with your application or site and remove anything that doesn't make the tasks at hand easier to perform. Glossy sites are good, but glossy sites that are usable are *great*.

Using the Slide Effects

jQuery has a set of effects that slide elements on and off the screen. The methods for this are described in Table 10-4.

***Table 10-4.** Slide Effects Methods*

Method	Description

`slideDown()`
`slideDown((time, function)`
`slideDown(time, easing, function)`
	Show elements by sliding them down

`slideUp()`
`slideUp(time, function)`
`slideUp(time, easing, function)`
	Hide elements by sliding them up

`slideToggle()`
`slideToggle(time, function)`
`slideToggle(time, easing, function)`
	Toggle the visibility of elements by sliding them up and down

These methods animate an element in the vertical axis. The arguments to these methods are as for the basic effect. You can elect to provide a time span, an easing style, and a callback function. Listing 10-8 shows the slide effects in use.

Listing 10-8. Using the Slide Effects

```
...
<script type="text/javascript">
    $(document).ready(function() {
        $("<button>Toggle</button>").insertAfter("#buttonDiv button")
            .click(function(e) {
                $('h1').slideToggle("fast");
                e.preventDefault();
            });
    });
</script>
...
```

In this script, I use the `slideToggle` method to toggle the visibility of the `h1` element. You can see the effect in Figure 10-7.

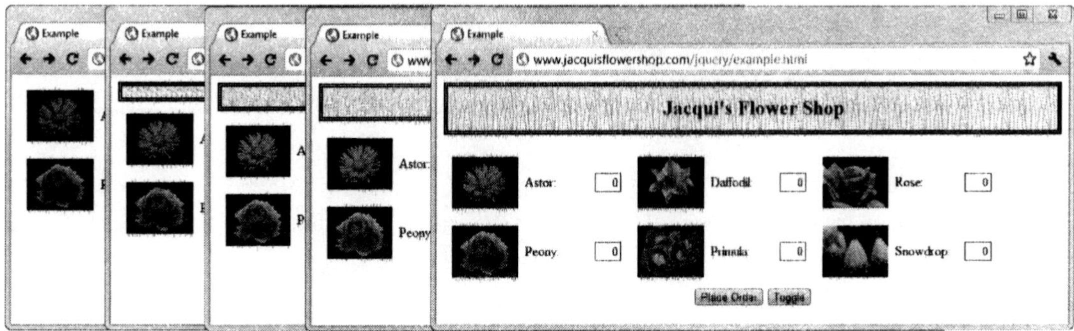

Figure 10-7. Using the slide effect to reveal an element

The figure shows the h1 element being made visible. The elements are clipped, rather than scaled, because jQuery creates the effect by manipulating the height of the element. You can see what I mean by this in Figure 10-8.

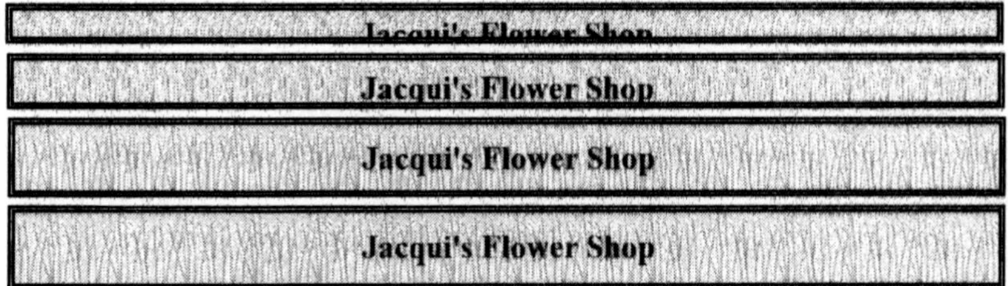

Figure 10-8. jQuery creating an effect by manipulating the height of the elements

This figure shows a close-up of the h1 element as it is made visible. You can see that the size of the text doesn't change, only the amount of it that is shown. However, this isn't true for images, because the browser scales them automatically. If you look really closely, you can see that the entire background image is always shown, but it is scaled down to fit the height.

Using the Fade Effects

The fade effect methods show and hide elements by reducing their opacity (or, if you prefer, increasing their transparency). The fade effect methods are described in Table 10-5.

***Table 10-5.** Fade Effects Methods*

Method	Description

`fadeOut()`
`fadeOut(timespan)`
`fadeOut(timespan, function)`
`fadeOut(timespan, easing, function)`
	Hide elements by decreasing opacity

`fadeIn()`
`fadeIn(timespan)`
`fadeIn(timespan, function)`
`fadeIn(timespan, easing, function)`
	Show elements by increasing opacity

`fadeTo(timespan, opacity)` `fadeTo(timespan, opacity, easing, function)`	Change the opacity to the specified level

`fadeToggle()`
`fadeToggle(timespan)`
`fadeToggle(timespan, function)`
`fadeToggle(timespan, easing, function)`
	Toggle the visibility of elements using opacity

The `fadeOut`, `fadeIn`, and `fadeToggle` methods are consistent with the other effect methods. You can provide a time span, an easing style, and a callback function, just as in the previous examples. Listing 10-9 demonstrates how to use fading.

Listing 10-9. Showing and Hiding Elements by Fading

```
...
<script type="text/javascript">
    $(document).ready(function() {
        $("<button>Toggle</button>").insertAfter("#buttonDiv button")
            .click(function(e) {
                $('img').fadeToggle();
                e.preventDefault();
            });
    });
</script>
...
```

I have applied the `fadeToggle` method to the `img` elements in the document, in part to demonstrate one of the limitations of this effect. Figure 10-9 shows what happens when you hide the elements.

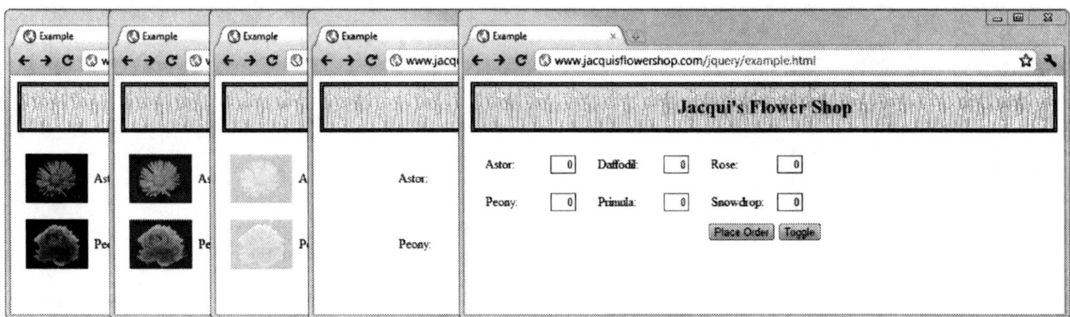

Figure 10-9. Using the fade effect

The fade effect operates only on opacity, unlike the other effects that change the size of the selected elements as well. This means you get a nice smooth fade effect until the elements are completely transparent, at which point jQuery hides them and the page snaps into a new layout. This last stage can be somewhat jarring if not used carefully.

Fading to a Specific Opacity

You can use the fadeTo method to fade elements to a particular opacity. The range of opacity values is a number within the range of 0 (completely transparent) to 1 (completely opaque). The visibility of the elements isn't changed, so you avoid the snap of the page layout I mentioned. Listing 10-10 shows the use of the fadeTo method.

Listing 10-10. Fading to a Specific Opacity

```
...
<script type="text/javascript">
    $(document).ready(function() {
        $("<button>Fade</button>").insertAfter("#buttonDiv button")
            .click(function(e) {
                $('img').fadeTo("fast", 0);
                e.preventDefault();
            });
    });
</script>
...
```

In this example, I have specified that the img elements should be faded until they are completely transparent. This has the same effect as the fadeOut method but doesn't hide the elements at the end of the transition. Figure 10-10 shows the effect.

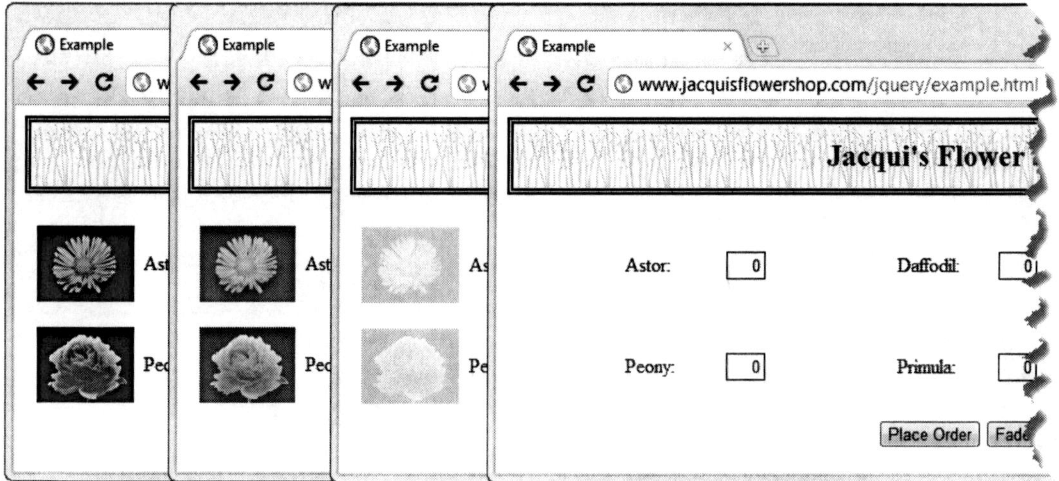

Figure 10-10. Fading out an element with the fadeTo method

You don't have to fade elements to the extremes of the opacity range. You can specify intermediate values as well, as Listing 10-11 demonstrates.

Listing 10-11. Fading to a Specific Opacity

```
...
<script type="text/javascript">
    $(document).ready(function() {
        $("<button>Fade</button>").insertAfter("#buttonDiv button")
            .click(function(e) {
                $('img').fadeTo("fast", 0.4);
                e.preventDefault();
            });
    });
</script>
...
```

You can see the effect in Figure 10-11.

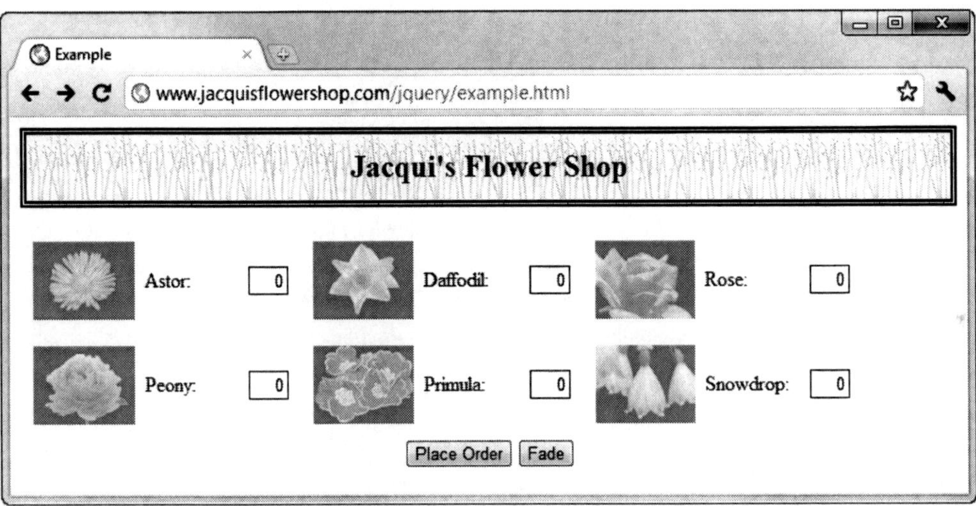

Figure 10-11. Fading to a specific opacity

Creating Custom Effects

jQuery doesn't limit you to the basic slide and fade effects. You can create your own as well. Table 10-6 shows the methods that you use for this.

Table 10-6. Custom Effects Methods

Method	Description

`animate(properties)`
`animate(properties, time)`
`animate(properties, time, function)`
`animate(properties, time, easing, function)`
	Animate one or more CSS properties, with an optional time span, easing style, and callback function

`animate(properties, options)`	Animates one or more CSS properties, specifying the options as a map

jQuery can animate any property that accepts a simple numeric value, for example, the `height` property.

■ **Note** Being able to animate numeric CSS properties means you can't animate colors. There are a few ways to address this. The first (and to my mind best) solution is to use jQuery UI, which I describe in Part IV of this book. If you don't want to use jQuery UI, then you might like to consider using the native browser support for CSS animations. The performance of these is pretty good, but the support is patchy currently and nonexistent in older browser versions. For details of CSS animation, see my book The *Definitive Guide to HTML5*, which is also published by Apress. The approach that I like least is using a jQuery plugin. Animating colors is difficult to get right, and I have yet to find a plugin that I am entirely satisfied with, but the most reliable I have found is available from `https://github.com/jquery/jquery-color`.

You supply a set of properties that you want to animate as a map object, and, if you want, you can do the same for the options you want to set. Listing 10-12 shows a custom animation.

Listing 10-12. Using a Custom Animation

```
...
<script type="text/javascript">
    $(document).ready(function() {

        $('form').css({"position": "fixed", "top": "70px", "z-index": "2"});
        $('h1').css({"position": "fixed", "z-index": "1", "min-width": "0"});

        $("<button>Animate</button>").insertAfter("#buttonDiv button")
            .click(function(e) {

                $('h1').animate({
                    height: $('h1').height() + $('form').height() + 10,
                    width: ($('form').width())
                });
```

```
                e.preventDefault();
            });
    });
</script>
...
```

In this example, I want to animate dimensions of the h1 element so that its background image extends behind the form element. Before I can do this, I need to make some changes to the CSS for the affected elements. I could do this using the style sheet I defined in Chapter 3, but since this is a book on jQuery, I have chosen to use JavaScript. To make the animation easier to manage, I have positioned both the form and h1 elements using the fixed mode and have used the z-index property to ensure that the h1 element is displayed below the form.

I have added a button to the document that calls the animate method when clicked. I have chosen to animate the height and width properties, using information obtained via other jQuery methods. You can see the effect of the animation in Figure 10-12.

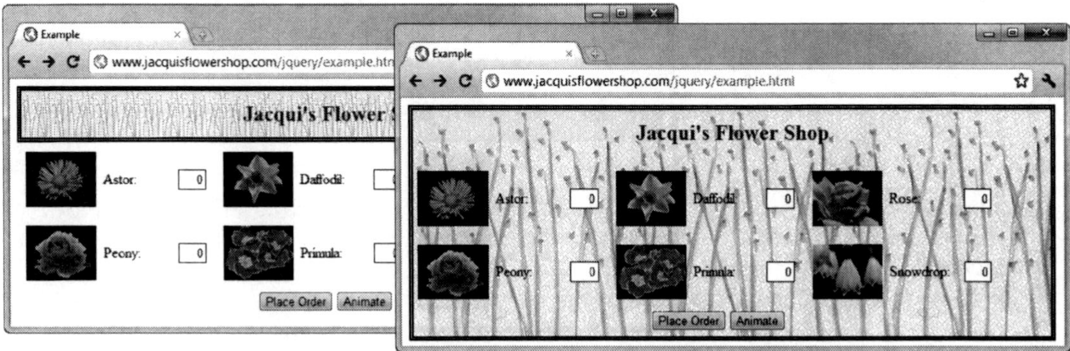

Figure 10-12. Performing a custom animation

I have shown only the start and end states in the figure, but jQuery provides a smooth transition just like with the other effects, and you can exert control other the transition by specifying a time span and an easing style.

Using Absolute Target Property Values

Notice that you specify only the final values for the animation. The start point for jQuery custom animations is the current values of the properties being animated. I used values I derived from other jQuery methods, but you have some other choices. First, and most obvious, is that you can use absolute values, as shown in Listing 10-13.

Listing 10-13. Performing a Custom Animation Using Absolute Values

```
...
<script type="text/javascript">
    $(document).ready(function() {

        $('form').css({"position": "fixed", "top": "70px", "z-index": "2"});
        $('h1').css({"position": "fixed", "z-index": "1", "min-width": "0"});

        $("<button>Animate</button>").insertAfter("#buttonDiv button")
            .click(function(e) {
                $('h1').animate({
                    left: 50,
                    height: $('h1').height() + $('form').height() + 10,
                    width: ($('form').width())
                });

                e.preventDefault();
            });
    });
</script>
...
```

In this example, I have added the `left` property to the animation, specifying an absolute value of 50 (which will be taken as 50 pixels). This shifts the `h1` element to the right. Figure 10-13 shows the outcome of the animation.

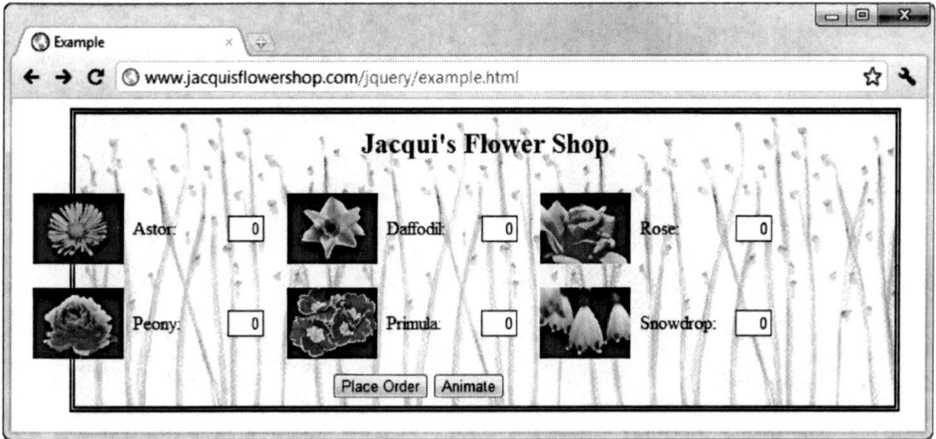

Figure 10-13. Creating a custom animation with a fixed final property value

Using Relative Target Property Values

You can also specify your animation targets using relative values. You specify an increase by prefixing a value with += and a decrease with -=. Listing 10-14 shows the use of relative values.

Listing 10-14. Using Relative Values in a Custom Animation Effect

```
...
<script type="text/javascript">
    $(document).ready(function() {

        $('form').css({"position": "fixed", "top": "70px", "z-index": "2"});
        $('h1').css({"position": "fixed", "z-index": "1", "min-width": "0"});

        $("<button>Animate</button>").insertAfter("#buttonDiv button")
            .click(function(e) {
                $('h1').animate({
                    height: +=100,
                    width: -=700
                });

                e.preventDefault();
            });
    });
...
```

Creating and Managing the Effect Queue

When you use effects, jQuery creates a queue of the animations that it has to perform and works its way through them. There are a set of methods you can use to get information about the queue or take control of it. These methods are described in Table 10-7.

***Table 10-7.** Effects Queue Methods*

Method	Description
`queue()`	Returns the queue of effects to be performed on the elements in the `jQuery` object
`queue(function)`	Adds a function to the end of the queue
`dequeue()`	Removes and executes the first item in the queue for the elements in the `jQuery` object

`stop()`
`stop(clear)`
`stop(clear, jumpToEnd)`
	Stop the current animation

`delay(time)`	Inserts a delay between effects in the queue

You create a queue of effects by chaining together calls to effect-related methods, as shown in Listing 10-15.

Listing 10-15. Creating an Effect Queue

```
...
<script type="text/javascript">
    $(document).ready(function() {

        $('form').css({"position": "fixed", "top": "70px", "z-index": "2"});
        $('h1').css({"position": "fixed", "z-index": "1", "min-width": "0"});

        var timespan = "slow";

        cycleEffects();

        function cycleEffects() {
                $('h1')
                .animate({left: "+=100"}, timespan)
                .animate({left: "-=100"}, timespan)
                .animate({height: 223,width: 700}, timespan)
                .animate({height: 30,width: 500}, timespan)
                .slideUp(timespan)
                .slideDown(timespan, cycleEffects);
        }
    });
</script>
...
```

This script in this example uses regular jQuery method chaining to string together a series of effects on the h1 element. The last effect uses the cycleEffects function as the callback, which starts the process over again. This is a pretty annoying sequence. It is hypnotic for a moment and then a little irritating, and then it tips right over into the kind of effect that brings on a headache. But it does create a queue of effects, which is what I need to demonstrate the queue features.

■ **Note** I could have used the callback functions to achieve the same effect, but that doesn't create the effect queue, because the function that starts the next animation isn't executed until the previous animation has completed. When you use regular method chaining, as in this example, all of the methods are evaluated, and the animation effects are placed in the queue. The limitation of using method chaining is that you are limited to working with the current selection. When using callbacks, you can string together sequences that involve entirely unrelated elements.

Displaying the Items in the Effect Queue

You can use the queue method to inspect the contents of the effects queue. This is not entirely helpful because the queue contains one of two types of data object. If an effect is being executed, then the corresponding item in the queue is the string value inprogress. If the effect is not being executed, the item in the queue is the function that will be invoked. The jQuery effects are all performed by the doAnimation function, and you can't inspect that to find out what is going to be animated. That said, inspecting the content is a good place to start with the queue, and Listing 10-16 shows how it can be done.

Listing 10-16. Inspecting the Contents of the Effect Queue

```
...
<script type="text/javascript">
    $(document).ready(function() {


        $('h1').css({"position": "fixed", "z-index": "1", "min-width": "0"});
        $('form').remove();
        $('<table border=1></table>')
            .appendTo('body').css({
                position: "fixed", "z-index": "2",
                "border-collapse": "collapse", top: 100
            });

        var timespan = "slow";

        cycleEffects();
        printQueue();

        function cycleEffects() {
                $('h1')
                .animate({left: "+=100"}, timespan)
                .animate({left: "-=100"}, timespan)
                .animate({height: 223,width: 700}, timespan)
                .animate({height: 30,width: 500}, timespan)
                .slideUp(timespan)
                .slideDown(timespan, cycleEffects);
        }

        function printQueue() {
            var q = $('h1').queue();
            var qtable = $('table');
            qtable.html("<tr><th>Queue Length:</th><td>" + q.length + "</td></tr>");
            for (var i = 0; i < q.length; i++) {
                var baseString = "<tr><th>" + i + ":</th><td>";
                if (q[i] == "inprogress") {
                    $('table').append(baseString + "In Progress</td></tr>");
                } else if (q[i].name == "") {
                    $('table').append(baseString + q[i] + "</td></tr>");
                } else {
                    $('table').append(baseString + q[i].name + "</td></tr>");
                }
            }
            setTimeout(printQueue, 500);
        }
    });
```

```
</script>
...
```

You don't need the form element in this example, so I have removed it from the DOM and replaced it with a simple table that I'll use to display the contents of the effect queue. I have added a repeating function called printQueue that calls the queue method and displays the number of items and a little detail about each of them in the table. As I say, the items in the queue are not especially useful in their own right, but they do give you an overall picture of what is going on. Figure 10-14 shows how jQuery progresses through the effects queue.

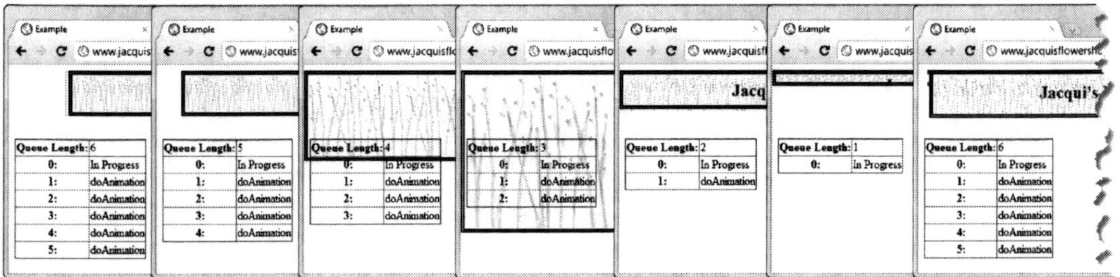

Figure 10-14. Inspecting the contents of the queue

This is an example that is hard to portray in static images. I recommend you load the document into a browser to see for yourself. When the cycleEffects function is first called, there are six items in the effects queue, the first of which is shown as being in progress. The others are instances of the doAnimation function. After each effect is completed, jQuery removes the item from the queue. At the end of the last effect, the cycleEffects function is called again, which puts back in the position of having six items in the queue.

Stopping Effects and Clearing the Queue

You can use the stop method to interrupt the effect that jQuery is currently performing. You can provide two optional arguments to this method, both of which are boolean values. If you pass true as the first argument, then all of the other effects are removed from the queue and will not be performed. If you pass true as the second argument, then the CSS properties that are being animated will be set to their target values.

The default value for both arguments is false, which means that only the current effect is removed from the queue and that the properties that were being animated are left at the values they were set to at the moment the effect was interrupted. If you don't clear the queue, jQuery will move on to the next effect and begin executing it as normal. Listing 10-17 provides an example of using the stop method.

■ **Tip** When you call the stop method, any callback associated with the current effect will not be executed. When you use the stop method to clear the queue, no callback associated with any of the effects in the queue will be executed.

Listing 10-17. Using the stop Method

```
...
<script type="text/javascript">
    $(document).ready(function() {


        $('h1').css({"position": "fixed", "z-index": "1", "min-width": "0"});
        $('form').remove();
        $('<table border=1></table>')
            .appendTo('body')
            .css({
                position: "fixed", "z-index": "2",
                "border-collapse": "collapse", top: 100
            });

        $('<button>Stop</button><button>Start</button>')
          .appendTo($('<div/>').appendTo("body")
            .css({position: "fixed", "z-index": "2",
                "border-collapse": "collapse", top: 100, left:200
            })).click(function(e) {
                $(this).text() == "Stop" ? $('h1').stop(true, true) : cycleEffects();
            });

        var timespan = "slow";

        cycleEffects();
        printQueue();

        function cycleEffects() {
                $('h1')
                .animate({left: "+=100"}, timespan)
                .animate({left: "-=100"}, timespan)
                .animate({height: 223,width: 700}, timespan)
                .animate({height: 30,width: 500}, timespan)
                .slideUp(timespan)
                .slideDown(timespan, cycleEffects);
        }

        function printQueue() {
            var q = $('h1').queue();
            var qtable = $('table');
            qtable.html("<tr><th>Queue Length:</th><td>" + q.length + "</td></tr>");
            for (var i = 0; i < q.length; i++) {
                var baseString = "<tr><th>" + i + ":</th><td>";
                if (q[i] == "inprogress") {
                    $('table').append(baseString + "In Progress</td></tr>");
                } else if (q[i].name == "") {
                    $('table').append(baseString + q[i] + "</td></tr>");
                } else {
                    $('table').append(baseString + q[i].name + "</td></tr>");
```

```
                }
            }
            setTimeout(printQueue, 500);
        }
    });
</script>
...
```

To demonstrate the stop method, I have added two buttons to the document. When the Stop button is clicked, I call the stop method, passing in two true arguments. This has the effect of clearing the rest of the effect queue and snapping the element to the target values for the property that was being animated. Since callback functions are not invoked when the stop method is used, the loop of cycleEffects method calls is broken, and animation is brought to a halt. When the Start button is clicked, the cycleEffects method is called and the animation resumes.

■ **Tip** Clicking the Start button when the animations are running doesn't confuse jQuery. It just adds the effects used by the cycleEffects method to the effects queue. The use of callbacks means that the size of the queue will jump around a little, but in terms of the animations, everything continues as normal.

Inserting a Delay into the Queue

You can use the delay method to introduce a pause between two effects in the queue. The argument to this method is the number of milliseconds that the delay should last for. Listing 10-18 shows the use of this method.

Listing 10-18. Using the delay Method

```
...
<script type="text/javascript">
    $(document).ready(function() {


        $('h1').css({"position": "fixed", "z-index": "1", "min-width": "0"});
        $('form').remove();
        $('<table border=1></table>')
            .appendTo('body')
            .css({
                position: "fixed", "z-index": "2",
                "border-collapse": "collapse", top: 100
            });

        $('<button>Stop</button><button>Start</button>')
          .appendTo($('<div/>').appendTo("body")
            .css({position: "fixed", "z-index": "2",
                "border-collapse": "collapse", top: 100, left:200
            })).click(function(e) {
                $(this).text() == "Stop" ? $('h1').stop(true, true) : cycleEffects();
```

```
        });

    var timespan = "slow";

    cycleEffects();
    printQueue();

    function cycleEffects() {
            $('h1')
            .animate({left: "+=100"}, timespan)
            .animate({left: "-=100"}, timespan)
            .delay(1000)
            .animate({height: 223,width: 700}, timespan)
            .animate({height: 30,width: 500}, timespan)
            .delay(1000)
            .slideUp(timespan)
            .slideDown(timespan, cycleEffects);
    }

    function printQueue() {
        var q = $('h1').queue();
        var qtable = $('table');
        qtable.html("<tr><th>Queue Length:</th><td>" + q.length + "</td></tr>");
        for (var i = 0; i < q.length; i++) {
            var baseString = "<tr><th>" + i + ":</th><td>";
            if (q[i] == "inprogress") {
                $('table').append(baseString + "In Progress</td></tr>");
            } else if (q[i].name == "") {
                $('table').append(baseString + q[i] + "</td></tr>");
            } else {
                $('table').append(baseString + q[i].name + "</td></tr>");
            }
        }
        setTimeout(printQueue, 500);
    }
  });
</script>
...
```

This script introduces two one-second delays in the sequence of animation effects. The `delay` method uses an anonymous function to handle the delay, so you'll see the following code in the queue inspection table in the document:

```
function (next, runner) {
    var timeout = setTimeout(next, time);
    runner.stop = function () {
        clearTimeout(timeout);
    };
}
```

I have formatted the code to make it easier to read, but you don't have to understand how it functions. Just know what it means when you find it in the queue.

Inserting Functions into the Queue

You can add your own functions into the queue using the queue method, and they will be executed just as the standard effect methods are. You can use this feature to start other animations, gracefully exit a chain of animations based on an external variable, or, well, do anything that you need. Listing 10-19 contains an example.

Listing 10-19. Inserting a Custom Function into the Queue

```
...
<script type="text/javascript">
    $(document).ready(function() {

        $('form').css({"position": "fixed", "top": "70px", "z-index": "2"});
        $('h1').css({"position": "fixed", "z-index": "1", "min-width": "0"});

        var timespan = "slow";

        cycleEffects();

        function cycleEffects() {
                $('h1')
                .animate({left: "+=100"}, timespan)
                .animate({left: "-=100"}, timespan)
                .queue(function() {
                    $('img').fadeTo(timespan, 0).fadeTo(timespan, 1);
                    $(this).dequeue();
                })
                .animate({height: 223,width: 700}, timespan)
                .animate({height: 30,width: 500}, timespan)
                .slideUp(timespan)
                .slideDown(timespan, cycleEffects);
        }
    });
</script>
...
```

The this variable is set to the jQuery object that the method was called on. This is useful because you must make sure to call the dequeue method at some point in your function in order to move the queue onto the next effect or function. In this example, I used the queue method to add a function that fades the img elements to fully transparent and back.

■ **Tip** The effects I added in the custom function are added to the effect queues for the img elements. Each element has its own queue, and you can manage them independently of one another. If you want to animate multiple properties on the same elements whose queue you are operating on, then you just use the animate method. Otherwise, your effects will just be added to the queue in sequence.

Alternatively, you can accept a single argument to the function, which is the next function in the queue. In this situation, you must invoke the function to move the queue to the next effect, as shown in Listing 10-20.

Listing 10-20. Using the Argument Passed to the Custom Function

```
...
<script type="text/javascript">
    $(document).ready(function() {

        $('form').css({"position": "fixed", "top": "70px", "z-index": "2"});
        $('h1').css({"position": "fixed", "z-index": "1", "min-width": "0"});

        var timespan = "slow";

        cycleEffects();

        function cycleEffects() {
                $('h1')
                .animate({left: "+=100"}, timespan)
                .animate({left: "-=100"}, timespan)
                .queue(function(nextFunction) {
                    $('img').fadeTo(timespan, 0).fadeTo(timespan, 1);
                    nextFunction();
                })
                .animate({height: 223,width: 700}, timespan)
                .animate({height: 30,width: 500}, timespan)
                .slideUp(timespan)
                .slideDown(timespan, cycleEffects);
        }
    });
</script>
...
```

■ **Tip** If you don't invoke the next function or call the `dequeue` method, then the effect sequence will stall.

Enabling and Disabling Effect Animations

You can disable the animation of effects by setting the value of the `$.fx.off` property to `true`, as shown in Listing 10-21.

Listing 10-21. Disabling Animations

```
<script type="text/javascript">
    $(document).ready(function() {

        $.fx.off = true;

        $('form').css({"position": "fixed", "top": "70px", "z-index": "2"});
        $('h1').css({"position": "fixed", "z-index": "1", "min-width": "0"});

        var timespan = "slow";

        cycleEffects();

        function cycleEffects() {
                $('h1').animate({left: "+=100"}, timespan)
                .delay(500)
                .animate({left: "-=100"}, timespan)
                .delay(500)
                .queue(function(nextFunction) {
                    $('img').fadeTo(timespan, 0).fadeTo(timespan, 1);
                    nextFunction();
                })
                .delay(500)
                .animate({height: 223,width: 700}, timespan)
                .delay(500)
                .animate({height: 30,width: 500}, timespan)
                .delay(500)
                .slideUp(timespan)
                .delay(500)
                .slideDown(timespan, setTimeout(cycleEffects, 1));
        }
    });
</script>
```

When animations are disabled, calls to effect methods cause the elements to snap to their target property values immediately. Time spans are ignored, and there are no intermediate animations. On a modern computer, the browser can snap between these states so quickly that they are invisible. It is for this reason that I have added all the calls to the delay method in the example. Without these calls, no changes are discernible. The other point to note is that looping sets of effects will quickly hit the call stack limit when animations are disabled. To avoid this, I have used the `setTimeout` method, as described earlier in this chapter.

Summary

In this chapter, I showed you how to use the jQuery effect features. The built-in effect methods are mostly for making elements visible and invisible in different ways, but you can go beyond this and animate any numeric CSS property. You can also dig into the effect queue and take more control over the sequence of effects that are applied to elements.

CHAPTER 11

Refactoring the Example: Part I

In the previous chapters, I showed you each functional area in isolation, including how to deal with events, how to manipulate the DOM, and so on. The real power and flexibility of jQuery arises when you combine these features. In this chapter, I am going to demonstrate the combination of features by refactoring the flower shop example document.

All of the changes that I make in this chapter are in the `script` element. I have not changed the underlying HTML of the example document. As with most jQuery features, there are many different routes to achieving the same result. The approaches I take in this chapter reflect the parts of jQuery that I like the most and the way that I tend to think about the DOM. You may have a different mental model and prefer different combinations of methods. It really doesn't matter, and there is no single correct way of using jQuery.

Reviewing the Example Document

I started this book with a very simple example document, a basic flower shop page. In the chapters that followed, you selected elements from the document, explored and rearranged its DOM, listened to events, and applied effects to its elements. Before you start to refactor the example, let's look back to where you started. Listing 11-1 shows the basic document.

Listing 11-1. The Basic Example Document

```
<!DOCTYPE html>
<html>
<head>
    <title>Example</title>
    <script src="jquery-1.7.js" type="text/javascript"></script>
    <link rel="stylesheet" type="text/css" href="styles.css"/>
    <script type="text/javascript">
        $(document).ready(function() {
             // jQuery statements will go here
        });
    </script>
</head>
<body>
    <h1>Jacqui's Flower Shop</h1>
    <form method="post">
        <div id="oblock">
            <div class="dtable">
                <div id="row1" class="drow">
```

```
                    <div class="dcell">
                        <img src="astor.png"/><label for="astor">Astor:</label>
                        <input name="astor" value="0" required />
                    </div>
                    <div class="dcell">
                        <img src="daffodil.png"/><label for="daffodil">Daffodil:</label>
                        <input name="daffodil" value="0" required />
                    </div>
                    <div class="dcell">
                        <img src="rose.png"/><label for="rose">Rose:</label>
                        <input name="rose" value="0" required />
                    </div>
                </div>
                <div id="row2"class="drow">
                    <div class="dcell">
                        <img src="peony.png"/><label for="peony">Peony:</label>
                        <input name="peony" value="0" required />
                    </div>
                    <div class="dcell">
                        <img src="primula.png"/><label for="primula">Primula:</label>
                        <input name="primula" value="0" required />
                    </div>
                    <div class="dcell">
                        <img src="snowdrop.png"/><label for="snowdrop">Snowdrop:</label>
                        <input name="snowdrop" value="0" required />
                    </div>
                </div>
            </div>
        </div>
        <div id="buttonDiv"><button type="submit">Place Order</button></div>
    </form>
</body>
</html>
```

I have highlighted the script element, because that's where you spend your time in this book. I have put in the ubiquitous jQuery handler for the ready event, but that's all. There are no other JavaScript statements. You can see how the unvarnished document appears in the browser in Figure 11-1.

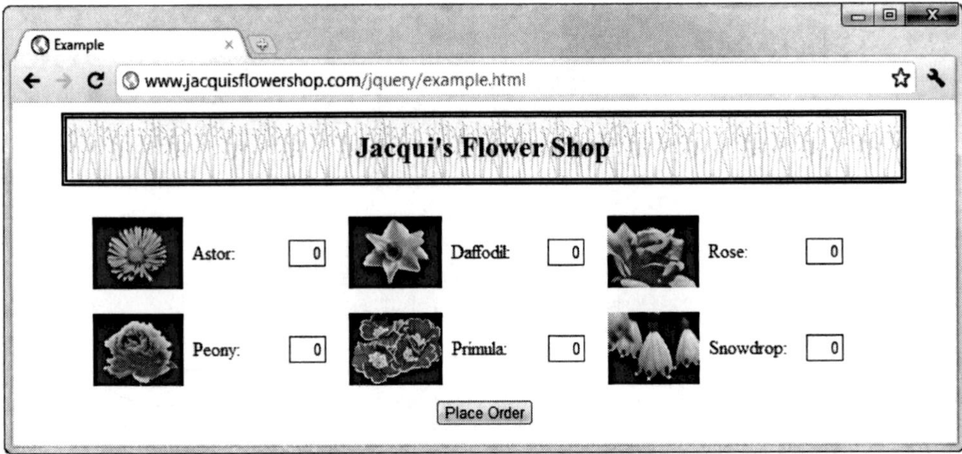

Figure 11-1. The basic example document

Adding Additional Flower Products

The first change I will make is to add some additional flowers to the shop. I want to do this to demonstrate how you can create elements in a loop and because it will enhance a different addition later in this chapter. Listing 11-2 shows the `script` element with the additions.

Listing 11-2. Adding Products to the Page

```
...
<script type="text/javascript">
    $(document).ready(function() {

        var fNames = ["Carnation", "Lily", "Orchid"];
        var fRow = $('<div id=row3 class=drow/>').appendTo('div.dtable');
        var fTemplate = $('<div class=dcell><img/><label/><input/></div>');
        for (var i = 0; i < fNames.length; i++) {
            fTemplate.clone().appendTo(fRow).children()
                .filter('img').attr('src', fNames[i] + ".png").end()
                .filter('label').attr('for', fNames[i]).text(fNames[i]).end()
                .filter('input').attr({name: fNames[i], value: 0, required: "required"})
        }
    });
</script>
...
```

I have defined the three additional types of flower (`Carnation`, `Lily`, and `Orchid`) and created a new `div` element that is assigned to the `drow` class and that I append to the existing `div` element that acts as a table in the CSS table layout model:

```
var fNames = ["Carnation", "Lily", "Orchid"];
var fRow = $('<div id=row3 class=drow/>').appendTo('div.dtable');
```

I then define a skeletal set of elements; these describe the structure of elements that I want for each product but don't contain any of the attributes that distinguish one flower from another:

```
var fTemplate = $('<div class=dcell><img/><label/><input/></div>');
```

I use the skeletal elements as a simple template, cloning them for each of the flowers I want to add and using the name of the flower to add the attributes and values:

```
for (var i = 0; i < fNames.length; i++) {
    fTemplate.clone().appendTo(fRow).children()
        .filter('img').attr('src', fNames[i] + ".png").end()
        .filter('label').attr('for', fNames[i]).text(fNames[i]).end()
        .filter('input').attr({name: fNames[i], value: 0, required: "required"})
}
```

I use the filter and end methods to narrow and broaden the selection and the attr method to set the attribute values. I end up with a fully populated set of elements for each new flower, inserted into the row-level div element, which in turn is inserted into the table-level element. You can see the effect in Figure 11-2.

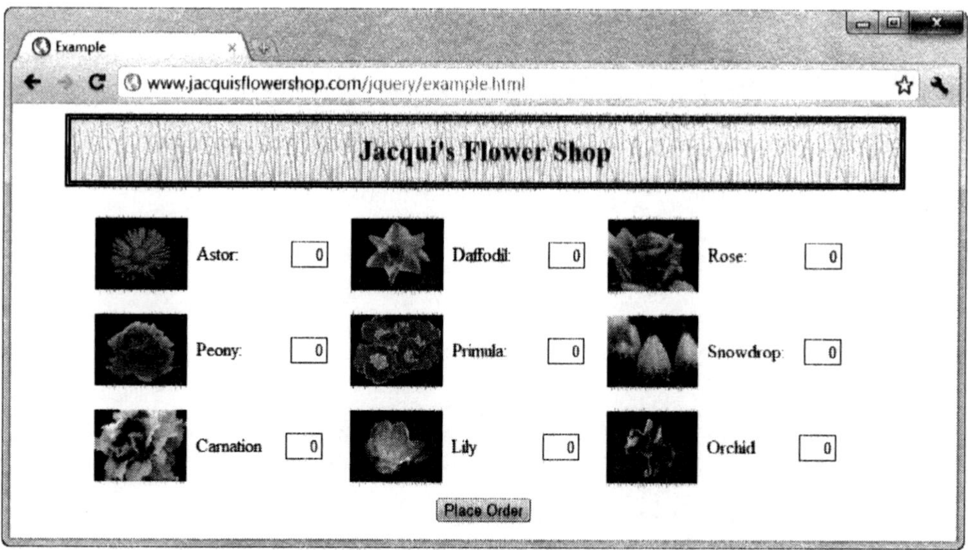

Figure 11-2. Adding new flowers to the page

One of the nice jQuery features that is evident in this example is the way you can select and navigate around elements that are not attached to the main document. The template elements are not part of the document when I clone them, but I can still use the children and filter methods to narrow down the selection.

Adding the Carousel Buttons

I am going to create a simple carousel that will let the user page through sets of flowers. To begin with, you need left and right buttons for the pagination. Listing 11-3 shows how I added them to the document.

Listing 11-3 Adding the Carousel Buttons

```
...
<script type="text/javascript">
    $(document).ready(function() {

        var fNames = ["Carnation", "Lily", "Orchid"];
        var fRow = $('<div id=row3 class=drow/>').appendTo('div.dtable');
        var fTemplate = $('<div class=dcell><img/><label/><input/></div>');
        for (var i = 0; i < fNames.length; i++) {
            fTemplate.clone().appendTo(fRow).children()
                .filter('img').attr('src', fNames[i] + ".png").end()
                .filter('label').attr('for', fNames[i]).text(fNames[i]).end()
                .filter('input').attr({name: fNames[i], value: 0, required: "required"})
        }

        $('<a id=left></a><a id=right></a>').prependTo('form')
            .css({
                "background-image": "url(leftarrows.png)",
                "float": "left",
                "margin-top": "15px",
                display: "block", width: 50, height: 50
            }).click(handleArrowPress).hover(handleArrowMouse)

        $('#right').css("background-image", "url(rightarrows.png)").appendTo('form');


        $('#oblock').css({float: "left", display: "inline", border: "thin black solid"});
        $('form').css({"margin-left": "auto", "margin-right": "auto", width: 885});

        function handleArrowMouse(e) {
        }

        function handleArrowPress(e) {

        }
    });
</script>
...
```

To start with, I define a pair of a elements, prepend them to the form element, and use the css method to apply values for a number of different properties:

```
$('<a id=left></a><a id=right></a>').prependTo('form')
    .css({
        "background-image": "url(leftarrows.png)",
```

```
        "float": "left",
        "margin-top": "15px",
        display: "block", width: 50, height: 50
}).click(handleArrowPress).hover(handleArrowMouse)
```

The key property is background-image, which I set to leftarrows.png. You can see this image in Figure 11-3.

Figure 11-3. The leftarrows.png image

This image contains three different arrows in a combined image. Each individual arrow is 50 pixels wide, and by setting the width and height properties to 50, I make sure that only one of the individual arrows is showing at any time.

I use the click and hover methods to define handler functions for the click, mouseenter, and mouseexit events:

```
$('<a id=left></a><a id=right></a>').prependTo('form')
    .css({
        "background-image": "url(leftarrows.png)",
        "float": "left",
        "margin-top": "15px",
        display: "block", width: 50, height: 50
}).click(handleArrowPress).hover(handleArrowMouse)
```

The handleArrowPress and handleArrowMouse functions are empty. I'll populate them in a moment. At this point, I have two arrow elements, both displaying left-facing arrows and both next to one another in the form element. I created and formatted the a elements together because most of the configuration is common, but now it is time to move and tailor the right button, which I do like this:

```
$('#right').css("background-image", "url(rightarrows.png)").appendTo('form');
```

I use the append method to move the element to the end of the form element and use the css method to change the background-image property to use the rightarrows.png. You can see this image in Figure 11-4.

Figure 11-4. The rightarrows.png image

Using combined images like this is a common technique, because it avoids the browser having to incur the overhead of making three different requests to the server to get three closely related images. You'll see how you can use this kind of image when I fill in the handleArrowMouse function shortly. You can see how the page looks in Figure 11-5.

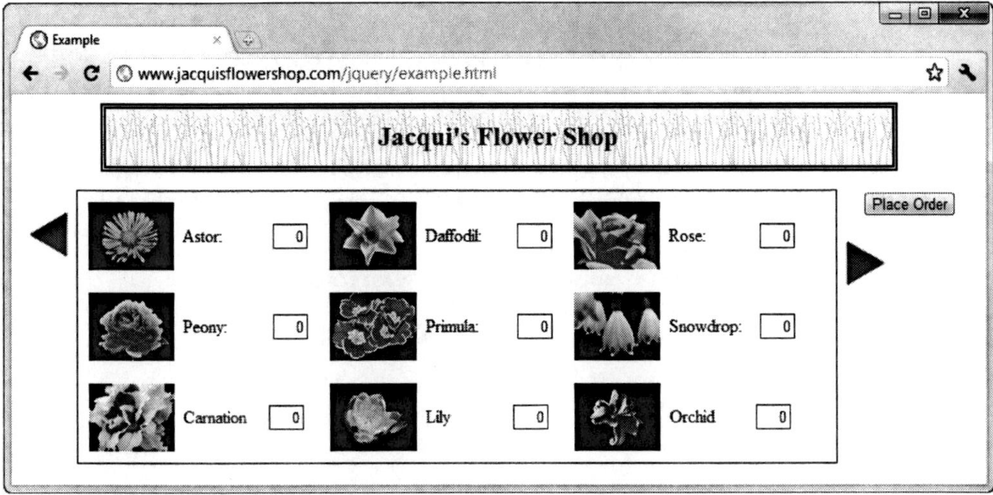

Figure 11-5. The intermediate state for the example document

Dealing with the Submit Button

As you can see from Figure 11-5, you are in an intermediate state. New features have appeared, but I have not properly accounted for them by dealing with some of the existing elements. The most significant of these is the Place Order button that submits the form. Listing 11-4 shows the additions to the script to deal with this element (and add a new feature).

Listing 11-4. Dealing with the Submit Button

```
...
<script type="text/javascript">
    $(document).ready(function() {

        var fNames = ["Carnation", "Lily", "Orchid"];
        var fRow = $('<div id=row3 class=drow/>').appendTo('div.dtable');
        var fTemplate = $('<div class=dcell><img/><label/><input/></div>');
        for (var i = 0; i < fNames.length; i++) {
            fTemplate.clone().appendTo(fRow).children()
                .filter('img').attr('src', fNames[i] + ".png").end()
                .filter('label').attr('for', fNames[i]).text(fNames[i]).end()
                .filter('input').attr({name: fNames[i], value: 0, required: "required"})
        }

        $('<a id=left></a><a id=right></a>').prependTo('form')
            .css({
                "background-image": "url(leftarrows.png)",
                "float": "left",
                "margin-top": "15px",
                display: "block", width: 50, height: 50
```

```
            }).click(handleArrowPress).hover(handleArrowMouse)

        $('#right').css("background-image", "url(rightarrows.png)").appendTo('form');

        $('h1').css({"min-width": "0", width: "95%",});
        $('#row2, #row3').hide();
        $('#oblock').css({float: "left", display: "inline", border: "thin black solid"});
        $('form').css({"margin-left": "auto", "margin-right": "auto", width: 885});

        var total = $('#buttonDiv')
            .prepend("<div>Total Items: <span id=total>0</span></div>")
            .css({clear: "both", padding: "5px"});
        $('<div id=bbox />').appendTo("body").append(total).css("clear: left");

        function handleArrowMouse(e) {
        }

        function handleArrowPress(e) {

        }
    });
</script>
...
```

To accommodate the changes in the layout caused by the carousel buttons, I have moved the div that contains the button element (it has an id of buttonDiv) to be inside a new div element, which, in turn, I have appended to the body element. This moves the button to a position where it returns to the bottom of the page. I have also added a div and a span element. These will be used to display the total number of products that the user has selected.

```
var total = $('#buttonDiv')
    .prepend("<div>Total Items: <span id=total>0</span></div>")
    .css({clear: "both", padding: "5px"});
$('<div id=bbox />').appendTo("body").append(total).css("clear: left");
```

The next change for this section is to hide two of the rows of products. This is so that you can reveal them to the user when they click the carousel buttons:

```
$('#row2, #row3').hide();
```

I have also tweaked the style of the h1 element to match the revised layout style:

```
$('h1').css({"min-width": "0", width: "95%",});
```

You can see the effect of these changes in Figure 11-6.

Figure 11-6. Dealing with the submit button and tidying the CSS

Implementing the Carousel Event Handler Functions

You are starting to see something emerge that is a little different from the document you started with. The next step is to implement the functions that handle events for the carousel buttons. First I am going to deal with the `mouseenter` and `mouseexit` events, which are handled by the `handleArrowMouse` function. Listing 11-5 shows the implementation of this function.

Listing 11-5. Handling the Arrow Button Mouse Events

```
...
function handleArrowMouse(e) {
   var propValue = e.type == "mouseenter" ? "-50px 0px" : "0px 0px";
   $(this).css("background-position", propValue);
}
...
```

The trick to dealing with combined images is to use the `background-position` property to shift the image so that only the part you want is visible. Although there are three images in my sets of arrows, I am going to use only two of them. The darkest image will be shown normally, and the middle image will be shown when the mouse is hovering over the element. You could use the remaining arrow to represent a button being clicked or being disabled, but I want to keep things simple. You can see the two states that the images represent in Figure 11-7.

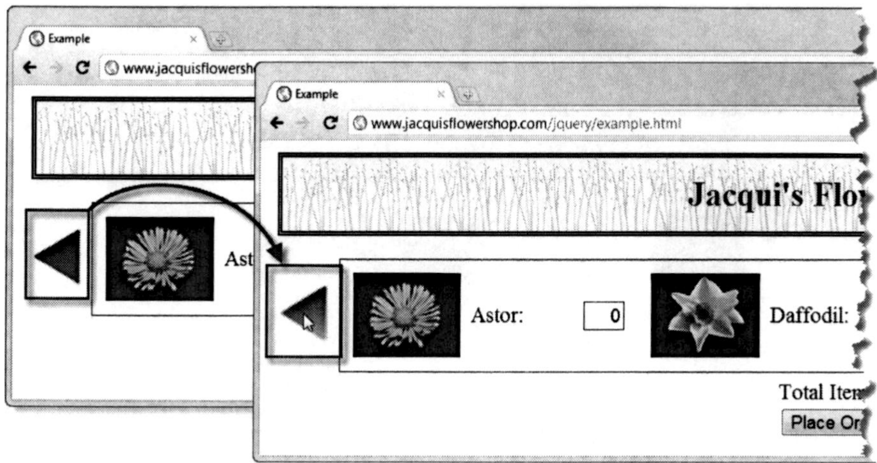

Figure 11-7. The two states of the arrow buttons

The handleArrowPress function is responsible for creating the carrousel effect, allowing the user to page through the rows of flowers. Listing 11-6 shows the implementation of this function.

Listing 11-6. Implementing the handleArrowPress Function

```
...
function handleArrowPress(e) {
    var elemSequence = ["row1", "row2", "row3"];
    var visibleRow = $('div.drow:visible');
    var visibleRowIndex = jQuery.inArray(visibleRow.attr("id"), elemSequence);

    var targetRowIndex;
    if (e.target.id == "left") {
        targetRowIndex = visibleRowIndex - 1;
        if (targetRowIndex < 0) {targetRowIndex = elemSequence.length -1};
    } else {
        targetRowIndex = (visibleRowIndex + 1) % elemSequence.length;
    }

    visibleRow.fadeOut("fast", function() {
        $('#' + elemSequence[targetRowIndex]).fadeIn("fast")});
}
...
```

The first three statements in this function set up the basic data you need:

```
var elemSequence = ["row1", "row2", "row3"];
var visibleRow = $('div.drow:visible');
var visibleRowIndex = jQuery.inArray(visibleRow.attr("id"), elemSequence);
```

The first statement defines the set of id attribute values for the row elements. The second statement uses jQuery to get the visible row. This is then used to determine the index of the visible row in the array of row id values. (I do this using the inArray utility method, which I explain in Chapter 33). So, you know which row is visible and where in your sequence of rows you are. Next, I figure out the index of the row that will be displayed next:

```
var targetRowIndex;
if (e.target.id == "left") {
    targetRowIndex = visibleRowIndex - 1;
    if (targetRowIndex < 0) {targetRowIndex = elemSequence.length -1};
} else {
    targetRowIndex = (visibleRowIndex + 1) % elemSequence.length;
}
```

In almost any other programming language, I could use the modulo operator to figure out the index of the next row to display, but there is a bug in the JavaScript implementation of modulo math, and it doesn't support negative values properly. So, if the user clicks the left button, I check for array bounds manually and do it using the % operator if the user clicks the right button. Once I have figured out the currently visible element and the element to display next, I use jQuery effects to animate a transition from one to the other:

```
visibleRow.fadeOut("fast", function() {
    $('#' + elemSequence[targetRowIndex]).fadeIn("fast")});
```

I have used the fadeOut and fadeIn methods because they work nicely with my CSS table-style layout. I use a callback in the first effect to trigger the second and perform both effects using the fast time span. There is no change in the static layout of the page, but the arrow buttons now take the user from one row of flowers to the next, as shown in Figure 11-8.

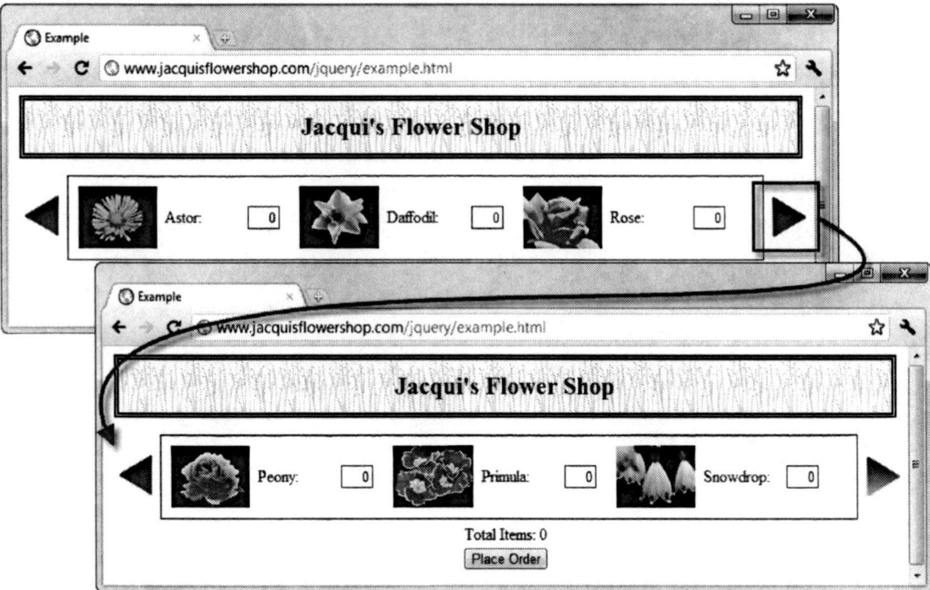

Figure 11-8. Providing a carousel of product rows

Totaling the Product Selection

The last change is to wire up the item total so that the total number of flowers selected in individual input fields is shown under the product carousel. Listing 11-7 shows the changes to the script.

Listing 11-7. Wiring Up the Product Total

```
...
<script type="text/javascript">
    $(document).ready(function() {

        var fNames = ["Carnation", "Lily", "Orchid"];
        var fRow = $('<div id=row3 class=drow/>').appendTo('div.dtable');
        var fTemplate = $('<div class=dcell><img/><label/><input/></div>');
        for (var i = 0; i < fNames.length; i++) {
            fTemplate.clone().appendTo(fRow).children()
                .filter('img').attr('src', fNames[i] + ".png").end()
                .filter('label').attr('for', fNames[i]).text(fNames[i]).end()
                .filter('input').attr({name: fNames[i], value: 0, required: "required"})
        }

        $('<a id=left></a><a id=right></a>').prependTo('form')
            .css({
                "background-image": "url(leftarrows.png)",
                "float": "left",
                "margin-top": "15px",
                display: "block", width: 50, height: 50
            }).click(handleArrowPress).hover(handleArrowMouse)

        $('#right').css("background-image", "url(rightarrows.png)").appendTo('form');

        $('h1').css({"min-width": "0", width: "95%",});
        $('#row2, #row3').hide();
        $('#oblock').css({float: "left", display: "inline", border: "thin black solid"});
        $('form').css({"margin-left": "auto", "margin-right": "auto", width: 885});

        var total = $('#buttonDiv')
            .prepend("<div>Total Items: <span id=total>0</span></div>")
            .css({clear: "both", padding: "5px"});
        $('<div id=bbox />').appendTo("body").append(total).css("clear: left");

        $('input').change(function(e) {
            var total = 0;
            $('input').each(function(index, elem) {
                total += Number($(elem).val());
            });
            $('#total').text(total);
        });

        function handleArrowMouse(e) {
           var propValue = e.type == "mouseenter" ? "-50px 0px" : "0px 0px";
```

```
            $(this).css("background-position", propValue);
        }

        function handleArrowPress(e) {
            var elemSequence = ["row1", "row2", "row3"];

            var visibleRow = $('div.drow:visible');
            var visibleRowIndex = jQuery.inArray(visibleRow.attr("id"), elemSequence);

            var targetRowIndex;

            if (e.target.id == "left") {
                targetRowIndex = visibleRowIndex - 1;
                if (targetRowIndex < 0) {targetRowIndex = elemSequence.length -1};
            } else {
                targetRowIndex = (visibleRowIndex + 1) % elemSequence.length;
            }
            visibleRow.fadeOut("fast", function() {
                $('#' + elemSequence[targetRowIndex]).fadeIn("fast")});
        }

    });
</script>
...
```

In this addition, I select the input element in the document and register a handler function that gets the value from each, sums it, and sets it as the content for the span element I added earlier. You can see the effect in Figure 11-9.

Figure 11-9. Displaying the product selection total

The total shows the sum of all of the input elements and not just the ones that are currently visible (although it would be a simple matter to use the other approach).

Disabling JavaScript

You have made some pretty sweeping changes to the example document, but you made all of those changes with jQuery. This means that if you have effectively created two tiers of document, one for JavaScript-enabled browsers and one for non-JavaScript browsers, Figure 11-10 shows what happens when you disable JavaScript and view the example document.

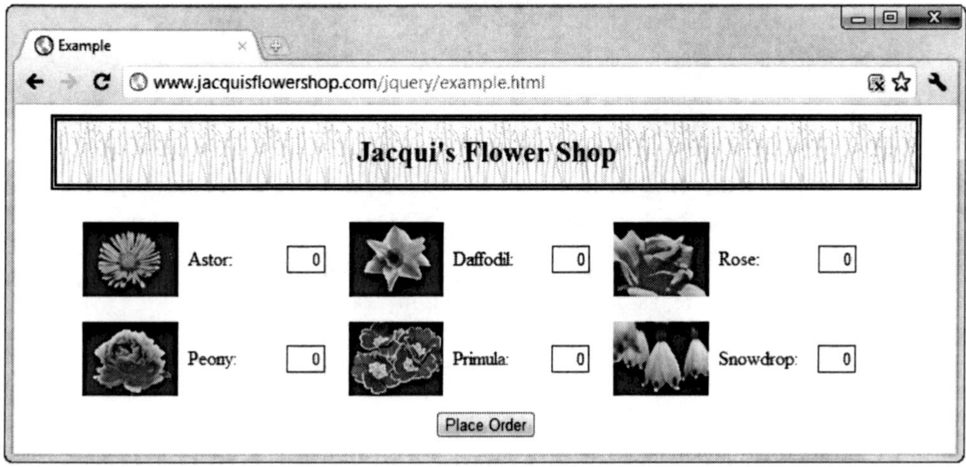

Figure 11-10. Disabling JavaScript and viewing the example document

You are back where you started from. With a little planning and forethought, you can offer non-JavaScript clients a set of functionality that still lets them interact with your page or application. This is generally a good idea; there are a lot of large corporations that manage IT centrally and disable JavaScript as a security precaution. (Well, sort of. When working for such organizations for many years, I came to believe that these policies didn't actually stop staff from using JavaScript; they simply created incentives to find loopholes ad workarounds.)

Summary

In this chapter, I showed you how to combine the techniques from previous chapters to refactor the example document. You added new content programmatically, you created a simple carousel of your products, and you created a total that displays the overall number of selected items. Along the way, you tweaked the DOM and CSS to accommodate these changes, all in a way that lets non-JavaScript browsers fall back to a document that remains useful.

In the next part of this book, I'll continue to build on this example, bringing in ever more jQuery features to flesh out the functionality. For the most part, I'll apply these to the original example document so as to focus on each feature in turn, but in Chapter 16 you'll refactor the document again to bring in more features.

PART 3

Working with Data and Ajax

CHAPTER 12

Using Data Templates

You will see your first jQuery plugin in this chapter; it is called the *jQuery Templates* plugin and it provides a way for you to use templates to easily generate HTML elements from JavaScript data objects.

I want to be very clear that this plugin is not actively developed or supported and has been deprecated by the jQuery team. That doesn't mean you shouldn't use it, but you should be aware of this fact before you incorporate this plugin into your projects. I'd recommend a more actively development alternative if I could find one that was anywhere as powerful and expressive as the jQuery Templates plugin, but even in an abandoned state this plugin is the best around.

This history of this plugin is rather odd. Microsoft and the jQuery team announced that three plugins developed by Microsoft had been accepted as "official" plugins, a status that had not been accorded to any other plugin. A while later, the jQuery team announced that the plugins were deprecated, that the official status was removed, and that there were plans to replace them with other functionality. A replacement for the template plugin would be created as part of jQuery UI (which I describe in Part IV of this book). Sadly, nothing has yet appeared, and the abandoned plugins are still available and widely used (especially in the case of the template plugin). Obviously, the decision about using abandoned code is a personal one, but I like the functionality that the template plugin provides, and I use it often. My thinking is that I can always dig into the source code and fix any serious problems and that the occasional need to work around minor problems is justified by the utility value of the template feature. Table 12-1 provides the summary for this chapter.

Table 12-1. *Chapter Summary*

Problem	Solution	Listing
Generate elements using a template.	Define a template in a `script` element and apply it through the `tmpl` method.	1–6
Assign the elements generated from a template to different parents.	Either split the source data and render the template twice or use the `slice` `filter` and `end` methods to divide up the generated elements.	7–9
Insert the result of an expression in a template.	Enclose the expression in the `${...}` template tag.	10
Access the data object in the template.	Use the `$data` variable.	11

Select elements within a template.	Use the jQuery $ function.	12
Pass options to the template.	Pass a map object to the `tmpl` method and use the `$item` variable to access the options as properties.	13
Render a nested template.	Use the `{{tmpl}}` template tag.	14–16
Create conditional regions in a template.	Use the `{{if}}` and `{{else}}` template tags.	17–19
Control template rendering for the items in an array.	Use the `{{each}}` template tag.	20, 21
Disable HTML-safe encoding of data values inserted into a template.	Use the `{{html}}` template tag.	22, 23
Re-render elements using different templates or data values.	Use the `$.tmplItem` method to obtain the template item object. Use the object's properties to modify the template or data and call the update method to regenerate the content.	24–26

Understanding the Problem That Templates Solve

Data templates solve a very specific problem: they allow you to programmatically generate elements from the properties and values of JavaScript objects. This is something you can do in other ways. In fact, I did something very similar in Chapter 11 when I created some elements to represent additional flowers in the example document. Listing 12-1 shows the relevant statements from that chapter.

Listing 12-1. Creating Elements Programmatically

```
...
<script type="text/javascript">
    $(document).ready(function() {

        var fNames = ["Carnation", "Lily", "Orchid"];
        var fRow = $('<div id=row3 class=drow/>').appendTo('div.dtable');
        var fTemplate = $('<div class=dcell><img/><label/><input/></div>');
        for (var i = 0; i < fNames.length; i++) {
            fTemplate.clone().appendTo(fRow).children()
                .filter('img').attr('src', fNames[i] + ".png").end()
                .filter('label').attr('for', fNames[i]).text(fNames[i]).end()
                .filter('input').attr({name: fNames[i], value: 0, required: "required"})
        }
    });
</script>
...
```

The problem with this approach is that it doesn't scale very well. As it is, the statements in the listing are already quite hard to read, and the complexity increases sharply for more complex elements. To my mind, the underlying issue of intelligibility arises because you are using JavaScript to solve a problem that is really about HTML elements. Handily, as I'll explain, the jQuery data templates library puts the emphasis back on HTML and, unless you want something very specialized, minimizes the amount of code you need to use to generate elements from data.

Taking a broader view, the need to integrate data into the document is a common issue to resolve. In my projects, it arises through two situations. The first is because I am working with some preexisting system that contains the data that drives my web application. I *could* obtain the data and integrate it into the document at the server—and there are some great technologies available to do this—but it means that my server farm spends a lot of time doing work that I could get the browser to do for me. If you have ever built and operated a high-volume web application, you know that the costs are substantial, and any opportunity to reduce the amount of processing required is taken seriously.

The second reason I need to integrate data into a document is that my web application is sourcing the data via Ajax in response to a user action. I will explain the jQuery support for Ajax fully in Chapters 14 and 15, but the short version is that you can obtain and display data from a server without reloading the entire page in the browser. It is a powerful technique that is very widely used, and the data template library works nicely with it.

Setting Up the jQuery Templates Library

Before you can use the jQuery template, you have to obtain the library and link to it in your document. You can download the library from `https://github.com/jquery/jquery-tmpl`. Decompress the archive file and copy either the `jquery.templ.js` file (for development) or the `jquery.teml.min.js` file (for deployment) to your web server, ideally to the same location as your main jQuery JavaScript file.

The next step is to add a `script` element to your example document that imports the template library, as shown in Listing 12-2.

Listing 12-2. Adding the Template Library to the Example Document

```
<!DOCTYPE html>
<html>
<head>
    <title>Example</title>
    <script src="jquery-1.7.js" type="text/javascript"></script>
    <script src="jquery.tmpl.js" type="text/javascript"></script>
    <link rel="stylesheet" type="text/css" href="styles.css"/>
    <script type="text/javascript">
        $(document).ready(function() {

            // example will go here

        });
    </script>
</head>
<body>
    <h1>Jacqui's Flower Shop</h1>
    <form method="post">
        <div id="oblock">
            <div class="dtable">
```

```
                <div id="row1" class="drow"></div>
                <div id="row2"class="drow"></div>
            </div>
        </div>
        <div id="buttonDiv"><button type="submit">Place Order</button></div>
    </form>
</body>
</html>
```

I'll use this listing as the example document for this chapter. Aside from the addition of the template library, you will notice that I have removed the individual flowers. You'll be using the template library to explore some different techniques for adding them back in. As a starting point, you can see how this document appears in Figure 12-1.

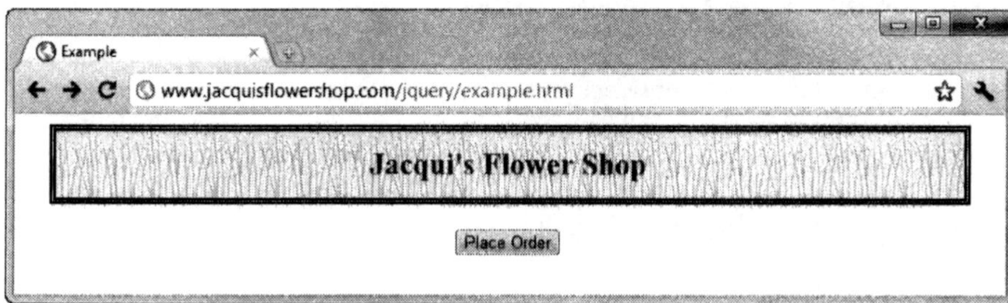

Figure 12-1. The starting example document

■ **Caution** Previously, I showed you how you could use jQuery to enhance and remodel a document while still leaving it functional for non-JavaScript users. In general, this is a very sensible approach, but one with which the techniques in this chapter are largely incompatible. The idea of using JavaScript to create elements from data using a template makes it hard to create a non-JavaScript equivalent. After all, if the document already contained the elements that result from the data, you wouldn't need to use the templates. I am a big fan of providing a fallback for non-JavaScript browsers, and I recommend you think carefully about the experience you offer to such users, even as I commend these template features to you for their convenience and utility.

A First Data Templates Example

The best way to start learning about data templates is to jump right in. Listing 12-3 demonstrates the basic template features. I have included the full HTML document in this listing because of the way you express templates using a `script` element, but I'll just show the relevant elements in future examples.

Listing 12-3. A First Data Templates Example

```
<!DOCTYPE html>
<html>
<head>
```

```
    <title>Example</title>
    <script src="jquery-1.7.js" type="text/javascript"></script>
    <script src="jquery.tmpl.js" type="text/javascript"></script>
    <link rel="stylesheet" type="text/css" href="styles.css"/>
    <script type="text/javascript">
        $(document).ready(function() {

            var data = [
                { name: "Astor", product: "astor", stocklevel: "10", price: 2.99},
                { name: "Daffodil", product: "daffodil", stocklevel: "12", price: 1.99},
                { name: "Rose", product: "rose", stocklevel: "2", price: 4.99},
                { name: "Peony", product: "peony", stocklevel: "0", price: 1.50},
                { name: "Primula", product: "primula", stocklevel: "1", price: 3.12},
                { name: "Snowdrop", product: "snowdrop", stocklevel: "15", price: 0.99},
            ];

            $('#flowerTmpl').tmpl(data).appendTo('#row1');

        });
    </script>
    <script id="flowerTmpl" type="text/x-jquery-tmpl">
        <div class="dcell">
            <img src="${product}.png"/>
            <label for="${product}">${name}:</label>
            <input name="${product}" data-price="${price}" data-stock="${stocklevel}"
                value="0" required />
        </div>
    </script>
</head>
<body>
    <h1>Jacqui's Flower Shop</h1>
    <form method="post">
        <div id="oblock">
            <div class="dtable">
                <div id="row1" class="drow"></div>
                <div id="row2"class="drow"></div>
            </div>
        </div>
        <div id="buttonDiv"><button type="submit">Place Order</button></div>
    </form>
</body>
</html>
```

In the sections that follow, I'll break down the example and explain each part. When the data is part of the document, it is known as *inline data*. The alternative is *remote data*, which is where you get the data from a server separately from the document. I'll demonstrate remote data later in the chapter, but it touches upon the jQuery support for Ajax, which is the topic of Chapters 14 and 15.

Defining the Data

The starting point for the example is the data, which in this case is an array of objects, each of which describes a single flower product. Listing 12-4 shows the relevant statements from the document.

Listing 12-4. Defining the Flower Data

```
...
var data = [
    { name: "Astor", product: "astor", stocklevel: "10", price: 2.99},
    { name: "Daffodil", product: "daffodil", stocklevel: "12", price: 1.99},
    { name: "Rose", product: "rose", stocklevel: "2", price: 4.99},
    { name: "Peony", product: "peony", stocklevel: "0", price: 1.50},
    { name: "Primula", product: "primula", stocklevel: "1", price: 3.12},
    { name: "Snowdrop", product: "snowdrop", stocklevel: "15", price: 0.99},
];
...
```

You express your data as one or more JavaScript objects. The jQuery template library is very flexible about the kind of objects that can be used as data, but the format shown in the template is the most commonly used because it corresponds to the JSON data format, which I explain in Chapter 14.

■ **Tip** JSON is important is because it is often used with Ajax, which I explain in Chapters 14 and 15.

For this example, the array contains six objects, each of which has a set of properties that describe a flower shop product: the display name, the product name, the stock level, and the price.

Defining the Template

As you might imagine, at the heart of the data template library is the *data template*. This is a set of HTML elements containing placeholders that correspond to aspects of the data objects. Listing 12-5 shows the template for this example.

Listing 12-5. Defining the Data Template

```
...
<script id="flowerTmpl" type="text/x-jquery-tmpl">
    <div class="dcell">
        <img src="${product}.png"/>
        <label for="${product}">${name}:</label>
        <input name="${product}" data-price="${price}" data-stock="${stocklevel}"
            value="0" required />
    </div>
</script>
...
```

The first thing to note about the template is that it is contained within a script element with a type attribute value of text/x-jquery-tmpl. The reason you do this is to stop the browser from interpreting the contents of the template as regular HTML. It is not essential, but it is very good practice and avoids a lot of potential problems.

The second thing to note is that when you define a template in a script element, you assign a name to the template using the id attribute. In this case, the template is called flowerTmpl. You need to know the name of the template when you apply it to your data.

The contents of the template will be applied to the objects in the data array in order to produce a set of HTML elements for each and every object. You can see that the structure of the template corresponds to the set of elements that I have used for the flower products in previous chapters. The key difference, of course, is the sections I have emphasized in the listings. These are the *data placeholders.*

When the template library processes the template, it replaces any data placeholders with the value of the property from the object being dealt with. So, for example, for the first object in the array, the template library will encounter the ${product} placeholder and replace it with the value of the product property, which is astor. So, this part of the template:

```
<img src="${product}.png"/>
```

is transformed into this:

```
<img src="astor.png"/>
```

Inserting data values is only one of the things you can do with a template. I'll explain the others later in the chapter.

Applying the Template

We bring the template together using the tmpl method. This allows you to specify the data you want to use and the template that should be applied to it. Listing 12-6 shows the use of this method in the listing.

Listing 12-6. Applying the Data Template

```
...
$('#flowerTmpl').tmpl(data).appendTo('#row1');
...
```

You use the jQuery $ function to select the element that contains the template and then call the tmpl method on the result, passing in the data that you want to be processed as the method argument.

The tmpl method returns a standard jQuery object that contains the elements produced from the template. In this case, I end up with a set of div elements, each of which contains an img, label, and input element that has been tailored for one of the objects in my data array. I use the appendTo method to insert the complete set as children to the row1 element. You can see the result in Figure 12-2.

Figure 12-2. Using data templates

Tweaking the Result

You don't quite get the desired result because all of the products are in a single line. But, since you are dealing with a jQuery object, you can slice and dice the elements as you usually would. Listing 12-7 shows how you can do this by operating on the `tmpl` method result.

Listing 12-7. Processing the Results from a Template

```
...
<script type="text/javascript">
    $(document).ready(function() {

    var data = [
        { name: "Astor", product: "astor", stocklevel: "10", price: 2.99},
        { name: "Daffodil", product: "daffodil", stocklevel: "12", price: 1.99},
        { name: "Rose", product: "rose", stocklevel: "2", price: 4.99},
        { name: "Peony", product: "peony", stocklevel: "0", price: 1.50},
        { name: "Primula", product: "primula", stocklevel: "1", price: 3.12},
        { name: "Snowdrop", product: "snowdrop", stocklevel: "15", price: 0.99},
    ];

    $('#flowerTmpl').tmpl(data)
        .slice(0, 3).appendTo('#row1').end().end().slice(3).appendTo("#row2");

    });
</script>
<script id="flowerTmpl" type="text/x-jquery-tmpl">
    <div class="dcell">
        <img src="${product}.png"/>
        <label for="${product}">${name}:</label>
        <input name="${product}" data-price="${price}" data-stock="${stocklevel}"
            value="0" required />
```

```
    </div>
</script>
...
```

In this example, I use the slice and end methods to narrow and broaden the selection and the appendTo method to add subsets of the elements generated from the template to different rows.

Notice that I have to call the end method twice in succession to unwind the narrowing caused by the slide and appendTo methods. This is perfectly functional, and I generally like using the end method to create single-statement operations, but I find the end().end() sequence dislikable. Instead, I would usually break down the steps into separate operations, as shown in Listing 12-8.

Listing 12-8. Splitting the Elements Using Multiple Statements

```
...
var templResult = $('#flowerTmpl').tmpl(data);
templResult.slice(0, 3).appendTo('#row1');
templResult.slice(3).appendTo("#row2"); ;
...
```

Either way, you get the same result, which is that the products are broken into two rows, each containing three flowers, as shown in Figure 12-3.

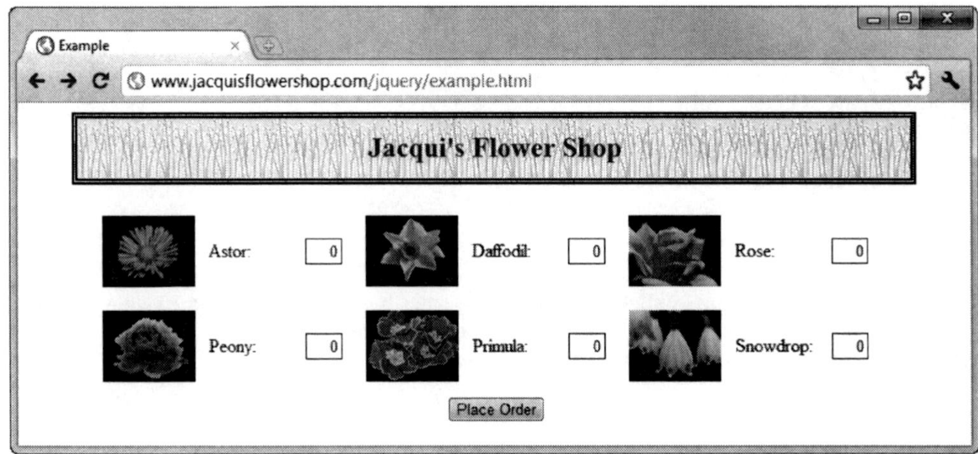

Figure 12-3. Tweaking the result to suit the layout

Tweaking the Input

The other approach you can take is to adjust the data that you pass to the tmpl method. Listing 12-9 shows how this can be done.

Listing 12-9. Using the Data to Adjust the Output from the Template

```
...
<script type="text/javascript">
    $(document).ready(function() {

        var data = [
            { name: "Astor", product: "astor", stocklevel: "10", price: 2.99},
            { name: "Daffodil", product: "daffodil", stocklevel: "12", price: 1.99},
            { name: "Rose", product: "rose", stocklevel: "2", price: 4.99},
            { name: "Peony", product: "peony", stocklevel: "0", price: 1.50},
            { name: "Primula", product: "primula", stocklevel: "1", price: 3.12},
            { name: "Snowdrop", product: "snowdrop", stocklevel: "15", price: 0.99},
        ];

        var template = $('#flowerTmpl');
        template.tmpl(data.slice(0, 3)).appendTo("#row1");
        template.tmpl(data.slice(3)).appendTo("#row2");

    });
</script>
<script id="flowerTmpl" type="text/x-jquery-tmpl">
    <div class="dcell">
        <img src="${product}.png"/>
        <label for="${product}">${name}:</label>
        <input name="${product}" data-price="${price}" data-stock="${stocklevel}"
            value="0" required />
    </div>
</script>
...
```

In this script, I solved the problem of allocating flowers to rows by using the template twice—once for each row. I used the split method so that I could feed a range of data objects to the template each time. The technique is different, but the result is the same, as shown in Figure 12-2.

Evaluating Expressions

You are not limited to just the property values from the data objects. You can place JavaScript expressions between the brace characters, and the template engine will evaluate them and insert the results into the HTML produced by the template. Listing 12-10 contains an example.

Listing 12-10. Evaluating an Expression in a Template

```
...
<script id="flowerTmpl" type="text/x-jquery-tmpl">

    <div class="dcell">
        <img src="${product}.png"/>
        <label for="${product}">${name}:</label>
        <input name="${product}" data-price="${price}" data-stock="${stocklevel}"
            value="${stocklevel > 0 ? 1: 0}" required />
```

```
    </div>
</script>
...
```

In this template, I use the JavaScript ternary operator to set the value attribute of the input element based on the stocklevel property. I place this expression between the brace characters, just as I did when I included a property value directly. If the stocklevel property is greater than zero, then the value attribute will be set to 1; otherwise, it will be zero. You can see the effect in Figure 12-4. All of the flowers except the peony have a stocklevel value greater than zero.

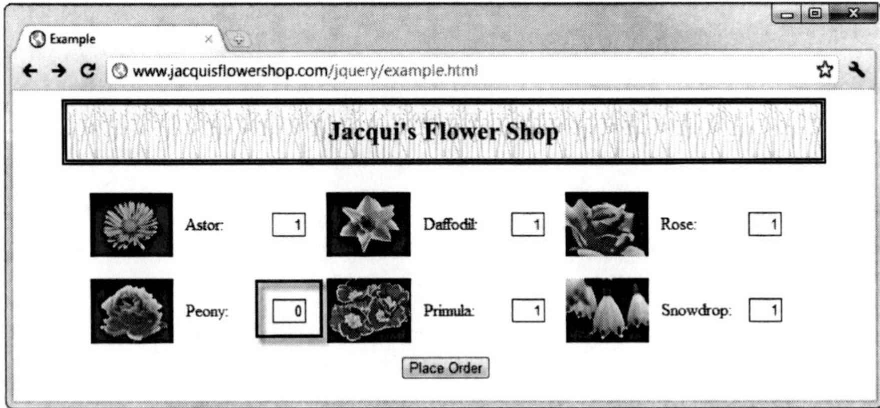

Figure 12-4. Evaluating an expression in a template

This example demonstrates the core template functionality in a nutshell: you combine data with a template to product DOM objects, which you then add to the document using core jQuery. You can use the values from the data directly or indirectly in expressions to generate content.

Using the Template Variables

Templates are not JavaScript scripts. Any content you add to the script is assumed to be part of the template and will be added to the output when the template is used. To help make templates more flexible, you are provided with a small number of context variables that you can use within the placeholder tags. These are described in Table 12-2 and explained in the following sections.

Table 12-2. *The Template Context Variables*

Variable	Description
`$data`	Returns the current data item
`$item`	Returns the current template item
`$`	The jQuery $ function

Using the Data Variable

The $data variable returns the data item to which the template is being applied. For the example in this chapter, $data will be set to each flower object in turn. In the previous listing, I used the ternary operator in a template. This is a perfectly acceptable technique, but I find that it is easy to end up with an unreadable template, which is part of the problem you want to avoid.

I like to keep the amount of code in a template to a bare minimum, and to do this, I like to combine the $data variable with the ability to call JavaScript functions from within the template. Listing 12-11 gives a demonstration.

Listing 12-11. Using the $data Variable in a Template

```
...
<script type="text/javascript">
    $(document).ready(function() {

        var data = [
            { name: "Astor", product: "astor", stocklevel: "10", price: 2.99},
            { name: "Daffodil", product: "daffodil", stocklevel: "12", price: 1.99},
            { name: "Rose", product: "rose", stocklevel: "2", price: 4.99},
            { name: "Peony", product: "peony", stocklevel: "0", price: 1.50},
            { name: "Primula", product: "primula", stocklevel: "1", price: 3.12},
            { name: "Snowdrop", product: "snowdrop", stocklevel: "15", price: 0.99},
        ];

        var template = $('#flowerTmpl');
        template.tmpl(data.slice(0, 3)).appendTo("#row1");
        template.tmpl(data.slice(3)).appendTo("#row2");

    });

    function stockDisplay(product) {
        return product.stocklevel > 0 ? 1 : 0;
    }

</script>
<script id="flowerTmpl" type="text/x-jquery-tmpl">
    <div class="dcell">
        <img src="${product}.png"/>
        <label for="${product}">${name}:</label>
        <input name="${product}" data-price="${price}" data-stock="${stocklevel}"
            value="${stockDisplay($data)}" required />
    </div>
</script>
...
```

In this example, I have defined a function called stockDisplay that produces the value that should be shown in the input element. The argument to the function is a data object, which I obtain within the template using the $data variable. For a simple ternary expression, the difference in legibility is minor, but you can imagine the difference for more complex expressions or where an expression is used several times in the same template.

■ **Caution** You must be careful where you define functions that will be called from a template. More specifically, the function must have been defined before the `tmpl` method is called. I tend to place these functions at the end of my `script` element, but if you want them inside your handler for the `ready` event, then make sure that the function is defined early. Equally, a common mistake is to define the function *inside* the template.

Using the jQuery $ Function in a Template

You can use the jQuery $ function in a template placeholder, but it is important to bear in mind that the elements that you are generating through the template are not yet attached to the document, so your jQuery selections won't reflect them. I rarely use this feature because my interest usually lies with the elements I am generating and the data behind them, but Listing 12-12 contains a simple demonstration.

Listing 12-12. Using the jQuery $ Function in a Template

```
...
<script type="text/javascript">
    $(document).ready(function() {

        $("<h2>Today's special offer: <span id=offer data-discount='0.50'>"
            + "50 cents off</span></h2>")
            .insertAfter('h1')
            .css({ color: "red", fontSize: "14pt", textAlign: "center" });

        var data = [
            { name: "Astor", product: "astor", stocklevel: "10", price: 2.99},
            { name: "Daffodil", product: "daffodil", stocklevel: "12", price: 1.99},
            { name: "Rose", product: "rose", stocklevel: "2", price: 4.99},
            { name: "Peony", product: "peony", stocklevel: "0", price: 1.50},
            { name: "Primula", product: "primula", stocklevel: "1", price: 3.12},
            { name: "Snowdrop", product: "snowdrop", stocklevel: "15", price: 0.99},
        ];

        var template = $('#flowerTmpl');
        template.tmpl(data.slice(0, 3)).appendTo("#row1");
        template.tmpl(data.slice(3)).appendTo("#row2");


    });

    function stockDisplay(product) {
        return product.stocklevel > 0 ? 1 : 0;
    }
</script>
<script id="flowerTmpl" type="text/x-jquery-tmpl">
    <div class="dcell">
        <img src="${product}.png"/>
        <label for="${product}">${name}:</label>
```

```
        <input name="${product}" data-price="${price - $('#offer').data('discount')}"
            data-stock="${stocklevel}" value="${stockDisplay($data)}" required />
    </div>
</script>
...
```

In this example, I have added an h2 element to the document that contains a span element, and the data-discount attribute on this element defines the discount that should be applied to the product prices. In the template, I use the jQuery $ function to locate the span element and the data method to read the value of the attribute (the data method is explained in Chapter 8). When the template is used to generate elements, the price specified in each data object is reduced by the discount amount.

I have included this example for completeness, but there is a lot about it that I don't like. First, using the $ function this way means I am searching the document for the span element for every data object that I process, which is a needless overhead. Second, I am back to including code in my template, which I'd much rather avoid. Third, handling this in a function would allow me to abstract the way in which the price is determined from the template. Still, all that said, you do have access to the $ function from within templates, and that may suit your coding style more than it does mine.

Using the Template Variable

The object returned by the $item variable performs several functions, which I'll explain as you go through the chapter. The first function is to provide you with a means of passing additional data between your jQuery script and the template. Listing 12-13 provides a demonstration. For details of other uses of this object, see the "Manipulating Templates from Event Handler Functions" section later in the chapter.

Listing 12-13. Passing Options to the Template via the $item Variable

```
...
<script type="text/javascript">
    $(document).ready(function() {

        $("<h2>Today's special offer: <span id=offer data-discount='0.50'>"
            + "50 cents off</span></h2>")
            .insertAfter('h1')
            .css({ color: "red", fontSize: "14pt", textAlign: "center" });

        var data = [
            { name: "Astor", product: "astor", stocklevel: "10", price: 2.99},
            { name: "Daffodil", product: "daffodil", stocklevel: "12", price: 1.99},
            { name: "Rose", product: "rose", stocklevel: "2", price: 4.99},
            { name: "Peony", product: "peony", stocklevel: "0", price: 1.50},
            { name: "Primula", product: "primula", stocklevel: "1", price: 3.12},
            { name: "Snowdrop", product: "snowdrop", stocklevel: "15", price: 0.99},
        ];

        var options = {
            discount: $('#offer').data('discount'),
            stockDisplay: function(product) {
                return product.stocklevel > 0 ? 1 : 0;
            }
```

```
        };
        var template = $('#flowerTmpl');
        template.tmpl(data.slice(0, 3), options).appendTo("#row1");
        template.tmpl(data.slice(3), options).appendTo("#row2");


    });

</script>
<script id="flowerTmpl" type="text/x-jquery-tmpl">
    <div class="dcell">
        <img src="${product}.png"/>
        <label for="${product}">${name}:</label>
        <input name="${product}" data-price="${price - $item.discount}"
            data-stock="${stocklevel}" value="${$item.stockDisplay($data)}" required />
    </div>
</script>
...
```

In this example, I create an object called `options` and define a property (`discount`) and a method (`stockDisplay`). I then pass this object as the second argument to the `tmpl` method. The properties and methods of the object are available through the `$item` variable in the template. So, when I want to read the value of the `discount` property, I do the following:

```
${price - $item.discount}
```

and when I want to call the `stockDisplay` function, I do this:

```
${$item.stockDisplay($data)}
```

You can see how I have used the `discount` property in the `options` object to tidy up the discount level that I previously obtained through the jQuery $ function. Not only do I like this code style better, but I search the document only once for the span element.

■ **Tip** Once again, notice how I refer to the template variables with the $ prefix: `$item` and `$data`. Also notice how the whole thing is wrapped in the `${...}` sequence that you started the chapter with. A common mistake is to omit one or other of the dollar signs.

Using Nested Templates

When building complex applications, it can be helpful to break down the overall template into smaller sections and compose them at runtime. As you'll see in later sections of this chapter, by composing templates in this way, you can get some finely tuned output. To start with the basics, Listing 12-14 shows how you can refer to one template from another.

Listing 12-14. Nesting Templates

```
...
<script type="text/javascript">
    $(document).ready(function() {

        $("<h2>Today's special offer: <span id=offer data-discount='0.50'>"
            + "50 cents off</span></h2>")
            .insertAfter('h1')
            .css({ color: "red", fontSize: "14pt", textAlign: "center" });

        var data = [
            { name: "Astor", product: "astor", stocklevel: "10", price: 2.99},
            { name: "Daffodil", product: "daffodil", stocklevel: "12", price: 1.99},
            { name: "Rose", product: "rose", stocklevel: "2", price: 4.99},
            { name: "Peony", product: "peony", stocklevel: "0", price: 1.50},
            { name: "Primula", product: "primula", stocklevel: "1", price: 3.12},
            { name: "Snowdrop", product: "snowdrop", stocklevel: "15", price: 0.99},
        ];

        var options = {
            discount: $('#offer').data('discount'),
            stockDisplay: function(product) {
                return product.stocklevel > 0 ? 1 : 0;
            }
        }
        var template = $('#flowerTmpl');
        template.tmpl(data.slice(0, 3), options).appendTo("#row1");
        template.tmpl(data.slice(3), options).appendTo("#row2");
    });

</script>
<script id="flowerTmpl" type="text/x-jquery-tmpl">
    <div class="dcell">
        <img src="${product}.png"/>
        <label for="${product}">${name}:</label>
        {{tmpl($data, $item) "#inputTmpl"}}
    </div>
</script>
<script id="inputTmpl" type="text/x-jquery-tmpl">
   <input name="${product}" data-price="${price - $item.discount}"
            data-stock="${stocklevel}" value="${$item.stockDisplay($data)}" required />
</script>
...
```

I have split the template into two in this example. The first template, `flowerTmpl`, is called for each item in the data array. This template calls the `inputTmpl` template in order to create the input element. You call another template using the `{{tmpl}}` tag, like this:

```
{{tmpl($data, $item) "#inputTmpl"}}
```

There are three arguments when using the {{tmpl}} tag. The first two are the data item to process and the options object, and these are placed in parentheses, as shown. The third argument is the template to use. This can be expressed as a selector (as I have done) or accessed via a variable or a function defined in a script.

Using Nested Templates on Arrays

If you pass a single value or object to a nested template, then the specified template is used just once, as in the previous example. However, if you pass an array of objects, then the template is used to generate elements for each item in the array, as shown in Listing 12-15.

Listing 12-15. Using a Nested Template on an Array

```
...
<script type="text/javascript">
    $(document).ready(function() {

        var data = [
            {
            rowid: "row1",
            flowers:
                [{ name: "Astor", product: "astor", stocklevel: "10", price: 2.99},
                { name: "Daffodil", product: "daffodil", stocklevel: "12", price: 1.99},
                { name: "Rose", product: "rose", stocklevel: "2", price: 4.99}]
            },
            {
            rowid: "row2",
            flowers:
                [{ name: "Peony", product: "peony", stocklevel: "0", price: 1.50},
                { name: "Primula", product: "primula", stocklevel: "1", price: 3.12},
                { name: "Snowdrop", product: "snowdrop", stocklevel: "15", price: 0.99}]
            }
        ];

        $('div.drow').remove();
        $('#rowTmpl').tmpl(data).appendTo('div.dtable');
    });

</script>
<script id="flowerTmpl" type="text/x-jquery-tmpl">
    <div class="dcell">
        <img src="${product}.png"/>
        <label for="${product}">${name}:</label>
        <input name="${product}" data-price="${price}"
            data-stock="${stocklevel}" value="${stocklevel}" required />
    </div>
</script>
<script id="rowTmpl" type="text/x-jquery-tmpl">
    <div id="${rowid}" class="drow">
        {{tmpl($data.flowers) '#flowerTmpl'}}
    </div>
```

```
</script>
...
```

To demonstrate this feature, I have refactored the data object so that it is an array that contains two objects. Each of these objects defines an rowid to be used as a row identifier and an array of three object representing flower products.

I remove the row-level div elements from the document and then use the rowTmpl template to process the data. This template generates a replacement row-level div for my CSS table-style layout and then uses the {{tmpl}} tag to process the array of flower objects, as follows:

```
<script id="rowTmpl" type="text/x-jquery-tmpl">
    <div id="${rowid}" class="drow">
        {{tmpl($data.flowers) '#flowerTmpl'}}
    </div>
</script>
```

Even though I have invoked the template only once, the template engine uses it to generate elements for every item in the array, which means that I end up with a cell-level element for each flower.

You might reasonably object to structuring the data to match the intended layout, so Listing 12-16 shows how you can slice and dice the original data format to get the same effect (because it is rare that data comes in a perfect format for immediate display).

Listing 12-16. Refactoring the Inline Data to Use Nested Templates

```
...
<script type="text/javascript">
    $(document).ready(function() {

        var originalData = [
            { name: "Astor", product: "astor", stocklevel: "10", price: 2.99},
            { name: "Daffodil", product: "daffodil", stocklevel: "12", price: 1.99},
            { name: "Rose", product: "rose", stocklevel: "2", price: 4.99},
            { name: "Peony", product: "peony", stocklevel: "0", price: 1.50},
            { name: "Primula", product: "primula", stocklevel: "1", price: 3.12},
            { name: "Snowdrop", product: "snowdrop", stocklevel: "15", price: 0.99},
        ];

        var itemsPerRow = 4;
        var slicedData = [];

        for (var i = 0, j = 0; i < originalData.length; i+= itemsPerRow, j++) {
            slicedData.push({
                rowid: "row" + j,
                flowers: originalData.slice(i, i + itemsPerRow)
            });
        }

        $('div.drow').remove();
        $('#rowTmpl').tmpl(slicedData).appendTo('div.dtable');
    });

</script>
```

```
<script id="flowerTmpl" type="text/x-jquery-tmpl">
    <div class="dcell">
        <img src="${product}.png"/>
        <label for="${product}">${name}:</label>
        <input name="${product}" data-price="${price}"
            data-stock="${stocklevel}" value="${stocklevel}" required />
    </div>
</script>
<script id="rowTmpl" type="text/x-jquery-tmpl">
    <div id="${rowid}" class="drow">
        {{tmpl($data.flowers) '#flowerTmpl'}}
    </div>
</script>
...
```

In this example, I allocate the elements to rows using a `for` loop and then pass the formatted data object to the `tmpl` method. The number of items per row is determined by the value of the `itemsPerRow` variable, which I have set to 4 in this example. You can see the result in Figure 12-5.

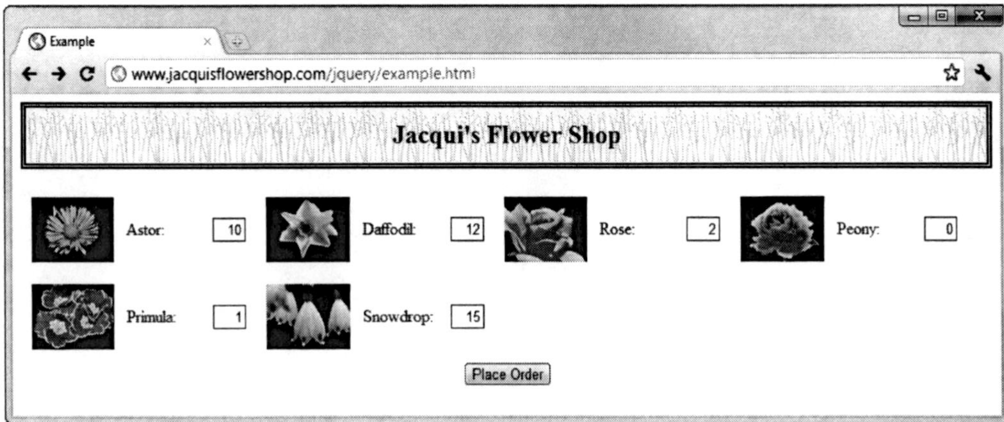

Figure 12-5. Formatting data to suit the templates

To an extent, I am simply pushing the complexity around the document. I either format the data or accept a more complex template. To my mind, this is unavoidable because the template engine can do only so much to help us. The correct balance between code complexity and template complexity will depend on the data format you are working with. My advice is to play around and try different approaches until you arrive at something that you can live with, that other people can understand, and that you are confident you can maintain in the future.

Using Conditional Templates

The template engine allows you to determine which portions of the template are used dynamically, based on a condition. You do this using the `{{if}}` and `{{/if}}` tags, as shown in Listing 12-17.

Listing 12-17. Selecting Parts of the Template Based on a Condition

```
...
<script type="text/javascript">
    $(document).ready(function() {

        var originalData = [
            { name: "Astor", product: "astor", stocklevel: "10", price: 2.99},
            { name: "Daffodil", product: "daffodil", stocklevel: "12", price: 1.99},
            { name: "Rose", product: "rose", stocklevel: "2", price: 4.99},
            { name: "Peony", product: "peony", stocklevel: "0", price: 1.50},
            { name: "Primula", product: "primula", stocklevel: "1", price: 3.12},
            { name: "Snowdrop", product: "snowdrop", stocklevel: "15", price: 0.99},
        ];

        var itemsPerRow = 3;
        var slicedData = [];

        for (var i = 0, j = 0; i < originalData.length; i+= itemsPerRow, j++) {
            slicedData.push({
                rowid: "row" + j,
                flowers: originalData.slice(i, i + itemsPerRow)
            });
        }

        $('div.drow').remove();
        $('#rowTmpl').tmpl(slicedData).appendTo('div.dtable');
    });

</script>
<script id="flowerTmpl" type="text/x-jquery-tmpl">
    {{if stocklevel > 0}}
        <div class="dcell">
            <img src="${product}.png"/>
            <label for="${product}">${name}:</label>
            <input name="${product}" data-price="${price}"
                data-stock="${stocklevel}" value="${stocklevel}" required />
        </div>
    {{/if}}
</script>
<script id="rowTmpl" type="text/x-jquery-tmpl">
    <div id="${rowid}" class="drow">
        {{tmpl($data.flowers) '#flowerTmpl'}}
    </div>
</script>
...
```

You specify a condition in the `{{if}}` tag, and if the condition evaluates to `true`, then the portion of the template until the `{{/if}}` tag is used. If the condition is `false`, then that part of the template is skipped. In this example, I check the value of the `stocklevel` property and skip the entire `flowerTmpl` template if the value is zero. This means the flower shop displays only those products that are in stock, as shown in Figure 12-6.

Figure 12-6. Rendering the template for in-stock items only

You can create more complex conditions by adding the {{else}} tag, which lets you define a region of the template that will be used if the condition specified by the {{if}} tag evaluates as false. Listing 12-18 gives an example.

Listing 12-18. Using the {{else}} Tag

```
...
<script type="text/javascript">
    $(document).ready(function() {

        var originalData = [
            { name: "Astor", product: "astor", stocklevel: "10", price: 2.99},
            { name: "Daffodil", product: "daffodil", stocklevel: "12", price: 1.99},
            { name: "Rose", product: "rose", stocklevel: "2", price: 4.99},
            { name: "Peony", product: "peony", stocklevel: "0", price: 1.50},
            { name: "Primula", product: "primula", stocklevel: "1", price: 3.12},
            { name: "Snowdrop", product: "snowdrop", stocklevel: "15", price: 0.99},
        ];

        var itemsPerRow = 3;
        var slicedData = [];

        for (var i = 0, j = 0; i < originalData.length; i+= itemsPerRow, j++) {
            slicedData.push({
                rowid: "row" + j,
                flowers: originalData.slice(i, i + itemsPerRow)
            });
        }
```

```
        $('div.drow').remove();
        $('#rowTmpl').tmpl(slicedData).appendTo('div.dtable');
    });

</script>
<script id="flowerTmpl" type="text/x-jquery-tmpl">
    {{if stocklevel > 0}}
        <div class="dcell">
            <img src="${product}.png"/>
            <label for="${product}">${name}:</label>
            <input name="${product}" data-price="${price}"
                data-stock="${stocklevel}" value="${stocklevel}" required />
        </div>
    {{else}}
         <div class="dcell">
            <img src="${product}.png" style="opacity:0.5"/>
            <span style="color: grey">${name} (No stock)</span>
        </div>
    {{/if}}
</script>
<script id="rowTmpl" type="text/x-jquery-tmpl">
    <div id="${rowid}" class="drow">
        {{tmpl($data.flowers) '#flowerTmpl'}}
    </div>
</script>
...
```

In this example, I display one set of elements for products that are in stock and another set of elements for those that are out of stock. You can go further and put a condition in the {{else}} tag to create the equivalent of an else...if condition, as shown in Listing 12-19.

Listing 12-19. Applying a Condition to an {{else}} Tag

```
...
<script id="flowerTmpl" type="text/x-jquery-tmpl">
    {{if stocklevel > 5}}
        <div class="dcell">
            <img src="${product}.png"/>
            <label for="${product}">${name}:</label>
            <input name="${product}" data-price="${price}"
                data-stock="${stocklevel}" value="${stocklevel}" required />
        </div>
    {{else stocklevel > 0}}
        <div class="dcell">
            <img src="${product}.png"/>
            <label style="color:red" for="${product}">${name}: (Low Stock)</label>
            <input name="${product}" data-price="${price}"
                data-stock="${stocklevel}" value="${stocklevel}" required />
        </div>
    {{else}}
         <div class="dcell">
```

```
            <img src="${product}.png" style="opacity:0.5"/>
            <span style="color: grey">${name} (No stock)</span>
        </div>
    {{/if}}
</script>
...
```

In this script, I display different sets of elements for the products for which you have more than five items in stock—those products with less stock and those with none at all. I have only slightly differentiated the elements generated for each condition, but you can use this feature to produce completely different content. And, of course, you can make a call to other templates as required. You can see the effect of this script in Figure 12-7.

Figure 12-7. Using conditional statements in templates

Controlling Iteration Over Arrays

The {{each}} template tag lets you exert control over how arrays of data items are processed in a template. This is an alternative approach to using calls to nested templates, which I showed you earlier in the chapter. Listing 12-20 shows how the {{each}} tag is used.

Listing 12-20. Using the {{each}} Template Tag

```
...
<script type="text/javascript">
    $(document).ready(function() {

        var originalData = [
            { name: "Astor", product: "astor", stocklevel: "10", price: 2.99},
            { name: "Daffodil", product: "daffodil", stocklevel: "12", price: 1.99},
            { name: "Rose", product: "rose", stocklevel: "2", price: 4.99},
            { name: "Peony", product: "peony", stocklevel: "0", price: 1.50},
```

```
            { name: "Primula", product: "primula", stocklevel: "1", price: 3.12},
            { name: "Snowdrop", product: "snowdrop", stocklevel: "15", price: 0.99},
        ];

        var itemsPerRow = 3;
        var slicedData = [];

        for (var i = 0, j = 0; i < originalData.length; i+= itemsPerRow, j++) {
            slicedData.push({
                rowid: "row" + j,
                flowers: originalData.slice(i, i + itemsPerRow)
            });
        }

        $('div.drow').remove();
        $('#flowerTmpl').tmpl(slicedData).appendTo('div.dtable');
    });

    function stockDisplay(product) {
        return product.stocklevel > 0 ? 1 : 0;
    }

</script>
<script id="flowerTmpl" type="text/x-jquery-tmpl">
    <div id="${rowid}" class="drow">
        {{each flowers}}
            <div class="dcell">
                <img src="${product}.png"/>
                <label for="${product}">${$index} ${name}: </label>
                <input name="${product}" value="${stockDisplay($value)}" required />
            </div>
        {{/each}}
    </div>
</script>
...
```

The content between the {{each}} and {{/each}} tags is rendered once for each item in the specified array. Within the {{each}} and {{/each}} tags, you can refer to individual properties as you would normally. You can refer to the current item in the array using the `$value` variable and the index of the current item using the `$index` variable.

■ **Tip** You can specify different names for `$index` and `$value` by providing arguments to the `{{each}}` tag. For example, if you wanted `$i` instead of `$index` and `$v` instead of `$value`, you would write `{{each($i, $v) flowers}}`.

Iterating Over the Result of an Expression

If you provide an expression to the {{each}} tag, then the content up until {{/each}} will be rendered once for each item in the expression result. Listing 12-21 shows this technique, where I filter the set of data items to remove those that are low or out of stock.

Listing 12-21. Using an Expression with the {{each tag}}

```
...
<script type="text/javascript">
    $(document).ready(function() {

        var originalData = [
            { name: "Astor", product: "astor", stocklevel: "10", price: 2.99},
            { name: "Daffodil", product: "daffodil", stocklevel: "12", price: 1.99},
            { name: "Rose", product: "rose", stocklevel: "2", price: 4.99},
            { name: "Peony", product: "peony", stocklevel: "0", price: 1.50},
            { name: "Primula", product: "primula", stocklevel: "1", price: 3.12},
            { name: "Snowdrop", product: "snowdrop", stocklevel: "15", price: 0.99},
        ];

        var itemsPerRow = 3;
        var slicedData = [];

        for (var i = 0, j = 0; i < originalData.length; i+= itemsPerRow, j++) {
            slicedData.push({
                rowid: "row" + j,
                flowers: originalData.slice(i, i + itemsPerRow)
            });
        }

        $('div.drow').remove();
        $('#flowerTmpl').tmpl(slicedData).appendTo('div.dtable');
    });

    function stockDisplay(product) {
        return product.stocklevel > 0 ? 1 : 0;
    }

    function filterLowStock(flowers) {
        var result = [];
        for (var i = 0; i < flowers.length; i++) {
            if (flowers[i].stocklevel > 2) { result.push(flowers[i]) }
        }
        return result;
    }
</script>
<script id="flowerTmpl" type="text/x-jquery-tmpl">
    <div id="${rowid}" class="drow">
        {{each filterLowStock(flowers)}}
            <div class="dcell">
```

```
                <img src="${product}.png"/>
                <label for="${product}">${name}: </label>
                <input name="${product}" value="${stockDisplay($value)}" required />
            </div>
        {{/each}}
    </div>
</script>
...
```

I call the `filterLowStock` function from the `{{each}}` tag, which limits the number of items that are iterated over. You can see the result in Figure 12-8.

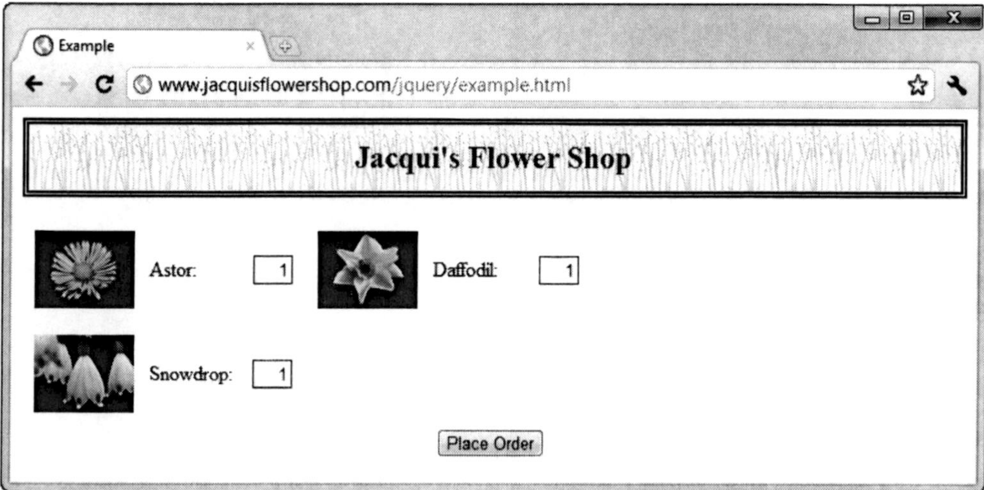

Figure 12-8. Using an expression with an {{each}} tag

Disabling HTML Encoding

By default, the template engine encodes the values that you insert into a template to make them safe to display in a web page. This means characters such as < and > are replaced or encoded so that they are not interpreted as denoting an HTML element. This is usually useful, but if you are dealing with data that contains HTML markup, then it causes a problem. Listing 12-22 provides a demonstration.

Listing 12-22. Working with Data That Contains HTML Markup

```
...
<script type="text/javascript">
    $(document).ready(function() {

        var data = [
            { name: "Astor", product: "astor", elem: "<img src=astor.png/>"},
            { name: "Daffodil", product: "daffodil", elem: "<img src=daffodil.png/>"},
            { name: "Rose", product: "rose", elem: "<img src=rose.png/>"},
            { name: "Peony", product: "peony", elem: "<img src=peony.png/>" },
```

```
            { name: "Primula", product: "primula", elem: "<img src=primula.png/>" },
            { name: "Snowdrop", product: "snowdrop", elem: "<img src=snowdrop.png/>" },
        ];

        var templResult = $('#flowerTmpl').tmpl(data);
        templResult.slice(0, 3).appendTo('#row1');
        templResult.slice(3).appendTo("#row2"); ;
    });
</script>
<script id="flowerTmpl" type="text/x-jquery-tmpl">
    <div class="dcell">
        ${elem}
        <label for="${product}">${name}: </label>
        <input name="${product}" value="0" required />
    </div>
</script>
...
```

In this example, each data item contains a property whose value is the HTML element that displays an image for the product. In the template, I display the content of this property by referring to the property name, `${elem}`. You can see the issue in Figure 12-9.

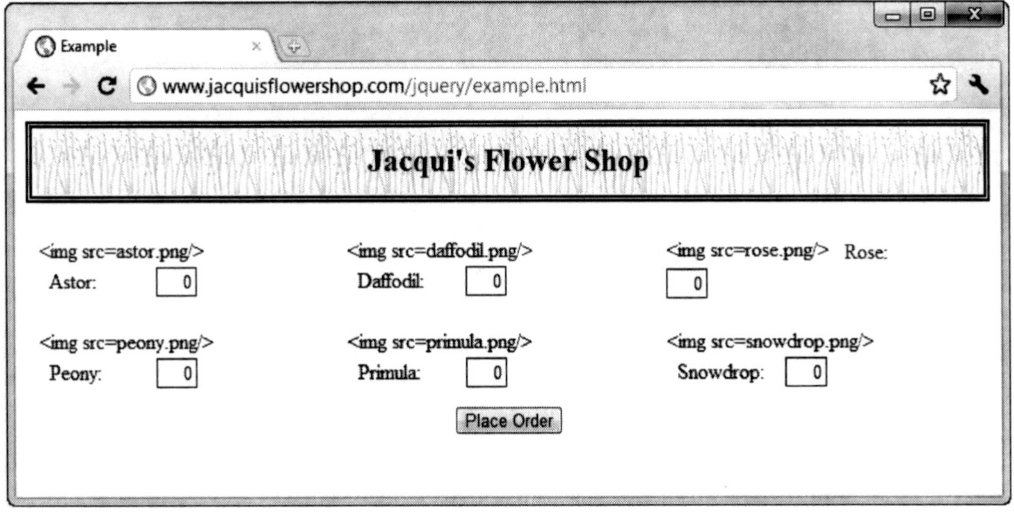

Figure 12-9. The effect of encoding HTML content from a data object

You can avoid this problem by using the `{{html}}` tag, which tells the template engine that the content you are working with should be displayed as is. Listing 12-23 shows the application of this tag.

■ **Caution** Use this tag carefully and never trust content that has been submitted by users. It is very easy for malicious content to be injected into your page, including scripts that can override the event handlers of your own code.

Listing 12-23. Using the {{html}} Tag

```
...
<script id="flowerTmpl" type="text/x-jquery-tmpl">
    <div class="dcell">
        {{html elem}}
        <label for="${product}">${name}: </label>
        <input name="${product}" value="0" required />
    </div>
</script>
...
```

You use the {{html}} tag with the value that you want to insert into the template, and the encoding sequence is skipped.

■ **Caution** I'm not kidding. Be careful about the data that you insert into the template using this tag. It can be incredibly dangerous if you cannot guarantee that the data is absolutely benign. Don't forget that your own colleagues might be capable of malicious modifications, especially that weird guy in the operations team. He's never liked you. He's probably plotting to get at your data even now. Trust no one.

Manipulating Templates from Event Handler Functions

You can go back to the template that was used to create an element and make changes. You can change the template, change the data or options that were used to generate the template, or even modify the elements that were generated by the template the first time around. The most common reason for doing this is to change part of the document in response to a user action, which means you are usually performing these tasks from within an event handler function, as demonstrated by Listing 12-24.

Listing 12-24. Changing the Template Used to Render a Data Item

```
...
<style type="text/css">
    .bigview {
        border: medium solid black;
        position: relative;
        top: -10px;
        left: -10px;
        background-color: white;
```

```
    }
    .bigview > img {
        width: 160px;
        height: 120px;
    }
</style>
<script type="text/javascript">
    $(document).ready(function() {

        var data = [
            { name: "Astor", product: "astor", stocklevel: "10", price: "2.99"},
            { name: "Daffodil", product: "daffodil", stocklevel: "12", price: "1.99"},
            { name: "Rose", product: "rose", stocklevel: "2", price: "4.99"},
            { name: "Peony", product: "peony", stocklevel: "0", price: "1.50"},
            { name: "Primula", product: "primula", stocklevel: "1", price: "3.12"},
            { name: "Snowdrop", product: "snowdrop", stocklevel: "15", price: "0.99"},
        ];

        var templResult = $('#flowerTmpl').tmpl(data);
        templResult.slice(0, 3).appendTo('#row1');
        templResult.slice(3).appendTo("#row2"); ;

        $('div.dcell').mouseenter(handleMouse);

        function handleMouse(e) {
            var tmplItem = $.tmplItem(this);
            var template = e.type == "mouseenter" ? "#flowerTmplSel" : "#flowerTmpl";
            tmplItem.tmpl = $(template).template();
            tmplItem.update();
            $('div.dcell').unbind()
                .bind(e.type == "mouseenter" ? "mouseleave" : "mouseenter", handleMouse);
        }
    });
</script>
<script id="flowerTmpl" type="text/x-jquery-tmpl">
    <div class="dcell">
        <img src="${product}.png"/>
        <label for="${product}">${name}: </label>
        <input name="${product}" value="0" required />
    </div>
</script>
<script id="flowerTmplSel" type="text/x-jquery-tmpl">
    <div class="dcell bigview">
        <img src="${product}.png"/>
        {{if $data.stocklevel > 0}}
            Stock: ${stocklevel} Price: $${price}
        {{else}}
            (Out of stock)
        {{/if}}
    </div>
</script>
...
```

This example required a detailed explanation. There is a surprising amount going on and some potential problems for the unwary. The baseline of this example is pretty simple. You have an inline data object that is rendered using the `flowerTmpl` template.

After rendering the content, I use the `mouseenter` method to register the `handleMouse` function as a handler for the elements that match the `div.dcell` elements. These are the top-level elements that the template has rendered.

When the mouse enters one of these `div` elements, the `handleMouse` function is executed. The first thing I do in this function is obtain the template item associated with the element that triggered the event:

```
var tmplItem = $.tmplItem(this);
```

This is the same kind of object that you can obtain using the `$item` variable inside the template (as described earlier in the chapter), but the object is a lot more useful here. Table 12-3 shows the properties of the template item object.

Table 12-3. *Properties of the Template Item Object*

Name	Description
`nodes`	The set of `HTMLElement` objects that were generated by the template. The hierarchy of objects is preserved, so only the top-level elements are returned by this property.
`data`	The data object used to render the element.
`tmpl`	The template used to generate the selected element.
`parent`	The parent template, if the element was generated from a nested template.
`<option properties>`	The properties defined by the `options` object (if used) are available directly on this object.

Returning to the example, I select the template I want to use to display the selected element based on the event type. If the mouse has entered the element, then I select the `flowerTmplSel` template:

```
var template = e.type == "mouseenter" ? "#flowerTmplSel" : "#flowerTmpl";
```

I then use the tmpl property of the template item to associate the template with the data item:

```
tmplItem.tmpl = $(template).template();
```

In thinking about what is happening here, it helps to understand that the template engine remembers how it generated the content that you are now trying to change. It keeps a record of the data object *and* the template you used. This is a neat trick, and it works even when you use condition and nested templates. By using the `tmpl` property, I am telling the template engine that I want to use a different template to generate content for the data item that was originally used to generate the element that triggered the event you are now processing (you might need to read this sentence a couple of times to parse it properly).

When you have finished making changes, you call the update method on the template item to re-render the content using the new values (in this case, the new template):

```
tmplItem.update();
```

You can see how this new template is applied in Figure 12-10.

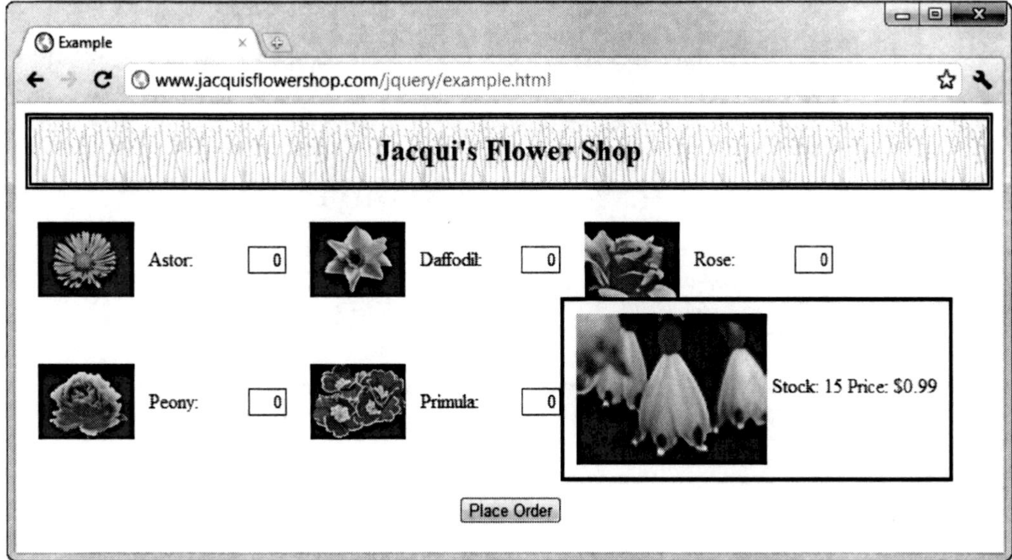

Figure 12-10. Using a different template when the mouse is over an element

The last statement in the handleMouse function is as follows:

```
$('div.dcell').unbind().bind(e.type == "mouseenter" ? "mouseleave" : "mouseenter",
    handleMouse);
```

When you change the template, the elements that were previous generated are removed from the document and replaced by those generated by the new template. This means that any event handlers are removed as well. There is an unfortunate interaction between the template library and the core jQuery library, which means that the live method (described in Chapter 9) doesn't work properly and so you must take care to add back the handlers you require.

Changing the Data Used by a Template

You can modify the data used by a template and have the template engine regenerate the elements using the new values. Listing 12-25 provides an example.

Listing 12-25. Modifying the Data Used by a Template

```
...
<script type="text/javascript">
    $(document).ready(function() {

        var data = [
            { name: "Astor", product: "astor", stocklevel: "10", price: "2.99"},
            { name: "Daffodil", product: "daffodil", stocklevel: "12", price: "1.99"},
            { name: "Rose", product: "rose", stocklevel: "2", price: "4.99"},
            { name: "Peony", product: "peony", stocklevel: "0", price: "1.50"},
            { name: "Primula", product: "primula", stocklevel: "1", price: "3.12"},
            { name: "Snowdrop", product: "snowdrop", stocklevel: "15", price: "0.99"},
        ];

        var templResult = $('#flowerTmpl').tmpl(data);
        templResult.slice(0, 3).appendTo('#row1');
        templResult.slice(3).appendTo("#row2"); ;

        $('<button>Modify Data</button>').prependTo("#buttonDiv").click(function(e) {
            var item = $.tmplItem($('div.dcell').first());
            item.data.product = "orchid";
            item.data.name = "Orchid";
            item.update();
            e.preventDefault();
        });
    });
</script>
<script id="flowerTmpl" type="text/x-jquery-tmpl">
    <div class="dcell">
        <img src="${product}.png"/>
        <label for="${product}">${name}: </label>
        <input name="${product}" value="0" required />
    </div>
</script>
...
```

In this example, I add a button to the document. When the button is clicked, I obtain the template item for the first element that matches the `div.dcell` selector and then use the data property to make changes to the data objects:

```
var item = $.tmplItem($('div.dcell').first());
item.data.product = "orchid";
item.data.name = "Orchid";
```

I then call the update method to regenerate the content using the new values. You can see the effect in Figure 12-11.

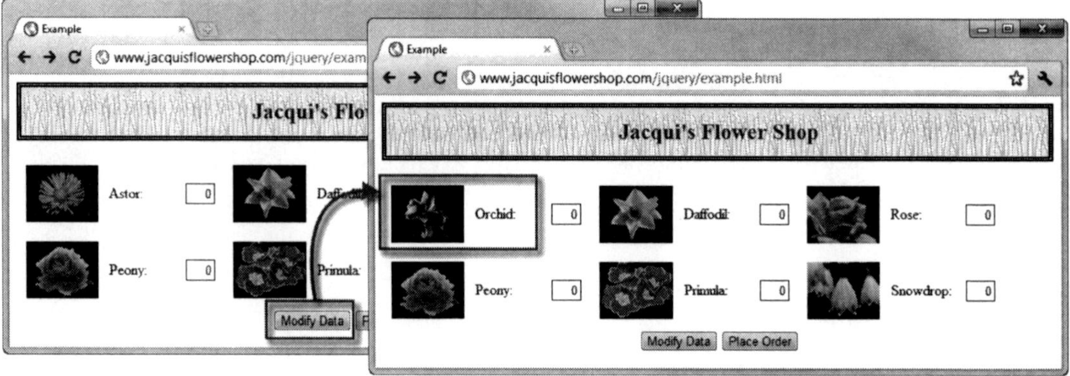

Figure 12-11. Changing the data associated with a template

If you still have a reference to the original data object, you can achieve the same effect by applying changed directly, as shown in Listing 12-26.

Listing 12-26. Changing the Values of the Data Object Directly

```
...
<script type="text/javascript">
    $(document).ready(function() {

        var data = [
            { name: "Astor", product: "astor", stocklevel: "10", price: "2.99"},
            { name: "Daffodil", product: "daffodil", stocklevel: "12", price: "1.99"},
            { name: "Rose", product: "rose", stocklevel: "2", price: "4.99"},
            { name: "Peony", product: "peony", stocklevel: "0", price: "1.50"},
            { name: "Primula", product: "primula", stocklevel: "1", price: "3.12"},
            { name: "Snowdrop", product: "snowdrop", stocklevel: "15", price: "0.99"},
        ];

        var templResult = $('#flowerTmpl').tmpl(data);
        templResult.slice(0, 3).appendTo('#row1');
        templResult.slice(3).appendTo("#row2"); ;

        data[0].name = "Orchid";
        data[0].product = "orchid";

        $('<button>Modify Data</button>').prependTo("#buttonDiv").click(function(e) {
            var item = $.tmplItem($('div.dcell').first()).update();
            e.preventDefault();
        });
    });
</script>
...
```

Summary

In this chapter, I introduced the jQuery template library, which gives you a nice set of features for translating JavaScript data into HTML elements without getting bogged down in a mass of nasty code. Even though the status of this plugin is uncertain, it is still extremely useful and widely used, and although it is not perfect, I recommend its use because it is so very convenient and powerful.

CHAPTER 13

Working with Forms

In this chapter, I will show you the support that jQuery provides for working with HTML forms. In part, I will recap the form-related events and the jQuery methods you can use to manage them, but most of this chapter is dedicated to a plugin that provides a great mechanism for validating the values that users enter into a form before it is submitted to a server. If you have written any kind of form-based web application, you will have realized that users will enter all sorts of data into a form, so validation is an important process.

I begin this chapter by introducing the `Node.js` server script that you will use in this part of the book. For this chapter, the script doesn't do a great deal other than show you the data values that were entered into the form, but in later chapters you'll start to rely on `Node.js` a little more. Table 13-1 provides the summary for this chapter.

***Table 13-1.** Chapter Summary*

Problem	Solution	Listing
Set up the `Node.js` server.	Use the script listed in this chapter (and included in the source code that accompanies this book).	1, 2
Respond to the focus being gained or lost by a `form` element.	Use the `focus` and `blur` methods.	3
Respond to changes in the value that the user has entered into a `form` element.	Use the `change` method.	4
Respond to (and interrupt) the user submitting the form.	Use the `submit` method.	5, 6
Validate the values in a form.	Use the validation plugin.	7
Configure the validation plugin.	Pass a map object to the `validate` method.	8
Define and apply validation rules using a class.	Use the `addClassRules` and `addClass` methods.	9–12

Apply validation rules directly to elements.	Use the `rules` method.	13, 14
Apply validation rules using element names.	Add a `rules` property to the `options` object.	15
Apply validation rules using element attributes.	Define attributes that correspond to individual validation checks.	16
Define custom messages for rules applied via element names and attributes.	Add a `message` property to the options object, set to a map object that defines the custom messages.	17, 18
Define custom messages for rules applied directly to elements.	Include a map object defining the messages as an argument to the `rules` method.	19
Create a custom validation check.	Use the `addMethod` method.	20, 21
Format the validation messages.	Use the `highlight`, `unhighlight`, `errorElement`, and `errorClass` properties of the `options` object.	22–26
Use a validation summary.	Use the `errorContainer` and `errorLabelContainer` properties.	27

Preparing the Node.js Server

In this chapter, you will be using `Node.js` to receive and process form data from the browser. I don't want to get drawn into the details of how `Node.js` functions, but one of the reasons that I selected it for this book was because `Node.js` is built around JavaScript, which means you can use the same skills for server-side programming as you do for client-side programming.

■ **Tip** If you want to re-create the example in this chapter, then you should see Chapter 1 for details of how to obtain `Node.js` and the additional module that I rely on. You can download the server-side script along with all of the HTML documents from Apress.com.

Listing 13-1 shows the server-side script that you will use in this chapter. I present this as a black box and explain only the inputs and output.

Listing 13-1. The formserver.js Node.js Script

```
var http = require('http');
var querystring = require('querystring');

http.createServer(function (req, res) {
    console.log("[200 OK] " + req.method + " to " + req.url);

    if (req.method == 'POST') {
        var dataObj = new Object();
        var contentType = req.headers["content-type"];
        var fullBody = '';

        if (contentType) {
            if (contentType.indexOf("application/x-www-form-urlencoded") > -1) {
                req.on('data', function(chunk) { fullBody += chunk.toString();});
                req.on('end', function() {
                    res.writeHead(200, "OK", {'Content-Type': 'text/html'});
                    res.write('<html><head><title>Post data</title></head><body>');
                    res.write('<style>th, td {text-align:left; padding:5px; color:black}\n');
                    res.write('th {background-color:grey; color:white; min-width:10em}\n');
                    res.write('td {background-color:lightgrey}\n');
                    res.write('caption {font-weight:bold}</style>');
                    res.write('<table border="1"><caption>Form Data</caption>');
                    res.write('<tr><th>Name</th><th>Value</th>');
                    var dBody = querystring.parse(fullBody);
                    for (var prop in dBody) {
                    res.write("<tr><td>" + prop + "</td><td>" + dBody[prop] + "</td></tr>");
                    }
                    res.write('</table></body></html>');
                    res.end();
                });
            }
        }
    }
}).listen(80);
console.log("Ready on port 80");
```

To run this script, I enter the following at the command line:

```
node.exe formserver.js
```

The command will be different if you are using another operating system. See the `Node.js` documentation for details. To demonstrate the `Node.js` functionality you'll use in this chapter, you need to turn to your example document, which is shown in Listing 13-2.

Listing 13-2. The Example Document for This Chapter

```
<!DOCTYPE html>
```

```
<html>
<head>
    <title>Example</title>
    <script src="jquery-1.7.js" type="text/javascript"></script>
    <script src="jquery.tmpl.js" type="text/javascript"></script>
    <link rel="stylesheet" type="text/css" href="styles.css"/>
    <script type="text/javascript">
        $(document).ready(function() {

            var data = [
               { name: "Astor", product: "astor", stocklevel: "10", price: "2.99"},
               { name: "Daffodil", product: "daffodil", stocklevel: "12", price: "1.99"},
               { name: "Rose", product: "rose", stocklevel: "2", price: "4.99"},
               { name: "Peony", product: "peony", stocklevel: "0", price: "1.50"},
               { name: "Primula", product: "primula", stocklevel: "1", price: "3.12"},
               { name: "Snowdrop", product: "snowdrop", stocklevel: "15", price: "0.99"},
            ];

            var templResult = $('#flowerTmpl').tmpl(data);
            templResult.slice(0, 3).appendTo('#row1');
            templResult.slice(3).appendTo("#row2");

        });
    </script>
    <script id="flowerTmpl" type="text/x-jquery-tmpl">
        <div class="dcell">
            <img src="${product}.png"/>
            <label for="${product}">${name}: </label>
            <input name="${product}" value="0" required />
        </div>
    </script>
</head>
<body>
    <h1>Jacqui's Flower Shop</h1>
    <form method="post" action="http://node.jacquisflowershop.com/order">
        <div id="oblock">
            <div class="dtable">
                <div id="row1" class="drow">
                </div>
                <div id="row2"class="drow">
                </div>
            </div>
        </div>
        <div id="buttonDiv"><button type="submit">Place Order</button></div>
    </form>
</body>
</html>
```

The individual product elements are generated using data templates (as described in Chapter 12). I have specified a value for the action attribute of the form element, which means it will post to the following URL:

```
http://node.jacquisflowershop.com/order
```

I am using two different servers. The first server (`www.jacquisflowershop.com`) is the one you have been using throughout this book. It delivers the static content such as HTML documents, scripts files, and images. For me, this is Microsoft's IIS 7.5, but you can use any server that appeals to you (I use IIS because a lot of my books are about Microsoft web programming technologies, and I already have a server set up and ready to go).

The second server (`node.jacquisflowershop.com`) runs `Node.js` (using the script shown previously), and when you submit the `form` in the example document, this is where the data will be sent. In this chapter, you don't care a great deal about what the server does with the data it receives. You are focused on the form itself. In Figure 13-1, you can see that I have entered some values into the `input` elements in the document.

Figure 13-1. Entering data into the input elements

When I click the Place Order button, the form is submitted to the `Node.js` server, and a simple response is sent back to the browser, as shown in Figure 13-2.

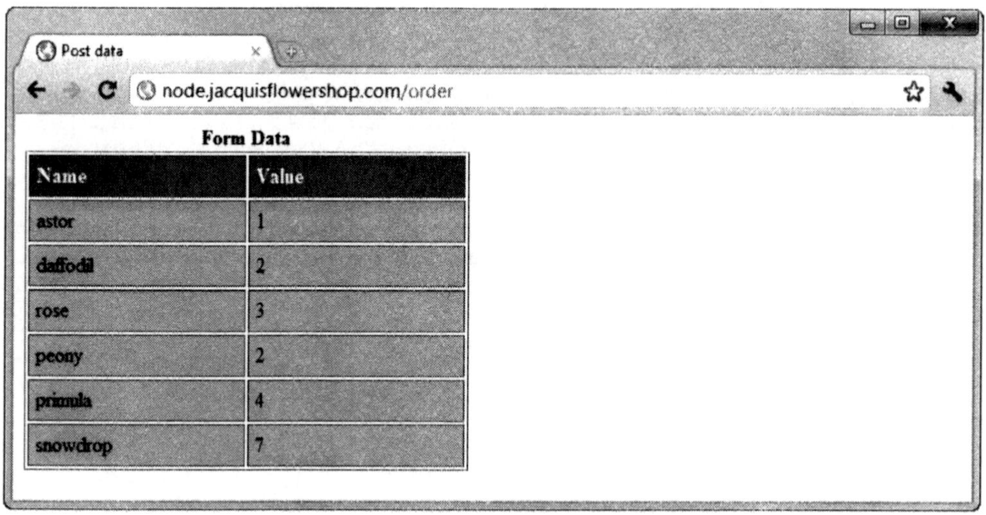

Figure 13-2. The response from the Node.js server

I know this is not a very interesting response, but you just need somewhere to send the data for now, and I don't want to get drawn off-track into the world of server development.

Recapping the Form Event Methods

As I mentioned in Chapter 9, there are a set of jQuery methods that deal with form-related events. It is worth recapping these now that you are specifically looking at forms. Table 13-2 describes the methods and the events to which they correspond.

■ **Tip** Don't forget that jQuery defines a set of extension selectors that match form elements. See Chapter 5 for details.

***Table 13-2.** The jQuery Form-Event Methods*

Method	Event	Description
`blur(function)`	`blur`	Triggered when a `form` element loses the focus
`change(function)`	`change`	Triggered when the value of a `form` element changes
`focus(function)`	`focus`	Triggered when the focus is given to a `form` element

select(function)	select	Triggered when the user selects text within a form element
submit(function)	submit	Triggered when the user wants to submit the form

Dealing with Form Focus

The blur and focus methods allow you to respond to changes in the focus. A common use for these features is to help the user by emphasizing which element has the focus (and thus which element will receive input from the keyboard). Listing 13-3 provides a demonstration.

Listing 13-3. Managing Form Element Focus

```
...
<script type="text/javascript">
$(document).ready(function() {
    var data = [
       { name: "Astor", product: "astor", stocklevel: "10", price: "2.99"},
       { name: "Daffodil", product: "daffodil", stocklevel: "12", price: "1.99"},
       { name: "Rose", product: "rose", stocklevel: "2", price: "4.99"},
       { name: "Peony", product: "peony", stocklevel: "0", price: "1.50"},
       { name: "Primula", product: "primula", stocklevel: "1", price: "3.12"},
       { name: "Snowdrop", product: "snowdrop", stocklevel: "15", price: "0.99"},
    ];

    var templResult = $('#flowerTmpl').tmpl(data);
    templResult.slice(0, 3).appendTo('#row1');
    templResult.slice(3).appendTo("#row2");

    $('input').focus(handleFormFocus).blur(handleFormFocus);

    function handleFormFocus(e) {
        var borderVal = e.type == "focus" ? "medium solid green" : "";
        $(this).css("border", borderVal);
    }

});
</script>...
```

In this example, I select all of the input elements and register the handleFormFocus function as the handler for both the focus and blur events. The function applies a green border when an element gains the focus and removes it when the focus is lost. You can see the effect in Figure 13-3.

Figure 13-3. Emphasizing the focused element

Notice that I used the `input` selector. In other words, I selected the elements by tag. jQuery provides the extension selector `:input` (I described the extension selectors in Chapter 5). This extension selector matches elements more broadly in some browsers, and in particular, it will match button elements that are capable of submitting the form, which means if you use the extension selector, your border will be applied to the `button` as well as the actual `input` elements. You can see the difference when the button is focused in Figure 13-4.

Figure 13-4. The difference between the input and :input selectors

Which selector you use is a matter for personal preference, but it is useful to be aware of the difference.

Dealing with Value Changes

The change event is triggered when the user changes the value in a `form` element. This is a particularly useful event if you are providing cumulative information based on the values in the form. Listing 13-4 shows how you can use this event to track the total number of items selected in the flower shop document. This is the same approach I took when I refactored the example at the end of Part II of this book.

Listing 13-4. Responding to the Change Event

```
...
<script type="text/javascript">
$(document).ready(function() {
    var data = [
       { name: "Astor", product: "astor", stocklevel: "10", price: "2.99"},
       { name: "Daffodil", product: "daffodil", stocklevel: "12", price: "1.99"},
       { name: "Rose", product: "rose", stocklevel: "2", price: "4.99"},
       { name: "Peony", product: "peony", stocklevel: "0", price: "1.50"},
       { name: "Primula", product: "primula", stocklevel: "1", price: "3.12"},
       { name: "Snowdrop", product: "snowdrop", stocklevel: "15", price: "0.99"},
    ];

    var templResult = $('#flowerTmpl').tmpl(data);
    templResult.slice(0, 3).appendTo('#row1');
    templResult.slice(3).appendTo("#row2");

    $('input').focus(handleFormFocus).blur(handleFormFocus);

    function handleFormFocus(e) {
        var borderVal = e.type == "focus" ? "medium solid green" : "";
        $(this).css("border", borderVal);
    }

    var total = $('#buttonDiv')
        .prepend("<div>Total Items: <span id=total>0</span></div>")
        .css({clear: "both", padding: "5px"});
    $('<div id=bbox />').appendTo("body").append(total).css("clear: left");

    $('input').change(function(e) {
        var total = 0;
        $('input').each(function(index, elem) {
            total += Number($(elem).val());
        });
        $('#total').text(total);
    });
});
</script>
...
```

In this example, I respond to the change event by totaling the values in all of the `input` elements and displaying the result in the span element that I had previously added to the document.

■ **Tip** Notice that I use the `val` method to get the value from the `input` elements.

Dealing with Form Submission

A lot of the more advanced activities you can perform with forms arise from the way you can prevent the browser's default form mechanism from working. Listing 13-5 provides a simple demonstration.

Listing 13-5. Intercepting the Form Submission

```
...
<script type="text/javascript">
$(document).ready(function() {
    var data = [
        { name: "Astor", product: "astor", stocklevel: "10", price: "2.99"},
        { name: "Daffodil", product: "daffodil", stocklevel: "12", price: "1.99"},
        { name: "Rose", product: "rose", stocklevel: "2", price: "4.99"},
        { name: "Peony", product: "peony", stocklevel: "0", price: "1.50"},
        { name: "Primula", product: "primula", stocklevel: "1", price: "3.12"},
        { name: "Snowdrop", product: "snowdrop", stocklevel: "15", price: "0.99"},
    ];

    var templResult = $('#flowerTmpl').tmpl(data);
    templResult.slice(0, 3).appendTo('#row1');
    templResult.slice(3).appendTo("#row2");

    $('form').submit(function (e) {
        if ($('input').val() == 0) {
            e.preventDefault();
        }
    });
});
</script>...
```

In this script, I register an inline function for the `submit` event. This event will be triggered when the user clicks the Place Order button. If the value of the first `input` element is `0`, I call the `preventDefault` method to interrupt the default action of the form, which is to submit the data to the server. For any other value, the form is submitted.

■ **Tip** As an alternative, you can return `false` from the function to achieve the same effect.

There are ways in which the form can be programmatically submitted. You can use the jQuery `submit` method without any arguments, and you can use the `submit` method, which is defined for `form` elements by the HTML5 specification. Listing 13-6 shows both approaches in use.

Listing 13-6. Explicitly Submitting a Form

```
...
<script type="text/javascript">
$(document).ready(function() {
    var data = [
        { name: "Astor", product: "astor", stocklevel: "10", price: "2.99"},
        { name: "Daffodil", product: "daffodil", stocklevel: "12", price: "1.99"},
        { name: "Rose", product: "rose", stocklevel: "2", price: "4.99"},
        { name: "Peony", product: "peony", stocklevel: "0", price: "1.50"},
        { name: "Primula", product: "primula", stocklevel: "1", price: "3.12"},
        { name: "Snowdrop", product: "snowdrop", stocklevel: "15", price: "0.99"},
    ];

    var templResult = $('#flowerTmpl').tmpl(data);
    templResult.slice(0, 3).appendTo('#row1');
    templResult.slice(3).appendTo("#row2");

    $('form').submit(function (e) {
        if ($('input').val() == 0) {
            e.preventDefault();
        }
    });

    $('<button>DOM API</button>').appendTo('#buttonDiv').click(function (e) {
        document.getElementsByTagName("form")[0].submit();
        e.preventDefault();
    });

    $('<button>jQuery Method</button>').appendTo('#buttonDiv').click(function (e) {
        $('form').submit();
        e.preventDefault();
    });
});
</script>...
```

I have added two buttons to the document. The one that uses the jQuery submit method ends up calling your handler function, and if the value of the first input element is zero, the form won't be submitted. However, the button that uses the DOM API and calls the submit method defined by the form element bypasses your event handler, and the form will always be submitted.

■ **Tip** My advice is to stick to the jQuery methods, of course, but if you do use the DOM method, at least you will understand the results you get.

Validating Form Values

The main reason for interrupting and preventing the browser from submitting data to the server is that you want to *validate* the values that a user has entered into the form. At some point, every web programmer realizes that users will type any old crap into an `input` element. There are an infinite number of different values you might have to process, but in my experience there are only a few reasons why the user gives you something unexpected in a form.

The first reason is that the user doesn't understand what data you are after. You might have asked for the name on the credit card, but the user might have entered their card number, for example.

The second reason is that the user doesn't want to give you the information you have requested and is just trying to get through the form as quickly as possible. They'll enter anything that will move them to the next stage in the process. If you have a lot of new users whose e-mail address is `a@a.com`, then you know that this is the problem.

The third reason is that you are asking for information the user doesn't have, such as asking a UK resident which state they live in. (We don't have states here. I am looking at you, NPR. No donation for you.)

The final reason is that the user has made a genuine mistake, typically a typo. For example, I am a quick but inaccurate typist, and I often type my surname as `Freman` instead of `Freeman`, missing out an e.

There is nothing you can do about typos, but the way that you deal with the other three reasons can make the difference between creating a smooth and seamless application and something that annoys and angers users.

I don't want to get into a long rant about the design of web forms, but I do want to say that the best way of approaching this issue is to focus on what the user is trying to achieve. And when things go wrong, try to see the problem (and the required resolution) the way the user sees it. Your users don't know about how you have built your systems, and they don't know about your business processes; they just want to get something done. Everyone can be happy if you keep the focus on the task the user is trying to complete and don't needlessly punish them when they don't give you the data you want.

jQuery provides you with all the tools you need to create your own system to validate data values, but I recommend a different approach. One of the most popular jQuery plugins is called Validation, and as you guess from the name, it handles form validation.

■ **Caution** What I am discussing in this chapter is *client-side validation*. This is a complement to rather than a replacement for *server-side validation*, where you check the data as it is received by the server. Client-side validation is for the benefit of the *user*: to stop them from having to make repeated submissions to the server to discover and correct data errors. Server-side validation is for the benefit of the *application* and ensures that bad data doesn't cause problems. You must use both: it is trivial to bypass client-side validation, and it does not provide reliable protection for your application.

You can download the Validation plugin from `http://bassistance.de/jquery-plugins/jquery-plugin-validation` or use the version that I included in the source code download for this book (available at Apress.com). Listing 13-7 shows the use of this plugin.

■ **Tip** There are a lot of different configuration options for the validation plugin. In this chapter, I have focused on those that are most frequently used and that cover the broadest range of situations. If they don't suit you, I suggest exploring some of the other options, which are described in the documentation available in the plugin download.

Listing 13-7. Using the Form Validation Plugin

```
<!DOCTYPE html>
<html>
<head>
    <title>Example</title>
    <script src="jquery-1.7.js" type="text/javascript"></script>
    <script src="jquery.tmpl.js" type="text/javascript"></script>
    <script src="jquery.validate.js" type="text/javascript"></script>
    <link rel="stylesheet" type="text/css" href="styles.css"/>
    <style type="text/css">
        div.errorMsg {color: red}
        .invalidElem {border: medium solid red}
    </style>
    <script type="text/javascript">
    $(document).ready(function() {

            var data = [
                { name: "Astor", product: "astor", stocklevel: "10", price: "2.99"},
                { name: "Daffodil", product: "daffodil", stocklevel: "12", price: "1.99"},
                { name: "Rose", product: "rose", stocklevel: "2", price: "4.99"},
                { name: "Peony", product: "peony", stocklevel: "0", price: "1.50"},
                { name: "Primula", product: "primula", stocklevel: "1", price: "3.12"},
                { name: "Snowdrop", product: "snowdrop", stocklevel: "15", price: "0.99"},
            ];

            var templResult = $('#flowerTmpl').tmpl(data);
            templResult.slice(0, 3).appendTo('#row1');
            templResult.slice(3).appendTo("#row2");

            $('form').validate({
                highlight: function(element, errorClass) {
                    $(element).add($(element).parent()).addClass("invalidElem");
                },
                unhighlight: function(element, errorClass) {
                    $(element).add($(element).parent()).removeClass("invalidElem");
                },
                errorElement: "div",
                errorClass: "errorMsg"
            });

            $.validator.addClassRules({
                flowerValidation: {
```

```
                    min: 0
                }
            })

            $('input').addClass("flowerValidation").change(function(e) {
                $('form').validate().element($(e.target));
            });

    });
    </script>
    <script id="flowerTmpl" type="text/x-jquery-tmpl">
        <div class="dcell">
            <img src="${product}.png"/>
            <label for="${product}">${name}: </label>
            <input name="${product}" value="0" required />
        </div>
    </script>
</head>
<body>
    <h1>Jacqui's Flower Shop</h1>
    <form method="post" action="http://node.jacquisflowershop.com/order">
        <div id="oblock">
            <div class="dtable">
                <div id="row1" class="drow">
                </div>
                <div id="row2"class="drow">
                </div>
            </div>
        </div>
        <div id="buttonDiv"><button type="submit">Place Order</button></div>
    </form>
</body>
</html>
```

■ **Note** HTML5 includes support for some basic form validation. It is a good start, but it is pretty basic, and there are still some significant differences in the way that browsers interpret the specification. Until the scope, richness, and consistency of the HTML5 features improves, I recommend sticking with jQuery for form validation.

Importing the JavaScript File

The first thing you have to do is bring the template plugin into the document, as follows:

```
...
<script src="jquery.validate.js" type="text/javascript"></script>
...
```

I have used the debug version of the file, but there is a minimized version available as well, and some, but not all, of the CDN services host this file because it is so popular.

Configuring the Validation

The next step is to configure the validation of the form element, which you do by calling the validate method on the form elements on which you want to perform validation. The argument to the validate method is a map object that contains configuration settings, as shown in Listing 13-8.

Listing 13-8. Configuring the Validation

```
...
$('form').validate({
    highlight: function(element, errorClass) {
        $(element).add($(element).parent()).addClass("invalidElem");
    },
    unhighlight: function(element, errorClass) {
        $(element).add($(element).parent()).removeClass("invalidElem");
    },
    errorElement: "div",
    errorClass: "errorMsg"
});
...
```

I have specified values for four options (highlight, unhighlight, errorElement, and errorClass); I'll come back to these later in the chapter and explain their meaning.

Defining the Validation Rules

A lot of the flexibility of the validation plugin comes from the way that you can quickly and easily define rules to test for valid input. There are various ways of associating rules with elements. The one I tend to use works through classes. You define a set of rules and associate them with a class, and when the form is validated, the rules are applied to any form element that is a member of the specified class. I created only a single rule in the example, as shown in Listing 13-9.

Listing 13-9. Defining a Validation Rule

```
...
$.validator.addClassRules({
    flowerValidation: {
        min: 0
    }
})
...
```

In this case, I have created a new rule that will be applied to form elements that are members of the flowerValidation class. The rule is that the value should be equal to or greater than 0. I have expressed the condition in the rule using min. This is just one of a number of convenient predefined checks that the validation plugin provides, and I'll describe all of them later in the chapter.

Applying the Validation Rules

You associate the validation rules with the elements in the form by adding the element to the class you specified in the previous step. This gives you the ability to tailor the validation for different kinds of element in a form. For this example, all of the elements are to be treated the same, so I use jQuery to select all of the input elements and add them to the `flowerValidation` class, as shown in Listing 13-10.

Listing 13-10. Adding the Input Elements to the Class Associated with Validation

```
...
$('input').addClass("flowerValidation").change(function(e) {
    $('form').validate().element($(e.target));
});
...
```

I have also used a function bound to the change event to explicitly validate the element whose value has changed. This makes sure the user gets immediate feedback if they correct an error. You can see the effect of the validation plugin in Figure 13-5. To create this figure, I entered `-1` in the input field and clicked the Place Order button.

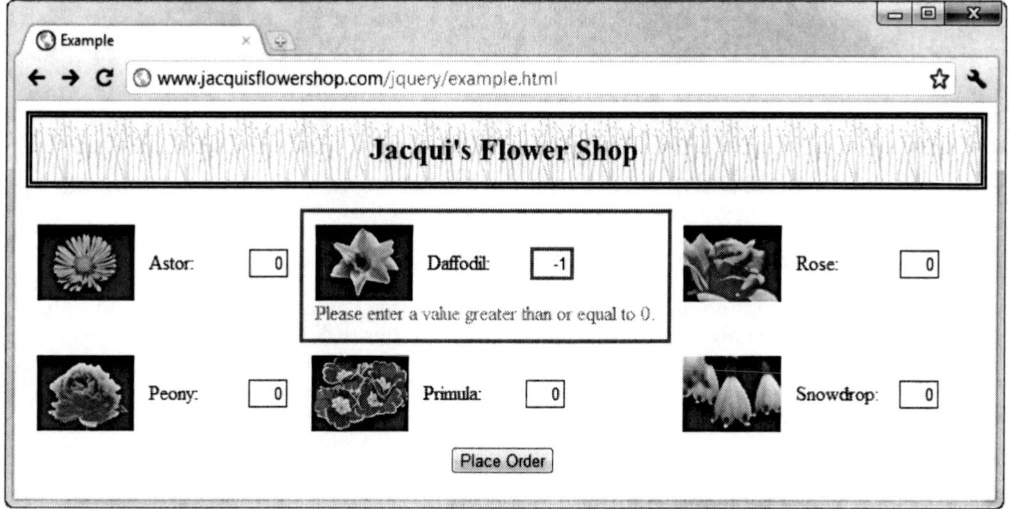

Figure 13-5. Using the validation plugin

■ **Tip** The text of the message shown to the user is generated by the validation plugin. I show you how to customize these messages later in the chapter.

Much like the homegrown validation I showed you earlier, the user can't submit the form until the problem has been resolved, but this time, the user can see which value or values are problematic and is given guidance as to how the problems can be resolved. (I accept that the message is a bit generic, but I'll show you how to change that later in the chapter.)

Using the Validation Checks

The Validation plugin supports a wide range of checks that you can use to validate form values. You saw the `min` check in the previous example. This ensures that the value is greater to or equal to a specified numeric value. Table 13-3 describes the set of checks you can perform.

Table 13-3. *Validation Plugin Checks*

Checks	Description
`creditcard: true`	The value must contain a credit card number.
`date: true`	The value must be a valid JavaScript date.
`digits: true`	The value must contain only digits.
`email: true`	The value must be a valid e-mail address.
`max: maxVal`	The value must be at least as large as `maxVal`.
`maxlength: length`	The value must contain no more than `length` characters.
`min: minVal`	The value must be at least as large as `minVal`.
`minlength: length;`	The value must contain at least `length` characters.
`number: true`	The value must be a decimal number.
`range: [minVal, maxVal]`	The value must be between `minVal` and `maxVal`.
`rangelength: [minLen, maxLen]`	The value must contain at least `minLen` and no more than `maxLen` characters.
`required: true;`	A value is required.
`url: true`	The value must be a URL.

You can associate multiple rules together in a single rule. This allows you to perform complex validations in a compact and expressive way.

■ **Tip** Included in the validation plugin distribution is a file called `additional-methods.js`. This file defines some additional checks, including U.S. and U.K. phone numbers, IPv4 and IPv6 addresses, and some additional date, e-mail, and URL formats.

You can apply these checks to your elements in several ways. I describe each in the sections that follow.

■ **Note** The Validation plugin also supports *remote validation*, where the data the user has entered into a field is checked using a remote server. This is useful when you need to check with data that cannot be distributed to the client, because it would be either insecure or impractical (such as checking that a username hasn't already been used). I demonstrate remote validation in Chapter 16, after I introduce the features it relies on in Chapters 14 and 15.

Applying Validation Rules via Classes

The technique I find myself using most frequently is applying checks through classes. This is the approach I took in the example. You are not limited to a single check, though. You can apply multiple checks together to validate different aspects of the value that the user provides, as demonstrated in Listing 13-11.

Listing 13-11. Combining Multiple Checks in a Single Rule

```
...
<script type="text/javascript">
$(document).ready(function() {

        var data = [
            { name: "Astor", product: "astor", stocklevel: "10", price: "2.99"},
            { name: "Daffodil", product: "daffodil", stocklevel: "12", price: "1.99"},
            { name: "Rose", product: "rose", stocklevel: "2", price: "4.99"},
            { name: "Peony", product: "peony", stocklevel: "0", price: "1.50"},
            { name: "Primula", product: "primula", stocklevel: "1", price: "3.12"},
            { name: "Snowdrop", product: "snowdrop", stocklevel: "15", price: "0.99"},
        ];

        var templResult = $('#flowerTmpl').tmpl(data);
        templResult.slice(0, 3).appendTo('#row1');
        templResult.slice(3).appendTo("#row2");


    $('form').validate({
        highlight: function(element, errorClass) {
```

```
            $(element).add($(element).parent()).addClass("invalidElem");
        },
        unhighlight: function(element, errorClass) {
            $(element).add($(element).parent()).removeClass("invalidElem");
        },
        errorElement: "div",
        errorClass: "errorMsg"
    });

    $.validator.addClassRules({
        flowerValidation: {
            required: true,
            digits: true,
            min: 0,
            max: 100
        }
    })

    $('input').addClass("flowerValidation").change(function(e) {
        $('form').validate().element($(e.target));
    });

});
</script>
...
```

In this example, I have combined the `required`, `digits`, `min`, and `max` checks to ensure that the user provides a value that comprises only digits and that falls within the range of 0 to 100.

Notice that I associate the rule with the class using the `addClassRules` method. The argument to this method is one or more sets of checks and the class name they are to be applied to. As shown, you call the `addClassRules` method on the `validator` property of the main jQuery $ function.

Each validated `form` element is assessed individually, which means the user can be presented with different error messages for different problems, as shown in Figure 13-6.

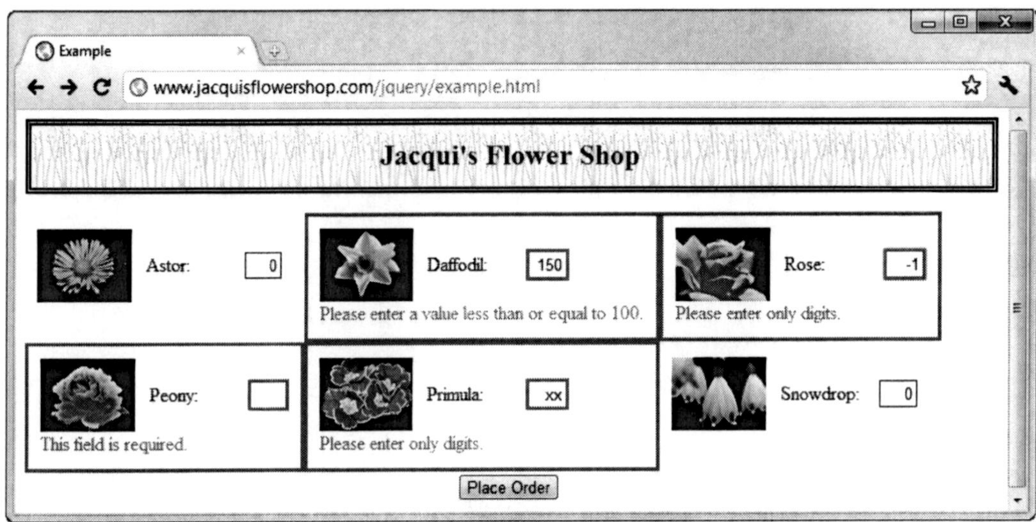

Figure 13-6. Applying multiple validation checks to form elements

I have entered several values that will fail one of the checks. It is important to note that the checks are performed in the order you defined them in the rule. If you look at the error message for the `Rose` product, you will see that it has failed the `digits` check. If you rearrange the order of the checks, you can get a different error. Listing 13-12 shows the revised order.

Listing 13-12. Changing the Order in Which Checks Are Applied

```
...
$.validator.addClassRules({
    flowerValidation: {
        required: true,
        min: 0,
        max: 100,
        digits: true
    }
})
...
```

In this example, I have moved the digits check to the end of the rule. If I enter `-1` into a form field now, it is the `min` check that will fail, as demonstrated by Figure 13-7.

Figure 13-7. Changing the order in which the checks are applied during validation

Applying Validation Rules Directly to Elements

The next technique allows you to apply rules to a single element, as shown in Listing 13-13.

Listing 13-13. Applying Validation Rules to the Elements in a Selection

```
...
<script type="text/javascript">
$(document).ready(function() {

        var data = [
            { name: "Astor", product: "astor", stocklevel: "10", price: "2.99"},
            { name: "Daffodil", product: "daffodil", stocklevel: "12", price: "1.99"},
            { name: "Rose", product: "rose", stocklevel: "2", price: "4.99"},
            { name: "Peony", product: "peony", stocklevel: "0", price: "1.50"},
            { name: "Primula", product: "primula", stocklevel: "1", price: "3.12"},
            { name: "Snowdrop", product: "snowdrop", stocklevel: "15", price: "0.99"},
        ];

        var templResult = $('#flowerTmpl').tmpl(data);
        templResult.slice(0, 3).appendTo('#row1');
        templResult.slice(3).appendTo("#row2");


    $('form').validate({
        highlight: function(element, errorClass) {
            $(element).add($(element).parent()).addClass("invalidElem");
        },
        unhighlight: function(element, errorClass) {
```

```
            $(element).add($(element).parent()).removeClass("invalidElem");
        },
        errorElement: "div",
        errorClass: "errorMsg"
    });

    $.validator.addClassRules({
        flowerValidation: {
            required: true,
            min: 0,
            max: 100,
            digits: true,
        }
    })

    $('#row1 input').each(function(index, elem) {
        $(elem).rules("add", {
            min: 10,
            max: 20
        })
    });

    $('input').addClass("flowerValidation").change(function(e) {
        $('form').validate().element($(e.target));
    });

});
</script>
...
```

Notice that you call the rules method on a jQuery object, passing in the string add and a map object with the checks you want to perform and their arguments. The rules method operates on only the first element in the selection, so you have to use the each method if you want to apply the rules more broadly. In this case, I selected all of the input elements that are descendants of the row1 element and applied a set of checks.

■ **Tip** You can remove rules from elements by replacing add with remove when you call the rules method.

Rules that are applied to elements using the rules methods are evaluated before those applied using a class. For my example, this means the input elements on the top row will be checked using a min value of 10 and a max value of 20, while the other input elements will use values of 0 and 100, respectively. You can see the effect of this in Figure 13-8.

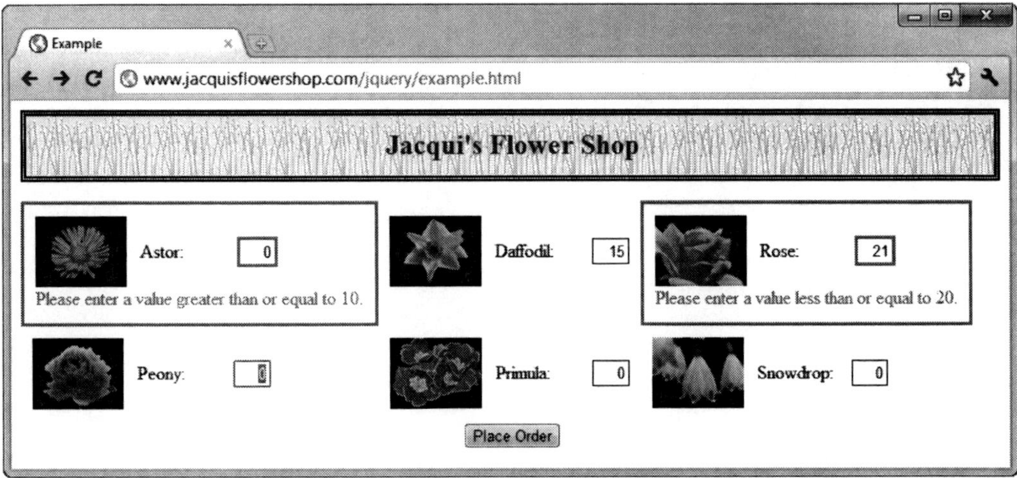

Figure 13-8. Applying rules directly to elements

Because you are dealing with each element individually, you can tailor the checks. Listing 13-14 gives an example.

Listing 13-14. Tailoring Checks for Elements

```
...
<script type="text/javascript">
$(document).ready(function() {

    var data = [
        { name: "Astor", product: "astor", stocklevel: "10", price: "2.99"},
        { name: "Daffodil", product: "daffodil", stocklevel: "12", price: "1.99"},
        { name: "Rose", product: "rose", stocklevel: "2", price: "4.99"},
        { name: "Peony", product: "peony", stocklevel: "0", price: "1.50"},
        { name: "Primula", product: "primula", stocklevel: "1", price: "3.12"},
        { name: "Snowdrop", product: "snowdrop", stocklevel: "15", price: "0.99"},
    ];

    var templResult = $('#flowerTmpl').tmpl(data);
    templResult.slice(0, 3).appendTo('#row1');
    templResult.slice(3).appendTo("#row2");


    $('form').validate({
        highlight: function(element, errorClass) {
            $(element).add($(element).parent()).addClass("invalidElem");
        },
        unhighlight: function(element, errorClass) {
            $(element).add($(element).parent()).removeClass("invalidElem");
        },
        errorElement: "div",
```

```
        errorClass: "errorMsg"
    });

    $('input').each(function(index, elem) {
        var rules = {
            required: true,
            min: 0,
            max: data[index].stocklevel,
            digits: true
        }
        if (Number(data[index].price) > 3.00) {
            rules.max--;
        }
        $(elem).rules("add", rules);
    });

    $('input').change(function(e) {
        $('form').validate().element($(e.target));
    });

});
</script>
...
```

In this example, I tailor the value of the `max` check using the data object that I added to the document to generate elements using the template. The value for the `max` check is set based on the `stocklevel` property and adjusted down if the price is greater than $3. When you have data like this, you are able to perform much more useful validation. You can see the effect of this change in Figure 13-9.

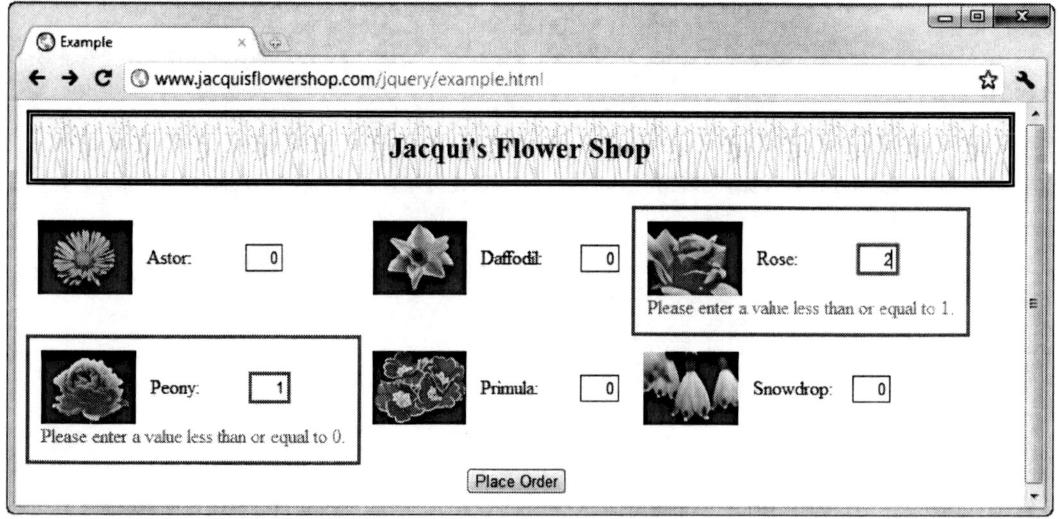

Figure 13-9. Setting different values for validation checks based on data

Applying Validation Rules via the Element Name Attribute

You can apply validation rules to elements based on the value of the name attribute. Nothing in the HTML specification requires the name attribute value to be unique, and a single value is often used to categorize a group of form elements. In my flower shop example document, each name is different and corresponds to a specific product. Either way, you can create rules that correspond to a name attribute value and rules that apply to all elements assigned that value. Listing 13-15 gives a demonstration.

Listing 13-15. Assigning Validation Rules Based on Element Name

```
...

<script type="text/javascript">
$(document).ready(function() {

    var data = [
        { name: "Astor", product: "astor", stocklevel: "10", price: "2.99"},
        { name: "Daffodil", product: "daffodil", stocklevel: "12", price: "1.99"},
        { name: "Rose", product: "rose", stocklevel: "2", price: "4.99"},
        { name: "Peony", product: "peony", stocklevel: "0", price: "1.50"},
        { name: "Primula", product: "primula", stocklevel: "1", price: "3.12"},
        { name: "Snowdrop", product: "snowdrop", stocklevel: "15", price: "0.99"},
    ];

    var templResult = $('#flowerTmpl').tmpl(data);
    templResult.slice(0, 3).appendTo('#row1');
    templResult.slice(3).appendTo("#row2");

    var rulesList = new Object();
    for (var i = 0; i < data.length; i++) {
        rulesList[data[i].product] = {
            min: 0,
            max: data[i].stocklevel,
        }
    }

    $('form').validate({
        highlight: function(element, errorClass) {
            $(element).add($(element).parent()).addClass("invalidElem");
        },
        unhighlight: function(element, errorClass) {
            $(element).add($(element).parent()).removeClass("invalidElem");
        },
        errorElement: "div",
        errorClass: "errorMsg",
        rules: rulesList
    });

    $('input').change(function(e) {
        $('form').validate().element($(e.target));
    });
```

```
});
</script>
...
```

You add rules that rely on element names using the rules property of the configuration object you pass to the validate method when you set up form validation. Notice that I have used just the data object to create the set of rules (and also notice that the product property in the data object is used to generate the name attribute on the input elements). I tend not to use this approach, since I would rather work directly with the elements in the document, but this technique can be handy if you have a data object and want to set up validation before the form elements have been added to the document.

Applying Validation Rules Using Element Attributes

The final way you can apply checks to attributes is to use elements. The validation plugin checks form elements to see whether they define attributes that correspond to the name of the built-in checks, so an element that defines a required attribute is assumed to need the required check. Listing 13-16 provides a demonstration.

Listing 13-16. Performing Validation Using Element Attributes

```
...
<script type="text/javascript">
$(document).ready(function() {

    var data = [
        { name: "Astor", product: "astor", stocklevel: "10", price: "2.99"},
        { name: "Daffodil", product: "daffodil", stocklevel: "12", price: "1.99"},
        { name: "Rose", product: "rose", stocklevel: "2", price: "4.99"},
        { name: "Peony", product: "peony", stocklevel: "0", price: "1.50"},
        { name: "Primula", product: "primula", stocklevel: "1", price: "3.12"},
        { name: "Snowdrop", product: "snowdrop", stocklevel: "15", price: "0.99"},
    ];

    var templResult = $('#flowerTmpl').tmpl(data);
    templResult.slice(0, 3).appendTo('#row1');
    templResult.slice(3).appendTo("#row2");


    $('form').validate({
        highlight: function(element, errorClass) {
            $(element).add($(element).parent()).addClass("invalidElem");
        },
        unhighlight: function(element, errorClass) {
            $(element).add($(element).parent()).removeClass("invalidElem");
        },
        errorElement: "div",
        errorClass: "errorMsg",
    });

    $('input').change(function(e) {
```

```
        $('form').validate().element($(e.target));
    });

});
</script>
<script id="flowerTmpl" type="text/x-jquery-tmpl">
    <div class="dcell">
        <img src="${product}.png"/>
        <label for="${product}">${name}: </label>
        <input name="${product}" value="0" required min="0" max="${stocklevel}"/>
    </div>
</script>
...
```

I like this technique when it is used in conjunction with a data template, but I find it clutters up a document when applied to statically defined elements, because the same attributes are applied to elements over and over again.

Specifying Validation Messages

The validation plugin defines a default error message for all of the built-in checks, but these are generic and not always useful to the user. As a simple example, if you set a `max` check with a value of `10` and the user enters `20` in the field, then the error message will be as follows:

```
Please enter a value less than or equal to 12
```

This message describes the constraint you have applied on a `form` element, but it doesn't provide any guidance to the user as to why there is a limit. Fortunately, you can change these messages to provide some additional context and tailor the message to your needs. The method you use to change the messages depends on how you created the validation rule in the first place. You can't change the messages when you apply rules using a class, but in the following sections I describe how to define messages for the other techniques.

Specifying Messages for Attribute and Name Validation

When you rely on the `name` attribute or on check attributes to associate rules with elements, you can change the messages by adding a `messages` property to the `options` object that you pass to the `validate` method when you set up validation. Listing 13-17 provides a demonstration.

Listing 13-17. Using the messages Property on the options Object

```
...
<script type="text/javascript">
$(document).ready(function() {

    var data = [
        { name: "Astor", product: "astor", stocklevel: "10", price: "2.99"},
        { name: "Daffodil", product: "daffodil", stocklevel: "12", price: "1.99"},
        { name: "Rose", product: "rose", stocklevel: "2", price: "4.99"},
        { name: "Peony", product: "peony", stocklevel: "0", price: "1.50"},
        { name: "Primula", product: "primula", stocklevel: "1", price: "3.12"},
```

```
        { name: "Snowdrop", product: "snowdrop", stocklevel: "15", price: "0.99"},
    ];

    var templResult = $('#flowerTmpl').tmpl(data);
    templResult.slice(0, 3).appendTo('#row1');
    templResult.slice(3).appendTo("#row2");


    $('form').validate({
        highlight: function(element, errorClass) {
            $(element).add($(element).parent()).addClass("invalidElem");
        },
        unhighlight: function(element, errorClass) {
            $(element).add($(element).parent()).removeClass("invalidElem");
        },
        errorElement: "div",
        errorClass: "errorMsg",
        messages: {
            rose: {
                max: "We don't have that many roses in stock!"
            },
            peony: {
                max: "We don't have that many peonies in stock!"
            }
        }
    });

    $('input').change(function(e) {
        $('form').validate().element($(e.target));
    });

});
</script>
...
```

You can see the structure of the object that you provide as the value for the messages property. You define a property using the name of the element you are interested in and set the value of this property to be a map between the check and the new message you want to use. In this example, I have changed the message for the max check on the elements with the names of rose and peony. You can see the effect in Figure 13-10. Both of these elements are shown with a tailored validation message.

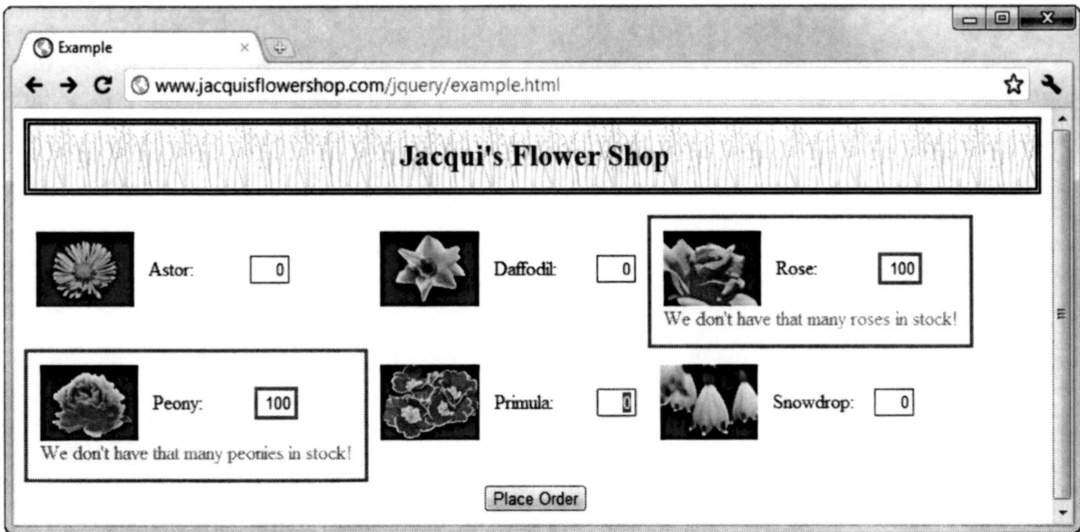

Figure 13-10. Changes messages via the options object

The syntax for setting up these validation messages can be highly duplicative, so I tend to create an object with the messages I want programmatically, as shown in Listing 13-18.

Listing 13-18. Defining Custom Messages Programmatically

```
...
<script type="text/javascript">
$(document).ready(function() {

    var data = [
        { name: "Astor", product: "astor", stocklevel: "10", price: "2.99"},
        { name: "Daffodil", product: "daffodil", stocklevel: "12", price: "1.99"},
        { name: "Rose", product: "rose", stocklevel: "2", price: "4.99"},
        { name: "Peony", product: "peony", stocklevel: "0", price: "1.50"},
        { name: "Primula", product: "primula", stocklevel: "1", price: "3.12"},
        { name: "Snowdrop", product: "snowdrop", stocklevel: "15", price: "0.99"},
    ];

    var templResult = $('#flowerTmpl').tmpl(data);
    templResult.slice(0, 3).appendTo('#row1');
    templResult.slice(3).appendTo("#row2");

    var customMessages = new Object();
    for (var i = 0; i < data.length; i++) {
        customMessages[data[i].product] = {
            max: "We only have " + data[i].stocklevel + " in stock"
        }
    }
```

```
    $('form').validate({
        highlight: function(element, errorClass) {
            $(element).add($(element).parent()).addClass("invalidElem");
        },
        unhighlight: function(element, errorClass) {
            $(element).add($(element).parent()).removeClass("invalidElem");
        },
        errorElement: "div",
        errorClass: "errorMsg",
        messages: customMessages
    });

    $('input').change(function(e) {
        $('form').validate().element($(e.target));
    });

});
</script>
...
```

In this example, I incorporate the stocklevel property from the data objects to give a more meaningful message to the user.

Specifying Messages for Per-Element Validation

When you apply rules to individual elements, you can pass in a messages object that defines the messages you want for your checks. Listing 13-19 shows how this is done.

Listing 13-19. Specifying Messages for Rules Applied on a Per-Element Basis

```
...
<script type="text/javascript">
$(document).ready(function() {

    var data = [
        { name: "Astor", product: "astor", stocklevel: "10", price: "2.99"},
        { name: "Daffodil", product: "daffodil", stocklevel: "12", price: "1.99"},
        { name: "Rose", product: "rose", stocklevel: "2", price: "4.99"},
        { name: "Peony", product: "peony", stocklevel: "0", price: "1.50"},
        { name: "Primula", product: "primula", stocklevel: "1", price: "3.12"},
        { name: "Snowdrop", product: "snowdrop", stocklevel: "15", price: "0.99"},
    ];

    var templResult = $('#flowerTmpl').tmpl(data);
    templResult.slice(0, 3).appendTo('#row1');
    templResult.slice(3).appendTo("#row2");

    $('form').validate({
        highlight: function(element, errorClass) {
            $(element).add($(element).parent()).addClass("invalidElem");
```

```
        },
        unhighlight: function(element, errorClass) {
            $(element).add($(element).parent()).removeClass("invalidElem");
        },
        errorElement: "div",
        errorClass: "errorMsg",
    });

    $('input').each(function(index, elem) {
        $(elem).rules("add", {
            min: 10,
            max: 20,
            messages: {
                max: "You only have " + data[index].stocklevel + " in stock"
            }
        })
    }).change(function(e) {
        $('form').validate().element($(e.target));
    });

});
</script>
...
```

Once again, I have used the stockvalue property to define the message. For simplicity, I have assumed that the input elements are ordered in the same way that the data items are ordered. You can see the effect of these messages in Figure 13-11.

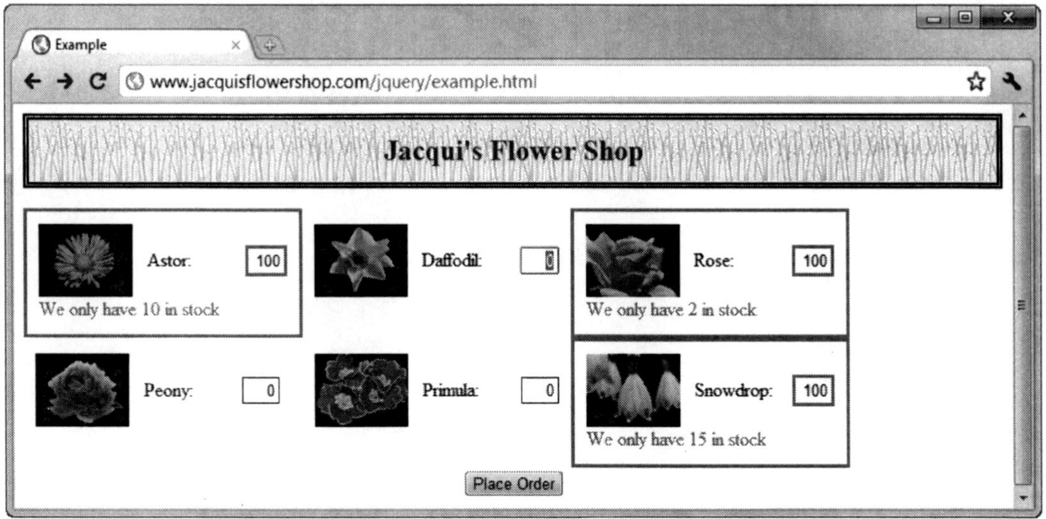

Figure 13-11. Specifying messages that are derived from the data object

Creating a Custom Check

You can create a custom validation check if the built-in ones don't suit your needs. This is a relatively simple process that means you can closely relate validation to the structure and nature of your web application. Listing 13-20 provides a demonstration.

Listing 13-20. Creating a Custom Validation Check

```
...
<script type="text/javascript">
$(document).ready(function() {

    var data = [
        { name: "Astor", product: "astor", stocklevel: "10", price: "2.99"},
        { name: "Daffodil", product: "daffodil", stocklevel: "12", price: "1.99"},
        { name: "Rose", product: "rose", stocklevel: "2", price: "4.99"},
        { name: "Peony", product: "peony", stocklevel: "0", price: "1.50"},
        { name: "Primula", product: "primula", stocklevel: "1", price: "3.12"},
        { name: "Snowdrop", product: "snowdrop", stocklevel: "15", price: "0.99"},
    ];

    var templResult = $('#flowerTmpl').tmpl(data);
    templResult.slice(0, 3).appendTo('#row1');
    templResult.slice(3).appendTo("#row2");

    $('form').validate({
        highlight: function(element, errorClass) {
            $(element).add($(element).parent()).addClass("invalidElem");
        },
        unhighlight: function(element, errorClass) {
            $(element).add($(element).parent()).removeClass("invalidElem");
        },
        errorElement: "div",
        errorClass: "errorMsg",
    });

    $.validator.addMethod("stock", function(value, elem, args) {
        return Number(value) < Number(args);
    }, "We don't have that many in stock");

    $('input').each(function(index, elem) {
        $(elem).rules("add", {
            min: 0,
            stock: data[index].stocklevel
        })
    }).change(function(e) {
        $('form').validate().element($(e.target));
    });

});
</script>
```

...

You define a custom check using the addMethod method, which is called on the validator property of the $ function. The arguments to this method are the name you want to assign the check, a function that is used to perform validation, and a message to show if validation fails. In this example, I have defined a check called stock.

Defining the Validation Function

The arguments to the custom validation function are the value entered by the user, the HTMLElement object representing the form element, and any arguments that were specified when the check is applied to an element for validation, like this:

```
...
$(elem).rules("add", {
    min: 0,
    stock: data[index].stocklevel
})
...
```

When I applied the rule, I specified the value of a stocklevel property as the argument to the check. This is passed as is to the custom validation function:

```
function(value, elem, args) {
    return Number(value) <= Number(args);
}
```

You signal if the value is valid through the result you return from the function. If the value is valid, you return true. If not, you return false. The value and the arguments are presented as strings, which means I have to use the Number type to ensure that JavaScript compares the values as numbers. For my function, a value is valid if it is smaller than or equal to the argument.

Defining the Validation Message

You can specify the message that is displayed in two ways. The first is as a string, which is what I used in the earlier example. The other way to specify a message is with a function, allowing you to create messages with a lot more context. Listing 13-21 provides a demonstration.

Listing 13-21. Creating a Message for a Custom Check Using a Function

```
...
<script type="text/javascript">
$(document).ready(function() {

    var data = [
        { name: "Astor", product: "astor", stocklevel: "10", price: "2.99"},
        { name: "Daffodil", product: "daffodil", stocklevel: "12", price: "1.99"},
        { name: "Rose", product: "rose", stocklevel: "2", price: "4.99"},
        { name: "Peony", product: "peony", stocklevel: "0", price: "1.50"},
        { name: "Primula", product: "primula", stocklevel: "1", price: "3.12"},
        { name: "Snowdrop", product: "snowdrop", stocklevel: "15", price: "0.99"},
```

```
        ];

        var templResult = $('#flowerTmpl').tmpl(data);
        templResult.slice(0, 3).appendTo('#row1');
        templResult.slice(3).appendTo("#row2");

        $('form').validate({
            highlight: function(element, errorClass) {
                $(element).add($(element).parent()).addClass("invalidElem");
            },
            unhighlight: function(element, errorClass) {
                $(element).add($(element).parent()).removeClass("invalidElem");
            },
            errorElement: "div",
            errorClass: "errorMsg",
        });

        $.validator.addMethod("stock", function(value, elem, args) {
            return Number(value) <= Number(args);
        }, function(args) {
            return "We only have " + args + " in stock"
        });

        $('input').each(function(index, elem) {
            $(elem).rules("add", {
                min: 0,
                stock: data[index].stocklevel
            })
        }).change(function(e) {
            $('form').validate().element($(e.target));
        });

    });
</script>
...
```

The argument to the function is the argument you provide when applying the rule. This is the value of the stocklevel property in this example. You can see the effect in Figure 13-12.

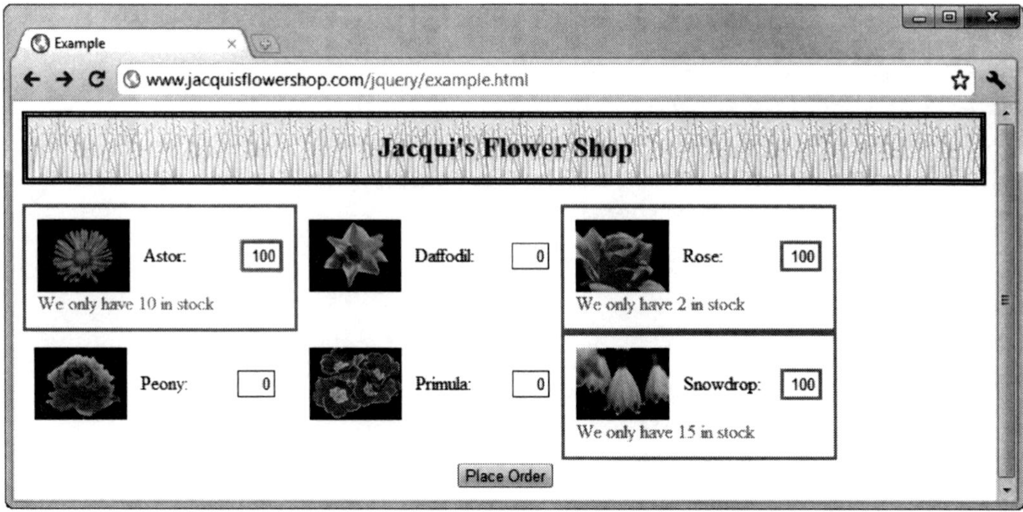

Figure 13-12. Defining error messages for custom checks using a function

Formatting the Validation Error Display

To my mind, one of the best features of the validation plugin is the wide range of ways that you can configure how validation error messages are displayed to the user. In the examples so far in this chapter, I have relied on the configuration options highlighted in Listing 13-22.

Listing 13-22. The Configuration Options for Formatting the Validation Errors

```
...
$(document).ready(function() {

    var data = [
        { name: "Astor", product: "astor", stocklevel: "10", price: "2.99"},
        { name: "Daffodil", product: "daffodil", stocklevel: "12", price: "1.99"},
        { name: "Rose", product: "rose", stocklevel: "2", price: "4.99"},
        { name: "Peony", product: "peony", stocklevel: "0", price: "1.50"},
        { name: "Primula", product: "primula", stocklevel: "1", price: "3.12"},
        { name: "Snowdrop", product: "snowdrop", stocklevel: "15", price: "0.99"},
    ];

    var templResult = $('#flowerTmpl').tmpl(data);
    templResult.slice(0, 3).appendTo('#row1');
    templResult.slice(3).appendTo("#row2");

    $('form').validate({
        highlight: function(element, errorClass) {
            $(element).add($(element).parent()).addClass("invalidElem");
        },
        unhighlight: function(element, errorClass) {
```

```
            $(element).add($(element).parent()).removeClass("invalidElem");
        },
        errorElement: "div",
        errorClass: "errorMsg",
    });

    $.validator.addMethod("stock", function(value, elem, args) {
        return Number(value) <= Number(args);
    }, function(args) {
        return "We only have " + args + " in stock"
    });

    $('input').each(function(index, elem) {
        $(elem).rules("add", {
            min: 0,
            stock: data[index].stocklevel
        })
    }).change(function(e) {
        $('form').validate().element($(e.target));
    });

});
</script>
...
```

I have relied on four different configuration options, but they are tightly coupled together. I explain the significance of each in the following sections.

Setting the Class for Invalid Elements

The errorClass option allows you to set a class that will be associated with invalid values. This class is applied to error messages when they are added to the document. In my examples, I specify a class called errorMsg, for which there is a corresponding selector in the style element, as shown in Listing 13-23.

Listing 13-23. The style Element for the Example Document

```
...
<style type="text/css">
    div.errorMsg {color: red}
    .invalidElem {border: medium solid red}
</style>
...
```

I have simply set the color property so that the validation text is shown in red.

Setting the Error Message Element

Error messages are inserted into the document as the immediate next sibling of the form element that contains the invalid value. By default, the error message text is contained within a label element. This didn't suit me in the examples, because the external style sheet contains a selector that matches all label elements within the cell-level div elements in the CSS table layout and applied a style that prevented the text from displaying properly. To address this, I used the errorElement option to specify that a div element be used instead, as shown in Listing 13-24.

Listing 13-24. Specifying the Element That Will Be Used for the Error Message

```
...
$('form').validate({
    highlight: function(element, errorClass) {
        $(element).add($(element).parent()).addClass("invalidElem");
    },
    unhighlight: function(element, errorClass) {
        $(element).add($(element).parent()).removeClass("invalidElem");
    },
    errorElement: "div",
    errorClass: "errorMsg",

});
...
```

Setting the Highlighting for Invalid Elements

The highlight and unhighlight options let you specify functions to use to highlight elements that contain invalid values. The arguments to the functions are the HTMLElement object representing the invalid element and whatever class you specified using the errorClass option. As you can see in the highlighted statements in Listing 13-25, I ignore the second attribute but use the HTMLElement object to create a jQuery selection, navigate to the parent element, and add it to the invalidElem class.

Listing 13-25. Controlling the Element Highlight

```
...
$('form').validate({
    highlight: function(element, errorClass) {
        $(element).add($(element).parent()).addClass("invalidElem");
    },
    unhighlight: function(element, errorClass) {
        $(element).add($(element).parent()).removeClass("invalidElem");
    },
    errorElement: "div",
    errorClass: "errorMsg",

});
...
```

The function specified by the unhighlight option is called when the user has corrected the problem and the element contains a valid value. I use this opportunity to remove the class I added in the other function. The invalidElem class corresponds to a selector in the style element contained in the document, as shown in Listing 13-26.

Listing 13-26. The Style Used for Highlighting Element

```
...
<style type="text/css">
    div.errorMsg {color: red}
    .invalidElem {border: medium solid red}
</style>
...
```

You can select and manipulate elements in these functions in any way you like. I have applied a border to the parent element to demonstrate the freedom you have in the DOM, but I could have operated directly on the element itself or on another part of the document entirely had I preferred.

Using a Validation Summary

You can present the user with a single list of all the validation errors, rather than add individual messages next to each element. This can be useful if the structure or layout of your document can't easily flex to accommodate additional elements. Listing 13-27 shows how you can create a validation summary.

Listing 13-27. Using a Validation Summary

```
...
<script type="text/javascript">
$(document).ready(function() {

    var data = [
        { name: "Astor", product: "astor", stocklevel: "10", price: "2.99"},
        { name: "Daffodil", product: "daffodil", stocklevel: "12", price: "1.99"},
        { name: "Rose", product: "rose", stocklevel: "2", price: "4.99"},
        { name: "Peony", product: "peony", stocklevel: "0", price: "1.50"},
        { name: "Primula", product: "primula", stocklevel: "1", price: "3.12"},
        { name: "Snowdrop", product: "snowdrop", stocklevel: "15", price: "0.99"},
    ];

    var plurals = {
        astor: "Astors",
        daffodil: "Daffodils",
        rose: "Roses",
        peony: "Peonies",
        primula: "Primulas",
        snowdrop: "Snowdrops"
    }

    var templResult = $('#flowerTmpl').tmpl(data);
    templResult.slice(0, 3).appendTo('#row1');
    templResult.slice(3).appendTo("#row2");

    $('<div id=errorSummary>Please correct the following errors:</div>')
        .append('<ul id="errorsList"></ul>').hide().insertAfter('h1');
```

```
    $('form').validate({
        highlight: function(element, errorClass) {
            $(element).addClass("invalidElem");
        },
        unhighlight: function(element, errorClass) {
            $(element).removeClass("invalidElem");
        },
        errorContainer: '#errorSummary',
        errorLabelContainer: '#errorsList',
        wrapper: 'li',
        errorElement: "div"
    });

    $.validator.addMethod("stock", function(value, elem, args) {
        return Number(value) <= Number(args.data.stocklevel);
    }, function(args) {
        return "You requested " + $(args.element).val() + " "
            + plurals[args.data.product] + " but you only have "
            + args.data.stocklevel + " in stock";
    });

    $('input').each(function(index, elem) {
        $(elem).rules("add", {
            min: 0,
            stock: {
                index: index,
                data: data[index],
                element: elem
            }
        })
    }).change(function(e) {
        $('form').validate().element($(e.target));
    });

});
</script>
...
```

For this example, I am going to work backward and show you the result before explaining how I get there. Figure 13-13 shows the validation summary being displayed.

Figure 13-13. Using a validation summary

Preparing the Validation Messages

The first issue to solve when using a validation summary is that the context that is implied by placing an error message next to a `form` element is lost; you have to put some additional work into the error messages so that they make sense. To start with, I defined an object that contained the plurals of the flower names:

```
var plurals = {
    astor: "Astors",
    daffodil: "Daffodils",
    rose: "Roses",
    peony: "Peonies",
    primula: "Primulas",
    snowdrop: "Snowdrops"
}
```

I use these values to generate a specific error message using the function feature of the custom check, like this:

```
$.validator.addMethod("stock", function(value, elem, args) {
    return Number(value) <= Number(args.data.stocklevel);
}, function(args) {
    return "You requested " + $(args.element).val() + " "
```

```
        + plurals[args.data.product] + " but you only have "
        + args.data.stocklevel + " in stock";
});
```

The link between these two stages is the argument object that I specify when applying the custom check to the form elements. The built-in checks have simple arguments, but you can create complex objects and pass whatever data suits you:

```
$('input').each(function(index, elem) {
    $(elem).rules("add", {
        min: 0,
        stock: {
            index: index,
            data: data[index],
            element: elem
        }
    })
}).change(function(e) {
    $('form').validate().element($(e.target));
});
```

I don't have access to all of the objects I would like in the message-generating functions, so I pass them via the argument. In this case, I have passed the index, the data array, and the element itself, all of which I use to piece together the message to display to the user.

Creating the Validation Summary

You are responsible for adding the element that will contain the validation summary and adding it to the document. I have added a div element that contains an ul element. My goal is to create an unnumbered list showing each error:

```
$('<div id=errorSummary>Please correct the following errors:</div>')
    .append('<ul id="errorsList"></ul>').hide().insertAfter('h1');
```

I have included some text in the div element. This will be displayed above the list of errors. I have emphasized the call to the hide method. You are responsible for making sure the element isn't visible. This isn't compulsory. The element can be visible all of the time, but I think it is good practice only to show a validation summary when there are errors for the user to resolve.

Now that you have all the pieces in place, you can turn to the options that you use to configure the validation summary:

```
$('form').validate({
    highlight: function(element, errorClass) {
        $(element).addClass("invalidElem");
    },
    unhighlight: function(element, errorClass) {
        $(element).removeClass("invalidElem");
    },
    errorContainer: '#errorSummary',
    errorLabelContainer: '#errorsList',
    wrapper: 'li',
    errorElement: "div"
```

```
});
```

I have tightened the focus of the hightlight and unhighlight functions so that only the input element is highlighted, but the important options are highlighted.

The errorContainer option specifies a selector that will be made visible when there are validation errors to display. In my case, this is the element with the errorSummary ID (the div element).

The errorLabelContainer option specifies the element into which the individual error messages will be inserted. For my example, this is the ul element, since I want my messages displayed as a list.

The wrapper option specifies an element into which the validation message will be inserted. This is really useful only if you want a list display. Finally, the errorElement specifies the element that will contain the error text. This is the label element by default, but I have switched to div elements to make the formatting easier. The result of these options is the validation summary that is shown in Figure 13-13.

The validation plugin removes messages when the user resolves an issue, and when there are no issues at all, the user can submit the form. Figure 13-14 shows the validation summary after two of the three errors from the last figure have been resolved.

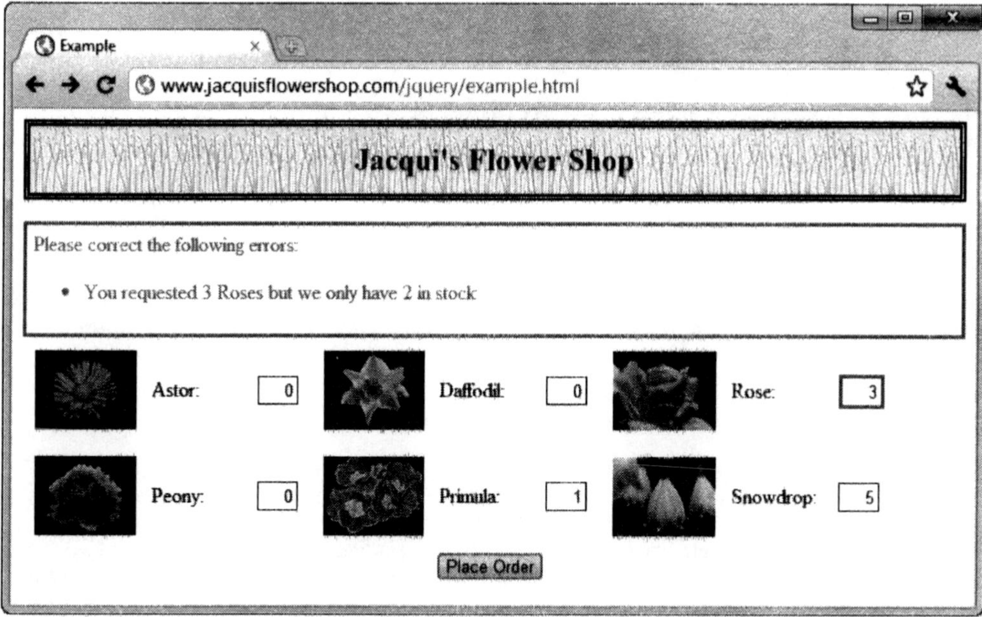

Figure 13-14. A validation summary showing fewer error messages

The choice between inline messages and validation summaries is a personal one and is usually driven by the structure of the document. The good news is that the validation plugin is very flexible, and it usually doesn't take much work to define and apply validation that is closely tailored to your needs.

Summary

In this chapter, I showed you the support that jQuery provides for forms. I began by recapping the form-related event methods and explained the roles that the most important ones play in the life of an HTML form. Most of the chapter was spent covering the Validation plugin, which provides flexible and extensible support for validating the values that users enter into a form and providing the means for resolving any problems before the data is submitted to the server.

CHAPTER 14

Using Ajax: Part I

Ajax stands for Asynchronous JavaScript and XML but is generally a word in its own right these days. Ajax allows you to make requests to the server asynchronously, meaning, in short, that your request happens in the background and doesn't prevent the user from interacting with the content in your HTML document. The most common use for Ajax is to submit data from a `form` element. The advantage of doing this is that the browser doesn't have to load a new document to display the server's response, and you can use the standard jQuery functions to display the data within the document seamlessly.

The Ajax support that I'll be using in this chapter is built into the core jQuery library, although I do briefly describe a useful plugin at the end of the chapter. jQuery doesn't reinvent Ajax but rather makes the existing browser Ajax API easier to use.

In this chapter, I am going to describe the *shorthand* and *convenience* Ajax methods. These are simpler methods that make using Ajax relatively quick and easy. In Chapter 15, I describe the low-level jQuery Ajax API on which these methods are based. However, as you'll see, the low-level API isn't *that* low-level, and the main reason for its use is when the shorthand and convenience methods don't do quite what you want. Table 14-1 provides the summary for this chapter.

***Table 14-1.** Chapter Summary*

Problem	Solution	Listing
Perform an asynchronous HTTP `GET` request.	Use the `get` method.	1–3
Process the data obtained from an Ajax `GET` request.	Pass a function to the `get` method.	4
Perform an Ajax request in response to a user action.	Call the `get` method within an event handler.	5
Request JSON data from the server.	Use the `get` method and receive an object in the argument function.	6, 7
Send data to the server as part of a `GET` request.	Pass a JavaScript object as an argument to the `get` method.	8
Perform an asynchronous HTTP `POST` request.	Use the `post` method.	9, 10

Send nonform data in a POST request.	Pass any JavaScript object as an argument to the post method.	11
Override the data type specified by the server in the response to an Ajax request.	Pass the expected type as an argument to the get or post methods.	12–13
Avoid the most common Ajax pitfall.	Don't treat Ajax requests as though they were synchronous.	14
Use the convenience methods to make GET requests for specific data types.	Use the load, getScript, or getJSON method.	15–18
Easily enable Ajax for form elements.	Use the Ajax Forms plugin.	19

Using the Ajax Shorthand Methods

Although Ajax is usually associated with posting form data, it can actually be used a lot more widely. I am going to start introducing Ajax by performing some simpler tasks, starting with some different ways that you can obtain data from the server without using forms at all.

jQuery defines a set of *Ajax shorthand methods*, which are convenient wrappers around the core Ajax functions and which allow you to quickly and simply perform common Ajax tasks. In the sections that follow, I introduce you to the shorthand methods for retrieving data from the server using HTTP GET requests.

(BRIEFLY) UNDERSTANDING ASYNCHRONOUS TASKS

If you are new to Ajax, let me provide a simple explanation of asynchronous requests. This is important because they are so central to Ajax that the first letter in the acronym stands for *asynchronous*. Most of the time, you are used to writing synchronous code. You define a block of statements that perform some task, and then you wait while the browser executes them. When the last statement has been executed, you know the task has been performed. During the execution, the browser doesn't let the user interact with the content in any way.

When you perform an asynchronous task, you are telling the browser that you want something done in the background. The phrase "in the background" is something of a catchall, but in essence you are saying "Do this thing without preventing the user from interacting with the document and tell me when you have done it." In the case of Ajax, you are telling the browser to communicate with the server and tell you when the request has been completed. This communication is handled through *callback functions*. You give jQuery one or more functions that will be called when the task is complete. There will be a function to deal with a successful request, and there can be other functions for other outcomes, such as errors.

The advantage of asynchronous requests is that they allow you to create a rich HTML document that can be seamlessly updated using responses from the server without interrupting the user's interaction and without having to make the user wait while the browser loads a new document.

The disadvantage is that you have to think through your code very carefully. You can't predict when an asynchronous request will be completed, and you can't make assumptions about the outcome. Further, the use of callback functions tends to create more complex code that can punish the unwary programmer who makes assumptions about the outcome or timeliness of a request.

Performing an Ajax GET Request

To begin, you are going to use Ajax to perform an HTTP GET request to load a fragment of HTML that you can add to your document. Listing 14-1 shows the example document that you will be working with.

Listing 14-1. The Example Document

```
<!DOCTYPE html>
<html>
<head>
    <title>Example</title>
    <script src="jquery-1.7.js" type="text/javascript"></script>
    <script src="jquery.tmpl.js" type="text/javascript"></script>
    <script src="jquery.validate.js" type="text/javascript"></script>
    <link rel="stylesheet" type="text/css" href="styles.css"/>
    <script type="text/javascript">
        $(document).ready(function() {
            // script will go here
        });
    </script>
</head>
<body>
    <h1>Jacqui's Flower Shop</h1>
    <form method="post" action="http://node.jacquisflowershop.com/order">
        <div id="oblock">
            <div class="dtable">
                <div id="row1" class="drow">
                </div>
                <div id="row2"class="drow">
                </div>
            </div>
        </div>
        <div id="buttonDiv"><button type="submit">Place Order</button></div>
    </form>
</body>
</html>
```

This is similar to the examples you have seen previously, but there are no elements to describe the products and no data item or templates to generate them. Instead, I have created a separate file called flowers.html, which I have placed next to the example document (which is called example.html in the source code download for this book). Listing 14-2 shows the content of flowers.html.

Listing 14-2. The flowers.html File

```
...
<div>
    <img src="astor.png"/><label for="astor">Astor:</label>
    <input name="astor" value="0" required />
</div>
<div>
    <img src="daffodil.png"/><label for="daffodil">Daffodil:</label>
    <input name="daffodil" value="0" required />
</div>
<div>
    <img src="rose.png"/><label for="rose">Rose:</label>
    <input name="rose" value="0" required />
</div>
<div>
    <img src="peony.png"/><label for="peony">Peony:</label>
    <input name="peony" value="0" required />
</div>
<div>
    <img src="primula.png"/><label for="primula">Primula:</label>
    <input name="primula" value="0" required />
</div>
<div>
    <img src="snowdrop.png"/><label for="snowdrop">Snowdrop:</label>
    <input name="snowdrop" value="0" required />
</div>
...
```

These are the same elements you have been using in previous chapters, except that they are not assigned to rows and I have removed the class attribute from the div elements. I have made these changes only so that I can show you how to work with the elements once you load them. There is no technical reason for doing this. Notice that this isn't a complete HTML document, just a fragment.

You can now use the jQuery support for Ajax to bring the HTML fragment into the main HTML document. This might seem like an odd thing to do, but you are simulating a common situation where different pieces of content are produced by different systems and need to be stitched together to create a complex document or web application. I am using only one server in this example for simplicity, but it is easy to imagine that the information about the products is coming from elsewhere. In fact, in later examples, I will introduce Node.js in order to show you how to deal with multiple servers. That is all to come. For the moment, let's look at the basic jQuery Ajax support and use it to deal with the flowers.html file. Listing 14-3 shows how you can do this.

Listing 14-3. Using jQuery Ajax Support with an HTML Fragment

```
...
<script type="text/javascript">
$(document).ready(function() {
    $.get("flowers.html",
        function(data) {
            var elems = $(data).filter('div').addClass("dcell");
            elems.slice(0, 3).appendTo('#row1');
```

```
            elems.slice(3).appendTo("#row2");
    });
});
</script>
...
```

I used the get method and provided two arguments. The first argument is the URL that you want to load. In this case, I have specified `flowers.html`, which will be interpreted as being a URL that is relative to the URL from which the main document was loaded.

The second argument is a function that will be invoked if the request is successful. As I mentioned in the sidebar, Ajax relies heavily on callback functions because the requests are performed asynchronously. jQuery passes the data from the server response as the argument to the function.

When you load a document that contains this script, the `flowers.html` file is loaded from the server, the HTML fragment it contains is parsed into element, and then they are added to the document. Figure 14-1 shows the result.

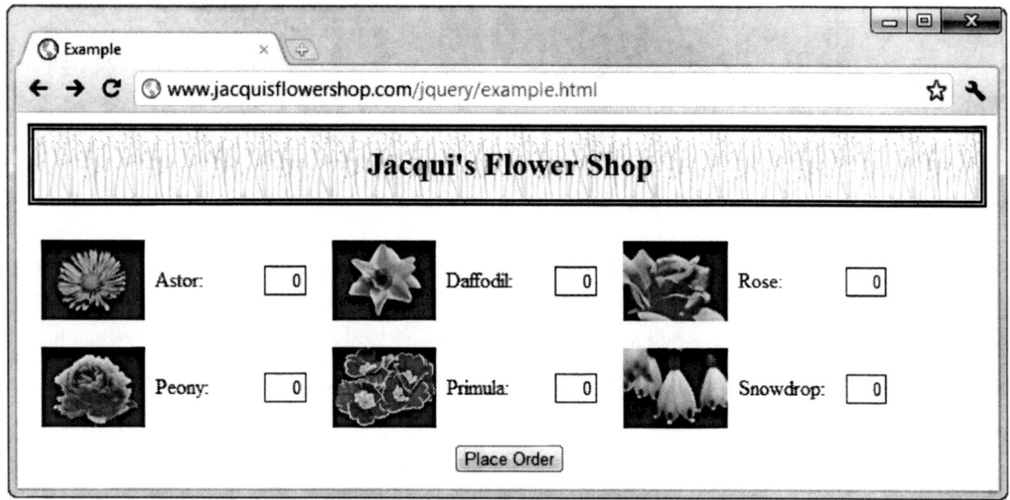

Figure 14-1. The effect of using Ajax

OK, so I admit that you ended up with the same result you saw when the elements or data was inline, but how the path you took to get there is worth exploring. Let's dig into the detail.

■ **Tip** Although I have used the `get` method to load HTML, it can be used to obtain any kind of data from the server.

Processing the Response Data

The argument passed to the success function is the data that the server has sent back an in answer to our request. In this example, you get back the content of the `flowers.html` file, which is an HTML fragment.

To make this into something I can use with jQuery, I passed the data into the jQuery $ function so that it would be parsed and a hierarchy of HTMLElement objects generated, as shown in Listing 14-4.

Listing 14-4. Processing the Data Obtained from the Server

```
...
<script type="text/javascript">
$(document).ready(function() {
    $.get("flowers.html",
        function(data) {
            var elems = $(data).filter('div').addClass("dcell");
            elems.slice(0, 3).appendTo('#row1');
            elems.slice(3).appendTo("#row2");
    });
});
</script>
...
```

As I mentioned previously, I left out the class attributes from the div elements. You can see that I add them back in using the standard jQuery addClass method. Once the data has been passed to the $ function, then you can use the jQuery object that is returned as you would any other. I go on to add the elements to the document using the slice and appendTo methods, as I have in previous chapters.

■ **Tip** Notice that I have used the filter method to select only the div elements generated from the data. When parsing the data, jQuery assumes that the carriage-return characters that I added between the div elements in the flowers.html file for structure are text content and creates text elements for them. To avoid this, you can either ensure that there are no carriage returns in the documents you request or use the filter method to remove then.

Making the Effect Easier to See

The statements that trigger the Ajax request are executed in response to the ready event (which I described in Chapter 9). This makes it hard to visualize how using Ajax is any different from using inline data. To make it more obvious, I have added a button to the document, and the Ajax request will be performed only when this button is clicked. You can see the changes in Listing 14-5.

Listing 14-5. Making an Ajax Request in Response to a Button Press

```
...
<script type="text/javascript">
$(document).ready(function() {
    $('<button>Ajax</button>').appendTo('#buttonDiv').click(function(e) {
        $.get("flowers.html",
            function(data) {
                var elems = $(data).filter("div").addClass("dcell");
                elems.slice(0, 3).appendTo('#row1');
                elems.slice(3).appendTo("#row2");
```

```
            });
            e.preventDefault();
        });
});
</script>
...
```

Now the flowers.html document isn't loaded until the button is clicked, and each time that it is clicked, additional elements are added to the document, as shown in Figure 14-2. Notice that I have called the preventDefault method on the Event object that is passed to my event handler function. Since the button element is contained with a form element, the default action is to submit the form to the server.

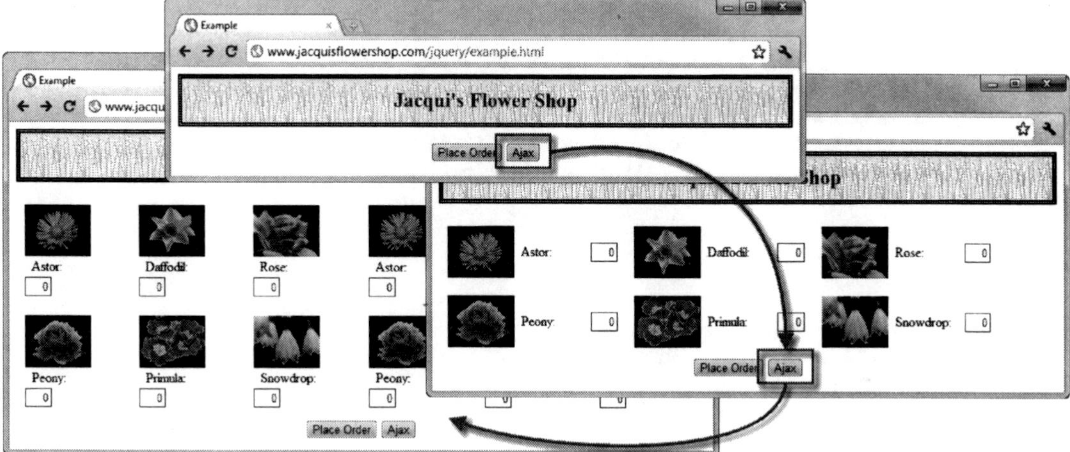

Figure 14-2. Using Ajax in response to a button press

Getting Other Kinds of Data

You are not limited to using the get method just for HTML. You can obtain any kind of data from the server. Of particular interest is JSON, because of the way that jQuery helpfully processes the data for you. Back when Ajax started to be widely adopted, XML was seen as the data format of choice, so much so that the *X* in Ajax stands for XML. I am not going to go into the details XML, but it tends to be verbose, hard to read, and relatively time- and resource-consuming to generate and process.

In recent years, XML has been largely replaced by the JavaScript Object Notation (JSON), which is a simpler data format and is exceptionally easy to work with in JavaScript code (as the name suggests). For this example, I have created a file called mydata.json and saved it alongside the example.html file on the web server. Listing 14-6 shows the contents of mydata.json.

Listing 14-6. The Contents of mydata.json

```
[{"name":"Astor","product":"astor","stocklevel":"10","price":"2.99"},
 {"name":"Daffodil","product":"daffodil","stocklevel":"12","price":"1.99"},
 {"name":"Rose","product":"rose","stocklevel":"2","price":"4.99"},
```

```
{"name":"Peony","product":"peony","stocklevel":"0","price":"1.50"},
{"name":"Primula","product":"primula","stocklevel":"1","price":"3.12"},
{"name":"Snowdrop","product":"snowdrop","stocklevel":"15","price":"0.99"}]
```

The file contains the data for the flower shop products, and as you can see, JSON data is identical to the way you represent data inline in JavaScript code. This is one of the reasons that JSON has replaced XML for web applications. To load and process this data using Ajax, you can use the get method, as shown in Listing 14-7.

Listing 14-7. Using the get Method to Obtain JSON Data

```
...
<script type="text/javascript">
$(document).ready(function() {
    $('<button>Ajax</button>').appendTo('#buttonDiv').click(function(e) {
        $.get("mydata.json", function(data) {
            var template = $('#flowerTmpl');
            template.tmpl(data.slice(0, 3)).appendTo("#row1");
            template.tmpl(data.slice(3)).appendTo("#row2");
        });
        e.preventDefault();
    });
});
</script>
<script id="flowerTmpl" type="text/x-jquery-tmpl">
    <div class="dcell">
        <img src="${product}.png"/>
        <label for="${product}">${name}:</label>
        <input name="${product}" data-price="${price}" data-stock="${stocklevel}"
            value="0" required />
    </div>
</script>
...
```

In this example, I request the JSON data file in response to the button click. The data retrieved from the server is passed to a function, just as with the HTML fragment. I have used the data template plugin (described in Chapter 12) to process the data and generate HTML elements from it and then the slice and appendTo method to insert the elements into the document. Notice that I didn't have to do anything to convert the JSON string to a JavaScript object. jQuery does this for me automatically.

■ **Tip** Some web servers (and this includes Microsoft IIS 7.5, which I have used for this book) will not return content to browsers if they don't recognize the file extension or data format. To make this example work with IIS, I have to add a new mapping between the file extension (.json) and the MIME type for JSON data (application/json). Until I did this, IIS would return 404 – Not Found errors when mydata.json was requested.

Providing Data to GET Requests

You can send data to the server as part of your GET requests, which are the kind of requests made by the get, load, getScript, and getJSON methods. You do this by passing a data object to the shorthand method you are using. Listing 14-8 provides an example.

Listing 14-8. Sending Data as Part of a GET Request

```
...
<script type="text/javascript">
$(document).ready(function() {

    var requestData = {
        country: "US",
        state: "New York"
    }

    $.get("flowers.html", requestData,
        function(responseData) {
            var elems = $(responseData).filter('div').addClass("dcell");
            elems.slice(0, 3).appendTo('#row1');
            elems.slice(3).appendTo("#row2");
    });

});
</script>
...
```

The data you provide is appended to the specified URL as a query string. For this example, this means you request the following:

```
http://www.jacquisflowershop.com/jquery/flowers.html?country=US&state=New+York
```

The server can use the data you provide to tailor the content that is returned. You might have different flower sections for different states, for example.

GET AND POST: PICK THE RIGHT ONE

You might be tempted to send in form data using a GET request. Be careful. The rule of thumb is that GET requests should be used for all read-only information retrieval, while POST requests should be used for any operation that changes the application state.

In standards-compliance terms, GET requests are for safe interactions (having no side effects besides information retrieval), and POST requests are for unsafe interactions (making a decision or changing something). These conventions are set by the World Wide Web Consortium (W3C), at www.w3.org/Provider/Style/URI.

So, you can use GET requests to send form data to the server, but not for operations that change state. Many web developers learned this the hard way in 2005 when Google Web Accelerator was released to the public. This application prefetched all the content linked from each page, which is legal within HTTP because GET requests should be safe. Unfortunately, many web developers had ignored the HTTP conventions and placed simple links to "delete item" or "add to shopping cart" in their applications. Chaos ensued.

One company believed its content management system was the target of repeated hostile attacks, because all its content kept getting deleted. They later discovered that a search-engine crawler had hit upon the URL of an administrative page and was crawling all the delete links.

Performing an Ajax POST Request

Now that you have seen how to get data from the server, you can turn your attention to how you send it, that is to say, how you post form data to the server. Once again, there is a shorthand method: post, which makes posting a form very simple. Before you look at that method, you need to set up your server, which means turning once again to Node.js and understanding how to work within a security feature that browsers apply to Ajax POST requests.

Preparing Node.js to Receive Form Data

For this part of the chapter, you need a server script that will receive data sent from the browser using the HTTP POST method, perform some simple operation on the data that has been sent, and generate a response. Listing 14-9 shows the Node.js script this section.

Listing 14-9. The Node.js Script for Posting Data

```
var http = require('http');
var url = require('url');
var querystring = require('querystring');

http.createServer(function (req, res) {
    console.log("[200 OK] " + req.method + " to " + req.url);

    if (req.method == 'OPTIONS') {
        res.writeHead(200, "OK", {
            "Access-Control-Allow-Headers": "Content-Type",
            "Access-Control-Allow-Methods": "*",
            "Access-Control-Allow-Origin": "*"
            });
        res.end();

    } else if (req.method == 'POST') {
        var dataObj = new Object();
        var contentType = req.headers["content-type"];
        var fullBody = '';

        if (contentType) {
            if (contentType.indexOf("application/x-www-form-urlencoded") > -1) {
                req.on('data', function(chunk) { fullBody += chunk.toString();});
                req.on('end', function() {
                    var dBody = querystring.parse(fullBody);
```

```
                    writeResponse(req, res, dBody,
                        url.parse(req.url, true).query["callback"])
                });
            } else {
                req.on('data', function(chunk) { fullBody += chunk.toString();});
                req.on('end', function() {
                    dataObj = JSON.parse(fullBody);
                    var dprops = new Object();
                    for (var i = 0; i < dataObj.length; i++) {
                        dprops[dataObj[i].name] = dataObj[i].value;
                    }
                    writeResponse(req, res, dprops);
                });
            }
        }
    } else if (req.method == "GET") {
        var data = url.parse(req.url, true).query;
        writeResponse(req, res, data, data["callback"])
    }
    console.log("Ready on port 80");
}).listen(80);

function writeResponse(req, res, data, jsonp) {
    var total = 0;
    for (item in data) {
        if(item != "_" && data[item] > 0) {
            total += Number(data[item]);
        } else {
            delete data[item];
        }
    }
    data.total = total;
    jsonData = JSON.stringify(data);
    if (jsonp) {
        jsonData = jsonp + "(" + jsonData + ")";
    }

    res.writeHead(200, "OK", {
        "Content-Type": "application/json",
        "Access-Control-Allow-Origin": "*"});
    res.write(jsonData);
    res.end();
}
```

I saved this script to a file called `formserver.js`. The easiest way to get this script is to download the source code that accompanies this book and that is freely available from Apress.com. I run the script by entering the following at the command prompt:

```
node.exe formserver.js
```

This script processes the data sent by the browser and creates a JSON response. I could have returned HTML from this script, but JSON is more compact and often simpler to work with. The JSON object I return is very simple: an object that contains the total number of products that the user has selected and the number of each of them for which a value was specified. So, for example, if I selected one astor, two daffodils, and three roses, the JSON response sent back by the Node.js script would be as follows:

```
{"astor":"1","daffodil":"2","rose":"2","total":5}
```

The previous JSON I showed you represented an array of objects, but this server script returns just a single object whose properties correspond to the selected flowers. The total property contains the sum of the individual selections. I appreciate that this is hardly the most valuable activity a server can perform, but I want to keep our focus on using Ajax rather than server-side development.

Understanding Cross-Origin Ajax Requests

If you look at the Node.js script, you will see that when I write the response to the browser, I set an HTTP header, like this:

```
Access-Control-Allow-Origin: http://www.jacquisflowershop.com
```

By default, browsers limit scripts to making make Ajax requests within the same *origin* as the document that contains them. An origin is the combination of the protocol, hostname, and port components of a URL. If two URLs have the same protocol, hostname, and port, then they are within the same origin. If any of the three components is different, then they are in different origins.

■ **Tip** This policy is intended to reduce the risks of a *cross-site scripting* (CSS) attack, where the browser (or user) is tricked into executing a malicious script. CSS attacks are outside the scope of this book, but there is a nice Wikipedia article at http://en.wikipedia.org/wiki/Cross-site_scripting that provides a good introduction to the topic.

Table 14-2 shows how a number of URLs compare to the URL of the main example document, which is www.jacquisflowershop.com/jquery/example.html.

***Table 14-2.** Comparing URLs*

URL	Origin Comparison
http://www.jacquisflowershop.com/apps/mydoc.html	Same origin
https://www.jacquisflowershop.com/apps/mydoc.html	Different origin; protocol differs
http://www.jacquisflowershop.com:81/apps/mydoc.html	Different origin; port differs
http://node.jacquisflowershop.com/order	Different origin; host differs

In my configuration, I have two servers. `www.jacquisflowershop.com` handles the static content, and `node.jacquisflowershop.com` runs `Node.js`. As you can see from the table, a document from the first server has a different origin to the second. When you want to make a request from one origin to another, it is known as a *cross-origin request*.

The problem with this policy is that it is a blanket ban; there are no cross-origin requests. This has led to the use of some very ugly tricks to trick the browser into making requests that contravene the policy. Fortunately, there is now a legitimate means of making cross-origin requests, defined in the *Cross-Origin Resource Sharing* (CORS) specification. I am only going to describe CORS briefly. For complete details, see the full CORS standard at `www.w3.org/TR/cors`.

■ **Tip** The CORS specification is reasonably recent. It is supported by the current generation of browsers, but older browsers will simply ignore cross-origin requests. A more established approach is to use JSONP, which I describe in the "Working with JSONP" section.

The way that CORS works is that the browser contacts the second server (the `Node.js` server for us) and includes an `Origin` header in the request. The value of this header is the origin of the document that has led to the request being made.

If the server recognizes the origin and wants to allow the browser to make a cross-origin request, then it adds the `Access-Control-Allow-Origin` header, setting the value to match the `Origin` header from the request. If the response doesn't contain this header, then the browser discards the response.

■ **Tip** Supporting CORS means that the browser has to apply the cross-origin security policy after it has contacted the server and has obtained the response header, meaning that the request is made even if the response is discarded because the required header is missing or specified a different domain. This is a very different approach from browsers that don't implement CORS and that simply block the request, never contacting the server.

In the `Node.js` script, I manually set the `Access-Control-Allow-Origin` header to my trusted origin `www.jacquisflowershop.com`, but you could easily use the value of the `Origin` header in the request to follow a more sophisticated decision process. You can also set the `Access-Control-Allow-Origin` header to an asterisk (*), which means that cross-origin requests from *any* origin will be permitted. This is fine for the purposes of testing, but you should think carefully about the security implications before using this setting in a production application.

Using the post Method to Submit Form Data

So, now that you have prepared the server and understood CORS, you are in a position to use the `post` method to send form data to the server, as shown by Listing 14-10.

Listing 14-10. Sending Data with the post Method

```
...
<script type="text/javascript">
$(document).ready(function() {

    $('button').get(0).disabled = true;

    $.getJSON("mydata.json", function(data) {
        var template = $('#flowerTmpl');
        template.tmpl(data.slice(0, 3)).appendTo("#row1");
        template.tmpl(data.slice(3)).appendTo("#row2");
        $('button').get(0).disabled = false;
    });

    $('button').click(function(e) {
        var formData = $('form').serialize();

        $.post("http://node.jacquisflowershop.com/order", formData,
            function(data) {
                processServerResponse(data);
            })

        e.preventDefault();
    })

    function processServerResponse(data) {
        var inputElems = $('div.dcell').hide();

        for (var prop in data) {
            var filtered = inputElems.has('input[name=' + prop + ']')
                .appendTo("#row1").show();
        }

        $('#buttonDiv, #totalDiv').remove();
        $('#totalTmpl').tmpl(data).appendTo('body');
    }
});
</script>
<script id="totalTmpl" type="text/x-jquery-tmpl">
    <div id="totalDiv" style="clear: both; padding: 5px">
        <div style="text-align: center">Total Items: <span id=total>${total}</span></div>
        <div id="buttonDiv"><button type="submit">Place Order</button></div>
    </div>
</script>
<script id="flowerTmpl" type="text/x-jquery-tmpl">
    <div class="dcell">
        <img src="${product}.png"/>
        <label for="${product}">${name}:</label>
        <input name="${product}" data-price="${price}" data-stock="${stocklevel}"
```

```
            value="0" required />
    </div>
</script>
...
```

This example looks more complicated than it really is. I start by using the getJSON method to obtain the mydata.json file that contains details of the flower products and then use a data template to generate elements and add them to the document. This gives you the starting point that you have come to know and love, as shown in Figure 14-3.

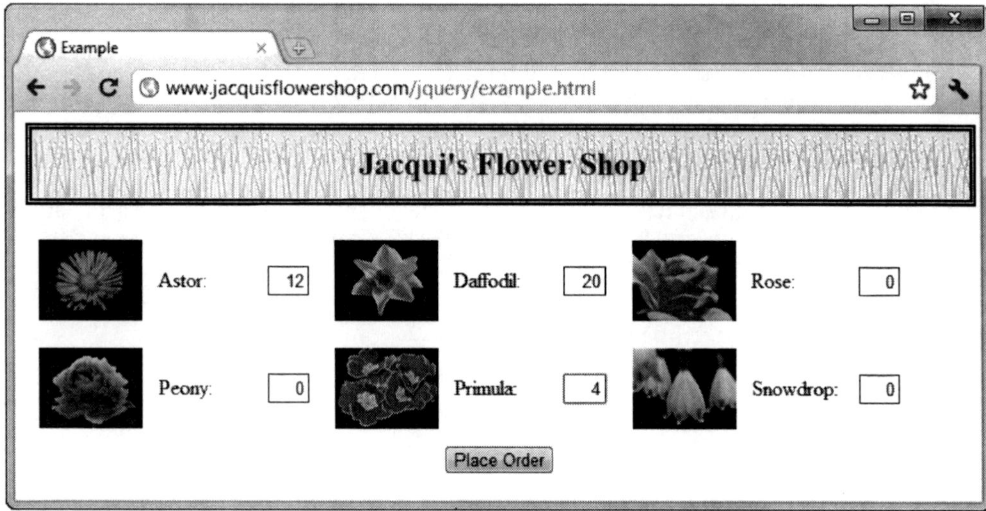

Figure 14-3. The starting point for sending data to the server

You can see that I have entered some values into the input elements: 12 astors, 20 daffodils, and 4 primulas. I use the click method to register a function that will be called when the button element is clicked, like this:

```
$('button').click(function(e) {
    var formData = $('form').serialize();

    $.post("http://node.jacquisflowershop.com/order", formData,
        function(data) {
            processServerResponse(data);
        })

    e.preventDefault();
})
```

The first thing that I do is to call the serialize method on the form element. This is a very helpful method that works its way through all of the form elements and creates a URL-encoded string that you can send to the server.

■ **Tip** Notice that I call the `preventDefault` method on the `Event` object that is passed to my handler function for the click event. I need to do this to stop the browser posting the form in the regular way, that is, by sending the data and loading the response as a new document.

For the values I entered, the `serialize` method generates a string like this:

```
astor=12&daffodil=20&rose=0&peony=0&primula=4&snowdrop=0
```

I use the `serialize` method because the `post` method sends data in the URL-encoded format (although this can be changed by using the `ajaxSetup` global event handler method, which I describe in Chapter 15). Once I have the data from the input elements, I call the `post` method to initiate the Ajax request.

The arguments to the `post` method are the URL that I want to send the data to (which need not be the same as the URL specified by the `action` attribute of the `form` element), the data I want to send, and a function to call if the request is successful. In this example, I take the response from the server and pass it to the `processServerResponse` function, which is defined as follows:

```
function processServerResponse(data) {
    var inputElems = $('div.dcell').hide();

    for (var prop in data) {
        var filtered = inputElems.has('input[name=' + prop + ']')
            .appendTo("#row1").show();
    }

    $('#buttonDiv, #totalDiv').remove();
    $('#totalTmpl').tmpl(data).appendTo('body');
}
```

I hide all of the cell-level `div` elements in the CSS layout (which are members of the `dcell` class) and then display those that correspond to the properties in the JSON object from the server. I also use a data template to generate a display for the total number of selected items. These are both activities you could have performed on the client, but the point here is that you obtained the data through an Ajax `POST` request. You can see the result in Figure 14-4.

Figure 14-4. The effect of processing the data returned from the Ajax POST request

You can see how easy it is to submit form data to the server (and, of course, how easy it is to process the response, especially if it is JSON).

■ **Tip** If you don't get the response shown in the figure, then the likely cause is that your CORS header isn't being set to the correct domain in the Node.js script.

Sending Other Data Using the post Method

Although the post method is usually used to submit form data, you can actually send any data you like. You just need to create an object that contains your data, call the serialize method to format the data properly, and then pass it to the post method. This can be a useful technique if you are collecting data from the user without using a form or if you want to be selective about the form elements that you include in the POST request. Listing 14-11 shows how you can use the post method in this way.

Listing 14-11. Using the post Method to Send Nonform Data to the Server

```
...
<script type="text/javascript">
$(document).ready(function() {

    $('button').click(function(e) {
        var requestData = {
            apples: 2,
            oranges: 10
        };

        $.post("http://node.jacquisflowershop.com/order", requestData,
            function(responseData) {
```

```
                alert(JSON.stringify(responseData));
            })
        e.preventDefault();
    })
});
</script>
...
```

In this script, I create an object and define properties explicitly. I pass this object to the post method and use the alert method to display the response from the server. (The server doesn't really care what kind of data it gets from the browser; it will just try to add up the values and generate a total.) You can see the dialog box that is shown in Figure 14-5.

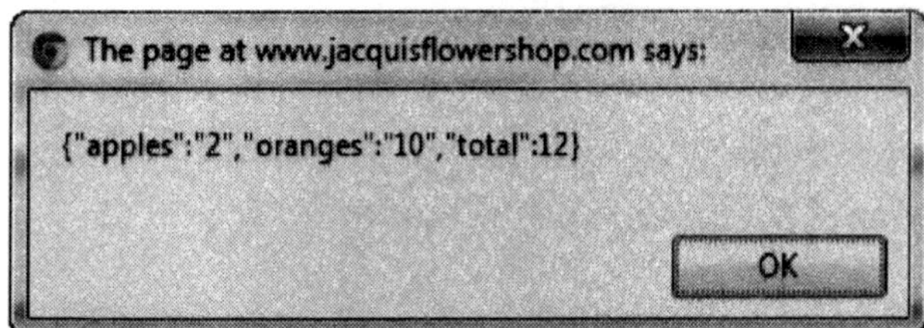

Figure 14-5. The response from the server for some nonform data

---

■ **Tip** The JSON response from the server is automatically transformed into a JavaScript object by jQuery. I used the JSON.stringify method (which is supported by most browsers) to turn it back into a string so that I could display it in the dialog box.

Specifying the Expected Data Type

When you use the get and post methods, jQuery has to figure out what kind of data the server is sending back in response to your request. It can be anything from HTML to a JavaScript file. To do this, jQuery relies on the information that the server provides in the response, particularly the Content-Type header. For the most part, this works very well, but on occasion jQuery needs a little help. This is usually because the server is specifying the wrong MIME type for the data in the response.

You can override the information that the server provides and can tell jQuery what data you are expecting by passing an additional argument to the get or post methods. This argument can be one of the following values:

- xml
- json
- jsonp
- script
- html

- `text`

Listing 14-12 shows how you can specify the expected data type for the get method.

Listing 14-12. Specifying the Expected Data Type

```
...
<script type="text/javascript">
$(document).ready(function() {

    $.get("mydata.json",
        function(responseData) {
            console.log(JSON.stringify(responseData));
    }, "json");

});
</script>
...
```

You specify the data type as the last argument to the shorthand methods. In this example, I have told jQuery that I am expecting JSON data. It doesn't matter what the server says the content type is. jQuery will not treat the response as JSON. In this example, I write the response to the console, which produces the following output:


```
[{"name":"Astor","product":"astor","stocklevel":"10","price":"2.99"},
 {"name":"Daffodil","product":"daffodil","stocklevel":"12","price":"1.99"},
 {"name":"Rose","product":"rose","stocklevel":"2","price":"4.99"},
 {"name":"Peony","product":"peony","stocklevel":"0","price":"1.50"},
 {"name":"Primula","product":"primula","stocklevel":"1","price":"3.12"},
 {"name":"Snowdrop","product":"snowdrop","stocklevel":"15","price":"0.99"}]
```


This is the same content that I put into the `mydata.json` file, which is, of course, what you hoped would happen. The problem with specifying the data type is that you have to be right. If the data is actually of a different type, then you can have some problems, as demonstrated in Listing 14-13.

Listing 14-13. Specifying the Wrong Kind of Data

```
...
<script type="text/javascript">
$(document).ready(function() {
    $.get("flowers.html",
        function(responseData) {
            console.log(JSON.stringify(responseData));
    }, "json");

});
</script>
...
```

In this example, I have requested a file that contains HTML but told jQuery that it should treat it as JSON. The problem here is that when dealing with JSON, jQuery automatically creates a JavaScript object from the data, which it can't do with HTML. The Ajax request ends in the following error:

```
SyntaxError: Unexpected token <
```

■ **Tip** I'll show you how to detect Ajax errors in Chapter 15.

Avoiding the Most Common Ajax Pitfall

Before you go any further, I want to show you the most common problem that web programmer makes with Ajax, which is to treat the asynchronous request as though it were synchronous. Listing 14-14 gives an example of the problem.

Listing 14-14. A Common Ajax Mistake

```
...
<script type="text/javascript">
$(document).ready(function() {
    $('<button>Ajax</button>').appendTo('#buttonDiv').click(function(e) {
        e.preventDefault();

        var elems;

        $.get("flowers.html", function(data) {
            elems = $(data).filter("div").addClass("dcell");
        });

        elems.slice(0, 3).appendTo('#row1');
        elems.slice(3).appendTo("#row2");

    });
});
</script>
...
```

In this example, I have defined a variable called elems, which is then used by the Ajax callback function to assign the result of the server request. I then use the slice and appendTo methods to add the elements that I have obtained from the server to the document. If you run this example, you will see that no elements are added to the document, and depending on your browser, you will see an error message displayed on the console. Here is the message shown by Google Chrome:

```
Uncaught TypeError: Cannot call method 'slice' of undefined
```

The issue here is that the statements in the script element are not executed in the order in which they are written. The problem is that I have assumed that the following sequence will occur:

1. Define the elems variable.
2. Get the data from the server and assign it to the elems variable.

3. Slice the elements in the elems variable and add them to the document.

What really happens is this:

1. Define the elems variable.
2. Start the asynchronous request to the server.
3. Slice the elements in the elems variable and add them to the document.

And, at some point in the near future, this happens:

1. Receive the request from the server.
2. Process the data and assign it to the elems variable.

In short, you get the error message because you called the slice methods on a variable that doesn't contain any elements. The worst thing about this mistake is that sometimes the code actually works. This is because the Ajax response completes so quickly that the variable contains the data you expect before you come to process it (this is typically the case when the data is cached by the browser or you perform some complex operations between starting the Ajax request and trying to operate on the data). You now know what to look for whether you see this kind of behavior from your code.

Using the Type-Specific Convenience Methods

jQuery provides three convenience methods that make dealing with particular types of data a little more convenient. These methods are described and demonstrated in the sections that follow.

Getting an HTML Fragment

The load method will *only* obtain HTML data, which allows you to request an HTML fragment, process the response to create a set of elements, and insert those elements in the document in a single step. Listing 14-15 shows how you can use the load method.

Listing 14-15. Using the Load Shorthand Method

```
...
<script type="text/javascript">
$(document).ready(function() {
    $('<button>Ajax</button>').appendTo('#buttonDiv').click(function(e) {
        $('#row1').load("flowers.html");
        e.preventDefault();
    });
});
</script>
...
```

You call the load method on the element in the document that you want to insert the new elements into and pass the URL as a method argument. If the request is successful and the response from the server contains valid HTML, then the elements will be inserted at the specified location, as shown in Figure 14-6.

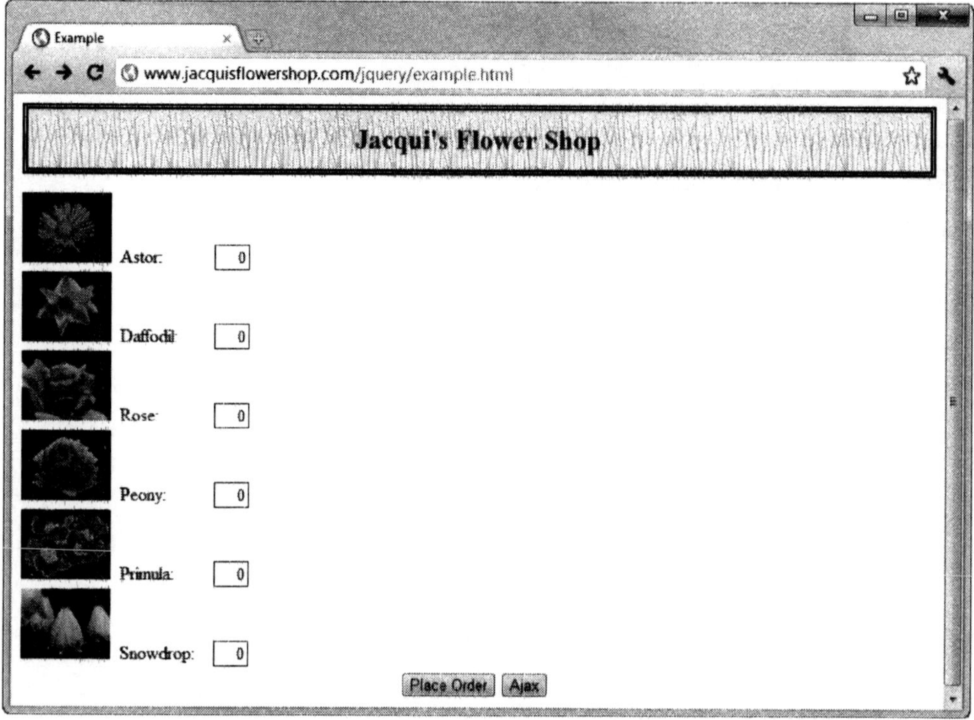

Figure 14-6. Adding elements to the document using the load method

You can see that the elements from the `flower.html` file have all been added to the document, but because they lack the `class` attribute, they are not properly added to the CSS table layout that the main document uses. For this reason, the `load` method is most useful when all of the elements are to be inserted in a single location, and you don't need to modify them before they are added.

Getting and Executing Scripts

The `getScript` method loads a JavaScript file and then executes the statements it contains. To demonstrate this method, I have created a file called `myscript.js` and saved it alongside `example.html` on my web server. Listing 14-16 shows the contents of this file.

Listing 14-16. The Contents of the myscript.js File

```
var flowers = [
    ["Astor", "Daffodil", "Rose"],
    ["Peony", "Primula", "Snowdrop"],
    ["Carnation", "Lily", "Orchid"]
]

$('<div id=row3 class=drow/>').appendTo('div.dtable');
```

```
var fTemplate = $('<div class=dcell><img/><label/><input/></div>');

for (var row = 0; row < flowers.length; row++) {
    var fNames = flowers[row];

    for (var i = 0; i < fNames.length; i++) {
        fTemplate.clone().appendTo("#row" + (row + 1)).children()
            .filter('img').attr('src', fNames[i] + ".png").end()
            .filter('label').attr('for', fNames[i]).text(fNames[i]).end()
            .filter('input').attr({name: fNames[i], value: 0})
    }
}
```

These statements generate three rows of elements that describe the flowers. I have generated these elements using loops so I don't have to get involved defining templates (although, in general, I would much rather use data templates as described in Chapter 12).

The most important thing to realize when dealing with scripts like this is that the state of the document may change between you initiating the Ajax request and the `script` statements being executed. Listing 14-17 contains a script from the main document that uses the `getScript` method but that also modifies the DOM before the Ajax request can complete.

Listing 14-17. Requesting and Executing Scripts with the getScript Method

```
...
<script type="text/javascript">
$(document).ready(function() {
    $('<button>Ajax</button>').appendTo('#buttonDiv').click(function(e) {
        $.getScript("myscript.js");
        $('#row2').remove();

        e.preventDefault();
    });
});
</script>
...
```

You call the `getScript` method on the main `$` function and just pass the URL of the JavaScript file you want to use as the argument. If the server can provide the file and if it contains valid JavaScript statements, then the code will be executed.

■ **Tip** The `getScript` method can be used for any script file, but I find it especially useful for loading and executing scripts that are not central to a web application's functionality, like tracker or geolocation scripts. The user doesn't care if I am able to accurately locate their location for my site statistics, but they do care when loading and executing the script makes them wait. By using the `getScript` method, I can get the information I require without making it annoying. To be very clear, I am not suggesting that you do anything that is hidden from the user, only that you defer loading and executing legitimate functionality that the user is unlikely to value more than their time.

In this example, after I start the Ajax request with the getScript method, I use the remove method to remove the row2 element from the document. This element is used by the myscript.js file to insert some of the new elements. These elements are quietly discarded because the selector for the row2 ID doesn't match anything in the document. You can see the effect in Figure 14-7. Depending on the circumstances, you can view this as a robust design that does its best in the face of document changes or an annoyance that quietly disposes of elements. Either way, it pays not to make too many assumptions about the state of the document in your external JavaScript files.

Figure 14-7. The effect of a document change during an Ajax request

Getting JSON Data

The getJSON method obtains a JSON object from the server. This is perhaps the least useful of the three convenience methods because it doesn't do anything more with the data than the basic get method. Listing 14-18 shows the use of the getJSON method.

Listing 14-18. Using the getJSON Method

```
...
<script type="text/javascript">
$(document).ready(function() {
    $('<button>Ajax</button>').appendTo('#buttonDiv').click(function(e) {
        $.getJSON("mydata.json", function(data) {
            var template = $('#flowerTmpl');
            template.tmpl(data.slice(0, 3)).appendTo("#row1");
            template.tmpl(data.slice(3)).appendTo("#row2");
        });
        e.preventDefault();
    });
});
</script>
<script id="flowerTmpl" type="text/x-jquery-tmpl">
    <div class="dcell">
        <img src="${product}.png"/>
        <label for="${product}">${name}:</label>
        <input name="${product}" data-price="${price}" data-stock="${stocklevel}"
            value="0" required />
    </div>
</script>
...
```

In this example, I request the JSON data file in response to the `button` click. The data retrieved from the server is passed to a function, much as with the get method that I showed you earlier in the chapter. I have used the data template plugin (described in Chapter 12) to process the data and generate HTML elements from it and then the `slice` and `appendTo` method to insert the elements into the document. Notice that you are passed a JavaScript object as the argument to the function. You don't have to do anything to convert from the JSON format into an object because jQuery takes care of this for you.

Working with JSONP

JSONP is an alternative to CORS and works around the same-origin restriction on Ajax requests. It relies on the fact that the browser will allow you to load JavaScript code from any server, which is how the `script` element works when you specify a `src` attribute. To begin with, define a function in the document that will process the data, like this:

```
...
function processJSONP(data) {
    //...do something with the data...
}
...
```

You then make a request to the server where the query string includes your form data and a `callback` property, set to the name of the function you just defined, like this:

```
http://node.jacquisflowershop.com/order?callback=processJSONP&astor=1
    &daffodil=2&rose=2&peony=0&primula=0&snowdrop=0
```

The server, which needs to understand how JSONP works, generates the JSON data as normal and then creates a JavaScript statement that calls the function you created and passes in the data as an argument, like this:

```
processJSONP({"astor":"1","daffodil":"2","rose":"2","total":5})
```

The server also sets the content type of the response to be `text/javascript`, which tells the browser that it has received some JavaScript statements and should execute them. This has the effect of invoking the method you defined earlier, passing in the data sent by the server. In this way, you neatly sidestep the same-domain issues without using CORS.

■ **Caution** Cross-origin requests are restricted for good reason. Don't use JSONP casually. It can create some serious security problems.

---

jQuery has very convenient support for JSONP. All you have to do is use the `getJSON` method and specify a URL that contains `callback=?` in the query string. jQuery creates a function with a random name and uses this when communicating to the server, meaning you don't have to modify your code at all. Listing 14-19 demonstrates how to make a JSONP request.

Listing 14-19. Making a JSONP Request Using the getJSON Method

```
...
<script type="text/javascript">
    $(document).ready(function() {

        $('button').get(0).disabled = true;

        $.getJSON("mydata.json", function(data) {
            var template = $('#flowerTmpl');
            template.tmpl(data.slice(0, 3)).appendTo("#row1");
            template.tmpl(data.slice(3)).appendTo("#row2");
            $('button').get(0).disabled = false;
        });

        $('button').click(function(e) {
            var formData = $('form').serialize();

            $.getJSON("http://node.jacquisflowershop.com/order?callback=?",
                    formData, processServerResponse)

            e.preventDefault();
        })

        function processServerResponse(data) {
            var inputElems = $('div.dcell').hide();
            for (var prop in data) {
                var filtered = inputElems.has('input[name=' + prop + ']')
                    .appendTo("#row1").show();
```

```
            }
            $('#buttonDiv, #totalDiv').remove();
            $('#totalTmpl').tmpl(data).appendTo('body');
        }
    });
</script>
...
```

Using the Ajax Forms Plugin

So far, I have been using the built-in jQuery support for Ajax. As I mentioned previously, one of the strengths of jQuery is the ease with which it can be extended to add new functionality and the vibrant world of plugins that this leads to. To finish this chapter, I am going to briefly describe a useful form-related plugin.

If you are interested in using Ajax solely to post form data to a server, then you might like the Ajax Forms plugin, which you can get from `www.malsup.com/jquery/form`. This is a plugin that makes using Ajax on forms extremely simple, as Listing 14-20 demonstrates.

Listing 14-20. Using the Ajax Forms Plugin

```
<!DOCTYPE html>
<html>
<head>
    <title>Example</title>
    <script src="jquery-1.7.js" type="text/javascript"></script>
    <script src="jquery.tmpl.js" type="text/javascript"></script>
    <script src="jquery.validate.js" type="text/javascript"></script>
    <script src="jquery.form.js" type="text/javascript"></script>
    <link rel="stylesheet" type="text/css" href="styles.css"/>
    <script type="text/javascript">
        $(document).ready(function() {

            $.getScript("myscript.js");

            $('form').ajaxForm(function(data) {
                console.log(JSON.stringify(data))
            });
        });
    </script>
</head>
<body>
    <h1>Jacqui's Flower Shop</h1>
    <form method="post" action="http://node.jacquisflowershop.com/order">
        <div id="oblock">
            <div class="dtable">
                <div id="row1" class="drow">
                </div>
                <div id="row2"class="drow">
                </div>
            </div>
        </div>
```

```
        <div id="buttonDiv"><button type="submit">Place Order</button></div>
    </form>
</body>
</html>
```

In this example, I have added the jquery.form.js script file to the document (this is included in the download for the plugin) and, in the script element, called the ajaxForm method on the form element. The argument to the ajaxForm method is a callback function, and this provides me with access to the response from the server. This is a neat and simple approach to basic Ajax forms, right down to the fact that the URL to post the form to is taken from the form element itself.

This plugin does a lot more, and it even includes some support for basic form validation, but if you get to the point where you want to start taking control of your Ajax requests, then I suggest using the low-level Ajax features that I describe in Chapter 15. But for quick and simple situations, this plugin is convenient and well-designed.

Summary

In this chapter, I introduced you to the shorthand and convenience methods that jQuery provides for Ajax. I have shown you how to use the get and post methods to make asynchronous HTTP GET and POST requests, how to work with JSON data, and how to use the convenience methods that deal with specific data types. Along the way, I have shown you the most common Ajax pitfall, explained cross-origin requests, and showed how to deal with them and briefly introduced a jQuery plugin, which makes it even easier to use Ajax with forms that the shorthand methods. In the next chapter, I'll show you the low-level API, although you'll see that it isn't really that low-level and is actually quite pleasant to use.

CHAPTER 15

Using Ajax: Part II

In this chapter, I show you how to use the low-level jQuery Ajax API. The term *low-level* implies that you are rooting around in the guts of the request, but that really isn't the case. The methods I describe in this chapter are not as convenient as those in Chapter 14, but with just a little more effort you can configure the request so that it meets your needs when the configuration used by the shorthand and convenience methods doesn't quite do the job. Table 15-1 provides the summary for this chapter.

***Table 15-1.** Chapter Summary*

Problem	Solution	Listing
Make an Ajax call with the low-level API.	Use the `ajax` method.	1
Get details of the request in a way that is similar to the native `XMLHttpRequest` object.	Use the `jqXHR` method.	2
Specify the URL for an Ajax request.	Use the `url` setting.	3
Specify the HTTP method for a request.	Use the `type` setting.	4
Respond to successful requests.	Use the `success` setting.	5
Respond to unsuccessful requests.	Use the `error` setting.	6
Respond to completed requests, regardless of success or errors.	Use the `complete` setting.	7, 8
Configure a request before it is sent.	Use the `beforeSend` setting.	9
Specify multiple functions to handle successful, unsuccessful, or completed requests.	Specify an array of functions for the `success`, `error`, or `complete` setting.	10
Specify the element that will be assigned to the `this` variable in the functions for the `success`, `error`, and `complete` settings.	Use the `context` setting.	11

Respond to events for all Ajax requests.	Use the global event methods.	12
Specify whether a request will lead to global events being triggered.	Use the `global` setting.	13
Set the timeout for a request.	Use the `timeout` setting.	14
Add headers to the request.	Use the `headers` setting.	14
Specify the content type being set to the server.	Use the `contentType` header.	15
Specify whether a request will be performed synchronously or asynchronously.	Use the `async` setting.	16
Ignore data that has not been changed.	Use the `ifModified` setting.	17
Respond to the HTTP status code sent by the server.	Use the `statusCode` setting.	18
Clean up the response data.	Use the `dataFilter` setting.	19
Control how data is converted.	Use the `converters` setting.	20
Define a common configuration for all Ajax requests.	Use the `ajaxSetup` method.	21
Dynamically change the configuration for individual requests.	Use the `ajaxPrefilter` method.	22

Making a Simple Ajax Request with the Low-Level API

Making a request with the low-level API isn't much more complicated than using the shorthand and convenience methods I showed you in Chapter 14. The difference is that you can configure many different aspects of the request and get a lot more information about the request that is being performed. The method that is at the heart of the low-level API is `ajax`, and Listing 15-1 provides a simple demonstration of its use.

Listing 15-1. Using the ajax Method

```
<!DOCTYPE html>
<html>
<head>
    <title>Example</title>
    <script src="jquery-1.7.js" type="text/javascript"></script>
    <script src="jquery.tmpl.js" type="text/javascript"></script>
    <script src="jquery.validate.js" type="text/javascript"></script>
```

```
    <link rel="stylesheet" type="text/css" href="styles.css"/>
    <script type="text/javascript">
        $(document).ready(function() {
        $.ajax("mydata.json",{
                success: function(data) {
                    var template = $('#flowerTmpl');
                    template.tmpl(data.slice(0, 3)).appendTo("#row1");
                    template.tmpl(data.slice(3)).appendTo("#row2");
                }
            });
        });
    </script>
    <script id="flowerTmpl" type="text/x-jquery-tmpl">
        <div class="dcell">
            <img src="${product}.png"/>
            <label for="${product}">${name}:</label>
            <input name="${product}" data-price="${price}" data-stock="${stocklevel}"
                value="0" required />
        </div>
    </script>
</head>
<body>
    <h1>Jacqui's Flower Shop</h1>
    <form method="post" action="http://node.jacquisflowershop.com/order">
        <div id="oblock">
            <div class="dtable">
                <div id="row1" class="drow">
                </div>
                <div id="row2"class="drow">
                </div>
            </div>
        </div>
        <div id="buttonDiv"><button type="submit">Place Order</button></div>
    </form>
</body>
</html>
```

You use the ajax method by passing the URL that you want to request and a map object whose properties define a set of key/value pairs, each of which configures a setting for the request.

■ **Note** This chapter relies on the same Node.js script used in Chapter 14.

In this example, my object has one setting: the success setting specifies the function to call if the request is successful. In this example, I request the mydata.json file from the server and use it with a data template to create and insert elements into the document, just as I did in the previous chapter with the shorthand methods. By default, the ajax method makes an HTTP get request, which means that the example is equivalent to using the get or getJSON method, which I showed you in Chapter 14. I'll show you how to configure POST requests later in this chapter.

Lots of settings are available, and I explain them throughout the rest of the chapters, in addition to some useful methods that jQuery provides to make using Ajax easier.

Understanding the jqXHR Object

The result of the `ajax` method is a `jqXHR` object, which you can use to get details about the request and interact with it. The `jqXHR` is a superset of the `XMLHttpRequest` object that underpins browser support for Ajax and has been adapted to work with the jQuery *deferred object* features that I describe in Chapter 35.

For most Ajax operations, you can simply ignore the `jqXHR` object, which is exactly what I suggest you do. The `jqXHR` object is useful when you need more information about the response from the server than would otherwise be available. You can also use the `jqXHR` object to configure the Ajax request, but this is more easily done using the settings for the `ajax` method. Table 15-2 describes the members of the `jqXHR` object.

Table 15-2. *The jqXHR Members*

Member	Description
`readyState`	Returns the progress of the request through its life cycle from unsent (value 0) to complete (value 4)
`status`	Returns the HTTP status code sent back by the server
`statusText`	Returns the text description of the status code
`responseXML`	Returns the response if it is an XML document
`responseText`	Returns the response as a string
`setRequestHeader(name, value)`	Sets a header on the request (this is more easily done using the `headers` setting)
`getAllResponseHeaders()`	Returns all of the headers in the response as a single string
`getResponseHeader(name)`	Returns the value of the specified response header
`abort()`	Terminates the request

You see the `jqXHR` object in a few places. The first is as the result from the `ajax` method, as demonstrated by Listing 15-2.

Listing 15-2. Using the jqXHR Object

```
...
<script type="text/javascript">
    $(document).ready(function() {

        var jqxhr = $.ajax("mydata.json",{
            success: function(data) {
                var template = $('#flowerTmpl');
                template.tmpl(data.slice(0, 3)).appendTo("#row1");
                template.tmpl(data.slice(3)).appendTo("#row2");
            }
        });

        var timerID = setInterval(function() {
            console.log("Status: " + jqxhr.status + " " + jqxhr.statusText);
            if (jqxhr.readyState == 4) {
                console.log("Request completed: " + jqxhr.responseText);
                clearInterval(timerID);
            }
        }, 100);
    });
</script>
...
```

In this example, I assign the result from the ajax method and then use the setInterval method to write information about the request to the console every 100 milliseconds. Using the result of the ajax method doesn't change the fact that the request is performed asynchronously, so caution is required when working with the jqXHR object. I use the readyState property to check the status of the request (the value of 4 indicates the request has completed) and write the response from the server to the console. This script produces the following output (although you might see something slightly different based on your browser configuration):

```
Status: 200 OK

Request completed: [{"name":"Astor","product":"astor","stocklevel":"10","price":"2.99"},
{"name":"Daffodil","product":"daffodil","stocklevel":"12","price":"1.99"},
{"name":"Rose","product":"rose","stocklevel":"2","price":"4.99"},
{"name":"Peony","product":"peony","stocklevel":"0","price":"1.50"},
{"name":"Primula","product":"primula","stocklevel":"1","price":"3.12"},
{"name":"Snowdrop","product":"snowdrop","stocklevel":"15","price":"0.99"}]
```

I rarely use the jqXHR object at all and never when it is the result of the ajax method. jQuery starts the Ajax request automatically when the ajax method is called, so I don't find the ability to configure the request useful. If I want to work with the jqXHR object (typically to get additional information about the response from a server), then I usually do so through the event handler settings that I describe in the "Handling Ajax Events" section later in the chapter. They give me a context regarding the status of the request and mean that I don't have to poll for request status.

Setting the Request URL

The url setting is one of the most important available, allowing you to specify the URL for the request. You can use this setting as an alternative to passing the URL as an argument to the ajax method, as shown in Listing 15-3.

Listing 15-3. Using the url Setting

```
...
<script type="text/javascript">
    $(document).ready(function() {
        $.ajax({
            url: "mydata.json",
            success: function(data) {
                var template = $('#flowerTmpl');
                template.tmpl(data.slice(0, 3)).appendTo("#row1");
                template.tmpl(data.slice(3)).appendTo("#row2");
            }
        });
    });
</script>
...
```

Making a POST Request

You set the type of HTTP request you want to make using the type setting. The default is to make GET requests, as in the previous example. Listing 15-4 shows using the ajax method to create a POST request and submit form data to the server.

Listing 15-4. Creating a POST Request with the ajax Method

```
...
<script type="text/javascript">
    $(document).ready(function() {

        $.ajax({
            url: "mydata.json",
            success: function(data) {
                var template = $('#flowerTmpl');
                template.tmpl(data.slice(0, 3)).appendTo("#row1");
                template.tmpl(data.slice(3)).appendTo("#row2");
            }
        });

        $('button').click(function(e) {
            $.ajax({
                url: $('form').attr("action"),
                data: $('form').serialize(),
                type: 'post',
                success: processServerResponse
```

```
            })
            e.preventDefault();
        })

        function processServerResponse(data) {
            var inputElems = $('div.dcell').hide();
                for (var prop in data) {
                var filtered = inputElems.has('input[name=' + prop + ']')
                    .appendTo("#row1").show();
            }
            $('#buttonDiv, #totalDiv').remove();
            $('#totalTmpl').tmpl(data).appendTo('body');
        }
    });
</script>
<script id="totalTmpl" type="text/x-jquery-tmpl">
    <div id="totalDiv" style="clear: both; padding: 5px">
        <div style="text-align: center">Total Items: <span id=total>${total}</span></div>
        <div id="buttonDiv"><button type="submit">Place Order</button></div>
    </div>
</script>
...
```

I have used several settings in addition to type. To specify the target for the POST request, I used the url setting, which I described earlier. In this example, I take the url from the target of the form element in the document. I specify the data to send using the data setting that I set by using the serialize method, which I described in Chapter 33.

GOING BEYOND GET AND POST

You can use the type setting to specify any HTTP method, but you may have difficulty using anything other than GET or POST. This is because many firewalls and application servers are configured to discard other kinds of request. If you want to use other HTTP methods, then you can make a POST request, but add the X-HTTP-Method-Override header, setting it to the method you want to use, like this:

```
X-HTTP-Method-Override: PUT
```

This convention is widely supported by web application frameworks and is a common way of creating *RESTful web applications*, which you can learn more about at http://en.wikipedia.org/wiki/Representational_state_transfer. See the "Setting Timeouts and Headers" section for details of how to set a header on a jQuery Ajax request.

Handling Ajax Events

Several settings let you specify handler functions for events that are triggered through the life of an Ajax request. These are the means by which you specify the callback functions that are so central to Ajax requests. You already saw one of these in the success setting in the previous example. Table 15-3 lists the event-related settings and describes each of them.

Table 15-3. The Ajax Event Settings

Setting	Description
beforeSend	Specifies a function that will be called before the Ajax request is started
complete	Specifies a function that will be called when the Ajax request succeeds or fails
error	Specifies a function that will be called when the Ajax request fails
success	Specifies a function that will be called when the Ajax request succeeds

■ **Tip** The settings described in Table 15-3 are related to local events, meaning that they deal with individual Ajax requests. You can also use a series of *global events*, which I describe in the "Using the Global Ajax Events" section later in this chapter.

Dealing with Successful Requests

When I demonstrated the use of the success property, I omitted a couple of arguments from the function. They are a status message describing the result of the request and a jqXHR object. Listing 15-5 shows the use of a function that accepts these arguments.

Listing 15-5. Receiving All of the Arguments to a Success Function

```
...
<script type="text/javascript">
    $(document).ready(function() {

        $.ajax("mydata.json",{
            success: function(data, status, jqxhr) {

                console.log("Status: " + status);

                console.log("jqXHR Status: " + jqxhr.status + " " + jqxhr.statusText);
                console.log(jqxhr.getAllResponseHeaders());

                var template = $('#flowerTmpl');
                template.tmpl(data.slice(0, 3)).appendTo("#row1");
                template.tmpl(data.slice(3)).appendTo("#row2");
            }
        });
    });
</script>
...
```

The status argument is a string that describes the outcome of the request. The function that we specify using the success setting is executed only for successful results, and so this argument generally has the value success. The exception is when you use the ifModified setting, which I describe in the "Ignoring Unmodified Data" section later in the chapter.

The callback functions for Ajax events follow the same pattern, and this argument is more useful some of the other events.

The final argument is a jqXHR object. You don't have to poll the status of the request before working with the jqXHR object since you know the function is executed only when the request has successfully completed. In this example, I have used the jqXHR object to get the status information and the headers that the server has included in the response and write them to the console. This example produces the following result (although you will see a different set of headers depending on the web server you are using):

```
Status: success
jqXHR Status: 200 OK

Date: Sat, 22 Oct 2011 09:19:03 GMT
X-Powered-By: ASP.NET
Content-Length: 437
Last-Modified: Wed, 19 Oct 2011 12:49:28 GMT
Server: Microsoft-IIS/7.5
ETag: "c2d4ec895d8ecc1:0"
Content-Type: application/json
Cache-Control: no-cache
Accept-Ranges: bytes
```

Dealing with Errors

You use the error setting to specify a function to be called when a request fails. Listing 15-6 provides a demonstration.

Listing 15-6. Using the error Setting

```
...
<style type="text/css">
    .error {color: red; border: medium solid red; padding: 4px;
            margin: auto; width: 200px; text-align: center}
</style>
<script type="text/javascript">
    $(document).ready(function() {

        $.ajax("NoSuchFile.json",{
            success: function(data, status, jqxhr) {
                var template = $('#flowerTmpl');
                template.tmpl(data.slice(0, 3)).appendTo("#row1");
                template.tmpl(data.slice(3)).appendTo("#row2");
            },
            error: function(jqxhr, status, errorMsg) {
                $('<div class=error/>')
```

```
                    .text("Status: " + status + " Error: " + errorMsg)
                    .insertAfter('h1');
                }
            });
        });
    </script>
    ...
```

In this example, I have requested a file called NoSuchFile.json, which doesn't exist on the web server, thus guaranteeing that the request will fail and the function I have specified with the error setting will be invoked. The arguments to the function are a jqXHR object, a status message, and the error message from the server response. In the error function I add a div element to the document showing the value of the status and errorMsg arguments, as shown in Figure 15-1.

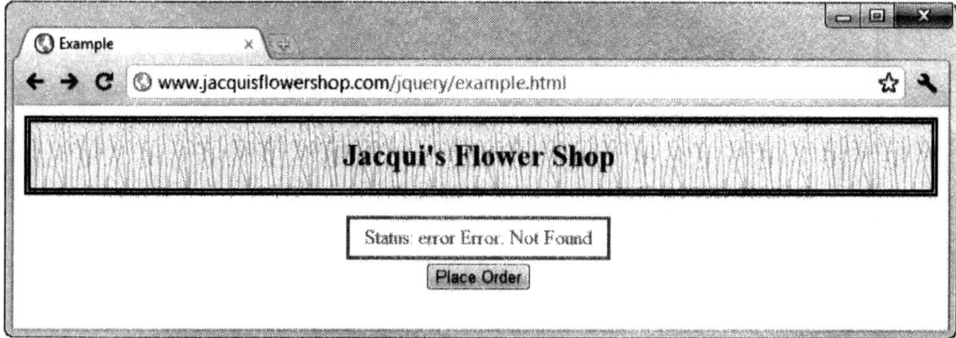

Figure 15-1. Displaying an error message

The status argument can be one of the values shown in Table 15-4.

Table 15-4. *The error status values*

Setting	Description
abort	Indicates that the request was aborted (using the jqXHR object)
error	Indicates a general error, usually reported by the server
parsererror	Indicates that the data returned by the server could not be parsed
timeout	Indicates that the request timed out before the server responded

The errorMsg argument varies based on the status. When the status is error, then errorMsg will be set to the text portion of the response from the server. So, in this example, the response from the server was 404 Not Found, and so errorMsg is set to Not Found.

When the status is timeout, the value of errorMsg will also be timeout. You can specify the period before a request times out using the timeout setting, which I describe in the "Setting Timeouts and Headers" section later in this chapter.

When the status is parsererror, then errorMsg will contain details of the problem. This error occurs when data is badly formed or the server returns the wrong MIME type for the data. You can override the data type using the dataType setting. Finally, when the request is abort, both the status and the errorMsg values will be abort.

■ **Tip** Although I have displayed the status and errorMsg values in the document, this is generally unhelpful to the user, since the messages require some understanding of what's happening inside the web application and they contain no instructions about how the problem might be resolved.

Dealing with Completed Requests

You can use the complete setting to specify a function that will be called when the Ajax request completes, irrespective of whether it succeeds or fails. Listing 15-7 provides a demonstration.

Listing 15-7. Using the Complete Setting

```
...
<script type="text/javascript">
    $(document).ready(function() {

        $.ajax("mydata.json",{
            success: function(data, status, jqxhr) {
                var template = $('#flowerTmpl');
                template.tmpl(data.slice(0, 3)).appendTo("#row1");
                template.tmpl(data.slice(3)).appendTo("#row2");
            },
            error: function(jqxhr, status, errorMsg) {
                $('<div class=error/>')
                    .text("Status: " + status + " Error: " + errorMsg)
                    .insertAfter('h1');
            },
            complete: function(jXHR, status) {
                console.log("Completed: " + status);
            }
        });
    });
</script>
...
```

The function specified by the complete setting is called after the functions specified by the success and error settings. You get a lot less prepackaged information from jQuery in this function, although you do get a wider range of values for the status argument, as shown in Table 15-5.

Table 15-5. The Ajax Event Settings

Setting	Description
abort	Indicates that the request was aborted (using the jqXHR object)
error	Indicates a general error, usually reported by the server
notmodified	Indicates that the requested content has not been modified since it was last requested (see the "Ignoring Unmodified Data" section for more details)
parsererror	Indicates that the data returned by the server could not be parsed
success	Indicates that the request completed successfully
timeout	Indicates that the request timed out before the server responded

You might be tempted to use the complete setting to specify a single function that can handle all outcomes of a request, but doing so means you don't benefit from the way that jQuery processes data and errors. A better approach is to use the success and error settings and carefully organize the arguments on the common function, as shown in Listing 15-8.

Listing 15-8. Using a Single Function to Handle All Request Outcomes

```
...
<script type="text/javascript">
    $(document).ready(function() {

        $.ajax("mydata.json",{
            success: function(data, status, jqxhr) {
                handleResponse(status, data, null, jqxhr);
            },
            error: function(jqxhr, status, errorMsg) {
                handleResponse(status, null, errorMsg, jqxhr);
            }
        });

        function handleResponse(status, data, errorMsg, jqxhr) {
            if (status == "success") {
                var template = $('#flowerTmpl');
                template.tmpl(data.slice(0, 3)).appendTo("#row1");
                template.tmpl(data.slice(3)).appendTo("#row2");
            } else {
                $('<div class=error/>')
                    .text("Status: " + status + " Error: " + errorMsg)
                    .insertAfter('h1');
            }
        }
```

```
    });
</script>
...
```

Configuring Requests Before They Are Sent

The beforeSend setting lets you specify a function that will be called before the request is started. This gives you an opportunity to do any last-minute configuration, supplementing or overriding the settings you passed to the ajax method (which can be useful if you are using the same settings object for multiple requests). Listing 15-9 demonstrates the use of this setting.

Listing 15-9. Using the beforeSend Setting

```
...
<script type="text/javascript">
    $(document).ready(function() {

        $.ajax({
            success: function(data, status, jqxhr) {
                handleResponse(status, data, null, jqxhr);
            },
            error: function(jqxhr, status, errorMsg) {
                handleResponse(status, null, errorMsg, jqxhr);
            },
            beforeSend: function(jqxhr, settings) {
                settings.url = "mydata.json";
            }
        });

        function handleResponse(status, data, errorMsg, jqxhr) {
            if (status == "success") {
                var template = $('#flowerTmpl');
                template.tmpl(data.slice(0, 3)).appendTo("#row1");
                template.tmpl(data.slice(3)).appendTo("#row2");
            } else {
                $('<div class=error/>')
                    .text("Status: " + status + " Error: " + errorMsg)
                    .insertAfter('h1');
            }
        }

    });
</script>
...
```

The arguments to the function are the jqXHR object (which can be helpful for setting the request headers or for aborting the request before it is started) and the settings object that you passed to the ajax method. In this example, I used the url setting to specify the URL for the Ajax request.

Specifying Multiple Event Handler Functions

I have shown using just one function to respond to the Ajax request events, but you set the success, error, complete, and beforeStart settings to an array of functions, each of which will be executed when the corresponding event is triggered. Listing 15-10 provides a simple demonstration.

Listing 15-10. Specifying Multiple Event Handling Functions

```
...
<script type="text/javascript">
    $(document).ready(function() {

        $.ajax("mydata.json", {
            success: [processData, reportStatus]
        });

        function processData(data, status, jqxhr) {
            var template = $('#flowerTmpl');
            template.tmpl(data.slice(0, 3)).appendTo("#row1");
            template.tmpl(data.slice(3)).appendTo("#row2");
        }

        function reportStatus(data, status, jqxhr) {
            console.log("Status: " + status + " Result code: " + jqxhr.status);
        }
    });
</script>
...
```

In this example, I have set the success setting to an array of two functions, one of which uses the data to add elements to the document and the other of which prints information to the console.

■ **Tip** You can also use the jqXHR object to register event listeners as part of the general jQuery for deferred objects, which I describe in Chapter 35.

Setting the Context for Events

The context setting lets you specify an element that will be assigned to the this variable when an event function is enabled. This can be useful for easily targeting elements in the document without having to select them in the handler function. Listing 15-11 gives a demonstration.

Listing 15-11. Using the context Setting

```
...
<script type="text/javascript">
    $(document).ready(function() {

        $.ajax("mydata.json", {
            context: $('h1'),
            success: function(data, status, jqxhr) {
                var template = $('#flowerTmpl');
                template.tmpl(data.slice(0, 3)).appendTo("#row1");
                template.tmpl(data.slice(3)).appendTo("#row2");
            },
            complete: function(jqxhr, status) {
                var color = status == "success" ? "green" : "red";
                this.css("border", "thick solid " + color);
            }
        });
    });
</script>
...
```

In this example, I set the `context` setting to the jQuery object containing the `h1` elements in the document. In the complete function, I use the `css` method on the jQuery object (which I refer to as `this`) to set the border for the selected elements (or element, since there is only one in the document), varying the color based on the status of the request.

■ **Tip** You can assign any object using the `context` setting, and so you are responsible for ensuring that you do appropriate things with it. For example, if you set the context to be an `HTMLElement` object, then you must be sure to pass the object to the `$` function before calling any jQuery methods on it.

Using the Global Ajax Events

In addition to the per-request events that I described in the previous chapter, jQuery also defines a set of *global events,* which you can use to monitor all Ajax queries that are made by your application. Table 15-6 shows the methods available for global events.

Table 15-6. jQuery Ajax Event Methods

Method	Description
`ajaxComplete(function)`	Registers a function to be called when an Ajax request completes (irrespective of whether it was successful)
`ajaxError(function)`	Registers a function to be called when an Ajax requests encounters an error
`ajaxSend(function)`	Registers a function to be called before an Ajax request commences
`ajaxStart(function)`	Registers a function to be called when an Ajax request starts
`ajaxStop(function)`	Registers a function to be called when all Ajax requests complete
`ajaxSuccess(function)`	Registers a function to be called when an Ajax request succeeds

You use these methods on any element in the document, just as you do with the regular event methods I described in Chapter 9. You pass the function that you want to be executed when the corresponding event occurs. The `ajaxStart` and `ajaxStop` methods do not pass any arguments to their functions. The other methods provide the following arguments:

- An `Event` object describing the event
- A `jqXHR` object describing the request
- The settings object that contains the configuration for the request

The `ajaxError` method passes an additional argument to the function, which is the description of the error that has occurred.

■ **Tip** The jQuery documentation states that the functions passed to the `ajaxComplete` and `ajaxSuccess` methods are provided with an `XMLHttpRequest` object rather a `jqXHR` object. This is not true; all of the functions that take arguments are given a `jqXHR`.

There are two important things to remember about these methods. The first is that the functions will be triggered for events from *all* Ajax requests, which means you have to be careful to ensure that you are not making assumptions that are true only for a specific request. The second thing to remember is that you need to call these methods before you start making Ajax requests to ensure that the functions are properly triggered. If you call the global methods after calling the `ajax` method, you run the risk that the Ajax request will have finished before jQuery can properly register your event handler functions. Listing 15-12 provides a demonstration of using the global Ajax event methods.

Listing 15-12. Using the Global Ajax Event Methods

```
...
<style type="text/css">
    .ajaxinfo {color: blue; border: medium solid blue; padding: 4px;
            margin: auto; margin-bottom:2px; width: 200px; text-align: center}
</style>
<script type="text/javascript">
    $(document).ready(function() {

        $('<div class=ajaxinfo ><label for="globalevents">Events:<input type="checkbox"'
         + 'id="globalevents" name="globalevents" checked></label></div>')
            .insertAfter('h1');
        $('<div id="info" class=ajaxinfo/>').text("Ready").insertAfter('h1');

        $(document)
            .ajaxStart(function() {
                displayMessage("Ajax Start")
            })
            .ajaxSend(function(event, jqxhr, settings) {
                displayMessage("Ajax Send: " + settings.url)
            })
            .ajaxSuccess(function(event, jqxhr, settings) {
                displayMessage("Ajax Success: " + settings.url)
            })
            .ajaxError(function(event, jqxhr, settings, errorMsg) {
                displayMessage("Ajax Error: " + settings.url)
            })
            .ajaxComplete(function(event, jqxhr, settings) {
                displayMessage("Ajax Complete: " + settings.url)
            })
            .ajaxStop(function() {
                displayMessage("Ajax Stop")
            })

        function displayMessage(msg) {
           $('#info').queue(function() {
                $(this).fadeTo("slow", 0).queue(function() {
                        $(this).text(msg).dequeue()
                    }).fadeTo("slow", 1).dequeue();
           })
        }

        $('button').click(function(e) {
            $('#row1, #row2').children().remove();
            $.ajax("mydata.json", {
                global: $('#globalevents:checked').length > 0,
                success: function(data, status, jqxhr) {
                    var template = $('#flowerTmpl');
                    template.tmpl(data.slice(0, 3)).appendTo("#row1");
```

```
                    template.tmpl(data.slice(3)).appendTo("#row2");
                }
            });
            e.preventDefault();
        })
    });
</script>
...
```

In this example, I have registered functions for all of the global Ajax events. These functions call the `displayMessage` function and show which event has been triggered. Because Ajax requests can complete very quickly, I have used the effects queue to slow down the transition from one message to another so you can see the sequence clearly (this doesn't slow down the Ajax request, just the display of the event messages). Finally, so that you can control the start of the sequence, I have added a handle for the `button` element's `click` event, which begins the Ajax request. You can see the status display in Figure 15-2.

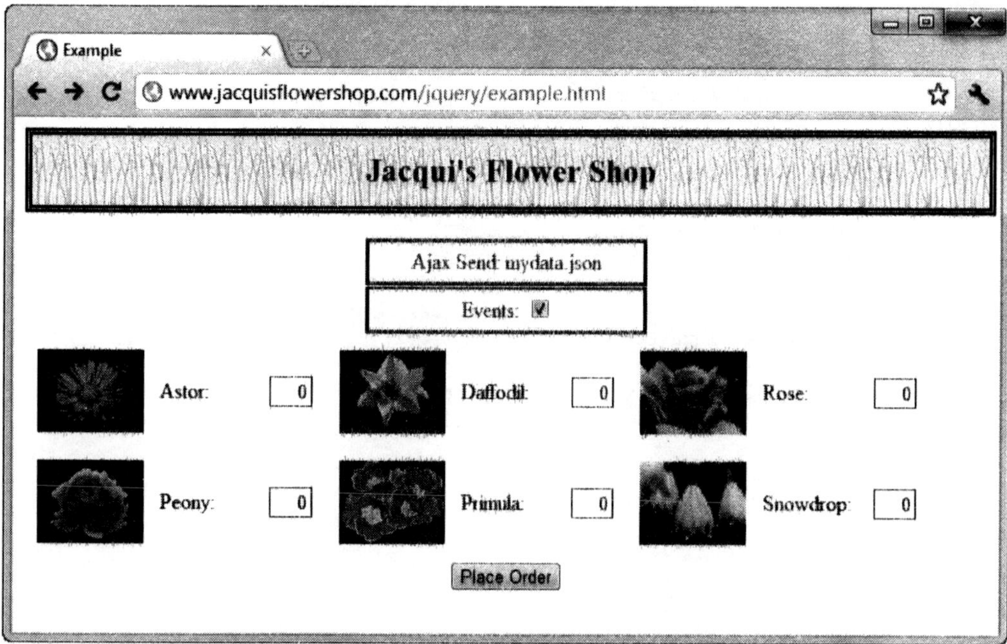

Figure 15-2. Displaying the global Ajax events

Controlling Global Events

You will notice that I have added a check box to the document. In the call to the `ajax` function, I use the check box to set the value of the `global` setting, as shown in Listing 15-13.

Listing 15-13. Using the global Setting

```
$.ajax("mydata.json", {
    global: $('#globalevents:checked').length > 0,
    success: function(data, status, jqxhr) {
        var template = $('#flowerTmpl');
        template.tmpl(data.slice(0, 3)).appendTo("#row1");
        template.tmpl(data.slice(3)).appendTo("#row2");
    }
});
```

When the `global` setting is false, the Ajax request doesn't generate the global Ajax events. You can try this yourself using the example. Uncheck the box and click the button, and you will see that the Ajax request is performed without any status information being shown.

Configuring the Basic Settings for an Ajax Request

There are a group of settings that allow you to perform some basic configuration of the Ajax request. These are the least interesting of the settings available, and they are largely self-evident. Table 15-7 shows the settings I am referring to, and I demonstrate a small number of these settings in the sections that follow.

Table 15-7. *Basic Request Configuration Settings*

Setting	Description
`accepts`	Sets the value of the `Accept` request header, which specifies the MIME types that the browser will accept. By default, this is determined by the `dataType` setting.
`cache`	If set to `false`, the content from the request will not be cached by the server. By default, the `script` and `jsonp` data types are not cached, but everything else is.
`contentType`	Sets the `Content-Type` header for the request.
`dataType`	Specifies the data type that is expected from the server. When this setting is used, jQuery will ignore the information provided by the server about the response type. See Chapter 14 for details of how this works.
`headers`	Specifies additional headers and values to add to the request; see the following discussion for a demonstration.
`jsonp`	Specifies a string to use instead of a callback when making JSONP requests. This requires coordination with the server. See Chapter 14 for details about JSONP.
`jsonpCallback`	Specifies the name for the callback function, replacing the randomly generated name that jQuery uses by default. See Chapter 14 for details of JSONP.
`password`	Specifies a password to use in response to an authentication challenge.

scriptCharset	When requesting JavaScript content, tells jQuery that the script is encoded with the specified character set.
timeout	Specifies the timeout (in milliseconds) for the request. If the request times out, then the function specified by the error setting will be called with a status of timeout.
username	Specifies a username to use in response to an authentication challenge.

Setting Timeouts and Headers

Users are often not aware of Ajax requests happening, so setting a timeout period is a good way of avoiding leaving the user hanging around waiting for a process they don't even know is happening to complete. Listing 15-14 shows how you can set a timeout on a request.

Listing 15-14. Setting Timeouts

```
...
<script type="text/javascript">
    $(document).ready(function() {

        $.ajax("mydata.json", {
            timeout: 5000,
            headers: {
                "X-HTTP-Method-Override": "PUT"
            },
            success: function(data, status, jqxhr) {
                var template = $('#flowerTmpl');
                template.tmpl(data.slice(0, 3)).appendTo("#row1");
                template.tmpl(data.slice(3)).appendTo("#row2");
            },
            error: function(jqxhr, status, errorMsg) {
                console.log("Error: " + status);
            }
        });
    });
</script>
...
```

In this example, I have used the timeout setting to specify a maximum duration for the request of five seconds. If the request hasn't completed in that time, then the function specified by the error setting will be executed, with a status value of error.

■ **Caution** The timer starts as soon as the request is passed to the browser, and most browsers put limits on the number of concurrent requests. This means you run the risk of timing out requests before they even start. To avoid this, you must have some awareness of the limits of the browser and the volume and expected duration of any other Ajax requests that are in progress.

In this listing, I also used the headers setting to add a header to the request, like this:

```
...
headers: {
    "X-HTTP-Method-Override": "PUT"
},
...
```

You specify additional headers using a map object. The header in the example is the one I mentioned in the "Making a POST Request" section earlier in the chapter. This header can be useful for creating a RESTful web application, as long as it is properly understood by the server.

Sending JSON Data to the Server

It can be useful to send JSON to the server; it is a compact and expressive data format and easy to generate from JavaScript objects. You use the contentType setting to specify the Content-Type header in the request, which tells the server what kind of data is being sent. You can see an example of sending JSON data in Listing 15-15.

Listing 15-15. Sending JSON to the Server

```
...
<script type="text/javascript">
    $(document).ready(function() {

        $.ajax("mydata.json", {
            success: function(data, status, jqxhr) {
                var template = $('#flowerTmpl');
                template.tmpl(data.slice(0, 3)).appendTo("#row1");
                template.tmpl(data.slice(3)).appendTo("#row2");
            }
        });

        $('button').click(function(e) {
            $.ajax({
                url: $('form').attr("action"),
                contentType: "application/json",
                data: JSON.stringify($('form').serializeArray()),
                type: 'post',
                success: processServerResponse
            })
```

```
            e.preventDefault();
        })

        function processServerResponse(data) {
            var inputElems = $('div.dcell').hide();
                for (var prop in data) {
                var filtered = inputElems.has('input[name=' + prop + ']')
                    .appendTo("#row1").show();
            }
            $('#buttonDiv, #totalDiv').remove();
            $('#totalTmpl').tmpl(data).appendTo('body');
        }
    });
</script>
...
```

I have used the contentType setting to specify a value of application/json, which is the MIME type for JSON. I could have sent any object to the server, but I wanted to demonstrate how you can express form data as JSON, which is like this:

```
...
data: JSON.stringify($('form').serializeArray()),
...
```

I select the form element and call the serializeArray method; this creates an array of objects, each of which has a name property and a value property representing one of the input elements in the form. I then use the JSON.stringify method to convert this into a string like this:

```
[{"name":"astor","value":"1"}, {"name":"daffodil","value":"1"},
 {"name":"rose","value":"1"}, {"name":"peony","value":"1"},
 {"name":"primula","value":"1"},{"name":"snowdrop","value":"1"}]
```

And you have a convenient array of JSON objects that you can send to the server. The Node.js script that I am using for this chapter is able to parse and process this object.

Using More Advanced Configuration Settings

In the sections that follow, I describe the most interesting and useful of the advanced settings that you can apply to an Ajax request. I find that I don't use these often, but they are invaluable when I need them. They provide some fined-grained control over how jQuery deals with Ajax.

Making the Request Synchronously

The async setting specifies whether the request will be performed asynchronously. A value of true, which is the default, means that it will; a value of false means that the request will be performed synchronously.

When the request is performed synchronously, the ajax method behaves like a normal function, and the browser will wait for the request to complete before moving on to execute other statements in the script. Listing 15-16 gives an example.

Listing 15-16. Making a Synchronous Request

```
...
<script type="text/javascript">
    $(document).ready(function() {
        var elems;

        $.ajax("flowers.html", {
            async: false,
            success: function(data, status, jqxhr) {
                elems = $(data).filter("div").addClass("dcell");
            }
        });

        elems.slice(0, 3).appendTo('#row1');
        elems.slice(3).appendTo("#row2");
    });
</script>
...
```

This is the same request that I showed you in Chapter 14 to demonstrate the most common pitfall when using Ajax, updated to use the low-level API. The difference in this case is that the async setting is false, and so the browser won't get to the statements that call the slice and appendTo methods until the request has been completed and the results are assigned to the elems variable (assuming that the request completed successfully). Making synchronous calls using the Ajax method is an odd thing to do, and I recommend you consider why your web application needs to do this.

■ **Tip** Do not use synchronous calls because you find making asynchronous calls arduous; I appreciate that using callbacks and making sure you don't make assumptions about the outcome of requests can be tiresome, but it really is worth the time to get your head around this approach to web programming.

Ignoring Unmodified Data

You can use the ifModified setting to receive data only if the response has changed since the last time you queried it; this is determined by the Last-Modified header in the response. If you need to request the same data repeatedly in response to a user action, you often end up processing the server response and modifying the document just to present the user with whatever was already there. The default value for this setting is false, which tells jQuery to ignore the header and always give you the data.

Listing 15-17 provides a demonstration of using this setting.

Listing 15-17. Using the ifModified Setting

```
...
<script type="text/javascript">
    $(document).ready(function() {
```

```
        $('button').click(function(e) {
            $.ajax("mydata.json", {
                ifModified: true,
                success: function(data, status) {
                    if (status == "success") {
                        $('#row1, #row2').children().remove();
                        var template = $('#flowerTmpl');
                        template.tmpl(data.slice(0, 3)).appendTo("#row1");
                        template.tmpl(data.slice(3)).appendTo("#row2");
                    } else if (status == "notmodified") {
                        $('img').css("border", "thick solid green");
                    }
                }
            });
            e.preventDefault();
        })
    });
</script>
...
```

In this example, the value of the ifModified setting is true. The success function is always called, but if the content has not been modified since I last requested it, then the data argument will be undefined and the status argument will be notmodified. In this example, I perform different actions based on the status argument. If the argument is success, then I use the data argument to add elements to the document. If the argument is notmodified, then I use the css method to add a border to the img elements already in the document.

I make the call to the ajax method in response to the click event from the button element. This allows me to make the same request repeatedly to demonstrate the effect of the ifModified setting, which you can see in Figure 15-3.

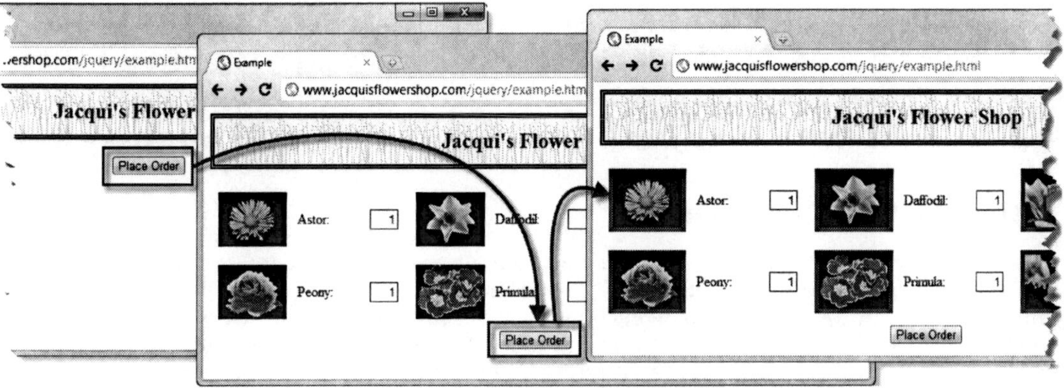

Figure 15-3. Using the ifModified setting

This can be a very useful setting, but I recommend being careful with its use. If you are making a request as a consequence of a user action (say, a button press), there is possibility that the user is pressing the button because the previous request didn't perform the way it was supposed to perform. Imagine that you request the data but the success method contains a bug that doesn't properly update the document with the content; the user is pressing the button to try to get the document to display properly. By using the `ifModified` setting unwisely, you can end up ignoring the user action, forcing the user to take more serious steps to resolve the problem.

Dealing with the Response Status Code

The `statusCode` setting allows you to respond to the different status codes that are returned in HTTP responses. You can use this feature as an alternative to the `success` and `error` settings or as a complement. Listing 15-18 shows how you can use the `statusCode` setting on its own.

Listing 15-18. Using the statusCode Setting

```
...
<style type="text/css">
    .error {color: red; border: medium solid red; padding: 4px;
            margin: auto; width: 200px; text-align: center}
</style>
<script type="text/javascript">
    $(document).ready(function() {

        $.ajax({
            url: "mydata.json",
            statusCode: {
                200: handleSuccessfulRequest,
                404: handleFailedRequest,
                302: handleRedirect
            }
        });

        function handleSuccessfulRequest(data, status, jqxhr) {
            $('#row1, #row2').children().remove();
            var template = $('#flowerTmpl');
            template.tmpl(data.slice(0, 3)).appendTo("#row1");
            template.tmpl(data.slice(3)).appendTo("#row2");
        }

        function handleRedirect() {
            // this function will neber be called
        }

        function handleFailedRequest(jqxhr, status, errorMsg) {
            $('<div class=error>Code: ' + jqxhr.status + ' Message: '
                + errorMsg + '</div>').insertAfter('h1');
        }
    });
</script>
...
```

You use the `statusCode` setting with an object that maps between HTTP status codes and the functions you want executed when they are returned to the server. In this example, I have defined three functions and associated them with the status codes 200, 404, and 302.

The arguments passed to the functions depend on whether the status code reflects a successful request or an error. If the code represents a success (such as 200), then the arguments are the same as for the success-setting function. Otherwise (such as the 404 code, which indicates the requested file can't be found), the arguments are the same as for the error-setting function.

Notice that I have also added a map for the 302 code. This is sent back to the browser when the server wants to redirect you to another URL. jQuery automatically follows redirections until it receives some content or encounters an error. This means that my function for the 302 code won't ever be called.

■ **Tip** The 304 code, indicating that content has not been modified since it was last requested, is generated only if the `ifModified` setting has been used. Otherwise, jQuery sends a 200 code instead. See the previous section for information about the `ifModified` setting.

As you can see, this feature doesn't quite expose all of the status codes directly. I find this feature useful when I am debugging interactions between the browser and the server, typically to find out why jQuery isn't behaving quite the way I would like. When I do this, I use the `statusCode` setting to complement the `success` and `error` settings and print out information to the console. When using these settings together, the `success` or `error` function will be executed before those specified by the `statusCode` setting.

Cleaning Up the Response Data

The `dataFilter` setting allows you to specify a function that will be called to process the data returned by the server. This is a very useful feature when the server sends you data that isn't quite what you need, either because the formatting isn't perfect or because it contains data that you don't want processed. I find this setting useful when working with Microsoft ASP.NET servers that can append extra data into JSON data. The `dataFilter` settings lets me remove this data with very little effort. Listing 15-19 shows the use of the `dataFilter` setting.

Listing 15-19. Using the dataFilter Setting

```
...
<script type="text/javascript">
    $(document).ready(function() {

            $.ajax({
                url: "mydata.json",
                success: function(data, status, jqxhr) {
                    $('#row1, #row2').children().remove();
                    var template = $('#flowerTmpl');
                    template.tmpl(data.slice(0, 3)).appendTo("#row1");
                    template.tmpl(data.slice(3)).appendTo("#row2");
                },
                dataType: "json",
                dataFilter: function(data, dataType) {
                    if (dataType == "json") {
                        var filteredData = $.parseJSON(data);
```

```
                        filteredData.shift();
                        return JSON.stringify(filteredData.reverse());
                    } else {
                        return data;
                    }
                }
            });
        });
</script>
...
```

The function is passed the data received from the server and the value of the `dataType` setting. If the `dataType` setting has not been used, then the second function argument will be `undefined`. Your job in this function is to return the filtered data. In this example, I focus on the `json` data type, as follows:

```
...
var filteredData = $.parseJSON(data);
filteredData.shift();
return JSON.stringify(filteredData.reverse());
...
```

To keep this example simple, I am doing something that is slightly redundant. First, I convert the JSON data into a JavaScript array by using the jQuery `parseJSON` data (this is one of the jQuery utility methods I describe in Chapter 33). I then use the `shift` method to remove the first item in the array and use the `reverse` method to reverse the order of the remaining items.

The redundancy comes because you have to return a string from the function, so I call the `JSON.stringify` method, knowing that jQuery will convert the data into a JavaScript object before calling the `success` function. Still, that aside, you can see that I am able to remove an element in the array, and I could have performed any other kind of processing that I needed. You can see the effect of this function in Figure 15-4.

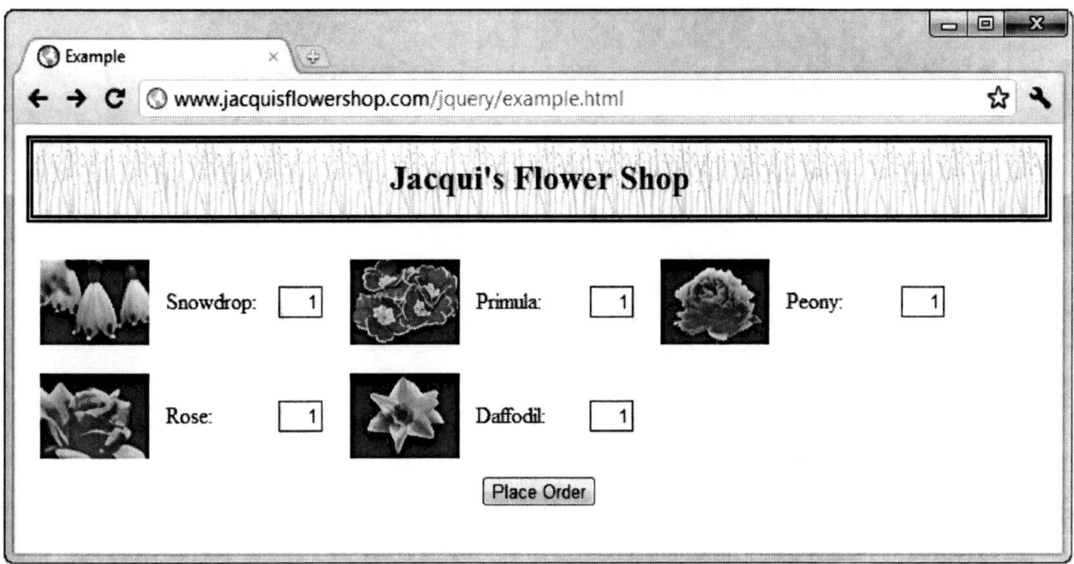

Figure 15-4. Removing an item and reversing the order of the data using the dataFilter setting

Managing Data Conversion

I have saved one of my favorite settings until last. You will have noticed that jQuery does some handy conversions when it receives certain data types. As an example, when jQuery receives some JSON data, it presents the success function with a JavaScript object, rather than the raw JSON string.

You can control these conversions using the converters setting. The value for this setting is an object that maps between data types and functions that are used to process them. Listing 15-20 shows how you can use this setting to automatically parse HTML data into a jQuery object.

Listing 15-20. Using the converters Setting

```
...
<script type="text/javascript">
    $(document).ready(function() {

        $.ajax({
            url: "flowers.html",
            success: function(data, status, jqxhr) {
                var elems = data.filter('div').addClass("dcell");
                elems.slice(0, 3).appendTo('#row1');
                elems.slice(3).appendTo("#row2");
            },
            converters: {
                "text html": function(data) {
                    return $(data);
                }
            }
```

```
        });
    });
</script>
...
```

In this example, I have registered a function for the text html type. Notice that you use a space between the components of the MIME type (as opposed to text/html). The function is passed the data that has been received from the server and returns the converted data. In this case, I simply pass the HTML fragment that is contained in the flowers.html file to the jQuery $ function and return the result. This means I can call all the usual jQuery methods on the object passed as the data argument to the success function.

■ **Tip** The data types don't always match the MIME types that are returned by the server. For example, application/json is usually presented as "text json" to the converters method.

It is easy to get carried away with these converters. I always try to avoid the temptation to do more in these functions than I should. For example, I am sometimes tempted to take JSON data, apply a data template, and pass the resulting HTML elements back. And although this is a nice trick, it can catch you out if someone else tries to extend your coding or you need to unwind heavy processing to get at the raw data later.

Setting Up and Filtering Ajax Requests

Now that you have seen the ajax method and the settings that are available, you can turn your attention to a couple of additional methods that jQuery provides to make configuring requests simpler.

Defining Default Settings

The ajaxSetup method lets you specify the settings that will be used for every Ajax request, freeing you from having to define all of the settings you are interested in for each and every request. Listing 15-21 shows this method in use.

Listing 15-21. Using the ajaxSetup Method

```
...
<script type="text/javascript">
    $(document).ready(function() {

        $.ajaxSetup({
            timeout: 15000,
            global: false,
            error: function(jqxhr, status, errorMsg) {
                $('<div class=error/>')
                    .text("Status: " + status + " Error: " + errorMsg)
                    .insertAfter('h1');
            },
```

```
            converters: {
                "text html": function(data) {
                    return $(data);
                }
            }
        });

        $.ajax({
            url: "flowers.html",
            success: function(data, status, jqxhr) {
                var elems = data.filter('div').addClass("dcell");
                elems.slice(0, 3).appendTo('#row1');
                elems.slice(3).appendTo("#row2");
            },
        });
    });
</script>
...
```

You call the ajaxSetup method against the jQuery $ function, just as you do for the ajax method. The argument to the ajaxSetup is an object that contains the settings you want to use as the defaults for all your Ajax requests. In this example, I define defaults for the timeout, global, error, and converters settings. Once I have called the ajaxSetup method, I only have to define values for those settings for which I haven't provided a default value or whose value I want to change. This can be a useful time-saver if you are making a lot of Ajax requests that have similar configurations.

■ **Tip** The settings specified by the ajaxSetup method also affect requests made by the convenience and shorthand methods I showed you in Chapter 14. This can be a nice way of combining the detailed control that comes with the low-level API with the simplicity of the convenience methods.

Filtering Requests

The ajaxSetup method defines a baseline configuration that is applied to all Ajax requests. You can use the ajaxPrefilter method if you want to dynamically tailor the settings for requests individually. Listing 15-22 contains a demonstration of using this method.

Listing 15-22. Using the ajaxPrefilter Method

```
...
<script type="text/javascript">
    $(document).ready(function() {

        $.ajaxSetup({
            timeout: 15000,
            global: false,
            error: function(jqxhr, status, errorMsg) {
                $('<div class=error/>')
```

```
                .text("Status: " + status + " Error: " + errorMsg)
                .insertAfter('h1');
        },
        converters: {
            "text html": function(data) {
                return $(data);
            }
        }
    })

    $.ajaxPrefilter("json html", function(settings, originalSettings, jqxhr) {
        if (originalSettings.dataType == "html") {
            settings.timeout = 2000;
        } else {
            jqxhr.abort();
        }
    })

    $.ajax({
        url: "flowers.html",
        dataType: "html",
        success: function(data, status, jqxhr) {
            var elems = data.filter('div').addClass("dcell");
            elems.slice(0, 3).appendTo('#row1');
            elems.slice(3).appendTo("#row2");
        },
    });
});
</script>
...
```

The function that you specify will be executed for each new Ajax request. The arguments passed to the function are the settings for the request (which includes any defaults you have set using ajaxSetup); the original settings passed to the Ajax method (which excludes any default values) and to the jqXHR object for the request. You make changes to the object passed as the first argument, as shown in the example. In this script, if a dataType setting has been specified in the settings passed to the Ajax method, I set the timeout to be two seconds. For all other requests, I call the abort method on the jqXHR object to prevent the request from being sent.

Summary

In this chapter, I showed you the low-level jQuery Ajax interface that, as I hope you agree, isn't that much harder to work with than the convenience and shorthand methods I showed you in Chapter 14. For a modicum of additional effort, you can control many aspects of the way that the Ajax request is processed, giving you endless ways in which you can tweak the process to your needs and preferences.

CHAPTER 16

Refactoring the Example: Part II

I have introduced some very rich features in this part of the book, and as before, I want to bring them together to give a broader view of jQuery. I am not going to try to preserve a workable non-JavaScript structure in this chapter, since all of the features I am adding to the example rely heavily on JavaScript.

Reviewing the Refactored Example

In Chapter 11, you used the core jQuery features to refactor the example to include DOM manipulation, effects, and events. Listing 16-1 shows the document you ended up with, which will be the starting point for this chapter as you integrate the features from this part of the book.

There are a number of points in the script where I insert elements dynamically. Rather than making these static, I am going to leave them as they are so that you can focus on adding the new features.

Listing 16-1. The Starting Point for This Chapter

```
<!DOCTYPE html>
<html>
<head>
    <title>Example</title>
    <script src="jquery-1.7.js" type="text/javascript"></script>
    <link rel="stylesheet" type="text/css" href="styles.css"/>
    <style type="text/css">
        a.arrowButton {
            background-image: url(leftarrows.png); float: left;
            margin-top: 15px; display: block; width: 50px; height: 50px;
        }
        #right {background-image: url(rightarrows.png)}
        h1 { min-width: 0px; width: 95%; }
        #oblock { float: left; display: inline; border: thin black solid; }
        form { margin-left: auto; margin-right: auto; width: 885px; }
        #bbox {clear: left}
    </style>
    <script type="text/javascript">
        $(document).ready(function() {

            var fNames = ["Carnation", "Lily", "Orchid"];
            var fRow = $('<div id=row3 class=drow/>').appendTo('div.dtable');
            var fTemplate = $('<div class=dcell><img/><label/><input/></div>');
            for (var i = 0; i < fNames.length; i++) {
```

```
                    fTemplate.clone().appendTo(fRow).children()
                        .filter('img').attr('src', fNames[i] + ".png").end()
                        .filter('label').attr('for', fNames[i]).text(fNames[i]).end()
                        .filter('input').attr({name: fNames[i],
                                              value: 0, required: "required"})
                }

                $('<a id=left></a><a id=right></a>').prependTo('form')
                    .addClass("arrowButton").click(handleArrowPress).hover(handleArrowMouse);
                $('#right').appendTo('form');

                $('#row2, #row3').hide();

                var total = $('#buttonDiv')
                    .prepend("<div>Total Items: <span id=total>0</span></div>")
                    .css({clear: "both", padding: "5px"});
                $('<div id=bbox />').appendTo("body").append(total);

                $('input').change(function(e) {
                    var total = 0;
                    $('input').each(function(index, elem) {
                        total += Number($(elem).val());
                    });
                    $('#total').text(total);
                });

                function handleArrowMouse(e) {
                   var propValue = e.type == "mouseenter" ? "-50px 0px" : "0px 0px";
                   $(this).css("background-position", propValue);
                }

                function handleArrowPress(e) {
                    var elemSequence = ["row1", "row2", "row3"];

                    var visibleRow = $('div.drow:visible');
                    var visibleRowIndex = jQuery.inArray(visibleRow.attr("id"),elemSequence);

                    var targetRowIndex;

                    if (e.target.id == "left") {
                        targetRowIndex = visibleRowIndex - 1;
                        if (targetRowIndex < 0) {targetRowIndex = elemSequence.length -1};
                    } else {
                        targetRowIndex = (visibleRowIndex + 1) % elemSequence.length;
                    }
                    visibleRow.fadeOut("fast", function() {
                        $('#' + elemSequence[targetRowIndex]).fadeIn("fast")});
                }
            });
        </script>
    </head>
    <body>
```

```
    <h1>Jacqui's Flower Shop</h1>
    <form method="post" action="http://node.jacquisflowershop.com/order">
        <div id="oblock">
            <div class="dtable">
                <div id="row1" class="drow">
                    <div class="dcell">
                        <img src="astor.png"/><label for="astor">Astor:</label>
                        <input name="astor" value="0" />
                    </div>
                    <div class="dcell">
                        <img src="daffodil.png"/><label for="daffodil">Daffodil:</label>
                        <input name="daffodil" value="0"/>
                    </div>
                    <div class="dcell">
                        <img src="rose.png"/><label for="rose">Rose:</label>
                        <input name="rose" value="0" />
                    </div>
                </div>
                <div id="row2"class="drow">
                    <div class="dcell">
                        <img src="peony.png"/><label for="peony">Peony:</label>
                        <input name="peony" value="0" />
                    </div>
                    <div class="dcell">
                        <img src="primula.png"/><label for="primula">Primula:</label>
                        <input name="primula" value="0" />
                    </div>
                    <div class="dcell">
                        <img src="snowdrop.png"/><label for="snowdrop">Snowdrop:</label>
                        <input name="snowdrop" value="0" />
                    </div>
                </div>
            </div>
        </div>
        <div id="buttonDiv"><button type="submit">Place Order</button></div>
    </form>
</body>
</html>
```

This isn't quite the same as the document in Chapter 11. I have tidied up a lot of the CSS additions by adding a style element, rather than using the css method on individual selections. You can see how this document appears in Figure 16-1, and, of course, Chapter 11 breaks down the set of changes I applied to the document to get this far.

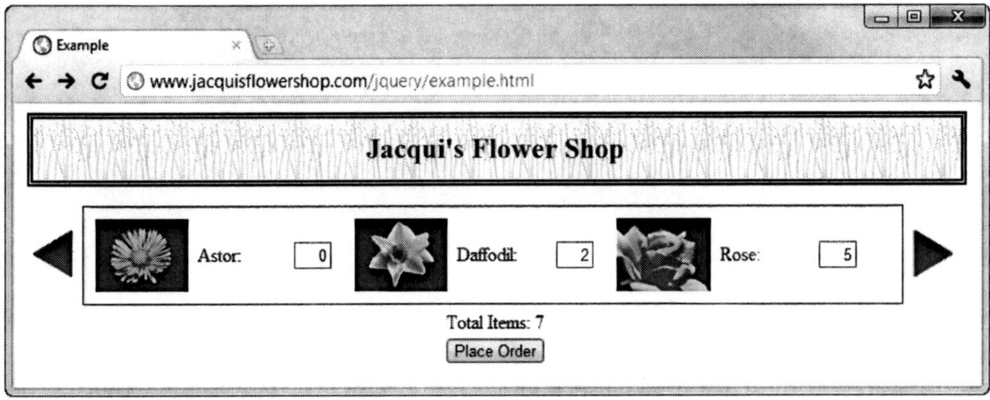

Figure 16-1. The starting point for the example document in this chapter

Updating the Node.js Script

Before you get started with the jQuery features, you need to upgrade your server-side script. These additions are to enrich the data that is sent back when a form is submitted and to support a new validation feature. Listing 16-2 shows the new script.

Listing 16-2. The Revised Node.js Script

```
var http = require('http');
var url = require('url');
var querystring = require('querystring');

http.createServer(function (req, res) {
    console.log("Request: " + req.method + " to " + req.url);

    if (req.method == 'OPTIONS') {
        res.writeHead(200, "OK", {
            "Access-Control-Allow-Headers": "Content-Type",
            "Access-Control-Allow-Methods": "*",
            "Access-Control-Allow-Origin": "*"
            });
        res.end();

    } else if (req.method == 'POST') {
        var dataObj = new Object();
        var contentType = req.headers["content-type"];
        var fullBody = '';

        if (contentType) {
            if (contentType.indexOf("application/x-www-form-urlencoded") > -1) {
                req.on('data', function(chunk) { fullBody += chunk.toString();});
                req.on('end', function() {
                    var dBody = querystring.parse(fullBody);
```

```
                writeResponse(req, res, dBody,
                    url.parse(req.url, true).query["callback"])
            });
        } else {
            req.on('data', function(chunk) { fullBody += chunk.toString();});
            req.on('end', function() {
                dataObj = JSON.parse(fullBody);
                var dprops = new Object();
                for (var i = 0; i < dataObj.length; i++) {
                    dprops[dataObj[i].name] = dataObj[i].value;
                }
                writeResponse(req, res, dprops);
            });
        }
    }
} else if (req.method == "GET") {
    var data = url.parse(req.url, true).query;
    writeResponse(req, res, data, data["callback"])
}

}).listen(80);
console.log("Ready on port 80");

var flowerData = {
    astor: { price: 2.99, stock: 10, plural: "Astors"},
    daffodil: {price: 1.99, stock: 10, plural: "Daffodils"},
    rose: {price: 4.99, stock: 2, plural: "Roses"},
    peony: {price: 1.50, stock: 3, plural: "Peonies"},
    primula: {price: 3.12, stock: 20, plural: "Primulas"},
    snowdrop: {price: 0.99, stock: 5, plural: "Snowdrops"},
    carnation: {price: 0.50, stock: 1, plural: "Carnations"},
    lily: {price: 1.20, stock: 2, plural: "Lillies"},
    orchid: {price: 10.99, stock: 5, plural: "Orchids"}
}

function writeResponse(req, res, data, jsonp) {
    var jsonData;
    if (req.url == "/stockcheck") {
        for (flower in data) {
            if (flowerData[flower].stock >= data[flower]) {
                jsonData = true;
            } else {
                jsonData = "We only have " + flowerData[flower].stock + " "
                    + flowerData[flower].plural + " in stock";
            }
            break;
        }
        jsonData = JSON.stringify(jsonData);
    } else {
        var totalCount = 0;
        var totalPrice = 0;
        for (item in data) {
```

```
            if(item != "_" && data[item] > 0) {
                var itemNum = Number(data[item])
                totalCount += itemNum;
                totalPrice += (itemNum * flowerData[item].price);
            } else {
                delete data[item];
            }
        }
        data.totalItems = totalCount;
        data.totalPrice = totalPrice.toFixed(2);

        jsonData = JSON.stringify(data);
        if (jsonp) {
            jsonData = jsonp + "(" + jsonData + ")";
        }
    }
    res.writeHead(200, "OK", {
        "Content-Type": jsonp ? "text/javascript" : "application/json",
        "Access-Control-Allow-Origin": "*"});
    res.write(jsonData);
    res.end();
}
```

The response to the browser now includes the total prices for the items selected using the `form` elements and submitted to the server, returning a JSON result like this:

```
{"astor":"1","daffodil":"2","rose":"4","totalItems":7,"totalPrice":"26.93"}
```

I saved this script to a file called `formserver.js`. The easiest way to get this script is to download the source code that accompanies this book and that is freely available from Apress.com. I run the script by entering the following at the command prompt:

```
node.exe formserver.js
```

Preparing for Ajax

To being with, I am going to add some basic elements and styles that I will use to display any Ajax request errors and set up the basic configuration that will apply to all of my Ajax requests. Listing 16-3 shows the changes to the document.

Listing 16-3. Setting Up the Support for Ajax Requests and Error Handling

```
...
<style type="text/css">
    a.arrowButton {
        background-image: url(leftarrows.png); float: left;
        margin-top: 15px; display: block; width: 50px; height: 50px;}
    #right {background-image: url(rightarrows.png)}
    h1 { min-width: 0px; width: 95%; }
    #oblock { float: left; display: inline; border: thin black solid; }
```

```
    form { margin-left: auto; margin-right: auto; width: 885px; }
    #bbox {clear: left}
    #error {color: red; border: medium solid red; padding: 4px; margin: auto;
        width: 300px; text-align: center; margin-bottom: 5px}
</style>
<script type="text/javascript">
    $(document).ready(function() {

        $.ajaxSetup({
            timeout: 5000,
            converters: {
                "text html": function(data) {
                    return $(data);
                }
            }
        })

        $(document).ajaxError(function(e, jqxhr, settings, errorMsg) {
            $('#error').remove();
            var msg = "An error occurred. Please try again"
            if (errorMsg == "timeout") {
                msg = "The request timed out. Please try again"
            } else if (jqxhr.status == 404) {
                    msg = "The file could not be found";
            }
            $('<div id=error/>').text(msg).insertAfter('h1');
        }).ajaxSuccess(function() {
            $('#error').remove();
        })

        var fNames = ["Carnation", "Lily", "Orchid"];
        var fRow = $('<div id=row3 class=drow/>').appendTo('div.dtable');
        var fTemplate = $('<div class=dcell><img/><label/><input/></div>');
        for (var i = 0; i < fNames.length; i++) {
            fTemplate.clone().appendTo(fRow).children()
                .filter('img').attr('src', fNames[i] + ".png").end()
                .filter('label').attr('for', fNames[i]).text(fNames[i]).end()
                .filter('input').attr({name: fNames[i],
                                       value: 0, required: "required"})
        }

        $('<a id=left></a><a id=right></a>').prependTo('form')
            .addClass("arrowButton").click(handleArrowPress).hover(handleArrowMouse);
        $('#right').appendTo('form');

        $('#row2, #row3').hide();

        var total = $('#buttonDiv')
            .prepend("<div>Total Items: <span id=total>0</span></div>")
            .css({clear: "both", padding: "5px"});
        $('<div id=bbox />').appendTo("body").append(total);
```

```
        $('input').change(function(e) {
            var total = 0;
            $('input').each(function(index, elem) {
                total += Number($(elem).val());
            });
            $('#total').text(total);
        });

        function handleArrowMouse(e) {
           var propValue = e.type == "mouseenter" ? "-50px 0px" : "0px 0px";
           $(this).css("background-position", propValue);
        }

        function handleArrowPress(e) {
            var elemSequence = ["row1", "row2", "row3"];

            var visibleRow = $('div.drow:visible');
            var visibleRowIndex = jQuery.inArray(visibleRow.attr("id"),elemSequence);

            var targetRowIndex;

            if (e.target.id == "left") {
                targetRowIndex = visibleRowIndex - 1;
                if (targetRowIndex < 0) {targetRowIndex = elemSequence.length -1};
            } else {
                targetRowIndex = (visibleRowIndex + 1) % elemSequence.length;
            }
            visibleRow.fadeOut("fast", function() {
                $('#' + elemSequence[targetRowIndex]).fadeIn("fast")});
        }
    });
</script>
...
```

I have used the global Ajax events to set up a simple display for errors. When an error occurs, new elements are added to the screen with a description of the problem. The error messages that I show are derived from the information I get from jQuery, but I have kept things simple. In a real web application, these messages should be more descriptive and provide suggestions for basic resolution if possible. I have used the global events so that I am able to use the success and error setting on individual requests without having to worry about concatenating arrays of functions. You can see an example of a simple error in Figure 16-2.

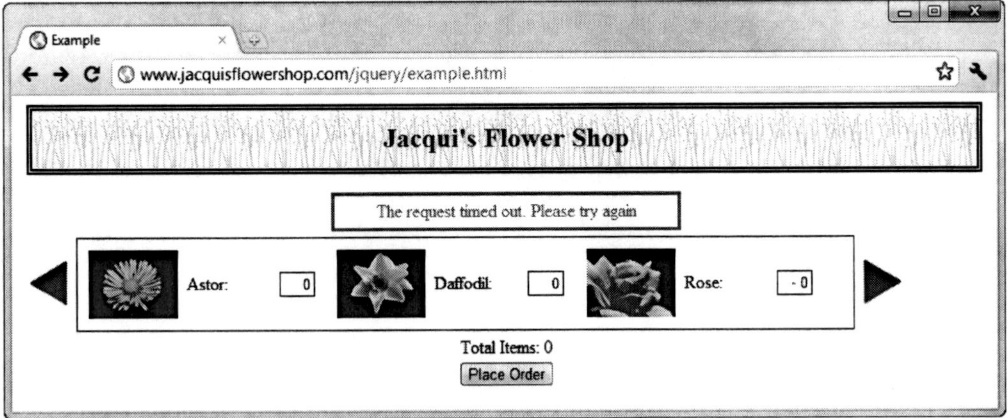

Figure 16-2. Displaying an error message for Ajax

The error is displayed until a successful request is made or another error occurs, at which point the elements are removed from the document.

In addition to the events, I used the `ajaxSetup` method to define values for the `timeout` setting and to provide a converter for HTML fragments so that they are automatically processed by jQuery.

Sourcing the Product Information

The next change I am going to make is to remove the existing product elements and the loop that adds three additional flowers to the list, replacing them with a couple of Ajax calls and a data template. First, however, I have created a new file called `additionalflowers.json`, which is shown in Listing 16-4.

Listing 16-4. The Contents of the Additionalflowers.json File

```
[{"name":"Carnation","product":"carnation"},
 {"name":"Lily","product":"lily"},
 {"name":"Orchid","product":"orchid"}]
```

This file contains a basic JSON description of the additional products I want to display. I am going to get the main set of products as an HTML fragment and then add to the set by processing the JSON data. Listing 16-5 shows the changes.

Listing 16-5. Setting Up the Products via HTML and JSON Obtained via Ajax

```
<!DOCTYPE html>
<html>
<head>
    <title>Example</title>
    <script src="jquery-1.7.js" type="text/javascript"></script>
    <script src="jquery.tmpl.js" type="text/javascript"></script>
    <link rel="stylesheet" type="text/css" href="styles.css"/>
    <style type="text/css">
        a.arrowButton {
```

```
            background-image: url(leftarrows.png); float: left;
            margin-top: 15px; display: block; width: 50px; height: 50px;}
        #right {background-image: url(rightarrows.png)}
        h1 { min-width: 0px; width: 95%; }
        #oblock { float: left; display: inline; border: thin black solid; }
        form { margin-left: auto; margin-right: auto; width: 885px; }
        #bbox {clear: left}
        #error {color: red; border: medium solid red; padding: 4px; margin: auto;
            width: 300px; text-align: center; margin-bottom: 5px}
    </style>
    <script type="text/javascript">
        $(document).ready(function() {

            $.ajaxSetup({
                timeout: 5000,
                converters: {
                    "text html": function(data) { return $(data); }
                }
            })

            $(document).ajaxError(function(e, jqxhr, settings, errorMsg) {
                $('#error').remove();
                var msg = "An error occurred. Please try again"
                if (errorMsg == "timeout") {
                    msg = "The request timed out. Please try again"
                } else if (jqxhr.status == 404) {
                        msg = "The file could not be found";
                }
                $('<div id=error/>').text(msg).insertAfter('h1');
            }).ajaxSuccess(function() {
                $('#error').remove();
            })

            $('#row2, #row3').hide();

            $.get("flowers.html", function(data) {
                var elems = data.filter('div').addClass("dcell");
                elems.slice(0, 3).appendTo('#row1');
                elems.slice(3).appendTo("#row2");
            })

            $.getJSON("additionalflowers.json", function(data) {
                $('#flowerTmpl').tmpl(data).appendTo("#row3");
            })

            $('<a id=left></a><a id=right></a>').prependTo('form')
                .addClass("arrowButton").click(handleArrowPress).hover(handleArrowMouse);
            $('#right').appendTo('form');

            var total = $('#buttonDiv')
                .prepend("<div>Total Items: <span id=total>0</span></div>")
                .css({clear: "both", padding: "5px"});
```

```
            $('<div id=bbox />').appendTo("body").append(total);

            $('input').change(function(e) {
                var total = 0;
                $('input').each(function(index, elem) {
                    total += Number($(elem).val());
                });
                $('#total').text(total);
            });

            function handleArrowMouse(e) {
               var propValue = e.type == "mouseenter" ? "-50px 0px" : "0px 0px";
               $(this).css("background-position", propValue);
            }

            function handleArrowPress(e) {
                var elemSequence = ["row1", "row2", "row3"];

                var visibleRow = $('div.drow:visible');
                var visibleRowIndex = jQuery.inArray(visibleRow.attr("id"),elemSequence);

                var targetRowIndex;

                if (e.target.id == "left") {
                    targetRowIndex = visibleRowIndex - 1;
                    if (targetRowIndex < 0) {targetRowIndex = elemSequence.length -1};
                } else {
                    targetRowIndex = (visibleRowIndex + 1) % elemSequence.length;
                }
                visibleRow.fadeOut("fast", function() {
                    $('#' + elemSequence[targetRowIndex]).fadeIn("fast")});
            }
        });
    </script>
    <script id="flowerTmpl" type="text/x-jquery-tmpl">
        <div class="dcell">
            <img src="${product}.png"/>
            <label for="${product}">${name}:</label>
            <input name="${product}" value="0" />
        </div>
    </script>
</head>
<body>
    <h1>Jacqui's Flower Shop</h1>
    <form method="post" action="http://node.jacquisflowershop.com/order">
        <div id="oblock">
            <div class="dtable">
                <div id="row1" class="drow"></div>
                <div id="row2" class="drow"></div>
                <div id="row3" class="drow"></div>
            </div>
        </div>
```

```
        <div id="buttonDiv"><button type="submit">Place Order</button></div>
    </form>
</body>
</html>
```

I have used the Ajax shorthand methods to get the HTML fragment and the JSON data I need to create the rows. It may not be obvious from the script, but one of the nice things about the shorthand method is that they are just wrappers around calls to the low-level API, and this means that the settings you apply via the `ajaxSetup` method apply just as they do when you use the `ajax` method directly.

In addition to the calls to the get and `getJSON` methods, I have added a simple data template so I can process the JSON simply and easily. There is no change to the appearance of the document, but the source of the content has changed.

Adding Form Validation

The next stage is to add some validation to your input elements. Listing 16-6 shows the additions that are required.

Listing 16-6. Adding Form Validation

```
<!DOCTYPE html>
<html>
<head>
    <title>Example</title>
    <script src="jquery-1.7.js" type="text/javascript"></script>
    <script src="jquery.tmpl.js" type="text/javascript"></script>
    <script src="jquery.validate.js" type="text/javascript"></script>
    <link rel="stylesheet" type="text/css" href="styles.css"/>
    <style type="text/css">
        a.arrowButton {
            background-image: url(leftarrows.png); float: left;
            margin-top: 15px; display: block; width: 50px; height: 50px;}
        #right {background-image: url(rightarrows.png)}
        h1 { min-width: 0px; width: 95%; }
        #oblock { float: left; display: inline; border: thin black solid; }
        form { margin-left: auto; margin-right: auto; width: 885px; }
        #bbox {clear: left}
        #error {color: red; border: medium solid red; padding: 4px; margin: auto;
            width: 300px; text-align: center; margin-bottom: 5px}
        .invalidElem {border: medium solid red}
        #errorSummary {border: thick solid red; color: red; width: 350px; margin: auto;
            padding: 4px; margin-bottom: 5px}
    </style>
    <script type="text/javascript">
        $(document).ready(function() {

            $.ajaxSetup({
                timeout: 5000,
                converters: {
                    "text html": function(data) { return $(data); }
                }
```

```
})

$(document).ajaxError(function(e, jqxhr, settings, errorMsg) {
    $('#error').remove();
    var msg = "An error occurred. Please try again"
    if (errorMsg == "timeout") {
        msg = "The request timed out. Please try again"
    } else if (jqxhr.status == 404) {
            msg = "The file could not be found";
    }
    $('<div id=error/>').text(msg).insertAfter('h1');
}).ajaxSuccess(function() {
    $('#error').remove();
})

$('#row2, #row3').hide();

var flowerReq = $.get("flowers.html", function(data) {
    var elems = data.filter('div').addClass("dcell");
    elems.slice(0, 3).appendTo('#row1');
    elems.slice(3).appendTo("#row2");
})

var jsonReq = $.getJSON("additionalflowers.json", function(data) {
    $('#flowerTmpl').tmpl(data).appendTo("#row3");
})

$('<div id=errorSummary>Please correct the following errors:</div>')
    .append('<ul id="errorsList"></ul>').hide().insertAfter('h1');

$('form').validate({
    highlight: function(element, errorClass) {
        $(element).addClass("invalidElem");
    },
    unhighlight: function(element, errorClass) {
        $(element).removeClass("invalidElem");
    },
    errorContainer: '#errorSummary',
    errorLabelContainer: '#errorsList',
    wrapper: 'li',
    errorElement: "div"
});

var plurals = {
    astor: "Astors", daffodil: "Daffodils", rose: "Roses",
    peony: "Peonies", primula: "Primulas", snowdrop: "Snowdrops",
    carnation: "Carnations", lily: "Lillies", orchid: "Orchids"
}

$.when(flowerReq, jsonReq).then(function() {
    $('input').each(function(index, elem) {
```

```
        $(elem).rules("add", {
            required: true,
            min: 0,
            digits: true,

            messages: {
              required: "Please enter a number for " + plurals[elem.name],
              digits: "Please enter a number for " + plurals[elem.name],
              min: "Please enter a positive number for " + plurals[elem.name]
            }
        })
    }).change(function(e) {
        if ($('form').validate().element($(e.target))) {
            var total = 0;
            $('input').each(function(index, elem) {
                total += Number($(elem).val());
            });
            $('#total').text(total);
        }
    });
});

$('<a id=left></a><a id=right></a>').prependTo('form')
    .addClass("arrowButton").click(handleArrowPress).hover(handleArrowMouse);
$('#right').appendTo('form');

var total = $('#buttonDiv')
    .prepend("<div>Total Items: <span id=total>0</span></div>")
    .css({clear: "both", padding: "5px"});
$('<div id=bbox />').appendTo("body").append(total);

function handleArrowMouse(e) {
   var propValue = e.type == "mouseenter" ? "-50px 0px" : "0px 0px";
   $(this).css("background-position", propValue);
}

function handleArrowPress(e) {
    var elemSequence = ["row1", "row2", "row3"];

    var visibleRow = $('div.drow:visible');
    var visibleRowIndex = jQuery.inArray(visibleRow.attr("id"),elemSequence);

    var targetRowIndex;

    if (e.target.id == "left") {
        targetRowIndex = visibleRowIndex - 1;
        if (targetRowIndex < 0) {targetRowIndex = elemSequence.length -1};
    } else {
        targetRowIndex = (visibleRowIndex + 1) % elemSequence.length;
    }
    visibleRow.fadeOut("fast", function() {
```

```
                $('#' + elemSequence[targetRowIndex]).fadeIn("fast")});
            }
        });
    </script>
    <script id="flowerTmpl" type="text/x-jquery-tmpl">
        <div class="dcell">
            <img src="${product}.png"/>
            <label for="${product}">${name}:</label>
            <input name="${product}" value="0" />
        </div>
    </script>
</head>
<body>
    <h1>Jacqui's Flower Shop</h1>
    <form method="post" action="http://node.jacquisflowershop.com/order">
        <div id="oblock">
            <div class="dtable">
                <div id="row1" class="drow"></div>
                <div id="row2" class="drow"></div>
                <div id="row3" class="drow"></div>
            </div>
        </div>
        <div id="buttonDiv"><button type="submit">Place Order</button></div>
    </form>
</body>
</html>
```

In this listing, I have imported the JavaScript library for the validation plugin and defined some basic styles that will be used to display validation errors. I then call the `validate` method on the `form` element to set up form validation, specifying a single validation summary. This approach is straight out of Chapter 13.

Now, the use of Ajax to generate elements for the flower products gives me a problem. These are, of course, asynchronous calls, so I can't make assumptions about the presence of the input elements in the document in the statements that follow the Ajax calls. This is the common pitfall I described in Chapter 14, and if the browser executes my selection of the input elements before both Ajax requests are complete, then I won't match any elements (because they have yet to be created and added to the document), and my validation setup will fail. To get around this, I have used the `when` and `then` methods, which are part of the jQuery deferred objects feature that I describe in Chapter 35. Here are the relevant statements:

```
...
$.when(flowerReq, jsonReq).then(function() {
    $('input').each(function(index, elem) {
        $(elem).rules("add", {
            required: true,
            min: 0,
            digits: true,
            messages: {
              required: "Please enter a number for " + plurals[elem.name],
              digits: "Please enter a number for " + plurals[elem.name],
              min: "Please enter a positive number for " + plurals[elem.name]
            }
```

```
            })
        }).change(function(e) {
            if ($('form').validate().element($(e.target))) {
                var total = 0;
                $('input').each(function(index, elem) {
                    total += Number($(elem).val());
                });
                $('#total').text(total);
            }
        });
});
...
```

I don't want to get ahead of myself, but the jqXHR objects that are returned by all of the Ajax methods can be passed as arguments to the when method, and if both requests are successful, then the function passed to the then method will be executed.

I set up my form validation in the function I pass to the then method, selecting the input elements and adding the validation rules I require to each of them. I have specified that values are required, that they must be digits, and that the minimum acceptable value is zero. I have defined custom messages for each check, and these refer to an array of plural flower names to help them make sense to the user.

Since I have the input elements selected, I take the opportunity to provide a handler function for the change event, which is triggered when the value entered into the field changes. Notice that I call the element method, like this:

```
...
if ($('form').validate().element($(e.target))) {
...
```

This triggers validation on the changed element, and the result from the method is a Boolean indicating the validity of the entered value. By using this in an if block, I can avoid adding invalid values to my running total of selected items.

Adding Remote Validation

The validation I performed in the previous example and that I described in Chapter 13 are examples of *local validation*, which is to say that the rules and the data required to enforce them are available within the document.

The validation plugin also supports *remote validation*, where the value entered by the user is sent to the server and the rules are applied there. This is useful when you don't want to send the data to the browser because there is too much of it, because doing so would be insecure, or because you want to perform validation against the latest data.

■ **Caution** Some caution is required when using remote validation because the load it can place on a server is significant. In this example, I perform a remote validation every time the user changes the value of an input element, but in a real application this is likely to generate a lot of requests. A more sensible approach is usually to perform remote validation only as a precursor to submitting the form.

I didn't explain remote validation in Chapter 13 because it relies on JSON and Ajax, and I didn't want to get into those topics too early. Listing 16-7 shows the addition of remote validation to the example document, where I use it to ensure that the user is unable to order more items than the server records as being in stock.

Listing 16-7. Performing Remote Validation

```
...
$.when(flowerReq, jsonReq).then(function() {
    $('input').each(function(index, elem) {
        $(elem).rules("add", {
            required: true,
            min: 0,
            digits: true,
            remote: {
                url: "http://node.jacquisflowershop.com/stockcheck",
                type: "post",
                global: false
            },
            messages: {
              required: "Please enter a number for " + plurals[elem.name],
              digits: "Please enter a number for " + plurals[elem.name],
              min: "Please enter a positive number for " + plurals[elem.name]
            }
        })
    }).change(function(e) {
        if ($('form').validate().element($(e.target))) {
            var total = 0;
            $('input').each(function(index, elem) {
                total += Number($(elem).val());
            });
            $('#total').text(total);
        }
    });
});
...
```

Setting remote validation is easy now that you have seen the jQuery support for Ajax. We specify the check as `remote` and set it to be a standard Ajax settings object. In this example, I have used the `url` setting to specify the URL will be called to perform the remote validation, the `type` setting to specify that I want a `POST` request, and the `global` setting to disable global events.

I have disabled global events because I don't want errors making the validation request to be treated as general errors that the user can do something about. Instead, I want them to fail quietly, on the basis that the server will perform further validation when the form is submitted (the `Node.js` script doesn't perform any validation, but it is important that real web applications do, as I mentioned in Chapter 13).

The validation plugin uses your Ajax setting to make a request to the specified URL, sending the `name` of the `input` element and the value that the user has entered. If the response from the server is the word `true`, then the value is valid. Any other response is considered to be an error message that will be displayed to the user. You can see how these messages are used in Figure 16-3.

Figure 16-3. Displaying remote validation messages

Submitting the Form Data Using Ajax

Submitting the values in the form is exceptionally simple, and Listing 16-8 shows the same technique that I used in Chapter 15.

Listing 16-8. Submitting the Form Using Ajax

```
...
<style type="text/css">
    a.arrowButton {
        background-image: url(leftarrows.png); float: left;
        margin-top: 15px; display: block; width: 50px; height: 50px;}
    #right {background-image: url(rightarrows.png)}
    h1 { min-width: 0px; width: 95%; }
    #oblock { float: left; display: inline; border: thin black solid; }
    form { margin-left: auto; margin-right: auto; width: 885px; }
    #bbox {clear: left}
    #error {color: red; border: medium solid red; padding: 4px; margin: auto;
        width: 300px; text-align: center; margin-bottom: 5px}
    .invalidElem {border: medium solid red}
    #errorSummary {border: thick solid red; color: red; width: 350px; margin: auto;
        padding: 4px; margin-bottom: 5px}
    #popup {
        text-align: center; position: absolute; top: 100px;
        left: 0px; width: 100%; height: 1px; overflow: visible; visibility: visible;
        display: block }
```

```
    #popupContent { color: white; background-color: black; font-size: 14px ;
        font-weight: bold; margin-left: -75px; position: absolute; top: -55px;
        left: 50%; width: 150px; height: 60px; padding-top: 10px; z-index: 2;
    }
</style>
<script type="text/javascript">
    $(document).ready(function() {

        $('<div id="popup"><div id="popupContent"><img src="progress.gif"'
            + 'alt="progress"/><div>Placing Order</div></div></div>')
            .appendTo('body');

        $.ajaxSetup({
            timeout: 5000,
            converters: {
                "text html": function(data) { return $(data); }
            }
        })

        $(document).ajaxError(function(e, jqxhr, settings, errorMsg) {
            $('#error').remove();
            var msg = "An error occurred. Please try again"
            if (errorMsg == "timeout") {
                msg = "The request timed out. Please try again"
            } else if (jqxhr.status == 404) {
                    msg = "The file could not be found";
            }
            $('<div id=error/>').text(msg).insertAfter('h1');
        }).ajaxSuccess(function() {
            $('#error').remove();
        })

        $('#row2, #row3, #popup').hide();

        var flowerReq = $.get("flowers.html", function(data) {
            var elems = data.filter('div').addClass("dcell");
            elems.slice(0, 3).appendTo('#row1');
            elems.slice(3).appendTo("#row2");
        })

        var jsonReq = $.getJSON("additionalflowers.json", function(data) {
            $('#flowerTmpl').tmpl(data).appendTo("#row3");
        })

        var plurals = {
            astor: "Astors", daffodil: "Daffodils", rose: "Roses",
            peony: "Peonies", primula: "Primulas", snowdrop: "Snowdrops",
            carnation: "Carnations", lily: "Lillies", orchid: "Orchids"
        }

        $('<div id=errorSummary>Please correct the following errors:</div>')
            .append('<ul id="errorsList"></ul>').hide().insertAfter('h1');
```

```
$('form').validate({
    highlight: function(element, errorClass) {
        $(element).addClass("invalidElem");
    },
    unhighlight: function(element, errorClass) {
        $(element).removeClass("invalidElem");
    },
    errorContainer: '#errorSummary',
    errorLabelContainer: '#errorsList',
    wrapper: 'li',
    errorElement: "div"
});

$.when(flowerReq, jsonReq).then(function() {
    $('input').each(function(index, elem) {
        $(elem).rules("add", {
            required: true,
            min: 0,
            digits: true,
            remote: {
                url: "http://node.jacquisflowershop.com/stockcheck",
                type: "post",
                global: false
            },
            messages: {
              required: "Please enter a number for " + plurals[elem.name],
              digits: "Please enter a number for " + plurals[elem.name],
              min: "Please enter a positive number for " + plurals[elem.name]
            }
        })
    }).change(function(e) {
        if ($('form').validate().element($(e.target))) {
            var total = 0;
            $('input').each(function(index, elem) {
                total += Number($(elem).val());
            });
            $('#total').text(total);
        }
    });
});

$('button').click(function(e) {
    e.preventDefault();

    var formData = $('form').serialize();
    $('body *').not('#popup, #popup *').css("opacity", 0.5);
    $('input').attr("disabled", "disabled");
    $('#popup').show();
    $.ajax({
        url: "http://node.jacquisflowershop.com/order",
        type: "post",
```

```
                data: formData,
                complete: function() {
                    setTimeout(function() {
                    $('body *').not('#popup, #popup *').css("opacity", 1);
                    $('input').removeAttr("disabled");
                    $('#popup').hide();
                    }, 1500);
                }
            })
        })

        $('<a id=left></a><a id=right></a>').prependTo('form')
            .addClass("arrowButton").click(handleArrowPress).hover(handleArrowMouse);
        $('#right').appendTo('form');

        var total = $('#buttonDiv')
            .prepend("<div>Total Items: <span id=total>0</span></div>")
            .css({clear: "both", padding: "5px"});
        $('<div id=bbox />').appendTo("body").append(total);

        function handleArrowMouse(e) {
           var propValue = e.type == "mouseenter" ? "-50px 0px" : "0px 0px";
           $(this).css("background-position", propValue);
        }

        function handleArrowPress(e) {
            var elemSequence = ["row1", "row2", "row3"];
            var visibleRow = $('div.drow:visible');
            var visibleRowIndex = jQuery.inArray(visibleRow.attr("id"),elemSequence);
            var targetRowIndex;
            if (e.target.id == "left") {
                targetRowIndex = visibleRowIndex - 1;
                if (targetRowIndex < 0) {targetRowIndex = elemSequence.length -1};
            } else {
                targetRowIndex = (visibleRowIndex + 1) % elemSequence.length;
            }
            visibleRow.fadeOut("fast", function() {
                $('#' + elemSequence[targetRowIndex]).fadeIn("fast")});
        }
    });
</script>
...
```

I've gone beyond just making an Ajax POST request because I want to provide some additional context for how these requests can be handled in real projects. To start with, I have added an element that is positioned above all of the other elements in the document and tells the user that their order is being placed. Here are the CSS and jQuery statements that create this effect:

```
...
#popup {
    text-align: center; position: absolute; top: 100px;
    left: 0px; width: 100%; height: 1px; overflow: visible; visibility: visible;
```

```
    display: block }
#popupContent { color: white; background-color: black; font-size: 14px ;
    font-weight: bold; margin-left: -75px; position: absolute; top: -55px;
    left: 50%; width: 150px; height: 60px; padding-top: 10px; z-index: 2;
}
...
$('<div id="popup"><div id="popupContent"><img src="progress.gif"'
    + 'alt="progress"/><div>Placing Order</div></div></div>')
    .appendTo('body');
...
```

It is surprisingly hard to create an element that looks like a pop-up and that is properly positioned on the screen, and you can see that the amount of CSS required to make it work is significant. The HTML elements are surprisingly simple by comparison, and the HTML that is generated looks like this when properly formatted:

```
<div id="popup">
    <div id="popupContent">
        <img src="progress.gif" alt="progress">
        <div>Placing Order</div>
    </div>
</div>
```

The img element I have specified (progress.gif) is an animated GIF image. There are a number of web sites that will generate progress images to your specification, and I used one of them. If you don't want to create your own, then use the one from this example that is included in the source code download for this book (available without charge at Apress.com). You can see how these elements appear in Figure 16-4, where I have removed the other elements for clarity.

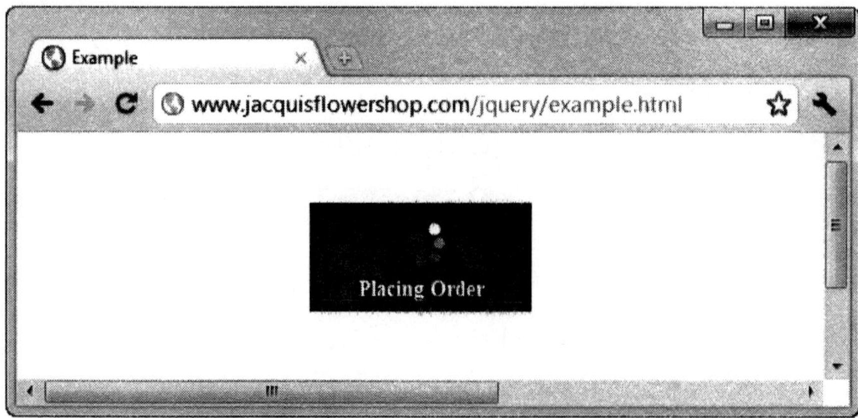

Figure 16-4. Showing progress to the user

I hide these elements initially because it makes no sense to show the user a progress display until they actually place the order:

```
$('#row2, #row3, #popup').hide();
```

With these elements in place and hidden, you can turn to the form submission. I register a handler function for the click event for the button element, as follows:

```
...
$('button').click(function(e) {
    e.preventDefault();

    var formData = $('form').serialize();
    $('body *').not('#popup, #popup *').css("opacity", 0.5);
    $('input').attr("disabled", "disabled");
    $('#popup').show();
    $.ajax({
        url: "http://node.jacquisflowershop.com/order",
        type: "post",
        data: formData,
        complete: function() {
            setTimeout(function() {
                $('body *').not('#popup, #popup *').css("opacity", 1);
                $('input').removeAttr("disabled");
                $('#popup').hide();
            }, 1500);
        }
    })
})
...
```

Before starting the Ajax request, I show the pop-up elements and make all of the other elements partially transparent. I also disable the input elements by adding the disabled attribute. I do this because I don't want the user to be able to change the value of any of the input elements while I am sending the data to the user:

```
...
$('body *').not('#popup, #popup *').css("opacity", 0.5);
$('input').attr("disabled", "disabled");
$('#popup').show();
...
```

The problem with disabling the input elements is that their values won't be included in the data sent to the server. The serialize method will include values only from input elements that are *successful controls*, as defined by the HTML specification; this excludes those elements that are disabled or don't have a name attribute. I could iterate through the input elements myself and get the values anyway, but it is simpler to gather the data to send before disabling the elements, like this:

```
var formData = $('form').serialize();
```

I have used the complete setting to restore the interface to its normal state by making all of the elements opaque, removing the disabled attribute from the input elements and hiding the pop-up elements. I have introduced an artificial 1.5-second delay after the request has completed before restoring the interface, like this:

```
...
complete: function() {
    setTimeout(function() {
        $('body *').not('#popup, #popup *').css("opacity", 1);
```

```
            $('input').removeAttr("disabled");
            $('#popup').hide();
        }, 1500);
    }
...
```

I would not do this in a real web application, but for demonstration purposes when the development machine and the server are on the same LAN, this is useful to emphasize the transition. You can see how the browser appears during the Ajax request in Figure 16-5.

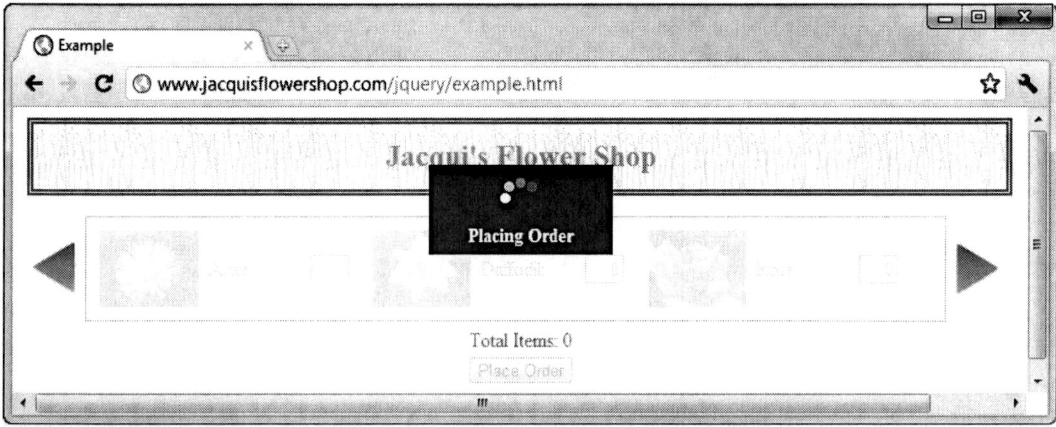

Figure 16-5. The browser during the form submission request

Processing the Server Response

All that remains is to do something useful with the data that you get back from the server. For this chapter, I am going to use a simple table. You will learn about creating rich user interfaces with jQuery UI in the next part of this book, and I don't want to have to do by hand what I can do much more elegantly with the UI widgets. You can see the finished result in Figure 16-6.

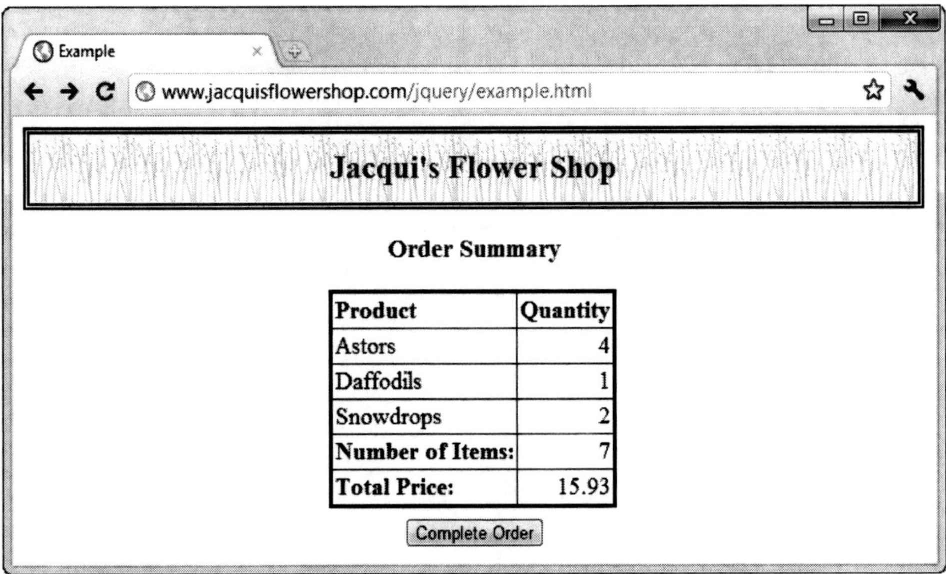

Figure 16-6. Displaying the order summary

Listing 16-9 shows the complete document that supports this enhancement.

Listing 16-9. Processing the Response from the Server

```
<!DOCTYPE html>
<html>
<head>
    <title>Example</title>
    <script src="jquery-1.7.js" type="text/javascript"></script>
    <script src="jquery.tmpl.js" type="text/javascript"></script>
    <script src="jquery.validate.js" type="text/javascript"></script>
    <link rel="stylesheet" type="text/css" href="styles.css"/>
    <style type="text/css">
        a.arrowButton {
            background-image: url(leftarrows.png); float: left;
            margin-top: 15px; display: block; width: 50px; height: 50px;}
        #right {background-image: url(rightarrows.png)}
        h1 { min-width: 0px; width: 95%; }
        #oblock { float: left; display: inline; border: thin black solid; }
        #orderForm { margin-left: auto; margin-right: auto; width: 885px; }
        #bbox {clear: left}
        #error {color: red; border: medium solid red; padding: 4px; margin: auto;
            width: 300px; text-align: center; margin-bottom: 5px}
        .invalidElem {border: medium solid red}
        #errorSummary {border: thick solid red; color: red; width: 350px; margin: auto;
            padding: 4px; margin-bottom: 5px}
        #popup {
```

```
            text-align: center; position: absolute; top: 100px;
            left: 0px; width: 100%; height: 1px; overflow: visible; visibility: visible;
            display: block }
        #popupContent { color: white; background-color: black; font-size: 14px ;
            font-weight: bold; margin-left: -75px; position: absolute; top: -55px;
            left: 50%; width: 150px; height: 60px; padding-top: 10px; z-index: 2;
        }
        #summary {text-align: center}
        table {border-collapse: collapse; border: medium solid black; font-size: 18px;
            margin: auto; margin-bottom: 5px;}
        th {text-align: left}
        th, td {padding: 2px}
        tr > td:nth-child(1) {text-align: left}
        tr > td:nth-child(2) {text-align: right}
    </style>
    <script type="text/javascript">
        $(document).ready(function() {

            $('<div id="popup"><div id="popupContent"><img src="progress.gif"'
                + 'alt="progress"/><div>Placing Order</div></div></div>')
                .appendTo('body');

            $.ajaxSetup({
                timeout: 5000,
                converters: {
                    "text html": function(data) { return $(data); }
                }
            })

            $(document).ajaxError(function(e, jqxhr, settings, errorMsg) {
                $('#error').remove();
                var msg = "An error occurred. Please try again"
                if (errorMsg == "timeout") {
                    msg = "The request timed out. Please try again"
                } else if (jqxhr.status == 404) {
                        msg = "The file could not be found";
                }
                $('<div id=error/>').text(msg).insertAfter('h1');
            }).ajaxSuccess(function() {
                $('#error').remove();
            })

            $('#row2, #row3, #popup, #summaryForm').hide();

            var flowerReq = $.get("flowers.html", function(data) {
                var elems = data.filter('div').addClass("dcell");
                elems.slice(0, 3).appendTo('#row1');
                elems.slice(3).appendTo("#row2");
            })

            var jsonReq = $.getJSON("additionalflowers.json", function(data) {
                $('#flowerTmpl').tmpl(data).appendTo("#row3");
```

```
})

var plurals = {
    astor: "Astors", daffodil: "Daffodils", rose: "Roses",
    peony: "Peonies", primula: "Primulas", snowdrop: "Snowdrops",
    carnation: "Carnations", lily: "Lillies", orchid: "Orchids"
}

$('<div id=errorSummary>Please correct the following errors:</div>')
    .append('<ul id="errorsList"></ul>').hide().insertAfter('h1');

$('#orderForm').validate({
    highlight: function(element, errorClass) {
        $(element).addClass("invalidElem");
    },
    unhighlight: function(element, errorClass) {
        $(element).removeClass("invalidElem");
    },
    errorContainer: '#errorSummary',
    errorLabelContainer: '#errorsList',
    wrapper: 'li',
    errorElement: "div"
});

$.when(flowerReq, jsonReq).then(function() {
    $('input').each(function(index, elem) {
        $(elem).rules("add", {
            required: true,
            min: 0,
            digits: true,
            remote: {
                url: "http://node.jacquisflowershop.com/stockcheck",
                type: "post",
                global: false
            },
            messages: {
              required: "Please enter a number for " + plurals[elem.name],
              digits: "Please enter a number for " + plurals[elem.name],
              min: "Please enter a positive number for " + plurals[elem.name]
            }
        })
    }).change(function(e) {
        if ($('#orderForm').validate().element($(e.target))) {
            var total = 0;
            $('input').each(function(index, elem) {
                total += Number($(elem).val());
            });
            $('#total').text(total);
        }
    });
});
```

```
$('#orderForm button').click(function(e) {
    e.preventDefault();

    var formData = $('#orderForm').serialize();
    $('body *').not('#popup, #popup *').css("opacity", 0.5);
    $('input').attr("disabled", "disabled");
    $('#popup').show();
    $.ajax({
        url: "http://node.jacquisflowershop.com/order",
        type: "post",
        data: formData,
        dataType: "json",
        dataFilter: function(data, dataType) {
            data = $.parseJSON(data);

            var cleanData = {
                totalItems: data.totalItems,
                totalPrice: data.totalPrice
            };
            delete data.totalPrice; delete data.totalItems;
            cleanData.products = [];
            for (prop in data) {
                cleanData.products.push({
                    name: plurals[prop],
                    quantity: data[prop]
                })
            }
            return cleanData;
        },
        converters: {"text json": function(data) { return data;}},
        success: function(data) {
            processServerResponse(data);
        },
        complete: function() {
            $('body *').not('#popup, #popup *').css("opacity", 1);
            $('input').removeAttr("disabled");
            $('#popup').hide();
        }
    })
})

function processServerResponse(data) {
    if (data.products.length > 0) {
        $('body > *:not(h1)').hide();
        $('#summaryForm').show();
        $('#productRowTmpl').tmpl(data.products).appendTo('tbody');
        $('#totalitems').text(data.totalItems);
        $('#totalprice').text(data.totalPrice);
    } else {
        var elem = $('input').get(0);
            var err = new Object();
```

```
                    err[elem.name] = "No products selected";
                $('#orderForm').validate().showErrors(err);
                $(elem).removeClass("invalidElem");
            }
        }

        $('<a id=left></a><a id=right></a>').prependTo('#orderForm')
            .addClass("arrowButton").click(handleArrowPress).hover(handleArrowMouse);
        $('#right').appendTo('#orderForm');

        var total = $('#buttonDiv')
            .prepend("<div>Total Items: <span id=total>0</span></div>")
            .css({clear: "both", padding: "5px"});
        $('<div id=bbox />').appendTo("body").append(total);

        function handleArrowMouse(e) {
           var propValue = e.type == "mouseenter" ? "-50px 0px" : "0px 0px";
           $(this).css("background-position", propValue);
        }

        function handleArrowPress(e) {
            var elemSequence = ["row1", "row2", "row3"];
            var visibleRow = $('div.drow:visible');
            var visibleRowIndex = jQuery.inArray(visibleRow.attr("id"),elemSequence);
            var targetRowIndex;
            if (e.target.id == "left") {
                targetRowIndex = visibleRowIndex - 1;
                if (targetRowIndex < 0) {targetRowIndex = elemSequence.length -1};
            } else {
                targetRowIndex = (visibleRowIndex + 1) % elemSequence.length;
            }
            visibleRow.fadeOut("fast", function() {
                $('#' + elemSequence[targetRowIndex]).fadeIn("fast")});
        }
    });
</script>
<script id="flowerTmpl" type="text/x-jquery-tmpl">
    <div class="dcell">
        <img src="${product}.png"/>
        <label for="${product}">${name}:</label>
        <input name="${product}" value="0" />
    </div>
</script>
  <script id="productRowTmpl" type="text/x-jquery-tmpl">
    <tr><td>${name}</td><td>${quantity}</td></tr>
</script>
</head>
<body>
    <h1>Jacqui's Flower Shop</h1>
    <form id="orderForm" method="post" action="http://node.jacquisflowershop.com/order">
        <div id="oblock">
            <div class="dtable">
```

```
                <div id="row1" class="drow"></div>
                <div id="row2" class="drow"></div>
                <div id="row3" class="drow"></div>
            </div>
        </div>
        <div id="buttonDiv"><button type="submit">Place Order</button></div>
    </form>
    <form id="summaryForm" method="post" action="">
        <div id="summary">
            <h3>Order Summary</h3>
            <table border="1">
                <thead>
                    <tr><th>Product</th><th>Quantity</th>
                </thead>
                <tbody>
                </tbody>
                <tfoot>
                    <tr><th>Number of Items:</th><td id="totalitems"></td></tr>
                    <tr><th>Total Price:</th><td id="totalprice"></td></tr>
                </tfoot>
            </table>
            <div id="buttonDiv2"><button type="submit">Complete Order</button></div>
        </div>
    </form>
</body>
</html>
```

I'll break down the changes I made step by step.

Adding the New Form

The first thing that I did was add a new form to the static HTML part of the document, like this:

```
...
<form id="summaryForm" method="post" action="">
    <div id="summary">
        <h3>Order Summary</h3>
        <table border="1">
            <thead>
                <tr><th>Product</th><th>Quantity</th>
            </thead>
            <tbody>
            </tbody>
            <tfoot>
                <tr><th>Number of Items:</th><td id="totalitems"></td></tr>
                <tr><th>Total Price:</th><td id="totalprice"></td></tr>
            </tfoot>
        </table>
        <div id="buttonDiv2"><button type="submit">Complete Order</button></div>
    </div>
</form>
...
```

This is the heart of the new functionality. When the user submits their product selection to the server, the table in this form will be used to display the data you get back from the Ajax request.

■ **Tip** I had been using the `$('form')` selector in previous examples, but since they are two forms in the document now, I have gone through and switched these references to the use the `form` element's `id` attribute values.

I don't want to display the new form immediately, so I added it to the list of elements that I hide in the script, like this:

```
$('#row2, #row3, #popup, #summaryForm').hide();
```

And, as you might expect by now, when there are new elements, there is new CSS to style them, as follows:

```
...
#summary {text-align: center}
table {border-collapse: collapse; border: medium solid black; font-size: 18px;
    margin: auto; margin-bottom: 5px;}
th {text-align: left}
th, td {padding: 2px}
tr > td:nth-child(1) {text-align: left}
tr > td:nth-child(2) {text-align: right}
...
```

These styles ensure that the table is displayed in the middle of the browser window and the text in various columns is aligned to the correct edge.

Completing the Ajax Request

The next step was to complete the call to the ajax request, like this:

```
...
$('#orderForm button').click(function(e) {
    e.preventDefault();

    var formData = $('#orderForm').serialize();
    $('body *').not('#popup, #popup *').css("opacity", 0.5);
    $('input').attr("disabled", "disabled");
    $('#popup').show();
    $.ajax({
        url: "http://node.jacquisflowershop.com/order",
        type: "post",
        data: formData,
        dataType: "json",
        dataFilter: function(data, dataType) {
            data = $.parseJSON(data);
```

```
                var cleanData = {
                    totalItems: data.totalItems,
                    totalPrice: data.totalPrice
                };
                delete data.totalPrice; delete data.totalItems;
                cleanData.products = [];
                for (prop in data) {
                    cleanData.products.push({
                        name: plurals[prop],
                        quantity: data[prop]
                    })
                }
                return cleanData;
            },
            converters: {"text json": function(data) { return data;}},
            success: function(data) {
                processServerResponse(data);
            },
            complete: function() {
                $('body *').not('#popup, #popup *').css("opacity", 1);
                $('input').removeAttr("disabled");
                $('#popup').hide();
            }
        })
})
...
```

I removed the explicit delay in the `complete` function and added the `dataFilter`, `converters`, and `success` settings to the request.

I use the `dataFilters` setting to provide a function that transforms the JSON data I get from the server into something more useful. The server sends me a JSON string like this:

```
{"astor":"4","daffodil":"1","snowdrop":"2","totalItems":7,"totalPrice":"15.93"}
```

I parse the JSON data and restructure it so that I get this:

```
{"totalItems":7,
 "totalPrice":"15.93",
 "products":[{"name":"Astors","quantity":"4"},
             {"name":"Daffodils","quantity":"1"},
             {"name":"Snowdrops","quantity":"2"}]
}
```

This format has two advantages. The first is that it is better suited for use with data templates because I can pass the `products` property to the `tmpl` method. The second is that I can check whether the user has selected any elements with `products.length`. These are two quite minor advantages, but I wanted to integrate as many of the features from the earlier chapters as possible. Notice that I have also replaced the name of the product (`orchid`, for example) with the plural name (`Orchids`).

Having already parsed the JSON data into a JavaScript object (using the `parseJSON` method, which I describe in Chapter 33), I want to disable the built-in converter, which will try to do the same thing. To that end, I have defined a custom converter for JSON, which just passes the data through without modification:

```
...
converters: {"text json": function(data) { return data;}}
...
```

Processing the Data

For the success setting in the ajax method call, I specified the processServerResponse function, which I defined as follows:

```
...
function processServerResponse(data) {
    if (data.products.length > 0) {
        $('body > *:not(h1)').hide();
        $('#summaryForm').show();
        $('#productRowTmpl').tmpl(data.products).appendTo('tbody');
        $('#totalitems').text(data.totalItems);
        $('#totalprice').text(data.totalPrice);
    } else {
        var elem = $('input').get(0);
            var err = new Object();
            err[elem.name] = "No products selected";
        $('#orderForm').validate().showErrors(err);
        $(elem).removeClass("invalidElem");
    }
}
...
```

If the data from the server contains product information, then I hide all of the elements in the document that I don't want (including the original form element and the additions I made in the script) and show the new form. I populate the table using the following data template:

```
<script id="productRowTmpl" type="text/x-jquery-tmpl">
  <tr><td>${name}</td><td>${quantity}</td></tr>
</script>
```

This is a very simple template and produces a table row for each selected product. Finally, I set contents of the cells that display the total price and item count using the text method:

```
$('#totalitems').text(data.totalItems);
$('#totalprice').text(data.totalPrice);
```

However, if the data from the server doesn't contain any product information (which indicates that the user has left all of the input element values as zero), then I do something very different. First I select the first of the input elements, like this:

```
var elem = $('input').get(0);
```

I then create an object that contains a property whose name is the name value of the input element and whose value is a message to the user. I then call the validate method on the form element and the showErrors method on the result, like this:

```
var err = new Object();
err[elem.name] = "No products selected";
$('#orderForm').validate().showErrors(err);
```

This allows me to manually inject an error into the validation system and take advantage of all of the structure and formatting that I put in place earlier. I have to provide the name of an element so that the validation plugin can highlight where the error occurs, which is not ideal, as you can see in Figure 16-7.

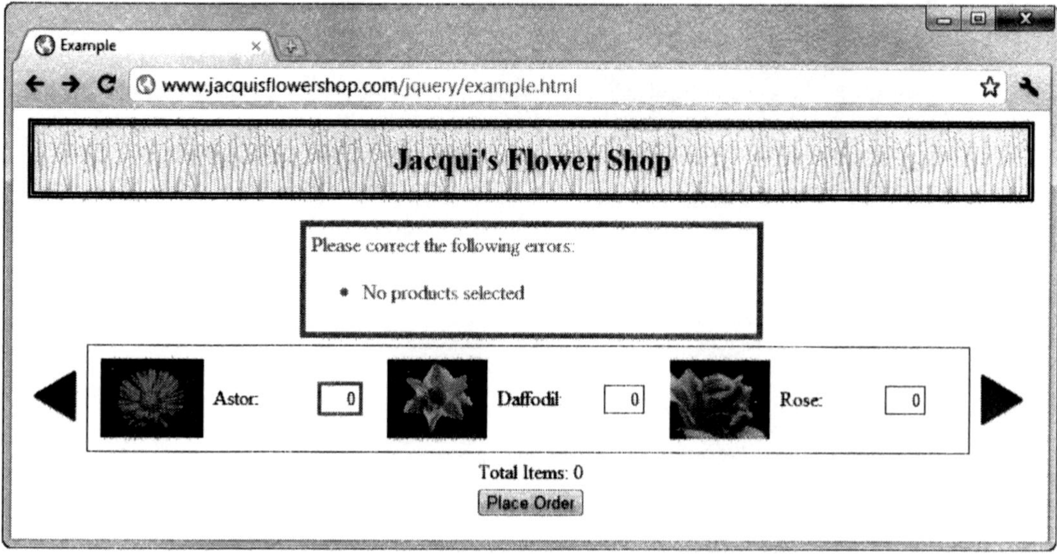

Figure 16-7. Display the selection error

I am displaying a general message, but the highlighting is applied to just one input element. To deal with this, I remove the class that the validation plugin uses for highlighting, like this:

```
$(elem).removeClass("invalidElem");
```

This produces the effect shown in Figure 16-8.

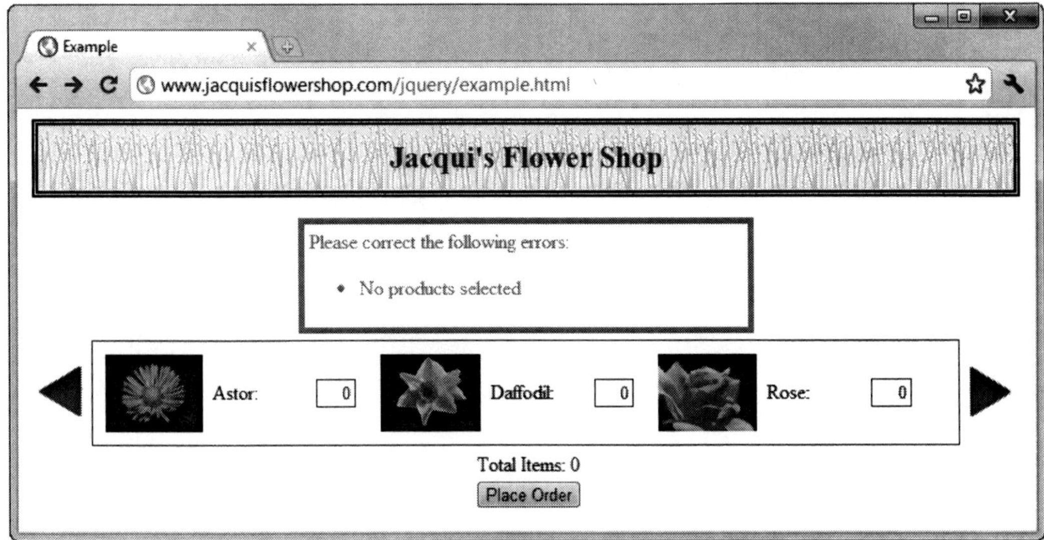

Figure 16-8. Removing the highlighting from the element associated with the error

Summary

In this chapter, I refactored the example to bring together the themes and features covered in this part of the book. I used Ajax widely (using both the shorthand and low-level methods), applied a pair of data templates, and used the validation plugin to check values locally and remotely (and to display an error manually).

In the next part of the book, you will turn your attention to jQuery UI, and the next time that you refactor the example document, it will have a very different appearance.

PART 4

Using jQuery UI

CHAPTER 17

Setting Up jQuery UI

Downloading and installing jQuery UI is slightly more complicated than for other JavaScript libraries. It is not burdensome, but it requires some explanation, which is what I cover in this chapter. For this book, you only need to get set up for development, but I have also included details of how to install the minimized files that are suitable for production deployment and details of how to use jQuery UI through a content distribution network.

Obtaining jQuery UI

The process for downloading jQuery UI is a little more complex than for other JavaScript libraries, but it is worth the effort. There are five main areas of functionality in jQuery UI, and you create a custom download that includes and configures each of them. In this part of the book, I'll be showing you all of the jQuery UI features, but for a real web application you can omit the parts you don't need and create a smaller library for browsers to download.

Tip jQuery UI isn't the only UI toolkit that is based on jQuery, although it is by far the most popular. An alternative is jQuery Tools, which is open source and can be downloaded without any license or restrictions from `http://flowplayer.org/tools`. There are also some commercial alternatives such as jQWidgets (`www.jqwidgets.com`) and Wijmo (`http://wijmo.com`). And, of course, there is jQuery Mobile, which I describe in Part V of this book.

Deciding on a Theme

Before you build your custom jQuery UI library, you need to decide on a theme. jQuery UI is endlessly configurable, and you can change the appearance of every aspect of every feature that you use. In fact, there are so many choices that it can be somewhat overwhelming. The jQuery UI web site includes a tool for creating custom themes, but there is also a gallery of predefined themes that you can choose to make life easier.

To start, go to `http://jqueryui.com` and click the Themes button. This loads the ThemeRoller page, which consists of a display of jQuery UI widgets and a panel on the left that lets you configure the theme settings, as shown in Figure 17-1.

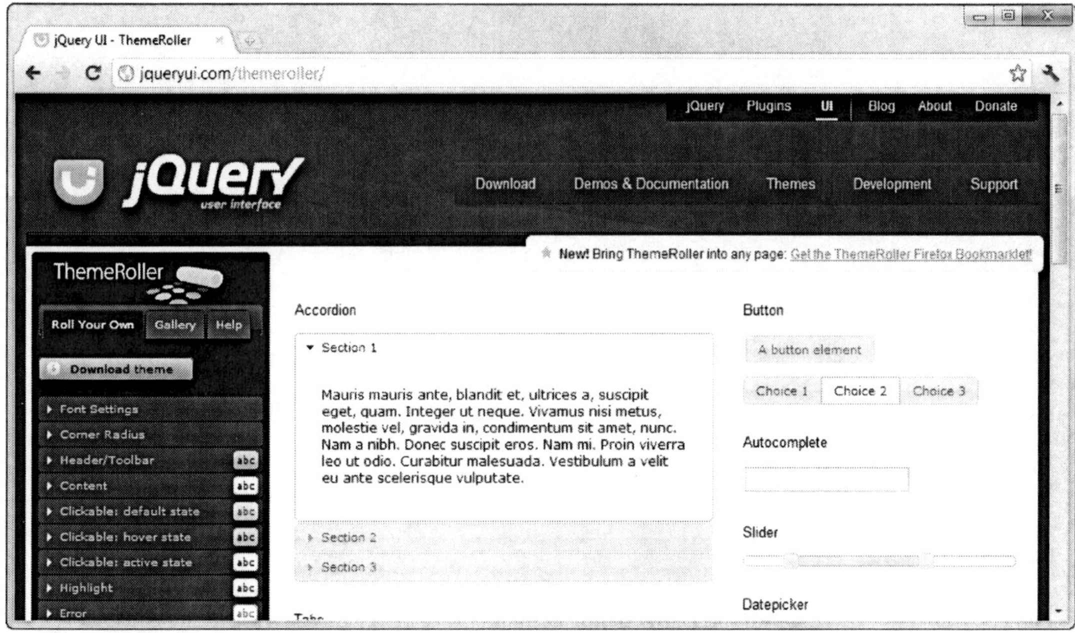

Figure 17-1. The jQuery UI web site theme page

If you have a certain visual style that you need to follow to make jQuery UI fit in with the rest of a site or application, then the Roll Your Own tab (which is selected by default) is for you. You can change every aspect of the CSS that is used by jQuery UI.

The predefined themes are available on the Gallery tab. As I write this, 24 themes are available in the gallery, and they range from the understated and subtle to the bright and garish. As you click each gallery theme, the widgets in the rest of the page are updated to show you what your application will look like, as shown in Figure 17-2.

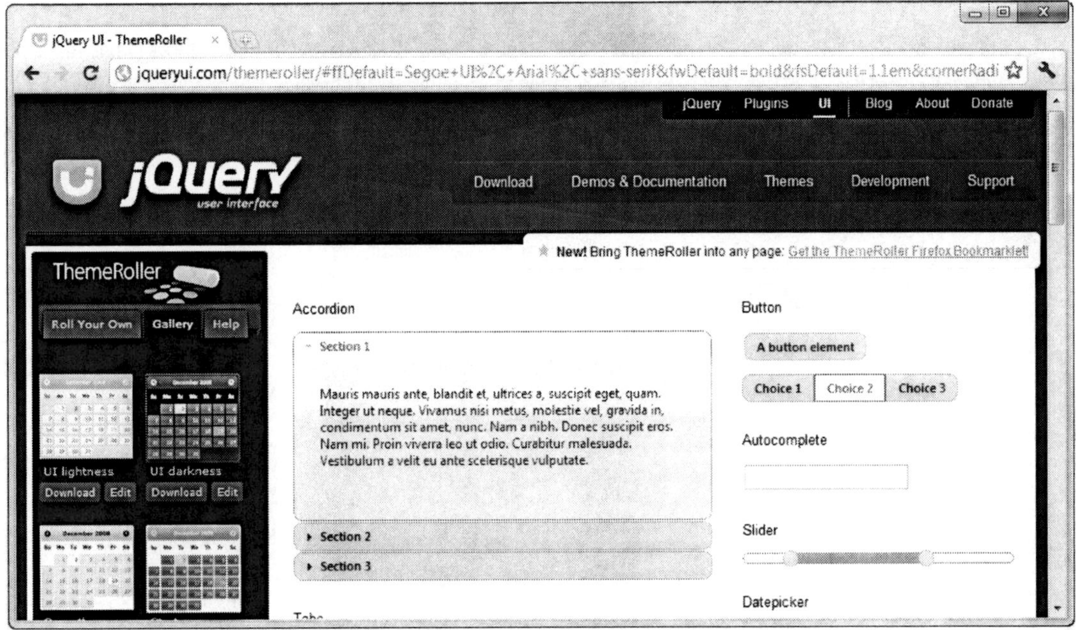

Figure 17-2. The gallery showing the Sunny theme

The default theme for jQuery UI is called UI lightness, but it doesn't have enough contrast to show up well on a book page, so I will be using the Sunny theme, which shows up a little better. You don't need to do anything with the theme at the moment, other than to remember which one you want to use. The themes don't look that good when printed, but they have a very different appearance on the screen, and I recommend you look through the list until you find one you like.

■ **Tip** You don't have to select the same theme that I will be using, but if you pick a different one, you will obviously get results that look different from mine.

Creating the jQuery UI Custom Download

Now that you have a theme in mind, you can create your jQuery UI download. Click the Download button at the top of the page to move to the Build Your Download page. This page has a list of jQuery UI components, broken into four functional groups: UI Core, Interactions, Widgets, and Effects.

By selecting only the features that you require for a project, it is possible to create a set of smaller files for the browser to download. I think this a nice idea, but it is something that I tend not to use. My view is that the best way to reduce the bandwidth required to deliver jQuery UI is to rely on a content distribution network, which I show you how to do later in this chapter.

For this chapter, you will need all of the components, so make sure that all of the components are checked.

■ **Tip** Some of the components in the list depend on others, but you don't have to worry about this when you build a custom jQuery UI library. When you enable a component, any other component it depends on is also loaded.

The next step is to select the theme you want. The selector for this in on the right side of the page, as shown in Figure 17-3.

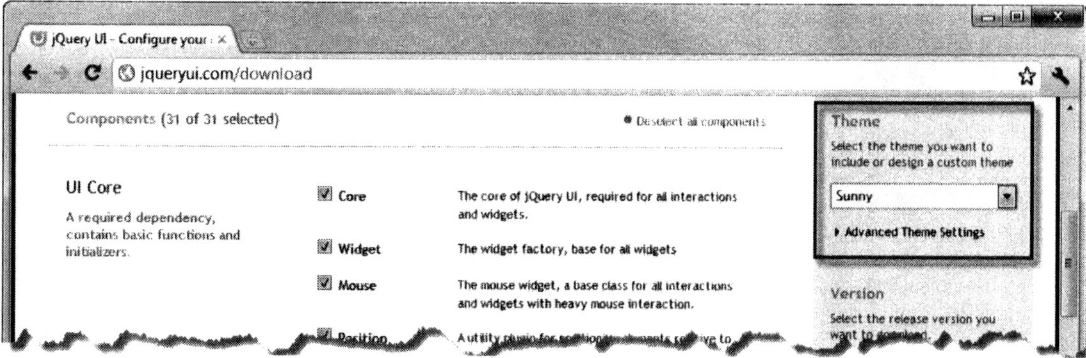

Figure 17-3. Selecting the theme

■ **Tip** You can also choose the version of jQuery UI to include in the library download. You will need the *stable* release for this chapter, which works with all versions of jQuery after 1.3.2.

Once you have selected all of the components, selected the theme you want, and selected the stable version, click the Download button to download the customized jQuery UI library.

Installing jQuery UI for Development

The jQuery UI download contains all the files that you need for development and production. For this book, you will use the development files that include the uncompressed source code. This makes it easy to look into the internals of jQuery UI if you have a problem. You need to copy the following into the folder that contains your example files:

- The `development-bundle\ui\jquery-ui-1.8.16.custom.js` file
- The `development-bundle\themes\sunny\jquery-ui-1.8.16.custom.css` file
- The `development-bundle\themes\sunny\images` folder

You will notice that there are JavaScript and CSS files for individual components and features in the ui and themes folders. You don't need to use them, but they can be helpful if you need to work with only a limited set of jQuery UI features.

■ **Tip** The name of the JavaScript and CSS files include the version number of the release that was downloaded. For me, this is version 1.8.16. jQuery UI is actively developed, and you may have downloaded a later release than 1.8.16.

Adding jQuery UI to an HTML Document

All that remains is to add jQuery UI to your HTML document. You can do this by adding script and link elements that refer to the JavaScript and CSS files that you just copied, as shown in Listing 17-1. You don't need to refer directly to the images directory. As long as the images directory and the CSS file are in the same place, jQuery UI will be able to find the resources it needs.

Listing 17-1. Adding jQuery UI to an HTML Document

```
<!DOCTYPE html>
<html>
<head>
    <title>Example</title>
    <script src="jquery-1.7.js" type="text/javascript"></script>
    <script src="jquery-ui-1.8.16.custom.js" type="text/javascript"></script>
    <link rel="stylesheet" type="text/css" href="styles.css"/>
    <link rel="stylesheet" type="text/css" href="jquery-ui-1.8.16.custom.css"/>
    <script type="text/javascript">
        $(document).ready(function() {
            $('a').button();
        });
    </script>
</head>
<body>
    <a href="http://apress.com">Visit Apress</a>
</body>
</html>
```

■ **Tip** jQuery UI depends on jQuery. You must have added jQuery to a document in order to use jQuery UI. jQuery UI is not a stand-alone library.

The document shown in the listing includes a simple test that allows you to check that jQuery UI has been added properly. If you view this in the document, you should see a distinct button like the one in

Figure 17-4. Don't worry about the call to the `button` method in the script element in the listing. I'll explain what this does and how it works in Chapter 18.

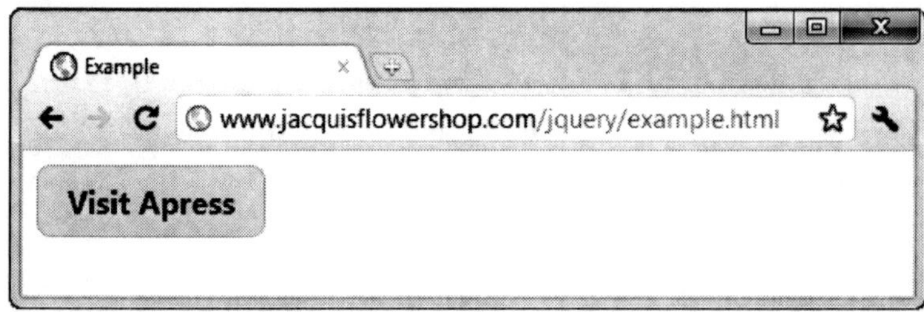

Figure 17-4. Checking that jQuery UI has been added to the document correctly

If you have not properly specified the path to either of the two files, then you will see a simple a element instead, as illustrated by Figure 17-5.

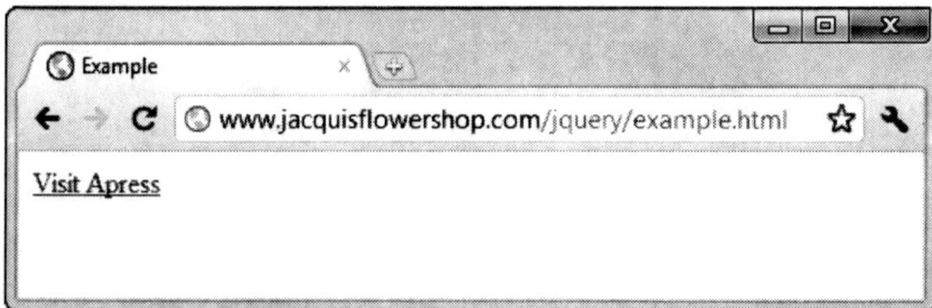

Figure 17-5. Identifying a problem importing jQuery UI into a document

Installing jQuery UI for Production

When you have finished developing your web application and are ready to deploy it, you can use the minimized files that are included in the download. These files are smaller but harder to read for debugging purposes. To use the production files, you must copy the following into your web server directory:

- The `js\jquery-ui-1.8.16.custom.min.js` file
- The `css\sunny\jquery-ui-1.8.16.custom.css` file
- The `css\sunny\images` folder

The `images` directory and CSS file are the same as for the development version; only the JavaScript file changes. You only have to copy these files for a clean installation.

Using jQuery UI via a Content Distribution Network

I touched upon using a CDN for jQuery in Chapter 5. If this is an approach that appeals to you, you will be pleased to learn that you can do the same with jQuery UI. Both Google and Microsoft host the jQuery UI files on their CDNs. For this example, I'll use the Microsoft service, because it hosts the standard themes as well as the jQuery UI JavaScript.

To use a CDN, you just need the URLs to the files you want. For the Microsoft service, go to www.asp.net/ajaxlibrary/cdn.ashx to get started. If you scroll down the page, you will see a link for jQuery UI releases, broken down by version. Click the link for the version you are using (for me, the latest version is 1.8.16). You will see the URLs for the regular and minimized version of the jQuery UI library file. For my version, the URL for the minimized file is as follows:

http://ajax.aspnetcdn.com/ajax/jquery.ui/1.8.16/jquery-ui.min.js.

The rest of the page shows each of the predefined jQuery UI themes, with the URL for the theme CSS shown underneath. The URL for the Sunny theme is as follows:

http://ajax.aspnetcdn.com/ajax/jquery.ui/1.8.16/themes/sunny/jquery-ui.css

To use these files on the CDN, you simply place the URLs in the script and link elements that refer to the local jQuery UI files, as shown in Listing 17-2.

Listing 17-2. Using jQuery UI via a CDN

```
<!DOCTYPE html>
<html>
<head>
    <title>Example</title>
    <script src="jquery-1.7.js" type="text/javascript"></script>
    <script src="http://ajax.aspnetcdn.com/ajax/jquery.ui/1.8.16/jquery-ui.min.js"
      type="text/javascript"></script>
    <link rel="stylesheet" type="text/css" href="styles.css"/>
    <link rel="stylesheet" type="text/css"
      href="http://ajax.aspnetcdn.com/ajax/jquery.ui/1.8.16/themes/sunny/jquery-ui.css"/>
    <script type="text/javascript">
        $(document).ready(function() {
            $('a').button();
        });
    </script>
</head>
<body>
    <a href="http://apress.com">Visit Apress</a>
</body>
</html>
```

Once again, you can tell whether you have the correct URLs by loading the document and seeing whether the browser displays a button similar to the one in Figure 17-4.

Summary

In this chapter, I showed you the steps required to create a jQuery UI download. There is a lot of flexibility in the features you include and the default appearance jQuery UI imparts on your web application. I particularly like the ThemeRoller application. It is an elegant way of creating a completely customized theme to fit into an existing visual scheme, which is ideal for adding jQuery UI to corporate-branded sites.

In the next chapter, you'll start to look at the different jQuery UI features, starting with the most popular functional area: widgets.

CHAPTER 18

Using the Button, Progress Bar, and Slider Widgets

Now that you have configured, downloaded, and installed jQuery UI, you can start to look at the widgets it contains. These are the major functional blocks of jQuery UI, and although there are other features (such as effects, which I describe in Chapter 34), it is the widgets that jQuery UI is known for.

In this chapter, I describe the three simplest widgets: the button, progress bar, and sliders. All widgets have some common characteristics: settings, methods, and events. Mastering one widget provides a solid foundation for working with all of them, so I spend some time at the start of this chapter providing some overall context.

It is hard to tie all of the widgets into the flower shop example, so you will find that many of the examples in this part of the book are small, self-contained HTML documents that demonstrate a single widget. You'll return to the flower shop example in Chapter 25 when you refactor it to include jQuery UI. Table 18-1 provides the summary for this chapter.

Table 18-1. *Chapter Summary*

Problem	Solution	Listing
Create a jQuery UI button.	Select an element and use the `button` method.	1
Configure a button element.	Pass a map object to the `button` method or use the `option` method.	2, 3
Use icons in jQuery UI buttons.	Use the `icons` setting.	4
Use a custom image in a jQuery UI button.	Set the content of the button to be an `img` element.	5
Remove the jQuery UI button widget.	Use the `destroy` method.	6
Enable or disable the jQuery UI button.	Use the `enable` or `disable` method.	7
Refresh the state of a jQuery UI button to reflect a programmatic change to the underlying element.	Use the `refresh` method.	8

Respond to a jQuery UI button being created.	Specify a function for the `create` event.	9
Create uniform buttons from different kinds of element.	Create jQuery UI buttons from `input`, `button`, or a element.	10
Create a toggle button.	Create a jQuery UI from a check box.	11
Create a button set.	Use the `buttonset` method.	12, 13
Create a jQuery UI progress bar.	Use the `progressbar` method.	14
Get or set the progress shown to the user.	Use the `value` method.	15
Animate a jQuery UI progress bar.	Use an animated GIF for the `background-image` property in the CSS `ui-progressbar-value` class.	16
Respond to changes in the progress bar.	Specify functions for the `create`, `change`, or `complete` event.	17
Create a jQuery UI slider.	Use the `slider` method.	18
Change the orientation of a jQuery UI slider.	Use the `orientation` setting.	19, 20
Animate the movement of the handle when the user clicks the slider.	Use the `animate` setting.	21
Create a jQuery UI slider that allows the user to specify a range of values.	Use the `range` and `values` settings.	22
Control a jQuery UI slider programmatically.	Use the `value` or `values` methods.	23
Respond to changes in the slider handle positions.	Handle the `start`, `stop`, `change`, or `slide` event.	24

Using the jQuery UI Button

The first widget you will look at provides a good introduction into the world of jQuery UI. The button widget is relatively simple but has a transformational effect on HTML documents. The button widget applies the jQuery UI theme to button and a elements. This means that the size, shape, font, and color of the element is transformed to match the theme you selected when you created your custom jQuery UI theme. Applying jQuery UI widgets is very simple, as Listing 18-1 shows.

Listing 18-1. A Simple HTML Document

```
<!DOCTYPE html>
<html>
<head>
    <title>Example</title>
    <script src="jquery-1.7.js" type="text/javascript"></script>
    <script src="jquery.tmpl.js" type="text/javascript"></script>
    <script src="jquery-ui-1.8.16.custom.js" type="text/javascript"></script>
    <link rel="stylesheet" type="text/css" href="styles.css"/>
    <link rel="stylesheet" type="text/css" href="jquery-ui-1.8.16.custom.css"/>
    <script type="text/javascript">
        $(document).ready(function() {
            $.ajax("mydata.json",{
                    success: function(data) {
                        var template = $('#flowerTmpl');
                        template.tmpl(data.slice(0, 3)).appendTo("#row1");
                        template.tmpl(data.slice(3)).appendTo("#row2");
                    }
                });

            $('button').button();
        });
    </script>
    <script id="flowerTmpl" type="text/x-jquery-tmpl">
        <div class="dcell">
            <img src="${product}.png"/>
            <label for="${product}">${name}:</label>
            <input name="${product}" data-price="${price}" data-stock="${stocklevel}"
                value="0" required />
        </div>
    </script>
</head>
<body>
    <h1>Jacqui's Flower Shop</h1>
    <form method="post" action="http://node.jacquisflowershop.com/order">
        <div id="oblock">
            <div class="dtable">
                <div id="row1" class="drow">
                </div>
                <div id="row2"class="drow">
                </div>
            </div>
        </div>
        <div id="buttonDiv"><button type="submit">Place Order</button></div>
    </form>
</body>
</html>
```

To apply the button widget, you use jQuery to select the elements you want to transform and call the button method. jQuery UI takes care of the rest. You can see the effect in Figure 18-1. Notice that you apply the button method to a jQuery selection object. The integration between jQuery and jQuery UI is very close, and it means that using jQuery UI is generally a natural extension of using the core jQuery techniques that I showed you in the earlier parts of this book.

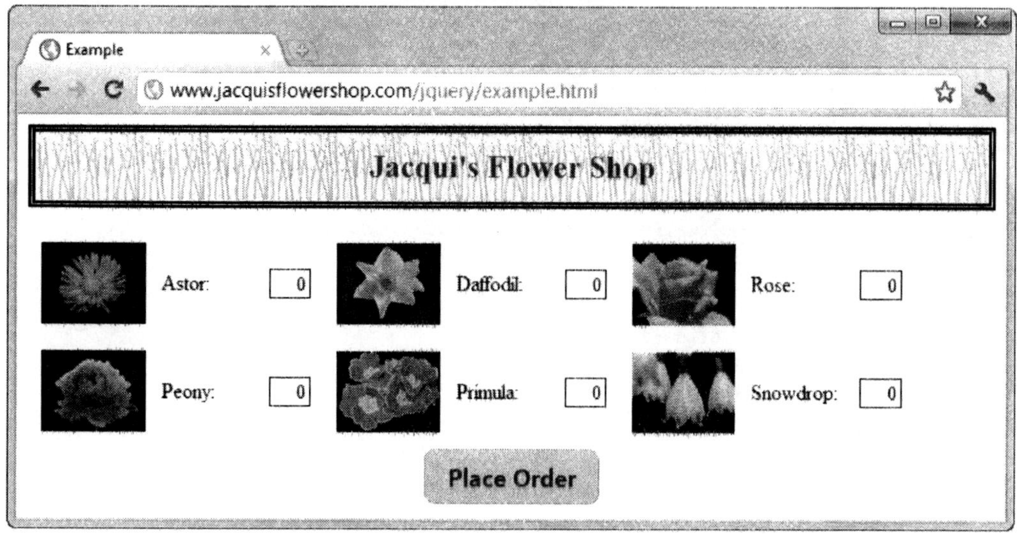

Figure 18-1. Applying the Button widget

Like all of the jQuery UI widgets, the button shown in the figure is a series of CSS styles applied to the existing HTML element. The `button` method transforms the element from this:

```
<button type="submit">Place Order</button>
```

to this:

```
<button type="submit" class="ui-button ui-widget ui-state-default ui-corner-all
    ui-button-text-only" role="button" aria-disabled="false">
        <span class="ui-button-text">Place Your Order</span>
</button>
```

This is a nice approach because it lets you work normally with the HTML element without having to worry about whether you are applying jQuery UI widgets to them.

Configuring the Button

The jQuery UI button widget can be configured via settings properties, allowing you to apply some control over the way that the button is created. These properties are described in Table 18-2.

***Table 18-2.** The Settings Properties for the Button Widget*

Property	Description
`disabled`	Gets or sets the disabled state of the button. A `true` value indicates that the button is disabled. jQuery UI doesn't take into account the state of the

	underlying HTML element.
text	Gets or sets whether the button will display text. This setting is ignored if icons is false.
icons	Gets or sets whether the button will display an icon.
label	Gets or sets the text that is displayed by the button.

You can apply these settings in two ways. The first is using a map object when you call the button methods, as highlighted in Listing 18-2.

Listing 18-2. Configuring the Button Widget Using a Map Object

```
...
<script type="text/javascript">
    $(document).ready(function() {

        $.ajax("mydata.json", {
                success: function(data, status) {
                    var template = $('#flowerTmpl');
                    template.tmpl(data.slice(0, 3)).appendTo("#row1");
                    template.tmpl(data.slice(3)).appendTo("#row2");
                }
            });

        $('button').button({
            label: "Place Your Order",
            disabled: true
        });

        $('button').button("option", "disabled", false);
    });
</script>
...
```

I have set the text that the button displays with the label setting and used the disabled setting to disable the button. This is the approach to use when defining the initial configuration for a widget and follows the style you saw most recently for configuring Ajax requests.

Listing 18-2 also shows the technique you use to define a new value for a setting property after the widget has been created, which is as follows:

```
$('button').button("option", "disabled", false);
```

You call the button method again, but with three arguments. The first argument is option, the second argument is the setting you want to change, and the third argument is the new value for the setting. This statement example sets false as the value for the disabled setting, undoing the value I passed in via the map object when I created the widget.

You can combine these techniques so that you call the button method with a first argument of option and a map object as the second argument. This allows you to apply multiple settings in one go, as shown in Listing 18-3.

Listing 18-3. Using the option Argument with a Map Object

```
...
<script type="text/javascript">
    $(document).ready(function() {

        $.ajax("mydata.json", {
                success: function(data, status) {
                    var template = $('#flowerTmpl');
                    template.tmpl(data.slice(0, 3)).appendTo("#row1");
                    template.tmpl(data.slice(3)).appendTo("#row2");
                }
            });

        $('button').button()

        $('button').button("option", {
            label: "Place Your Order",
            disabled: false
        });

        console.log("Enabled? " + $('button').button("option", "disabled"));
    });
</script>
...
```

You use the same slightly ugly syntax to read the value of a setting. In this case, you call the `button` method with two arguments. The first is `option`, and the second is the setting whose value you want to get, as this statement shows:

```
console.log("Enabled? " + $('button').button("option", "disabled"));
```

This statement reads the value of the `disabled` setting and writes it to the console, producing the following output for this example:

```
Enabled? false
```

Using jQuery UI Icons in Buttons

The jQuery UI themes include a range of icons that you can use for any purpose, including displaying them in buttons. Listing 18-4 shows the use of icons in a jQuery UI button.

Listing 18-4. Displaying an Icon in a Button

```
...
$('button').button({
    icons: {
        primary: "ui-icon-star",
        secondary: "ui-icon-circle-arrow-e"
    }
```

```
});
...
```

You use the icons setting to specify which icons will be displayed. The button widget has two positions for icons. The primary icon is displayed to the left of the text, and the secondary icon is displayed to the right of the text. As the listing demonstrates, you use an object that has primary and secondary properties to specify the icons you want. You can omit either property to display just a single icon. The icons themselves are quite small, as you can see in Figure 18-2.

Figure 18-2. Displaying icons in a button

You specify icons using classes that are defined in the jQuery UI CSS file. There are 173 different icons available, which is too many to list in this chapter. The easiest way to figure out the name of the icon you want is to go to http://jqueryui.com, select the Themes page, and scroll to the bottom of the page. You will see all of the icons listed in a grid, and moving the mouse button over each icon reveals the class name to use for the icon, as shown in Figure 18-3.

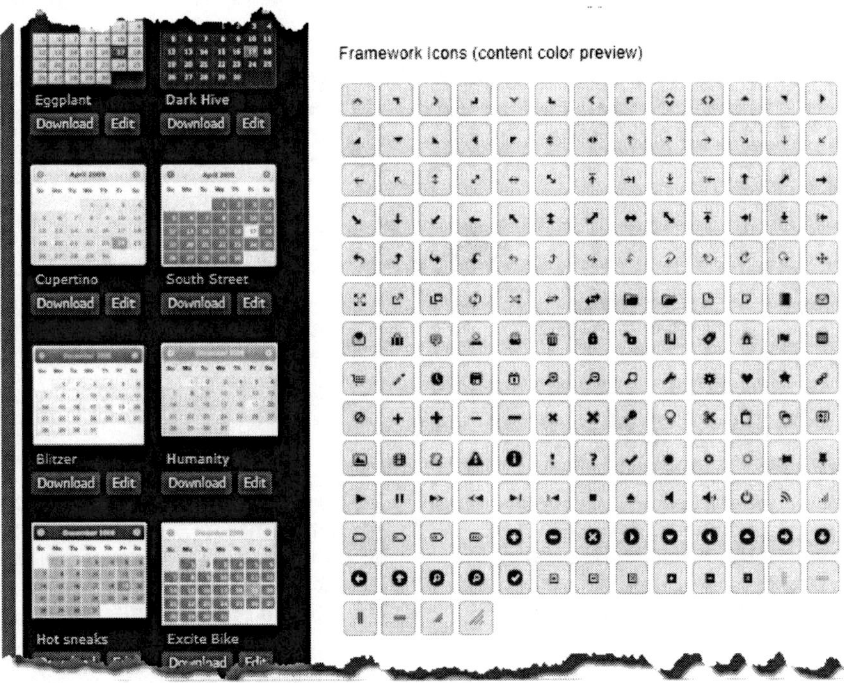

Figure 18-3. The jQuery UI icon grid

■ **Tip** The name that pops up on the web page has a leading period that must be omitted to be used with the icons setting. So, for example, if you hover the mouse over the first icon in the grid, `.ui-icon-caret-1-n` will pop up. To use this icon with a button, set the primary or secondary property to `ui-icon-caret-1-n`.

Using a Custom Image

I don't find the jQuery UI icons all that useful; they are usually too small for my needs. You can use a couple of techniques to display a different image in a jQuery UI button. The first is to insert an `img` element inside the `button` element to which you intend to apply jQuery UI. The jQuery UI button is very good at respecting the content of the underlying `button` element, and as long as you use an image with a transparent background, you don't have to worry about making the image match the theme. Listing 18-5 gives a simple demonstration.

Listing 18-5. Using a Custom Image with a jQuery UI Button

```
...
$('button')
    .text("")
    .append("<img src=rightarrows.png width=100 height=30 />")
    .button();
...
```

You can use the `text` setting to stop the jQuery UI button from displaying the content of the underlying button element only if the `icons` setting is `true`. If I don't want text *and* I don't want to use a jQuery UI icon, then I can use the jQuery `text` method to set the content to an empty string. I then use the `append` method to insert an `img` element and call the `button` method to create a jQuery UI button. You can see the result in Figure 18-4.

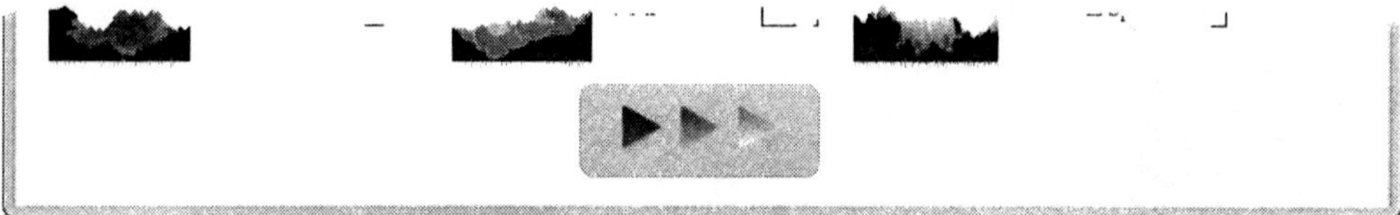

Figure 18-4. Showing a custom image in a button

Using the Button Methods

The jQuery UI widgets also define methods, which you can use to control the widget once it has been created. These are not true methods because you have to pass specific arguments to the `button` method, just as you did to change the value of settings earlier in the chapter. I am going to refer to them as methods, since that is the jQuery UI terminology. Table 18-3 shows the different methods you can use and the effect each has.

Table 18-3. Button Methods

Method	Description
`button("destroy")`	Returns the HTML element to its original state
`button("disable")`	Disables the button
`button("enable")`	Enables the button
`button("option")`	Sets one or more options; see the "Configuring the Button" section
`button("refresh")`	Refreshes the button; see the "Refreshing the State of a jQuery UI Button" section

Removing the Widget

The `destroy` method removes the jQuery UI widget from the HTML element, returning it to its original state. Listing 18-6 shows an example.

Listing 18-6. Using the destroy Method

```
...
<script type="text/javascript">
    $(document).ready(function() {

        $.ajax("mydata.json", {
                success: function(data, status) {
                    var template = $('#flowerTmpl');
                    template.tmpl(data.slice(0, 3)).appendTo("#row1");
                    template.tmpl(data.slice(3)).appendTo("#row2");
                }
            });

        $('button').button().click(function(e) {
            $('button').button("destroy");
            e.preventDefault();
        })
    });
</script>
...
```

In this example, I have used the click method to register a handler function for the button. Notice that you do this just as you did in Chapter 9 and that you don't have to make any special accommodation for the jQuery UI additions. I call the `destroy` method in the function, meaning that clicking the button causes it to disable itself. You can see the effect in Figure 18-5.

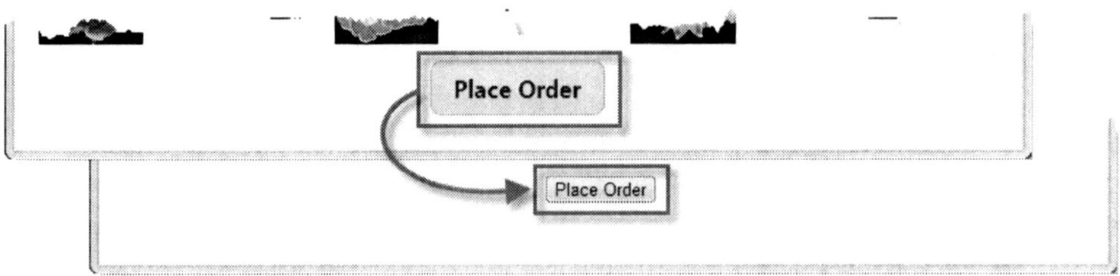

Figure 18-5. Destroying the jQuery UI button widget

Enabling and Disabling the Button

The enable and disable methods let you change the status of the jQuery UI button, as shown in Listing 18-7.

Listing 18-7. Enabling and Disabling a Button

```
...
<script type="text/javascript">
    $(document).ready(function() {

        $.ajax("mydata.json", {
                success: function(data, status) {
                    var template = $('#flowerTmpl');
                    template.tmpl(data.slice(0, 3)).appendTo("#row1");
                    template.tmpl(data.slice(3)).appendTo("#row2");
                }
            });

        $('<span>Enabled:<span><input type=checkbox checked />').prependTo('#buttonDiv');
        $(':checkbox').change(function(e) {
            $('button').button(
                $(':checked').length == 1 ? "enable" : "disable"
            )
        });

        $('button').button();
    });
</script>
...
```

In this script I have inserted a check box into the document and used the change method to register a function that will be called when the box is checked or unchecked. I call the enable and disable methods to change the state of the button to match the check box. You can see the effect in Figure 18-6.

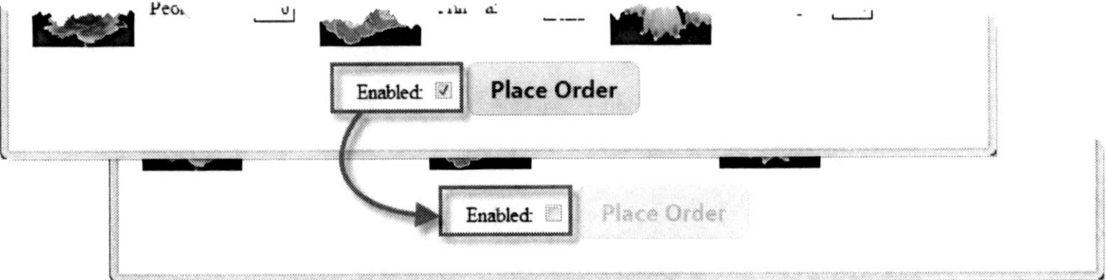

Figure 18-6. Enabling and disabling a jQuery UI button

Refreshing the State of a jQuery UI Button

The `refresh` method updates the state of the jQuery UI button to reflect any changes in the underlying HTML element. This can be useful for reflecting programmatic changes, like the ones shown in Listing 18-8.

Listing 18-8. Refreshing the jQuery UI Button

```
...
<script type="text/javascript">
    $(document).ready(function() {

        $.ajax("mydata.json", {
                success: function(data, status) {
                    var template = $('#flowerTmpl');
                    template.tmpl(data.slice(0, 3)).appendTo("#row1");
                    template.tmpl(data.slice(3)).appendTo("#row2");
                }
            });

        $('<span>Enabled:<span><input type=checkbox checked />').prependTo('#buttonDiv');
        $(':checkbox').change(function(e) {
            var buttons = $('button');
            if ($(':checked').length == 1) {
                buttons.removeAttr("disabled");
            } else {
                buttons.attr("disabled", "disabled");
            }
            buttons.button("refresh");
        });

        $('button').button();
    });
</script>
...
```

In this example, I use the check box to trigger adding and removing the disabled attribute from the HTML button element. This change isn't automatically detected by jQuery UI, so I call the refresh method to bring everything back in sync.

Using the Button Event

The jQuery UI widgets define events that you can use in addition to those of the underlying element. The button widget defines a single event called create, which is triggered when you create a jQuery UI button. As with the methods, you deal with events by using predefined arguments passed to the jQuery UI method, which is button in this case. Listing 18-9 shows how you can use the create event.

Listing 18-9. Using the jQuery UI Button create Event

```
...
<script type="text/javascript">
    $(document).ready(function() {
        $('button').button({
            create: function(e) {
                $(e.target).click(function(ev) {
                    ev.preventDefault();
                    alert("Button was pressed");
                })
            }
        });
    });
</script>
...
```

In this example, I use the create event to set up a function to respond to the click event on the button. I don't find the create event very useful and generally find that anything that can be done in response to this event can be done in a way that is more in keeping with the broader jQuery approach.

Creating Different Types of Button

The button method is sensitive to the kind of element it is applied to. The basic behavior, a regular button, is created when you call the button method on button elements, on a elements, or on input elements whose types are set to submit, reset, or button. Listing 18-10 shows all of these elements being transformed into jQuery UI buttons.

Listing 18-10. Creating Standard Buttons

```
<!DOCTYPE html>
<html>
<head>
    <title>Example</title>
    <script src="jquery-1.7.js" type="text/javascript"></script>
    <script src="jquery-ui-1.8.16.custom.js" type="text/javascript"></script>
    <link rel="stylesheet" type="text/css" href="jquery-ui-1.8.16.custom.css"/>
    <script type="text/javascript">
        $(document).ready(function() {
```

```
            $('.jqButton').click(function(e) {
               e.preventDefault();
               $(this).button();
            });
        });
    </script>
</head>
<body>
    <form>
        <input class="jqButton" type="submit" id="inputSubmit" value="Submit">
        <input class="jqButton" type="reset" id="inputReset" value="Reset">
        <input class="jqButton" type="button" id="inputButton" value="Input Button">
        <button class="jqButton">Button Element</button>
        <a class="jqButton" href="http://apress.com">A Element</a>
    </form>
</body>
</html>
```

In this simple document, I have defined one of each of the elements I described. I have used the click method so that each element is transformed into a jQuery UI button when it is clicked. You can see the transformation in Figure 18-7.

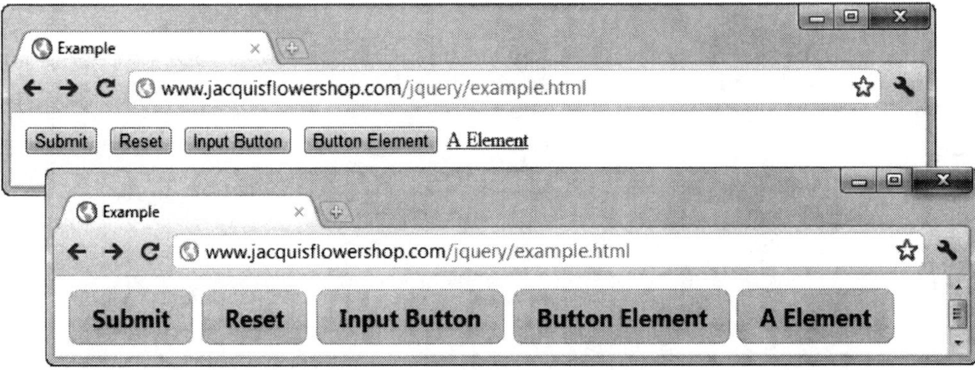

Figure 18-7. Creating standard jQuery UI buttons

Creating a Toggle Button

If you call the button method on an input element whose type is set to checkbox, then you get a toggle button. A toggle button is switched on or off when you click it, following the checked and unchecked states of the underlying element. Listing 18-11 provides a demonstration.

Listing 18-11. Applying jQuery UI to a Check Box

```
<!DOCTYPE html>
<html>
<head>
    <title>Example</title>
    <script src="jquery-1.7.js" type="text/javascript"></script>
    <script src="jquery-ui-1.8.16.custom.js" type="text/javascript"></script>
    <link rel="stylesheet" type="text/css" href="jquery-ui-1.8.16.custom.css"/>
    <script type="text/javascript">
        $(document).ready(function() {
            $('.jqButton').button();
        });
    </script>
</head>
<body>
    <form>
        <input class="jqButton" type="checkbox" id="toggle">
        <label for="toggle">Toggle Me</label>
    </form>
</body>
</html>
```

To create a jQuery UI button from a check box, you must have an input element and a matching label element, as shown in the listing. jQuery UI creates a button that has the same appearance as a basic button but that toggles its state when clicked. You can see the effect in Figure 18-8.

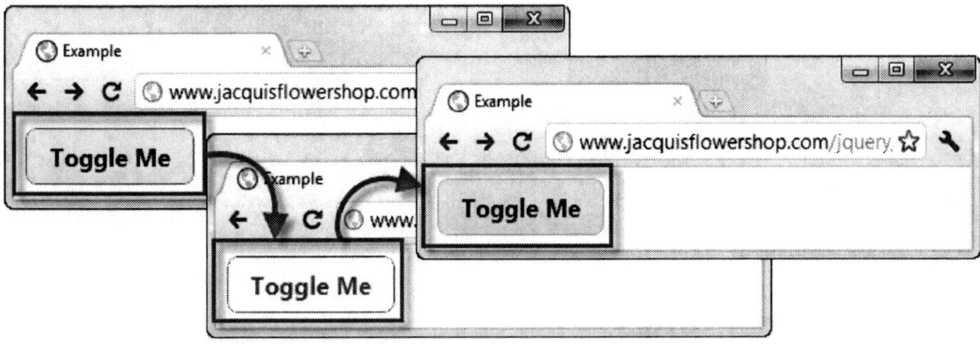

Figure 18-8. Creating a toggle button from a check box

Remember that jQuery UI doesn't change the underlying element, so the check box is still treated the same way by the browser when included in forms. The change of state is reflected using the checked attribute, just as it would be without jQuery UI.

Creating a Button Set

You can use the buttonset method to create jQuery UI buttons from radio button elements, as shown in Listing 18-12.

Listing 18-12. Creating a Button Set

```
<!DOCTYPE html>
<html>
<head>
    <title>Example</title>
    <script src="jquery-1.7.js" type="text/javascript"></script>
    <script src="jquery-ui-1.8.16.custom.js" type="text/javascript"></script>
    <link rel="stylesheet" type="text/css" href="jquery-ui-1.8.16.custom.css"/>
    <script type="text/javascript">
        $(document).ready(function() {
            $('#radioDiv').buttonset();
        });
    </script>
</head>
<body>
    <form>
        <div id="radioDiv">
            <input type="radio" name="flower" id="rose" checked />
                <label for="rose">Rose</label>
            <input type="radio" name="flower" id="lily"/><label for="lily">Lily</label>
            <input type="radio" name="flower" id="iris"/><label for="iris">Iris</label>
        </div>
    </form>
</body>
</html>
```

Notice that I have selected the div element that contains the radio buttons in order to call the buttonset method. You don't call the button method on the individual input elements. You can see the effect of the buttonset method in Figure 18-9.

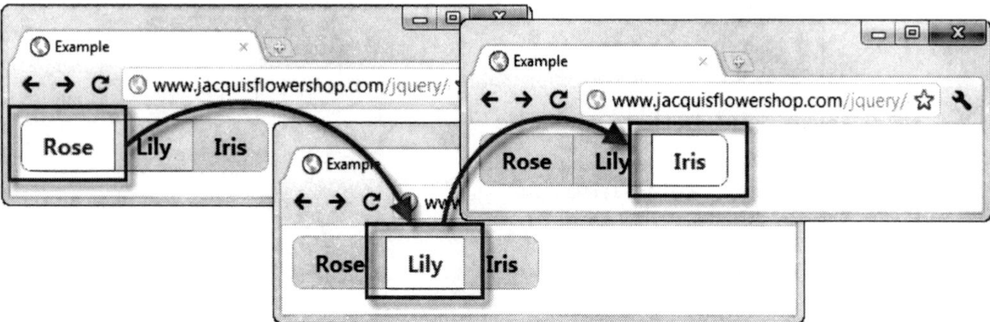

Figure 18-9. Creating a button set

As with regular radio buttons, at most one of the buttons can be selected, allowing you to provide the user with a fixed set of choices in a way that is visually consistent with other jQuery UI buttons. Notice that jQuery UI emphases the relationship between the buttons in a set by applying different styling to the edges where buttons meet. This is shown more clearly in Figure 18-10.

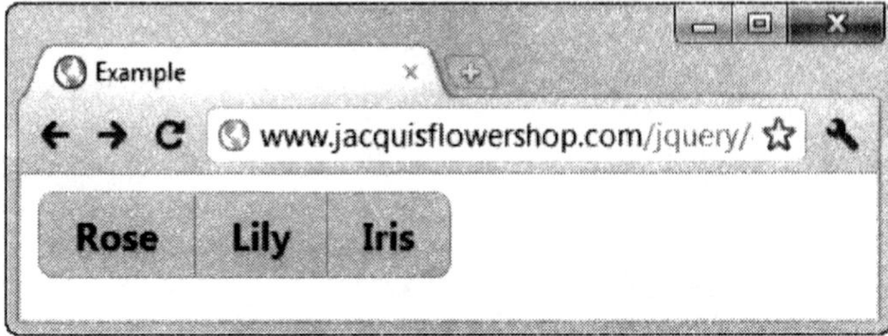

Figure 18-10. The jQuery UI styling for button sets

Creating Button Sets from Regular Buttons

You can use the buttonset method on any element that can be used with the regular button method. This has the effect of applying the *style* of a set of radio buttons but not the behavior so that each button works individually. Listing 18-13 shows this use of the buttonset method.

Listing 18-13. Creating a Button Set from Regular Buttons

```
<!DOCTYPE html>
<html>
<head>
    <title>Example</title>
    <script src="jquery-1.7.js" type="text/javascript"></script>
    <script src="jquery-ui-1.8.16.custom.js" type="text/javascript"></script>
    <link rel="stylesheet" type="text/css" href="jquery-ui-1.8.16.custom.css"/>
    <script type="text/javascript">
        $(document).ready(function() {
            $('#radioDiv').buttonset();
        });
    </script>
</head>
<body>
    <form>
        <div id="radioDiv">
            <input type="submit" value="Submit"/>
            <input type="reset" value="Reset"/>
            <input type="button" value="Press Me"/>
            <a href="http://apress.com">Visit Apress</a>
        </div>
    </form>
</body>
</html>
```

Any suitable element in the div container will be transformed into a button, and the adjoining edges will be styled just as with the radio button, as you can see in Figure 18-11.

Figure 18-11. Creating a button set from regular buttons

■ **Tip** Be careful when using this technique. It can be confusing to the user, especially if you are using radio buttons elsewhere in the same document or web application.

Using the jQuery UI Progress Bar

Now that you've used the button to understand the basic structure of a jQuery UI widget, you can begin to look at the other widgets that jQuery UI supports, starting with the progress bar.

The progress bar allows you to show the user progress in completing a task. The progress bar is designed only to show *determinate* tasks, where you can give the user an accurate indication of how far you are through the task as a percentage. The alternative is an *indeterminate* task, where you don't have visibility of what's happening and you just need to tell the user to wait (I showed you a simple indeterminate progress indicator in Chapter 16 when I used an animated image).

SHOWING USEFUL PROGRESS INFORMATION

There are no rules for the way widgets should be used in web applications, but the user expectations of controls such as progress bars are informed by the standards set by operating systems such as Windows and Mac OS. To help the user make sense of your progress bar, there are a couple of rules to follow.

First, only ever increment the progress. Don't be tempted to reduce the progress when the task has more steps than initially expected. The progress bar shows the percentage of a task that been completed and is not an estimate of the remaining time. If there are different possible paths for a task to follow, then show the most pessimistic progress. It is better to take a giant leap in progress rather than confuse the user.

Second, don't loop around the progress bar more than once. If you have enough information to show the user reasonably accurate completion information, then you should be using an indeterminate progress indicator. When the progress nears 100 percent, the user expects the task to complete. If the progress bar then resets and starts to build up again, you have simply confused the user and made the use of the progress bar meaningless.

Creating the Progress Bar

You create a progress bar by calling selecting a div element and calling the progressbar method, as shown in Listing 18-14.

Listing 18-14. Creating a Progress Bar

```
<!DOCTYPE html>
<html>
<head>
    <title>Example</title>
    <script src="jquery-1.7.js" type="text/javascript"></script>
    <script src="jquery-ui-1.8.16.custom.js" type="text/javascript"></script>
    <link rel="stylesheet" type="text/css" href="jquery-ui-1.8.16.custom.css"/>
    <script type="text/javascript">
        $(document).ready(function() {
            $('#progressDiv').progressbar({
                value: 21
            });
        });
    </script>
</head>
<body>
    <div id="progressDiv"></div>
</body>
</html>
```

In this example, the document contains a div element with an id of progressDiv. To create a progress bar, you must use an empty div element. If there are any contents, they affect the layout of the widget. I select the progressDiv element and call the progressbar method, passing in a map object to provide the initial configuration. The progress bar supports two settings, which are described in Table 18-4.

***Table 18-4.** The Settings for the Progress Bar Widget*

Setting	Description
disabled	If true, the progress bar will be disabled. The default value is false.
value	Sets the percentage complete displayed to the user. The default is zero.

In the example, I specified an initial value of 21 percent, and you can see the effect in Figure 18-12.

Figure 18-12. Creating a progress bar

Using the Progress Bar Methods

The progress bar widget defines a number of methods, which are in the same style as for the button. In other words, you call the `progressbar` method, and the first argument specifies the method you want. Table 18-5 describes the available methods.

***Table 18-5.** Progress Bar Methods*

Method	Description
`progressbar("destroy")`	Returns the `div` element to its original state
`progressbar("disable")`	Disables the progress bar
`progressbar("enable")`	Enables the progress bar
`progressbar("option")`	Sets one or more options; see the "Configuring the Button" section for details of configuring a jQuery UI widget
`progressbar("value", value)`	Gets and sets the value displayed by the progress bar

Most of these methods work in the same way as for the button widget, so I am not going to demonstrate them again. The exception is the `value` method, which lets you get and set the value that is displayed by the progress bar. Listing 18-15 demonstrates the use of this method.

Listing 18-15. Using the Progress Bar Value Method

```
<!DOCTYPE html>
<html>
<head>
    <title>Example</title>
    <script src="jquery-1.7.js" type="text/javascript"></script>
    <script src="jquery-ui-1.8.16.custom.js" type="text/javascript"></script>
    <link rel="stylesheet" type="text/css" href="jquery-ui-1.8.16.custom.css"/>
    <script type="text/javascript">
        $(document).ready(function() {

            $('#progressDiv').progressbar({
```

```
                value: 21
            });

            $('button').click(function(e) {
                var divElem = $('#progressDiv');
                var currentProgress = divElem.progressbar("value");
                    divElem.progressbar("value",
                        this.id == "decr" ? currentProgress - 10 :
                                                    currentProgress + 10)
            })
        });
    </script>
</head>
<body>
    <div id="progressDiv"></div>
    <button id="decr">Decrease</button>
    <button id="incr">Increase</button>
</body>
</html>
```

I have added a pair of button elements in this example that I used to increase or decrease the value displayed by the progress bar. Each press of a button changes the value by 10 percent, and you can see the effect in Figure 18-13.

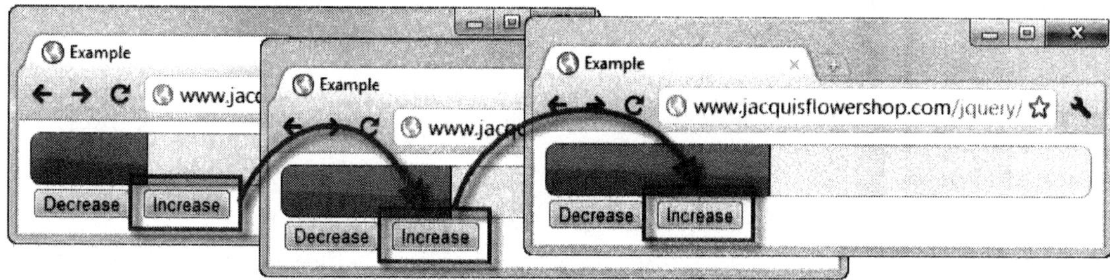

Figure 18-13. Using the value method to change the progress displayed

---

■ **Tip** The value method will return a number between 0 and 100 even if you have set the value to a greater or smaller number. This means you can rely on the progress bar to check the magnitude of the values you specify rather than having to do it yourself.

Animating the Progress Bar

The appearance of the progress bar is pretty basic, although it is consistent with the rest of the jQuery UI theme. When you create a progress bar, jQuery UI adds a div element to the document and adds a number of classes to the new div and the one you used for the progressbar method. The HTML that is generated looks like this:

```
<div id="progressDiv" class="ui-progressbar ui-widget ui-widget-content ui-corner-all"
     role="progressbar" aria-valuemin="0" aria-valuemax="100" aria-valuenow="10">
     <div class="ui-progressbar-value ui-widget-header ui-corner-left"
         style="width: 10%; ">
     </div>
</div>
```

The ui-progressbar-value class affects the element that jQuery UI has added to display the progress value, and the ui-progressbar class affects the outer div element that you started with. You can take advantage of these classes to create a progress bar that uses an animated GIF image for the progress value, as shown in Listing 18-16.

Listing 18-16. Using an Animated GIF Image with a Progress Bar

```
<!DOCTYPE html>
<html>
<head>
    <title>Example</title>
    <script src="jquery-1.7.js" type="text/javascript"></script>
    <script src="jquery-ui-1.8.16.custom.js" type="text/javascript"></script>
    <link rel="stylesheet" type="text/css" href="jquery-ui-1.8.16.custom.css"/>
    <style type="text/css">
        .ui-progressbar-value {
            background-image: url(progress-animation.gif);
        }
        .ui-progressbar {
            height: 22px
        }
    </style>
    <script type="text/javascript">
        $(document).ready(function() {
            $('#progressDiv').progressbar({
                value: 75
            });
        });
    </script>
</head>
<body>
    <div id="progressDiv"></div>
</body>
</html>
```

You can use the background-image CSS property to specify the image that will be used by the inner div element. In this case, I have specified an image called progress-animation.gif, which is a simple animated GIF image from the jQuery UI web site. It is difficult to show the effect of an animated GIF in a screenshot, but Figure 18-14 shows a single frame of the animation.

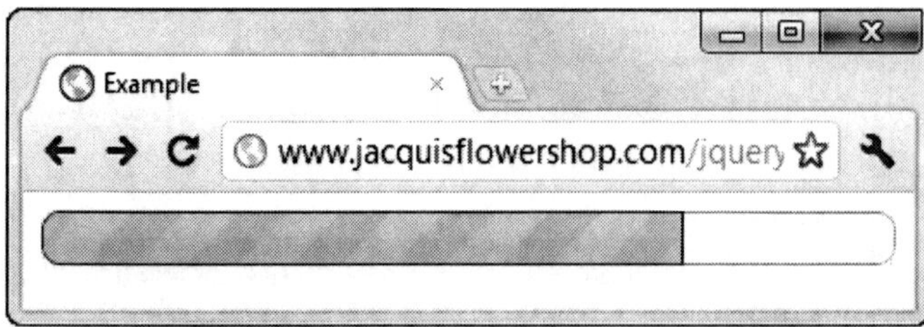

Figure 18-14. Using an animated image for a progress bar

There are a couple of points to note when using an image like this. The first is that you are responsible for selecting an image that matches the rest of the theme. jQuery UI doesn't manipulate the image in any way. The second is that you have to pay attention to the height of the image. By default, a jQuery UI progress bar is `2em` high, which can cause problems with smaller images. To address this, you can set the `height` property for the `ui-progressbar` class to match the image you are using. In the example, my image is 22 pixels high. If you don't manage the height, you can end up with a border above and below the image, as shown in Figure 18-15.

Figure 18-15. An image that is less than 2em high

Using the Progress Bar Events

The jQuery UI progress bar widget defines three events, as described in Table 18-6.

Table 18-6. *Progress Bar Events*

Event	Description
`create`	Triggered when the progress bar is created
`change`	Triggered when the value of the progress bar changes
`complete`	Triggered when the value of the progress bar is set to 100

Listing 18-17 shows the events in use.

Listing 18-17. Using the Progress Bar Events

```
<!DOCTYPE html>
<html>
<head>
    <title>Example</title>
    <script src="jquery-1.7.js" type="text/javascript"></script>
    <script src="jquery-ui-1.8.16.custom.js" type="text/javascript"></script>
    <link rel="stylesheet" type="text/css" href="jquery-ui-1.8.16.custom.css"/>
    <style type="text/css">
        .ui-progressbar-value {
            background-image: url(progress-animation.gif);
        }
        .ui-progressbar {
            height: 22px
        }
    </style>
    <script type="text/javascript">
        $(document).ready(function() {

            $('button').button();

            $('#progressDiv').progressbar({
                value: 75,
                create: function(e) {
                    $('#progVal').text($('#progressDiv').progressbar("value"));
                },
                complete: function(e) {
                    $('#incr').button("disable")
                },
                change: function(e) {
                    if ($(this).progressbar("value") < 100) {
                        $('#incr').button("enable")
                    }
                    $('#progVal').text($('#progressDiv').progressbar("value"));
                }
            });

            $('button').click(function(e) {
                var divElem = $('#progressDiv');
                var currentProgress = divElem.progressbar("value");
                    divElem.progressbar("value",
                        this.id == "decr" ? currentProgress - 10 :
                                                        currentProgress + 10)
            })
        });
    </script>
</head>
<body>
    <div id="progressDiv"></div>
    <button id="decr">Decrease</button>
```

```
    <button id="incr">Increase</button>
    Progress: <span id="progVal"></span>%
</body>
</html>
```

In this example, I have added a span element that I use to display the numeric progress value. I use the create event to set the initial value.

■ **Tip** Notice that I have used the same map object for the settings and events of the progress bar. This isn't required, but it does allow you to completely create and configure a widget in a single method call.

I use the complete event to disable the Increase button when the progress reaches 100% and the change event to ensure that the button is enabled for other values. I also use this event to update the contents of the span element. You can see the effect in Figure 18-16.

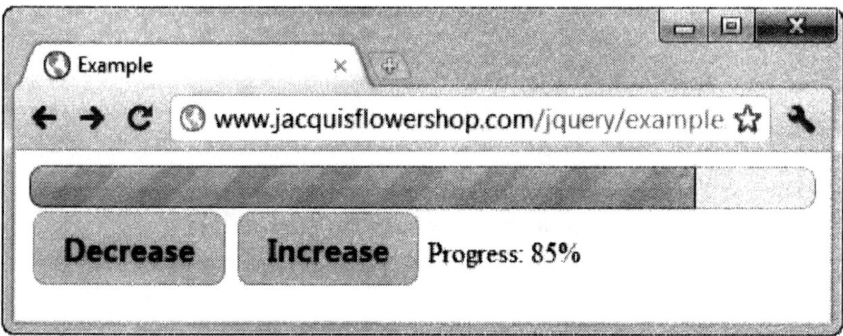

Figure 18-16. Responding to the progress bar events

■ **Tip** There are a couple of things to remember when using the events. First, the complete event fires every time the value is set to 100 or greater. This means the event can fire multiple times if you repeatedly set the value to 100, for example. Second, both the change and complete events are triggered for values of 100 or more, so you have to be able to deal with both when you complete the progress update.

Using the jQuery UI Slider

The slider widget creates sliders out of elements in the HTML document. You create sliders using the slider method, as shown in Listing 18-18. Sliders are useful when you want the user to select a value in a given range.

Listing 18-18. Creating a Slider

```
<!DOCTYPE html>
<html>
<head>
    <title>Example</title>
    <script src="jquery-1.7.js" type="text/javascript"></script>
    <script src="jquery-ui-1.8.16.custom.js" type="text/javascript"></script>
    <link rel="stylesheet" type="text/css" href="jquery-ui-1.8.16.custom.css"/>
    <script type="text/javascript">
        $(document).ready(function() {

            $('#slider').slider();

        });
    </script>
</head>
<body>
    <div id="slider"></div>
</body>
</html>
```

The slider is themed consistently with the other jQuery UI widgets and allows the user to use the mouse or arrow keys to move the slider handle up and down the scale. You can see how the basic slider appears in Figure 18-17.

Figure 18-17. A basic jQuery UI slider

Configuring the Slider

A with all jQuery UI widgets, the slider widget defines a number of settings that you can use to configure the appearance and behavior of sliders. These settings are described in Table 18-7. In the sections that follow, I show you how to use these settings to configure the widget.

Table 18-7. *The Settings for the Slider Widget*

Setting	Description
animate	When true, animates the slider when the user clicks a position outside of the handle. The default is false.

disabled	Disables the slider when set to true. The default is false.
max	Defines the maximum value for the slider. The default is 100.
min	Defines the minimum value for the slider. The default is 0.
orientation	Defines the orientation for the slider. See the following example for details.
range	Used with the values setting to create a multihandle slider.
step	Defines the interval that the slider moves between the min and max values.
value	Defines the value that the slider represents.
values	Used with the range setting to create a multihandle slider.

■ **Tip** The min and max values are exclusive, meaning that if you set a min value of 0 and a max value of 100, the user can select values between 1 and 99.

Changing the Slider Orientation

By default, sliders are horizontal, but you can use the orientation setting to create vertical sliders as well. Listing 18-19 provides a simple demonstration.

Listing 18-19. Using the orientation Setting

```
<!DOCTYPE html>
<html>
<head>
    <title>Example</title>
    <script src="jquery-1.7.js" type="text/javascript"></script>
    <script src="jquery-ui-1.8.16.custom.js" type="text/javascript"></script>
    <link rel="stylesheet" type="text/css" href="jquery-ui-1.8.16.custom.css"/>
    <style type="text/css">
        #hslider, #vslider { margin: 10px}
    </style>
    <script type="text/javascript">
        $(document).ready(function() {

            $('#hslider').slider({
                value: 35
            });

            $('#vslider').slider({
```

```
                orientation: "vertical",
                value: 35
            })

        });
    </script>
</head>
<body>
    <div id="hslider"></div>
    <div id="vslider"></div>
</body>
</html>
```

In this example, I have created two sliders, one of which has the orientation setting of vertical. I have also added a style element so that I can apply a margin to the slider elements to keep them apart. You control the size and position of sliders (and any jQuery UI widget) by styling the underlying element (which is why div elements work best; they can be readily manipulated with CSS). You can see the sliders in Figure 18-18. Notice that I used the value setting to set the initial position of the handle.

Figure 18-18. Creating vertical and horizontal sliders

Although I am keeping the options and methods separate, I could have written the previous example differently to make better use of the underlying jQuery functionality, as shown in Listing 18-20.

Listing 18-20. Making Better Use of jQuery

```
<!DOCTYPE html>
<html>
<head>
    <title>Example</title>
    <script src="jquery-1.7.js" type="text/javascript"></script>
    <script src="jquery-ui-1.8.16.custom.js" type="text/javascript"></script>
    <link rel="stylesheet" type="text/css" href="jquery-ui-1.8.16.custom.css"/>
    <style type="text/css">
        #hslider, #vslider { margin: 10px}
    </style>
    <script type="text/javascript">
```

```
        $(document).ready(function() {
            $('#hslider, #vslider').slider({
                value: 35,
                orientation: "vertical"
            }).filter('#hslider').slider('option', 'orientation', 'horizontal');
        });
    </script>
</head>
<body>
    <div id="hslider"></div>
    <div id="vslider"></div>
</body>
</html>
```

It is a minor point, but I don't want you to forget that jQuery UI is built on and tightly integrated with jQuery, and you can use all of the selections and manipulations you saw earlier in the book.

■ **Tip** Notice that I set the initial orientation to vertical and then changed it to horizontal. As I write this, there is a minor bug with the slider where changing the orientation to vertical after the slider has been created causes the handle to be misaligned.

Animating the Slider

The animate setting enables smooth handle movement when the user clicks the slider at the point they want the handle to move to (as opposed to moving the slider itself). You can enable the default animation by setting animate to true, set a speed for the animation by using fast or slow, or specify the number of milliseconds that the animation should last for. Listing 18-21 shows the use of the animate setting.

Listing 18-21. Using the animate Setting

```
<!DOCTYPE html>
<html>
<head>
    <title>Example</title>
    <script src="jquery-1.7.js" type="text/javascript"></script>
    <script src="jquery-ui-1.8.16.custom.js" type="text/javascript"></script>
    <link rel="stylesheet" type="text/css" href="jquery-ui-1.8.16.custom.css"/>
    <style type="text/css">
        #slider {margin: 10px}
    </style>
    <script type="text/javascript">
        $(document).ready(function() {
            $('#slider').slider({
                animate: "fast"
            });
        });
```

```
    </script>
</head>
<body>
    <div id="slider"></div>
</body>
</html>
```

In this example, I have set the `animate` setting to `fast`. It is hard to show animations in a screenshot, but Figure 18-19 shows what the `animate` setting does.

Figure 18-19. Animating the movement of the handle

This screenshot shows the slider just before I clicked the mouse button. If I had not enabled animations, then the handle would just snap instantly to the location I clicked, immediately setting the new value for the slider. But since I have enabled animations, the slider will gracefully move to its new position in a less jarring way. However, like any effect or animation, you don't want to over-egg the effect, which is why I have selected the `fast` option. This is an example that you need to play with to see the full result. I recommend downloading the source code that accompanies this book if you don't want to type in the code and HTML. It is freely available from Apress.com and contains all of the examples in this book.

Creating a Range Slider

A range slider has two handles and lets the user specify a range. For example, you might want to let the user express the price range they are willing to pay for products so that you can filter anything else out. Listing 18-22 demonstrates creating a range slider.

Listing 18-22. Creating a Range Slider

```
<!DOCTYPE html>
<html>
<head>
    <title>Example</title>
    <script src="jquery-1.7.js" type="text/javascript"></script>
    <script src="jquery-ui-1.8.16.custom.js" type="text/javascript"></script>
    <link rel="stylesheet" type="text/css" href="jquery-ui-1.8.16.custom.css"/>
    <style type="text/css">
        #slider { margin: 10px}
    </style>
    <script type="text/javascript">
        $(document).ready(function() {
```

```
            $('#slider').slider({
                values: [35, 65],
                range: true,
                create: displaySliderValues,
                slide: displaySliderValues
            })

            function displaySliderValues() {
                $('#lower').text($('#slider').slider("values", 0));
                $('#upper').text($('#slider').slider("values", 1));
            }
        });
    </script>
</head>
<body>
    <div id="slider"></div>
    <div>Lower Value: <span id="lower">
        </span> Upper Value: <span id="upper"></span></div>
</body>
</html>
```

To create a range slider, you must set the range setting to true and set the value setting to an array that contains the initial lower and upper bounds of the range. (When using a regular slider, you use the value setting, and when using a range slider, you use the values setting.) In this example, I have set the bounds to 35 and 65. You can see the effect in Figure 18-20.

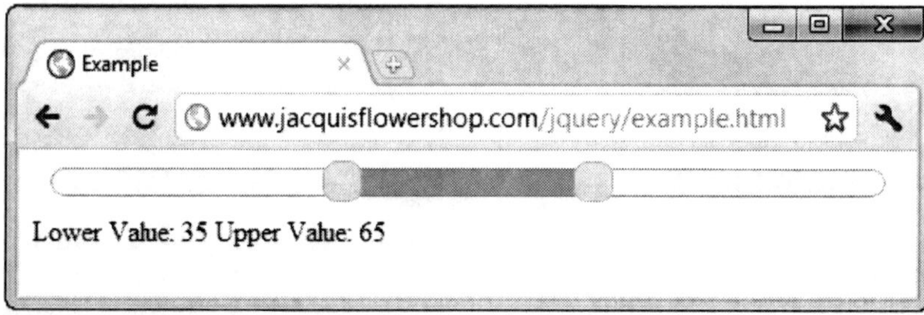

Figure 18-20. Creating a range slider

I have added a handler function for the create and slide events. I'll get to the events supported by the slider later in this chapter, but I wanted to demonstrate how you obtain the position of the handles in a range slider. You do this through the values method, specifying the index of the slider you are interested in, like this:

```
$('#slider').slider("values", 0);
```

The index is zero-based, so the previous fragment gets the value for the handle that represents the lower bound of the range. I have used the events to set the contents of two span elements.

Using the Slider Methods

The slider defines the same set of basic methods that all jQuery UI widgets define, plus a couple that let you set either a single value or the range of values to be shown. The methods are described in Table 18-8.

***Table 18-8.** Slider Methods*

Method	Description
`slider("destroy")`	Returns the underlying element to its original state
`slider("disable")`	Disables the slider
`slider("enable")`	Enables the slider
`slider("option")`	Sets one or more options; see the "Configuring the Button" section for details of configuring a jQuery UI widget
`slider("value", value)`	Gets or sets the value for a regular slider
`slider("values", [values])`	Gets or sets the values for a range slider

Listing 18-23 shows how you can use the value and values methods to control a slider programmatically.

Listing 18-23. Controlling Sliders Programmatically

```
<!DOCTYPE html>
<html>
<head>
    <title>Example</title>
    <script src="jquery-1.7.js" type="text/javascript"></script>
    <script src="jquery-ui-1.8.16.custom.js" type="text/javascript"></script>
    <link rel="stylesheet" type="text/css" href="jquery-ui-1.8.16.custom.css"/>
    <style type="text/css">
        #slider, #rangeslider, *.inputDiv { margin: 10px}
        label {width: 80px; display: inline-block; margin: 4px}
    </style>
    <script type="text/javascript">
        $(document).ready(function() {

            $('#slider').slider({
               value: 50,
               create: function() {
                    $('#slideVal').val($('#slider').slider("value"));
               }
            });

            $('#rangeslider').slider({
                values: [35, 65],
```

```
                range: true,
                create: function() {
                    $('#rangeMin').val($('#rangeslider').slider("values", 0));
                    $('#rangeMax').val($('#rangeslider').slider("values", 1));
                }
            })

            $('input').change(function(e) {
                switch (this.id) {
                    case "rangeMin":
                    case "rangeMax":
                        var index = (this.id == "rangeMax") ? 1 : 0;
                        $('#rangeslider').slider("values", index, $(this).val())
                        break;
                    case "slideVal":
                        $('#slider').slider("value", $(this).val())
                        break;
                }
            })
        });
    </script>
</head>
<body>
    <div id="rangeslider"></div>
    <div class="inputDiv">
        <label for="rangeMin">Range Min: </label><input id="rangeMin" />
        <label for="rangeMax">Range Max: </label><input id="rangeMax" />
    </div>
    <div id="slider"></div>
    <div class="inputDiv">
        <label for="slideVal">Slide Val: </label><input id="slideVal" />
    </div>
</body>
</html>
```

This document contains two sliders. There are also three input elements that allow the values for the handles to be specified without moving the handles themselves. You can see the layout of the document in Figure 18-21.

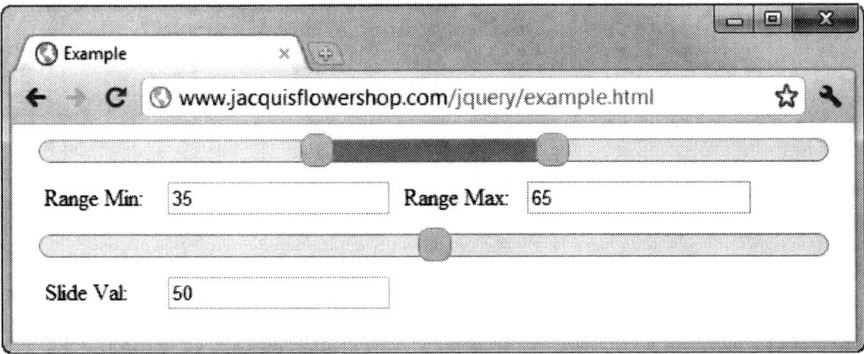

Figure 18-21. Controlling sliders programmatically

I have used jQuery to select the `input` elements in order to apply the `change` method so that my function is executed whenever the value of one of the `input` elements is changed. I then `switch` on the `id` attribute of the changed element and use the `value` or `values` methods to set the position of the handles. The relationship is one-way, meaning that moving the handles doesn't update the `input` elements. I'll show you how to do this in the next section when you turn to the events supported by the slider.

Using Slider Events

Table 18-9 shows the events that the slider supports. The best feature of these events is the support for both `change` and `stop`, which allows you to differentiate between new values created by the user moving the handle and values that you set programmatically.

Table 18-9. *Slider Events*

Event	Description
`create`	Triggered when the slider is created
`start`	Triggered when the user starts sliding the handle
`slide`	Triggered for every mouse move while the handle is sliding
`change`	Triggered when the user stops sliding the handle or when the value is changed programmatically
`stop`	Triggered when the user stops sliding the handle

Listing 18-24 shows the use of slider events to create a bidirectional relationship between the sliders and the input elements from the example in the previous section. This allows you to tie together programmatic support and user interaction to manage the sliders.

Listing 18-24. Using Slider Events to Create a Bidirectional Relationship Between Sliders and Inputs

```
<!DOCTYPE html>
<html>
<head>
    <title>Example</title>
    <script src="jquery-1.7.js" type="text/javascript"></script>
    <script src="jquery-ui-1.8.16.custom.js" type="text/javascript"></script>
    <link rel="stylesheet" type="text/css" href="jquery-ui-1.8.16.custom.css"/>
    <style type="text/css">
        #rangeslider, *.inputDiv { margin: 10px}
        label {width: 80px; display: inline-block; margin: 4px}
    </style>
    <script type="text/javascript">
        $(document).ready(function() {

            $('#rangeslider').slider({
                values: [35, 65],
                range: true,
                create: setInputsFromSlider,
                slide: setInputsFromSlider,
                stop: setInputsFromSlider
            })

            function setInputsFromSlider() {
                $('#rangeMin').val($('#rangeslider').slider("values", 0));
                $('#rangeMax').val($('#rangeslider').slider("values", 1));
            }

            $('input').change(function(e) {
                var index = (this.id == "rangeMax") ? 1 : 0;
                $('#rangeslider').slider("values", index, $(this).val())
            })
        });
    </script>
</head>
<body>
    <div id="rangeslider"></div>
    <div class="inputDiv">
        <label for="rangeMin">Range Min: </label><input id="rangeMin" />
        <label for="rangeMax">Range Max: </label><input id="rangeMax" />
    </div>
</body>
</html>
```

I removed one of the sliders to simplify the example. I already had all the code I needed because I set the values of the input elements in response to the create event. To enable this to work with the other events, I extracted the statements into a new function and used it to handle the create, slide, and stop events. Now the slider handles are moved when new values are entered into the input elements, and the values in the input elements are updated when the slider is moved. You can see how the document appears in Figure 18-22, but this is an example that requires interaction to see the full effect.

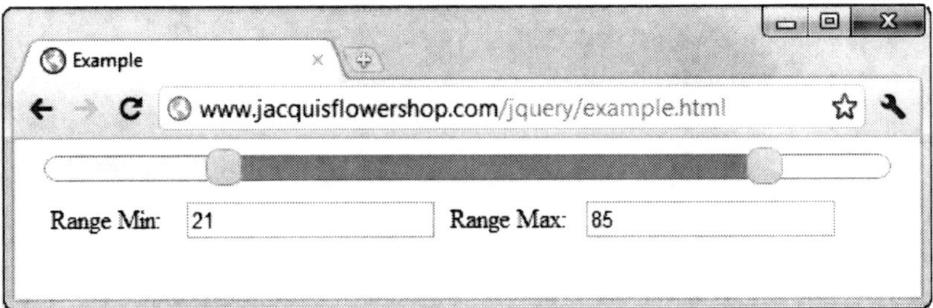

Figure 18-22. Responding to slider events

Summary

In this chapter, I introduced you to the first three jQuery UI widgets: the button, the progress bar, and the slider. Each widget follows the same basic structure. There is a single method that creates and configures the widget as well as letting you supply functions that will respond to its events. Some methods and events are common to each widget, but there are unique additions as well that expose the special functionality that some widgets offer. Now that I have gotten the basics out of the way, I'll show you some more flexible and complex widgets in the chapters that follow.

CHAPTER 19

Using the Autocomplete and Accordion Widgets

In this chapter, I describe the jQuery UI autocomplete and accordion widgets. These are more complex than the widgets I showed you in Chapter 18, but they follow the same pattern of settings, methods, and events as all jQuery UI widgets. They are highly configurable, flexible, and clever user interface controls, and used wisely, they can significantly enhance the appearance and usability of your documents and web applications. Table 19-1 provides the summary for this chapter.

Table 19-1. *Chapter Summary*

Problem	Solution	Listing
Add the jQuery UI autocomplete feature to an `input` element.	Use the `autocomplete` method.	1, 2
Obtain autocomplete suggestions from a remote server.	Set the `source` setting to a URL.	3–5
Generate autocomplete suggestions dynamically.	Specify a function for the `source` setting.	6
Control the autocomplete feature programmatically.	Use the `search` and `close` methods.	7
Receive notification of the selected autocomplete item.	Use the `focus`, `select`, and `change` events.	8
Override the default autocomplete action.	Override the default action for the `select` event.	9
Create a jQuery UI accordion widget.	Use the `accordion` method.	10
Set the height of the accordion based on the size of the content elements.	Use the `autoHeight` setting.	11, 12
Set the height of the accordion based on the size of the parent element.	Use the `fillSpace` setting.	13

Change the action that the user has to perform to activate a content element.	Use the event setting.	14
Set the active content element in a jQuery UI accordion.	Use the active and collapsible settings.	15, 16
Change the icons used by an accordion.	Use the icons setting.	17
Change the active content element in an accordion.	Use the activate method.	18
Receive notifications when the active element in an accordion changes.	Handle the change or changestart event.	19

Using jQuery UI Autocomplete

The autocomplete widget provides suggestions to the user as they enter values into an input element. Used well, this widget can be a helpful timesaver to the user, speeding up data entry and reducing errors. In the sections that follow, I'll show you how to create, configure, and use the jQuery UI autocomplete widget.

Creating the Autocomplete Element

You use the autocomplete method on an input element to create an autocompleting control. Listing 19-1 demonstrates the use of the method to set up basic autocompletion.

Listing 19-1. Creating an Autocompleting Input Element

```
<!DOCTYPE html>
<html>
<head>
    <title>Example</title>
    <script src="jquery-1.7.js" type="text/javascript"></script>
    <script src="jquery-ui-1.8.16.custom.js" type="text/javascript"></script>
    <link rel="stylesheet" type="text/css" href="jquery-ui-1.8.16.custom.css"/>
    <script type="text/javascript">
        $(document).ready(function() {

            var flowers = ["Astor", "Daffodil", "Rose", "Peony", "Primula", "Snowdrop",
                           "Poppy", "Primrose", "Petuna", "Pansy"];

            $('#acInput').autocomplete({
                source: flowers
            })
        });
    </script>
</head>
<body>
```

```
    <form>
        <div class="ui-widget">
            <label for="acInput">Flower Name: </label><input id="acInput"/>
        </div>
    </form>
</body>
</html>
```

The autocomplete method works just like the other jQuery UI methods you have seen, with the exception that you must pass in a map object containing a value for the source setting. This setting specifies where the autocomplete entries will come from. In this example, I have used a simple array of values. Figure 19-1 illustrates the way that the autocomplete feature is presented to the user.

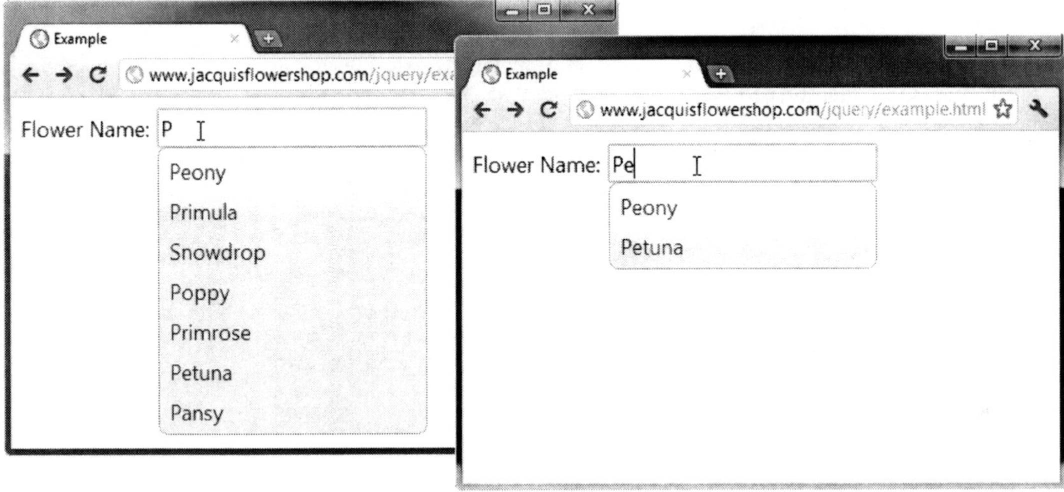

Figure 19-1. A basic jQuery UI autocomplete element

There are two screenshots in the figure. The first shows what happens when I type the letter *P*. As you can see, a list of the data items that contain the letter *P* are shown. This includes all of the flower names that start with *P* but also includes Snowdrop as well. In the second screenshot, I have typed *Pe*, and jQuery UI shows only the items that contain that combination of letters. The user can continue to type their entry or select one from the autocomplete list. The autocomplete feature doesn't enforce any kind of validation, and the user can enter any value into the input element, not just those that are defined by the source setting.

Notice that I have not sorted the items in the array that I used for the source setting. This is done automatically by jQuery UI. You can use a range of different data sources for the autocomplete values, which I demonstrate later in this chapter.

■ **Tip** In the document, I put the input element and its label inside a div element that belongs to the ui-widget class. This sets the CSS font properties for the label and input elements to match those used by the autocomplete pop-up. I'll explain more about how you can use the jQuery UI CSS classes in Chapter 34 (and I give a quick demonstration in Chapter 25).

Using an Object Array as the Data Source

An alternative approach is to use an array of objects, rather than just strings. This allows you to separate the label that is displayed in the pop-up menu from the value that is inserted into the input element. Listing 19-2 provides a demonstration.

Listing 19-2. Using an Array of Objects for Autocompletion

```
<!DOCTYPE html>
<html>
<head>
    <title>Example</title>
    <script src="jquery-1.7.js" type="text/javascript"></script>
    <script src="jquery-ui-1.8.16.custom.js" type="text/javascript"></script>
    <link rel="stylesheet" type="text/css" href="jquery-ui-1.8.16.custom.css"/>
    <style type="text/css">
        button {margin-bottom: 5px}
    </style>
    <script type="text/javascript">
        $(document).ready(function() {

            var flowers = [{label: "Astor (Purple)", value: "Astor"},
                {label: "Daffodil (White)", value: "Daffodil"},
                {label: "Rose (Pink)", value: "Rose"},
                {label: "Peony (Pink)", value: "Peony"}]

            $('#acInput').autocomplete({
                source: flowers
            })

        });
    </script>
</head>
<body>
    <form>
        <div class="ui-widget">
            <label for="acInput">Flower Name: </label><input id="acInput"/>
        </div>
```

```
    </form>
</body>
</html>
```

When you use an array of objects, the autocomplete feature looks for properties called `label` and `value`. The `label` property is used to create the pop-up list, and the `value` entry is inserted into the `input` element if the item is selected. In this example, I have added some color information to the labels, which is not included in the values. You can see the effect in Figure 19-2.

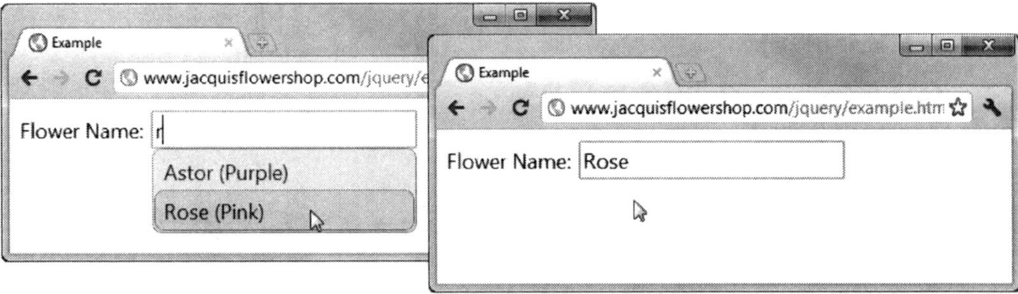

Figure 19-2. Using an array of objects to separate labels from values

Configuring Autocomplete

The autocomplete feature supports a number of settings that let you control different aspects of its functionality. These settings are described in Table 19-2. In the sections that follow, I show you how to use these settings to configure the widget.

Table 19-2. *Autocomplete Settings*

Setting	Description
`appendTo`	Specifies the element that the pop-up menu should be appended to. The default is the body element.
`autoFocus`	If set to `true`, the first item in the list will be given the focus, meaning that the user can select this item by pressing the Return key. The default is `false`.
`delay`	Specifies the delay (in milliseconds) after a keystroke after which the autocomplete data is updated. The default is `300`.
`disabled`	Disables the autocomplete feature when set to `true`. This setting does not affect the underlying `input` element. The default is `false`.
`minLength`	Specifies the minimum number of characters that the user has to type before the autocomplete menu is displayed. The default is `1`.
`source`	Specifies the source of items to be added to the autocomplete menu. There is no default for this setting, which must be specified when calling the `autocomplete` method.

Using a Remote Data Source

The most interesting autocomplete setting is source because you can use it to work with a wide range of different kinds of data to populate the pop-up menu. I used a JavaScript array in the previous example, which is fine for simple static lists of data. For more complex situations, you can get the list of matching items from a server. All you have to do is specify the URL that will generate the data, as shown in Listing 19-3.

Listing 19-3. Using a Remote Data Source

```
<!DOCTYPE html>
<html>
<head>
    <title>Example</title>
    <script src="jquery-1.7.js" type="text/javascript"></script>
    <script src="jquery-ui-1.8.16.custom.js" type="text/javascript"></script>
    <link rel="stylesheet" type="text/css" href="jquery-ui-1.8.16.custom.css"/>
    <script type="text/javascript">
        $(document).ready(function() {

            $('#acInput').autocomplete({
                source: "http://node.jacquisflowershop.com/auto"
            })
        });
    </script>
</head>
<body>
    <form>
        <div class="ui-widget">
            <label for="acInput">Flower Name: </label><input id="acInput"/>
        </div>
    </form>
</body>
</html>
```

When jQuery UI needs the list of items for the pop-up autocomplete menu, it will make an HTTP GET request to the specified URL. The characters that the user has typed so far are included in the request query string using the key term. So, for example, is the user has typed the letter *s*, then jQuery UI will request the following URL:

```
http://node.jacquisflowershop.com/auto?term=s
```

If the user then types the letter *n*, then jQuery UI will request the following:

```
http://node.jacquisflowershop.com/auto?term=sn
```

This technique is useful when there are a lot of data items and you don't want to send them all to the client. It can also be useful when the list of items changes dynamically and you want to make sure the user benefits from the latest data available.

The server is responsible for taking the term value from the query string and returning a JSON string representing the array of items to display to the user. Listing 19-4 shows a simple Node.js script that does just that.

Listing 19-4. The Node.js Script to Support Remote Autocompletion

```
var http = require('http');
var url = require('url');

http.createServer(function (req, res) {
    console.log("[200 OK] " + req.method + " to " + req.url);

    var flowers = ["Astor", "Daffodil", "Rose", "Peony", "Primula", "Snowdrop",
                   "Poppy", "Primrose", "Petuna", "Pansy"];

    req.on('end', function() {
        var matches = [];
        var term = url.parse(req.url, true).query["term"];

        if (term) {
            var pattern = new RegExp("^" + term, "i");
            for (var i = 0; i < flowers.length; i++) {
                if (pattern.test(flowers[i])) {
                    matches.push(flowers[i]);
                }
            }
        } else {
            matches = flowers;
        }

        res.writeHead(200, "OK", {
            "Content-Type": "application/json",
            "Access-Control-Allow-Origin": "*"});
        res.write(JSON.stringify(matches));
        res.end();
    });

}).listen(80);
console.log("Ready on port 80");
```

This script uses the same set of flower names as in the previous example and returns those that match the term sent by the browser. I have changed the search slightly so that only those names that start with the term are returned. For example, if jQuery UI sends a request like this:

```
http://node.jacquisflowershop.com/auto?term=p
```

then the `Node.js` server will return the following JSON:

```
["Peony","Primula","Poppy","Primrose","Petuna","Pansy"]
```

Because I am matching at the start of the flower name, Snowdrop is omitted from the list, as you can see in Figure 19-3.

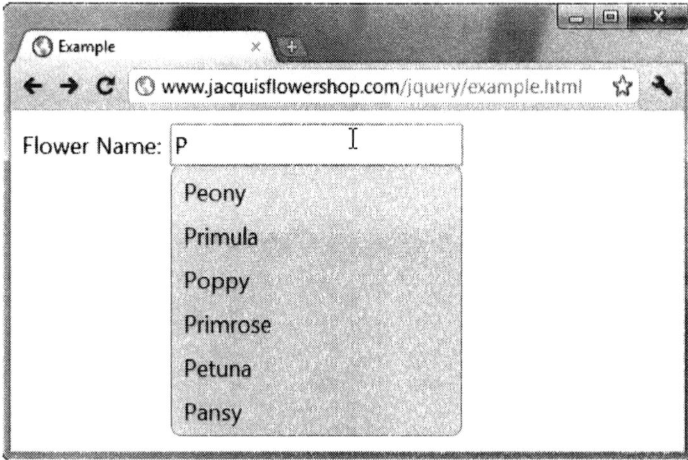

Figure 19-3. Obtaining autocomplete entries from a remote server

This is a really nice technique, but it can generate a lot of requests to the server. This isn't important in my example because I am performing only a simple search and my server and browser are on the same network. But for complex searches, across a wide-area network that can suffer delays, the load on the server can become an issue.

The best way to manage the rate at which autocomplete requests are made is to use the `minLength` and `delay` settings. The `minLength` setting specifies the number of characters that the user has to type before jQuery UI makes an autocomplete request to the server. You can use this setting such that you only request data from the server after several characters have been entered, by which time you have enough information to narrow the scope of your search.

The `delay` setting specifies the amount of time after a key press that the autocomplete information will be requested. You can use this setting to prevent requests from being made when the user is typing quickly. So, if the user types *s* and *n*, you can avoid hitting the server for the `s` list and then immediately doing so again for the `sn` list. By combining these settings, you can reduce the number of requests and still provide the user with guidance when it is needed. Listing 19-5 shows the uses of these settings.

Listing 19-5. Using the delay and minLength Settings to Reduce Server Requests

```
<!DOCTYPE html>
<html>
<head>
    <title>Example</title>
    <script src="jquery-1.7.js" type="text/javascript"></script>
    <script src="jquery-ui-1.8.16.custom.js" type="text/javascript"></script>
    <link rel="stylesheet" type="text/css" href="jquery-ui-1.8.16.custom.css"/>
    <script type="text/javascript">
        $(document).ready(function() {

            $('#acInput').autocomplete({
                source: "http://node.jacquisflowershop.com/auto",
                minLength: 3,
                delay: 1000
```

```
            })
        });
    </script>
</head>
<body>
    <form>
        <div class="ui-widget">
            <label for="acInput">Flower Name: </label><input id="acInput"/>
        </div>
    </form>
</body>
</html>
```

In this example, the initial request to the server won't be made until the user has entered three characters *and* has not typed any additional characters for one second.

Using a Function as the Data Source

You can use a function to create a truly customized source for autocomplete entries. You assign the function to the source setting, and it is called each time the autocomplete feature needs to display items to the user. Listing 19-6 provides a demonstration.

Listing 19-6. Using a Function to Generate Autocomplete Items

```
<!DOCTYPE html>
<html>
<head>
    <title>Example</title>
    <script src="jquery-1.7.js" type="text/javascript"></script>
    <script src="jquery-ui-1.8.16.custom.js" type="text/javascript"></script>
    <link rel="stylesheet" type="text/css" href="jquery-ui-1.8.16.custom.css"/>
    <style type="text/css">
        button {margin-bottom: 5px}
    </style>
    <script type="text/javascript">
        $(document).ready(function() {

            var flowers = ["Astor", "Daffodil", "Rose", "Peony", "Primula", "Snowdrop",
                           "Poppy", "Primrose", "Petuna", "Pansy"];

            $('#acInput').autocomplete({
                source: function(request, response) {
                    var term = request.term;
                    var pattern = new RegExp("^" + term, "i");

                    var results = $.map(flowers, function(elem) {
                        if (pattern.test(elem)) {
                            return elem;
                        }
                    })
                    response(results);
```

```
                }
            })
        });
    </script>
</head>
<body>
    <form>
        <div class="ui-widget">
            <label for="acInput">Flower Name: </label><input id="acInput"/>
        </div>

    </form>
</body>
</html>
```

Two arguments are passed to the function. The first argument is an object that has a single property called `term`. The value of this property is the string of characters that the user has entered into the `input` element. The second argument is a function that you call when you have generated the list of autocomplete items that you want to show to the user. The argument to this function is an array of strings or objects.

In this example, I have reproduced the server-side functionality from the previous listing, and I generate an array containing those items that start with the specified term.

■ **Tip** I processed the contents of the array using the jQuery `map` utility method, which I describe in Chapter 33.

I then pass the results back to jQuery UI by passing the array as an argument to the response function, like this:

```
response(results);
```

This is an odd way to process the results, but it works well enough, and the user is shown the items you generate, and you get the same effect as for the `Node.js` example.

Using the Autocomplete Methods

The jQuery UI autocomplete feature supports a number of methods that you can use to manipulate the autocomplete process. These methods are described in Table 19-3.

Table 19-3. *Autocomplete Methods*

Method	Description
`autocomplete("close")`	Closes the autocomplete menu.
`autocomplete("destroy")`	Removes the autocomplete functionality from the input element.
`autocomplete("disable")`	Disables autocompletion.

`autocomplete("enable")`	Enables autocompletion.
`autocomplete("option")`	Sets one or more options.
`autocomplete("search", value)`	Explicitly triggers autocompletion using the specified value. If no value argument is provided, then the contents of the input element are used.

The two methods that are unique to the autocomplete feature are `search` and `close`, which you can use to explicitly start and end the autocomplete process, as demonstrated in Listing 19-7.

Listing 19-7. Using the search and close Methods

```
<!DOCTYPE html>
<html>
<head>
    <title>Example</title>
    <script src="jquery-1.7.js" type="text/javascript"></script>
    <script src="jquery-ui-1.8.16.custom.js" type="text/javascript"></script>
    <link rel="stylesheet" type="text/css" href="jquery-ui-1.8.16.custom.css"/>
    <style type="text/css">
        button {margin-bottom: 5px}
    </style>
    <script type="text/javascript">
        $(document).ready(function() {

            var flowers = ["Astor", "Daffodil", "Rose", "Peony", "Primula", "Snowdrop",
                           "Poppy", "Primrose", "Petuna", "Pansy"];

            $('#acInput').autocomplete({
                source: flowers,
                minLength: 0,
                delay: 0
            })

            $('button').click(function(e) {
                e.preventDefault();
                switch (this.id) {
                    case "close":
                        $('#acInput').autocomplete("close");
                        break;
                    case "input":
                        $('#acInput').autocomplete("search");
                        break;
                    default:
                        $('#acInput').autocomplete("search", this.id);
                        break;
                }
            })
        });
```

```
    </script>
</head>
<body>
    <form>
        <button id="s">S</button>
        <button id="p">P</button>
        <button id="input">Input Content</button>
        <button id="close">Close</button>
        <div class="ui-widget">
            <label for="acInput">Flower Name: </label><input id="acInput"/>
        </div>

    </form>
</body>
</html>
```

In this example, I have added some button elements and used the click method to set up different autocomplete method calls. When the buttons marked *S* or *P* are pressed, I call the search method, passing in the selected letter as the search value. This triggers the autocomplete feature using the selected letter, irrespective of the contents of the input element, as shown in Figure 19-4.

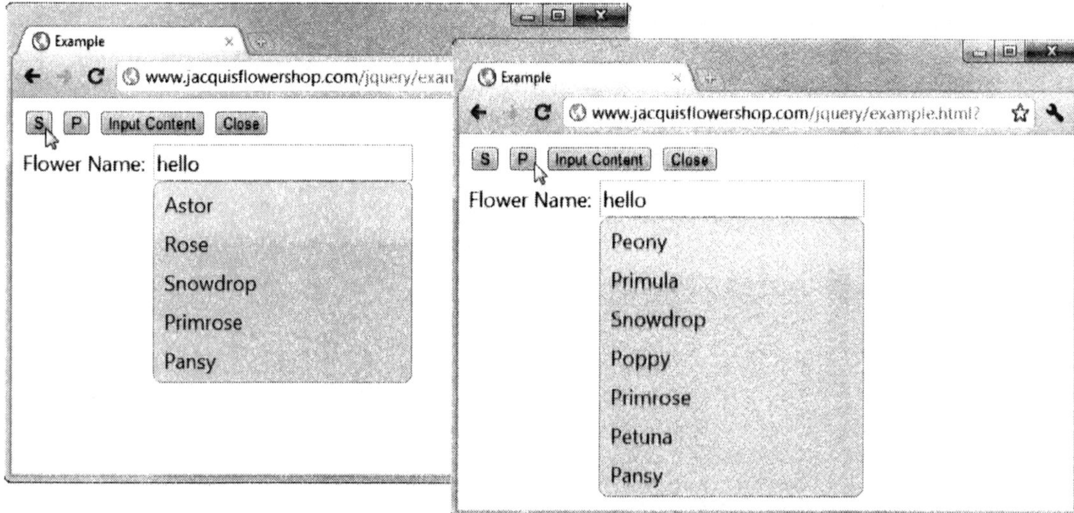

Figure 19-4. Using the search method with a search term

As you can see in the figure, the pop-up menu displays the entries that contain the letter from the button even though the input element contains the word hello.

The Input Content button triggers the autocomplete feature using whatever characters are contained in the input element. When I configured the autocomplete, I specified a minLength value of 0, which means that all of the items will be displayed in the list when I click the Input Content button, as shown in Figure 19-5. If the user had entered any characters in the input box, then the results would have been limited to items that contained that string.

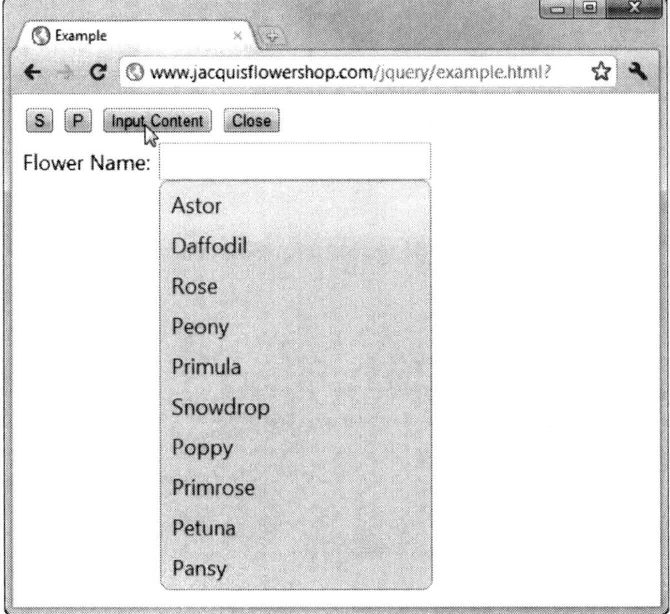

Figure 19-5. Searching using the contents of the input element

The final button, Close, calls the `close` method that dismisses the pop-up menu.

Using the Autocomplete Events

A number of events are triggered by the autocomplete feature, as described in Table 19-4.

***Table 19-4.** Autocomplete Events*

Event	Description
`change`	Triggered when the focus leaves the `input` element after the value has changed
`close`	Triggered when the pop-up menu is closed
`create`	Triggered when the autocomplete is created
`focus`	Triggered when an item in the pop-up menu gains the focus
`open`	Triggered when the pop-up menu is displayed
`search`	Triggered before the list of autocomplete items is generated or requested
`select`	Triggered when an item is selected from the menu

Getting Details of the Selected Item

jQuery UI provides additional information about an event through a second argument, typically called `ui`. For the `change`, `focus`, and `select` events, jQuery UI gives the `ui` object an `item` property that returns an object describing the selected or focused item from the pop-up menu. Listing 19-8 shows how you can use this feature to get information about the item.

Listing 19-8. Using the ui Object in Event Handlers

```
<!DOCTYPE html>
<html>
<head>
    <title>Example</title>
    <script src="jquery-1.7.js" type="text/javascript"></script>
    <script src="jquery-ui-1.8.16.custom.js" type="text/javascript"></script>
    <link rel="stylesheet" type="text/css" href="jquery-ui-1.8.16.custom.css"/>
    <script type="text/javascript">
        $(document).ready(function() {

            var flowers = ["Astor", "Daffodil", "Rose", "Peony", "Primula", "Snowdrop",
                           "Poppy", "Primrose", "Petuna", "Pansy"];

            $('#acInput').autocomplete({
                source: flowers,
                focus: displayItem,
                select: displayItem,
                change: displayItem
            })

            function displayItem(event, ui) {
                $('#itemLabel').text(ui.item.label)
            }
        });
    </script>
</head>
<body>
    <form>
        <div class="ui-widget">
            <label for="acInput">Flower Name: </label><input id="acInput"/>
            Item Label: <span id="itemLabel"></span>
        </div>
    </form>
</body>
</html>
```

In this example, I have added a span element that I use to display the `label` property of the selected object. jQuery UI creates objects with `label` and `value` properties even when you use a simple string array for the source setting, so you always need to read one of these properties from the `ui.item` object. In this example, I use the same function to display the item from the `focus`, `select`, and `change` events. You can see the effect in Figure 19-6.

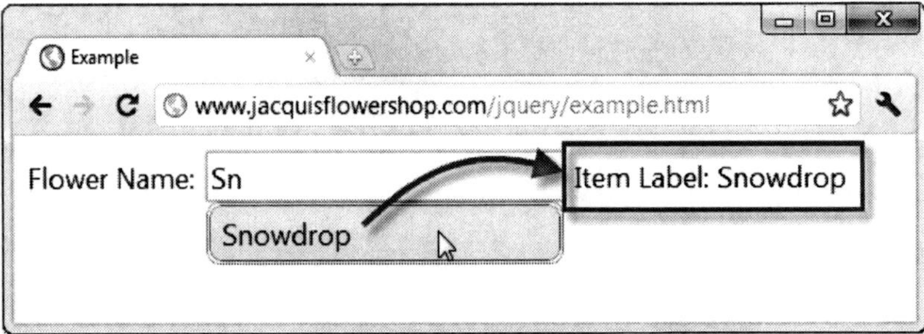

Figure 19-6. Getting the details of the selected item

Overriding the Default Select Action

The select event has a default action, which is to replace the contents of the input element with the contents of the value property of the item selected from the pop-up menu. This is exactly what you want most of the time, but you can use this event to either supplement the default action or prevent it entirely and do something different. Listing 19-9 contains an example of supplementing the default by setting the value of a related field.

■ **Tip** I described default actions for events in Chapter 9.

Listing 19-9. Overriding the Default Action of the select Event

```
<!DOCTYPE html>
<html>
<head>
    <title>Example</title>
    <script src="jquery-1.7.js" type="text/javascript"></script>
    <script src="jquery-ui-1.8.16.custom.js" type="text/javascript"></script>
    <link rel="stylesheet" type="text/css" href="jquery-ui-1.8.16.custom.css"/>
    <script type="text/javascript">
        $(document).ready(function() {

            var flowers = ["Astor", "Daffodil", "Rose"];

            var skus = { Astor: 100, Daffodil: 101, Rose: 102};

            $('#acInput').autocomplete({
                source: flowers,
                select: function(event, ui) {
                    $('#sku').val(skus[ui.item.value]);
                }
            })
```

```
        });
    </script>
</head>
<body>
    <form>
        <div class="ui-widget">
            <label for="acInput">Flower Name: </label><input id="acInput"/>
            <label for="sku">Stock Keeping Unit: </label><input id="sku"/>
        </div>
    </form>
</body>
</html>
```

When the select event is triggered, my handler function uses the ui argument to get the value of the selected item and set the value of a related field. In this case, the stock keeping unit, which is obtained from the skus object. In this way, I can help the user by providing default values for other fields based on the initial selection. This can be helpful in lots of situations, especially when selecting items such as shipping addresses. You can see the result in Figure 19-7, although this is an example where you should load a browser to get the full effect. The HTML for this document and all of the other examples in this book is available in the source code download that is freely available at Apress.com.

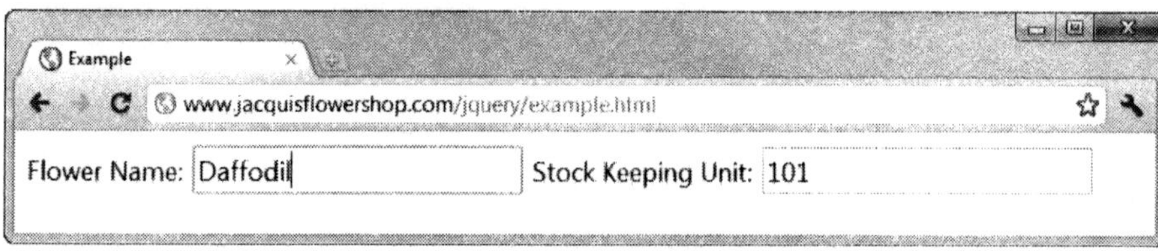

Figure 19-7. Using the select event to populate another field

Using the jQuery UI Accordion

The accordion widget takes a set of content elements and presents them so that at most one is visible to the user. The visible content is hidden when the user selects another, creating an effect that is reminiscent of the bellows in the musical instrument.

Accordions are great for presenting content that can be broken into discrete sections and where you don't want to overwhelm the user by displaying it all at once. Ideally, the individual content sections share some overarching theme that can be expressed using simple headers.

Creating the Accordion

As you might expect by now, you create the jQuery UI accordion widget using the accordion method. Listing 19-10 provides an example of creating an accordion.

Listing 19-10. Creating an Accordion

```
<!DOCTYPE html>
<html>
<head>
    <title>Example</title>
```

```
    <script src="jquery-1.7.js" type="text/javascript"></script>
    <script src="jquery.tmpl.js" type="text/javascript"></script>
    <script src="jquery-ui-1.8.16.custom.js" type="text/javascript"></script>
    <link rel="stylesheet" type="text/css" href="styles.css"/>
    <link rel="stylesheet" type="text/css" href="jquery-ui-1.8.16.custom.css"/>
    <style type="text/css">
        #accordion {margin: 5px}
        .dcell img {height: 60px}
    </style>
    <script type="text/javascript">
        $(document).ready(function() {
            var data = [{"name":"Astor","product":"astor"},
                        {"name":"Daffodil","product":"daffodil"},
                        {"name":"Rose","product":"rose"},
                        {"name":"Peony","product":"peony"},
                        {"name":"Primula","product":"primula"},
                        {"name":"Snowdrop","product":"snowdrop"},
                        {"name":"Carnation","product":"carnation"},
                        {"name":"Lily","product":"lily"},
                        {"name":"Orchid","product":"orchid"}];

            var elems = $('#flowerTmpl').tmpl(data);
            elems.slice(0, 3).appendTo("#row1");
            elems.slice(3, 6).appendTo("#row2");
            elems.slice(6).appendTo("#row3");

            $('#accordion').accordion();

            $('button').button();
        });
    </script>
    <script id="flowerTmpl" type="text/x-jquery-tmpl">
        <div class="dcell">
            <img src="${product}.png"/>
            <label for="${product}">${name}:</label>
            <input name="${product}" value="0" />
        </div>
    </script>
</head>
<body>
    <h1>Jacqui's Flower Shop</h1>
    <form method="post" action="http://node.jacquisflowershop.com/order">
        <div id="accordion">
            <h2><a href="#">Row 1</a></h2>
            <div id="row1"></div>
            <h2><a href="#">Row 2</a></h2>
            <div id="row2"></div>
            <h2><a href="#">Row 3</a></h2>
            <div id="row3"></div>
        </div>
        <div id="buttonDiv"><button type="submit">Place Order</button></div>
    </form>
```

```
</body>
</html>
```

The most important part of this example is the content of the div element whose id is accordion:

```
<div id="accordion">

    <h2><a href="#">Row 1</a></h2>
    <div id="row1"></div>

    <h2><a href="#">Row 2</a></h2>
    <div id="row2"></div>

    <h2><a href="#">Row 3</a></h2>
    <div id="row3"></div>

</div>
```

I have changed the formatting to make the structure more obvious. The top-level div element is the one you will target with the accordion method. When you do this, jQuery UI looks at the contents of the div for header elements (the h1 to h6 elements) and breaks up the content so that each header is associated with the element that follows it. In this case, I have used h2 elements as headers, each of which is followed by a div element. I use the data template plugin to populate these div elements with details of the products offered by the flower shop.

Notice that I have added an a element within each h2 element. This is the means by which you specify the title for each content section. You can see how jQuery UI transforms the top-level div element and its contents in Figure 19-8.

■ **Tip** Setting the href attribute to # is a common technique when defining a elements that are going to be used solely for JavaScript. I have used this approach because it makes the example simpler, but I generally recommend using jQuery to insert the a elements dynamically so that they don't interfere with non-JavaScript users.

Figure 19-8. A jQuery UI accordion

When the accordion is created, the first content section is displayed while the others are hidden. The content of the a elements are used as the labels for each section, and clicking a label triggers closes the current section and opens the selected one (there is a nice animation effect during the transition that I can't show using screenshots). You can see the effect of clicking the headers in Figure 19-9.

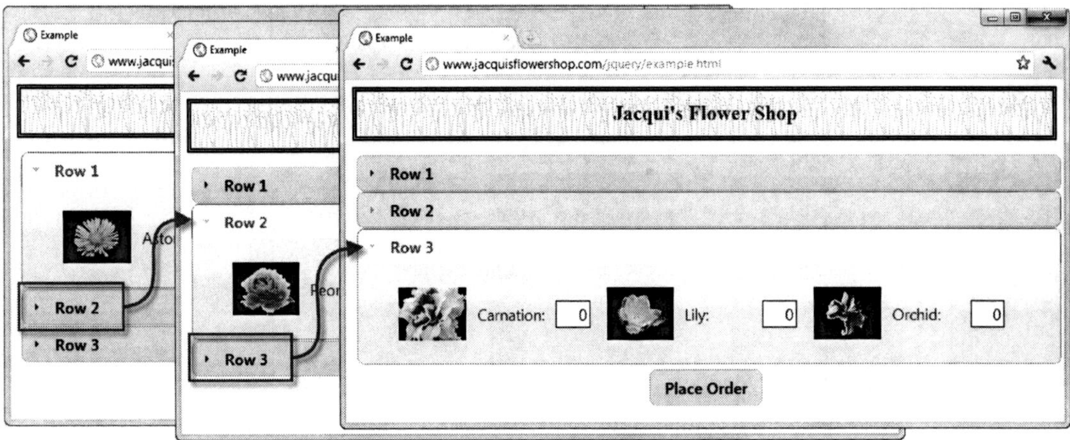

Figure 19-9. The accordion transitions

Configuring the Accordion

The accordion supports a number of settings that can be used to fine-tune it behavior. These settings are described in Table 19-5. In the sections that follow, I show you how to use these settings to configure the widget.

***Table 19-5.** Accordion Settings*

Setting	Description
`active`	Gets or sets the content element to be displayed. The default is to initially display the `first` content element.
`animated`	Specifies the animation that will be used during the transition from one content element to another. The default is `slide`. See Chapter 34 for details of the jQuery UI animations.
`autoHeight`	When `true`, uses the height of the tallest content element for all such elements. The default is `true`.
`clearStyle`	When `true`, the accordion clears the height and overflow CSS properties at the end of the transition animation. The default is `false`.
`collapsible`	When `true`, all of the content sections can be collapsed. The default is `false`.
`disabled`	When `true`, the accordion is disabled. The default is `false`.
`event`	Specifies the event from the header element that triggers the transition to another content element. The default is `click`.
`fillSpace`	When `true`, the accordion fills the height of the parent element. The default is `false`, meaning that the height of the accordion is derived by the content elements.
`header`	Specifies which elements will be used as headers.
`icons`	Specifies the icons used in the accordion.

Setting the Height of the Accordion

You can set the height of the accordion in various ways, based on either the height of the content elements or the height of the parent element. The most common technique is to rely on the default, which is defined by the `autoHeight` setting. This setting, which is set to `true` by default, sets all of the content elements to be the same height (the height of the tallest content element) and sizes the accordion based on that.

This is the approach I used in the previous example, although some caution is required when using content elements that contain images, especially when the `img` elements are inserted into the document using jQuery. The problem is that the call to the `accordion` method can be made before all of the images are loaded, which causes jQuery UI to get misleading information from the browser about the height of the content elements. In my example document, the height of the content `div` elements is 55 pixels before the images are loaded and 79 pixels when they are loaded. You can tell whether you have hit this problem when the accordion shows unexpected scrollbars to display the content, as shown in Figure 19-10.

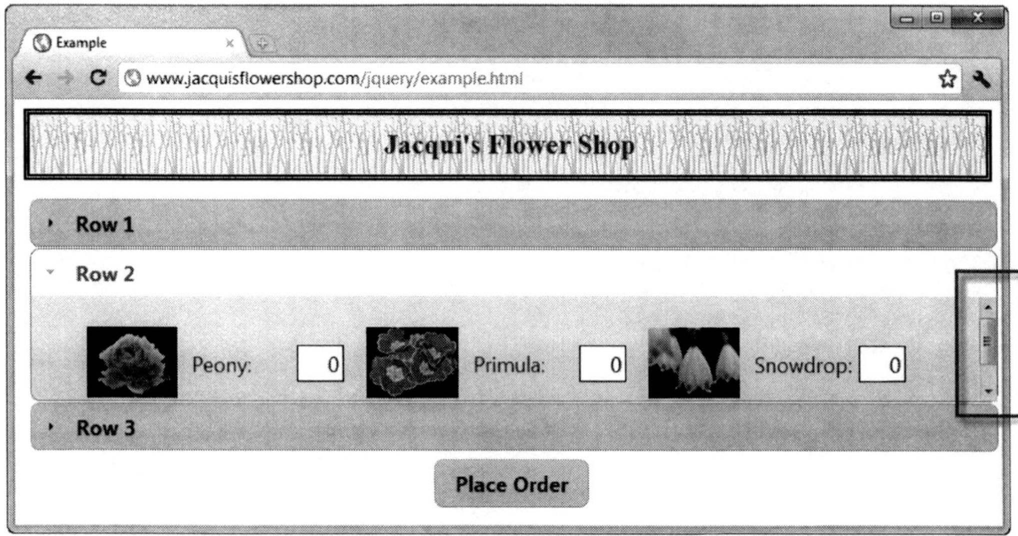

Figure 19-10. Problems caused by incorrect height information

jQuery UI doesn't detect the change in the content element's height when the images are loaded and ends up displaying the content incorrectly. To address this, you need to provide information about the height that the content elements will be once all of the external resources are loaded. There are lots of ways of doing this, and in the example, I chose to set the CSS `height` property for the `img` elements in a `style` element, as follows:

```
...
<style type="text/css">
    #accordion {margin: 5px}
    .dcell img {height: 60px}
</style>
...
```

Image issues aside, the `autoHeight` setting is useful when you want consistent heights for each of the content elements, but it can lead to some unappealing visuals when there is a large disparity between the sizes of the content elements. Listing 19-11 shows a script that inserts the product information elements in a slightly different way.

Listing 19-11. An Accordion with a Large Height Differential

```
...
<script type="text/javascript">
    $(document).ready(function() {
        var data = [{"name":"Astor","product":"astor"},
                    {"name":"Daffodil","product":"daffodil"},
                    {"name":"Rose","product":"rose"},
                    {"name":"Peony","product":"peony"},
                    {"name":"Primula","product":"primula"},
                    {"name":"Snowdrop","product":"snowdrop"},
                    {"name":"Carnation","product":"carnation"},
                    {"name":"Lily","product":"lily"},
                    {"name":"Orchid","product":"orchid"}];

        var elems = $('#flowerTmpl').tmpl(data);
        elems.slice(0, 3).appendTo("#row1");
        elems.slice(3, 6).appendTo("#row2");
        elems.slice(6).appendTo("#row3");

        $('<h2><a href=#>All</a></h2><div id=row0></div>').prependTo('#accordion')
            .filter('div').append($('#row1, #row2, #row3').clone())

        $('#accordion').accordion();

        $('button').button();
    });
</script>
...
```

To create an extra-high content element, I have used jQuery to clone the existing content div elements and insert them into a new content element, creating an element that displays all of the products. This new element is three times the height of the others, which causes the accordion to display a lot of empty space when the smaller content elements are displayed. You can see how this appears in Figure 19-11.

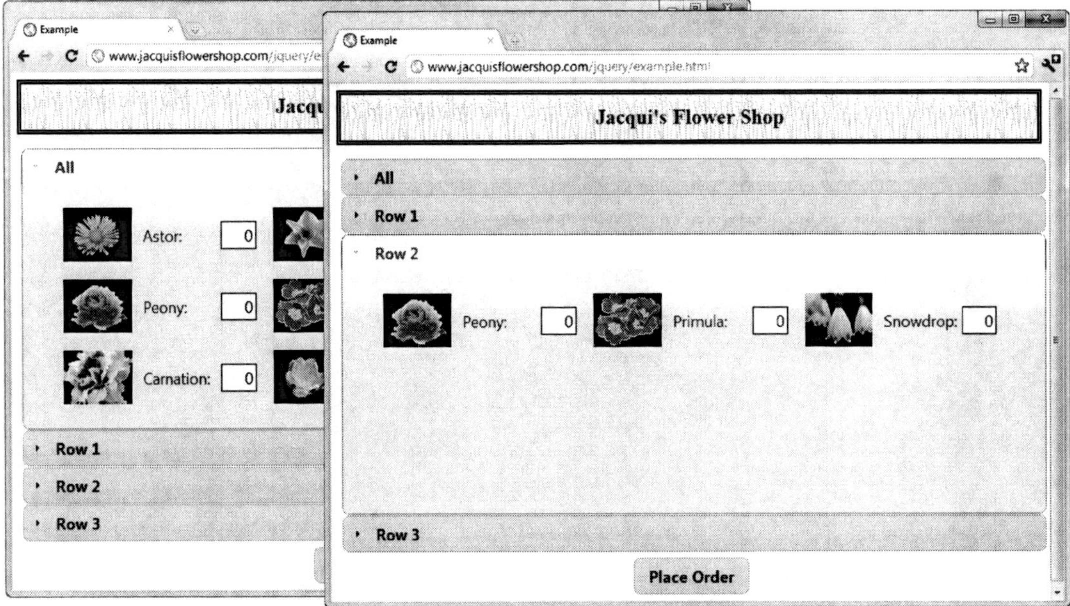

Figure 19-11. The effect of the autoHeight feature with a large height difference

If a large expanse of empty space doesn't suit your application, then you can simple change the `autoHeight` setting to `false`, as shown in Listing 19-12.

Listing 19-12. Disabling the autoHeight Feature

```
...
$('#accordion').accordion({
    autoHeight: false
});
...
```

The accordion will now change its height dynamically as part of the transition between content elements. You can see the effect in Figure 19-12.

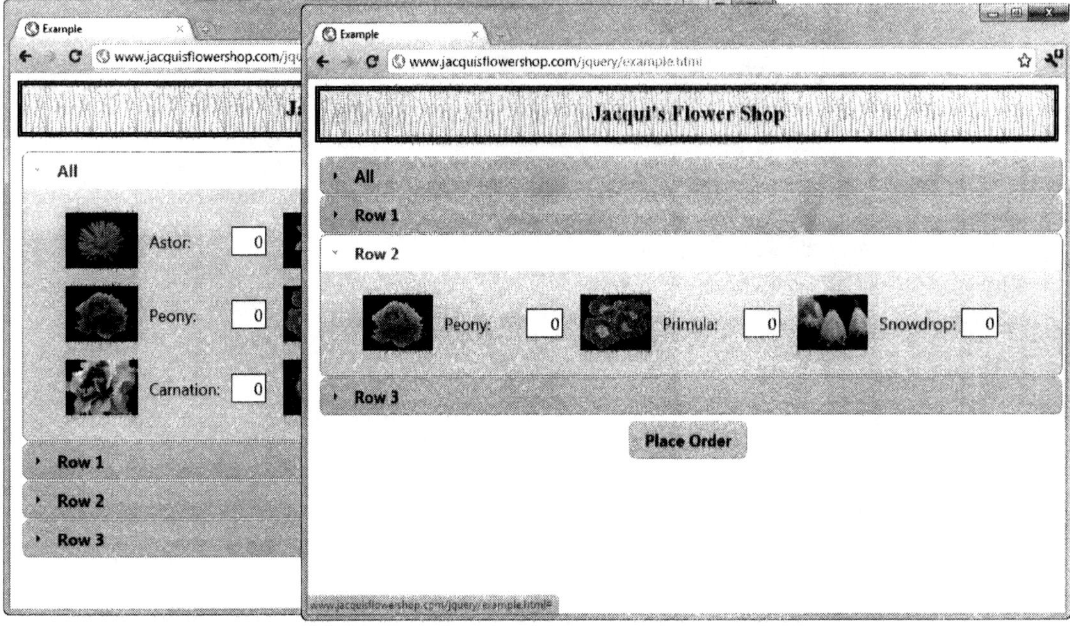

Figure 19-12. The accordion resizing itself to accomodate different content heights

This is a neater approach to displaying the content, but it does mean that the layout of the page changes as the accordion resizes itself. This can be annoying to users, especially if key controls are constantly moving around the screen.

Using the Parent to Determine the Height of the Accordion

An entirely different approach is to set the size of the accordion so that it simply fills its parent element. I find this most useful when I am working with content that is generated dynamically such that I don't have a good handle on the size and I don't want the layout to be adjusted. You can size the accordion this way through the `fillSpace` setting, as shown in Listing 19-13.

Listing 19-13. Sizing the Accordion to Fill the Parent Element

```
...
<script type="text/javascript">
    $(document).ready(function() {
        var data = [{"name":"Astor","product":"astor"},
                    {"name":"Daffodil","product":"daffodil"},
                    {"name":"Rose","product":"rose"},
                    {"name":"Peony","product":"peony"},
                    {"name":"Primula","product":"primula"},
                    {"name":"Snowdrop","product":"snowdrop"},
                    {"name":"Carnation","product":"carnation"},
                    {"name":"Lily","product":"lily"},
```

```
                {"name":"Orchid","product":"orchid"}];

        var elems = $('#flowerTmpl').tmpl(data);
        elems.slice(0, 3).appendTo("#row1");
        elems.slice(3, 6).appendTo("#row2");
        elems.slice(6).appendTo("#row3");

        $('<h2><a href=#>All</a></h2><div id=row0></div>').prependTo('#accordion')
            .filter('div').append($('#row1, #row2, #row3').clone())

        $('#accordion').wrap('<div style="height:300px"></div>');

        $('#accordion').accordion({
            fillSpace: true
        })

        $('button').button();
    });
</script>
...
```

In this example, I have wrapped the accordion element in a new parent div element that has a fixed size of 300 pixels. When I call the accordion method, I set fillSpace to true. If the parent is smaller than a content element, then the accordion adds a scrollbar. If the parent is larger than a content element, then some padding is added. You can see the application of the scrollbar in Figure 19-13. This arises because the content element that displays all of the flowers is taller than the 300 pixels of the parent element.

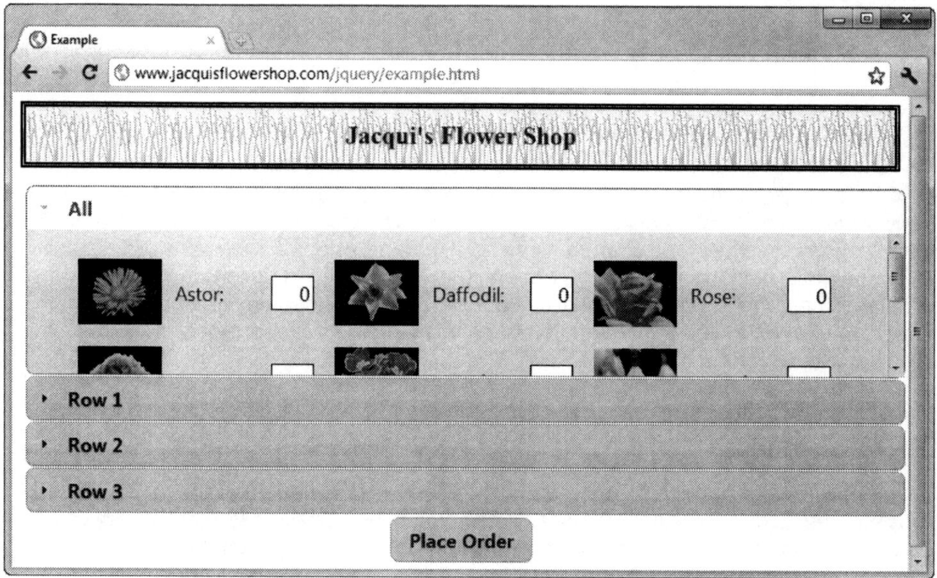

Figure 19-13. Using the accordion to fill the height of the pareent

Changing the Event Type

By default, the user opens and closes content elements by clicking them. You can customize this behavior through the event setting, as shown in Listing 19-14.

Listing 19-14. Using the event Setting

```
...
<script type="text/javascript">
    $(document).ready(function() {
        var data = [{"name":"Astor","product":"astor"},
                    {"name":"Daffodil","product":"daffodil"},
                    {"name":"Rose","product":"rose"},
                    {"name":"Peony","product":"peony"},
                    {"name":"Primula","product":"primula"},
                    {"name":"Snowdrop","product":"snowdrop"},
                    {"name":"Carnation","product":"carnation"},
                    {"name":"Lily","product":"lily"},
                    {"name":"Orchid","product":"orchid"}];

        var elems = $('#flowerTmpl').tmpl(data);
        elems.slice(0, 3).appendTo("#row1");
        elems.slice(3, 6).appendTo("#row2");
        elems.slice(6).appendTo("#row3");

        $('#accordion').accordion({
            event: "mouseover"
        })

        $('button').button();
    });
</script>
...
```

In this example, I have used the event setting to specify that content elements should be opened in response to the mouseover event (which I described in Chapter 9). The effect of this change is that as soon as the mouse pointer enters the label for a content element, jQuery UI opens the element and displays its content. I can't show this effect in a screenshot, but I recommend you load this example to see how it works. It is a neat feature, but I recommend it is used carefully. Users are generally quick to grasp the idea of clicking the icon to open a section of content, but responding to mouse events can make for a twitchy and surprising user experience.

Selecting the Active Header

The default behavior of the accordion is to initially show the first content element to the user. You can change this behavior using the active setting. You can set active to be a selector string, a jQuery object, an HTMLElement object, or a number. For the selector and jQuery object, the first matching element is used, and the number is used as a zero-based index. Listing 19-15 shows the use of a selector string.

Listing 19-15. Using the Active Setting

```
<!DOCTYPE html>
<html>
<head>
    <title>Example</title>
    <script src="jquery-1.7.js" type="text/javascript"></script>
    <script src="jquery.tmpl.js" type="text/javascript"></script>
    <script src="jquery-ui-1.8.16.custom.js" type="text/javascript"></script>
    <link rel="stylesheet" type="text/css" href="styles.css"/>
    <link rel="stylesheet" type="text/css" href="jquery-ui-1.8.16.custom.css"/>
    <style type="text/css">
        #accordion {margin: 5px}
        .dcell img {height: 60px}
    </style>
    <script type="text/javascript">
        $(document).ready(function() {
            var data = [{"name":"Astor","product":"astor"},
                        {"name":"Daffodil","product":"daffodil"},
                        {"name":"Rose","product":"rose"},
                        {"name":"Peony","product":"peony"},
                        {"name":"Primula","product":"primula"},
                        {"name":"Snowdrop","product":"snowdrop"},
                        {"name":"Carnation","product":"carnation"},
                        {"name":"Lily","product":"lily"},
                        {"name":"Orchid","product":"orchid"}];

            var elems = $('#flowerTmpl').tmpl(data);
            elems.slice(0, 3).appendTo("#row1");
            elems.slice(3, 6).appendTo("#row2");
            elems.slice(6).appendTo("#row3");

            $('#accordion').accordion({
                active: "#row2header"
            })

            $('button').button();
        });
    </script>
    <script id="flowerTmpl" type="text/x-jquery-tmpl">
        <div class="dcell">
            <img src="${product}.png"/>
            <label for="${product}">${name}:</label>
            <input name="${product}" value="0" />
        </div>
    </script>
</head>
<body>
    <h1>Jacqui's Flower Shop</h1>
    <form method="post" action="http://node.jacquisflowershop.com/order">
        <div id="accordion">
```

```
            <h2><a href="#">Row 1</a></h2>
            <div id="row1"></div>
            <h2 id="row2header"><a href="#">Row 2</a></h2>
            <div id="row2"></div>
            <h2><a href="#">Row 3</a></h2>
            <div id="row3"></div>
        </div>
        <div id="buttonDiv"><button type="submit">Place Order</button></div>
    </form>
</body>
</html>
```

The important thing to remember when using the active setting is that the selector applies to the header elements. For this example, that's the h2 elements and not the div or a element. I have added an id attribute to one of the h2 elements and used this as the selector string. The effect is that the accordion opens the row 2 content element initially, as shown in Figure 19-14.

Figure 19-14. Selecting the initial content element to display

You can also have no content initially active by setting active to false. If you do this, you must also set the collapsible setting to true. This disables the default policy that one content element must always be visible. Listing 19-16 shows the application of these settings.

Listing 19-16. Disabling the Initially Active Content Element

```
...
$('#accordion').accordion({
    active: false,
    collapsible: true
})
...
```

You can see the effect of these settings in Figure 19-15.

Figure 19-15. The accordion with no initially active content element

The accordion works normally, with the exception that there is no initially active content element and that all of the content elements can be closed. This is a useful technique when screen estate is limited and the content in the accordion is not of primary interest to the user.

Changing the Accordion Icons

You can use the `icons` setting to change the icons used in the accordion content headers. Listing 19-17 provides an example.

Listing 19-17. Changing the Icons Used by the Accordion

```
...
$('#accordion').accordion({
    collapsible: true,
    icons: {
        header: "ui-icon-zoomin",
        headerSelected: "ui-icon-zoomout"
    }
})
...
```

You set `icons` to be an object that has `header` and `headerSelected` properties. The first property specifies the icon to use when the content element is closed, and the second specifies the icon to use when it is open. I tend to use this setting in conjunction with the `collapsible` setting because it gives a more natural feel when using icons that suggest that user can perform an action. You can see how these icons appear in Figure 19-16.

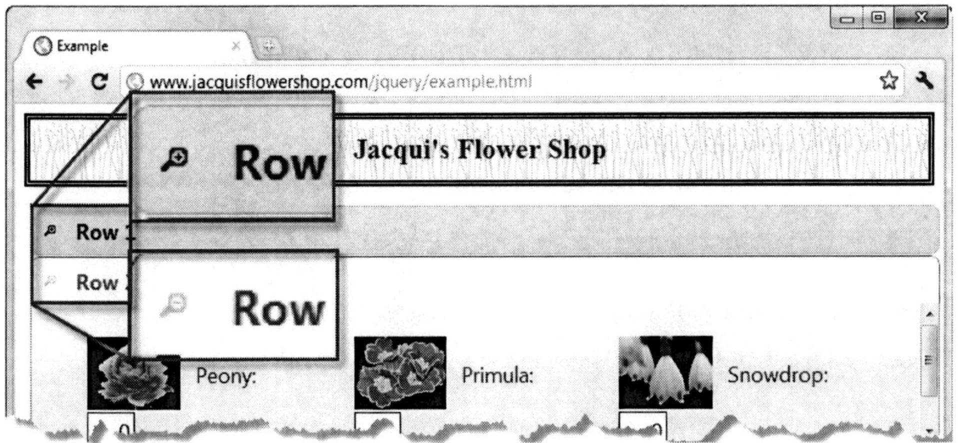

Figure 19-16. Using custom icons for the accordion section headers

Using the Accordion Methods

The jQuery UI accordion defines a number of methods. Most are the standard methods shared by all jQuery UI widgets, but there are two that allow you to control the accordion programmatically. Table 19-6 describes the methods available.

Table 19-6. *Accordion Methods*

Method	Description
`accordion("destroy")`	Removes the accordion functionality from the `input` element
`accordion("disable")`	Disables the accordion
`accordion("enable")`	Enables the accordion
`accordion("option")`	Sets one or more options
`accordion("activate", index)`	Opens the specified content element (the index is zero-based)
`accordion("resize")`	Resizes the accordion when the `fillSpace` setting is used and the size of the parent element changes

The `resize` method is best used with the jQuery UI *resizable* feature, which I described in Chapter 24. That leaves us only with the `activate` method to explore in this chapter, as all of the other methods are common among all jQuery UI widgets, and I explained how they work in Chapter 18. The `activate` method allows you to control the accordion programmatically, as Listing 19-18 demonstrates.

Listing 19-18. Controlling an Accordion Using the activate Method

```
...
<script type="text/javascript">
    $(document).ready(function() {
        var data = [{"name":"Astor","product":"astor"},
                    {"name":"Daffodil","product":"daffodil"},
                    {"name":"Rose","product":"rose"},
                    {"name":"Peony","product":"peony"},
                    {"name":"Primula","product":"primula"},
                    {"name":"Snowdrop","product":"snowdrop"},
                    {"name":"Carnation","product":"carnation"},
                    {"name":"Lily","product":"lily"},
                    {"name":"Orchid","product":"orchid"}];

        var elems = $('#flowerTmpl').tmpl(data);
        elems.slice(0, 3).appendTo("#row1");
        elems.slice(3, 6).appendTo("#row2");
        elems.slice(6).appendTo("#row3");

        $('#accordion').accordion({
            active: false,
            collapsible: true
        })

        $('button').hide();
        var ids = ["2", "1", "0", "None"];
        for (var i = 0; i < ids.length; i++) {
            $('<button id=' + ids[i] + '>' + ids[i] + '</button>').insertAfter('h1')
        }

        $('button').button().click(function(e) {
            if (this.id == "None") {
                $('#accordion').accordion("activate", false);
            } else {
                $('#accordion').accordion("activate", Number(this.id));
            }
        });
    });
</script>
...
```

In this script, I have added buttons that correspond to the index of each content element as well as one marked None. You can see the effect in Figure 19-17.

Figure 19-17. Adding buttons to control accordion activation

When the user clicks one of the numbered buttons, the corresponding content element is activated. I achieve this by using the activate method, as follows:

```
$('#accordion').accordion("activate", Number(this.id));
```

The final argument to the method is the id attribute of the button. You can also use a final argument of false to deactivate all of the content elements, like this:

```
$('#accordion').accordion("activate", false);
```

The false value will work only if collapsible has been set to true; otherwise, it is ignored.

Using the Accordion Events

The jQuery UI accordion widget supports the three events shown in Table 19-7.

***Table 19-7.** Accordion Events*

Event	Description
create	Triggered when the accordion is created
change	Triggered after the active content element changes
changestart	Triggered before the active content element changes

You can use the changestart and change events to monitor the transition between active content elements, as shown in Listing 19-19.

Listing 19-19. Using the change event

```
script type="text/javascript">
    $(document).ready(function() {
        var data = [{"name":"Astor","product":"astor"},
                    {"name":"Daffodil","product":"daffodil"},
                    {"name":"Rose","product":"rose"},
                    {"name":"Peony","product":"peony"},
                    {"name":"Primula","product":"primula"},
                    {"name":"Snowdrop","product":"snowdrop"},
                    {"name":"Carnation","product":"carnation"},
                    {"name":"Lily","product":"lily"},
                    {"name":"Orchid","product":"orchid"}];

        var elems = $('#flowerTmpl').tmpl(data);
        elems.slice(0, 3).appendTo("#row1");
        elems.slice(3, 6).appendTo("#row2");
        elems.slice(6).appendTo("#row3");

        $('#accordion').accordion({
            active: false,
            collapsible: true,
            change: handleAccordionChange
        })

        function handleAccordionChange(event, ui) {

            var contentElems = $('#accordion').children('div');

            if (ui.oldContent.length) {
                 var oldIndex =  contentElems.index(ui.oldContent);
                $('button[id=' + oldIndex + ']').button("enable");
            } else {
                $('button[id=None]').button("enable");
            }
            if (ui.newContent.length) {
                 var newIndex =  contentElems.index(ui.newContent);
                $('button[id=' + newIndex + ']').button("disable");
            } else {
                $('button[id=None]').button("disable");
            }
        }

        $('button').hide();
        var ids = ["2", "1", "0", "None"];
        for (var i = 0; i < ids.length; i++) {
            $('<button id=' + ids[i] + '>' + ids[i] + '</button>').insertAfter('h1')
        }

        $('button').button().click(function(e) {
```

```
            if (this.id == "None") {
                $('#accordion').accordion("activate", false);
            } else {
                $('#accordion').accordion("activate", Number(this.id));
            }
        });
    });
</script>
```

In this script, I use the change event to respond to the active content element being changed. I enable and disable the dynamically added buttons so that the button that corresponds to the active content element is always disabled. If there are no active elements, then the None button is disabled. When you use the change or changestart event, jQuery UI passes information to you about the active elements via an additional argument to the handler function, just as for the autocomplete widget. This additional argument, usually called ui, defines the properties shown in Table 19-8.

***Table 19-8.** The Properties of the ui Object for the change and changestart Events*

Name	Description
newHeader	The header element for the newly active content element
oldHeader	The header element for the previously active content element
newContent	The newly active content element
oldContent	The previously active content element

In the example, I use the newContent and oldContent properties in conjunction with the index method to work out the position of the old and new content elements. This value corresponds to the id attribute of the buttons, which allows you to enable and disable the correct elements. You can see the result that handling the events in this way has on the buttons in Figure 19-18.

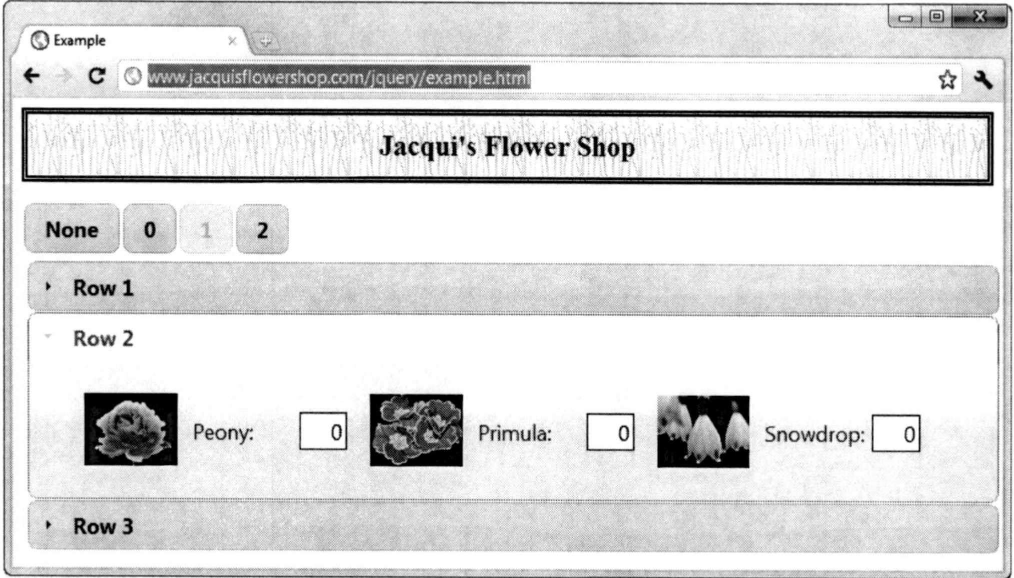

Figure 19-18. Using accordion events to control button states

Summary

In this chapter, I showed you the jQuery UI autocomplete and accordion widgets. These follow the same basic pattern you saw in Chapter 19 but offer richer functionality and a wider range of configuration options to customize the widgets so that they fit neatly into your web application model.

CHAPTER 20

Using the Tabs Widget

This chapter is dedicated to the tabs widget. The tabs widget is superficially similar to the accordion that I described in Chapter 19 but offers a lot more functionality and opportunities for customization. In common with the earlier widget chapters, I'll start with details of how to create the widget and then show you the settings, methods, and events that are supported. I finish this chapter with an example of how you can use the tabs widget to present forms to users in sections, which is a useful technique for dealing with long forms that require a lot of data input. Table 20-1 provides the summary for this chapter.

Table 20-1. *Chapter Summary*

Problem	Solution	Listing
Create a tabs widget.	Define a label and content element structure and call the `tabs` method.	1
Get the content for a tab via Ajax.	Set the `href` attribute for the tab a element to the HTML document that should be displayed in the content panel.	2, 3
Use JSON content in a tab.	Use the `ajaxOptions` setting to employ the Ajax `dataType` and `dataFilter` features.	4, 5
Deal with errors in Ajax requests for tab content.	Use the `ajaxOptions` setting to define a handler function for the Ajax error event.	6
Display a message to the user while content is being loaded via Ajax.	Add a `span` to the tab `a` element and use the `spinner` setting.	7, 8
Disable individual tabs.	Use the `disabled` setting.	9
Change the event that activates a tab.	Use the `event` setting.	10
Allow all of the tabs to be deactivated.	Use the `collapsible` setting.	11

Add or remove tabs programmatically.	Use the add or remove method.	12–14
Change the element that is used for new content panels.	Use the panelTemplate setting.	15
Force remote content to be loaded.	Use the load method.	16
Change the content panel or source for a tab.	Use the url method.	17
Cycle through tabs automatically.	Use the rotate method.	18, 19
Display a form across multiple tabs.	Partition the form using div elements, add a label structure, and call the tabs method.	20–22
Validate the content of a form displayed in multiple tabs.	Use the show and select events.	23

Creating the Tabs

You create jQuery UI tabs using the tabs method. As with the accordion widget, you need a particular structure of HTML elements in order to correctly apply the tab method. Listing 20-1 shows an example of this structure.

Listing 20-1. Creating jQuery UI Tabs

```
<!DOCTYPE html>
<html>
<head>
    <title>Example</title>
    <script src="jquery-1.7.js" type="text/javascript"></script>
    <script src="jquery.tmpl.js" type="text/javascript"></script>
    <script src="jquery-ui-1.8.16.custom.js" type="text/javascript"></script>
    <link rel="stylesheet" type="text/css" href="styles.css"/>
    <link rel="stylesheet" type="text/css" href="jquery-ui-1.8.16.custom.css"/>
    <script type="text/javascript">
        $(document).ready(function() {
            var data = [{"name":"Astor","product":"astor"},
                        {"name":"Daffodil","product":"daffodil"},
                        {"name":"Rose","product":"rose"},
                        {"name":"Peony","product":"peony"},
                        {"name":"Primula","product":"primula"},
                        {"name":"Snowdrop","product":"snowdrop"},
                        {"name":"Carnation","product":"carnation"},
                        {"name":"Lily","product":"lily"},
```

```
                    {"name":"Orchid","product":"orchid"}];

            var elems = $('#flowerTmpl').tmpl(data);
            elems.slice(0, 3).appendTo("#tab1");
            elems.slice(3, 6).appendTo("#tab2");
            elems.slice(6).appendTo("#tab3");

            $('#tabs').tabs();

            $('button').button();
        });
    </script>
    <script id="flowerTmpl" type="text/x-jquery-tmpl">
        <div class="dcell">
            <img src="${product}.png"/>
            <label for="${product}">${name}:</label>
            <input name="${product}" value="0" />
        </div>
    </script>
</head>
<body>
    <h1>Jacqui's Flower Shop</h1>
    <form method="post" action="http://node.jacquisflowershop.com/order">
        <div id="tabs">
            <ul>
                <li><a href="#tab1">Row 1</a>
                <li><a href="#tab2">Row 2</a>
                <li><a href="#tab3">Row 3</a>
            </ul>
            <div id="tab1"></div>
            <div id="tab2"></div>
            <div id="tab3"></div>
        </div>
        <div id="buttonDiv"><button type="submit">Place Order</button></div>
    </form>
</body>
</html>
```

The element that you select for use with the tabs method needs to contain two kinds of element. The first is the *content elements*, which are those elements whose contents should appear inside the tabs. The second kind of element is the *structure elements*, which give the jQuery UI tab widget the information it needs to create the tab structure.

You use the div element to contain the content. In this example, I have used three div elements, each of which will hold one row of flower product information, just as in earlier examples, as follows:

```
<div id="tab1"></div>
<div id="tab2"></div>
<div id="tab3"></div>
```

It is important that each content element has an id attribute so that the jQuery UI tab widget can find the right element to display. For the structure, you use li elements, each of which must contain an a element, like this:

```
<ul>
    <li><a href="#tab1">Row 1</a>
    <li><a href="#tab2">Row 2</a>
    <li><a href="#tab3">Row 3</a>
</ul>
```

The number of li items defines the number of tabs. The content of the a element is used as the tab label, and the href attribute specifies which content element the tab relates to.

■ **Tip** I used the data templates plugin to generate the tab content dynamically because it lets me show the required structure more clearly. The content can be defined statically or, as I explain in the next section, obtained dynamically from the server.

You can see how the structure in the example is transformed into a set of tabs in Figure 20-1.

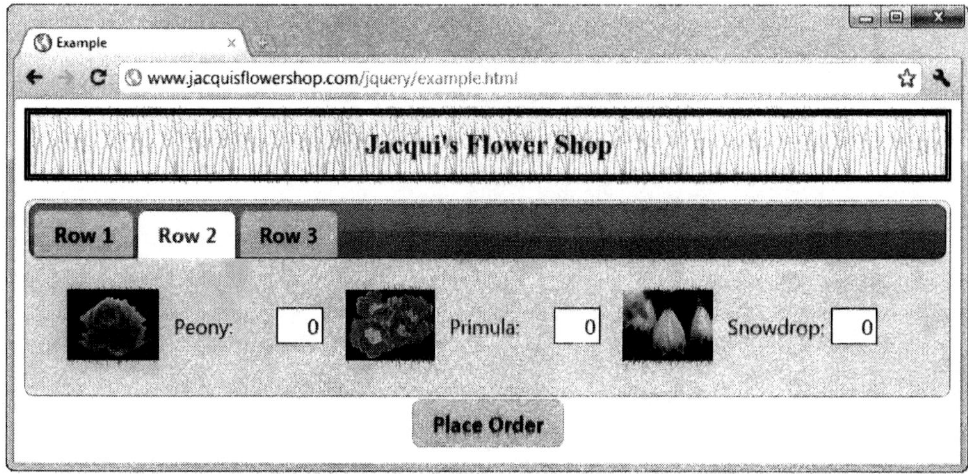

Figure 20-1. Creating jQuery UI tabs

Tabs are a familiar user interface metaphor. Clicking a tab causes jQuery UI to display the corresponding content element. As with the accordion, the tabs widget allows you to present a lot of content in a relatively compact manner, allowing the user to focus on what is important to them. This means you have to think carefully about how the tabs and their content relate to one another. Your goal is to group your content to minimize the amount of switching the user has to do between tabs to find what they are looking for. As with any user interface, this requires a solid understanding of the task that the user is performing and how their workflow (and not your systems) operates.

Getting Tab Content with Ajax

One of the nice features of the tab widget is the ability to obtain tab content via Ajax. To do this, you simply specify a URL as the href attribute for the appropriate a element. To demonstrate this feature, I have created an HTML document called tabflowers.html, the contents of which are shown in Listing 20-2. A tab that gets its content via Ajax is known as a *remote tab.*

Listing 20-2. The Contents of the tabflowers.html File

```
<div>
    <div class="dcell">
        <img src="astor.png"/><label for="astor">Astor:</label>
        <input name="astor" value="0" />
    </div>
    <div class="dcell">
        <img src="daffodil.png"/><label for="daffodil">Daffodil:</label>
        <input name="daffodil" value="0" />
    </div>
    <div class="dcell">
        <img src="rose.png"/><label for="rose">Rose:</label>
        <input name="rose" value="0" />
    </div>
</div>
<div>
    <div class="dcell">
        <img src="peony.png"/><label for="peony">Peony:</label>
        <input name="peony" value="0" />
    </div>
    <div class="dcell">
        <img src="primula.png"/><label for="primula">Primula:</label>
        <input name="primula" value="0" />
    </div>
    <div class="dcell">
        <img src="snowdrop.png"/><label for="snowdrop">Snowdrop:</label>
        <input name="snowdrop" value="0" />
    </div>
</div>
```

I have used the same structure and content as for the generated content elements in order to keep the example simple. Listing 20-3 shows how you can use the tabflowers.html file as the content for a tab.

Listing 20-3. Obtaining the Content of a Tab via Ajax

```
...
<body>
    <h1>Jacqui's Flower Shop</h1>
    <form method="post" action="http://node.jacquisflowershop.com/order">
        <div id="tabs">
            <ul>
                <li><a href="tabflowers.html">Ajax Content</a>
```

```
                <li><a href="#tab1">Row 1</a>
                <li><a href="#tab2">Row 2</a>
                <li><a href="#tab3">Row 3</a>
            </ul>
            <div id="tab1"></div>
            <div id="tab2"></div>
            <div id="tab3"></div>
        </div>
        <div id="buttonDiv"><button type="submit">Place Order</button></div>
    </form>
</body>
...
```

You modify the element structure rather than use settings for the tabs method. In this example, I have added a new tab called Ajax Content and specified the URL of the content that should be loaded. You can see the effect in Figure 20-2.

■ **Tip** You don't need to create a content element for a remote tab. This is done for you automatically by the tabs widget.

Figure 20-2. Getting the contents of a tab via Ajax

■ **Tip** By default, you can load only HTML documents into tabs via Ajax, but in the "Configuring Ajax Requests" section, I'll show you how you can achieve the same result with JSON.

Configuring the jQuery UI Tabs

At first glance, the tabs may look like a vertical variation of the accordion widget that I showed you in Chapter 19. There are some common characteristics, but you have a wider number of configuration options and settings when you use tabs. Table 20-2 describes the settings that are supported by the jQuery UI tabs widget. In the sections that follow, I show you how to use these settings to configure the widget.

***Table 20-2.** Tabs Settings*

Setting	Description
`ajaxOptions`	Gets or sets the configuration to use for Ajax requests.
`cache`	When `true`, the response from Ajax requests is cached so that subsequent activation of the tab doesn't result in further Ajax queries. The default is `false`, meaning that an Ajax request is made each time a remote tab is activated.
`collapsible`	When `true`, the user can unselect all of the tabs. The default is `false`, such that one tab is always active.
`disabled`	When set to `true` or `false`, this setting disables or enables the tab widget. When set to an array of numbers, this setting disables the tabs at the specified indices.
`event`	Gets or sets the event, which causes a tab to become active. The default is `click`, meaning that the user clicks the mouse to activate a tab.
`fx`	Specifies the effects used to animate activating and deactivating tabs. The default is `null`, meaning that no effects are used. I explain the jQuery UI effects in Chapter 34.
`panelTemplate`	Specifies the template from which programmatically created content elements are generated. The default is to use an empty `div` element. See the "Adding and Removing Tabs" section for details of adding tabs programmatically.
`selected`	Gets or set the index of the active tab.
`spinner`	Gets or sets the text shown to the user while remote tabs load their content. See the "Using the Ajax Spinner Message" section for details of how to use the spinner.
`tabTemplate`	Specifies the template from which programmatically created structure elements are generated. See the "Adding and Removing Tabs" section for details of adding tabs programmatically.

Configuring Ajax Requests

The `ajaxOptions` setting allows you to provide a map object containing the configuration that will be used when making Ajax requests for remote tabs. You can specify all of the settings that I described in Chapters 14 and 15. I most frequently use the `ajaxOptions` setting so that I can generate content for remote tabs with JSON rather than regular HTML. Listing 20-4 shows the content of the mydata.json file, which I will use to demonstrate this technique. This is the same file you first used in Chapter 14.

Listing 20-4. The Contents of the mydata.json File

```
[{"name":"Astor","product":"astor","stocklevel":"10","price":"2.99"},
 {"name":"Daffodil","product":"daffodil","stocklevel":"12","price":"1.99"},
 {"name":"Rose","product":"rose","stocklevel":"2","price":"4.99"},
 {"name":"Peony","product":"peony","stocklevel":"0","price":"1.50"},
 {"name":"Primula","product":"primula","stocklevel":"1","price":"3.12"},
 {"name":"Snowdrop","product":"snowdrop","stocklevel":"15","price":"0.99"}]
```

Now that you have the source data, you can turn to the ajaxOptions setting, as shown in Listing 20-5.

Listing 20-5. Using the ajaxOptions Setting to Work with JSON

```
...
$('#tabs').tabs({
    ajaxOptions: {
        dataType: "html",
        dataFilter: function(result){
            var data = $.parseJSON(result).slice(0, 3);
            return $('<div></div>')
                .append($('#flowerTmpl').tmpl(data)).html();
        }
    }
});
...
```

I need to use two of the Ajax configuration options to get the right result. The first is dataFilter, which allows you to parse the JSON data (using the parseJSON method, which I describe in Chapter 33), apply a data template, slice the array of HTML elements, and then return the content as an HTML string. This is standard stuff, and I showed you how it all worked in Chapters 14 to 16.

The second setting is dataType. Since the server informs the browser that the content is JSON (through the HTTP Content-Type header), the jQuery Ajax feature encounters problems when trying to deal with the HTML string that my dataFilter function generates. To resolve this, I use the dataType setting to tell jQuery that it is working with HTML, even though the server has reported JSON.

Of course, to take advantage of these changes, I also have to specify the JSON file as the source for the remote tab, as follows:

```
...
<ul>
    <li><a href="mydata.json">Ajax Content</a>
    <li><a href="#tab1">Row 1</a>
    <li><a href="#tab2">Row 2</a>
    <li><a href="#tab3">Row 3</a>
</ul>
...
```

Now the jQuery UI tabs widget will request my JSON file, my ajaxOptions settings will transform the JSON to HTML using a data template, and the result will be displayed in the panel of the remote tab, as you can see in Figure 20-3.

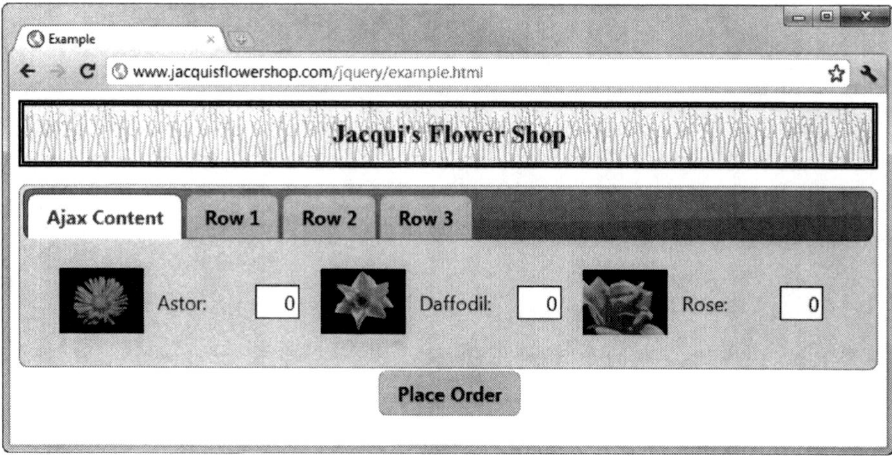

Figure 20-3. Using JSON to generate content for remote tabs

Dealing with Ajax Errors

By default, the jQuery UI tabs widget deals with Ajax problems by quietly ignoring them, which is far from ideal. Fortunately, you can apply your jQuery Ajax know-how in combination with the `ajaxOptions` setting to inform the user when something goes wrong. Listing 20-6 provides a demonstration.

Listing 20-6. Reporting a Remote Tab Ajax Error to the User

```
...
$('#tabs').tabs({
    ajaxOptions: {
        dataType: "html",
        dataFilter: function(result){
            var data = $.parseJSON(result).slice(0, 3);
            return $('<div></div>')
                .append($('#flowerTmpl').tmpl(data)).html();
        },
        error: function(jqxr, status, index, anchor) {
           $(anchor.hash).text("Sorry. There was an error loading the content");
        }
    }
});
...
```

The tabs widget passes an extra argument to the error function in addition to those used by the regular jQuery Ajax feature. This argument is the a element used as the header for the remote tab that has encountered an error. To create an error, I have changed the name of the file that I specified for the remote content, as follows:

```
<ul>
    <li><a href="mydata.jsonX">Ajax Content</a>
    <li><a href="#tab1">Row 1</a>
    <li><a href="#tab2">Row 2</a>
    <li><a href="#tab3">Row 3</a>
</ul>
```

There is no such file, so you can be sure that the tabs widget will encounter a problem. When you use a remote tab, the tabs widget creates a content element dynamically, and it looks something like this:

```
<div id="ui-tabs-1" class="ui-tabs-panel ui-widget-content ui-corner-bottom"></div>
```

The tabs widget generates a unique value for the id attribute, which I have shown in bold. The href that I used to specify the URL for the remote content is changed to match the id of the newly created content element, like this:

```
<li class="ui-state-default ui-corner-top ui-tabs-selected ui-state-active">
    <a href="#ui-tabs-1">Ajax Content</a>
</li>
```

It is the a element that is passed to your error function via the ajaxOptions setting. This means you can use the hash property defined by the DOM object that represents a element to get the id of the content element and then use the jQuery text method to display a message to the user, like this:

```
$(anchor.hash).text("Sorry. There was an error loading the content");
```

You can see the effect in Figure 20-4. You don't have to display the error in the content element, but I think it is the most natural place for most web applications, largely because this is where the user will be expecting the content advertised by the tab label to be.

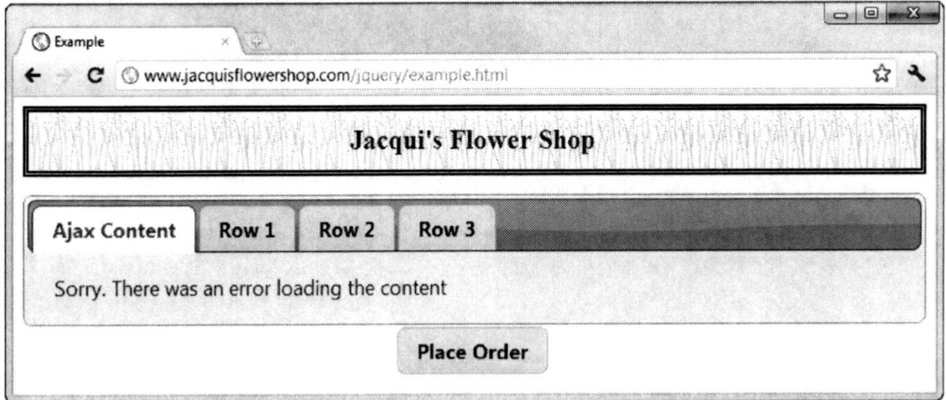

Figure 20-4. Displaying an error message to the user

Using the Ajax Spinner Message

The tabs widget will display a message to the user in the label of a remote tab while the content is being loaded. To enable this feature, you need to wrap the contents of the a element in a span, as shown in Listing 20-7.

Listing 20-7. Enabling the Ajax Spinner

```
...
<ul>
    <li><a href="tabflowers.html"><span>Ajax Content<span></a>
    <li><a href="#tab1">Row 1</a>
    <li><a href="#tab2">Row 2</a>
    <li><a href="#tab3">Row 3</a>
</ul>
...
```

For the duration of the Ajax request, the tabs widget will replace the tab label with a *spinner* message, which is "Loading..." by default (to be precise, the default is the HTML string `<em>Working…</em>`). You can see the effect in Figure 20-5.

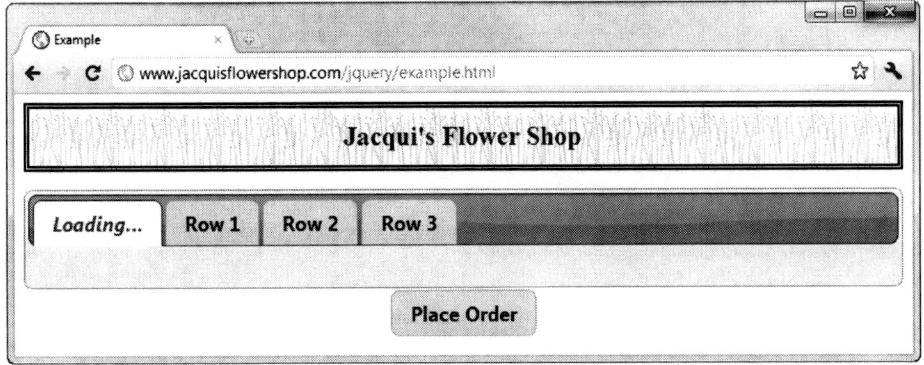

Figure 20-5. The jQuery UI tabs widget displaying the spinner message

---

■ **Tip** It is very important that the span element contain the text of the message. A common mistake is to leave the span element empty so that the spinner message is displayed before or after the tab label. The tab widget will add the spinner message when loading starts but will be unable to remove it when the request has completed.

You can change the message through the spinner setting, as shown in Listing 20-8.

Listing 20-8. Using the spinner Setting to Change the Message Displayed to Users

```
...
$('#tabs').tabs({
    spinner: "<em>Working...</em>"
});
...
```

Be careful when using long spinner messages. They are more expressive, but the tabs widget will simply resize the tab label to accommodate whatever the spinner setting specifies, which means that the label will suddenly grow when the request starts and then suddenly shrink again when the request finishes. You can get a sense of what I mean in Figure 20-6.

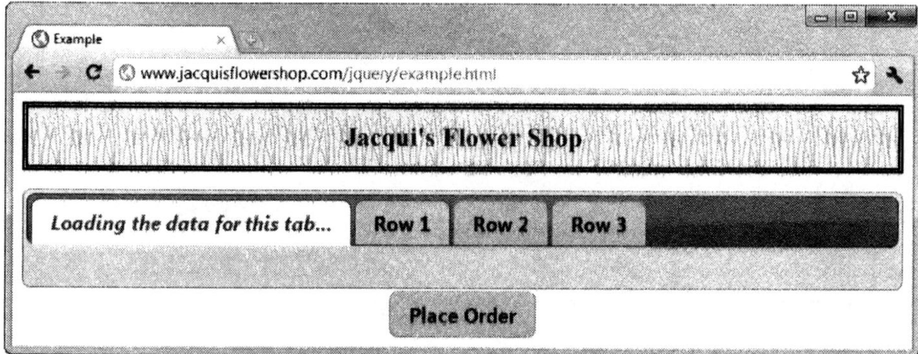

Figure 20-6. The tabs widget resizes the tab label to accommodate long spinner messages.

Disabling Individual Tabs

The disable setting works on the whole tabs widget if you use boolean values, but you can enable and disable individual tabs by using an array of numbers. Listing 20-9 provides a demonstration.

Listing 20-9. Enabling and Disabling Individual Tabs

```
<!DOCTYPE html>
<html>
<head>
    <title>Example</title>
    <script src="jquery-1.7.js" type="text/javascript"></script>
    <script src="jquery.tmpl.js" type="text/javascript"></script>
    <script src="jquery-ui-1.8.16.custom.js" type="text/javascript"></script>
    <link rel="stylesheet" type="text/css" href="styles.css"/>
    <link rel="stylesheet" type="text/css" href="jquery-ui-1.8.16.custom.css"/>
    <style type="text/css"> #buttonDiv {margin: 5px}</style>
    <script type="text/javascript">
        $(document).ready(function() {

            $('#tabs').tabs({
                select: function(event, ui) {
```

```
                $('input:checkbox').button("enable")
                    .filter('#cb' + ui.index).button("disable")
            }
        });

        $('input:checkbox').button().click(function() {
            var disabledPositions = [];
            $('input:checkbox[checked]').each(function(index, elem) {
                disabledPositions.push($(this).data("index"));
            })
            $('#tabs').tabs("option", "disabled", disabledPositions)
        });
    });
</script>
</head>
<body>
    <h1>Jacqui's Flower Shop</h1>
    <form method="post" action="http://node.jacquisflowershop.com/order">
        <div id="tabs">
            <ul>
                <li><a href="#tab1">Tab 1</a>
                <li><a href="#tab2">Tab 2</a>
                <li><a href="#tab3">Tab 3</a>
            </ul>
            <div id="tab1">This is the content for tab 1</div>
            <div id="tab2">This is the content for tab 2</div>
            <div id="tab3">This is the content for tab 3</div>
        </div>
        <div id="buttonDiv">
            <label for="cb0">Tab 1</label>
                <input type="checkbox" id="cb0" data-index=0 disabled>
            <label for="cb1">Tab 2</label><input type="checkbox" id="cb1" data-index=1>
            <label for="cb2">Tab 3</label><input type="checkbox" id="cb2" data-index=2>
        </div>
    </form>
</body>
</html>
```

In this document, I have created a tabs widget with static content and added a set of check boxes that I have transformed into jQuery UI toggle buttons. When a button is clicked, the corresponding tab is enabled or disabled. I have also used the select event so that I disable the toggle button for the active tab when it changes. (I explain the tabs events later in this chapter.) You can see the effect in Figure 20-7.

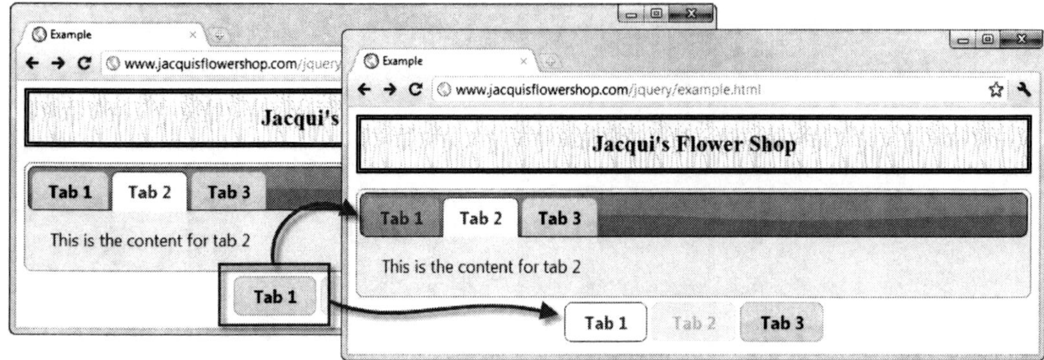

Figure 20-7. Disabling and enabling tabs in response to button clicks

Changing the Event Trigger

The tabs widget responds to the click event by default, meaning that users must click a tab to activate it. You can use the event setting to specify a different event to respond to. This is most useful for responding to mouse events, as shown in Listing 20-10.

Listing 20-10. Changing the Event That Activates a Tab

```
<!DOCTYPE html>
<html>
<head>
    <title>Example</title>
    <script src="jquery-1.7.js" type="text/javascript"></script>
    <script src="jquery.tmpl.js" type="text/javascript"></script>
    <script src="jquery-ui-1.8.16.custom.js" type="text/javascript"></script>
    <link rel="stylesheet" type="text/css" href="styles.css"/>
    <link rel="stylesheet" type="text/css" href="jquery-ui-1.8.16.custom.css"/>
    <style type="text/css"> #buttonDiv {margin: 5px}</style>
    <script type="text/javascript">
        $(document).ready(function() {

            $('#tabs').tabs({
                event: "mouseover"
            });
        });
    </script>
</head>
<body>
    <h1>Jacqui's Flower Shop</h1>
    <form method="post" action="http://node.jacquisflowershop.com/order">
        <div id="tabs">
            <ul>
                <li><a href="#tab1">Tab 1</a>
                <li><a href="#tab2">Tab 2</a>
                <li><a href="#tab3">Tab 3</a>
```

```
        </ul>
        <div id="tab1">This is the content for tab 1</div>
        <div id="tab2">This is the content for tab 2</div>
        <div id="tab3">This is the content for tab 3</div>
    </div>
  </form>
</body>
</html>
```

In this example, I specified the mouseover event, which means that the tabs widget will switch between tabs as the mouse moves across the tab labels.

■ **Tip** I recommend using this approach sparingly, just as I did for the same setting of the accordion widget. It is visually appealing effect, but it creates an annoying effect, forcing the user to take care not to move the mouse away from the label of the tab they want to interact with.

Using Collapsible Tabs

You can create a sort of hybrid between tabs and accordions by using the collapsible setting, as shown in Listing 20-11.

Listing 20-11. Using the collapsible Setting

```
...
<script type="text/javascript">
    $(document).ready(function() {

        $('#tabs').tabs({
            collapsible: true
        });
    });
</script>
...
```

When the collapsible setting is true, clicking the active tab collapses it just like an accordion content element. You can see the transition in Figure 20-8.

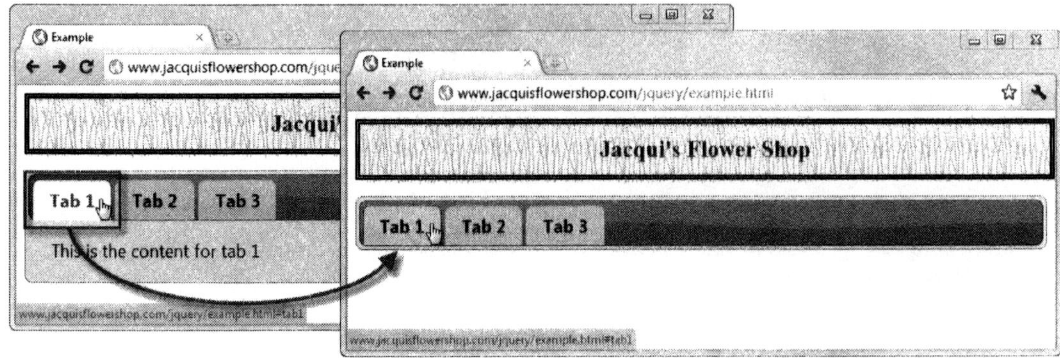

Figure 20-8. Collapsing the active tab

■ **Tip** I have included this setting for completeness, but it is one that I never use in my projects because I think the result is counterintuitive and confusing to users.

Using the jQuery UI Tabs Methods

Table 20-3 shows the methods that are supported by the jQuery UI tabs widget. I demonstrate the most useful of these in the sections that follow.

Table 20-3. *Tabs Methods*

Method	Description
`tabs("destroy")`	Removes the tab widget from the underlying HTML element.
`tabs("disable")`	Disables the entire widget or individual tabs. See the previous section for an example of using the corresponding setting.
`tabs("enable")`	Enables the entire widget or an individual tab.
`tabs("option")`	Changes one or more settings. See the "Configuring the Button" section in Chapter 18 for details of configuring a jQuery UI widget.
`tabs("add")`	Adds a new tab.
`tabs("remove")`	Removes a tab.
`tabs("select")`	Activates a tab.

tabs("load")	Explicitly loads the content of a tab.
tabs("url")	Changes the URL for a remote tab.
tabs("length")	Returns the number of tabs in the widget.
tabs("abort")	Aborts all active Ajax requests for remote tabs.
tabs("rotate")	Instructs the tab widget to cycle through the tabs.

Adding and Removing Tabs

You can add and remove tabs programmatically using the add and remove methods. This is useful when you are dealing with dynamic content or are generating tabs in response to user input. Listing 20-12 shows how you can use these methods.

Listing 20-12. Adding and Removing Tabs Programmatically

```
<!DOCTYPE html>
<html>
<head>
    <title>Example</title>
    <script src="jquery-1.7.js" type="text/javascript"></script>
    <script src="jquery.tmpl.js" type="text/javascript"></script>
    <script src="jquery-ui-1.8.16.custom.js" type="text/javascript"></script>
    <link rel="stylesheet" type="text/css" href="styles.css"/>
    <link rel="stylesheet" type="text/css" href="jquery-ui-1.8.16.custom.css"/>
    <style type="text/css"> #buttonDiv {margin: 5px}</style>
    <style type="text/css">
        input {width: 150px; text-align: left}
        #dc1 {margin: 5px}
    </style>
    <script type="text/javascript">
        $(document).ready(function() {

            $('#tabs').tabs();

            $('button').button().click(function(e) {
                var tabsElem = $('#tabs');
                if (this.id == "add") {
                    tabsElem.tabs("add", "tabflowers.html", $('#tabLabel').val());
                } else {
                    tabsElem.tabs("remove", tabsElem.tabs("option", "selected"))
                }
            })
        });
    </script>
</head>
<body>
```

```
    <h1>Jacqui's Flower Shop</h1>

    <div id="dc1" class="ui-widget">
        <label for="tabLabel">Tab Name: </label><input id="tabLabel"/>
        <button id="add">Add Tab</button>
        <button id="remove">Remove Active Tab</button>
    </div>

    <div id="tabs">
        <ul>
            <li><a href="#tab1">Tab 1</a>
            <li><a href="#tab2">Tab 2</a>
            <li><a href="#tab3">Tab 3</a>
        </ul>
        <div id="tab1">This is the content for tab 1</div>
        <div id="tab2">This is the content for tab 2</div>
        <div id="tab3">This is the content for tab 3</div>
    </div>
</body>
</html>
```

In this example, I have added an input element and a pair of button elements so that you can add new tabs and remove existing ones. You can see the additions in Figure 20-9.

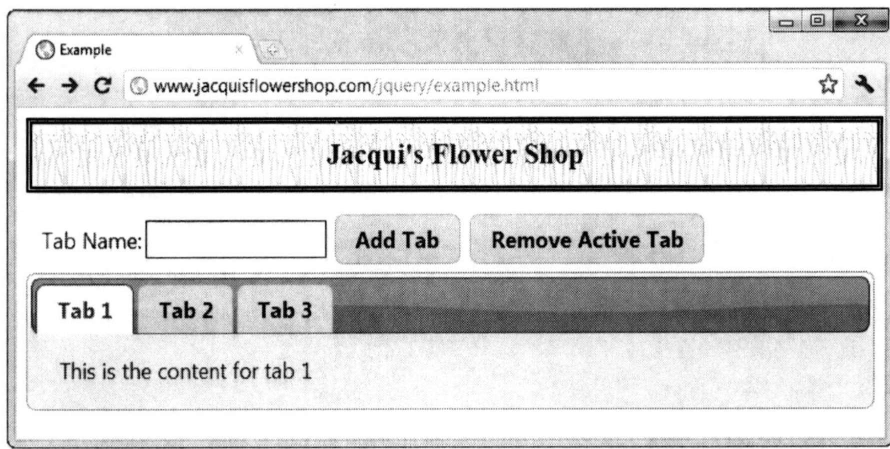

Figure 20-9. Additions to the document to programmatically add and remove tabs

When the user clicks the Remove Active Tab button, I get the index of the active tab using the selected setting and pass it as an argument to the remove method, like this:

```
tabsElem.tabs("remove", tabsElem.tabs("option", "selected"))
```

The tabs widget removes the tab at the specified index and activates the next tab. If the removed tab was the last tab in the widget, then the tab that is now last is activated.

When the Add Tab button is clicked, I call the tabs add method, like this:

```
tabsElem.tabs("add", "tabflowers.html", $('#tabLabel').val());
```

After the add argument comes the URL for the tab and then the label you want to use. In this case, I use the val method to get the contents of the input element. In the example, I set the URL to be the tabflowers.html document, which has the effect of creating a remote tab.

■ **Tip** The new tab is added as the last tab in the widget. To change this, you can supply an additional argument to the add method specifying the zero-based position into which the new tab should be inserted.

Figure 20-10 shows what happens if I type **New Tab** into the input element and click the Add Tab button.

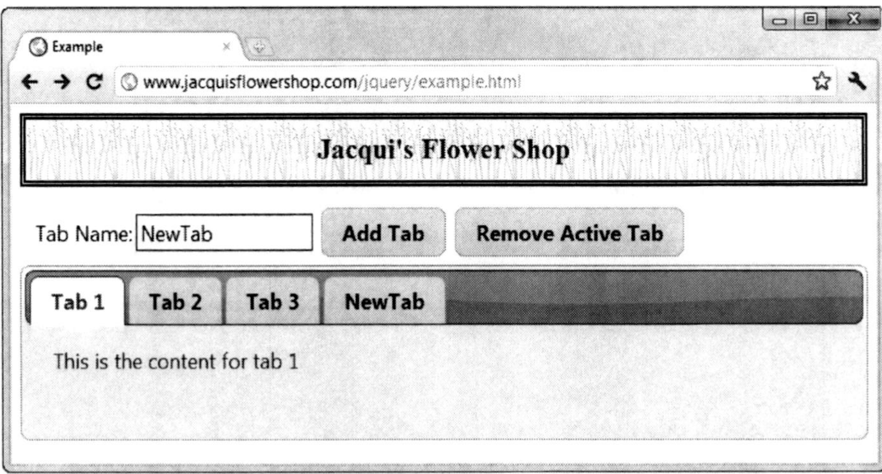

Figure 20-10. Adding a tab programmatically

The new tab isn't activated by default. The easiest way to activate a new tab is to handle the add event, as shown in Listing 20-13. I detail the event supported by the tabs widget later in this chapter, but the add event is useful in the context of the add method.

Listing 20-13. Automatically Activating a New Tab

```
...
<script type="text/javascript">
    $(document).ready(function() {

        $('#tabs').tabs({
            add: function(event, ui) {
                $(this).tabs("select", ui.index);
            }
        });

        $('button').button().click(function(e) {
```

```
            var tabsElem = $('#tabs');
            if (this.id == "add") {
                tabsElem.tabs("add", "tabflowers.html", $('#tabLabel').val());
            } else {
                tabsElem.tabs("remove", tabsElem.tabs("option", "selected"))
            }
        })
    });
</script>
...
```

The tabs widget provides you with information about the newly created tab through the ui object. The index property returns the index of the new tab, which I have used in conjunction with the select method to activate the tab as soon as it is created.

Adding Tabs with Static Content

You can also use the add event and the ui object to add tabs that contain static content, as shown in Listing 20-14.

Listing 20-14. Adding Tabs with Static Content

```
...
<script type="text/javascript">
    $(document).ready(function() {

        $('#tabs').tabs({
            add: function(event, ui) {
                $(this).tabs("select", ui.index);
                $(ui.panel).html("This is a <b>new</b> panel")
            }
        });

        var newTabCount = 0;

        $('button').button().click(function(e) {
            var tabsElem = $('#tabs');
            if (this.id == "add") {
                tabsElem.tabs("add", "#" + (newTabCount++), $('#tabLabel').val());
            } else {
                tabsElem.tabs("remove", tabsElem.tabs("option", "selected"))
            }
        })
    });
</script>
...
```

To create a static tab, you specify a fragment identifier as the URL, just as you do when defining the tab structure using HTML elements. It is important to ensure that the fragment is unique among tabs. The jQuery UI tabs widget has problems activating tabs programmatically if there are duplicates.

Static tabs are created without any content. Fortunately, the ui object that is passed to the add event function defines a property called panel that returns the HTML element that the tabs widget created during the call to the add method. You can add content to this panel using any jQuery technique. I used the html method to insert a simple message, like this:

```
$(ui.panel).html("This is a <b>new</b> panel")
```

You can see the effect in Figure 20-11.

Figure 20-11. Adding content to a newly added static tab

Another approach is to use the panelTemplate setting to change the template that the widget uses when creating new tabs. Listing 20-15 provides a demonstration.

Listing 20-15. Changing the Panel Template

```
...
<script type="text/javascript">
    $(document).ready(function() {

        $('#tabs').tabs({
            add: function(event, ui) {
                $(this).tabs("select", ui.index);
            },
            panelTemplate: "<div>This is the <b>default</b> content</div>"
        });

        var newTabCount = 0;

        $('button').button().click(function(e) {
            var tabsElem = $('#tabs');
            if (this.id == "add") {
                tabsElem.tabs("add", "#" + (newTabCount++), $('#tabLabel').val());
            } else {
                tabsElem.tabs("remove", tabsElem.tabs("option", "selected"))
```

```
            }
        })
    });
</script>
...
```

The default template is an empty div element. In this example, I have replaced this with a div element that contains a simple message. You can see the result in Figure 20-12. You can still use the add event to specify additional content or replace the default, of course, but replacing the template gives you a nice starting point for new tabs.

Figure 20-12. Defining default content for programmatically added static tabs

---

■ **Tip** You can also change the HTML used to create new tab labels. You do this through the `tabTemplate` setting, and the default is `<li><a href="#{href}"><span>#{label}</span></a></li>`. Notice the placeholders for the `href` and `label`. Change these to customize your labels.

Controlling Remote Tab Ajax Requests

You can use a number of methods to control the way that content is loaded for remote tabs. The one that I use most frequently is load, which immediately starts an Ajax request for the content in a tab. I find this useful when I am creating tabs dynamically and don't want the user to have to wait for the content to load and then activate the tab. Listing 20-16 shows the user of the load method.

Listing 20-16. Explicitly Loading the Content of a Remote Tab

```
...
<script type="text/javascript">
    $(document).ready(function() {
```

```
        $('#tabs').tabs({
            add: function(event, ui) {
                $(this).tabs("load", ui.index);
            },
            load: function(event, ui) {
                $(this).tabs("select", ui.index);
            }
        });

        $('button').button().click(function(e) {
            var tabsElem = $('#tabs');
            if (this.id == "add") {
                tabsElem.tabs("add", "tabflowers.html", $('#tabLabel').val());
            } else {
                tabsElem.tabs("remove", tabsElem.tabs("option", "selected"))
            }
        })
    });
</script>
...
```

The argument to the load method is the index of the remote tab you want to affect. In this case, I have used the load method in response to the add event, meaning that the content is loaded automatically when I add a new remote tab.

I have also used the load event. This event is triggered when the content for a remote tab has been loaded. I use this event to activate the tab when the Ajax request that I triggered with the load method has finished.

Changing the URL of a Remote Tab

The url method allows you to change the URL that is used to obtain content for a tab. The arguments for this method are the index of the tab you want to affect and the new URL you want to use. Listing 20-17 shows the use of this method.

Listing 20-17. Using the url Method to Change the Content Source for a Remote Tab

```
...
<script type="text/javascript">
    $(document).ready(function() {

        $('#tabs').tabs({
            add: function(event, ui) {
                $(this).tabs("load", ui.index);
            },
            load: function(event, ui) {
                $(this).tabs("select", ui.index);
            }
        });

        $('<button id=change>Change URL</button>').appendTo("#dc1");
```

```
        $('button').button().click(function(e) {
            var tabsElem = $('#tabs');
            switch (this.id) {
                case "add":
                    tabsElem.tabs("add", "tabflowers.html", $('#tabLabel').val());
                    break;
                case "remove":
                    tabsElem.tabs("remove", tabsElem.tabs("option", "selected"))
                    break;
                case "change":
                    var selectedIndex = tabsElem.tabs("option", "selected");
                    tabsElem.tabs("url", selectedIndex, "tabflowers.html");
                    tabsElem.tabs("load", selectedIndex);
                    break;
            }
        })
    });
</script>
...
```

In this script, I have added a Change URL button that calls the url method and changes the content location for the active tab. By changing the URL, you can switch a tab between local and remote content (it is harder to switch in the other direction because you need to associate the tab with a local HTML element).

When you change the URL to make a tab remote, the content won't be loaded until the user deactivates and reactivates the tab. To work around this, I call the load method to force an Ajax request immediately.

■ **Tip** jQuery UI will allow you only to change to URLs within the same origin. See Chapter 14 for a description of origins.

Automatically Cycling Through the Tabs

You can use the rotate method to automatically cycle through the tabs in the widget. This can be a very nice feature, especially if you have some visually striking content that the user might not see otherwise (I am thinking of a site I use to book vacations, which uses jQuery UI tabs to showcase stunning pictures of exotic locations). My example content is not as appealing, but I can still use it to demonstrate the method. See Listing 20-18 for a demonstration.

Listing 20-18. Cycling Through Tabs Automatically

```
<!DOCTYPE html>
<html>
<head>
    <title>Example</title>
    <script src="jquery-1.7.js" type="text/javascript"></script>
    <script src="jquery.tmpl.js" type="text/javascript"></script>
```

```
    <script src="jquery-ui-1.8.16.custom.js" type="text/javascript"></script>
    <link rel="stylesheet" type="text/css" href="styles.css"/>
    <link rel="stylesheet" type="text/css" href="jquery-ui-1.8.16.custom.css"/>
    <script type="text/javascript">
        $(document).ready(function() {
            var data = [{"name":"Astor","product":"astor"},
                        {"name":"Daffodil","product":"daffodil"},
                        {"name":"Rose","product":"rose"},
                        {"name":"Peony","product":"peony"},
                        {"name":"Primula","product":"primula"},
                        {"name":"Snowdrop","product":"snowdrop"},
                        {"name":"Carnation","product":"carnation"},
                        {"name":"Lily","product":"lily"},
                        {"name":"Orchid","product":"orchid"}];

            var elems = $('#flowerTmpl').tmpl(data);
            elems.slice(0, 3).appendTo("#tab1");
            elems.slice(3, 6).appendTo("#tab2");
            elems.slice(6).appendTo("#tab3");

            $('#tabs').tabs({
                fx: {
                    opacity: "toggle",
                    duration: "normal"
                }
            }).tabs("rotate", "5000", false);

            $('button').button();
        });
    </script>
    <script id="flowerTmpl" type="text/x-jquery-tmpl">
        <div class="dcell">
            <img src="${product}.png"/>
            <label for="${product}">${name}:</label>
            <input name="${product}" value="0" />
        </div>
    </script>
</head>
<body>
    <h1>Jacqui's Flower Shop</h1>
    <form method="post" action="http://node.jacquisflowershop.com/order">
        <div id="tabs">
            <ul>
                <li><a href="#tab1">Row 1</a>
                <li><a href="#tab2">Row 2</a>
                <li><a href="#tab3">Row 3</a>
            </ul>
            <div id="tab1"></div>
            <div id="tab2"></div>
            <div id="tab3"></div>
        </div>
        <div id="buttonDiv"><button type="submit">Place Order</button></div>
```

```
    </form>
</body>
</html>
```

The arguments for the rotate method are the number of milliseconds for which each tab should be shown and a Boolean that specifies whether the tabs will continue to cycle automatically after a user has explicitly activated a tab.

My recommendation is to transition between tabs slowly. The five seconds that I have specified in this example is a comfortable minimum direction. Any faster and you start to create a effect that is discomforting to users. Anything less than two seconds feels like a strobe effect and is distinctly unpleasant. I have added an animation effect to this example, which makes the transition between tabs less jarring. I explained the basic jQuery animations and effects in Chapter 10, and I describe the additional features added by jQuery UI in Chapter 34.

Resuming Tab Cycling Following User Interaction

The option to resume cycling the tabs after the user has activated one should always be false as far as I am concerned. The user has selected the tab they want to review, and by activating a tab, they have indicated that they understand the way that the content has been presented. By resuming cycling through the tabs, you run the risk of replacing the content that the user is studying with something they have already seen and discarded.

If you really must resume cycling the tabs, then I recommend doing so in a different way. Part of the problem with resuming via the rotate method is that cycling commences after the duration you specified. In my example, this means the user gets exactly five seconds to study the tab they activated before it is replaced with something else, which is just useless. Listing 20-19 shows how you can combine the rotate method with some of the tabs widget events to give the user a more graceful experience.

Listing 20-19. Resuming Tab Cycling in a More Elegant Way

```
...
<script type="text/javascript">
    $(document).ready(function() {
        var data = [{"name":"Astor","product":"astor"},
                    {"name":"Daffodil","product":"daffodil"},
                    {"name":"Rose","product":"rose"},
                    {"name":"Peony","product":"peony"},
                    {"name":"Primula","product":"primula"},
                    {"name":"Snowdrop","product":"snowdrop"},
                    {"name":"Carnation","product":"carnation"},
                    {"name":"Lily","product":"lily"},
                    {"name":"Orchid","product":"orchid"}];

        var elems = $('#flowerTmpl').tmpl(data);
        elems.slice(0, 3).appendTo("#tab1");
        elems.slice(3, 6).appendTo("#tab2");
        elems.slice(6).appendTo("#tab3");

        var displayDuration = 5000;
        var loadFactor = 5;
        var selectCount = 0;
```

```
        $('#tabs').tabs({
            fx: {
                opacity: "toggle",
                duration: "normal"
            },
            select: function() {
                var localCount = ++selectCount;
                setTimeout(function() {
                    if (localCount == selectCount) {
                        $('#tabs').tabs("rotate", displayDuration, false)
                    }
                }, displayDuration * loadFactor)
            }
        }).tabs("rotate", displayDuration, false);

        $('button').button();
    });
</script>...
```

In this script, I use the rotate method to set up tab cycling without the automatic resumption feature. I respond to the select event, which is triggered when the user activates a tab (but not when a tab is displayed as part of the rotation). In the handler function, I use the JavaScript setTimeout feature to invoke a function in the future. In this function I call the rotate method only if the user hasn't activated another tab since I initially responded to the select event.

I have expressed the period before I resume the rotation as a multiple of the display duration. In this example, the multiple is 5, and the display duration is 5000. This means each tab is displayed for 5 seconds and that rotation resumes 25 seconds after the user has last activated a tab. You should tune this multiple to suit your content such that the user has plenty of time to peruse the content of the activated tab.

■ **Caution** Use rotation only with content that does not require user interaction. If you are using tabs to contain HTML forms, for example, then you should never resume rotation once the user has started to enter data into the input elements.

Using the jQuery UI Tabs Events

I have already demonstrated some of the events that are supported by the jQuery UI tabs widget, but you can find the complete list in Table 20-4.

Table 20-4. Tabs Events

Event	Description
`create`	Triggered when the tabs widget is applied to an underlying HTML element
`select`	Triggered when the user activates a tab or when the `select` method is called
`load`	Triggered when the content for a remote tab has been loaded
`show`	Triggered whenever a tab is displayed to the user
`add`	Triggered when a tab is added to the widget
`remove`	Triggered when a tab is removed from the widget
`enable`	Triggered when a tab is enabled
`disable`	Triggered when a tab is disabled

The `select`, `show`, `load`, and `add` events are provided with a `ui` object that defines three properties that provide useful information about the event. These properties are described in Table 20-5. The `create`, `remove`, `enable`, and `disable` events don't provide this additional information.

Table 20-5. Properties of the ui Object Dispatched for Selected Tabs Events

Property	Description
`index`	The index of the tab
`panel`	The content `HTMLElement` object for the tab
`tab`	The content URL for the tab

I am going to focus on two particularly important events—`select` and `show`—and the difference between them. This difference provides the basis for using the tabs widget in some sophisticated settings. In this section, I am going to show you how to break up an HTML form and display sections of it in a series of tabs and then use the `select` and `show` events to perform validation in response to the user using the tabs to move through the sections of the form.

Using Tabs to Display a Form

This is a useful technique for making a long form more approachable while giving the user a sense of how far they have progressed through the form. To begin, Listing 20-20 shows the document that contains the form that you will use.

Listing 20-20. The Document That Contains a Form

```
<!DOCTYPE html>
<html>
<head>
    <title>Example</title>
    <script src="jquery-1.7.js" type="text/javascript"></script>
    <script src="jquery.tmpl.js" type="text/javascript"></script>
    <script src="jquery-ui-1.8.16.custom.js" type="text/javascript"></script>
    <link rel="stylesheet" type="text/css" href="styles.css"/>
    <link rel="stylesheet" type="text/css" href="jquery-ui-1.8.16.custom.css"/>
    <style type="text/css">
        #tab2 input, #tab3 input {width: 200px; text-align: left}
        #tab1, #tab2, #tab3 {padding: 10px}
        .fl {float: left}
        #buttonDiv {clear: both}
        #tabs, h1 {margin: 10px}
        .regLabel {width: auto}
    </style>
    <script type="text/javascript">
        $(document).ready(function() {
            var data = [{"name":"Astor","product":"astor"},
                        {"name":"Daffodil","product":"daffodil"},
                        {"name":"Rose","product":"rose"},
                        {"name":"Peony","product":"peony"}];

            var elems = $('#flowerTmpl').tmpl(data);
            elems.slice(0, 2).appendTo("#row1");
            elems.slice(2, 4).appendTo("#row2");

            var detailsData = [{name: "Name", hint: "Enter your name"},
                    {name: "Street", hint: "Enter your street"},
                    {name: "City", hint: "Enter your city"},
                    {name: "State", hint: "Enter your state"},
                    {name: "Zip", hint: "Enter your zip code"}];

            $('#detailsTmpl').tmpl(detailsData).appendTo("#tab2")
                .clone().appendTo("#tab3")

            $('button').button();
        });
    </script>
    <script id="flowerTmpl" type="text/x-jquery-tmpl">
        <div class="dcell ui-widget">
            <img src="${product}.png"/>
            <label for="${product}">${name}:</label>
            <input name="${product}" value="0"/>
        </div>
    </script>
    <script id="detailsTmpl" type="text/x-jquery-tmpl">
        <div class="ui-widget">
```

```
            <label for="${name}">${name}:</label>
            <input name="${name}"  placeholder="${hint}"/>
        </div>
    </script>
</head>
<body>
    <h1>Jacqui's Flower Shop</h1>
    <form method="post" action="http://node.jacquisflowershop.com/order">
        <div id="tabs" class="ui-widget">
            <ul>
                <li><a href="#tab1">1. Select Products</a>
                <li><a href="#tab2">2. Your Details</a>
                <li><a href="#tab3">3. Your Shipping Address </a>
            </ul>

            <div id="tab1">
                <h2>1. Select Products</h2>
                <div id="row1"></div>
                <div id="row2"></div>
            </div>
            <div id="tab2" class="fl"><h2>2. Your Details</h2></div>
            <div id="tab3" class="fl">
               <h2>3. Your Shipping Address</h2>
            </div>
        </div>
        <div id="buttonDiv"><button type="submit">Place Order</button></div>
    </form>
</body>
</html>
```

I have added some extra content and structure to the document to flesh out previous examples. There are fewer flower products, but I have added regions of the document to capture the user's personal and shipping details. You can see the basic form in Figure 20-13.

Figure 20-13. The multipart form for use with the tabs widget

There is nothing special about the form, other than it being well-suited for use with the jQuery UI tabs widget because it is neatly divided into distinct regions, each of which can be displayed in a tab.

I have added all of the content programmatically using the data templates plugin and a part of JavaScript arrays. You can see how I use the jQuery functionality I demonstrated in earlier chapters to generate elements from the data, clone them as required, and then add the results to the document. This isn't a requirement for using tabs to display forms, but in a book about jQuery, I like to use the core features as much as possible.

You can also see the `ul` element in the figure and the links that it contains that point to the content elements. I would usually hide this element, but I wanted to show you a nice side effect of the structure that the tabs widget uses for the labels. Because you create a list and each list contains a link, you can click the link to jump to that part of the document, and, if the link is to another file, then the browser will navigate to that document.

Applying the Tabs

You are now ready to create the tabs widget. Listing 20-21 shows the changes that are required in the script element. No changes are required anywhere else in the document.

Listing 20-21. Creating the Tabs Widget

```
...
<script type="text/javascript">
    $(document).ready(function() {
        var data = [{"name":"Astor","product":"astor"},
                    {"name":"Daffodil","product":"daffodil"},
                    {"name":"Rose","product":"rose"},
                    {"name":"Peony","product":"peony"}];

        var elems = $('#flowerTmpl').tmpl(data);
        elems.slice(0, 2).appendTo("#row1");
        elems.slice(2, 4).appendTo("#row2");

        var detailsData = [{name: "Name", hint: "Enter your name"},
                {name: "Street", hint: "Enter your street"},
                {name: "City", hint: "Enter your city"},
                {name: "State", hint: "Enter your state"},
                {name: "Zip", hint: "Enter your zip code"}];

        $('#detailsTmpl').tmpl(detailsData).appendTo("#tab2")
            .clone().appendTo("#tab3")

        $('.fl').removeClass("fl");
        $('#tabs').tabs().find("h2").remove();

        $('button').button()
    });
</script>
...
```

I remove the fl class that I used to position the content for the details and shipping address regions and remove the h2 elements that I was using for section headers. I then apply the tabs method, which uses the content elements as the basis for the tabs, as you can see in Figure 20-14.

Figure 20-14. Applying tabs to the form

Handling the Button Presses

To make the form easier to fill in using the tabs, I have registered a handler for the `click` event of the submit button. In this handler, I suppress the default action for the event and move to the next tab in the sequence until the last tab is reached. At this point, pressing the button submits the form to the server. Listing 20-22 shows the additions to the script.

Listing 20-22. Progressing Through the Form Using the Submit Button

```
...
$('button').button().click(function(e) {
    var tabsElem = $('#tabs');
    var activeTab = tabsElem.tabs("option", "selected");
    if (activeTab < (tabsElem.tabs("length") -1)) {
        e.preventDefault();
        tabsElem.tabs("select", activeTab + 1)
    }
});
...
```

I use the `selected` option and the `length` method to figure out where the user is in the sequence of tabs, and I use the `select` method to advance from one tab to another. I call the `preventDefault` method only when the user isn't on the final tab, which allows the form to be submitted at the end of the tab sequence.

Performing Validation

At the moment, the user can just jump to the last page and submit the form. To prevent this, I am going to apply some basic form validation. To keep this example simple, I am going to handle the validation manually, but for real projects I recommend using the validation plugin and the techniques I described in Chapter 13. Listing 20-23 shows the changes to the script to implement some basic validation and stop the user from jumping to the end of the tab sequence prematurely.

Listing 20-23. Preventing the User from Skipping Through the Tabs with Some Basic Validation

```
...
<script type="text/javascript">
    $(document).ready(function() {
        var data = [{"name":"Astor","product":"astor"},
                    {"name":"Daffodil","product":"daffodil"},
                    {"name":"Rose","product":"rose"},
                    {"name":"Peony","product":"peony"}];

        var elems = $('#flowerTmpl').tmpl(data);
        elems.slice(0, 2).appendTo("#row1");
        elems.slice(2, 4).appendTo("#row2");

        var detailsData = [{name: "Name", hint: "Enter your name"},
                {name: "Street", hint: "Enter your street"},
                {name: "City", hint: "Enter your city"},
                {name: "State", hint: "Enter your state"},
                {name: "Zip", hint: "Enter your zip code"}];

        $('#detailsTmpl').tmpl(detailsData).appendTo("#tab2")
            .clone().appendTo("#tab3")

        var visiblePanel;
        var visibleIndex;

        $('.fl').removeClass("fl");
        $('#tabs').tabs({
            show: function(event, ui) {
                visiblePanel = ui.panel;
                visibleIndex = ui.index;
            },
            select: function(event, ui) {
                if (ui.index > visibleIndex && !validateTab(visiblePanel)) {
                    event.preventDefault();
                }
            }
        }).find("h2").remove();


        function validateTab(contentPanel) {
            var valid = false;
            if (contentPanel.id == "tab1") {
```

```
                var productCount = 0;
                $('#tab1 input').each(function(index, elem) {
                    productCount += Number($(elem).val());
                })
                valid = (productCount > 0);
            } else {
                var emptyCount = 0;
                $(contentPanel).find("input").each(function(index, elem) {
                    if ($(elem).val() == "") {
                        emptyCount++;
                    }
                })
                valid = (emptyCount == 0);
            }
            if (!valid) {
                alert("Validation Problem!");
            }
            return valid;
        }

        $('button').button().click(function(e) {
            var tabsElem = $('#tabs');
            var activeTab = tabsElem.tabs("option", "selected");
            if (activeTab < (tabsElem.tabs("length") -1)) {
                e.preventDefault();
                tabsElem.tabs("select", activeTab + 1)
            }
        });
    });
</script>
...
```

The problem you face when trying to validate part of a form contained in a tab is that the tabs widget doesn't provide any convenient way to find the active content panel. You can dig through the CSS or the HTML elements created by the widget, but you expose yourself to problems if the jQuery UI team ever changes the way that the widget works.

I have used the show event to keep track of the active index and content panel. I have defined a pair of variables, like this:

```
...
var visiblePanel;
var visibleIndex;
...
```

I update these variables each time the show method is triggered:

```
...
show: function(event, ui) {
    visiblePanel = ui.panel;
    visibleIndex = ui.index;
},
...
```

I then use the select event to call my validation method:

```
select: function(event, ui) {
    if (ui.index > visibleIndex && !validateTab(visiblePanel)) {
        event.preventDefault();
    }
}
```

The difference between the select and show events is critical to this technique. The show event is triggered whenever the tabs widget displays a tab. This can be in response to user input, the select method being called, the initial creating of the widget, or the rotate setting being used. The show event will also be triggered if a new tab is displayed as a side effect of another operation. For example, disabling the active tab will trigger the show event when the tabs widget shows the next available enabled tab to the user. The select event will be triggered only when the user explicitly selects a tab or when the select method has been called.

This difference allows me to keep track of all tab changes using the show event and validate the user's input only in response to the select event.

Notice that I perform validation in the select handler function only if the user is moving forward through the tabs. I don't perform validation if the select event is triggered for a tab whose index is smaller than the index of the currently displayed tab. This allows the user to return to earlier tabs and change their entries.

Finally, notice how I stop the tab the user has selected by calling the preventDefault method on the Event object passed to the handler function. The default action for the select event is to display the selected tab, and by preventing this, I force the widget to stay on the current tab. You can see the effect of the validation in Figure 20-15. The validation in this example is trivial, and it just displays a dialog box if there is a problem. For a real project, you should use the validation plugin, as described in Chapter 13.

Figure 20-15. The alert box shown in response to a validation error

Summary

In this chapter, I showed you the jQuery UI tabs widget. This widget offers rich and complex functionality and can be used in a wide range of situations. I find myself using this widget a lot. It is flexible and completely customizable, and users are generally familiar with the idea of selectively revealing content contained in individual tabs, something that is not always the case with other widgets such as the accordion.

CHAPTER 21

Using the Datepicker Widget

This chapter focuses on the jQuery UI datepicker widget, which provides a convenient visual mechanism for helping users select dates. Getting date information from users as text is notoriously problematic because of the wide range of formats in which dates can be expressed. The datepicker widget can make it easier for the user to select a date and provide the information to you in a way that is more consistent and less prone to errors. Table 21-1 provides the summary for this chapter.

***Table 21-1.** Chapter Summary*

Problem	Solution	Listing
Create a pop-up jQuery UI datepicker.	Use the `datepicker` method on an `input` element.	1
Create an inline datepicker.	Use the `datepicker` method on a `span` or `div` element.	2
Specify the date displayed by the datepicker.	Use the `defaultDate` setting.	3
Specify an additional element that will be updated when the user selects a date.	Use the `altField` setting.	4
Change the action that causes a pop-up datepicker to appear.	Use the `showOn` setting.	5
Specify the text displayed in the datepicker trigger button.	Use the `buttonText` setting.	6
Show an image in place of the trigger button.	Use the `buttonImage` and `buttonImageOnly` settings.	7
Restrict the date selection.	Use the `constrainInput`, `minDate`, and `maxDate` settings.	8, 9
Display several months in the datepicker.	Use the `numberOfMonths` setting.	10–12

Enable drop-down menus to aid navigation to months and years.	Use the changeMonth and changeYear settings.	13
Show week information in the datepicker.	Use the showWeek and weekHeader settings.	14
Fill the date grid with dates from the previous and subsequent months.	Use the showOtherMonths and selectOtherMonths settings.	15
Display a button bar at the base of the datepicker.	Use the showButtonBar and gotoCurrent settings.	16
Show a formatting hint to the user.	Use the appendText setting (or the HTML5 placeholder feature).	17, 18
Get or set the date programmatically.	Use the getDate and setDate methods.	19
Show or hide a pop-up datepicker programmatically.	Use the show and hide events.	20
Respond to the user navigating to a new month or year.	Use the onChangeMonthYear event.	21
Respond to a pop-up datepicker closing.	Use the onClose event.	22
Localize the datepicker.	Use the jQuery UI i18n support.	23

Creating the Datepicker

You can use the datepicker in two basic ways. The most common is to attach the widget to an input element, using the datapicker method. There is no immediate visual change to the input, but when the element gains the focus (because the user either tabs from other elements or clicks the input field), the datepicker pops up to help the user select a date. This is known as a *pop-up* datepicker. Listing 21-1 shows how you create a pop-up datepicker.

Listing 21-1. Creating a Pop-up Datepicker

```
<!DOCTYPE html>
<html>
<head>
    <title>Example</title>
    <script src="jquery-1.7.js" type="text/javascript"></script>
    <script src="jquery-ui-1.8.16.custom.js" type="text/javascript"></script>
    <link rel="stylesheet" type="text/css" href="styles.css"/>
    <link rel="stylesheet" type="text/css" href="jquery-ui-1.8.16.custom.css"/>
    <style type="text/css">
        input {width: 200px; text-align: left}
```

```
    </style>
    <script type="text/javascript">
        $(document).ready(function() {
            $('#datep').datepicker();
        });
    </script>
</head>
<body>
    <h1>Jacqui's Flower Shop</h1>
    <form method="post" action="http://node.jacquisflowershop.com/order">
      <div class="ui-widget">
        <label for="datep">Date: </label><input id="datep"/>
      </div>
    </form>
</body>
</html>
```

You can see how focusing on the input element displays the datepicker in Figure 21-1.

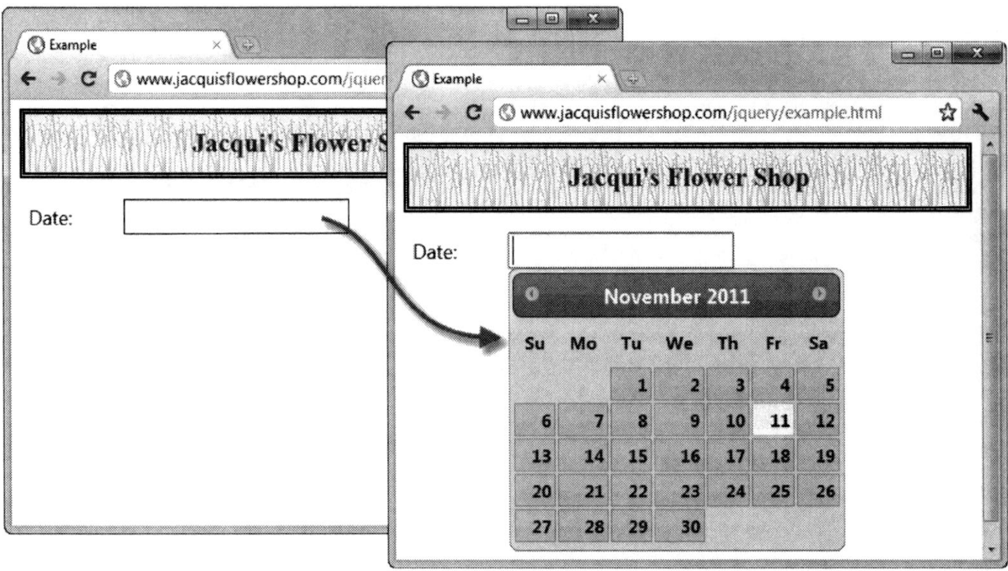

Figure 21-1. The datepicker pop ups up when the input element gains the focus.

When the datepicker pop-up is displayed, the user can choose to enter a date manually or use the datepicker window to select a date. The datepicker pop-up disappears when the `input` element loses the focus or when the user hits the Enter or Escape key.

Creating an Inline Datepicker

The other way to use the datepicker is to use it *inline*. To achieve this, you select a `div` or `span` element using jQuery and then call the `datepicker` method. An inline datepicker is visible whenever the underling element is visible. Listing 21-2 provides a demonstration of creating an inline datepicker.

Listing 21-2. Creating an Inline Datepicker

```
<!DOCTYPE html>
<html>
<head>
    <title>Example</title>
    <script src="jquery-1.7.js" type="text/javascript"></script>
    <script src="jquery-ui-1.8.16.custom.js" type="text/javascript"></script>
    <link rel="stylesheet" type="text/css" href="styles.css"/>
    <link rel="stylesheet" type="text/css" href="jquery-ui-1.8.16.custom.css"/>
    <style type="text/css">
        input {width: 200px; text-align: left; margin-right: 10px}
        #wrapper > * {float: left}
    </style>
    <script type="text/javascript">
        $(document).ready(function() {
            $('#inline').datepicker();
        });
    </script>
</head>
<body>
    <h1>Jacqui's Flower Shop</h1>
    <form method="post" action="http://node.jacquisflowershop.com/order">
      <div id="wrapper" class="ui-widget">
        <label for="datep">Date: </label><input id="datep"/><span id="inline"></span>
      </div>
    </form>
</body>
</html>
```

In this example, I have used a span element in the document and used this as the target of the datepicker method. You can see the effect in Figure 21-2.

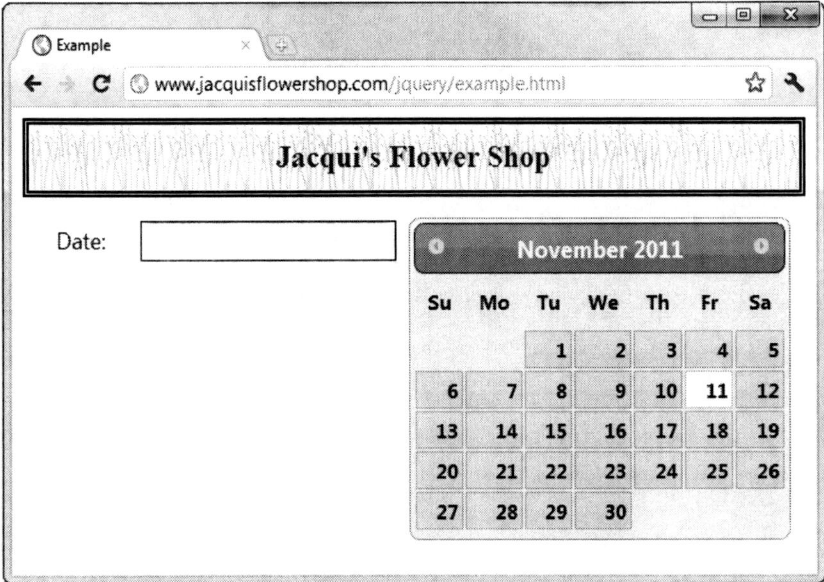

Figure 21-2. An inline datepicker

An inline datepicker can be useful when you don't want to work with pop-ups. There are some applications where dates are so important that it makes sense to display the datepicker all of the time, but in most cases hiding the pop-up until it is required is more sensible. The problem with hiding and showing an inline datepicker is that the layout of the document has to flex to accommodate the datepicker, which can cause presentation problems. For almost all situations, I find the pop-up datepicker to be more useful.

Configuring the Datepicker

If you have done any work with dates before, you will understand that they are very complicated to deal with. You see this complexity reflected in the large number of settings supported by the datepicker widget. In the following sections, I describe groups of related settings that can be used to configure the datepicker.

Setting Up the Basics

You can use some settings to configure the basic nature of the pop-up and inline datepickers. These are important because they allow you to control the integration of the datepicker widget into the document. Table 21-2 describes these settings.

Table 21-2. Basic Datepicker Settings

Setting	Description
`altField`	Specifies an additional field that will be updated with the data selection.
`buttonImageOnly`	Specifies that the image specified by `buttonImage` should be contained in an `img` element rather than a `button`. The default is `false`.
`buttonImage`	Specifies the URL of an image to use for the pop-up trigger button. Not used by default.
`buttonText`	Specifies the text for the pop-up trigger button. The default is an ellipsis (`...`).
`defaultDate`	Sets the date to highlight when the datepicker is displayed.
`disabled`	Specifies whether the datepicker widget is initially disabled. The default is `false`.
`showOn`	Specifies the trigger for displaying a pop-up datepicker. The default is `focus`.

Specifying the Default Date

The most basic setting is also one of the most useful. The `defaultDate` setting specifies the date that will be shown when the datepicker is displayed.

If you don't provide a value for the `defaultDate` setting, then the current date will be used. (This is, of course, the date as defined by the user's system. Time zones, date lines, and misconfiguration can all present the user with a different date from the one you might be expecting to appear.)

■ **Tip** This setting is used only if there isn't a `value` attribute for the `input` element. If there is, either because you have included the `value` attribute in the document or because the user has previously made a selection, then the datepicker uses this value.

If you don't want today's date, then you can choose from several different formats to express the date you want to start with. Table 21-3 shows the range of formats and values you can use.

Table 21-3. Formats and Values for the defaultDate Setting

Value/Format	Description
`null`	Use the current system date.
`Date` object	Use the value represented by the `Date` object.
`+days`, `-days`	Use the date that is the specified number of days from today. For example, `+3` means show three days from today, and `-2` means show the date two days ago.
`+1d +7w -1m +1y`	Use a date that is relative to today, expressed as a number of days (`d`), weeks (`w`), months (`m`), and years (`y`) in the future (`+`) or in the past (`-`). Positive and negative values can be mixed in a single date so that a value of `-1d +1m` used on November 12, 2011, selects the date December 11, 2011.

Listing 21-3 shows the use of the `defaultDate` setting to specify a date five years in the future.

Listing 21-3. Using the defaultDate Setting

```
...
<script type="text/javascript">
    $(document).ready(function() {
        $('#datep').datepicker({
            defaultDate: "+5y"
        });
    });
</script>
...
```

I am writing this chapter in November 2011, and you can see in Figure 21-3 that the `+5y` value for the `defaultDate` setting focuses the datepicker on November 2016.

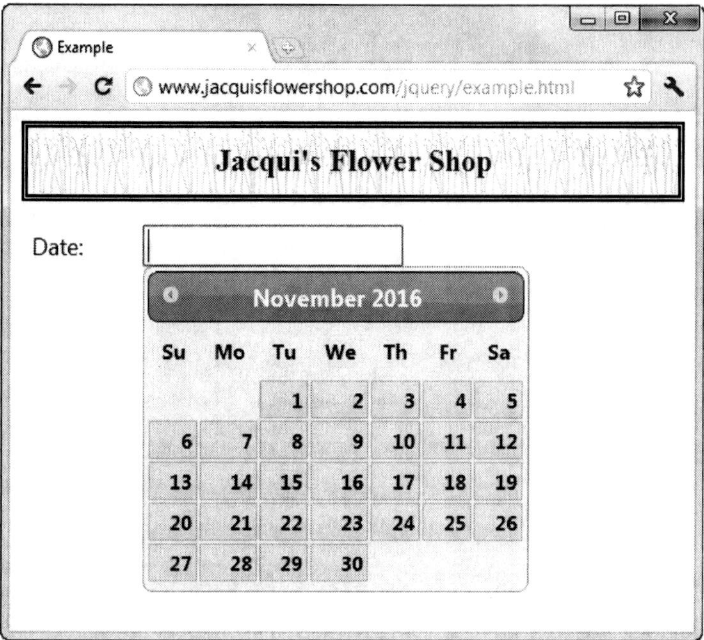

Figure 21-3. Displaying a future date using the defaultDate setting

You'll see this format for specifying relative dates again. It is a flexible format that gives a lot of precision. As in the example, you omit any interval that you don't want to change such that you can use `+5y` rather than `+0d +0w +0m +5y`. I also like the way you can mix and match negative and positive values for different intervals to zero in on the date you want.

Specifying the Alternate Element

The `altField` setting lets you specify an alternative `input` element that will be updated when a date selection is made. This is the easiest way of linking an element with an inline datepicker and can be a handy feature when using a pop-up. Listing 21-4 shows the use of the `altField` setting as a means of displaying the selection from an inline datepicker.

Listing 21-4. Using the altField Setting with an Inline Datepicker

```
...
<script type="text/javascript">
    $(document).ready(function() {
        $('#inline').datepicker({
            altField: "#datep"
        });
    });
</script>
...
```

In this example, I have used a selector string to identify the element I want to use, but the altField setting will also accept a jQuery object or a DOM HTMLElement object. The effect of this example is that the input element displays the date each time I make a selection using the datepicker.

Managing the Pop-up Trigger

The showOn setting lets you control what causes a pop-up datepicker to be shown to the user. There are three allowed values for this setting:

- focus: The pop-up is shown when the input element gains the focus. This is the default.
- button: The pop-up is shown when a button is clicked.
- both: The pop-up is shown when a button is clicked or when the input gains focus.

When you use the button or both value, the datepicker widget creates a button element and adds it to the document immediately after the input element. Listing 21-5 shows the use of the showOn setting.

Listing 21-5. Using the showOn Setting

```
...
<script type="text/javascript">
    $(document).ready(function() {
        $('#datep').datepicker({
            showOn: "both"
        });
    });
</script>
...
```

You can see the button element in Figure 21-4. Since I used the both value in this example, the pop-up will be displayed when the user either clicks the button or focuses on the input element.

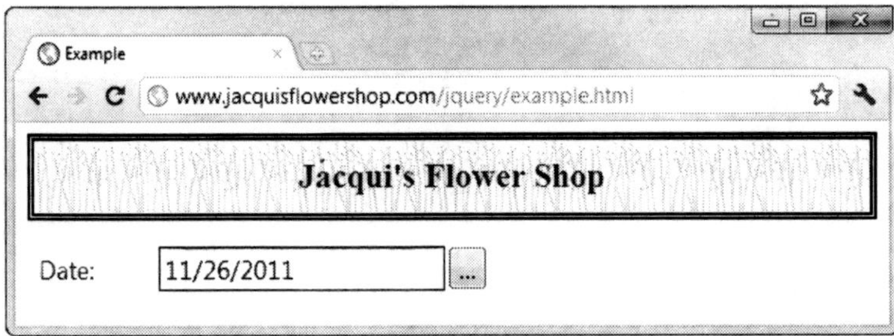

Figure 21-4. The button added in response to the showOn setting

---

■ **Tip** The button that the datepicker widget adds is not a jQuery UI button widget. If you want to keep your buttons consistent, then you will need to select the `button` element and call the jQuery UI `button` method, as described in Chapter 18.

You can format the `button` element using the `buttonImage` or `buttonText` setting. If you set `buttonImage` to a URL, the datepicker widget will use the image in the `button`. Alternatively, you can use the `buttonText` setting to set a phrase to replace the default content (which is `...`). Listing 21-6 shows the use of the `buttonText` setting.

Listing 21-6. Using the buttonText Setting

```
...
<script type="text/javascript">
    $(document).ready(function() {
        $('#datep').datepicker({
            showOn: "both",
            buttonText: "Select"
        });
    });
</script>
...
```

You can do without the button entirely if you use the `buttonImage` and `buttonTextOnly` settings together. This causes the datepicker to add an `img` element to the document rather than a button. Listing 21-7 provides a demonstration.

Listing 21-7. Using an Image Rather Than a Button

```
<!DOCTYPE html>
<html>
<head>
    <title>Example</title>
    <script src="jquery-1.7.js" type="text/javascript"></script>
    <script src="jquery-ui-1.8.16.custom.js" type="text/javascript"></script>
    <link rel="stylesheet" type="text/css" href="styles.css"/>
    <link rel="stylesheet" type="text/css" href="jquery-ui-1.8.16.custom.css"/>
    <style type="text/css">
        input {width: 200px; text-align: left}
        #dpcontainer * {vertical-align: middle}
        #dpcontainer img {width: 35px;}
    </style>
    <script type="text/javascript">
        $(document).ready(function() {
            $('#datep').datepicker({
                showOn: "both",
                buttonImage: "right.png",
                buttonImageOnly: true
            });
```

```
        });
    </script>
</head>
<body>
    <h1>Jacqui's Flower Shop</h1>
    <form method="post" action="http://node.jacquisflowershop.com/order">
      <div id="dpcontainer" class="ui-widget">
        <label for="datep">Date: </label><input id="datep"/>
      </div>
    </form>
</body>
</html>
```

In this example, I have specified an image called `right.png` and set `buttonImageOnly` to `true`. I have also added some CSS styles to the document to control the appearance of the image relative to the `label` and `input` elements. The datepicker widget isn't particularly smart about how it creates the `img` element, so you need to compensate to bring the style of the image in line with the rest of the document. You can see the effect of having an image rather than a button in Figure 21-5.

Figure 21-5. Using an image instead of a button with a pop-up datepicker

Managing the Date Selection

The purpose of the datepicker widget is to allow the user to select a date, but you often want to apply some constraints to the range of dates that are available for selection. Table 21-4 describes the settings that allow you to apply selection constraints to guide the user to a date you can work with.

Table 21-4. *Datepicker Settings for Managing Date Selection*

Setting	Description
`changeMonth`	When `true`, the datepicker displays a drop-down menu that allows direct navigation to a month. The default is `false`.
`changeYear`	When `true`, the datepicker displays a drop-down menu that allows direct navigation to a year. The default is `false`.

constrainInput	When true, limits the characters in the input element to those contained in a valid date. The default is true.
hideIfNoPrevNext	When true, the previous and next buttons are hidden, rather than disabled, when there are no selectable dates in the past or future relative to the displayed period. The default is false.
maxDate	Specifies the latest date that the user can select. The default is to allow the user to select any date.
minDate	Specifies the earliest date that the user can select. The default is to allow the user to select any date.
numberOfMonths	Specifies the number of months displayed by the datepicker. The default is 1.
showCurrentAtPos	Specifies where the current or default month is displayed in a multimonth datepicker. The default is 0.
stepMonths	Specifies the number of months that the display jumps when the previous and next buttons are clicked. The default is 1.
yearRange	Specifies the range of years that can be selected in the drop-down list that is enabled by the changeYear setting. The default is to display ten years before and ten years after the present year.

Limiting the Input Character and Date Range

When set to true, the constrainInput setting restricts the characters that can be entered into the input element to those that are contained in a valid date. The set of characters is dependent on the *localization configuration* you are using, which I talk more about in the "Localizing Date Selection" section later in this chapter. If you have not localized the datepicker widget, then you can expect the input element to be restricted so that the user can enter only numbers and the / character. This setting doesn't mean that the user can only enter valid dates because a value like 99/99/99 can be entered, but it can help reduce errors. The importance of this setting increases when the showOn setting is set to button because the pop-up won't automatically appear when the input element gains the focus. Users will typically select from the datepicker when it is presented to them but won't always realize that a button will display a picker. Every opportunity you give the user to enter a date directly sharply increases the chances you have to process a badly formatted value. Listing 21-8 shows the use of the constrainInput setting.

Listing 21-8 . Applying Basic Constraints to the Date Selection

```
<!DOCTYPE html>
<html>
<head>
    <title>Example</title>
    <script src="jquery-1.7.js" type="text/javascript"></script>
    <script src="jquery-ui-1.8.16.custom.js" type="text/javascript"></script>
```

```
    <link rel="stylesheet" type="text/css" href="styles.css"/>
    <link rel="stylesheet" type="text/css" href="jquery-ui-1.8.16.custom.css"/>
    <style type="text/css">
        input {width: 200px; text-align: left; margin-right: 10px}
        #wrapper > * {float: left}
    </style>
    <script type="text/javascript">
        $(document).ready(function() {
            $('#datep').datepicker({
                constrainInput: true,
                minDate: "-3",
                maxDate: "+1"
            });
        });
    </script>
</head>
<body>
    <h1>Jacqui's Flower Shop</h1>
    <form method="post" action="http://node.jacquisflowershop.com/order">
      <div id="wrapper" class="ui-widget">
        <label for="datep">Date: </label><input id="datep"/><span id="inline"></span>
      </div>
    </form>
</body>
</html>
```

The constrainInput setting is true by default, so I have added values for the minDate and maxDate settings as well, just to make the example a little more interesting. These settings allow you to specify the earliest and latest dates that the user can select. As with the defaultDate setting I showed you in the previous section, you can specify the dates for the minDate and maxDate settings as null (no date), a Date object, a number of days, or a relative date string. In this example, I used the number option that specifies the number of days relative to today. In Figure 21-6, you can see that the datepicker widget disables any date that the user cannot select.

Figure 21-6. Restricting the dates that the user can select

■ **Tip** Notice that the previous and next buttons are disabled automatically when they are not required. These are the buttons at the top left and top right of the datepicker that allow the user to move to the previous and next months. In Figure 21-6, all of the dates that the user can select are in the current month, so both of these buttons are disabled. You can hide, rather than disable, buttons in this situation by setting `hideIfNoPrevNext` to `true`.

The `minDate` need not be in past, the `maxDate` need not be in the future, and you don't have to provide values for both settings. If you need the user to pick a date for which there is some kind of lead time, you can specify a future date for the `minDate` setting to prevent dates from being selected that are inside the period you need to prepare, as shown in Listing 21-9.

Listing 21-9. Providing One Date Restriction to Create a Delay Window

```
...
<script type="text/javascript">
    $(document).ready(function() {
        $('#datep').datepicker({
            minDate: "+7"
        });
    });
</script>
...
```

In this example, I have specified that the user cannot select any date that occurs sooner than a week from today. There is no `maxDate` value, meaning that any future date after a week from now can be selected. You can see the result in Figure 21-7. Notice that the next button (which allows the user to navigate to the next month) is enabled in this figure, but the previous button is disabled (since there are no dates in the past that the user is allowed to select).

■ **Tip** The `minDate` and `maxDate` settings work in conjunction with the `defaultDate` setting, meaning that you can specify ranges of dates relative to a date that is not today.

Figure 21-7. Creating an open-ended date selection range

Creating a Multimonth Display

The datepicker setting allows you to specify how many months are displayed to the user through the `numberOfMonths` setting. You can specify either a number of months or a two-element array, which specifies the size of a grid of months. Listing 21-10 shows the array-based approach, which I find is most suited to inline datepickers because the grid is often too big to use as a pop-up (I'll explain why in a moment).

Listing 21-10. Using the numberofMonths Setting

```
...
<script type="text/javascript">
    $(document).ready(function() {
        $('#inline').datepicker({
            numberOfMonths: [1, 3]
        });
```

```
    });
</script>
...
```

In this example, I have specified a grid of one month high and three months wide. You can see the effect in Figure 21-8.

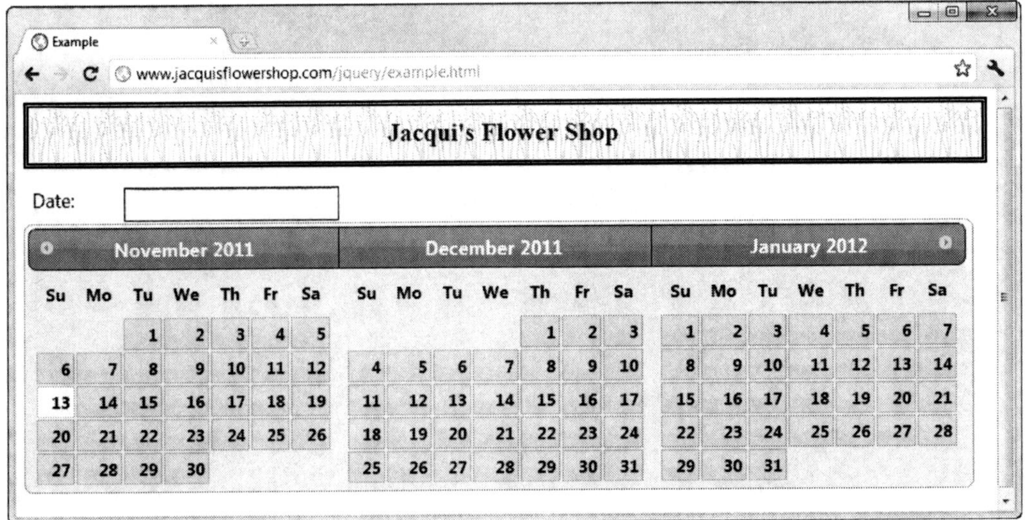

Figure 21-8. Displaying a grid of months

■ **Tip** The two-element array `[1, 3]` is equivalent to the numeric value `3`. When you provide a number for the `numberOfMonths` setting, the datepicker displays the specified number of months in a single row.

The reason that I rarely use this feature with pop-up datepickers is that a large grid requires assumptions about the size of the user's browser window and display. The datepicker pop-up isn't an operating system dialog box. It is a carefully formatted HTML element that is displayed as part of the HTML document. This means that when a large datepicker is displayed on a small screen or in a small browser window, much of the detail is displaced off the edge of the screen. Listing 21-11 shows a grid of months applied to a pop-up datepicker.

Listing 21-11. Using the numberOfMonths Setting with a Pop-up Datepicker

```
...
<script type="text/javascript">
    $(document).ready(function() {
        $('#datep').datepicker({
            numberOfMonths: [1, 3]
        });
```

```
    });
</script>
...
```

You can see the result in Figure 21-9. Not only are many of the available dates hidden from the user, but the next button (which allows the user to advance the displayed months) is off the screen as well.

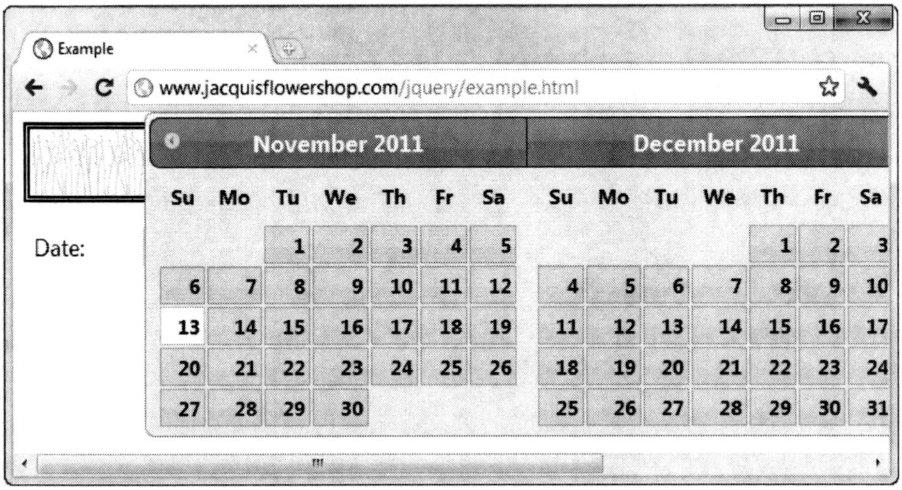

Figure 21-9. Displaying a large pop-up datepicker

You can change the position of the selected date in a multimonth datepicker using the `showCurrentAtPos` setting. As you can see in Figure 21-9, the default is to display the current month first, followed by the next two months in the future. The `showCurrentAtPos` setting takes a zero-based index value that specifies the location where the current month should be displayed. This is a very handy feature if you need to allow the user to select dates on either side of today. Listing 21-12 shows the use of this setting.

Listing 21-12. Using the showCurrentAtPos Setting

```
...
<script type="text/javascript">
    $(document).ready(function() {
        $('#inline').datepicker({
            numberOfMonths: 3,
            showCurrentAtPos: 1
        });
    });
</script>
...
```

I have specified that the current date should be shown in the middle of the three months shown by the datepicker. You can see the result in Figure 21-10.

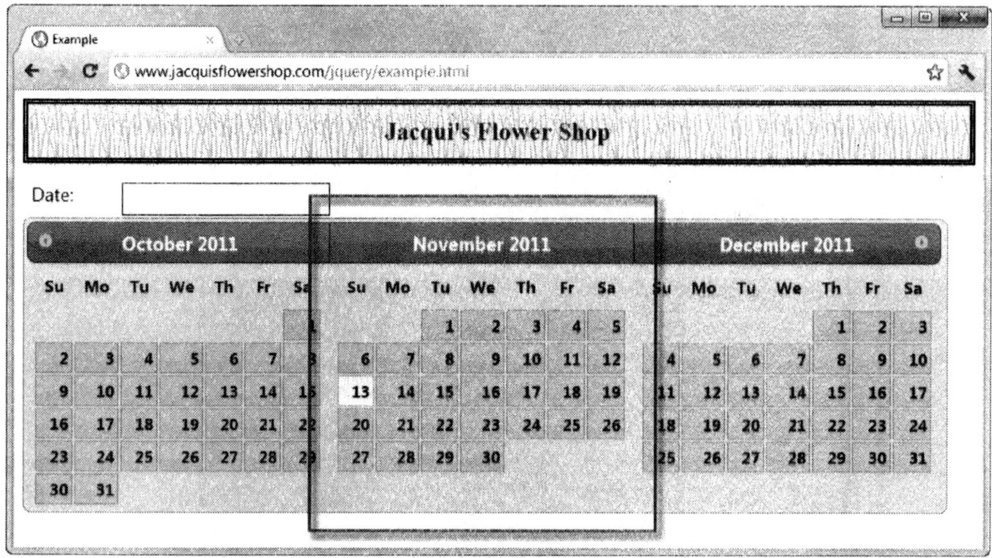

Figure 21-10. Specifying the location of the current month in a multimonth datepicker

Providing Direct Access to Months and Years

You can replace the month and year in the header of the datepicker header with drop-down menus that provide direct access to months and years. This can be a useful shortcut for users when there is a large date range to select from. The settings that control these features are `changeMonth` and `changeYear`. A `true` value for these settings enables the corresponding menu, and the menus can be enabled independently of one another. Listing 21-13 shows the use of these settings.

Listing 21-13. Providing Direct Access to Months and Years Through Drop-Down Menus

```
...
<script type="text/javascript">
    $(document).ready(function() {
        $('#datep').datepicker({
            changeMonth: true,
            changeYear: true,
            yearRange: "-1:+2"

        });
    });
</script>
...
```

In this script, I have enabled both drop-down menus. I have also used the `yearRange` setting to limit the range of years that the user can navigate to. In this example, I have specified a value of `-1:+2`, which means that the user can select one year back from today through to two years into the future. Since I am writing this chapter in 2011, the range of years that the user is presented with is 2010 to 2013. You can see how the menus are displayed (and how the year range appears) in Figure 21-10.

■ **Tip** You can also supply a range of actual years for the `yearRange` setting. I could have achieved the same result in Figure 21-11 with a value of `2010:2013`.

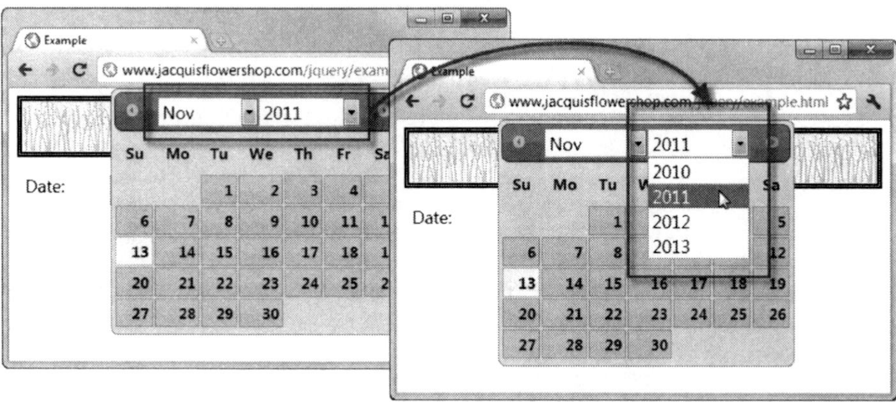

Figure 21-11. Providing the user with direct access to months and years

Managing the Appearance of the Datepicker

You can use a number of settings to tailor the appearance of the datepicker when it is displayed to the user. For general date selection purposes, the default appearance that you have seen in earlier examples is usually suitable, but the ability to tweak the appearance to suit the requirements of a web application is extremely useful. Table 21-5 describes the appearance-related settings.

Table 21-5. *Datepicker Settings for Controlling Appearance*

Setting	Description
`appendText`	Specifies a formatting hint that will be inserted into the document after the **`input`** element.
`closeText`	Specifies the text to use for the button in the button bar that dismisses a pop-up datepicker. The default is **`Done`**.
`currentText`	Specifies the text to use for the button in the button bar that returns to the current date. The default is **`Today`**.
`duration`	Specifies the speed or duration for the animation specified by the **`showAnim`** setting is performed. The default is **`normal`**. I described the

	jQuery UI animation effects in Chapter 34.
gotoCurrent	When **true**, the **Today** button in the button bar will return to the selected date rather than today's date. The default is **false**.
selectOtherMonths	When **true**, the dates shown as a result of the **showOtherMonths** setting can be selected. The default is **false**.
showAnim	Specifies the animation used to show and hide pop-up datepickers. I describe the jQuery UI animation effects in Chapter 34. The default is **show**.
showButtonPanel	When **true**, the datepicker displays a button bar allowing the user to jump to the current date and (when used with a pop-up) to dismiss the datepicker. The default is **false**.
showOptions	Specifies the options for the animation defined by the **showAnim** setting. I describe the jQuery UI animation effects in Chapter 34.
showOtherMonths	When **true**, the datepicker fills blanks in the date grid with dates from the previous and subsequent months. The default is **false**.
showWeek	When **true**, the datepicker displays a column showing week information. The default is **true**.
weekHeader	Sets the header for the week column enabled through the **showWeek** setting. The default is **Wk**.

Displaying Weeks

For some applications, knowing which week of the year a date falls in is essential. This is often the case in budget management applications, for example. The jQuery UI datepicker can display week information, configured through the showWeek and weekHeader settings, as shown in Listing 21-14.

Listing 21-14. Displaying Week Information in the Datepicker

```
...
<script type="text/javascript">
    $(document).ready(function() {
        $('#datep').datepicker({
            showWeek: true,
            weekHeader: "Week"
        });
    });
</script>
...
```

When the showWeek setting is true, the datepicker displays a column that shows week numbers. You can use the weekHeader setting to change the title of the week column from the default, Wk. In the example, I have enabled the week column and changed the title to Week. You can see the result in Figure 21-12.

Figure 21-12. Showing week information in the datepicker

Allowing Bleed Between Months

The datepicker displays only the dates in the current month by default. This means there are blank entries in the date grid before and after the range of dates. You can show dates from the previous and next months by using a value of true for the showOtherMonth setting, as shown in Listing 21-15.

Listing 21-15. Allowing Months to Bleed into One Another

```
...
<script type="text/javascript">
    $(document).ready(function() {
        $('#datep').datepicker({
            showOtherMonths: true
        });
    });
</script>
...
```

You can see the result in Figure 21-13. The dates from the other months cannot be selected unless selectOtherMonths is set to true.

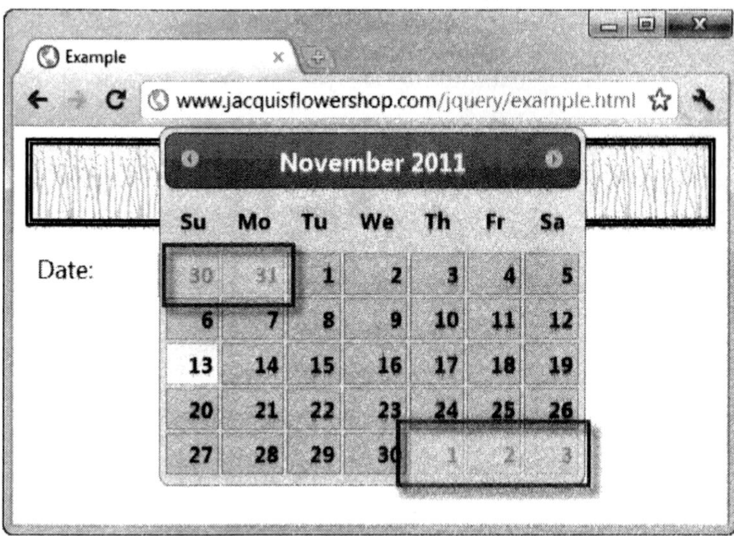

Figure 21-13. Showing dates from previous and subsequent months

Using the Button Bar

When `true`, the `showButtonBar` setting enables a button bar at the bottom of the datepicker window. When using a pop-up datepicker, the button bar contains Today and Done buttons. The Today button jumps back to the current date, and the Done button dismisses the pop-up. You can see the buttons Figure 21-14. When part of an inline datepicker, only the Today button is shown.

■ **Tip** You can change the text used for the Today and Done buttons using the `currentText` and `closeText` settings.

Figure 21-14. Showing the button bar

When true, the gotoCurrent setting will return the datepicker to the currently selected date rather than today's date. This is useful when you have configured the datepicker with the defaultDate setting. It doesn't always make sense to return to the current date if the purpose of the date selection is related to historical or future events. Listing 21-16 contains an example.

Listing 21-16. Using the gotoCurrent Setting

```
...
<script type="text/javascript">
    $(document).ready(function() {
        $('#datep').datepicker({
            showButtonPanel: true,
            gotoCurrent: true,
            defaultDate: "+1m +1y"
        }).val("12/25/2012");
    });
</script>
...
```

Note that the gotoCurrent setting causes the button to go to the selected date. In this example, this will be taken from the value attribute of the input element, but if the user selects another date and later opens the datepicker again, the button will return to the date the user selected, rather than the dates you specified.

Providing a Format Hint to the User

You can use the appendText setting to provide the user with a hint about the date format that you are expecting. Listing 21-17 provides a demonstration.

Listing 21-17. Using the appendText Setting to Provide a Format Hint

```
...
<script type="text/javascript">
    $(document).ready(function() {
        $('#datep').datepicker({
            appendText: '(mm/dd/yyyy)'
        });
    });
</script>
...
```

The datepicker inserts the text you specify into the document, as shown in Figure 21-15.

Figure 21-15. Using the appendText setting to provide a format hint to the user

This setting is most useful when you rely on a button to make the pop-up datepicker appear. When the user is free to enter the text without the datepicker, then the hint you give them about the format can significantly reduce the errors you have to deal with (which is good for you and less frustrating for the user).

Recently, I have started using the HTML5 placeholder attribute for input elements as a neater alternative to the datepicker appendTo setting. Listing 21-18 provides a demonstration.

Listing 21-18. Providing a Formatting Hint Using the HTML5 Placeholder Attribute

```
...
<script type="text/javascript">
    $(document).ready(function() {
        $('#datep').attr("placeholder", "mm/dd/yyyy").datepicker();
    });
</script>
...
```

Obviously, this requires the user to have an HTML5 browser, but the effect is more elegant. The user is presented with the format hint in grayed-out text that disappears as soon as they start typing. I prefer this because it is more closely associated the formatting hint with the input element, and it doesn't require space in the document layout. You can see how the placeholder is displayed in Google Chrome in Figure 21-16.

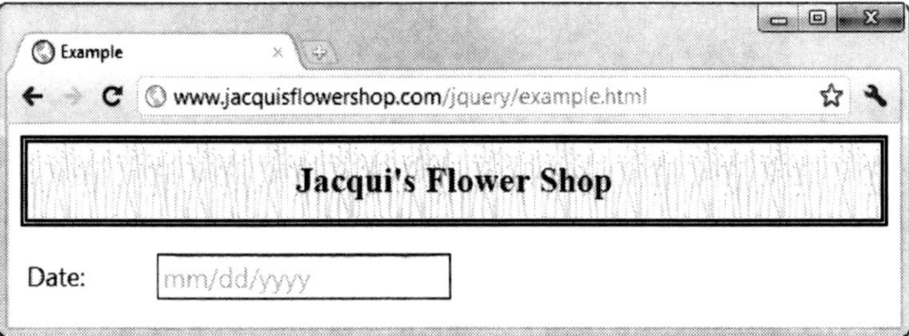

Figure 21-16. Using an HTML5 placeholder as a formatting hint

Using the Datepicker Methods

The datepicker widget supports the methods that are shown in Table 21-6.

***Table 21-6.** Accordion Methods*

Method	Description
`datepicker("destroy")`	Removes the datepicker from the underlying element
`datepicker("disable")`	Disables the datepicker
`datepicker("enable")`	Enables the datepicker
`datepicker("option")`	Sets one or more options for the datepicker
`datepicker("isDisabled")`	Returns `true` if the datepicker is disabled
`datepicker("hide")`	Hides a pop-up datepicker
`datepicker("show")`	Shows a pop-up datepicker
`datepicker("refresh")`	Refreshes a datepicker to reflects changes in the underlying element
`datepicker("getDate")`	Gets the selected date from the datepicker
`datepicker("setDate", date)`	Sets the selected date for the datepicker

Getting and Setting the Date Programmatically

I find that the getDate and setDate methods most useful when I am using multiple inline date pickers to allow the user to select a date range. In this situation, I don't want to display the selected dates in input elements. I want to display just the number of days between the first and second dates. Listing 21-19 provides a demonstration.

Listing 21-19. Using Two Datepickers to Select a Date Range

```
<!DOCTYPE html>
<html>
<head>
    <title>Example</title>
    <script src="jquery-1.7.js" type="text/javascript"></script>
    <script src="jquery-ui-1.8.16.custom.js" type="text/javascript"></script>
    <link rel="stylesheet" type="text/css" href="styles.css"/>
    <link rel="stylesheet" type="text/css" href="jquery-ui-1.8.16.custom.css"/>
    <style type="text/css">
        input {width: 200px; text-align: left; margin-right: 10px}
        #wrapper > * {float: left}
        #result {margin: auto; padding: 10px; width: 200px; clear: left}
    </style>
    <script type="text/javascript">
        $(document).ready(function() {

            $('#result').hide();

            $('#dateStart, #dateEnd').datepicker({
                minDate: "-7d",
                maxDate: "+7d",
                onSelect: function(date, datepicker) {
                    if (datepicker.id == "dateStart") {
                        $('#dateEnd').datepicker("setDate", date)
                            .datepicker("enable").datepicker("option", "minDate", date)
                    }

                    if (!$('#dateEnd').datepicker("isDisabled")) {
                        var startDate = $('#dateStart').datepicker("getDate");
                        var endDate = $('#dateEnd').datepicker("getDate");
                        var diff = endDate.getDate() - startDate.getDate();
                        $('#dayCount').text(diff).parent().show();
                    }
                }

            }).filter("#dateEnd").datepicker("disable");
        });
    </script>
</head>
<body>
    <h1>Jacqui's Flower Shop</h1>
    <form method="post" action="http://node.jacquisflowershop.com/order">
```

```
        <div id="wrapper" class="ui-widget">
          <label for="dateStart">Start: </label><span id="dateStart"></span>
          <label for="dateEnd">End: </label><span id="dateEnd"></span>
        </div>
        <div id="result" class="ui-widget">
          Number of Days: <span id="dayCount"></span>
        </div>
    </form>
</body>
</html>
```

There are two datepickers in this example, the second of which is disabled when the document is first loaded. I use the onSelect event (which I explain later in this chapter) to respond to the user making date selections. When the user makes a selection in the first datepicker, I use the setDate method to prepare the second datepicker and the getDate method to get the dates from both datepicker in order to work out the number of days between the first and second selected dates (to keep this example simple, I have done a simple comparison that assumes that both dates are in the same month). You can see how this document is displayed in the browser in Figure 21-17.

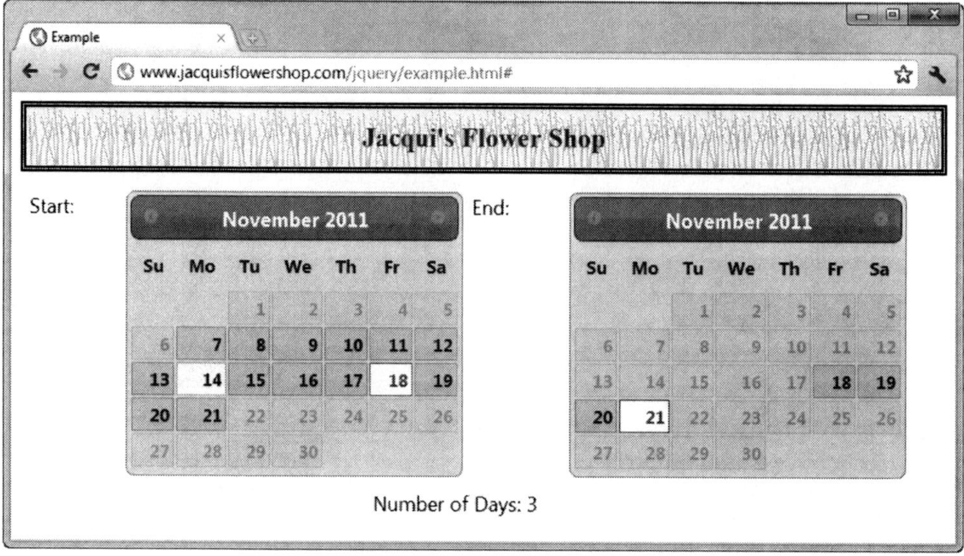

Figure 21-17. Using the getDate and setDate methods

Showing and Hiding Pop-up Datepickers Programmatically

You can use the show and hide methods to programmatically control the presence of a pop-up datepicker on the screen. This can be useful if you want to associate the datepicker with something other than the focus of the input element or the button that the datepicker widget creates. I am not much of a fan of letting the datepicker create a button in the document, so I occasionally find myself using these methods to control the datepicker from a button I have added myself, as demonstrated in Listing 21-20.

Listing 21-20. Using the Show and Hide Methods

```
<!DOCTYPE html>
<html>
<head>
    <title>Example</title>
    <script src="jquery-1.7.js" type="text/javascript"></script>
    <script src="jquery-ui-1.8.16.custom.js" type="text/javascript"></script>
    <link rel="stylesheet" type="text/css" href="styles.css"/>
    <link rel="stylesheet" type="text/css" href="jquery-ui-1.8.16.custom.css"/>
    <style type="text/css">
        input {width: 200px; text-align: left; margin-right: 10px}
        #wrapper > * {float: left}
        label {padding: 4px; text-align: right; width: auto}
    </style>
    <script type="text/javascript">
        $(document).ready(function() {

            $('#datep').datepicker();

            $('button').click(function(e) {
                e.preventDefault();
                $('#datep').datepicker("show");
                setTimeout(function() {
                    $('#datep').datepicker("hide");
                }, 5000)
            })

        });
    </script>
</head>
<body>
    <h1>Jacqui's Flower Shop</h1>
    <form method="post" action="http://node.jacquisflowershop.com/order">
      <div id="wrapper" class="ui-widget">
        <label for="datep">Date: </label><input id="datep"/><span id="inline"></span>
        <button>Datepicker</button>
      </div>
    </form>
</body>
</html>
```

I call the datepicker show method when the button is clicked. I don't often use the hide method because I want the user to be able to dismiss the pop-up when they have made a selection, but for completeness, I have used the setTimeout function so that the pop-up is programmatically dismissed five seconds after the button has been pressed.

Using the Datepicker Events

Like all jQuery UI widgets, the datepicker supports a set of events that allow you to receive notifications of important changes. These events are described in Table 21-7.

Table 21-7. Datepicker Events

Event	Description
create	Triggered when the datepicker is created
onChangeMonthYear	Triggered when the user moves to a different month or year
onClose	Triggered when a pop-up datepicker is closed
onSelect	Triggered when the user selects a date

I am not going to demonstrate the onSelect method again because I have already used it in a couple of examples, including the one in the previous section. I do want to mention that the arguments passed to the handler function for this event are a string representation of the selected date and the datepicker that has triggered the event.

Responding to a Month or Year Change

The onChangeMonthYear event allows you to respond when the user selects a new month or year, either from the drop-down menus enabled by the changeMonth and changeYear settings or through the previous and next buttons. Listing 21-21 shows how you can use this event to keep two datepickers consistent.

Listing 21-21. Using the onChangeMonthYear Event

```
<!DOCTYPE html>
<html>
<head>
    <title>Example</title>
    <script src="jquery-1.7.js" type="text/javascript"></script>
    <script src="jquery-ui-1.8.16.custom.js" type="text/javascript"></script>
    <link rel="stylesheet" type="text/css" href="styles.css"/>
    <link rel="stylesheet" type="text/css" href="jquery-ui-1.8.16.custom.css"/>
    <style type="text/css">
        input {width: 200px; text-align: left; margin-right: 10px}
        #wrapper > * {float: left}
    </style>
    <script type="text/javascript">
        $(document).ready(function() {

            $('#dateStart, #dateEnd').datepicker({
                onSelect: function(date, datepicker) {
                    if (datepicker.id == "dateStart") {
                        $('#dateEnd').datepicker("setDate", date)
```

```
                    }
                },
                onChangeMonthYear: function(year, month, datepicker) {
                    if (datepicker.id == "dateStart") {
                        var newDate = new Date();
                        newDate.setMonth(month -1);
                        newDate.setYear(year);
                        $('#dateEnd').datepicker("setDate", newDate);
                    }
                }
            })
        });
    </script>
</head>
<body>
    <h1>Jacqui's Flower Shop</h1>
    <form method="post" action="http://node.jacquisflowershop.com/order">
      <div id="wrapper" class="ui-widget">
        <label for="dateStart">Start: </label><span id="dateStart"></span>
        <label for="dateEnd">End: </label><span id="dateEnd"></span>
      </div>
    </form>
</body>
</html>
```

The three arguments to the function for this event are the displayed year, the displayed month, and the datepicker that triggered the event. The this variable is set to the input element for pop-up datepickers. When the user navigates to a new month or year on the first datepicker, I set the date on the second datepicker to keep them in sync.

Notice that the datepicker widget represents January as month 1 while the JavaScript Date object uses 0. This is why I have to make an ugly adjustment like this:

```
newDate.setMonth(month -1);
```

when I am creating the date I want displayed in the second datepicker.

Responding to the Pop-up Closing

You can use the onClose method to respond to the pop-up datepicker being closed. This event is triggered even when the user has not made a date selection. The arguments to the handler function are a string representation of the date (or the empty string if the user dismissed the datepicker without making a selection) and the datepicker that triggered the event. Listing 21-22 shows a simple response to this event.

Listing 21-22. Using the onClose Event

```
<!DOCTYPE html>
<html>
<head>
    <title>Example</title>
    <script src="jquery-1.7.js" type="text/javascript"></script>
    <script src="jquery-ui-1.8.16.custom.js" type="text/javascript"></script>
```

```
    <link rel="stylesheet" type="text/css" href="styles.css"/>
    <link rel="stylesheet" type="text/css" href="jquery-ui-1.8.16.custom.css"/>
    <style type="text/css">
        input {width: 200px; text-align: left; margin-right: 10px}
        #wrapper > * {float: left}
    </style>
    <script type="text/javascript">
        $(document).ready(function() {
            $('#datep').datepicker({
                onClose: function(date, datepicker) {
                    if (date != "") {
                        alert("Selected: " + date);
                    }
                }
            });
        });
    </script>
</head>
<body>
    <h1>Jacqui's Flower Shop</h1>
    <form method="post" action="http://node.jacquisflowershop.com/order">
      <div id="wrapper" class="ui-widget">
        <label for="datep">Date: </label><input id="datep"/>
      </div>
    </form>
</body>
</html>
```

In this example, I display an alert box to the user displaying the selection, if one has been made. I must admit that I have never found myself using this event in a real project; the onSelect event is the one that I find most useful.

Localizing Date Selection

The jQuery UI datepicker has some very comprehensive support for the different date formats that are used around the world. jQuery UI supports 61 localizations. To use them, you need to import an additional JavaScript script into your document and tell the datepicker which locale you want to use. Listing 21-23 provides an example.

Listing 21-23. Using the Localized Datepicker

```
<!DOCTYPE html>
<html>
<head>
    <title>Example</title>
    <script src="jquery-1.7.js" type="text/javascript"></script>
    <script src="jquery-ui-1.8.16.custom.js" type="text/javascript"></script>
    <script src="jquery-ui-i18n.js" type="text/javascript"></script>
    <link rel="stylesheet" type="text/css" href="styles.css"/>
    <link rel="stylesheet" type="text/css" href="jquery-ui-1.8.16.custom.css"/>
    <style type="text/css">
```

```
        input {width: 200px; text-align: left; margin-right: 10px}
        #wrapper > * {float: left}
    </style>
    <script type="text/javascript">
        $(document).ready(function() {
            $('#inline').datepicker($.datepicker.regional["es"]);
        });
    </script>
</head>
<body>
    <h1>Jacqui's Flower Shop</h1>
    <form method="post" action="http://node.jacquisflowershop.com/order">
      <div id="wrapper" class="ui-widget">
        <label for="datep">Date: </label><input id="datep"/><span id="inline"></span>
      </div>
    </form>
</body>
</html>
```

The `jquery-ui-i18n.js` file can be found in the `development-bundle/ui/i18n` folder of the customized jQuery UI download you created in Chapter 17. Copy this file into place alongside the main jQuery and jQuery UI script files and add the following to your document:

```
<script src="jquery-ui-i18n.js" type="text/javascript"></script>
```

You can specify the locale to use for the datepicker when you create it, as follows:

```
$('#inline').datepicker($.datepicker.regional["es"]);
```

This is a messy syntax, but it allows you to specify the localized formats you want. In this example, I have specified `es`, which means that I will be using the Spanish date formats. You can see the result in Figure 21-18.

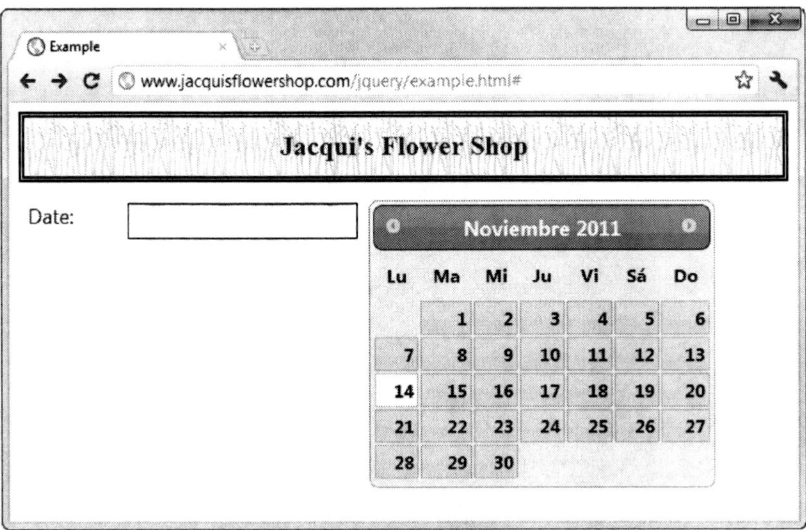

Figure 21-18. Localizing the date display

■ **Tip** You can create custom localizations if you need date conventions that are not currently supported by jQuery UI. See `http://docs.jquery.com/UI/Datepicker/Localization` for details.

My advice for localization is that it should be done properly or not at all. This means going far beyond just date formats and presenting the user with an interface that fully follows language, address, gender, currency, time, and every other local convention. Users find it jarring if you localize only part of a web application or following conventions inconsistently. To properly localize an application, you should hire an individual or a company that specializes in such work. There are so many ways to go wrong that you are doomed to fail without professional support.

If you find yourself trying to localize an application using Google Translate (which is not uncommon), then I recommend you just deliver the application using U.S. English and U.S. localization conventions. This limits your customer base to those who are familiar with U.S. variants on spelling, dates, currency, and so on, but at least you will avoid the train wreck that almost always arises when ad hoc localization is attempted.

Summary

In this chapter, I showed you the workings of the jQuery UI datepicker widget, which you can use to assist the user select dates. The datepicker is a very flexible widget that allows you to tailor the way that date selections are made and the appearance of the datepicker. My own experience with datepickers is that they are invaluable for reducing the number of formatting problems I have to deal with when requesting date information from users.

CHAPTER 22

Using the Dialog Widget

The jQuery UI dialog widget creates a floating window with a title and content area, similar to the kind of dialog you might see from a native application. Dialogs are useful for focusing the user's attention on an important event or message. However, as with any element that can obscure the document content, the dialog must be used sparingly and only when displaying the content inside the document layout isn't feasible. Table 22-1 provides the summary for this chapter.

Table 22-1. *Chapter Summary*

Problem	Solution	Listing
Create a jQuery UI dialog.	Select a `div` element with a `title` attribute and call the `dialog` method.	1
Prevent a dialog from being displayed as soon as it is created.	Set the `autoOpen` setting to `false`.	2
Prevent the user from resizing a dialog.	Set the `resizable` setting to `false`.	3
Change the initial position of a dialog.	Use the `position` setting.	4
Add one or more buttons to a dialog.	Use the `buttons` setting.	5
Prevent the user from dragging a dialog or moving it to the dialog stack.	Use the `draggable` and `stack` settings.	6
Create a model dialog.	Set the `modal` setting to `true`.	7, 8
Programmatically open and close a dialog.	Use the `open`, `close`, and `isOpen` methods.	9
Prevent a dialog from closing.	Return `false` in the handler function for the `beforeClose` event.	10
Respond to the user moving or changing the size of a dialog.	Respond to the `dragStart`, `dragStop`, `drag`, `resizeStart`, `resizeStop`, and `resize` events.	11

Creating the Dialog

You create a dialog box by using jQuery to select a div element and then calling the dialog method. The dialog widget is one that requires a specific structure of HTML elements in order to operate, although the structure is much simpler than the tabs widget requires, for example. Listing 22-1 shows a document that contains the required elements and a script that creates a dialog box.

Listing 22-1. Creating a Dialog Box Using jQuery UI

```
<!DOCTYPE html>
<html>
<head>
    <title>Example</title>
    <script src="jquery-1.7.js" type="text/javascript"></script>
    <script src="jquery-ui-1.8.16.custom.js" type="text/javascript"></script>
    <link rel="stylesheet" type="text/css" href="styles.css"/>
    <link rel="stylesheet" type="text/css" href="jquery-ui-1.8.16.custom.css"/>
    <script type="text/javascript">
        $(document).ready(function() {
            $('#dialog').dialog();
        });
    </script>
</head>
<body>
    <h1>Jacqui's Flower Shop</h1>
    <div id="dialog" title="Dialog Box">
      This is the content that will be displayed in the dialog box. This <b>content</b>
      can be <em>styled</em>.
    </div>
</body>
</html>
```

The dialog widget requires a div element that has a title attribute. The value of this attribute will be used in the title bar of the dialog box. The content of the div element will be used as the content for the dialog box, and, as the example shows, this content can contain other elements. When you call the dialog method with no settings, as I have done in the listing, the dialog box appears immediately. You can see how the dialog is presented by the browser in Figure 22-1.

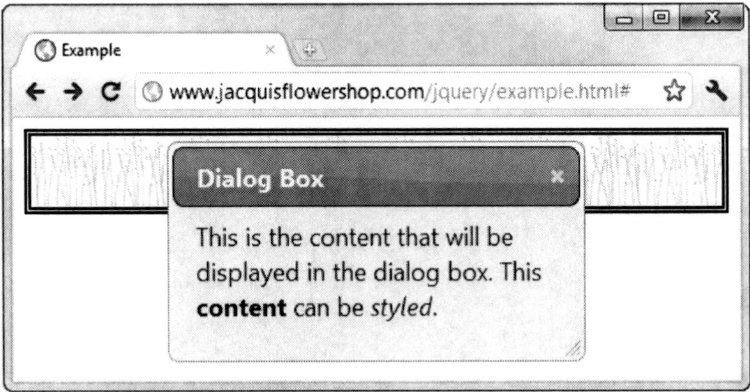

Figure 22-1. A simple dialog box

The dialog box is created through the clever use of HTML elements and is not created through the operating system. This means a jQuery UI dialog box doesn't behave in quite the same way as a native dialog box does. It doesn't show up when the user displays all of the open windows on the desktop, and it is possible to resize the browser window so that part (or all) of the jQuery UI dialog is obscured.

That being said, the jQuery UI team has done a pretty good job of making the dialog box as fully featured as possible. By clicking the title and dragging, the user can reposition the dialog within the browser window. The dialog can be resized using the drag handle as the bottom right of the window and dismissed by clicking the close button at the top right. And, since the jQuery UI dialog widget is constructed from HTML, it is styled using the jQuery UI theme you selected in Chapter 17, and it contains complex and styled HTML content.

I want to demonstrate a common usage of the dialog before I get into the details of the settings, methods, and events that the widget supports. When you call the `dialog` method with no arguments, the dialog widget appears immediately. This isn't usually that convenient. A more common scenario is that you want to create the dialog box when the document loads (so that the element structure isn't visible to the user) and then display the dialog box later in response to an event. Listing 22-2 shows how you can do this.

Listing 22-2. Deferring the Appearance of a jQuery UI Dialog Box

```
<!DOCTYPE html>
<html>
<head>
    <title>Example</title>
    <script src="jquery-1.7.js" type="text/javascript"></script>
    <script src="jquery-ui-1.8.16.custom.js" type="text/javascript"></script>
    <link rel="stylesheet" type="text/css" href="styles.css"/>
    <link rel="stylesheet" type="text/css" href="jquery-ui-1.8.16.custom.css"/>
    <script type="text/javascript">
        $(document).ready(function() {
            $('#dialog').dialog({
                autoOpen: false
            });

            $('button').button().click(function(e) {
```

```
                $('#dialog').dialog("open")
            })
        });
    </script>
</head>
<body>
    <h1>Jacqui's Flower Shop</h1>
    <div id="dialog" title="Dialog Box">
      This is the content that will be displayed in the dialog box. This <b>content</b>
      can be <em>styled</em>.
    </div>
    <button>Show Dialog</button>
</body>
</html>
```

You use the autoOpen setting to prevent the dialog from appearing immediately. When this setting is false, the HTML element structure is hidden from the user, but the dialog isn't displayed. When you are ready to display the dialog, you can call the open method. You can see how this works in Figure 22-2.

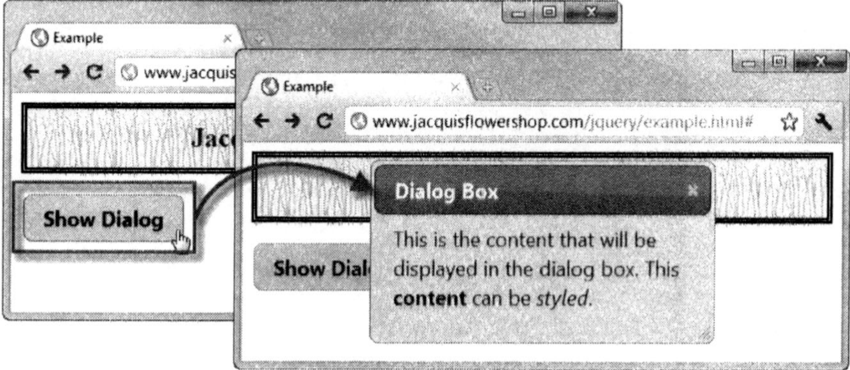

Figure 22-2. Deferring the appearance of a dialog box

Configuring the Dialog

The dialog widget supports a range of settings that allow you to customize the way that the dialog is presented to the user. I showed you the autoOpen setting in the previous section, but there many more, as described in Table 22-2.

***Table 22-2.** Dialog Settings*

Setting	Description
autoOpen	When true, the dialog is displayed as soon as it is created with the dialog method. The default is true.
buttons	Specifies the set of buttons to add to the dialog and the functions that will be invoked when those buttons are clicked. The default is to use no buttons.

closeOnEscape	When true, pressing the Escape key dismisses the dialog. The default is true.
draggable	When true, the user can click the dialog title and drag to move the dialog within the browser. The default is true.
height	Specifies the initial height of the dialog in pixels. The default is auto, which allows the dialog to size itself.
hide	Specifies the animation effect that is used to hide the dialog. See Chapter 34 for details of the jQuery UI effects.
maxHeight	Specifies the maximum height (in pixels) of the dialog. The default is false, which means that there is no size limit.
maxWidth	Specifies the maximum width (in pixels) of the dialog. The default is false, which means that there is no size limit.
minHeight	Specifies the minimum height (in pixels) of the dialog. The default is false, which means that there is no minimum size limit.
minWidth	Specifies the minimum width (in pixels) of the dialog. The default is false, which means that there is no minimum size limit.
modal	When true, the dialog is modal and the user cannot interact with the document until the dialog is dismissed. The default is false.
position	Specifies the initial position of the dialog. The default is center.
resizeable	When true, the dialog is displayed with a drag handle that allows the user to resize the dialog. The default is true.
show	Specifies the animation effect that is used to show the dialog. See Chapter 34 for details of the jQuery UI effects.
stack	When true, clicking a dialog brings it to the front of the screen. The default is true.
title	Specifies the title of the dialog.
width	Specifies the initial width of the dialog in pixels. The default is auto, which allows the dialog to size itself.

Configuring the Basic Dialog Appearance

The title setting allows you to create a dialog from a div element that doesn't have a title attribute. This can be useful if you are unable to control the generation of the elements that you want to use in the dialog. Listing 22-3 shows the application of the title setting.

Listing 22-3. Using the title Setting

```
<!DOCTYPE html>
<html>
<head>
    <title>Example</title>
    <script src="jquery-1.7.js" type="text/javascript"></script>
    <script src="jquery-ui-1.8.16.custom.js" type="text/javascript"></script>
    <link rel="stylesheet" type="text/css" href="styles.css"/>
    <link rel="stylesheet" type="text/css" href="jquery-ui-1.8.16.custom.css"/>
    <script type="text/javascript">
        $(document).ready(function() {
            $('#dialog').dialog({
                title: "Hello",
                resizable: false
            });
        });
    </script>
</head>
<body>
    <h1>Jacqui's Flower Shop</h1>
    <div id="dialog">
      This is the content that will be displayed in the dialog box. This <b>content</b>
      can be <em>styled</em>.
    </div>
</body>
</html>
```

I have also applied the resizable setting in this example. This setting controls the presence of the drag handle at the bottom right of the dialog. I prefer the cleaner appearance of a dialog without the drag handle, but I usually leave the resizable setting set to true because I like to leave the user with the opportunity to resize the dialog to accommodate the content. You can see how the browser shows the dialog in the example in Figure 22-3.

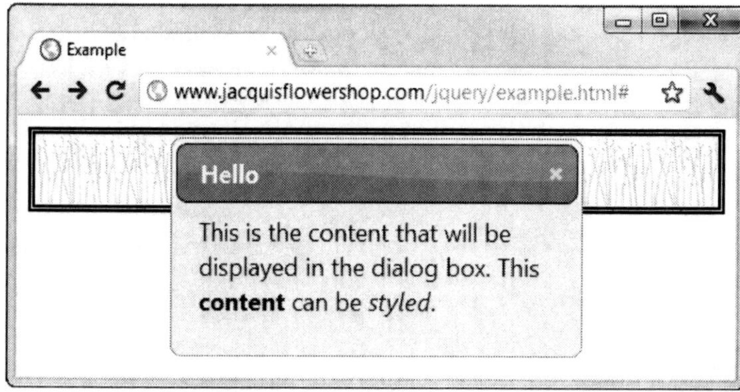

Figure 22-3. A dialog box with a custom title and no resize drag handle

Setting the Location of the Dialog

The `position` setting allows you to specify where the dialog will be displayed in the browser window. You can express the position using three different types of value, as described in Table 22-3.

Table 22-3. *Values for the position Setting*

Value	Description
`string`	A single string value, one of `center`, `left`, `right`, `top`, `bottom`
`[number, number]`	An two-element array, containing x, y coordinates from the top left of the window, e.g., `[10, 20]`
`[string, string]`	A two-element array, containing x, y position strings from the earlier list, e.g., `['left', 'top']`

The default position for a dialog is `center`. I find that this is generally the best position, but Listing 22-4 shows a dialog that is positioned using an array of string values.

Listing 22-4. Positioning the Dialog

```
...
<script type="text/javascript">
    $(document).ready(function() {
        $('#dialog').dialog({
            title: "Positioned Dialog",
            position: ["left", "top"]
        });
    });
</script>
...
```

Notice that the order of these string values requires that the x-position be specified first. This is counter to the way that you would typically describe the position in speech. I commonly reverse these values because in my head I want to position the dialog at the *top left* of the window, a position that must be specified as `[left, top]`. You can see how the dialog is positioned in Figure 22-4.

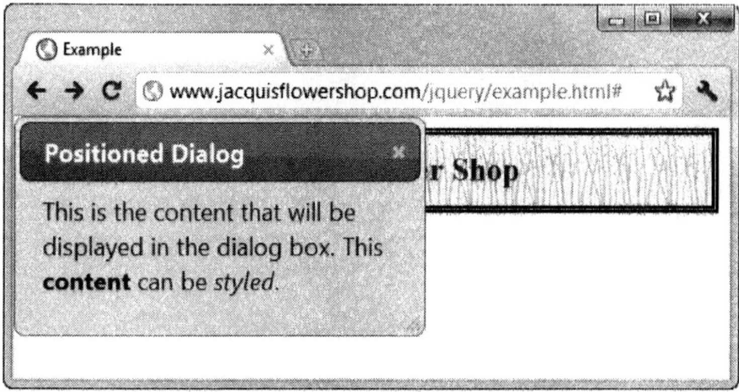

Figure 22-4. Specifying the position of the dialog

Adding Buttons to a Dialog

You can add buttons to a jQuery UI dialog using the `buttons` setting. The value of this setting is an array of objects, each of which has `text` and `click` properties. The value of the `text` property is used as the label for the button, and you provide a function as the value of `click` property, which will be invoked when the button is clicked. Listing 22-5 shows the use of this setting.

Listing 22-5. Adding Buttons to a Dialog

```
...
<script type="text/javascript">
    $(document).ready(function() {
        $('#dialog').dialog({
            title: "Dialog",
            buttons: [{text: "OK", click: function() {/* do something */}},
                      {text: "Cancel", click: function() {$(this).dialog("close")}}]

        });
    });
</script>
...
```

In this script, I have added two buttons. The function for the OK button doesn't do anything, but for the Cancel button, I close the dialog. Notice that I use the `this` variable in the jQuery selector within the `Cancel` function. This is set to the `div` element that was used to create the dialog. You can see how the buttons are displayed in Figure 22-5. This example uses the `close` method, which dismisses the dialog. I describe the dialog methods later in this chapter.

Figure 22-5. Adding buttons to a jQuery UI dialog

Dragging and Stacking Dialogs

The draggable setting determines whether the user can drag the dialog box within the browser window. This setting is true by default, and I recommend that you leave the setting unchanged. It allows the user to see the underlying content. This can be particularly important if you are showing a dialog to express some kind of error or problem. If the draggable setting is false, then the user won't be able to reposition the dialog box.

The draggable setting can also be important when you are using multiple dialogs in the same window. This is not something I recommend, but if you must display dialog boxes, you need to make sure the user can arrange them so that they can all be read. On small screens, they tend to pile up on top of each other. Another useful setting is stack, which brings a dialog to the front when it is clicked. This setting is also true by default. Listing 22-6 shows these settings in use.

Listing 22-6. Using the draggable and stack Settings

```
<!DOCTYPE html>
<html>
<head>
    <title>Example</title>
    <script src="jquery-1.7.js" type="text/javascript"></script>
    <script src="jquery-ui-1.8.16.custom.js" type="text/javascript"></script>
    <link rel="stylesheet" type="text/css" href="styles.css"/>
    <link rel="stylesheet" type="text/css" href="jquery-ui-1.8.16.custom.css"/>
<script type="text/javascript">
    $(document).ready(function() {
        $('.dialog').dialog({
            stack: true,
            draggable: true
        })
```

```
        $('#d1').dialog("option", "draggable", false);
        $('#d2').dialog("option", "stack", false);
    });
</script>
</head>
<body>
    <h1>Jacqui's Flower Shop</h1>
    <div id="d1" class="dialog" title="First Dialog">
      This is the first dialog
    </div>
    <div id="d2" class="dialog" title="Second Dialog">
      This is the second dialog
    </div>
    <div id="d3" class="dialog" title="Third Dialog">
      This is the third dialog
    </div>
</body>
</html>
```

I create three dialogs in this document. I disable the draggable setting for one of them and the stack setting for another. The result is shown in Figure 22-6, but you need to experiment with this example to really get a feel for how annoying the changes are.

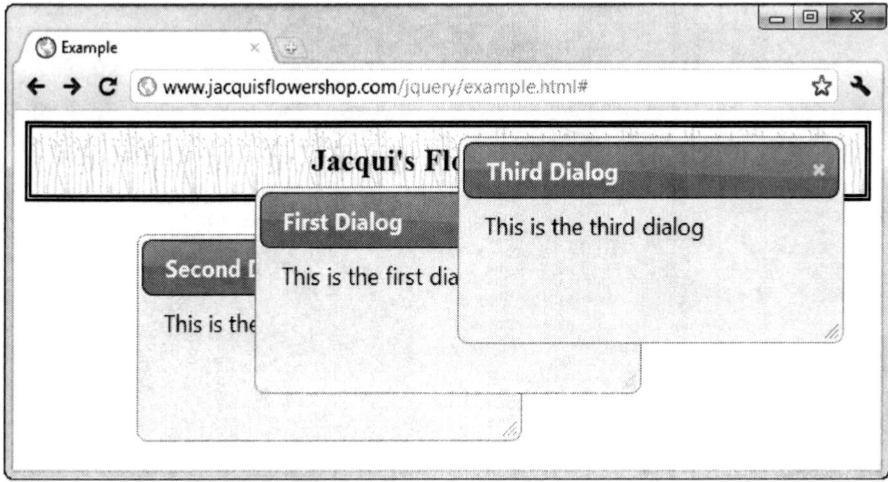

Figure 22-6. Disabling the draggable and stack settings

Creating Modal Dialogs

A modal dialog prevents the user from interacting with the elements in the document until the dialog has been dismissed. A value of true for the modal setting creates a modal dialog, as shown in Listing 22-7.

Listing 22-7. Creating a Modal Dialog

```
<!DOCTYPE html>
<html>
<head>
    <title>Example</title>
    <script src="jquery-1.7.js" type="text/javascript"></script>
    <script src="jquery-ui-1.8.16.custom.js" type="text/javascript"></script>
    <link rel="stylesheet" type="text/css" href="styles.css"/>
    <link rel="stylesheet" type="text/css" href="jquery-ui-1.8.16.custom.css"/>
    <script type="text/javascript">
        $(document).ready(function() {
            $('#dialog').dialog({
                buttons: [{text: "OK", click: function() {$(this).dialog("close")}}],
                modal: true,
                autoOpen: false
            })

            $('#show').button().click(function() {
                $('#dialog').dialog("open");
            })
        });
    </script>
</head>
<body>
    <h1>Jacqui's Flower Shop</h1>
    <div id="dialog" title="Modal Dialog">
      This is a modal dialog. Press OK to continue.
    </div>
    <button id="show">Show Dialog</button>
</body>
</html>
```

In this example, I have created a modal dialog that is not initially visible to the user. The dialog is shown in response to a button being clicked. You can see the effect in Figure 22-7. This example relies on the open and close methods, which show and dismiss the dialog. I explain all of the methods that the dialog widget supports later in this chapter.

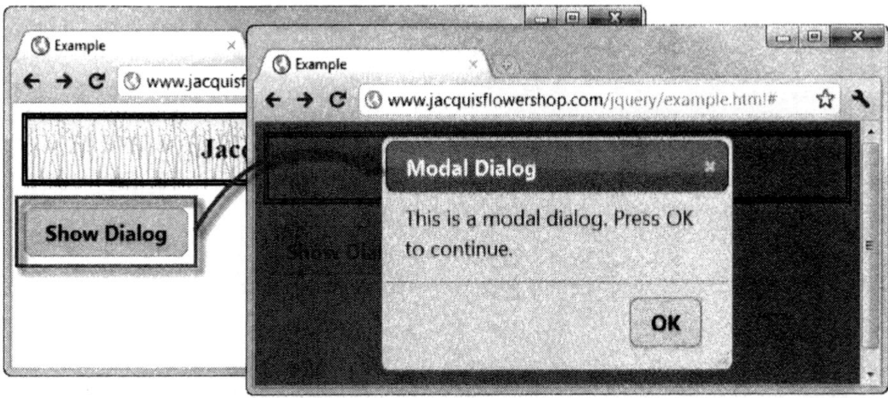

Figure 22-7. Displaying a modal dialog

When showing a modal dialog, jQuery UI places a dark layer behind the dialog but in front of the rest of the document. The document doesn't return to its original state until the dialog is dismissed. In this example, I have provided the user with an OK button that does this.

■ **Tip** When selecting the button you have added to the document to show the dialog, be careful not to use `$('button')` if you are also adding buttons to the dialog itself. This selector matches the buttons that you have added *and* those that are created by the `dialog` method, which means that the dialog buttons will end up with the same click handler as the button in the document, rather than the handlers specified by the `buttons` setting.

Showing a Form in a Modal Dialog

The benefit of a modal dialog is that it focuses the user's attention. You can use this to your advantage by displaying simple forms in modal dialogs, as shown in Listing 22-8.

Listing 22-8. Displaying a Form in a Model Dialog

```
<!DOCTYPE html>
<html>
<head>
    <title>Example</title>
    <script src="jquery-1.7.js" type="text/javascript"></script>
    <script src="jquery-ui-1.8.16.custom.js" type="text/javascript"></script>
    <script src="jquery.tmpl.js" type="text/javascript"></script>
    <link rel="stylesheet" type="text/css" href="styles.css"/>
    <link rel="stylesheet" type="text/css" href="jquery-ui-1.8.16.custom.css"/>
    <style type="text/css">
        #dialog input {width: 150px; margin: 5px; text-align: left}
        #dialog label {width: 100px}
```

```
        table {border-collapse: collapse; border: thin solid black; margin: 10px}
        #placeholder {text-align: center}
        #show {margin: 10px}
        td, th {padding: 5px; width: 100px}
    </style>
    <script type="text/javascript">
        $(document).ready(function() {
            $('#dialog').dialog({
                buttons: [{text: "OK", click: addDataToTable}],
                modal: true,
                autoOpen: false,
                width: 340
            })

            $('#show').button().click(function() {
                $('#dialog').dialog("open");
            })

            function addDataToTable() {
                var data = {
                    product: $('#product').val(),
                    color: $('#color').val(),
                    count: $('#count').val()
                }
                $('#placeholder').hide();
                $('#rowTmpl').tmpl(data).appendTo('#prods tbody');
                $('#dialog').dialog("close");
            }
        });
    </script>
    <script id="rowTmpl" type="text/x-jquery-tmpl">
        <tr><td>${product}</td><td>${color}</td><td>${count}</td></tr>
    </script>
</head>
<body>
    <h1>Jacqui's Flower Shop</h1>
    <div id="dialog" title="Enter Details" class="ui-widget">
        <div><label for="product">Product: </label><input id="product" /></div>
        <div><label for="color">Color: </label><input id="color" /></div>
        <div><label for="count">Quantity: </label><input id="count" /></div>
    </div>
    <table id="prods" class="ui-widget" border="1">
        <tr><th>Product</th><th>Color</th><th>Quantity</th></tr>
        <tr id="placeholder"><td colspan=3>No Products Selected</td></tr>
    </table>
    <button id="show">Add Product</button>
</body>
</html>
```

In this example, I have defined a simple set of input elements inside the div element that I use to create the modal dialog. When the user clicks the button in the document, the dialog is shown and gathers data from the user. When the user clicks the OK button (which I defined using the buttons setting), I collect the values from the input elements and use a data template to generate a new row for an HTML table. You can see the sequence in Figure 22-8.

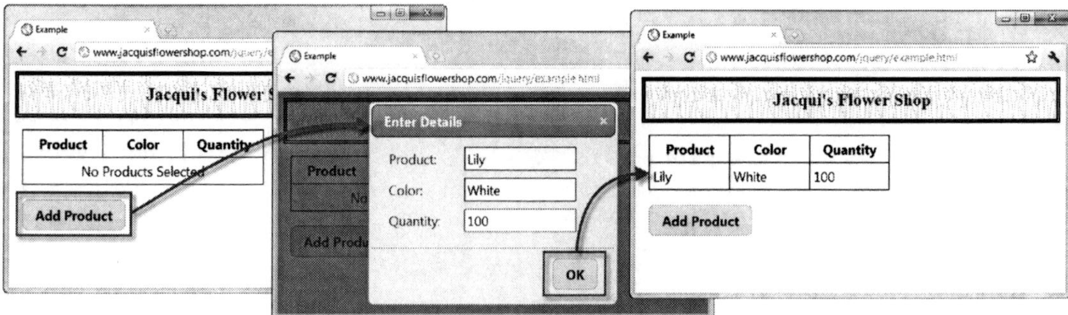

Figure 22-8. Using a modal dialog to capture input from the user

I have tried to keep this example simple, but you can readily apply the validation techniques I showed you in Chapter 13 to reduce the risk of data errors, and you can use the Ajax techniques I showed in Chapters 14 and 15 to submit the data entered by the user to a remote server.

Showing a form inside a modal dialog is a useful technique for simple forms only. You are at risk of confusing and annoying the user if you find yourself trying to combine tabs or accordions with a modal dialog. If a form represents a substantial effort to fill in, then it warrants being properly integrated into the document itself.

Using the Dialog Methods

The jQuery UI dialog widget supports the methods described in Table 22-4.

Table 22-4. *Dialog Methods*

Method	Description
`dialog("destroy")`	Removes the dialog widget from the underlying element
`dialog("disable")`	Disables the dialog
`dialog("enable")`	Enables the dialog
`dialog("option")`	Changes one or more settings
`dialog("close")`	Dismisses the dialog
`dialog("isOpen")`	Returns `true` if the dialog is visible
`dialog("moveToTop")`	Moves the dialog to the top of the stack
`dialog("open")`	Displays the dialog to the user

As you might expect, most of these methods allow you to manage a dialog programmatically. The methods that I find myself using most frequently are open and close, of course. Listing 22-9 shows the key methods in use.

Listing 22-9. Using the Dialog Methods

```
<!DOCTYPE html>
<html>
<head>
    <title>Example</title>
    <script src="jquery-1.7.js" type="text/javascript"></script>
    <script src="jquery-ui-1.8.16.custom.js" type="text/javascript"></script>
    <link rel="stylesheet" type="text/css" href="styles.css"/>
    <link rel="stylesheet" type="text/css" href="jquery-ui-1.8.16.custom.css"/>
    <script type="text/javascript">
        $(document).ready(function() {
            $('#d1, #d2').dialog({
                autoOpen: false,
                position: ["right", "top"]
            }).filter("#d2").dialog("option", "position", ["right", "bottom"])

            $('#t1, #t2').button().click(function (e) {
                var target = this.id == "t1" ? "#d1" : "#d2";
                if ($(target).dialog("isOpen")) {
                    $(target).dialog("close")
                } else {
                    $(target).dialog("open")
                }
            })
        });
    </script>
</head>
<body>
    <h1>Jacqui's Flower Shop</h1>
    <div id="d1" class="dialog" title="First Dialog" class="ui-widget">
        This is the first dialog
    </div>
    <div id="d2" class="dialog" title="Second Dialog" class="ui-widget">
        This is the second dialog
    </div>
    <div>
        <button id="t1">Toggle Dialog 1</button>
    </div>
    <button id="t2">Toggle Dialog 2</button>
</body>
</html>
```

This document includes two buttons that toggle the visibility of two dialogs. The visibility of each dialog is assessed using the isOpen method. Figure 22-9 shows the document displayed in the browser with both dialogs visible.

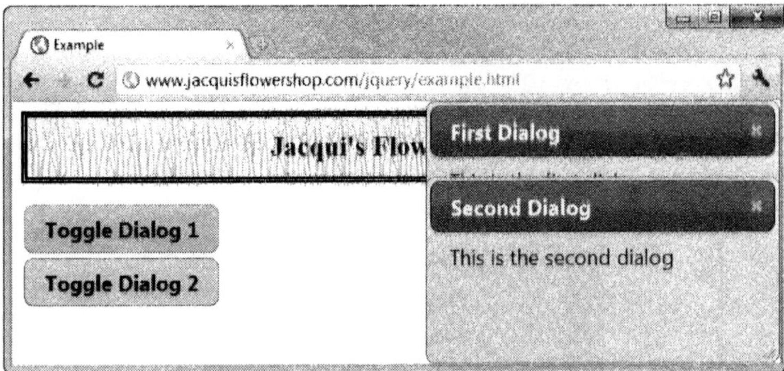

Figure 22-9. Toggling the visibility of dialogs using widget methods

Using the Dialog Events

The jQuery UI dialog widget supports the events described in Table 22-5. I describe some of the more useful events in the sections that follow.

***Table 22-5.** Dialog Events*

Event	Description
`create`	Triggered when the dialog widget is applied to an underlying HTML element.
`beforeClose`	Triggered when the dialog is about to close. Returning `false` from the handler function forces the dialog to remain open.
`open`	Triggered when the dialog is opened.
`focus`	Triggered when the dialog gains the focus.
`dragStart`	Triggered when the user starts to drag a dialog.
`drag`	Triggered for every mouse movement while a dialog is being dragged.
`dragStop`	Triggered when the user finishes dragging a dialog.
`resizeStart`	Triggered when the user beings resizing a dialog.
`resize`	Triggered for every mouse movement while a dialog is being resized.
`resizeStop`	Triggered when the user finishes resizing a dialog.
`close`	Triggered when a dialog is closed.

Keeping the Dialog Open

The beforeClose event allows you to receive notification that the user has requested that the dialog be closed. This can be because they have pressed the Escape key (if the closeOnEscape setting is true), clicked the close icon at the top-right of the dialog, or clicked a button you have added through the buttons setting.

Most of the time, you should respect the user's wishes and allow the dialog to close, but there are rare occasions when you require the user to perform some action using the dialog first or, as Listing 22-10 demonstrates, you require the dialog to be displayed for a certain period before allowing the user to continue.

Listing 22-10. Preventing a Dialog from Closing

```
<!DOCTYPE html>
<html>
<head>
    <title>Example</title>
    <script src="jquery-1.7.js" type="text/javascript"></script>
    <script src="jquery-ui-1.8.16.custom.js" type="text/javascript"></script>
    <link rel="stylesheet" type="text/css" href="styles.css"/>
    <link rel="stylesheet" type="text/css" href="jquery-ui-1.8.16.custom.css"/>
    <style type="text/css">
        input {width: 150px}
    </style>
    <script type="text/javascript">
        $(document).ready(function() {

            var canClose = false;
            var delay = 15;

            $('#dialog').dialog({
                modal: true,
                autoOpen: false,
                beforeClose: function() {
                    return canClose;
                },
                open: function() {
                    var count = delay;
                    var intID = setInterval(function() {
                        count--;
                        $('#time').text(count);
                        if (count == 0) {
                            clearInterval(intID)
                            canClose = true;
                            $('#dialog').dialog("close")
                        }
                    }, 1000)
                }
            })

            $('button').click(function(e) {
```

```
                $('#dialog').dialog("open")
            })

        });
    </script>
</head>
<body>
    <h1>Jacqui's Flower Shop</h1>

    <div class="ui-widget">
        <label for="user">Username: </label><input id="user"/>
        <label for="pass">Password: </label><input id="pass"/>
        <button id="send">Login</button>
    </div>
    <div id="dialog" title="Wrong Password">
        The password you entered was incorrect. Please try again in
        <span id="time">15</span> seconds.
    </div>
</body>
</html>
```

In this example, I have defined a par of `input` elements to collect a user name and password from the user. It doesn't matter what the user enters, however, because I respond to the `Login` button being clicked by displaying a Wrong Password modal dialog.

I respond to the open event by starting a repeating function that counts down from 15 seconds. During this period, I use the `beforeClose` event to prevent the user from closing the dialog. At the end of the 15 seconds, I call the close method and dismiss the dialog automatically. By combining the open and `beforeClose` events, I can ensure that the user immediately cannot try other user name or password combinations (well, at least not without reloading the HTML document, anyway).

Responding to Changing Sizes and Positions

The dialog widget provides a comprehensive set of events for tracking the dialog as it is resized or dragged. These are events that are usually not required but are handy to have in those rare situations where being able to track the changes becomes important. Listing 22-11 demonstrates using the `dragStart` and `dragStop` events to disable the `input` and `button` elements in a document while a dialog is being dragged.

Listing 22-11. Responding to a Dialog Being Dragged

```
<!DOCTYPE html>
<html>
<head>
    <title>Example</title>
    <script src="jquery-1.7.js" type="text/javascript"></script>
    <script src="jquery-ui-1.8.16.custom.js" type="text/javascript"></script>
    <link rel="stylesheet" type="text/css" href="styles.css"/>
    <link rel="stylesheet" type="text/css" href="jquery-ui-1.8.16.custom.css"/>
    <style type="text/css">
        input {width: 150px; text-align: left}
    </style>
```

```
    <script type="text/javascript">
        $(document).ready(function() {

            $('#dialog').dialog({
                autoOpen: true,
                dragStart: function() {
                    $('input, #send').attr("disabled", "disabled")
                },
                dragStop: function() {
                    $('input, #send').removeAttr("disabled")
                }
            })

            $('button').click(function(e) {
                $('#dialog').dialog("open")
            })
        });
    </script>
</head>
<body>
    <h1>Jacqui's Flower Shop</h1>

    <div class="ui-widget">
        <label for="user">Username: </label><input id="user"/>
        <label for="pass">Password: </label><input id="pass"/>
        <button id="send">Login</button>
    </div>
    <div id="dialog" title="Wrong Password">
        The password you entered was incorrect. Please try again in
        <span id="time">15</span> seconds.
    </div>
</body>
</html>
```

Summary

In this chapter, I showed you the jQuery UI dialog widget. Following the same format as the other widget chapters, I focused on the settings, methods, and events that the dialog widget supports. I showed you how to create modal and nonmodal dialogs, how to show and hide dialogs in response to events from other elements, and how to prevent a dialog from closing for a fixed period of time. I also showed you how you can use the dialog widget to present the user with simple forms, a technique that can create an elegant user experience when used appropriately.

CHAPTER 23

Using the Drag & Drop Interactions

In addition to the widgets I showed you in Chapters 18-22, jQuery UI also includes a set of *interactions.* These are lower-level building blocks that allow you to add functionality to your web application interface. In this chapter, I describe the *draggable* and *droppable* interactions, which you can use to add drag and drop to an HTML document.

The interactions follow the same basic structure as the widgets. They have settings, methods, and events. I will follow the same pattern in describing the interactions, but I'll be jumping around a little to accommodate the unique nature of some of the interactions.

It is hard to show the effect of applying the interactions using screenshots. They are, as the name suggests, dependent on interaction. I tried to give you the essence of what is happening, but to truly understand interactions you should experiment with them in the browser. All of the examples in this chapter (and every other chapter for that matter) are included in the free source code download that accompanies the book. If you want to avoid typing in the HTML and JavaScript, you can get everything you need at `www.apress.com`. Table 23-1 provides the summary for this chapter.

***Table 23-1.** Chapter Summary*

Problem	Solution	Listing
Apply the draggable interaction	Use the `draggable` method	1
Constrain the direction in which an element can be dragged	Use the `axis` setting	2
Limit the area in which the element can be dragged	Use the `containment` setting	3
Constrain dragging to the cells in a grid	Use the `grid` setting	4
Delay dragging for a period of time or for a number of pixels	Use the `delay` and `distance` settings	5
Respond to an element being dragged	Use the `start`, `drag`, and `stop` events	6
Apply the droppable interaction	Use the `droppable` method	7

Highlight a droppable element when an element is being dragged	Use the activate and deactivate events	8
Respond when a draggable element overlaps with a droppable element	Use the over and out events	9
Specify which draggable elements a droppable element will accept	Use the accept setting	10
Automatically apply CSS classes to a droppable element when dragging starts or overlaps	Use the activeClass and hoverClass settings	11
Changing the amount of overlap that will trigger the over event	Use the tolerance setting	12
Create groups of compatible draggable and droppable elements	Use the scope setting	13
Leave the draggable element in place during and after dragging	Use the helper setting	14, 15
Manipulate the helper element in response to a droppable event	Use the ui.helper property	16
Force the draggable element to snap to the edge of other elements	Use the snap, snapMode, and snapTolerance settings	17

Creating the Draggable Interaction

An element to which you apply the draggable interaction can be moved (dragged) around the browser window. The element appears in the initial document layout as normal, but the element's position changes if the user holds down the mouse button over the draggable element and then moves the mouse. Listing 23-1 provides a simple demonstration of the draggable interaction.

Listing 23-1. Using the draggable interaction

```
<!DOCTYPE html>
<html>
<head>
    <title>Example</title>
    <script src="jquery-1.7.js" type="text/javascript"></script>
    <script src="jquery-ui-1.8.16.custom.js" type="text/javascript"></script>
    <link rel="stylesheet" type="text/css" href="styles.css"/>
    <link rel="stylesheet" type="text/css" href="jquery-ui-1.8.16.custom.css"/>
    <style type="text/css">
        #draggable {font-size: x-large; border: thin solid black;
            width: 5em; text-align: center}
```

```
    </style>
    <script type="text/javascript">
        $(document).ready(function() {
            $('#draggable').draggable();
        });
    </script>
</head>
<body>
    <h1>Jacqui's Flower Shop</h1>
    <div id="draggable">
        Drag me
    </div>
</body>
</html>
```

In this example, I selected a div element and called the draggable method to create a draggable element. As Figure 23-1 shows, the element starts in its regular position but can be dragged anywhere in the browser window. Note that the other element in the document, the h1, is not affected by the draggable method.

Figure 23-1. Dragging an element around the browser window

■ **Tip** Being able to drag elements can be useful in its own right, but it becomes much more powerful when combined with the droppable interaction, which I describe in later in this chapter.

The draggable interaction is performed using some very clever HTML and CSS. This means that it works in pretty much any browser, but that draggable elements are not able to interact with the native drag and drop implemented by the user's operating system.

■ **Tip** HTML5 does include drag and drop that is usually implemented using the native mechanisms. I provide details and examples of the HTML5 mechanism in my book *The Definitive Guide to HTML5*, also published by Apress. If you are using the jQuery UI drag-and-drop mechanism, I recommend disabling the HTML5 equivalent to avoid confusion. To do this, set the `draggable` attribute to `false` on the `body` element in your document.

Configuring the Draggable Interaction

There are lots of ways you can configure the draggable interaction. Table 23-2 summarizes the most important settings available, which I demonstrate in the sections that follow.

■ **Tip** In the "Tuning Drag & Drop" section later in the chapter, I describe some additional settings that change the relationship between the draggable and droppable elements.

Table 23-2. *Draggable Settings*

Setting	Description
`axis`	Restricts the drag to a particular direction. The default is `false`, meaning no restriction, but you can also specify `x` (for the x-axis) and `y` (for the y-axis).
`containment`	Restricts the draggable element to a region of the screen. See Table 23-3 for details of the supported range of values. The default is `false`, meaning no restriction.
`delay`	Specifies a duration for which the user must drag the element before it moves. The default is `0`, meaning no delay.
`distance`	Specifies a distance that the user must drag the element from its initial position before it moves. The default is `1` pixel.
`grid`	Forces the draggable element to snap to a grid. The default is `false`, meaning no grid will be used.

Constraining the Drag Axis

There are several ways in which you can constrain the way an element can be dragged. The first is to use the axis setting, which allows you to limit dragging to either the x-axis or y-axis. Listing 23-2 provides an example.

Listing 23-2. Using the axis setting to constrain dragging

```
<!DOCTYPE html>
<html>
<head>
    <title>Example</title>
    <script src="jquery-1.7.js" type="text/javascript"></script>
    <script src="jquery-ui-1.8.16.custom.js" type="text/javascript"></script>
    <link rel="stylesheet" type="text/css" href="styles.css"/>
    <link rel="stylesheet" type="text/css" href="jquery-ui-1.8.16.custom.css"/>
    <style type="text/css">
        div.dragElement {font-size: large; border: thin solid black;
            width: 5em; text-align: center; background-color: lightgray; margin: 4px }
    </style>
    <script type="text/javascript">
        $(document).ready(function() {

            $('.dragElement').draggable({
                axis: "x"
            }).filter('#dragV').draggable("option", "axis", "y");

        });
    </script>
</head>
<body>
    <h1>Jacqui's Flower Shop</h1>
    <div id="dragV" class="dragElement">
        Drag Vertically
    </div>
    <div id="dragH" class="dragElement">
        Drag Horizontally
    </div>
</body>
</html>
```

In this example, I defined two `div` elements, selected them with jQuery, and called the `draggable` method. I use the settings object to define a value of `x` for both `div` elements initially, and then use the jQuery `filter` method to select the `dragV` element so that I can change the setting to `y` without having to make jQuery search the entire document again. The result is one `div` element that can be dragged only vertically and another that can be dragged only horizontally. You can see the effect in Figure 23-2.

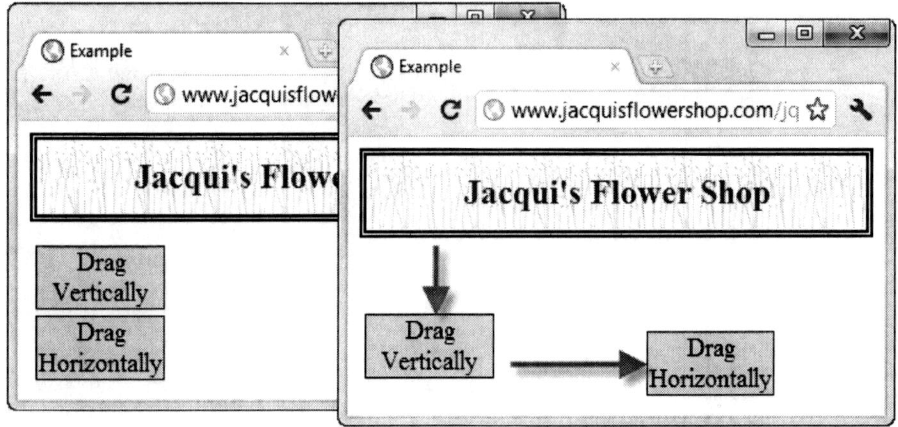

Figure 23-2. Constraining the direction in which an element can be dragged

Constraining the Drag Region

You can also limit the region of the screen in which an element can be dragged. You do this through the `containment` setting. This setting can be set using several value formats, as described in Table 23-3.

Table 23-3. *Values for the Containment Setting*

Value	Description
Selector	When you specify a selector string, the draggable element is constrained to the area occupied by the first matching element.
`HTMLElement`	The draggable element is constrained to the area occupied by the specified element.
`string`	You can specify the values `parent`, `document`, and `window` to restrict dragging.
Number Array	You can use a number array in the format `[x1, y1, x2, y2]` to restrict dragging to a region.

Listing 23-3 shows the use of the `containment` setting.

Listing 23-3. Using the containment setting

```
<!DOCTYPE html>
<html>
<head>
    <title>Example</title>
    <script src="jquery-1.7.js" type="text/javascript"></script>
    <script src="jquery-ui-1.8.16.custom.js" type="text/javascript"></script>
```

```
    <link rel="stylesheet" type="text/css" href="styles.css"/>
    <link rel="stylesheet" type="text/css" href="jquery-ui-1.8.16.custom.css"/>
    <style type="text/css">
        div.dragElement {font-size: large; border: thin solid black; padding: 4px;
            width: 5em; text-align: center; background-color: lightgray; margin: 4px }
        #container { border: medium double black; width: 400px; height: 150px}
    </style>
    <script type="text/javascript">
        $(document).ready(function() {

            $('.dragElement').draggable({
                containment: "parent"
            }).filter('#dragH').draggable("option", "axis", "x");

        });
    </script>
</head>
<body>
    <h1>Jacqui's Flower Shop</h1>
    <div id="container">
        <div id="dragH" class="dragElement">
            Drag Horizontally
        </div>
        <div class="dragElement">
            Drag within Parent
        </div>
    </div>
</body>
</html>
```

In this example, I constrained both div elements such that they can be dragged only within their parent element, which is a fixed-size div element. For one of the draggable div elements, I also applied the axis setting, meaning that it can be dragged only horizontally within the parent element. You can see the result in Figure 23-3.

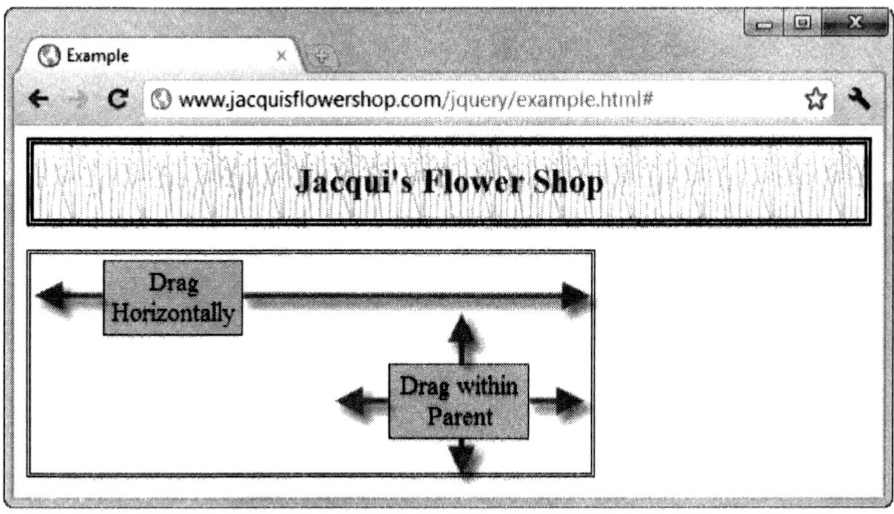

Figure 23-3. Restricting dragging to the parent element

Constraining Dragging to a Grid

The grid setting can be used to make a draggable element snap to a grid as it is dragged. The value for this setting is a two-element array specifying the width and the height of the grid in pixels. Listing 23-4 shows the grid setting in use.

Listing 23-4. Using the grid setting

```
<!DOCTYPE html>
<html>
<head>
    <title>Example</title>
    <script src="jquery-1.7.js" type="text/javascript"></script>
    <script src="jquery-ui-1.8.16.custom.js" type="text/javascript"></script>
    <link rel="stylesheet" type="text/css" href="styles.css"/>
    <link rel="stylesheet" type="text/css" href="jquery-ui-1.8.16.custom.css"/>
    <style type="text/css">
        #draggable {font-size: large; border: thin solid black; padding: 4px;
            width: 100px; text-align: center; background-color: lightgray; margin: 4px; }
    </style>
    <script type="text/javascript">
        $(document).ready(function() {
            $('#draggable').draggable({
                grid: [100, 50]
            })
        });
    </script>
</head>
<body>
```

```
    <h1>Jacqui's Flower Shop</h1>
    <div id="draggable">
        Drag Me
    </div>
</body>
</html>
```

In this example, I specified a grid in which the cells are 100 pixels wide and 50 pixels high. As you drag the element, it snaps from one (invisible) cell to the next, as shown in Figure 23-4.

Figure 23-4. Dragging an element with a grid

The snapping effect is hard to represent in a screenshot, and this is an example that particularly benefits from interaction.

■ **Tip** You can snap-to-grid in one direction only by specifying a value of 1 for the free-movement axis. For example, setting a value of `[100, 1]` forces the draggable element to snap to 100 pixel cells along the x-axis but allows free movement along the y-axis.

Delaying Dragging

There are two settings that allow you to delay the dragging action. You can use the `delay` setting to specify a time span so that the user has to drag the element for a number of milliseconds before the element starts to move. You can also use the `distance` setting, which makes the user make the drag motion for a certain number of pixels before the element begins to follow the mouse. Listing 23-5 shows both setting in use.

Listing 23-5. Using the delay and distance settings

```
<!DOCTYPE html>
<html>
<head>
    <title>Example</title>
    <script src="jquery-1.7.js" type="text/javascript"></script>
    <script src="jquery-ui-1.8.16.custom.js" type="text/javascript"></script>
    <link rel="stylesheet" type="text/css" href="styles.css"/>
    <link rel="stylesheet" type="text/css" href="jquery-ui-1.8.16.custom.css"/>
```

```
    <style type="text/css">
        #time, #distance {font-size: large; border: thin solid black; padding: 4px;
            width: 100px; text-align: center; background-color: lightgray; margin: 4px; }
    </style>
    <script type="text/javascript">
        $(document).ready(function() {
            $('#time').draggable({
                delay: 1000
            })

            $('#distance').draggable({
                distance: 150
            })
        });
    </script>
</head>
<body>
    <h1>Jacqui's Flower Shop</h1>
    <div id="time">Time Delay</div>
    <div id="distance">Distance</div>
</body>
</html>
```

I have two draggable div elements in this example, one of which I configured with the delay setting and the other with the distance setting.

When using the delay, the user has to continue dragging for the specified number of milliseconds before the element will begin to move. This is 1,000 milliseconds in the example. The user doesn't have to keep the mouse moving for this duration, but the mouse button has to be held down for the entire period and the mouse has to have been moved to start the dragging process. When the timespan has elapsed, the draggable element will snap to the location of the mouse pointer, subject to the grid, region, and axis constraints I showed you earlier.

The distance setting has a similar effect, but the user has to have moved the mouse pointer at least the specified number of pixels in any direction from the element's starting point. When the mouse has moved that far, the draggable element will snap to the current mouse location.

■ **Tip** If you apply both settings to a single element, the draggable element won't move until both conditions have been met—that is, the user has to have been dragging for the specified timespan *and* moved the mouse the specified number of pixels.

Using the Draggable Methods

The draggable interaction defines only the set of core methods you saw implemented by the widgets. There are no draggable-specific methods. Table 23-4 describes those that are available.

Table 23-4. Draggable Methods

Method	Description
`draggable("destroy")`	Removes the interaction from the element
`draggable("disable")`	Disables the draggable interaction
`draggable("enable")`	Enables the draggable interaction
`draggable("option")`	Changes one or more settings

Using the Draggable Events

The draggable interaction supports a simple set of events that notify you when an element is dragged. The events are described in Table 23-5.

Table 23-5. Draggable Events

Event	Description
`create`	Triggered when the draggable interaction is applied to an element
`start`	Triggered when dragging starts
`drag`	Triggered as the mouse moves during dragging
`stop`	Triggered when dragging stops

You respond to interaction events just as you do for widget events. Listing 23-6 demonstrates handling the `start` and `stop` events.

Listing 23-6. Using the draggable start and stop events

```
<!DOCTYPE html>
<html>
<head>
    <title>Example</title>
    <script src="jquery-1.7.js" type="text/javascript"></script>
    <script src="jquery-ui-1.8.16.custom.js" type="text/javascript"></script>
    <link rel="stylesheet" type="text/css" href="styles.css"/>
    <link rel="stylesheet" type="text/css" href="jquery-ui-1.8.16.custom.css"/>
    <style type="text/css">
        #draggable {font-size: large; border: thin solid black; padding: 4px;
            width: 100px; text-align: center; background-color: lightgray; margin: 4px; }
    </style>
    <script type="text/javascript">
```

```
        $(document).ready(function() {
            $('#draggable').draggable({
                start: function() {
                    $('#draggable').text("Dragging...")
                },
                stop: function() {
                    $('#draggable').text("Drag Me")
                }
            })
        });
    </script>
</head>
<body>
    <h1>Jacqui's Flower Shop</h1>
    <div id="draggable">
        Drag Me
    </div>
</body>
</html>
```

In this example, I use the `start` and `stop` events to change the contents of the element while it is being dragged. This is a benefit of the way that the draggable interaction (and all of the other jQuery UI interactions, for that matter) is implemented using HTML and CSS: you can use jQuery to modify the draggable element even when it is being moved around the screen. You can see the effect that this example creates in Figure 23-5.

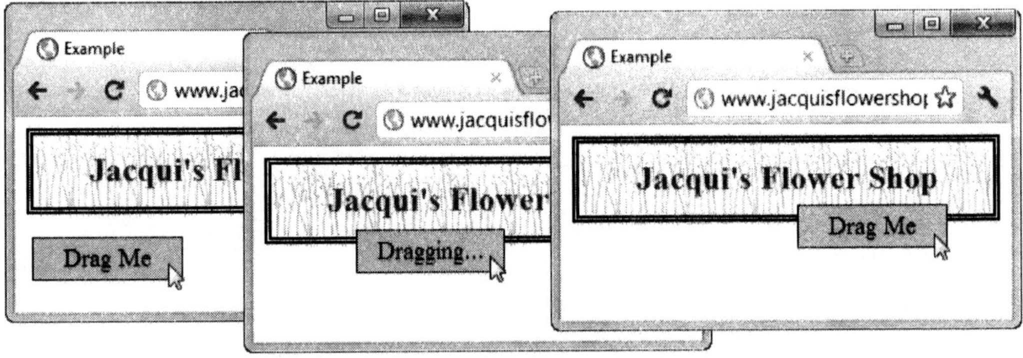

Figure 23-5. Using the draggable events to modify an element while it is being dragged

Using the Droppable Interaction

There are some occasions where just being able to drag an element can be useful, but the real utility of the draggable interaction arises when you combine it with the *droppable* interaction.

You create droppable elements using the `droppable` method, but to get any functionality, you need to provide handler functions for the events that the interaction defines. Table 23-6 describes the events that are available.

Table 23-6. Droppable Events

Event	Description
create	Triggered when the droppable interaction is applied
activate	Triggered when the user starts to drag a draggable element
deactivate	Triggered when the user stops dragging a draggable element
over	Triggered when the user drags a draggable element over the droppable element (but has not yet released the mouse button)
out	Triggered when the user drags a draggable element out of the droppable element
drop	Triggered when the user drops a draggable element on the droppable element

You can create a basic droppable element with just the drop event, as shown in Listing 23-7.

Listing 23-7. Creating a basic droppable interaction

```
<!DOCTYPE html>
<html>
<head>
    <title>Example</title>
    <script src="jquery-1.7.js" type="text/javascript"></script>
    <script src="jquery-ui-1.8.16.custom.js" type="text/javascript"></script>
    <link rel="stylesheet" type="text/css" href="styles.css"/>
    <link rel="stylesheet" type="text/css" href="jquery-ui-1.8.16.custom.css"/>
    <style type="text/css">
        #draggable, #droppable {font-size: large; border: thin solid black; padding: 4px;
            width: 100px; text-align: center; background-color: lightgray; margin: 4px;}
        #droppable {padding: 20px; position: absolute; right: 5px;}
    </style>
    <script type="text/javascript">
        $(document).ready(function() {
            $('#draggable').draggable();

            $('#droppable').droppable({
                drop: function() {
                    $('#draggable').text("Dropped")
                }
            });
        });
    </script>
</head>
<body>
    <h1>Jacqui's Flower Shop</h1>
    <div id="droppable">
```

```
            Drop Here
        </div>
        <div id="draggable">
            Drag Me
        </div>
</body>
</html>
```

I added a div element whose text content is Drop Here. I use jQuery to select this element and call the droppable method, passing in a settings object that defines a handler for the drop event. In response to this method, I change the text of the draggable element using the text method. This example creates the dullest possible drag-and-drop interaction, but it also provides a useful foundation to explain the way that the draggable and droppable interactions can be used together. You can see the different stages of the example in Figure 23-6.

Figure 23-6. Using simple drag and drop

This is pretty basic stuff. I drag the draggable element over the droppable element and let go. The draggable element stays where I left it, and its text content is changed in response to the drop event. In the sections that follow, I'll show you how to use the other droppable events to improve the experience.

Highlighting a Drop Target

You can use the activate and deactivate events to highlight the drop target when the user starts the drag motion. This is usually a very good idea, because it gives the user a clear signal which elements are part of the drag-and-drop model. Listing 23-8 provides an example.

Listing 23-8. Responding to the activate and deactivate events

```
...
<script type="text/javascript">
    $(document).ready(function() {
        $('#draggable').draggable();

        $('#droppable').droppable({
            drop: function() {
                $('#draggable').text("Dropped");
            },
            activate: function() {
                $('#droppable').css({
```

```
                    border: "medium double green",
                    backgroundColor: "lightGreen"
                });
            },
            deactivate: function() {
                $('#droppable').css("border", "").css("background-color", "");
            }
        });
    });
</script>
...
```

When the user starts dragging an element, my droppable element triggers the activate event and my handler function uses the `css` method to apply new values for the CSS `border` and `background-color` properties. This causes the drop target to light up, indicating to the user that the droppable element has a relationship to the element being dragged. I use the `deactivate` event to remove the CSS property values and return the droppable element to its original state when the user releases the mouse button. (This event is triggered whenever dragging stops, regardless of whether the user has dropped the draggable element on a droppable element.) You can see the effect in Figure 23-7.

Figure 23-7. Using the activate and deactivate events

Dealing with Overlapping Elements

You can refine your drag-and-drop technique by handling the `over` and `out` events. The `over` event is triggered when 50% of a draggable element is over any part of the droppable element. The `out` event is triggered when the elements no longer overlap. Listing 23-9 shows how you can respond to these events.

Listing 23-9. Using the over and out events

```
<script type="text/javascript">
    $(document).ready(function() {
        $('#draggable').draggable();

        $('#droppable').droppable({
            drop: function() {
                $('#draggable').text("Dropped");
            },
            over: function() {
```

```
                $('#droppable').css({
                    border: "medium double green",
                    backgroundColor: "lightGreen"
                });
            },
            out: function() {
                $('#droppable').css("border", "").css("background-color", "");
            }
        });
    });
</script>
```

I used the same event handler functions as in the previous example, but I associated them with the over and out events. The droppable element will show the border and background color when at least 50% of the draggable element overlaps with it, as shown in Figure 23-8.

■ **Tip** The 50% limit is known as the *tolerance*, and you can configure the droppable element with different tolerances, as I demonstrate in the "Changing the Overlap Tolerance" section later in this chapter.

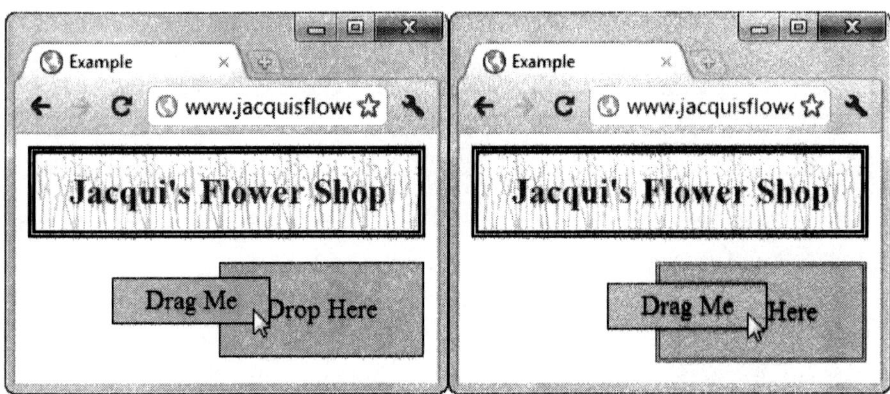

Figure 23-8. Responding to the over and out events

Configuring the Droppable Interaction

I broke away from the usual pattern in this part of the book because the events are so central to the droppable interaction. Of course, this interaction does have a number of settings you can use to change the way that it behaves, and these are described in Table 23-7.

■ **Tip** In the "Tuning Drag and Drop" section later in the chapter, I describe some additional settings that change the relationship between the draggable and droppable elements.

Table 23-7. Droppable Settings

Setting	Description
`disabled`	When `true`, the interaction is disabled initially. The default is `false`.
`accept`	Narrows the draggable elements that the droppable element will respond to. The default is *, which matches all elements.
`activeClass`	Specifies a class that will be applied in response to the `activate` event and removed in response to the `deactivate` event.
`hoverClass`	Specifies a class that will be applied in response to the over event and removed in response to the out event.
`tolerance`	Specifies the amount of overlap that has to occur before the on event is triggered.

Restricting Acceptable Draggable Elements

You can restrict the set of elements you are willing to receive with your droppable interaction by applying the accept setting. You use the `accept` setting by providing a selector as the value. This has the effect of triggering only the droppable events when a draggable element matches the selector. Listing 23-10 provides an example.

Listing 23-10. Restricting the acceptable elements

```
<!DOCTYPE html>
<html>
<head>
    <title>Example</title>
    <script src="jquery-1.7.js" type="text/javascript"></script>
    <script src="jquery-ui-1.8.16.custom.js" type="text/javascript"></script>
    <link rel="stylesheet" type="text/css" href="styles.css"/>
    <link rel="stylesheet" type="text/css" href="jquery-ui-1.8.16.custom.css"/>
    <style type="text/css">
        .draggable, #droppable {font-size: large; border: thin solid black; padding: 4px;
            width: 100px; text-align: center; background-color: lightgray; margin: 4px;}
        #droppable {padding: 20px; position: absolute; right: 5px;}
    </style>
    <script type="text/javascript">
        $(document).ready(function() {
            $('.draggable').draggable();
```

```
            $('#droppable').droppable({
                drop: function(event, ui) {
                    ui.draggable.text("Dropped");
                },
                activate: function() {
                    $('#droppable').css({
                        border: "medium double green",
                        backgroundColor: "lightGreen"
                    });
                },
                deactivate : function() {
                    $('#droppable').css("border", "").css("background-color", "");
                },
                accept: '#drag1'
            });
        });
    </script>
</head>
<body>
    <h1>Jacqui's Flower Shop</h1>
    <div id="droppable">
        Drop Here
    </div>
    <div id="drag1" class="draggable">
        Drag 1
    </div>
    <div id="drag2" class="draggable">
        Drag 2
    </div>
</body>
</html>
```

There are two draggable elements in this example, with the IDs drag1 and drag2. When creating the droppable element, I used the accept setting to specify that only the drag1 element should be accepted. When the drag1 element is dragged, you see the same effect as in the previous example. The activate, deactivate, over, out, and drop events are all fired at the appropriate moments. However, when you drag the drag2 element, it fails to match the selector I specified for the accept setting and those events don't fire. I can still drag the element around, but I can no longer drop it on the droppable element. You can see the effect in Figure 23-9.

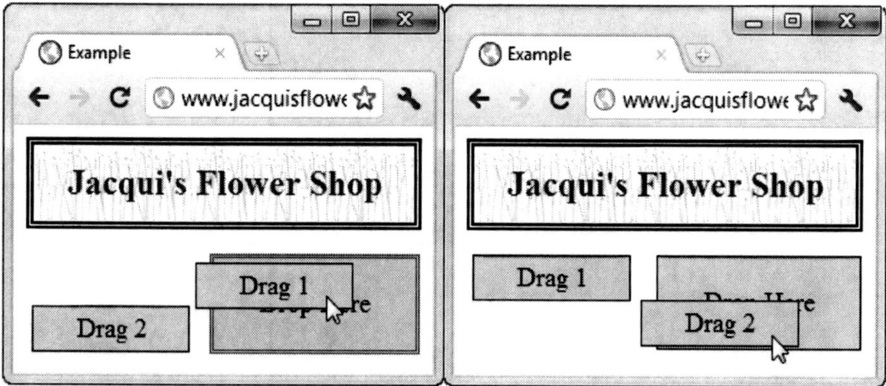

Figure 23-9. Using the accept setting

Notice that I changed the way I select the dropped element so that I can call the `text` method. When there was only one draggable element in the document, I just used the `id` attribute, like this:

```
$('#draggable').text("Dropped");
```

In this example, there are multiple draggable elements, so selecting by `id` won't work, because I'll always be changing the text on the same element, regardless of which one was dropped. Instead, I use the `ui` object, which jQuery UI provides as an additional argument to the event handling functions. The draggable property of the `ui` object returns a jQuery object that contains the element that the user is dragging or has dropped, allowing me to target that element like this:

```
ui.draggable.text("Dropped");
```

Highlighting the Droppable Using Classes

You can use the `activeClass` and `hoverClass` settings to change the appearance of the droppable element without using the `activate`, `deactivate`, `over`, and `out` events. Listing 23-11 provides a demonstration.

Listing 23-11. Using the activeClass and hoverClass settings

```
<!DOCTYPE html>
<html>
<head>
    <title>Example</title>
    <script src="jquery-1.7.js" type="text/javascript"></script>
    <script src="jquery-ui-1.8.16.custom.js" type="text/javascript"></script>
    <link rel="stylesheet" type="text/css" href="styles.css"/>
    <link rel="stylesheet" type="text/css" href="jquery-ui-1.8.16.custom.css"/>
    <style type="text/css">
        .draggable, #droppable {font-size: large; border: thin solid black; padding: 4px;
            width: 100px; text-align: center; background-color: lightgray; margin: 4px;}
        #droppable {padding: 20px; position: absolute; right: 5px;}
        #droppable.active {border: thick solid green}
```

```
        #droppable.hover {background-color: lightgreen}
    </style>
    <script type="text/javascript">
        $(document).ready(function() {
            $('.draggable').draggable();

            $('#droppable').droppable({
                drop: function(event, ui) {
                    ui.draggable.text("Dropped");
                },
                activeClass: "active",
                hoverClass: "hover"
            });
        });
    </script>
</head>
<body>
    <h1>Jacqui's Flower Shop</h1>
    <div id="droppable">
        Drop Here
    </div>
    <div class="draggable">
        Drag Me
    </div>
</body>
</html>
```

I defined two new CSS styles, which I have highlighted in the listing. I created classes that are specific to the id of the draggable element (for example, #draggable.active) so that they are more specific than the other styles I have been using (for example, #droppable) and so that they take precedence. See Chapter 3 for details of the rules by which CSS styles are applied to elements.

Having defined these styles, I then name them as the values to the activeClass and hoverClass settings. The droppable interaction takes care of adding and removing these classes from the droppable elements in response to the events. You can see the result in Figure 23-10.

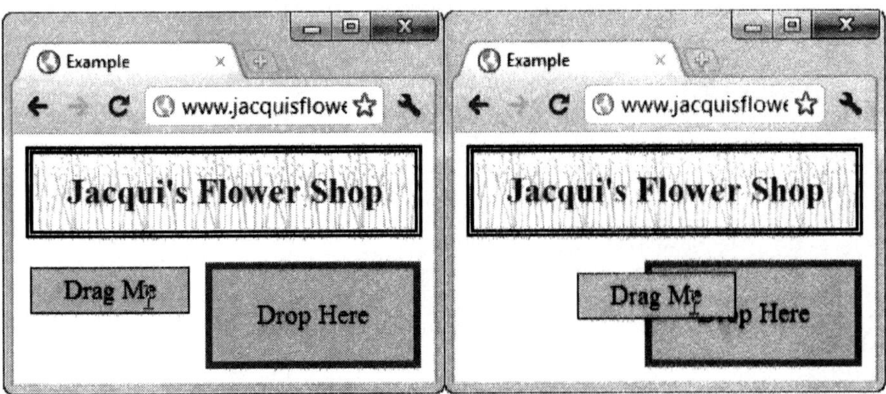

Figure 23-10. Using the activeClass and hoverClass settings

Changing the Overlap Tolerance

By default, the over event will trigger only when at least 50% of the draggable element overlaps with the droppable element. You can change this using the `tolerance` setting, which accepts the values shown in Table 23-8.

Table 23-8. *Tolerance Values*

Value	Description
`fit`	The dragged element must completely overlap the droppable element.
`intersect`	At last 50% of the dragged element must overlap the droppable element. This is the default.
`pointer`	The mouse pointer must be over the droppable element, regardless of where the user has grabbed the draggable element.
`touch`	The dragged element must overlap the droppable element by any amount.

The two values I use most frequently are `fit` and `touch`, because these represent the most readily understood approaches to the user. I use `fit` when I preserve the location of the dropped item and `touch` when I have the dropped item revert to its original location (something I'll demonstrate later in the chapter). Listing 23-12 shows the use of the `fit` and `touch` settings.

Listing 23-12. Changing the tolerance for draggable elements

```
<!DOCTYPE html>
<html>
<head>
    <title>Example</title>
    <script src="jquery-1.7.js" type="text/javascript"></script>
    <script src="jquery-ui-1.8.16.custom.js" type="text/javascript"></script>
    <link rel="stylesheet" type="text/css" href="styles.css"/>
    <link rel="stylesheet" type="text/css" href="jquery-ui-1.8.16.custom.css"/>
    <style type="text/css">
        .draggable, .droppable {font-size: large; border: thin solid black; padding: 4px;
            width: 100px; text-align: center; background-color: lightgray;}
        .droppable {margin-bottom: 10px; margin-right: 5px; height: 50px; width: 120px}
        #dropContainer {position: absolute; right: 5px;}
        div span {position: relative; top: 25%}
        .droppable.active {border: thick solid green}
        .droppable.hover {background-color: lightgreen}
    </style>
    <script type="text/javascript">
        $(document).ready(function() {

            $('.draggable').draggable();

            $('div.droppable').droppable({
                drop: function(event, ui) {
```

```
                    ui.draggable.text("Dropped");
                },
                activeClass: "active",
                hoverClass: "hover",
                tolerance: "fit"
            });

            $('#touchDrop').droppable("option", "tolerance", "touch");
        });
    </script>
</head>
<body>
    <h1>Jacqui's Flower Shop</h1>
    <div id="dropContainer">
        <div id="fitDrop" class="droppable">
            <span>Fit</span>
        </div>
        <div id="touchDrop" class="droppable">
            <span>Touch</span>
        </div>
    </div>
    <div class="draggable">
        <span>Drag Me</span>
    </div>
</body>
</html>
```

In this example, I created two droppable elements, one of which is configured with the `fit` value for the tolerance setting and the other with the `touch` value. There is a single draggable element, and Figure 23-11 shows the effect that the different values create. I took each screenshot at the moment that the over event triggered. Notice that the border I applied to the droppable elements is included when the `tolerance` setting is used to determine overlap.

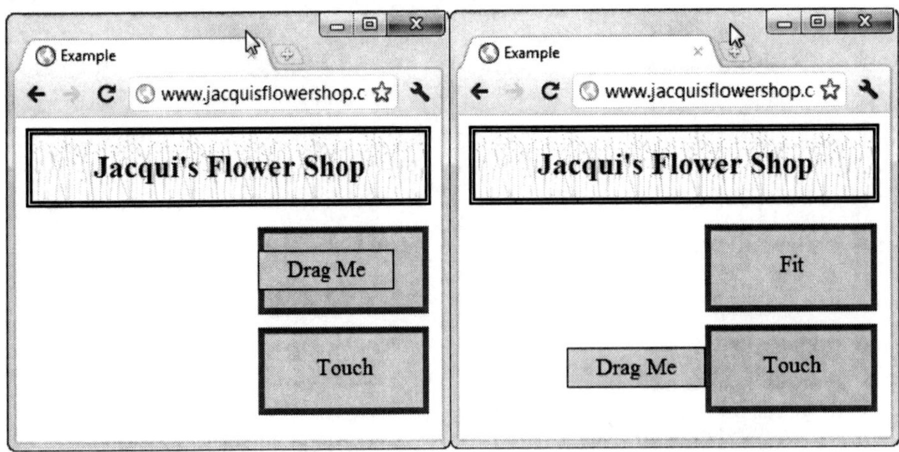

Figure 23-11. Using the fit and touch values for the tolerance setting

CAPTURING THE MOMENT AN EVENT IS TRIGGERED

You might be wondering how I captured these screenshots at the exact moment that the `over` event triggered. I used the JavaScript `debugger` keyword in my `script` element. Although it's not a part of the official language specification, browsers like Google Chrome and Firefox (with FireBug installed) have JavaScript debuggers that halt execution when they encounter `debugger` in a script (known as *breaking the debugger*). I added a handler for the `over` event, like this:

```
<script type="text/javascript">
    $(document).ready(function() {

        $('.draggable').draggable();

        $('div.droppable').droppable({
            drop: function(event, ui) {
                ui.draggable.text("Dropped");
            },
            activeClass: "active",
            hoverClass: "hover",
            tolerance: "fit",
            over: function() {
                debugger
            }
        });

        $('#touchDrop').droppable("option", "tolerance", "touch");
    });
</script>
```

When the `over` event triggers, the debugger breaks and no further execution of the script is possible until I tell the debugger to continue. This allowed me to get the screenshots you see in the figure at the point which the event triggered. The `debugger` keyword is generally useful, but it's especially so when working with events. Of course, it is vitally important that you remove all instances of `debugger` before users start to use your scripts.

Using the Droppable Methods

The droppable interaction defines only the set of core methods you saw implemented by the widgets. There are no interaction-specific methods. Table 23-9 describes those that are available.

Table 23-9. *Droppable Methods*

Method	Description
`droppable("destroy")`	Removes the interaction from the element
`droppable("disable")`	Disables the droppable interaction

droppable("enable")	Enables the droppable interaction
droppable("option")	Changes one or more settings

Tuning Drag and Drop

There are some additional settings you can use to fine-tune the way jQuery UI drag and drop works. In this section, I describe the settings and demonstrate their use.

Using Element Scope

Earlier in the chapter, I showed how the droppable accept setting can be used to filter the elements that will activate the drop zone. Using selectors works just fine for simple projects, but the selector can become overly complex and error prone if you have a lot of draggable elements to manage.

An alternative is to apply the scope setting on both the draggable and droppable elements. A draggable element will activate droppable elements with the same scope value. Listing 23-13 shows the scope setting in use.

■ **Tip** The scope setting can be combined with the accept setting in droppable elements. The droppable element will be activated only if the draggable element shares the same scope and matches the selector defined by the accept setting.

Listing 23-13. Using the scope setting

```
<!DOCTYPE html>
<html>
<head>
    <title>Example</title>
    <script src="jquery-1.7.js" type="text/javascript"></script>
    <script src="jquery-ui-1.8.16.custom.js" type="text/javascript"></script>
    <link rel="stylesheet" type="text/css" href="styles.css"/>
    <link rel="stylesheet" type="text/css" href="jquery-ui-1.8.16.custom.css"/>
    <style type="text/css">
        .draggable, .droppable {font-size: large; border: medium solid black;
            padding: 4px; width: 100px; text-align: center;
            background-color: lightgray; margin-bottom: 10px;}
        .droppable {margin-right: 5px; height: 50px; width: 120px}
        #dropContainer {position: absolute; right: 5px;}
        div span {position: relative; top: 25%}
        .droppable.active {border: medium solid green}
        .droppable.hover {background-color: lightgreen}
    </style>
    <script type="text/javascript">
        $(document).ready(function() {
```

```
            $('#apple').draggable({
                scope: "fruit"
            });
            $('#orchid').draggable({
                scope: "flower"
            });

            $('#flowerDrop').droppable({
                activeClass: "active",
                hoverClass: "hover",
                scope: "flower"
            });

            $('#fruitDrop').droppable({
                activeClass: "active",
                hoverClass: "hover",
                scope: "fruit"
            });
        });
    </script>
</head>
<body>
    <h1>Jacqui's Flower Shop</h1>
    <div id="dropContainer">
        <div id="flowerDrop" class="droppable">
            <span>Flowers</span>
        </div>
        <div id="fruitDrop" class="droppable">
            <span>Fruit</span>
        </div>
    </div>
    <div id="orchid" class="draggable">
        <span>Orchid</span>
    </div>
    <div id="apple" class="draggable">
        <span>Apple</span>
    </div>
</body>
</html>
```

In this example, I created two draggable elements and two droppable elements. When creating these elements, I assigned them to one of two `scope` values: `fruit` and `flower`. The result is that each draggable element will activate and be accepted only by the droppable element with the same scope, as shown in Figure 23-12.

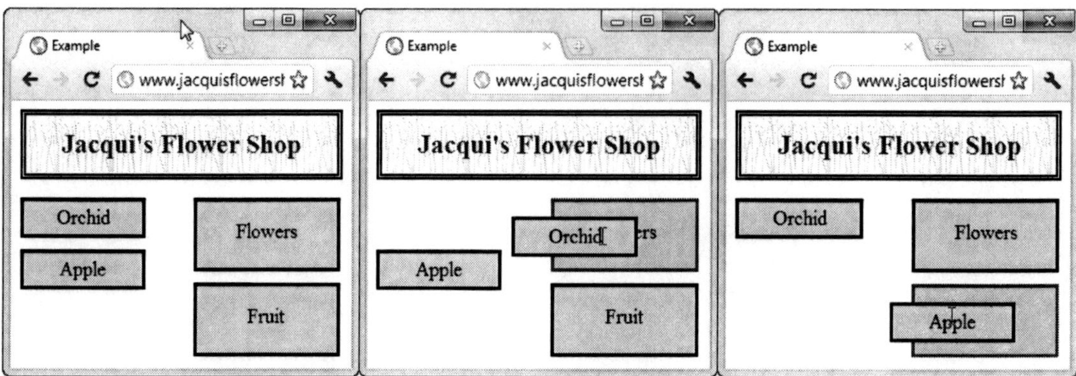

Figure 23-12. Grouping draggable and droppable elements by scope

---

■ **Tip** Notice that I defined the `scope` for each element in the initial call to the `draggable` and `droppable` methods, rather than using the `option` method. As I write this, there is a bug in jQuery UI where assigning a scope after the interaction has been created doesn't work.

Using a Helper Element

The helper setting allows you to specify an element that will be dragged in place of the draggable element, leaving the original draggable element in place. This is an entirely different effect from previous examples, where the draggable element has been moved from its original position. Listing 23-14 shows an example of using a helper element.

Listing 23-14. Using a large draggable element

```
<!DOCTYPE html>
<html>
<head>
    <title>Example</title>
    <script src="jquery-1.7.js" type="text/javascript"></script>
    <script src="jquery-ui-1.8.16.custom.js" type="text/javascript"></script>
    <link rel="stylesheet" type="text/css" href="styles.css"/>
    <link rel="stylesheet" type="text/css" href="jquery-ui-1.8.16.custom.css"/>
    <style type="text/css">
        .draggable, .droppable {font-size: large; border: medium solid black;
            padding: 4px; width: 150px; text-align: center;
            background-color: lightgray; margin-bottom: 10px;}
        .droppable {margin-right: 5px; height: 50px; width: 120px}
        #dropContainer {position: absolute; right: 5px;}
        div span {position: relative; top: 25%}
        .droppable.active {border: medium solid green}
        .droppable.hover {background-color: lightgreen}
```

```
    </style>
    <script type="text/javascript">
        $(document).ready(function() {

            $('div.draggable').draggable({
                helper: "clone"
            });

            $('#basket').droppable({
                activeClass: "active",
                hoverClass: "hover"
            });
        });
    </script>
</head>
<body>
    <h1>Jacqui's Flower Shop</h1>
    <div id="dropContainer">
        <div id="basket" class="droppable">
            <span>Basket</span>
        </div>
    </div>
    <div class="draggable">
        <img src="lily.png"/><label for="lily">Lily</label>
    </div>
</body>
</html>
```

The value clone tells jQuery UI to make a copy of the draggable element and all of its contents and use the result as the helper element. You can see the effect in Figure 23-13. The helper element is removed when the user drops it, leaving the draggable and droppable elements in their original positions.

Figure 23-13. A large draggable element

As the figure shows, the original draggable element remains in position and only the helper is moved across the screen to follow the user's mouse. Large draggable elements like the one in this example make it difficult for the user to see the underlying elements in the document, including the position of the droppable element. You can address this by providing a function as the value for the helper setting, as shown in Listing 23-15.

Listing 23-15. Using the helper setting

```
...
<script type="text/javascript">
    $(document).ready(function() {

        $('div.draggable').draggable({
            helper: function() {
                return $('<img src=lily.png />')
            }
        });

        $('#basket').droppable({
            activeClass: "active",
            hoverClass: "hover"
        });
    });
</script>
...
```

When the user starts to drag the element, jQuery UI calls the helper function and uses the element that it returns as the draggable item. In this case, I use jQuery to create an img element. You can see the effect in Figure 23-14.

Figure 23-14. Using a helper

The smaller image acts as a more compact stand-in for the draggable element, making it easier to see the rest of the document while dragging.

Manipulating the Helper Element

The ui object that jQuery UI passes to the droppable events contains a helper property, which you can use to manipulate the helper element as it is being dragged. Listing 23-16 shows the use of this property, tied to the over and out events.

Listing 23-16. Using the ui.helper property

```
...
<script type="text/javascript">
    $(document).ready(function() {

        $('div.draggable').draggable({
            helper: function() {
                return $('<img src=lily.png />')
            }
        });

        $('#basket').droppable({
            over: function(event, ui) {
                ui.helper.css("border", "thick solid green")
            },
            out: function(event, ui) {
                ui.helper.css("border", "")
            }
        });
    });
</script>
...
```

I use the over and out events and the ui.helper property to display a border on the helper element when it overlaps the droppable element. You can see the result in Figure 23-15.

Figure 23-15. Manipulating the helper element

Snapping to the Edges of Elements

You can make the draggable element snap to the edges of the elements that it passes over using the snap setting. The value for this setting is a selector. The draggable will snap to the edges of any element that it is near that matches the selector. Listing 23-17 shows the use of the snap setting.

Listing 23-17. Using the snap setting

```
<!DOCTYPE html>
<html>
<head>
    <title>Example</title>
    <script src="jquery-1.7.js" type="text/javascript"></script>
    <script src="jquery-ui-1.8.16.custom.js" type="text/javascript"></script>
    <link rel="stylesheet" type="text/css" href="styles.css"/>
    <link rel="stylesheet" type="text/css" href="jquery-ui-1.8.16.custom.css"/>
    <style type="text/css">
        #snapper, .draggable, .droppable {font-size: large; border: medium solid black;
            padding: 4px; width: 150px; text-align: center;
            background-color: lightgray; margin-bottom: 10px;}
        .droppable {margin-right: 5px; height: 50px; width: 120px}
        #dropContainer {position: absolute; right: 5px;}
        div span {position: relative; top: 25%}
        .droppable.active {border: medium solid green}
        .droppable.hover {background-color: lightgreen}
        #snapper {position: absolute; left: 35%; border: medium solid black;
            width: 180px; height: 50px}
    </style>
    <script type="text/javascript">
        $(document).ready(function() {

            $('div.draggable').draggable({
                snap: "#snapper, .droppable",
                snapMode: "both",
                snapTolerance: 50
            });

            $('#basket').droppable({
                activeClass: "active",
                hoverClass: "hover"
            });
        });
    </script>
</head>
<body>
    <h1>Jacqui's Flower Shop</h1>
    <div id="dropContainer">
        <div id="basket" class="droppable">
            <span>Basket</span>
        </div>
    </div>
```

```
    <div id="snapper"><span>Snap Here</span></div>
    <div class="draggable">
        <span>Drag Me</span>
    </div>
</body>
</html>
```

As the draggable element nears one of the matching elements, it jumps (snaps) so that the two closest edges touch. You can select any element to snap to, not just droppable elements. In the example, I added a div element and defined a value for the snap setting, which selects it and the droppable element in the document. It is pretty much impossible to show the effect of snapping using a screenshot, so I encourage you to experiment with this example in the browser.

There are a couple of supporting settings you can use to tweak the snapping behavior. The first is snapMode. This setting lets you specify which edges the draggable will snap to. The accepted values are inner (snap to the inner edges of the underlying element), outer (snap to the outer edges), and both (snap to all edges, which is the default value).

You use the snapTolerance setting to specify how far the draggable element has to be away from the target before it snaps into position. The default is 20, meaning 20 pixels. In the example, I specified a value of 50, which makes snapping occur from further away. Getting the right value for this setting is important. The user won't notice the snapping effect if the snapTolerance value is too small, and if the value is too large the draggable element starts leaping unexpectedly across the screen to snap to far-away elements

Summary

In this chapter, I introduced you to the two most important and useful of the jQuery UI interactions: draggable and droppable. I showed you how to apply and configure these interactions individually, how to respond to their events, and how to tune the way that they work together to get fine-grained control over the drag-and-drop experience you provide to your web application users.

CHAPTER 24

Using the Other Interactions

In this chapter, I describe the three remaining jQuery UI interactions: *sortable, selectable,* and *resizable.* These interactions are less used (and less useful) than draggable and droppable, which I described in Chapter 23. The interactions in this chapter can be useful, but they use models that are hard to highlight to the user. Because of that, they perform best as supplements to other, more conventional, approaches. Table 24-1 provides the summary for this chapter.

Table 24-1. *Chapter Summary*

Problem	Solution	Listing
Apply the sortable interaction	Select the container element, and call the sortable method	1
Obtain the order that the user created with a sortable interaction	Call the toArray or serialize method	2, 3
Enable dragging elements from one sortable item to another	Use the connectWith setting	4
Connect a draggable element with a sortable item	Use the connectToSortable setting on the draggable element	5
Specify which elements are sortable	Use the items setting	6
Style the empty space created while a sortable item is being dragged	Use the placeholder setting	7
Ignore a change in order	Use the cancel method	8
Refresh the set of elements in a sortable item	Use the refresh method	9
Get information about the sort operation in progress	Use the ui object provided to event handler functions	10

Apply the selectable interaction	Select the container element, and call the selectable method	11, 12
Prevent an element from being selected	Use the cancel method	13
Apply the resizable interaction	Use the resizable method	14
Resize multiple elements	Use the alsoResize setting	15, 16
Limit the size of a resizable element	Use the maxHeight, maxWidth, minHeight, and minWidth settings	17
Select the draggable edges and corners for a resizable element	Use the handles setting	18

Using the Sortable Interaction

The sortable interaction lets the user change the order of a set of elements by dragging them around. You apply the sortable interaction by selecting the element that contains the individual items that you want to sort and then calling the sortable method. Listing 24-1 contains a simple example.

Listing 24-1. Using the sortable interaction

```
<!DOCTYPE html>
<html>
<head>
    <title>Example</title>
    <script src="jquery-1.7.js" type="text/javascript"></script>
    <script src="jquery-ui-1.8.16.custom.js" type="text/javascript"></script>
    <link rel="stylesheet" type="text/css" href="styles.css"/>
    <link rel="stylesheet" type="text/css" href="jquery-ui-1.8.16.custom.css"/>
    <style type="text/css">
        div.sortable { width: 100px; background-color: lightgrey; font-size: large;
            float: left; margin: 4px; text-align: center; border: medium solid black;
            padding: 4px;}
    </style>
    <script type="text/javascript">
        $(document).ready(function() {
            $('#sortContainer').sortable();
        });
    </script>
</head>
<body>
    <h1>Jacqui's Flower Shop</h1>
    <div id="sortContainer">
        <div id="item1" class="sortable">Item 1</div>
        <div id="item2" class="sortable">Item 2</div>
        <div id="item3" class="sortable">Item 3</div>
```

```
    </div>
</body>
</html>
```

In this example, I created a number of div elements and assigned them to the sortable class. This class has no effect on the interaction, and I use it only to style the elements. To create the interaction, I select the parent div element (the one whose id is sortContainer) and call the sortable method. The result is that I can change the order of my three div elements simply by dragging them into a new position. You can see the effect in Figure 24-1 (although, like all of the examples in this chapter, you will get a better sense of what is happening by running the example in the browser).

Figure 24-1. Sorting items by dragging them

To demonstrate the sortable interaction, I dragged the element labeled Item 2 to the right of the browser window. Once I drag the element past the one labeled Item 3, jQuery UI rearranges the items so that they are in a new order. I only dragged an element one position, but you can move them around several positions at a time.

Getting the Sortable Order

At some point, you need to know the order that the user created by moving the elements around. To get this information, you can call the toArray method, which returns a JavaScript array of the id attribute values for the sorted elements. Listing 24-2 shows the addition of a button to the example that writes the current order to the console.

Listing 24-2. Obtaining the sorted element order

```
...
<script type="text/javascript">
    $(document).ready(function() {
        $('#sortContainer').sortable();

        $('<div id=buttonDiv><button>Get Order</button></div>').appendTo('body');
        $('button').button().click(function() {
            var order = $('#sortContainer').sortable("toArray");
            for (var i = 0; i < order.length; i++) {
                console.log("Position: " + i + " ID: " + order[i]);
            }
        })
    });
</script>
...
```

You can see the effect in Figure 24-2. When the button is pressed, I call the `toArray` method and enumerate the contents of the resulting array to the console.

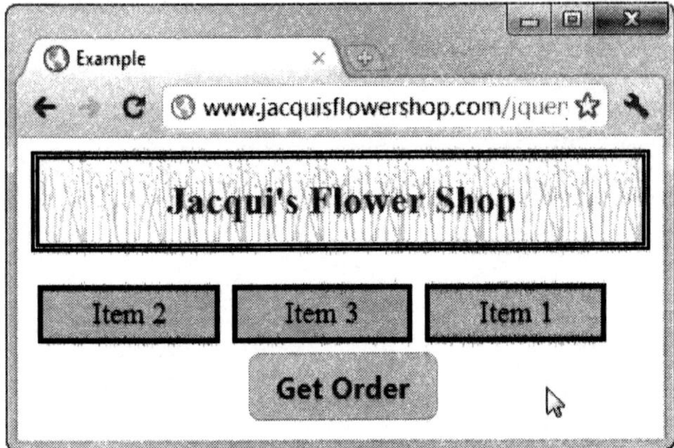

Figure 24-2. Adding a button to write out the sort order

For the order in the figure, pressing the button produces the following output:

```
Position: 0 ID: item2
Position: 1 ID: item3
Position: 2 ID: item1
```

You can also use the `serialize` method to generate a string that can easily be used with a form. Listing 24-3 provides an example.

Listing 24-3. Using the serialize method

```
<!DOCTYPE html>
<html>
<head>
    <title>Example</title>
    <script src="jquery-1.7.js" type="text/javascript"></script>
    <script src="jquery-ui-1.8.16.custom.js" type="text/javascript"></script>
    <link rel="stylesheet" type="text/css" href="styles.css"/>
    <link rel="stylesheet" type="text/css" href="jquery-ui-1.8.16.custom.css"/>
    <style type="text/css">
        div.sortable { width: 100px; background-color: lightgrey; font-size: large;
            float: left; margin: 4px; text-align: center; border: medium solid black;
            padding: 4px;}
            #buttonDiv {clear: both}
    </style>
    <script type="text/javascript">
        $(document).ready(function() {
            $('#sortContainer').sortable();
```

```
            $('<div id=buttonDiv><button>Get Order</button></div>').appendTo('body');
            $('button').button().click(function() {
                var formstring = $('#sortContainer').sortable("serialize");
                console.log(formstring);
            })
        });
    </script>
</head>
<body>
    <h1>Jacqui's Flower Shop</h1>
    <div id="sortContainer">
        <div id="item_1" class="sortable">Item 1</div>
        <div id="item_2" class="sortable">Item 2</div>
        <div id="item_3" class="sortable">Item 3</div>
    </div>
</body>
</html>
```

Notice that I had to change the id values of the sortable elements. The serialize method looks for a pattern of <key>_<index> when generating its string. The output for the order shown in Figure 24-2 is as follows:

```
item[]=2&item[]=3&item[]=1
```

Configuring the Sortable Interaction

The sortable interaction relies heavily on the draggable interaction I described in Chapter 23. This means that the options I described for that interaction (such as axis and tolerance) can be applied with the same effect to configure sortable interactions. I won't describe those settings again. Instead, Table 24-2 shows the settings that are unique to the sortable interaction and the most useful. I describe these settings in the sections that follow.

Table 24-2. *Sortable settings*

Setting	Description
connectWith	Specifies another sortable element to connect to so that items can be dragged between them. The default is false, meaning that there is no connection.
dropOnEmpty	When false, items cannot be dropped on a connected sortable interaction that contains no items. The default is true.
items	Specifies the items that will be sortable through a selector. The default is > *, which selects any descendant of the element on which the sortable method has been called.
placeholder	Specifies a class that will be assigned to the element that is created to preserve space while a sortable item is being dragged to a new location.

Connecting Sortable Interactions

The sortable feature I like most is the ability to connect two sortable interactions together, allowing items to be dragged between them. You achieve this using the connectWith setting, specifying a selector that matches the element you want to connect with. You can create a bidirectional connection by using the connectWith setting on both sortable elements, as shown in Listing 24-4.

Listing 24-4. Connecting sortable interactions together

```
<!DOCTYPE html>
<html>
<head>
    <title>Example</title>
    <script src="jquery-1.7.js" type="text/javascript"></script>
    <script src="jquery-ui-1.8.16.custom.js" type="text/javascript"></script>
    <link rel="stylesheet" type="text/css" href="styles.css"/>
    <link rel="stylesheet" type="text/css" href="jquery-ui-1.8.16.custom.css"/>
    <style type="text/css">
        div.sortable { width: 100px; background-color: lightgrey; font-size: large;
            margin: 4px; text-align: center; border: medium solid black; padding: 4px;}
        #fruitContainer {position: absolute; right:50px}
        #flowerContainer {position: absolute; left:50px}
        div.flower {background-color: lightgreen}
    </style>
    <script type="text/javascript">
        $(document).ready(function() {
            $('#fruitContainer').sortable({
                connectWith: '#flowerContainer'
            });
            $('#flowerContainer').sortable({
                connectWith: '#fruitContainer'
            });
        });
    </script>
</head>
<body>
    <h1>Jacqui's Flower Shop</h1>
    <div id="fruitContainer" class="sortContainer">
        <div id="fruit_1" class="sortable fruit">Apple</div>
        <div id="fruit_2" class="sortable fruit">Orange</div>
        <div id="fruit_3" class="sortable fruit">Banana</div>
        <div id="fruit_4" class="sortable fruit">Pear</div>
    </div>
    <div id="flowerContainer" class="sortContainer">
        <div id="flower_1" class="sortable flower">Astor</div>
        <div id="flower_2" class="sortable flower">Peony</div>
        <div id="flower_3" class="sortable flower">Lily</div>
        <div id="flower_4" class="sortable flower">Orchid</div>
    </div>
</body>
</html>
```

In this example, I created two groups of items and called the `sortable` method on their container element. I used the `connectwith` setting to associate each sortable with the other, and the result is shown in Figure 24-3.

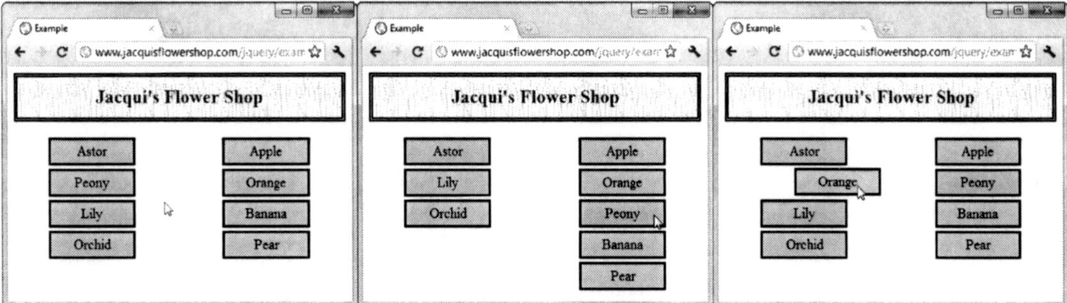

Figure 24-3. Dragging elements between connected sortable interactions

Connecting a Draggable Element with a Sortable Element

You can also connect a draggable element with a sortable one. You do this by applying the `connectToSortable` setting on the draggable element, specifying a selector that matches the draggable element you want to connect to. Listing 24-5 shows how this is done.

Listing 24-5. Connecting a draggable element and a sortable element

```
<!DOCTYPE html>
<html>
<head>
    <title>Example</title>
    <script src="jquery-1.7.js" type="text/javascript"></script>
    <script src="jquery-ui-1.8.16.custom.js" type="text/javascript"></script>
    <link rel="stylesheet" type="text/css" href="styles.css"/>
    <link rel="stylesheet" type="text/css" href="jquery-ui-1.8.16.custom.css"/>
    <style type="text/css">
        div.sortable { width: 100px; background-color: lightgrey; font-size: large;
            margin: 4px; text-align: center; border: medium solid black; padding: 4px;}
        #fruitContainer {position: absolute; right:50px}
        #flowerContainer {position: absolute; left:50px}
        div.flower {background-color: lightgreen}
    </style>
    <script type="text/javascript">
        $(document).ready(function() {
            $('#fruit_1').draggable({
                connectToSortable: '#flowerContainer',
                helper: "clone"
            });
            $('#flowerContainer').sortable();
        });
    </script>
```

```
</head>
<body>
    <h1>Jacqui's Flower Shop</h1>
    <div id="fruitContainer" class="sortContainer">
        <div id="fruit_1" class="sortable fruit">Apple</div>
    </div>
    <div id="flowerContainer" class="sortContainer">
        <div id="flower_1" class="sortable flower">Astor</div>
        <div id="flower_2" class="sortable flower">Peony</div>
        <div id="flower_3" class="sortable flower">Lily</div>
        <div id="flower_4" class="sortable flower">Orchid</div>
    </div>
</body>
</html>
```

In this example, I reduced the number of fruit items to one and made it draggable, connecting to the sortable list of flowers. The result is that the draggable item can be added to the sortable list, as shown in Figure 24-4. This setting works best when the helper setting for the draggable item is clone. It will work for other values, but an error will be reported.

Figure 24-4. Connecting a sortable item and a draggable item

Selecting the Sortable Items

You can be selective about which items in the container are sortable. You do this through the items setting, the value of which is a selector that matches the elements you want to enable sorting for. Elements that do not match the selector cannot be rearranged. Listing 24-6 provides a demonstration.

Listing 24-6. Selecting specific elements to be sortable

```
<!DOCTYPE html>
<html>
<head>
    <title>Example</title>
    <script src="jquery-1.7.js" type="text/javascript"></script>
    <script src="jquery-ui-1.8.16.custom.js" type="text/javascript"></script>
    <link rel="stylesheet" type="text/css" href="styles.css"/>
    <link rel="stylesheet" type="text/css" href="jquery-ui-1.8.16.custom.css"/>
    <style type="text/css">
        div.sortable { width: 100px; background-color: lightgrey; font-size: large;
            margin: 4px; text-align: center; border: medium solid black; padding: 4px;}
        #fruitContainer {position: absolute; right:50px}
        #flowerContainer {position: absolute; left:50px}
    </style>
    <script type="text/javascript">
        $(document).ready(function() {

            $('div.flower:even').css("background-color", "lightgreen")

            $('#flowerContainer').sortable({
                items: '.flower:even'
            });
        });
    </script>
</head>
<body>
    <h1>Jacqui's Flower Shop</h1>
    <div id="flowerContainer" class="sortContainer">
        <div id="flower_1" class="sortable flower">Astor</div>
        <div id="flower_2" class="sortable flower">Peony</div>
        <div id="flower_3" class="sortable flower">Lily</div>
        <div id="flower_4" class="sortable flower">Orchid</div>
    </div>
</body>
</html>
```

In this example, I used the items setting to specify that only the even-numbered elements in the container should be sortable. In Figure 24-5, the Astor and Lily elements can be sorted, but the Peony and Orchid elements won't respond to being dragged and remain in position.

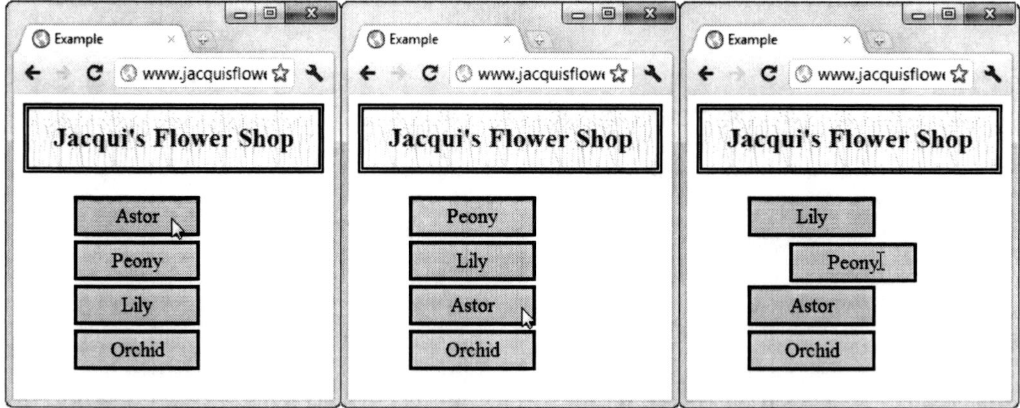

Figure 24-5. Selecting the items that can be sorted

There is an oddity you should be aware of when using the items setting, and I have shown it in the last frame of the figure. An element that doesn't match the selector cannot be dragged into a new position unless it has been dislodged by another element. So in the figure, I dragged the Astor element to a new position, which forces the Peony element to move. Once it is moved, the Peony element will respond to being dragged and sorted as though it matches the items selector.

Styling the Empty Space

While you are dragging an item into a new position, the space it leaves behind remains empty. You can apply a CSS class to this space through the placeholder setting. This can be a useful way to emphasize that the empty space is a drop target. Listing 24-7 shows the use of the placeholder setting.

Listing 24-7. Using the placeholder setting

```
<!DOCTYPE html>
<html>
<head>
    <title>Example</title>
    <script src="jquery-1.7.js" type="text/javascript"></script>
    <script src="jquery-ui-1.8.16.custom.js" type="text/javascript"></script>
    <link rel="stylesheet" type="text/css" href="styles.css"/>
    <link rel="stylesheet" type="text/css" href="jquery-ui-1.8.16.custom.css"/>
    <style type="text/css">
        div.sortable {width: 100px; background-color: lightgrey; font-size: large;
            margin: 4px; text-align: center; border: medium solid black; padding: 4px;}
        #flowerContainer {position: absolute; left:25%}
        .emptySpace {border: medium dotted red; height: 25px; margin: 4px}
    </style>
    <script type="text/javascript">
        $(document).ready(function() {
            $('#flowerContainer').sortable({
                placeholder: 'emptySpace'
```

```
            });
        });
    </script>
</head>
<body>
    <h1>Jacqui's Flower Shop</h1>
    <div id="flowerContainer" class="sortContainer">
        <div id="flower_1" class="sortable ">Astor</div>
        <div id="flower_2" class="sortable ">Peony</div>
        <div id="flower_3" class="sortable">Lily</div>
        <div id="flower_4" class="sortable">Orchid</div>
    </div>
</body>
</html>
```

In this example, I defined a CSS class called emptySpace, which defines sizes for the height and margin properties and defines a red dotted border. I specify this class using the placeholder setting and, as Figure 24-6 shows, when I drag an element to sort it, the space that it leaves behind is assigned to the emptySpace class.

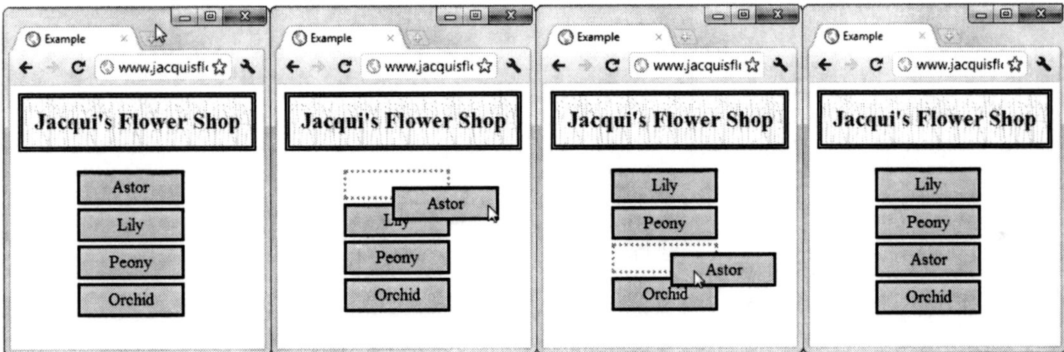

Figure 24-6. Using the placeholder setting

Using the Sortable Methods

The sortable interaction defines all of the standard jQuery UI methods, plus a few that are specific to working with sortable elements. Table 24-3 describes these methods.

Table 24-3. *Sortable Methods*

Method	Description
`sortable("destroy")`	Removes the interaction from the element
`sortable("disable")`	Disables the sortable interaction
`sortable("enable")`	Enables the sortable interaction

sortable("option")	Changes one or more settings
sortable("toArray")	Returns an array containing the sorted set of id attribute values (see the "Getting the Sortable Order" section earlier in the chapter for an example)
sortable("refresh")	Refreshes the sortable interaction
sortable("cancel")	Cancels a sort operation

Cancelling a Sort

You can use the cancel method to prevent elements from being sorted. This is something that should be done sparingly because it effectively ignores the actions that the user has taken. If you do cancel a sort, you should make sure the user knows why this happened. Listing 24-8 provides an example of using the cancel method in conjunction with the update event. The update event is triggered when the user releases the mouse button after having dragged an element to create a new sorted order. I describe the sortable events later in this chapter.

Listing 24-8. Using the cancel method

```
<!DOCTYPE html>
<html>
<head>
    <title>Example</title>
    <script src="jquery-1.7.js" type="text/javascript"></script>
    <script src="jquery-ui-1.8.16.custom.js" type="text/javascript"></script>
    <link rel="stylesheet" type="text/css" href="styles.css"/>
    <link rel="stylesheet" type="text/css" href="jquery-ui-1.8.16.custom.css"/>
    <style type="text/css">
        div.sortable {width: 100px; background-color: lightgrey; font-size: large;
            margin: 4px; text-align: center; border: medium solid black; padding: 4px;}
    </style>
    <script type="text/javascript">
        $(document).ready(function() {

            $('#error').dialog({autoOpen: false, modal: true})

            $('#flowerContainer').sortable({
                update: function() {
                    var sortedItems = $('#flowerContainer').sortable("toArray");
                    if (sortedItems[0] != "item_1") {
                        $('#error').dialog("open")
                        $('#flowerContainer').sortable("cancel")
                    }
                }
            });
        });
    </script>
</head>
```

```
<body>
    <div id="error">The King must be first</div>
    <h1>Jacqui's Flower Shop</h1>
    <div id="flowerContainer" class="sortContainer">
        <div id="item_1" class="sortable ">King</div>
        <div id="item_2" class="sortable ">Queen</div>
        <div id="item_3" class="sortable ">Jack</div>
        <div id="item_4" class="sortable">10</div>
    </div>
</body>
</html>
```

In this example, I call the cancel method if the new sorted order that the user has created means that the King element isn't in the first place in the list. I use the dialog widget, described in Chapter 22, to alert the user to the problem. Changes that affect the other sortable elements are allowed to continue.

Refreshing the Sortable Elements

The refresh method causes the sortable interaction to refresh its cache of the elements in the sortable container. Listing 24-9 shows how you can use this feature to add new sortable elements.

Listing 24-9. Adding new sortable elements

```
<!DOCTYPE html>
<html>
<head>
    <title>Example</title>
    <script src="jquery-1.7.js" type="text/javascript"></script>
    <script src="jquery-ui-1.8.16.custom.js" type="text/javascript"></script>
    <link rel="stylesheet" type="text/css" href="styles.css"/>
    <link rel="stylesheet" type="text/css" href="jquery-ui-1.8.16.custom.css"/>
    <style type="text/css">
        div.sortable {width: 100px; background-color: lightgrey; font-size: large;
            margin: 4px; text-align: center; border: medium solid black; padding: 4px;}
    </style>
    <script type="text/javascript">
        $(document).ready(function() {

            $('#flowerContainer').sortable();

            var itemCount = 2;

            $('button').click(function() {
                $('<div id=flower_' + (itemCount++) + ' class=sortable>Item ' +
                  itemCount + '</div>').appendTo('#flowerContainer');
                $('#flowerContainer').sortable("refresh");
            })
        });
    </script>
</head>
<body>
```

```
    <h1>Jacqui's Flower Shop</h1>
    <button>Add Sortable Item</button>
    <div id="flowerContainer" class="sortContainer">
        <div id="flower_1" class="sortable">Astor</div>
        <div id="flower_2" class="sortable">Peony</div>
    </div>
</body>
</html>
```

In this example, I added a `button` to the document that adds new items to the sortable container and calls the `refresh` method to make sure that the items are properly sortable.

Using the Sortable Events

The sortable interaction supports all of the events defined by the draggable interaction, which I described in Chapter 23. Table 24-4 describes the events that are unique to the sortable interaction.

Table 24-4. *Sortable Events*

Event	Description
`change`	Triggered when positions change while an element is being sorted by the user
`receive`	Triggered when an item is dragged to this sortable item from a connected one
`remove`	Triggered when an item is dragged from this sortable item to a connected one
`sort`	Triggered for each mouse move during a sort
`update`	Triggered when the user stops dragging an item and the order of items has changed

When triggering these events, jQuery UI provides additional information via a `ui` object argument, which has the properties shown in Table 24-5.

Table 24-5. *Sortable ui Object Properties*

Property	Description
`helper`	Returns the helper element
`position`	Returns the current position of the helper as an object with `top` and `left` properties
`item`	Returns a jQuery object containing the currently dragged item
`placeholder`	Returns a jQuery object containing the placeholder element
`sender`	Returns a jQuery object containing the connected sortable from which the element originates(this property is null when there is no connected sortable)

Listing 24-10 shows the use of the ui object with the sort and change events.

Listing 24-10. Using the change and sort events

```
<!DOCTYPE html>
<html>
<head>
    <title>Example</title>
    <script src="jquery-1.7.js" type="text/javascript"></script>
    <script src="jquery-ui-1.8.16.custom.js" type="text/javascript"></script>
    <link rel="stylesheet" type="text/css" href="styles.css"/>
    <link rel="stylesheet" type="text/css" href="jquery-ui-1.8.16.custom.css"/>
    <style type="text/css">
        div.sortable {width: 100px; background-color: lightgrey; font-size: large;
            margin: 4px; text-align: center; border: medium solid black; padding: 4px;}
        #flowerContainer {position: absolute; left:10px}
        #info {position: absolute; right: 10px; border: medium solid black; padding: 4px}
    </style>
    <script type="text/javascript">
        $(document).ready(function() {
            $('#flowerContainer').sortable({
                sort: function(event, ui) {
                    $('#itemId').text(ui.item.attr("id"))
                },
                change: function(event, ui) {
                    $('#pos').text($('#flowerContainer *').index(ui.placeholder))
                }
            });
        });
    </script>
</head>
<body>
    <h1>Jacqui's Flower Shop</h1>
    <div id="flowerContainer" class="sortContainer">
        <div id="flower_1" class="sortable ">Astor</div>
        <div id="flower_2" class="sortable ">Peony</div>
        <div id="flower_3" class="sortable">Lily</div>
        <div id="flower_4" class="sortable">Orchid</div>
    </div>
    <div id="info" class="ui-widget">
        <div>Item ID: <span id="itemId">None</span></div>
        <div>Pos: <span id="pos">None</span></div>
    </div>
</body>
</html>
```

I use the events to display information about the sorting operation. For the sort event, I read the ui.item property and get the id attribute of the element being dragged. For the change event, I use the ui.placeholder property, and I use the index method to figure out its position among the sortable elements.

Using the Selectable Interaction

The selectable interaction allows the user to select one or more elements, either by dragging the mouse or by clicking on individual elements. You apply the interaction through the `selectable` method as demonstrated in Listing 24-11.

Listing 24-11. Applying the selectable interaction

```
<!DOCTYPE html>
<html>
<head>
    <title>Example</title>
    <script src="jquery-1.7.js" type="text/javascript"></script>
    <script src="jquery-ui-1.8.16.custom.js" type="text/javascript"></script>
    <link rel="stylesheet" type="text/css" href="styles.css"/>
    <link rel="stylesheet" type="text/css" href="jquery-ui-1.8.16.custom.css"/>
    <style type="text/css">
        div.flower {width: 200px; background-color: lightgrey; font-size: large;
            margin: 4px; text-align: center; border: medium solid black; padding: 4px;}
        #flowerContainer {position: absolute; left:10px}
        div.ui-selected {border: medium solid green; background-color: lightgreen}
        div.ui-selecting {border: medium solid green}
    </style>
    <script type="text/javascript">
        $(document).ready(function() {
            $('#flowerContainer').selectable();
        });
    </script>
</head>
<body>
    <h1>Jacqui's Flower Shop</h1>
    <div id="flowerContainer">
        <div id="flower_1" class="flower">Astor</div>
        <div id="flower_2" class="flower">Peony</div>
        <div id="flower_3" class="flower">Lily</div>
        <div id="flower_4" class="flower">Orchid</div>
    </div>
</body>
</html>
```

You apply the selectable interaction to the element that contains the elements you want the user to be able to select. In this case, I use the same `div` elements I used for the sortable interaction earlier in the chapter. I select the container and call the `selectable` method like this:

```
$('#flowerContainer').selectable();
```

Although I have now applied the selectable interaction to my container, I need to define a pair of CSS styles for specific classes to give the user visual feedback. Here are the styles I associated with these classes:

```
div.ui-selected {border: medium solid green; background-color: lightgreen}
div.ui-selecting {border: medium solid green}
```

The selectable interaction applies these classes to my elements to reflect their selection status. The `ui.selecting` class is applied when the user is dragging the mouse to select the elements in a specific area, and the `ui-selected` class is applied when an element has been selected (either because the user has clicked on the element or because it was in the area covered by a mouse drag). I used simple styles that just apply green borders and backgrounds. You can see the effect of selecting elements by dragging the mouse in Figure 24-7.

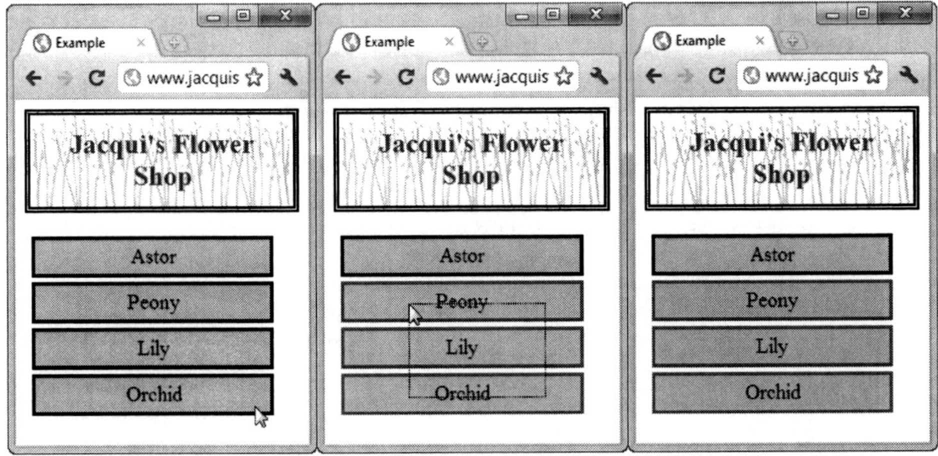

Figure 24-7. Selecting elements with a mouse

The user must start dragging the mouse within the container element to start the selection process. You can see the outline of the area that has been selected (known as the *marquee*) in the middle frame of the figure—at that point, jQuery UI has applied the `ui-selecting` class. When the mouse is released, the elements that the marquee overlaps are selected and the `ui-selected` class is applied, as shown in the last frame of the figure.

The user can also select elements by clicking on them. Multiple elements can be selected, and holding the Control/Meta key allows for noncontiguous selections. If you find that clicking causes a single selected element to toggle, you need the addition shown in Listing 24-12.

Listing 24-12. Enabling multiple element selection for the selectable interaction

```
<script type="text/javascript">
    $(document).ready(function() {
        $('#flowerContainer')
            .bind("mousedown", function(e) {e.metaKey = true;})
            .selectable();
    });
</script>
```

When the user presses down the mouse button, the `ui-selecting` class is applied. The `ui-selected` class is applied when the mouse button is released.

Configuring the Selectable Interaction

You can configure the selectable interaction using the settings described in Table 24-6.

Table 24-6. Selectable Settings

Setting	Description
`disabled`	When `true`, the interaction is initially disabled. The default is `false`.
`autoRefresh`	When `true`, the interaction refreshes the size and position of each of the selectable elements at the start of each select operation. The default is `true`.
`cancel`	A selector string that prevents matching elements from being selected.
`delay`	See the `delay` setting on the draggable interaction in Chapter 23.
`distance`	See the `distance` setting on the draggable interaction in Chapter 23.
`filter`	A selector used to match selectable elements in the container. The default is *, which matches all elements.

Most of these settings are self-evident or are the same as for other interactions. Of particular interest, though, is the `cancel` setting, which you can use to make elements unselectable by the user. Listing 24-13 provides a demonstration.

Listing 24-13. Using the cancel setting

```
...
<script type="text/javascript">
    $(document).ready(function() {
        $('#flowerContainer')
            .bind("mousedown", function(e) {e.metaKey = true;})
            .selectable({
                cancel: '#flower_3'
            });
    });
</script>
...
```

In this script, I use a selector that prevents the element with the ID of `flower_3` from being selected. This works well when the user is selecting elements by clicking on them, but it doesn't prevent selection by dragging. For this reason, use the `cancel` setting with care.

Using the Selectable Interaction Methods

The selectable interaction defines only one unique method, as described in Table 24-7. The other methods are those that are common to all widgets and interactions.

Table 24-7. Selectable Methods

Method	Description
`selectable("destroy")`	Removes the interaction from the element
`selectable("disable")`	Disables the selectable interaction
`selectable("enable")`	Enables the selectable interaction
`selectable("option")`	Changes one or more settings
`selectable("refresh")`	Refreshes the selectable interaction. This is the manual alternative to using `false` for the value of the `autoRefresh` setting.

Using the Selectable Interaction Events

The selectable interaction defines the events shown in Table 24-8.

Table 24-8. Selectable Methods

Event	Description
`create`	Triggered when the interaction is applied to an element.
`selected`	Triggered when an item has been selected. If multiple items have been selected, this event will be triggered once for each of them.
`selecting`	Triggered when the user has started the selection process (by pressing the mouse button or by dragging the mouse).
`unselected`	Triggered when an item has been unselected. If multiple items have been unselected, this event will be triggered once for each of them.
`unselecting`	Triggered when the user has started the unselection process by pressing the mouse button.

jQuery UI provides additional information for most of these events through a `ui` object. For the `selected` and `selecting` events, the `ui` object has a property called `selected`, which contains the `HTMLElement` corresponding to the element that has been (or is about to be) selected. For the `unselected` and `unselecting` events, the `ui` object has an `unselected` property that performs the same purpose.

Using the Resizable Interaction

The resizable interaction adds drag handles to elements that allow them to be resized by the user. Some browsers do this automatically with text areas, but the resizable interaction lets us apply this feature to any element in a document. Listing 24-14 shows the application of the resizable interaction that you perform using the resizable method.

Listing 24-14. Applying the resizable interaction

```
<!DOCTYPE html>
<html>
<head>
    <title>Example</title>
    <script src="jquery-1.7.js" type="text/javascript"></script>
    <script src="jquery-ui-1.8.16.custom.js" type="text/javascript"></script>
    <link rel="stylesheet" type="text/css" href="styles.css"/>
    <link rel="stylesheet" type="text/css" href="jquery-ui-1.8.16.custom.css"/>
    <style type="text/css">
        #astor, #lily {text-align: center; width: 150px; border: thin solid black;
            padding: 5px; float: left; margin: 20px}
        #astor img, #lily img {display: block; margin: auto}
    </style>
    <script type="text/javascript">
        $(document).ready(function() {
            $('#astor').resizable({
                alsoResize: "#astor img"
            });
        });
    </script>
</head>
<body>
    <h1>Jacqui's Flower Shop</h1>
    <div id="astor" class="ui-widget">
        <img src="astor.png" />
        Astor
    </div>
     <div id="lily" class="ui-widget">
        <img src="lily.png" />
        Lilly
    </div>
</body>
</html>
```

In this example, I created two div elements whose contents are an img and some text. I select one of these in the script and apply the resizable method (using the alsoResize setting, which I'll describe later in this chapter). jQuery UI adds a drag handle to the selected element, allowing me to resize it vertically and horizontally, as shown in Figure 24-8. In the figure, I increased the height of the element and reduced the width.

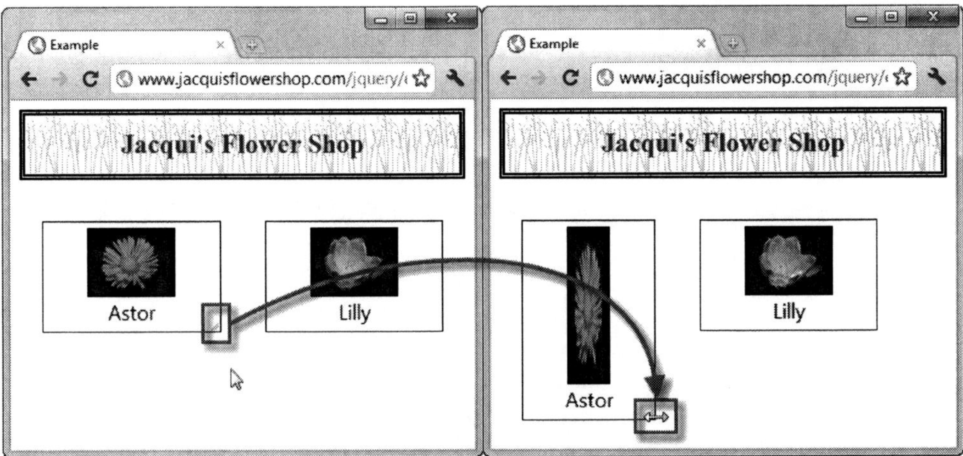

Figure 24-8. Using the drag handle to change the dimensions of a resizable element

Configuring the Resizable Interaction

You can configure the resizable interaction using the settings described in Table 24-9. The resizable interaction relies on the draggable interaction I described in Chapter 23. This means that, in addition to the settings described in the table, you can configure the resizable interaction using the draggable settings as well, including `delay`, `distance`, `grid`, and `containment`.

***Table 24-9.** Resizable Settings*

Setting	Description
`alsoResize`	A selector used to match elements that should be resized at the same time as the resizable element. The default is `false`, meaning no other elements are resized.
`aspectRatio`	When `true`, the element's aspect ratio is preserved when resized. The default is `false`.
`autoHide`	When `true`, the drag handles are visible only when the mouse hovers over the resizable element. The default is `false`.
`ghost`	When `true`, a semi-transparent helper element is drawn to show the user what the new size of the element will be. The default is `true`.
`handles`	Specifies where the drag handles will be placed on the resizable element. See later in this chapter for a list of supported values.
`maxHeight`	Specifies the maximum height that the element can be resized to. The default is `null`, meaning no limit.

maxWidth	Specifies the maximum width that the element can be resized to. The default is null, meaning no limit.
minHeight	Specifies the minimum height that the element can be resized to. The default is 10 pixels.
minWidth	Specifies the minimum width that the element can be resized to. The default is 10 pixels.

Resizing Related Elements

To my mind, `alsoResize` is the most useful setting for configuring the resizable interaction. It allows you to specify additional elements that will be resized along with the element to which you applied the `resizable` method. I use this mainly to ensure that content elements are resized in sync with their parent, as I demonstrated earlier in the chapter when I selected the `img` element to be resized with the `div`. First of all, it helps to understand what happens when you have content elements and don't use the `alsoResize` setting. Listing 24-15 sets the scene.

Listing 24-15. Resizing an element with content without the alsoResize setting

```
...
<script type="text/javascript">
    $(document).ready(function() {
        $('#astor').resizable();
    });
</script>
...
```

Without the `alsoResize` setting, only the `div` element will change size. The content elements will be left as they are. You can see what happens in Figure 24-9.

Figure 24-9. Resizing an element, but not its content

There are times when this is useful, but I find myself using the alsoResize setting almost every time I use the resizable interaction. For me, the neat thing about the alsoResize setting is that the matched elements are not limited to the contents of the element you are resizing. You can specify any element, as Listing 24-16 shows.

Listing 24-16. Resizing additional elements with the alsoResize setting

```
...
<script type="text/javascript">
    $(document).ready(function() {
        $('#astor').resizable({
            alsoResize: "#astor img, #lily, #lily img"
        });
    });
</script>
...
```

In this script, I broadened the selection to include the other div and img elements in the document. This means that when I resize the resizable div element, jQuery UI resizes four elements simultaneously. You can see the effect in Figure 24-10.

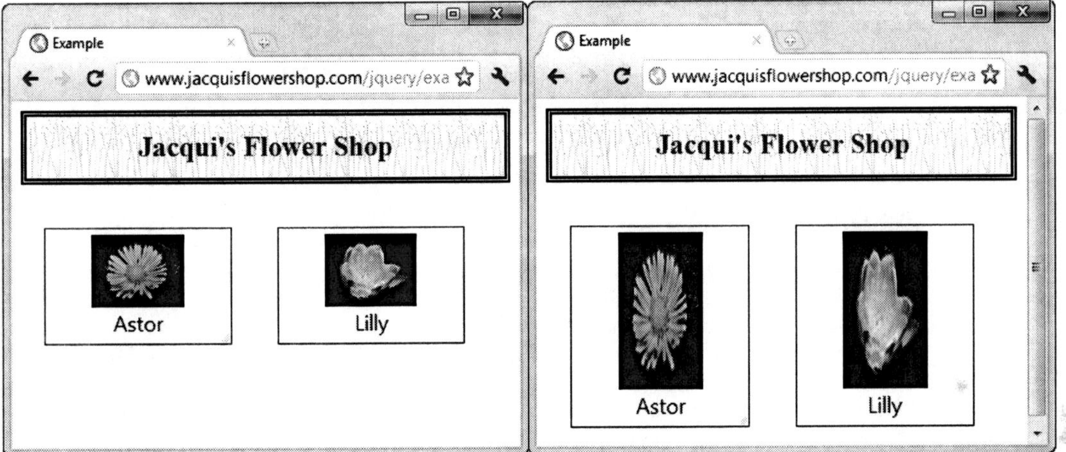

Figure 24-10. Resizing multiple elements

Constraining the Resizable Element Size

You can limit the size of resizable elements by applying the maxHeight, maxWidth, minHeight, and minWidth settings. The value for all four settings is a number of pixels or null, meaning that there is no limit. Listing 24-17 shows how you can use these settings.

■ **Tip** The default values for the `minWidth` and `minHeight` settings are 10 pixels. If the value is any smaller, jQuery UI cannot display the drag handles, which means the user would be unable to increase the size again. Use smaller values with caution.

Listing 24-17. Limiting the size of a resizable element

```
<script type="text/javascript">
    $(document).ready(function() {
        $('#astor').resizable({
            alsoResize: "#astor img",
            maxWidth: 200,
            maxHeight: 150
        });
    });
</script>
```

■ **Tip** You can also use the containment setting that is defined by the draggable interaction, which I described in Chapter 23. This allows you to limit the maximum size of a resizable element to the size of another element.

Positioning the Drag Handles

You can specify which edges and corners can be dragged through the `handles` setting. The value for this setting is either `all` (meaning that all edges and corners are draggable) or a combination of compass points (`n`, `e`, `s`, `w`, `ne`, `se`, `nw`, `sw`) to specify individual corners and edges.

You can specify multiple values, separated by commas. The default value for this setting is `e, s, se`, which means that the lower-right corner (`se`) and the right (`e`) and bottom (`s`) edges will be draggable. jQuery UI draws a diagonal drag handle only in the lower-right corner and only if you have specified `se` as part of the `handles` value. For all other edges and corners, the cursor will change to indicate that dragging is possible when the mouse hovers above the edge or corner. Listing 24-18 shows the use of the `handles` setting.

Listing 24-18. Using the handles setting

```
...
<script type="text/javascript">
    $(document).ready(function() {
        $('#astor').resizable({
            alsoResize: "#astor img"
        });

        $('#lily').resizable({
            alsoResize: "#lilyimg",
```

```
            handles: "n, s, e, w"
        });
    });
</script>
...
```

In this script, I made both div elements resizable and applied a custom set of drag handles to one of them. You can see how jQuery UI handles the visible drag handles and the cursor change in Figure 24-11.

Figure 24-11. Using the handles setting

Summary

In this chapter, I explained and demonstrated three of the jQuery UI interactions: sortable, selectable, and resizable. These are less commonly used than the draggable and droppable interactions I described in Chapter 23, but they can still be useful if applied carefully. As with all of the interactions, the main challenge is in making the user aware that he or she can drag, select, sort, or resize an element when there are no standardized visual cues in web applications. For that reason, the interactions should be used as supplements to other mechanisms for interacting with your application or document. This allows advanced users to discover the advantages of the interactions, while other users rely on more obvious and conventional techniques.

CHAPTER 25

Refactoring the Example: Part III

In this part of the book, I have introduced you to the jQuery UI widgets and interactions. These allow you to create rich web applications that are consistently themed and that can be endlessly configured and tweaked to meet your needs. In this chapter, I'll add some of these features to the example to demonstrate how they can fit together.

Reviewing the Refactored Example

When you last refactored the example, you were at the verge of re-creating some of the jQuery UI functionality that uses the core jQuery library. You can see where you got to in Figure 25-1.

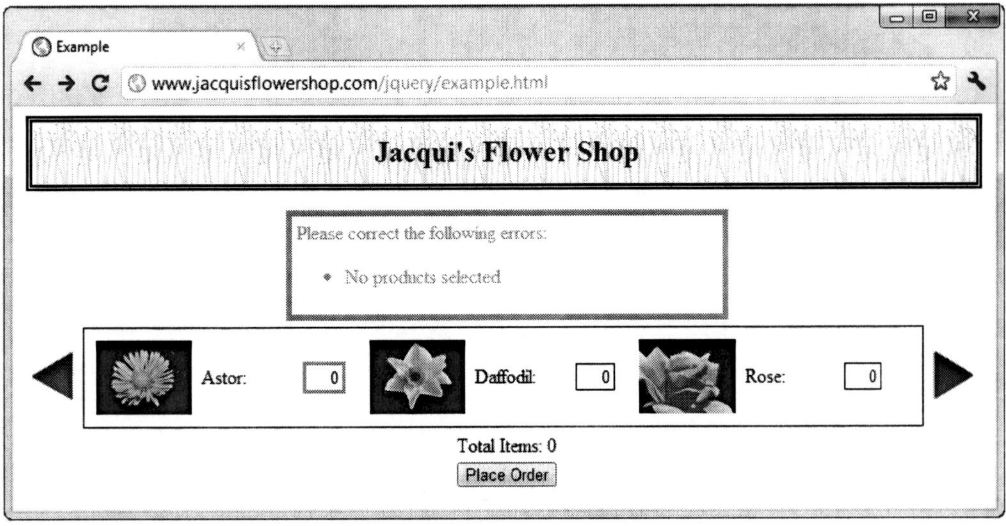

Figure 25-1. The previously refactored example document

The big additions in the previous part of the book included data templates, form validation, and Ajax, but you also added a simple product carousel that displayed the available products in a single row. I am going to use some of these features in this chapter, but my emphasis will be on applying jQuery UI. Listing 25-1 shows the starting point for this chapter.

Listing 25-1. The Starting Document for This Chapter

```
<!DOCTYPE html>
<html>
<head>
    <title>Example</title>
    <script src="jquery-1.7.js" type="text/javascript"></script>
    <script src="jquery-ui-1.8.16.custom.js" type="text/javascript"></script>
    <link rel="stylesheet" type="text/css" href="styles.css"/>
    <link rel="stylesheet" type="text/css" href="jquery-ui-1.8.16.custom.css"/>
    <script src="jquery.tmpl.js" type="text/javascript"></script>
    <script type="text/javascript">
        $(document).ready(function() {
            $.getJSON("mydata.json", function(data) {
                $('#flowerTmpl').tmpl(data).appendTo("#products");
            });
        });
    </script>
    <script id="flowerTmpl" type="text/x-jquery-tmpl">
        <div class="dcell">
            <img src="${product}.png"/>
            <label for="${product}">${name}:</label>
            <input name="${product}" value="0" />
        </div>
    </script>
</head>
<body>
    <h1>Jacqui's Flower Shop</h1>
    <form method="post" action="http://node.jacquisflowershop.com/order">
        <div id="products"></div>
        <div id="buttonDiv"><button type="submit">Place Order</button></div>
    </form>
</body>
</html>
```

In this document, I use the getJSON method to get the details of the products from a JSON file and generate elements using a date template. I add the product elements to a single div element, which has an id of products. You can see the starting point in Figure 25-2.

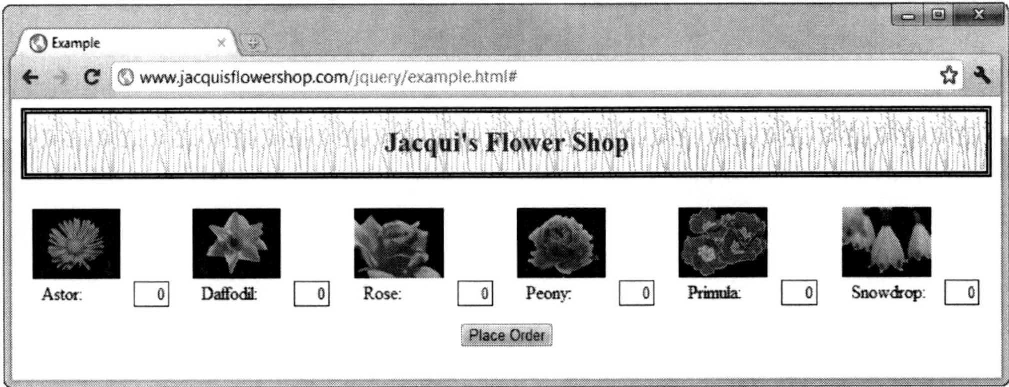

Figure 25-2. The starting document for this chapter

Displaying the Products

I am going to use an accordion to display the products to the user. I have only six products to deal with, but I am going to break them into groups of two and use jQuery to create the structure of elements that the accordion requires. Listing 25-2 shows the changes to the document.

Listing 25-2. Sorting and Structuring the Flower Elements

```
<!DOCTYPE html>
<html>
<head>
    <title>Example</title>
    <script src="jquery-1.7.js" type="text/javascript"></script>
    <script src="jquery-ui-1.8.16.custom.js" type="text/javascript"></script>
    <link rel="stylesheet" type="text/css" href="styles.css"/>
    <link rel="stylesheet" type="text/css" href="jquery-ui-1.8.16.custom.css"/>
    <script src="jquery.tmpl.js" type="text/javascript"></script>
    <style type="text/css">
        .dcell img {height: 60px}
    </style>
    <script type="text/javascript">
        $(document).ready(function() {
            $.getJSON("mydata.json", function(data) {
                var flowers = $('#flowerTmpl').tmpl(data);
                var rowCount = 1;
                for (var i = 0; i < flowers.length; i += 2) {
                    $("<h2><a href=#>" + data[i].name + " & " + data[i + 1].name
                      + "</a></h2>").appendTo("#products");
                    $("<div id='row" + (rowCount++) + "'></div>")
                        .appendTo("#products")
                        .append(flowers.slice(i, i + 2))
                }
                $('#products').accordion();
```

```
            });
        });
    </script>
    <script id="flowerTmpl" type="text/x-jquery-tmpl">
        <div class="dcell">
            <img src="${product}.png"/>
            <label for="${product}">${name}:</label>
            <input name="${product}" value="0" />
        </div>
    </script>
</head>
<body>
    <h1>Jacqui's Flower Shop</h1>
    <form method="post" action="http://node.jacquisflowershop.com/order">
        <div id="products"></div>
        <div id="buttonDiv"><button type="submit">Place Order</button></div>
    </form>
</body>
</html>
```

I have rewritten the function passed to the getJSON method to create the accordion, including constructing the element structure and calling the accordion method. The new implementation uses the JSON data object to extract the names of the flowers for the section titles but still uses the data template plugin to generate the HTML elements (that are then sliced and placed into wrapper div elements to suit the accordion). You can see how the document appears before and after the addition of the call to the accordion method in Figure 25-3.

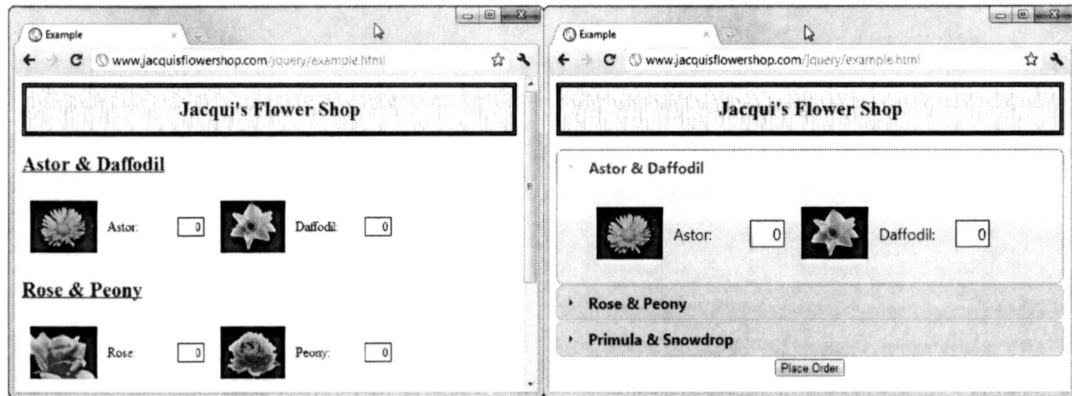

Figure 25-3. Creating the element structure and calling the accordion method

Adding the Shopping Basket

The next step is to add a simple shopping basket to show the user the selections they have made. Listing 25-3 shows the additions to the example document.

Listing 25-3. Adding the Shopping Basket

```
<!DOCTYPE html>
<html>
<head>
    <title>Example</title>
    <script src="jquery-1.7.js" type="text/javascript"></script>
    <script src="jquery-ui-1.8.16.custom.js" type="text/javascript"></script>
    <link rel="stylesheet" type="text/css" href="styles.css"/>
    <link rel="stylesheet" type="text/css" href="jquery-ui-1.8.16.custom.css"/>
    <script src="jquery.tmpl.js" type="text/javascript"></script>
    <style type="text/css">
        .dcell img {height: 60px}
        #basketTable {border: thin solid black; border-collapse: collapse}
        th, td {padding: 4px; width: 50px}
        td:first-child, th:first-child {width: 150px}
        #placeholder {text-align: center}
        #productWrapper {float: left; width: 65%}
        #basket {width: 30%; text-align: left; float: left; margin-left: 10px}
        #buttonDiv {clear: both}
    </style>
    <script type="text/javascript">
        $(document).ready(function() {
            $.getJSON("mydata.json", function(data) {
                var flowers = $('#flowerTmpl').tmpl(data);
                var rowCount = 1;
                for (var i = 0; i < flowers.length; i += 2) {
                    $("<h2><a href=#>" + data[i].name + " & " + data[i + 1].name
                      + "</a></h2>").appendTo("#products");
                    $("<div id='row" + (rowCount++) + "'></div>")
                        .appendTo("#products")
                        .append(flowers.slice(i, i + 2))
                }
                $('#products').accordion();

                $('input').change(function(event) {
                    $('#placeholder').hide();
                    var fname = $(this).attr("name");
                    var row = $('tr[id=' + fname + ']');
                    if (row.length == 0) {
                        $('#rowTmpl').tmpl({
                            name: fname,
                            val:  $(this).val(),
                            product: $(this).siblings("label").text()
                        }).appendTo("#basketTable").find("a").click(function() {
                            removeTableRow($(this).closest("tr"));
                            var iElem = $('#products').find("input[name=" + fname + "]")
                            $('#products').accordion("activate",
                                iElem.closest("div[id^=row]").prev())
                            iElem.val(0).select();
```

```
                    })
                } else if ($(this).val() != "0") {
                    row.children().eq(1).text($(this).val())
                } else {
                    removeTableRow(row)
                }
            })
        });

        function removeTableRow(row) {
            row.remove();
            if ($('#basketTable tbody').children(':visible').length == 1) {
                $('#placeholder').show();
            }
        }

    });
    </script>
    <script id="rowTmpl" type="text/x-jquery-tmpl">
        <tr id=${name}><td>${product}</td><td>${val}</td>
            <td><a href=#>Remove</a></td></tr>
    </script>
    <script id="flowerTmpl" type="text/x-jquery-tmpl">
        <div class="dcell">
            <img src="${product}.png"/>
            <label for="${product}">${name}:</label>
            <input name="${product}" value="0" />
        </div>
    </script>
</head>
<body>
    <h1>Jacqui's Flower Shop</h1>
    <form method="post" action="http://node.jacquisflowershop.com/order">
        <div id="productWrapper">
            <div id="products"></div>
        </div>
        <div id="basket" class="ui-widget">
            <table border=1 id="basketTable">
                <tr><th>Product</th><th>Quantity</th><th>Remove</th></tr>
                <tr id="placeholder"><td colspan=3>No Products</td></tr>
            </table>
        </div>
        <div id="buttonDiv"><button type="submit">Place Order</button></div>
    </form>
</body>
</html>
```

Wrapping the Accordion

I want to display the basket alongside the accordion. To do this, I have wrapped the element that I select for the accordion method in another div element, like this:

```
<div id="productWrapper">
    <div id="products"></div>
</div>
```

The accordion widget gets confused if it isn't set to occupy 100 percent of the parent element's width, so I add the wrapper element and then use the CSS `width` property to fix its size, as follows:

```
#productWrapper {float: left; width: 65%}
```

The accordion widget happily occupies 100 percent of the wrapper `div` element, which occupies only 65 percent of its parent element.

Adding the Table

I decided to display the basket using a `table` element, which I have added to the static elements in the document, as follows:

```
<div id="basket" class="ui-widget">
    <table border=1 id="basketTable">
        <tr><th>Product</th><th>Quantity</th><th>Remove</th></tr>
        <tr id="placeholder"><td colspan=3>No Products</td></tr>
    </table>
</div>
```

Just as for the accordion, I have put the `table` element inside a wrapper whose width I then set using CSS:

```
#basket {width: 30%; text-align: left; float: left; margin-left: 10px}
```

The `table` element contains a header row and a placeholder that spans the entire table. You can see the effect that is created in Figure 25-4.

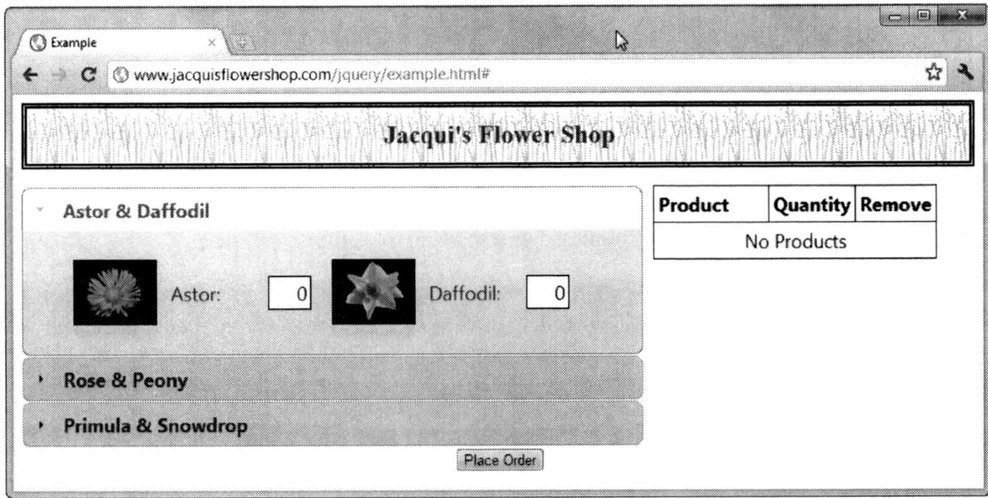

Figure 25-4. Adding the table to the document

Handling Input Value Changes

To link the table to the accordion, I listen to the change event on the input elements that I create in the getJSON function, like this:

```
$('input').change(function(event) {
    $('#placeholder').hide();
    var fname = $(this).attr("name");
    var row = $('tr[id=' + fname + ']');
    if (row.length == 0) {
        $('#rowTmpl').tmpl({
            name: fname,
            val:  $(this).val(),
            product: $(this).siblings("label").text()
        }).appendTo("#basketTable").find("a").click(function() {
            removeTableRow($(this).closest("tr"));
            var iElem = $('#products').find("input[name=" + fname + "]")
            $('#products').accordion("activate",
                iElem.closest("div[id^=row]").prev())
            iElem.val(0).select();
        })
    } else if ($(this).val() != "0") {
        row.children().eq(1).text($(this).val())
    } else {
        removeTableRow(row)
    }
})
```

A lot is going on in this function. When the user changes a value, I check to see whether there is already a row in the table for the corresponding product. If there is not, then I use the following template to create a new row:

```
<script id="rowTmpl" type="text/x-jquery-tmpl">
    <tr id=${name}><td>${product}</td><td>${val}</td>
    <td><a href=#>Remove</a></td></tr>
</script>
```

To get the values for this template, I use core jQuery methods to get information from the input element that triggered the event. I also want the display name for the product, which I obtain by navigating the DOM to find the nearby label element and reading its content, like this:

```
$(this).siblings("label").text()
```

I append the new row to the table. The placeholder row has already been hidden, back at the start of the function:

```
    $('#placeholder').hide();
```

You can see how newly added rows appear in Figure 25-5. The user enters a value in an input element, and a new row appears in the basket table when the focus changes.

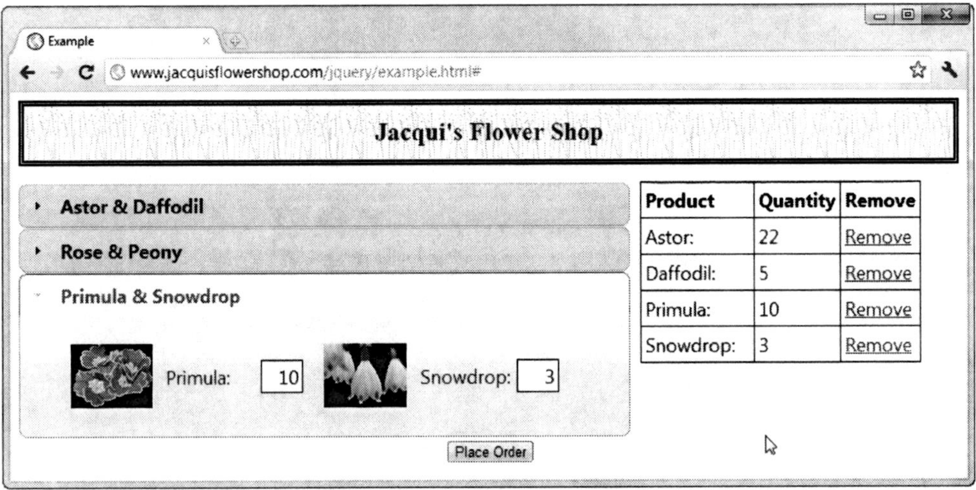

Figure 25-5. Adding rows to the basket table

Deleting Rows

You can see that I have added an a element to the table row as part of the data template. I register a handler for this element when I create the row from the data template, as follows:

```
...
}).appendTo("#basketTable").find("a").click(function() {
    removeTableRow($(this).closest("tr"));
    var iElem = $('#products').find("input[name=" + fname + "]")
    $('#products').accordion("activate",
        iElem.closest("div[id^=row]").prev())
    iElem.val(0).select();
})
...
```

The first thing I do is call the removeTableRow function, passing in the closest ancestor tr element to the a element. The removeTableRow function uses the remove method to remove the specified element from the document. It also restores the placeholder row in the table if there are no product-related rows, like this:

```
function removeTableRow(row) {
    row.remove();
    if ($('#basketTable tbody').children(':visible').length == 1) {
        $('#placeholder').show();
    }
}
```

Once the row has been deleted, I find the input element that is associated with the row in the product. I then navigate through the DOM to find the h2 element that is the immediate previous sibling to the div that contains the input element and pass this to the activate method of the accordion widget. This has the effect of opening the part of the accordion that contains the product that the user has just deleted from the basket. Finally, I set the value of the input element to zero and call the select method so that it is focused and the value is selected. You can see the effect in Figure 25-6 (although this is something that you really need to see in the browser to appreciate).

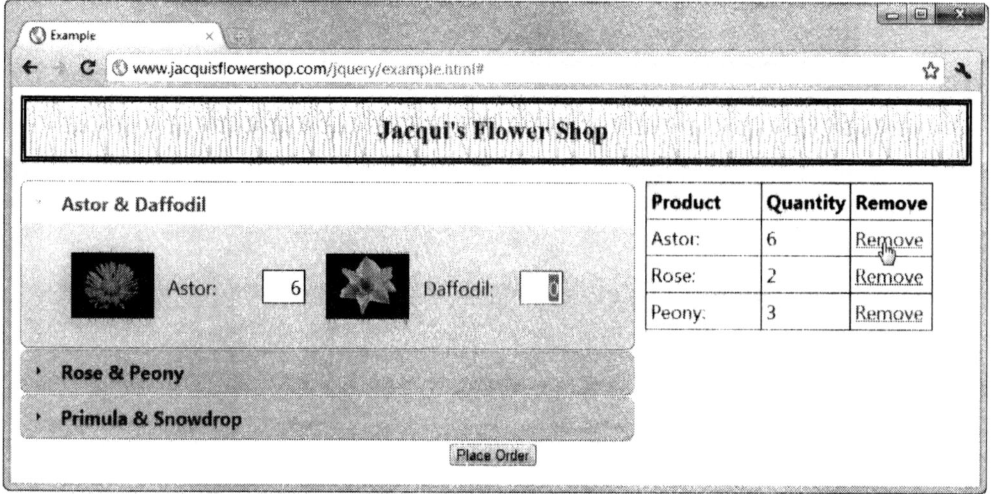

Figure 25-6. Focusing on an input element in the accordion when a table row is deleted

---

■ **Tip** I also delete rows when the user enters a value of zero in an input element for which there is a row in the table. I do this using the removeTableRow function so that the placeholder is shown if needed.

Updating Existing Rows

If there is already a row for the product, then the user is effectively changing the quantity that they want to order. Rather than remove and replace the row, I find it in the table and update the contents of the cell:

```
row.children().eq(1).text($(this).val())
```

The row variable is a jQuery object containing the tr element for the product in the table. I access the td element by position (using the index method) and then set its content using the text method.

Applying the Theme Style

The functionality of the basket is fine, but the appearance is terrible. Fortunately, jQuery UI provides a framework of CSS styles that you can apply to elements to give them the same visual appearance as applied to the widgets by your theme. Listing 25-4 shows some simple additions to the HTML elements in the document.

Listing 25-4. Applying the jQuery UI CSS Framework Styles to the table Element

```
...
<body>
    <h1>Jacqui's Flower Shop</h1>
    <form method="post" action="http://node.jacquisflowershop.com/order">
        <div id="productWrapper">
            <div id="products"></div>
        </div>
        <div id="basket" class="ui-widget ui-widget-content">
            <table border=0 id="basketTable">
                <tr class="ui-widget-header">
                    <th>Product</th><th>Quantity</th><th>Remove</th></tr>
                <tr id="placeholder"><td colspan=3>No Products</td></tr>
            </table>
        </div>
        <div id="buttonDiv"><button type="submit">Place Order</button></div>
    </form>
</body>
...
```

You may have noticed that I have used the `ui-widget` class in some of the examples in preceding chapters. This is the basic jQuery UI style, and it is applied to the outer container of sets of elements that require an appearance that is consistent with the jQuery UI widgets. The `ui-widget-content` class is used for elements that contain content, and the `ui-widget-header` is, as its name suggests, used for header elements.

■ **Tip** I describe the jQuery UI CSS framework classes in Chapter 34.

In addition to applying these classes, I disabled the border for the `table` element as follows:

```
#basketTable {border: none; border-collapse: collapse}
```

You can see the effect in Figure 25-7.

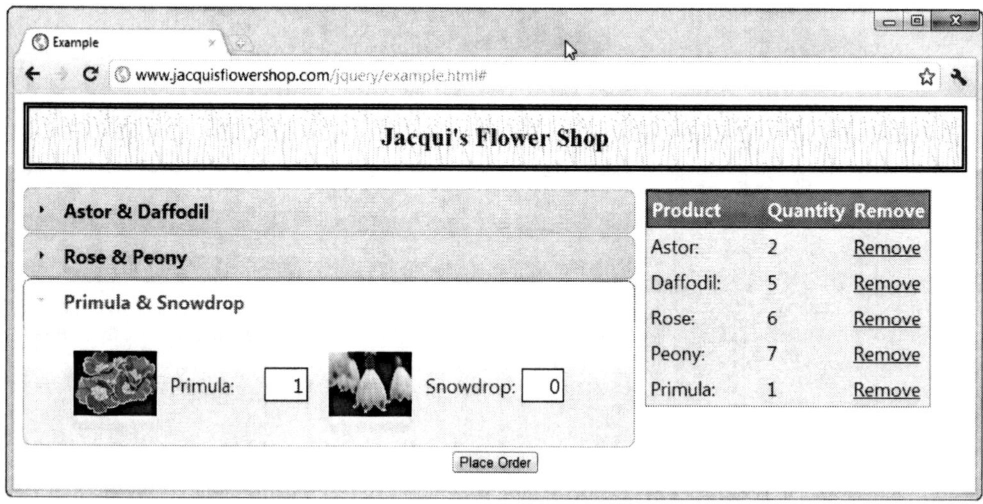

Figure 25-7. Applying the jQuery UI CSS framework classes to the table

Applying the CSS Framework More Widely

You can go further and apply the framework styles more widely. Listing 25-5 shows some useful additions to the document.

Listing 25-5. Applying the Framework Styles More Widely

```
...
<body>
    <div id="logoWrapper" class="ui-widget ui-widget-content ui-corner-all">
        <h1 id="logo">Jacqui's Flower Shop</h1>
    </div>
    <form method="post" action="http://node.jacquisflowershop.com/order">
        <div id="productWrapper">
            <div id="products"></div>
        </div>
        <div id="basket" class="ui-widget ui-widget-content">
            <table border=0 id="basketTable">
                <tr class="ui-widget-header">
                    <th>Product</th><th>Quantity</th><th>Remove</th></tr>
                <tr id="placeholder"><td colspan=3>No Products</td></tr>
            </table>
        </div>
        <div id="buttonDiv"><button type="submit">Place Order</button></div>
    </form>
</body>
...
```

I have placed the h1 element inside a div and applied several of the framework styles, including ui-corner-all, which creates the rounded corners that you can see in Figure 25-8. I also applied some new styles to this document to create the effect I wanted, overriding the styles in the `styles.css` file you have been using since Chapter 3:

```
<style type="text/css">
    .dcell img {height: 60px}
    #basketTable {border: none; border-collapse: collapse}
    th, td {padding: 4px; width: 50px}
    td:first-child, th:first-child {width: 150px}
    #placeholder {text-align: center}
    #productWrapper {float: left; width: 65%}
    #basket {width: 33%; text-align: left; float: left; margin-left: 10px;
        position: absolute; right: 10px}
    #buttonDiv {clear: both}
    #logo {font-size: 1.5em; background-size: contain; margin: 1px;
        border: none; color: inherit}
    #logoWrapper {margin-bottom: 5px}
</style>
```

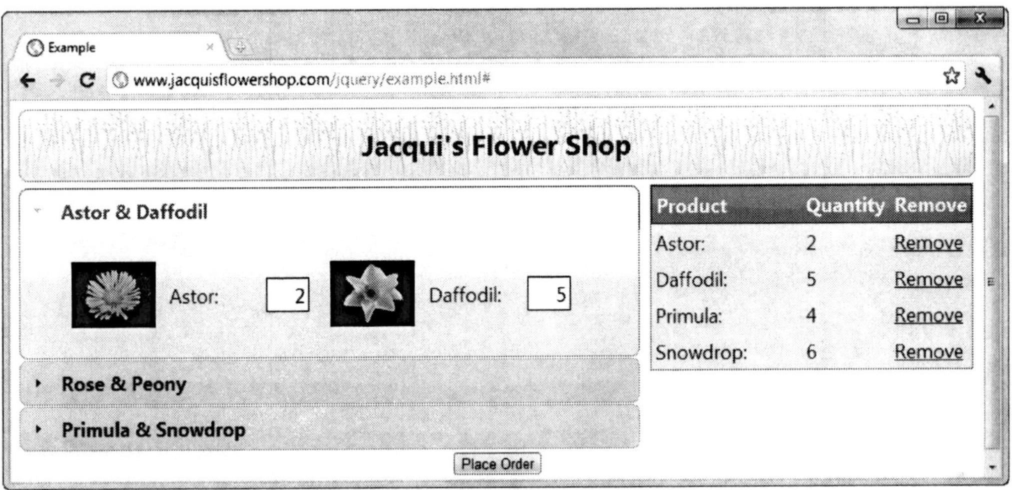

Figure 25-8. Applying the CSS framework styles to the document header

Applying Rounded Corners to the Table

Applying the `ui-corner-all` class to `table` elements causes some problems, as shown in Figure 25-9. You will notice that the `table` element doesn't have rounded corners. This is caused by an interaction between the jQuery UI CSS framework classes and the way that tables are handled in most browsers.

Figure 25-9. The effect of rounded corners on a table

To get around this problem, you need to change the table element, apply the jQuery UI CSS framework classes slightly differently, and define a new custom style. First, you need to modify the table, as shown in Listing 25-6.

Listing 25-6. Modifying the table Element to Support Rounded Corners

```
...
<form method="post" action="http://node.jacquisflowershop.com/order">
    <div id="productWrapper">
        <div id="products"></div>
    </div>
    <div id="basket" class="ui-widget ui-widget-content ui-corner-all">
        <table border=0 id="basketTable">
            <thead id="theader" class="ui-widget-header">
                <tr>
                    <th class="ui-corner-tl">Product</th>
                    <th>Quantity</th>
                    <th class="ui-corner-tr">Remove</th></tr>
            </thead>
            <tr id="placeholder"><td colspan=3>No Products</td></tr>
        </table>
    </div>
    <div id="buttonDiv"><button type="submit">Place Order</button></div>
</form>
...
```

I have added a thead element to the table, separating the header from the body rows. It is important to assign the thead element an id and to apply the ui-widget-header class. Since the header is part of the ui-widget-header class, you can remove it from the tr element.

Next, you apply the ui-corner-tl and ui-corner-tr classes to the outer cells in the header row. These classes create rounded corners for the top-left and top-right corners of the elements to which they are assigned. (I describe all of the jQuery UI CSS framework classes in Chapter 34.)

Next, you need to use the id you gave to the thead element to disable the CSS border property in the style element and do the same for the table element, like this:

```
...
<style type="text/css">
    .dcell img {height: 60px}
    #basketTable {border: none; border-collapse: collapse}
    th, td {padding: 4px; width: 50px}
    td:first-child, th:first-child {width: 150px}
    #placeholder {text-align: center}
    #productWrapper {float: left; width: 65%}
    #basket {width: 33%; text-align: left; float: left; margin-left: 10px;
```

```
        position: absolute; right: 10px}
    #buttonDiv {clear: both}
    #logo {font-size: 1.5em; background-size: contain; margin: 1px;
        border: none; color: inherit}
    #logoWrapper {margin-bottom: 5px}
    #theader {border: none}
</style>
...
```

Finally, you need to make a small tweak to the removeTableRow function. Now that you have separated the header row and placed it in a thead element, you have one fewer row in the tbody. Here is the change:

```
function removeTableRow(row) {
    row.remove();
    if ($('#basketTable tbody').children(':visible').length == 0) {
        $('#placeholder').show();
    }
}
```

■ **Tip** The tbody element is created automatically by the browser when the table element is parsed. It is an oddity of HTML that you don't have to specify this element (although you can if preferred)

With these changes, you have a table with rounded corners that matches the other elements in the document, as Figure 25-10 shows.

Figure 25-10. A table with rounded corners

Creating the jQuery UI Button

The next step is to relocate the button and transform it into a jQuery UI widget. Listing 25-7 shows the changes to the document.

Listing 25-7. Relocating and Transforming the Button

```
<!DOCTYPE html>
<html>
<head>
    <title>Example</title>
    <script src="jquery-1.7.js" type="text/javascript"></script>
    <script src="jquery-ui-1.8.16.custom.js" type="text/javascript"></script>
    <link rel="stylesheet" type="text/css" href="styles.css"/>
    <link rel="stylesheet" type="text/css" href="jquery-ui-1.8.16.custom.css"/>
    <script src="jquery.tmpl.js" type="text/javascript"></script>
    <style type="text/css">
        .dcell img {height: 60px}
        #basketTable {border: none; border-collapse: collapse}
        th, td {padding: 4px; width: 50px}
        td:first-child, th:first-child {width: 150px}
        #placeholder {text-align: center}
        #productWrapper {float: left; width: 65%}
        #basket {text-align: left;}
        #buttonDiv {clear: both; margin: 5px}
        #logo {font-size: 1.5em; background-size: contain; margin: 1px;
            border: none; color: inherit}
        #logoWrapper {margin-bottom: 5px}
        #theader {border: none}

    </style>
    <script type="text/javascript">
        $(document).ready(function() {
            $.getJSON("mydata.json", function(data) {
                var flowers = $('#flowerTmpl').tmpl(data);
                var rowCount = 1;
                for (var i = 0; i < flowers.length; i += 2) {
                    $("<h2><a href=#>" + data[i].name + " & " + data[i + 1].name
                      + "</a></h2>").appendTo("#products");
                    $("<div id='row" + (rowCount++) + "'></div>")
                        .appendTo("#products")
                        .append(flowers.slice(i, i + 2))
                }
                $('#products').accordion();

                $('input').change(function(event) {
                    $('#placeholder').hide();
                    var fname = $(this).attr("name");
                    var row = $('tr[id=' + fname + ']');
                    if (row.length == 0) {
                        $('#rowTmpl').tmpl({
```

```
                        name: fname,
                        val:  $(this).val(),
                        product: $(this).siblings("label").text()
                    }).appendTo("#basketTable").find("a").click(function() {
                        removeTableRow($(this).closest("tr"));
                        var iElem = $('#products').find("input[name=" + fname + "]")
                        $('#products').accordion("activate",
                            iElem.closest("div[id^=row]").prev())
                        iElem.val(0).select();
                    })
                } else if ($(this).val() != "0") {
                    row.children().eq(1).text($(this).val())
                } else {
                    removeTableRow(row)
                }
            })
        });

        $('#buttonDiv, #basket').wrapAll("<div />").parent().css({
             float: "left",
             marginLeft: "2px"
         })

         $('button').button()

        function removeTableRow(row) {
            row.remove();
            if ($('#basketTable tbody').children(':visible').length == 0) {
                $('#placeholder').show();
            }
        }
    });
  </script>
  <script id="rowTmpl" type="text/x-jquery-tmpl">
      <tr id=${name}><td>${product}</td><td>${val}</td>
          <td><a href=#>Remove</a></td></tr>
  </script>
  <script id="flowerTmpl" type="text/x-jquery-tmpl">
      <div class="dcell">
          <img src="${product}.png"/>
          <label for="${product}">${name}:</label>
          <input name="${product}" value="0" />
      </div>
  </script>
</head>
<body>
  <div id="logoWrapper" class="ui-widget ui-widget-content ui-corner-all">
      <h1 id="logo">Jacqui's Flower Shop</h1>
  </div>
  <form method="post" action="http://node.jacquisflowershop.com/order">
      <div id="productWrapper">
          <div id="products"></div>
```

```
        </div>
        <div id="basket" class="ui-widget ui-widget-content ui-corner-all">
            <table border=0 id="basketTable">
                <thead id="theader" class="ui-widget-header">
                    <tr>
                        <th class="ui-corner-tl">Product</th><th>Quantity</th>
                        <th class="ui-corner-tr">Remove</th></tr>
                </thead>
                <tr id="placeholder"><td colspan=3>No Products</td></tr>
            </table>
        </div>
        <div id="buttonDiv"><button type="submit">Place Order</button></div>
    </form>
</body>
</html>
```

I have wrapped the buttonDiv and basket elements in a new div element and adjusted some of the CSS styles to adjust the positioning of these elements. And, as Figure 25-11 shows, I call the button method to create a jQuery UI button.

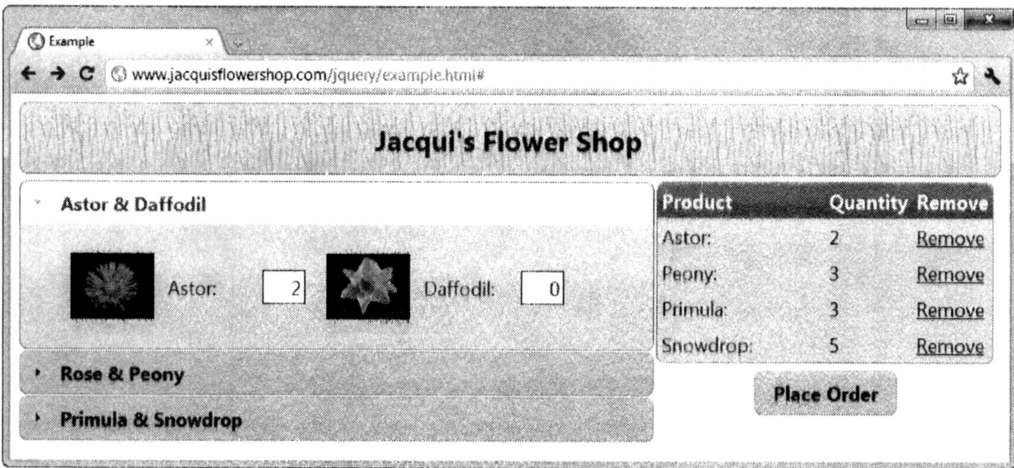

Figure 25-11. Repositioning and transforming the button element

Adding the Completion Dialog

When the user clicks the Place Order button, I want to collect some additional information from them. I showed you how to display a multipart form using tabs in Chapter 20, so for some variety, I'll use a dialog widget this time. Listing 25-8 shows the changes to the document for the dialog.

Listing 25-8. Adding the Dialog

```
<!DOCTYPE html>
<html>
<head>
```

```
<title>Example</title>
<script src="jquery-1.7.js" type="text/javascript"></script>
<script src="jquery-ui-1.8.16.custom.js" type="text/javascript"></script>
<link rel="stylesheet" type="text/css" href="styles.css"/>
<link rel="stylesheet" type="text/css" href="jquery-ui-1.8.16.custom.css"/>
<script src="jquery.tmpl.js" type="text/javascript"></script>
<style type="text/css">
    .dcell img {height: 60px}
    #basketTable {border: none; border-collapse: collapse}
    th, td {padding: 4px; width: 50px}
    td:first-child, th:first-child {width: 150px}
    #placeholder {text-align: center}
    #productWrapper {float: left; width: 65%}
    #basket {text-align: left;}
    #buttonDiv {clear: both; margin: 5px}
    #logo {font-size: 1.5em; background-size: contain; margin: 1px;
        border: none; color: inherit}
    #logoWrapper {margin-bottom: 5px}
    #theader {border: none}
    #completeDialog input {width: 150px; margin-left: 5px; text-align: left}
    #completeDialog label {width: 60px; text-align: right}
</style>
<script type="text/javascript">
    $(document).ready(function() {
        $.getJSON("mydata.json", function(data) {
            var flowers = $('#flowerTmpl').tmpl(data);
            var rowCount = 1;
            for (var i = 0; i < flowers.length; i += 2) {
                $("<h2><a href=#>" + data[i].name + " & " + data[i + 1].name
                  + "</a></h2>").appendTo("#products");
                $("<div id='row" + (rowCount++) + "'></div>")
                    .appendTo("#products")
                    .append(flowers.slice(i, i + 2))
            }
            $('#products').accordion();

            $('#products input').change(function(event) {
                $('#placeholder').hide();
                var fname = $(this).attr("name");
                var row = $('tr[id=' + fname + ']');
                if (row.length == 0) {
                    $('#rowTmpl').tmpl({
                        name: fname,
                        val:  $(this).val(),
                        product: $(this).siblings("label").text()
                    }).appendTo("#basketTable").find("a").click(function() {
                        removeTableRow($(this).closest("tr"));
                        var iElem = $('#products').find("input[name=" + fname + "]")
                        $('#products').accordion("activate",
                            iElem.closest("div[id^=row]").prev())
                        iElem.val(0).select();
                    })
```

```
                } else if ($(this).val() != "0") {
                    row.children().eq(1).text($(this).val())
                } else {
                    removeTableRow(row)
                }
            })
        });

        $('#buttonDiv, #basket').wrapAll("<div />").parent().css({
             float: "left",
             marginLeft: "2px"
         })

         $('button').button()

         $('#completeDialog').dialog({
            modal: true,
            buttons: [{text: "OK", click: sendOrder},
                      {text: "Cancel", click: function() {
                        $("#completeDialog").dialog("close");
                      }}]
        });

        function sendOrder() {

        }

        function removeTableRow(row) {
            row.remove();
            if ($('#basketTable tbody').children(':visible').length == 0) {
                $('#placeholder').show();
            }
        }
    });
</script>
<script id="rowTmpl" type="text/x-jquery-tmpl">
    <tr id=${name}><td>${product}</td><td>${val}</td>
        <td><a href=#>Remove</a></td></tr>
</script>
<script id="flowerTmpl" type="text/x-jquery-tmpl">
    <div class="dcell">
        <img src="${product}.png"/>
        <label for="${product}">${name}:</label>
        <input name="${product}" value="0" />
    </div>
</script>
</head>
<body>
    <div id="logoWrapper" class="ui-widget ui-widget-content ui-corner-all">
        <h1 id="logo">Jacqui's Flower Shop</h1>
    </div>
    <form method="post" action="http://node.jacquisflowershop.com/order">
```

```
        <div id="productWrapper">
            <div id="products"></div>
        </div>
        <div id="basket" class="ui-widget ui-widget-content ui-corner-all">
            <table border=0 id="basketTable">
                <thead id="theader" class="ui-widget-header">
                    <tr>
                        <th class="ui-corner-tl">Product</th><th>Quantity</th>
                        <th class="ui-corner-tr">Remove</th></tr>
                </thead>
                <tr id="placeholder"><td colspan=3>No Products</td></tr>
            </table>
        </div>
        <div id="buttonDiv"><button type="submit">Place Order</button></div>
    </form>
    <div id="completeDialog" title="Complete Purchase">
            <div><label for="name">Name: </label><input name="first" /></div>
            <div><label for="email">Email: </label><input name="email" /></div>
            <div><label for="city">City: </label><input name="city" /></div>
    </div>
</body>
</html>
```

I have added a div element with the content that will be displayed to the user in the body element, along with some CSS styles to override those that are in the styles.css file that is imported into the document using a link element. Here is the call to the dialog method that creates the dialog widget:

```
$('#completeDialog').dialog({
    modal: true,
    buttons: [{text: "OK", click: sendOrder},
        {text: "Cancel", click: function() {
        $("#completeDialog").dialog("close");
    }}]
});
```

I have created a modal dialog that has two buttons. Clicking the Cancel button will close the dialog. Clicking the OK button will call the sendOrder function. This function doesn't do anything at the moment.

As you will remember from Chapter 22, the dialog widget is open by default, which means that it is shown to the user as soon as it is created. You can see how it appears in Figure 25-12.

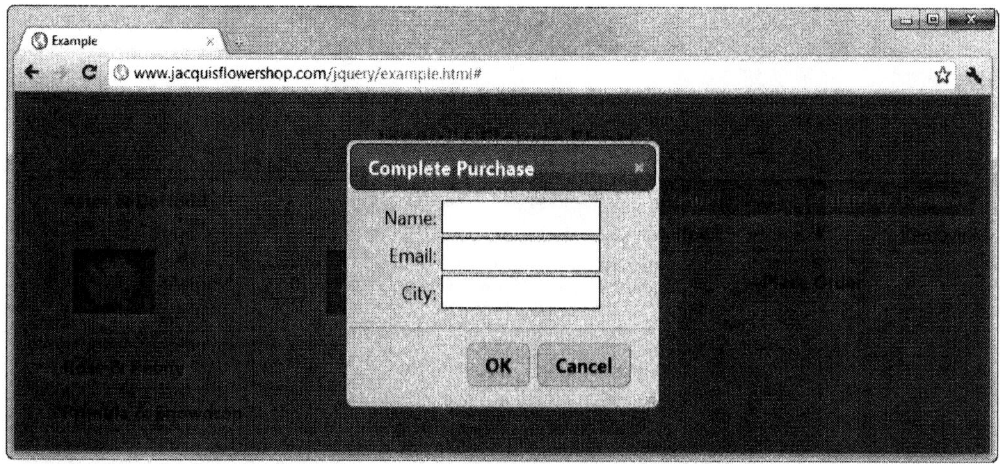

Figure 25-12. The dialog used to complete the purchase

■ **Tip** Notice that I have narrowed the selection when I set up the change event on the input elements. I limit the selection to exclude those input elements in the dialog. If I had not done this, entering a value in the Complete Purchase dialog would have added a new item in the basket.

Handling the Place Order Button Click

I don't want the user to see the dialog box until they click the Place Order button. I use the `autoOpen` setting to hide the dialog until it is needed and use the `click` method to handle the button click, as Listing 25-9 shows.

Listing 25-9. Hiding the Dialog and Handling the Button Click

```
...
<script type="text/javascript">
    $(document).ready(function() {
        $.getJSON("mydata.json", function(data) {
            var flowers = $('#flowerTmpl').tmpl(data);
            var rowCount = 1;
            for (var i = 0; i < flowers.length; i += 2) {
                $("<h2><a href=#>" + data[i].name + " & " + data[i + 1].name
                  + "</a></h2>").appendTo("#products");
                $("<div id='row" + (rowCount++) + "'></div>")
                    .appendTo("#products")
                    .append(flowers.slice(i, i + 2))
            }
            $('#products').accordion();
```

```
        $('input').change(function(event) {
            $('#placeholder').hide();
            var fname = $(this).attr("name");
            var row = $('tr[id=' + fname + ']');
            if (row.length == 0) {
                $('#rowTmpl').tmpl({
                    name: fname,
                    val:  $(this).val(),
                    product: $(this).siblings("label").text()
                }).appendTo("#basketTable").find("a").click(function() {
                    removeTableRow($(this).closest("tr"));
                    var iElem = $('#products').find("input[name=" + fname + "]")
                    $('#products').accordion("activate",
                        iElem.closest("div[id^=row]").prev())
                    iElem.val(0).select();
                })
            } else if ($(this).val() != "0") {
                row.children().eq(1).text($(this).val())
            } else {
                removeTableRow(row)
            }
        })
    });

    $('#buttonDiv, #basket').wrapAll("<div />").parent().css({
         float: "left",
         marginLeft: "2px"
     })

     $('button').button().click(function(e) {
        e.preventDefault();
        if ($('#placeholder:visible').length) {

            $('<div>Please select some products</div>').dialog({
                modal: true,
                buttons: [{text: "OK",
                    click: function() {$(this).dialog("close")}}]
            })
        } else {
            $('#completeDialog').dialog("open");
        }
     })

     $('#completeDialog').dialog({
        modal: true,
        autoOpen: false,
        buttons: [{text: "OK", click: sendOrder},
                  {text: "Cancel", click: function() {
                    $("#completeDialog").dialog("close");
                  }}]
```

```
        });

        function sendOrder() {

        }

        function removeTableRow(row) {
            row.remove();
            if ($('#basketTable tbody').children(':visible').length == 0) {
                $('#placeholder').show();
            }
        }
    });
</script>
...
```

When the user clicks the button, I check to see whether the placeholder element is visible. I do this using jQuery, using a selector that produces a jQuery object that will contain elements only if the placeholder is visible.

I am using the visibility of the placeholder as a proxy for the user having selected some products. The placeholder is hidden if there are any selections in the basket, and so a visible placeholder tells me that there are no selections.

▪ **Tip** This is a nice example of the way you can layer functionality in a document, but it does mean that my simple test for product selection depends on the implementation of the basket and will need to change if I ever modify the way that the basket works.

I create and display a dialog widget dynamically if the user clicks the button without having selected any products. You can see how this appears in Figure 25-13. If selections have been made, then the completion dialog is shown to capture the final information I want from the user.

Figure 25-13. Displaying a dialog if there is no product selection

Completing the Order

All that remains is to implement the sendOrder function. I have already shown you the different ways that you can send data to the server via Ajax, so to keep this chapter simple, I will simply collect the values from the various input elements and create a JSON object that can be sent to a server for processing. Listing 25-10 shows the additions to the document.

Listing 25-10. Completing the Order Process

```
...
function sendOrder() {
    var data = new Object();
    $('input').each(function(index, elem) {
        var jqElem = $(elem);
        data[jqElem.attr("name")] = jqElem.val();
    })
    console.log(JSON.stringify(data));
    $('#completeDialog').dialog("close");
    $('#products input').val("0");
    $('#products').accordion("activate", 0)
    $('#basketTable tbody').children(':visible').remove();
    $('#placeholder').show();
}
...
```

In this function I get the value from each of the input elements and add them as properties to an object that I then convert to JSON and write to the console.

More usefully, I then reset the document, closing the dialog, resetting the values of the input elements, switching to the first panel of the accordion, and resetting the basket. Figure 25-14 shows the document with some product selection. I'll use these to generate the JSON string.

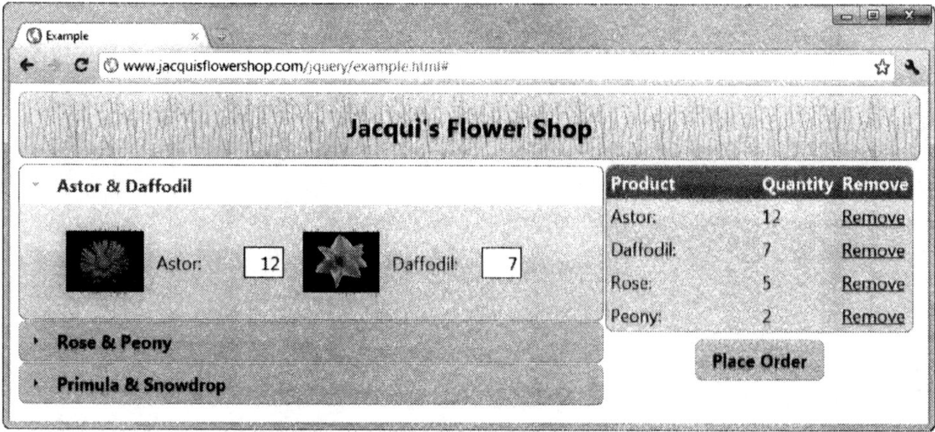

Figure 25-14. Selecting products using the example document

When I click the Place Order button, I am presented with the dialog requesting additional information, as shown in Figure 25-15.

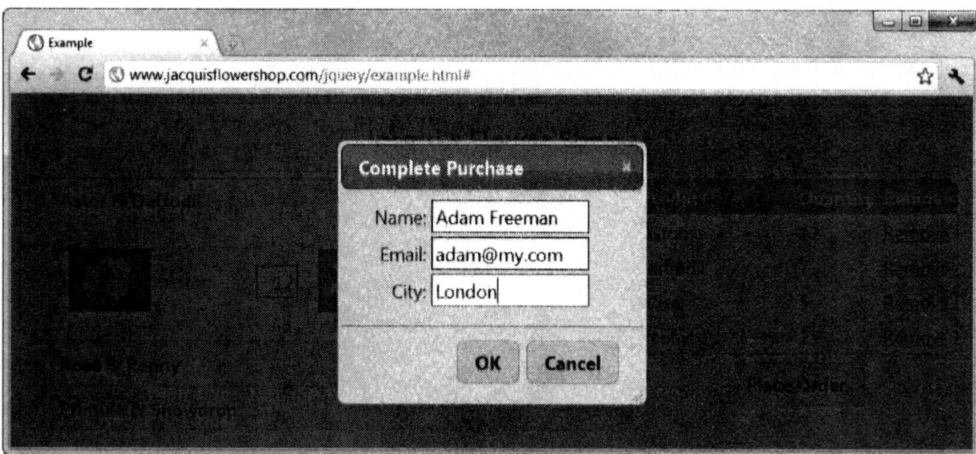

Figure 25-15. Providing additional information to complete the order

Finally, clicking the OK button generates the JSON and resets the document. The JSON for this example is as follows:

```
{"astor":"12","daffodil":"7","rose":"5","peony":"2","primula":"0","snowdrop":"0",
    "first":"Adam Freeman","email":"adam@my.com","city":"London"}
```

And, as Figure 25-16 shows, you are back where you started, ready to go through the process again.

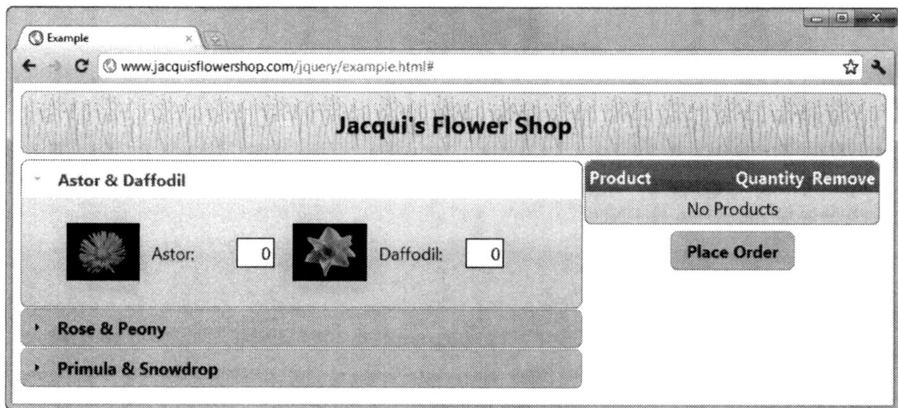

Figure 25-16. Resetting the document

Summary

In this chapter, I refactored the example document to incorporate features from jQuery UI. I added some of the widgets, such as accordion, dialog, and button, as well as gave an initial look at how you can apply the jQuery UI CSS framework classes to manage the appearance of other elements. I give more detail about these CSS classes in Chapter 34.

PART 5

Using jQuery Mobile

CHAPTER 26

Getting Started with jQuery Mobile

In this chapter, I show you how to obtain jQuery Mobile and add it to an HTML document. I also explain that jQuery Mobile takes a different approach to creating widgets and how you must adapt to accommodate this approach. Touch-enabled devices provide some unique challenges for web application developers, and I explain some of the core features that jQuery Mobile provides to help simplify the process and set out some general guidance for the development and testing of mobile web apps. Table 26-1 provides the summary for this chapter.

Table 26-1. *Chapter Summary*

Problem	Solution	Listing
Add jQuery Mobile to an HTML document.	Add a `script` element to import the jQuery and jQuery Mobile libraries and a `link` element to import the CSS.	1
Create a jQuery Mobile page.	Use the `data-role` attribute with a value of `page` .	2
Disable the browser virtual page.	Configure the viewport.	3
Defer the execution of custom JavaScript code until after jQuery Mobile has enhanced a document.	Use the `pageinit` event.	4
Simplify touch event handling.	Use the jQuery Mobile gesture and virtual mouse events.	5–7
Respond to changes in device orientation.	Handle the `orientationchange` event or use CSS media queries.	8, 9

Setting Up jQuery Mobile

To start this chapter, I'll show you how to obtain and install jQuery Mobile. jQuery Mobile is built on the foundation of jQuery and jQuery UI, so you'll see some common patterns that are consistent with the underlying libraries.

Obtaining jQuery Mobile

The first thing you need is jQuery Mobile, which is available from `http://jquerymobile.com`. As I write this, the current version of jQuery Mobile is 1.0, and you can get a zip file from the download page. For version 1.0, this is called `jquery.mobile-1.0.zip`.

■ **Tip** Just as with jQuery and jQuery UI, jQuery Mobile can be loaded via a content distribution network (CDN). I described CDNs in Chapter 5, and they can be a great idea for Internet-deployed web applications (but rarely for intranet applications). The jQuery Mobile download page includes details of the links you will require to use jQuery Mobile via a CDN.

Creating a Theme

jQuery Mobile supports a theme framework, which is like a simplified version of the one that jQuery UI uses. There is a default theme included in the jQuery Mobile package, but if you want to create a custom theme, you can do so at `http://jquerymobile.com/themeroller`. Using the ThemeRoller application generates a zip file that contains a CSS file to include in your web documents. I describe how to use the theme framework in Chapter 28, but I'll be using the default theme rather than creating a custom one. This is because the initial release of the theme creation tool is a little unstable—something that I hope has been resolved by the time you read this chapter.

Getting jQuery

You also need jQuery. Version 1.0 of jQuery Mobile is intended to work only with version 1.6.4 of jQuery. This is a temporary situation that I expect to be resolved by the time you read this book. To get an older release of jQuery, go to `http://jquery.com`, click the download link at the top of the page, and select Past Releases from the page contents.

Each release is available uncompressed or minified. For development projects, the uncompressed version is the most useful, since you can debug your own code as well as jQuery. Clicking the Uncompressed link will cause your browser to save a file called `jquery-1.6.4.js`.

■ **Tip** Even though jQuery Mobile is built on jQuery UI, you don't need to install the jQuery UI library. Everything you need is included in the jQuery Mobile download.

Installing jQuery Mobile

You need to copy four items into the directory from which you serve your web content. The first one is the `jquery-1.6.4.js` file that you got from `http://jquery.com`. The other three items are from the jQuery Mobile download:

- The jquery.mobile-1.0.js file (the jQuery Mobile JavaScript library)
- The jquery.mobile-1.0.css file (the CSS styles jQuery Mobile uses)
- The images directory (the jQuery Mobile icons)

Once all four items are in place, you can create an HTML document that uses jQuery Mobile. I called my file example.html, and I saved it in the same directory as the four items in the previous list. Listing 26-1 shows the contents of this file.

Listing 26-1. The Contents of example.html

```
<!DOCTYPE html>
<html>
<head>
    <title>Example</title>
    <meta name="viewport" content="width=device-width, initial-scale=1">
    <link rel="stylesheet" href="jquery.mobile-1.0.css" type="text/css" />
    <script type="text/javascript" src="jquery-1.6.4.js"></script>
    <script type="text/javascript" src="jquery.mobile-1.0.js"></script>
</head>
<body>
    <div data-role="page">
        <div data-role="header">
                <h1>Jacqui's Shop</h1>
        </div>
        <div data-role="content">
            This is Jacqui's Flower Shop
            <p><button>Press Me</button></p>
        </div>
   </div>
</body>
</html>
```

The elements that I have highlighted are required for jQuery Mobile. The two script elements import the jQuery and jQuery Mobile JavaScript libraries, and the link element imports the CSS that jQuery Mobile relies on. Since my HTML file is in the same directory as the JavaScript and CSS files, I am able to refer to these files simply by name.

■ **Tip** Ignore the rest of the document for the moment. I'll explain what the meta element does and how the contents of the body element are used shortly.

Understanding the jQuery Mobile Approach

Although jQuery Mobile is based on jQuery UI, there are some significant differences that you need to be aware of. Before you start digging into the capabilities of jQuery Mobile, I need to explain those differences to provide a context for the information in the following chapters.

TIERED SUPPORT

jQuery Mobile offers different levels of support for different mobile browsers. There are three grades of support available and a long list of the supported devices and browsers in each. At the high end, *A-grade* support provides the richest experience and implements all of the features that I describe in this part of the book.

B-grade support provides everything except Ajax navigation, which I describe in Chapter 27. This is still a good level of functionality, but the movement between pages in an application won't be as smooth as for an A-grade device.

The C-grade category is very basic. Only very old devices fall into this category, and jQuery Mobile is unable to provide much functionality for these devices.

Happily, most modern mobile devices fall into the A-grade category of support. You can see a detailed list of supported devices at `http://jquerymobile.com/demos/1.0/docs/about/platforms.html`.

Understanding Automatic Enhancement

The most striking difference when using jQuery Mobile is that widgets don't have to be created explicitly. When using jQuery UI, you use jQuery to select one or more elements and then apply a method such as `button` or `tabs` to create a specific jQuery UI widget in the document. If you look a Listing 26-1, you will notice that I have not added a `script` element to the document to create any widgets. The only `script` elements are there to import jQuery and jQuery Mobile libraries. And yet, as Figure 26-1 shows, you get formatted content. (This figure shows the Opera Mobile emulator that I use widely in this part of the book and that I introduce properly later in this chapter.)

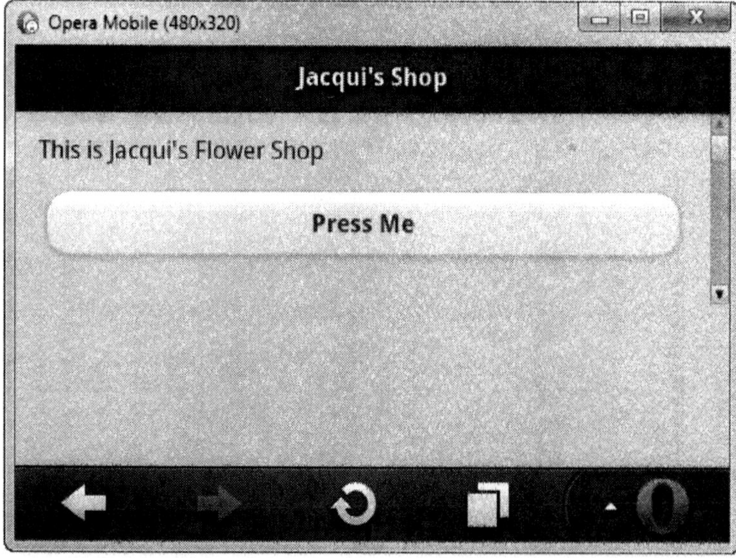

Figure 26-1. The example document

■ **Note** For many of the figures in this part of the book, I'll be using the Opera Mobile browser emulator, configured to a screen resolution of 480 by 320 pixels. This is a landscape resolution, which lets me pack more examples into each page, at a resolution that is pretty common for smartphones (although it does tend toward the small side compared with the latest models). This is a reasonable resolution to develop with, although I recommend testing real products at a wider range of common resolutions.

When you bring the jQuery Mobile library into a web page with a `script` element, the page is enhanced automatically. First jQuery Mobile looks for elements that have a `data-role` attribute. The value of these attributes tells jQuery Mobile what enhancements should be applied to the elements. Listing 26-2 highlights the `data-role` attributes in the example document.

■ **Tip** Attributes whose name begins with *data-* are known as *data attributes.* Data attributes have been an informal convention for defining custom attributes for some time and have been included in the official standard for HTML5.

Listing 26-2. The data-role Attributes in the Example Document

```
<!DOCTYPE html>
<html>
<head>
    <title>Example</title>
    <meta name="viewport" content="width=device-width, initial-scale=1">
    <link rel="stylesheet" href="jquery.mobile-1.0.css" type="text/css" />
    <script type="text/javascript" src="jquery-1.6.4.js"></script>
    <script type="text/javascript" src="jquery.mobile-1.0.js"></script>
</head>
<body>
    <div data-role="page">
        <div data-role="header">
                <h1>Jacqui's Shop</h1>
        </div>
        <div data-role="content">
            This is Jacqui's Flower Shop
            <p><button>Press Me</button></p>
        </div>
   </div>
</body>
</html>
```

One of the unusual features of jQuery Mobile is that a single HTML document can contain multiple pages (a feature that I demonstrate in Chapter 27). The page is the building block of a jQuery Mobile application. There is only one page in this example, and it is denoted by the `div` element whose `data-`

role value is page. Because the page is nested inside an HTML document, you also need to provide jQuery Mobile with additional information about the purpose of the elements contained within the page. There are two other data-role attributes, which tell jQuery Mobile which element contains the header information for page and which element contains the content. Table 26-2 summarizes the three data-role values in this example and their significance. You can readily correlate the div elements and their data-role values with the structure of the page shown in Figure 26-1.

■ **Tip** jQuery Mobile will automatically insert the wrapper for the content part of a page. This means that any elements that are not part of another section are treated as content, allowing you to skip explicitly defining an element for that section.

Table 26-2. Data-Role Attribute Values in the Example Document

Value	Description
page	Tells jQuery Mobile to treat the content of the element as a page
header	Tells jQuery Mobile that the element represents the page header
content	Tells jQuery Mobile that the element contains the content for the page

You don't have to take any explicit action to make jQuery Mobile find the elements with data-role attributes and generate a page. This all happens automatically when the HTML document is loaded. Some elements, such as button, are automatically styled (although, as I demonstrate in later chapters, you can configure most widgets using other data attributes).

■ **Tip** jQuery Mobile goes to great lengths to minimize the amount of custom JavaScript that is needed to create a mobile web application. In fact, it is possible to create simple applications without any custom JavaScript at all. This doesn't mean you can build jQuery Mobile applications for browsers that have JavaScript disabled, however. jQuery Mobile is a JavaScript library and requires JavaScript support to perform automatic enhancement of pages.

Understanding the Viewport

Although not part of jQuery Mobile, an important element to add to your HTML documents is the one highlighted in Listing 26-3.

Listing 26-3. The meta Element That Configures the Viewport

```
...
<head>
    <title>Example</title>
    <meta name="viewport" content="width=device-width, initial-scale=1">
    <link rel="stylesheet" href="jquery.mobile-1.0.css" type="text/css" />
    <script type="text/javascript" src="jquery-1.6.4.js"></script>
    <script type="text/javascript" src="jquery.mobile-1.0.js"></script>
</head>
...
```

I have highlighted the meta element whose name attribute is viewport. Many mobile browsers use a *virtual page* to display web content in order to improve compatibility with web sites that have been designed with desktop browsers in mind. This is generally a sensible idea because it provides the user with an overall sense of the page structure, even though the details are too small to read. Figure 26-2 shows the jQuery Mobile home page as it is displayed initially and zoomed so that the text is readable.

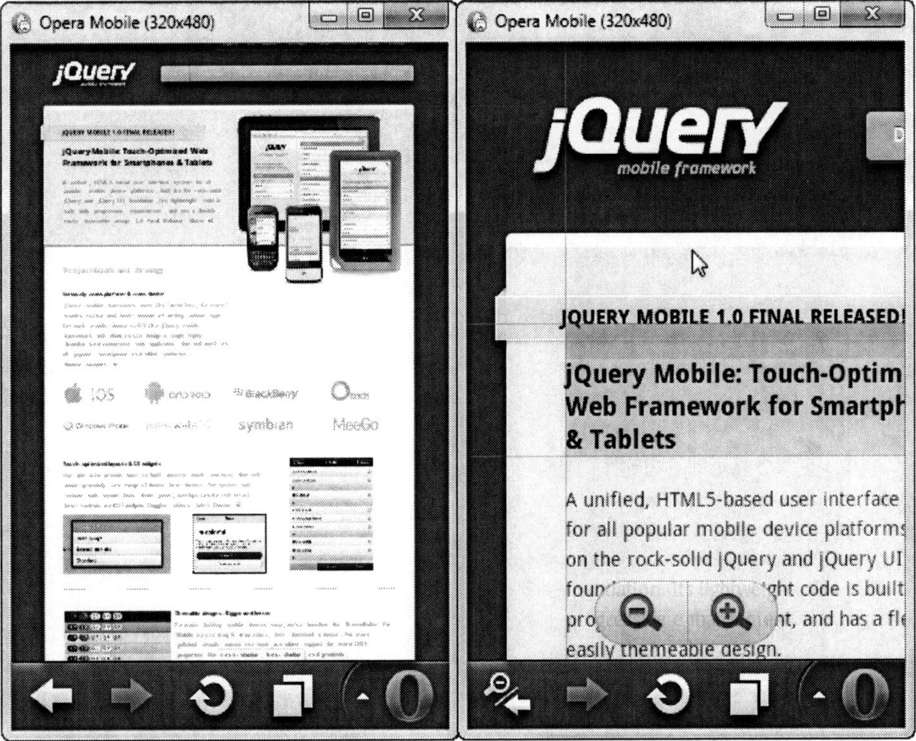

Figure 26-2. The mobile browser virtual page

The first frame shows the jQuery Mobile web site in a portrait orientation (which accentuates the effect). The text is too small to read, but mobile browsers have support for zooming in to regions of the page, as the second frame shows. The virtual page is a compromise, to be sure, but it's an understandable one given that relatively few web sites are tailored to mobile devices.

The problem is that the virtual page is applied without much discrimination and causes problems for jQuery Mobile applications. Figure 26-3 shows how the example document is displayed when the virtual page is used.

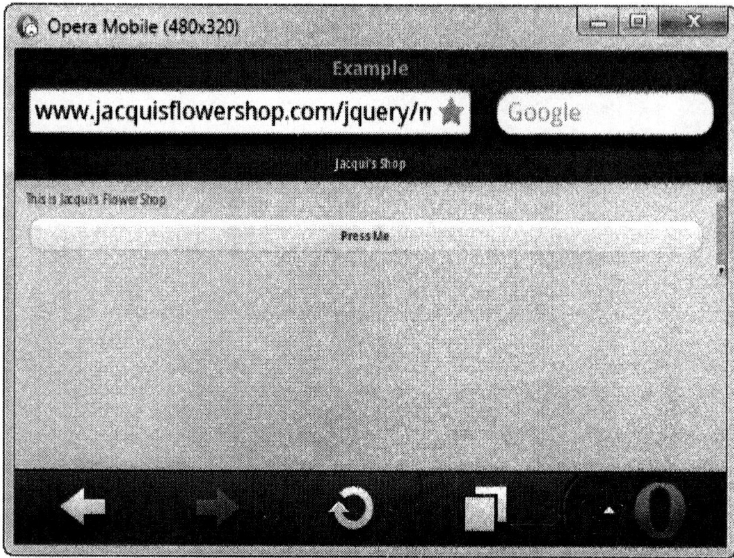

Figure 26-3. The example document displayed in a wide virtual page

As the figure demonstrates, the jQuery Mobile elements are displayed so small that they are unusable. The `meta` element in the example document tells the browser that the width of the page should be the width of the screen. This causes the browser to display your jQuery Mobile elements at a sensible size.

Understanding jQuery Mobile Events

There are two important pieces of information about events as they relate to jQuery Mobile. In the sections that follow, I describe each of them.

Understanding the pageinit Event

jQuery Mobile automatically enhances pages by registering its functions to handle the jQuery `ready` event that you have been relying on in earlier parts of the book. If you want to include custom JavaScript in a document, you have to take care not to have your code executed before jQuery Mobile has finished processing the document. This means you have to wait for a different event, called `pageinit`. This event is defined by jQuery Mobile, and it is triggered when jQuery Mobile has finished initializing the document. There is no convenient method like there is for the `ready` event, so you have to use the `bind` method to associate your function with the event, as demonstrated in Listing 26-4.

Listing 26-4. Using the pageinit Event

```
<!DOCTYPE html>
<html>
<head>
    <title>Example</title>
    <meta name="viewport" content="width=device-width, initial-scale=1">
    <link rel="stylesheet" href="jquery.mobile-1.0.css" type="text/css" />
    <script type="text/javascript" src="jquery-1.6.4.js"></script>
    <script type="text/javascript">
        $(document).bind("pageinit", function() {
            $('button').click(function() {
                console.log("Button pressed")
            })
        });
    </script>
    <script type="text/javascript" src="jquery.mobile-1.0.js"></script>
</head>
<body>
    <div data-role="page">
        <div data-role="header">
                <h1>Jacqui's Shop</h1>
        </div>
        <div data-role="content">
            This is Jacqui's Flower Shop
            <p><button>Press Me</button></p>
        </div>
   </div>
</body>
</html>
```

The arguments to the bind method are the name of the event you are interested in and the function that should be executed when the event is triggered. Your function will be executed only when the event is triggered for the element or elements you have selected and applied the bind method to.

In this example, I have used the bind method to register a function that will be executed when the pageinit event is triggered. Inside that function, I place the statements that I want performed when the document has been loaded and processed. In this case, I have used jQuery to select the button element in the document and used the click method to register another function that will be performed when the button is clicked, just as I have been doing throughout this book.

■ **Tip** Notice that I have inserted my new script element *before* the jQuery Mobile JavaScript library is imported into the document. This isn't essential for the pageinit event but is required for the mobileinit event that you use to change some jQuery Mobile settings (I demonstrate how to do this in Chapter 27). I find it a good idea to always put the custom code before the importing the jQuery Mobile library, even if I am only responding to the pageinit event.

Understanding Touch Events

There is a specification for touch events in a browser, but it is pretty low-level because there is a lot of variety in the touch interaction model. Some devices support multi-touch, for example, and there is wide variety in the way that touch gestures are interpreted. Table 26-3 describes these low-level touch events.

Table 26-3. *The Standard Touch Events*

Event	Description
`touchstart`	Triggered when the user touches the screen. For multi-touch devices, this event will be triggered each time a finger touches the screen.
`touchend`	Triggered when the user removes a finger from the screen.
`touchmove`	Triggered when the user holds a moves a finger while it is touching the screen.
`touchcancel`	Triggered when a touch sequence is disrupted. The meaning of this is device-specific, but a common example is when the user slides a finger off the edge of the screen.

The responsibility of interpreting these events and working out their significance falls to the web developer. It is a painful task that is fraught with errors and one that I recommend you avoid wherever possible. It's something that jQuery Mobile helps with, as I explain shortly.

■ **Tip** If you do want to get into the details of touch events, then you can find the specification at `www.w3.org/TR/touch-events`. This includes full descriptions of the events and the properties that are available for getting the detail of each touch interaction.

Most web sites have not been designed with touch events in mind. To support the widest possible range of web site scripts, the mobile browsers synthesize mouse events from the touch events. This means the browser triggers the touch events and then generates corresponding (fake) mouse events that represent the same actions, but as though they had been performed with a traditional mouse. Listing 26-5 contains a useful script that demonstrates how this is done.

Listing 26-5. Monitoring Touch and Synthesized Mouse Events

```
<!DOCTYPE html>
<html>
<head>
    <title>Event Test</title>
    <meta name="viewport" content="width=device-width, initial-scale=1">
    <link rel="stylesheet" href="jquery.mobile-1.0.css" type="text/css" />
    <script type="text/javascript" src="jquery-1.6.4.js"></script>
```

```
    <style type="text/css">
        table {border-collapse: collapse; border: medium solid black; padding: 4px}
        #placeholder {text-align: center}
        #countContainer * {display: inline; width:50px}
        th {width: 100px}
    </style>
    <script type="text/javascript">
        $(document).bind("pageinit", function() {
            var eventList = [
                "mousedown", "mouseup", "click", "mousecancel",
                "touchstart", "touchend", "touchmove", "touchcancel"]

            for (var i = 0; i < eventList.length; i++) {
                $('#pressme').bind(eventList[i], handleEvent)
            }

            $('#reset').bind("tap", function() {
                $('tbody').children().remove();
                $('#placeholder').show();
                startTime = 0;
            })
        });

        startTime = 0;
        function handleEvent(ev) {
            var timeDiff = startTime == 0 ? 0 : (ev.timeStamp - startTime);
            if (startTime == 0) {
                startTime = ev.timeStamp
            }
            $('#placeholder').hide();
            $('<tr><td>' + ev.type + '</td><td>' + timeDiff + '</td></tr>')
                .appendTo("tbody");
        }
    </script>
    <script type="text/javascript" src="jquery.mobile-1.0.js"></script>
</head>
<body>
    <div data-role="page">
        <div data-role="content">
            <div id="tcontainer" class="ui-grid-a">
                <div class="ui-block-a">
                    <button id="pressme">Press Me</button>
                    <button id="reset">Reset</button>
                </div>
                <div class="ui-block-b">
                    <table border=1>
                        <thead>
                            <tr><th>Event</th><th>Time</th></tr>
                            <tr id="placeholder"><td colspan=2>No Events</td><tr>
                        </thead>
                        <tbody></tbody>
                    </table>
```

```
                </div>
            </div>
        </div>
    </div>
</body>
</html>
```

There are two buttons and a table in this example. The Press Me button is wired up so that a selection of mouse and touch events are displayed in the table when the button is clicked. For each event, the event type and the number of milliseconds since the last event are shown. The Reset button clears the table and resets the timer. You can see the effect in Figure 26-4.

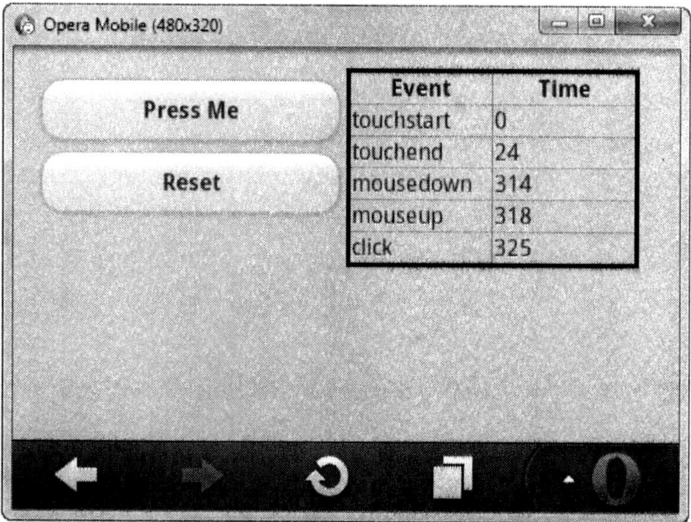

Figure 26-4. Observing the sequence of touch and mouse events

Table 26-4 shows the sequence of events and timings that arise when clicking the button in the Opera Mobile browser.

Table 26-4. *The Event Sequence from Opera Mobile*

Event	Relative Time
touchstart	0
touchend	24
mousedown	314
mouseup	318
click	325

You can see that the touchstart and touchend events are triggered first, responding to the moments when I touched and then released the screen. The browser then generates mousedown and mouseup events and then a click event. Notice that there is quite a delay between the touchend and mousedown events being triggered, roughly 300 milliseconds. This is enough of a delay to make relying on the synthesized events problematic because your web application will lag behind the user's touch interactions. Not all browsers have this problem, but it is common enough to be an issue, and I recommend you measure the latency on the browsers you intend to target.

Using the jQuery Mobile Gesture Methods

jQuery Mobile does two things to make working with events easier. The first is a set of gesture events that are triggered in response to certain sequences of low-level touch events, meaning that you don't have to analyze the touch sequence yourself to make sense of what gesture the user was making. These events are described in Table 26-5.

Table 26-5. *The Standard Touch Events*

Event	Description
tap	Triggered when the user touches the screen and then removes their finger in quick succession
taphold	Triggered after the user touches the screen, keeps their finger in place for about a second, and then releases
swipe	Triggered when the user performs a horizontal drag of at least 30 pixels with a vertical variation of less than 20 pixels within a one-second period
swipeleft	Triggered when the user swipes in the left direction
swiperight	Triggered when the user swipes in the right direction

These events make dealing with basic gestures very simple. Listing 26-6 adds these events to the timing example.

Listing 26-6. Adding the jQuery Mobile Gesture Events to the Timing Example

```
...
<script type="text/javascript">
    $(document).bind("pageinit", function() {
        var eventList = [
            "mousedown", "mouseup", "click", "mousecancel",
            "touchstart", "touchend", "touchmove", "touchcancel",
            "tap", "taphold", "swipe", "swipeleft", "swiperight"]

        for (var i = 0; i < eventList.length; i++) {
            $('#pressme').bind(eventList[i], handleEvent)
        }
```

```
        $('#reset').bind("tap", function() {
            $('tbody').children().remove();
            $('#placeholder').show();
            startTime = 0;
        })
    });

    startTime = 0;
    function handleEvent(ev) {
        var timeDiff = startTime == 0 ? 0 : (ev.timeStamp - startTime);
        if (startTime == 0) {
            startTime = ev.timeStamp
        }
        $('#placeholder').hide();
        $('<tr><td>' + ev.type + '</td><td>' + timeDiff + '</td></tr>')
            .appendTo("tbody");
    }
</script>
...
```

Figure 26-5 shows what happens when I click the button in the browser.

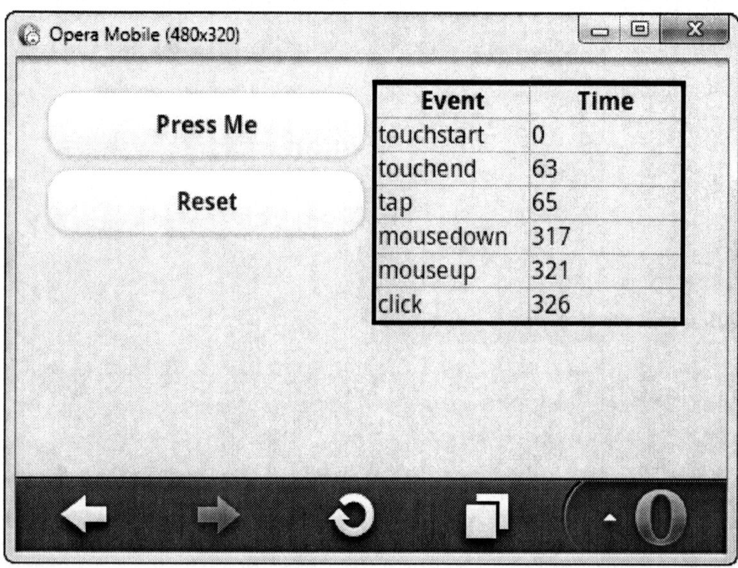

Figure 26-5. Adding the jQuery Mobile gesture events to the timing example

Table 26-6 shows the event sequence in an easy-to-read table. Since I am clicking a button, the only gesture event that appears is tap. The important thing to note is that the tap event is triggered quickly, within a couple of milliseconds of my releasing from the screen.

Table 26-6. The Event Sequence from Opera Mobile

Event	Relative Time
touchstart	0
touchend	63
tap	**65**
mousedown	317
mouseup	321
click	326

The nice thing about the gesture events is that jQuery Mobile will trigger them even in browsers that don't support touch events or that are running on devices without touch interfaces. Figure 26-6 shows the example running in the Google Chrome desktop browser.

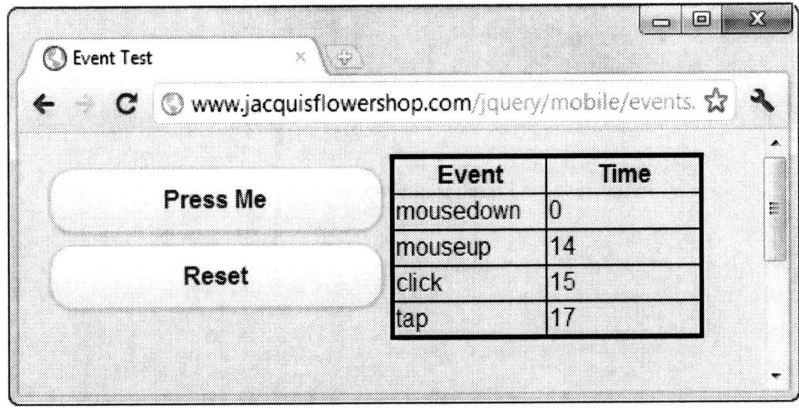

Figure 26-6. The event sequence in a desktop browser

Table 26-7 shows the sequence of events and their relative timings more clearly.

Table 26-7. The Event Sequence from Google Chrome

Event	Relative Time
mousedown	0
mouseup	14

click	15
tap	**17**

As you might expect, there are no touchstart and touchend events in this sequence, and the order of the events is different (because the mouse events are real, rather than synthesized). Even so, the tap event is still triggered, only two milliseconds after the click event.

I use the tap event instead of click in mobile web applications because it avoids the timing issue that comes from the synthesized events and because it is also generated on nontouch platforms.

Using the jQuery Mobile Virtual Mouse Events

Browsers are not required to synthesize mouse events, meaning that a web application that works on touch and nontouch devices should listen for both mouse events and touch events. For mobile browses that do synthesize events, you end up with touch and mouse events for each interaction. To help simplify this process, jQuery Mobile defines a set of virtual mouse events. When you register for these events, jQuery Mobile takes care of removing the duplicates and ensuring that the appropriate events are triggered, irrespective of whether you have touch support. Table 26-8 describes the virtual events.

Table 26-8. *The Standard Touch Events*

Event	Description
vmouseover	Triggered in response to mouseover events (there is no equivalent touch event because the user's finger isn't always in contact with the screen)
vmousedown	Triggered in response to touchstart or mousedown events
vmousemove	Triggered in response to touchmove or mousemove events
vmouseup	Triggered in response to touchend or mouseup events
vclick	Triggered in response to the click event
vmousecancel	Triggered in response to touchcancel or mousecancel events

The way that these events are generated creates a mouselike sequence, even on touch devices. To explain what I mean, I have added some of the virtual events to the timing example, as shown in Listing 26-7.

Listing 26-7. Adding the jQuery Mobile Virtual Events to the Timing Example

```
<script type="text/javascript">
    $(document).bind("pageinit", function() {
        var eventList = [
            "mousedown", "mouseup", "click", "mousecancel",
            "touchstart", "touchend", "touchmove", "touchcancel",
```

```
            "tap", "taphold", "swipe", "swipeleft", "swiperight",
            "vmouseover", "vmousedown", "vmouseup", "vclick", "vmousecancel"]

        for (var i = 0; i < eventList.length; i++) {
            $('#pressme').bind(eventList[i], handleEvent)
        }

        $('#reset').bind("tap", function() {
            $('tbody').children().remove();
            $('#placeholder').show();
            startTime = 0;
        })
    });

    startTime = 0;
    function handleEvent(ev) {
        var timeDiff = startTime == 0 ? 0 : (ev.timeStamp - startTime);
        if (startTime == 0) {
            startTime = ev.timeStamp
        }
        $('#placeholder').hide();
        $('<tr><td>' + ev.type + '</td><td>' + timeDiff + '</td></tr>')
            .appendTo("tbody");
    }
</script>
```

When I touch the screen, jQuery Mobile generates the vmouseover and vmousedown events. These don't have any meaning in a purely touch environment. If you are writing an application that works across platforms, then you might want to perform some action when the user moves the desktop mouse over an element. The triggering of the synthetic vmouseover event in response to the real touchstart allows you to perform the same action seamlessly for touch devices. You can see the result in Figure 26-7.

Figure 26-7. Adding the virtual events to the timing example

Table 26-9 shows the event and timing sequence in a more easily readable form. Although the `vclick` event is triggered long before the synthetic `click` event, this isn't always the case, and I do not recommend using `vclick` as a substitute for `click` as a way to address the event latency issue.

Table 26-9. *The Event Sequence from Google Chrome*

Event	Relative Time
touchstart	0
vmouseover	**1**
vmousedown	**2**
touchend	55
vmouseup	56
vclick	**58**
tap	58
mousedown	319
mouseup	331
click	333

■ **Caution** It is important not to make assumptions about the way that the real and virtual events are interleaved. This is because the event sequence on a nontouch device will be different. The order of the virtual events relative to one another will be the same; the intervening real events can change.

Responding to Device Orientation Changes

Most mobile browsers support an event called orientationchange, which is triggered every time the device is rotated through 90 degrees. To make your life easier, jQuery Mobile will synthesize the orientationevent when it is not supported by the browser. This is done by listening for changes in the window size and looking at the ratio of the new height and width values. Listing 26-8 shows how you can respond to this event.

Listing 26-8. Responding to Changes in Orientation

```
<!DOCTYPE html>
<html>
<head>
    <title>Example</title>
    <meta name="viewport" content="width=device-width, initial-scale=1">
    <link rel="stylesheet" href="jquery.mobile-1.0.css" type="text/css" />
    <script type="text/javascript" src="jquery-1.6.4.js"></script>
    <script type="text/javascript">
        $(document).bind("pageinit", function() {
            $(window).bind("orientationchange", function(e) {
                $('#status').text(e.orientation)
            })
            $('#status').text(jQuery.event.special.orientationchange.orientation())
        });
    </script>
    <script type="text/javascript" src="jquery.mobile-1.0.js"></script>
</head>
<body>
    <div data-role="page">
        <div data-role="header">
                <h1>Jacqui's Shop</h1>
        </div>
        <div data-role="content">
            <p>Device orientation is: <b><span id=status></span></b></p>
        </div>
    </div>
</body>
</html>
```

You must select the window object in order to bind to the orientationchange event. In this example, I change the text of a span element indicating the new orientation. This information is available through the orientation property of the Event object that is passed to the handler function.

jQuery Mobile also provides a method for determining the current orientation, as follows:

```
jQuery.event.special.orientationchange.orientation()
```

I use this method in the example to set the contents of the span element, since the `orientationchange` event isn't fired when the page is processed, only when the device is re-oriented subsequently.

If you don't have a real mobile device to test this example with, then you can use one of the emulators that I describe later in this chapter. Most of them have the ability to simulate a rotation, triggered by a particular key stroke or button press. For the Opera Mobile emulator that I am using, pressing Ctrl+Alt+R triggers the effect, which is shown in Figure 26-8.

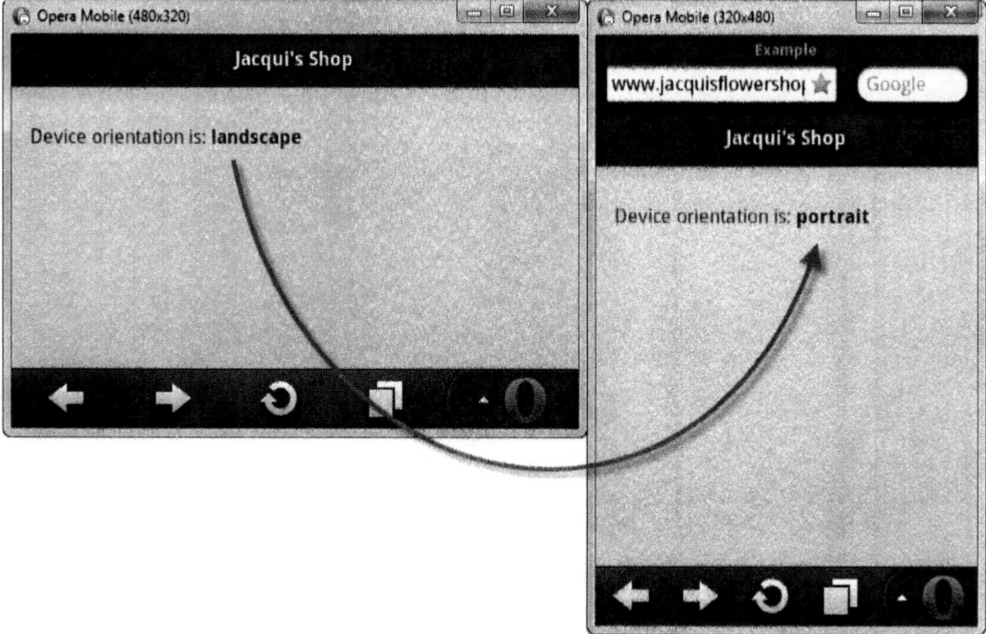

Figure 26-8. Responding to a change in orientation

The synthesized event that jQuery Mobile produces means you can get the same effect when you resize the window of a browser that doesn't support orientation changes, such as a desktop browser. In this case, the orientation is determined by the width and height of the window.

Using Media Queries to Manage Orientation

The `orientationchange` event allows you to respond to changes in orientation using JavaScript. An alternative approach is to use CSS, applying different styles to elements for each orientation, something you can achieve using a CSS *media query*. Listing 26-9 shows how this can be done.

Listing 26-9. Responding to Orientation Using CSS Media Queries

```
<!DOCTYPE html>
<html>
<head>
    <title>Example</title>
    <meta name="viewport" content="width=device-width, initial-scale=1">
    <link rel="stylesheet" href="jquery.mobile-1.0.css" type="text/css" />
    <script type="text/javascript" src="jquery-1.6.4.js"></script>
    <script type="text/javascript" src="jquery.mobile-1.0.js"></script>
    <style type="text/css">

        @media screen and (orientation:portrait) {
            #pstatus {display: none}
            #lstatus {display: inline}
        }

        @media screen and (orientation:landscape) {
            #pstatus {display: inline}
            #lstatus {display: none}
        }

    </style>
</head>
<body>
    <div data-role="page">
        <div data-role="header">
                <h1>Jacqui's Shop</h1>
        </div>
        <div data-role="content">
            <p>Device orientation is:
                <span id=pstatus><b>Portrait</b></span>
                <span id=lstatus><b>Landscape</b></span>
            </p>
        </div>
   </div>
</body>
</html>
```

CSS media queries allow you to define sets of styles that are applied under specific circumstances, in this case when the orientation is landscape or portrait. I use the CSS `display` property to show or hide elements, allowing me to create the same effect I had with JavaScript in the previous example. There is no need for any kind of synthesis in this situation. Media queries for orientation work equally well for desktop browsers and mobile browsers.

Working with Mobile Devices

Developing applications for mobile devices has some distinct differences from regular desktop development. In the sections that follow, I provide some guidance and information to help you get started and to highlight some of the key issues you will face.

IDENTIFYING MOBILE DEVICES

If you are offering an application to desktop and mobile users, you may want to tailor the interface you present. A common approach is to offer a jQuery UI interface to desktop browsers and a jQuery Mobile interface to mobile devices.

The difficulty is recognizing which browsers are running on mobile devices. There are various techniques for doing this, all of which are performed at the server, redirecting the browser to the appropriate HTML documents. I am not going to get into the detail of these, since they are outside the scope of this book. If you are new to this issue, then I suggest you look at `http://wurfl.sourceforge.net`, which contains a useful server-side component that can identify most mobile devices.

I recommend against automatically forcing the user to the mobile version of your application based on their browser. Some users prefer to use the desktop versions of applications, even on mobile devices, especially since mobile versions often have restricted functionality. My recommendation is to give the user a simple choice when they arrive at your site if you detect a mobile device and to make it easy to switch between the versions of your application even when the initial decision has been made.

Avoiding the Two Cardinal Sins of Mobile Development

There are two pitfalls to avoid when building web applications for mobile devices: *bad assumptions* and *unrealistic simulation.* Before you go any further, I will explain both and provide some context to help you avoid making some very common mistakes.

Avoiding Bad Assumptions

The market for mobile devices is extremely vibrant, relatively immature, and very poorly defined. When building web applications for desktops, there are some assumptions that are usually made (although they are often unstated). There is a general expectation about the minimum screen resolution, JavaScript support, the availability of certain plugins, and that the user will be able to point using a mouse and enter text using a keyboard.

That's not to say that these are reasonable assumptions. If you assume that JavaScript will be available, for example, then you eliminate potential customers who don't (or can't) enable JavaScript in their browser. You might decide that this is a good trade-off, that most users could enable JavaScript if they wanted, and that you'll just forgo users who don't meet the specification you require.

The situation in the mobile device market is much worse because the market is so fragmented. The desktop space may seem diverse, but a Mac, a Windows PC, and a Linux box all have quite a lot in common. The same can't be said for mobile devices, and assumptions about screen size, network connectivity, and input method will eliminate some very large segments of the market.

The World Is Not an iPhone

One of the worst assumptions I see made (and made often) is that the target market is the iPhone. The iPhone has been a wild success, but it isn't the totality of the mobile device market, and there are even variations between different iPhone models. A common target screen resolution is 320 by 480 pixels, which comes from the older iPhone models. A lot of devices have this resolution, but a growing amount do not. Using a fixed-screen resolution in your mobile application will simply eliminate users who have screens that are too small and annoy users who have paid a premium to get a higher-resolution device.

The World Is Not a Phone at All

Another common assumption is that the target market is mobile phones, ignoring the success of the tablet market. Not only do tablets have higher screen resolutions, but the way that people hold them and use them is different. To see what I mean, head to any coffee shop and watch the customers. My (entirely unscientific but consistent) observation is that the greater size of tablets makes them slightly awkward to hold and so they are usually propped up against something else. This means they are somewhat unstable, and dragging a finger across the screen makes the tablet wobble slightly (making accuracy a problem) and obscures a lot of the screen (because the user's hand and arm are over the tablet itself).

My point is that the nature of mobile devices dictates a lot about how they are used and what kind of interactions are sensible and desirable. The best way to figure this out is to observe people interacting with a range of devices. If you have money and time available, then a usability lab is a fantastic resource. But even if you are in a hurry and on a budget, an afternoon spent in Starbucks can provide some valuable insights.

The World Is Not Touch-Enabled

Not all mobile devices have touch screens. Some rely on a tiny mouse combined with a keyboard, and some have multiple input methods. One of my test machines is a small laptop that converts into a tablet. It has a touch screen as well as a full keyboard and mouse. Users expect to be able to use the best input method available to them, and making assumptions about the inputs available just leads to user frustration (which is why I rarely use the laptop/tablet combination device).

Mobile Bandwidth Is Not Free and Not Infinite

The price of network connectivity goes through cycles, driven by the kinds of activities that the users of the network perform. At the moment, network providers are struggling to fund and build enough network capacity to satisfy demand, especially in densely populated urban areas. Eventually, the cost of capacity will fall and bandwidth available will increase, but at the moment, network providers are charging a premium for data access and applying some low caps on the amount of data that a user can download in a month.

It is dangerous to assume that users are willing to dedicate a serious amount of their data to your web application. As a general rule, customers don't care as much about your application as you'd like them to care. It may hurt to hear, but it is almost always true. Your application fills your world, as it should, but it is just one of many to a user.

In Chapter 27, I show you how jQuery Mobile can prefetch the content for a web application before the user needs it. It is a great feature, but it should be used with caution because it assumes that the user is willing to spend bandwidth on content they may never need. The same goes for automatic and frequent data updates. Use sparingly, cautiously, and only when the user has explicitly indicated that your application should be a heavy user of their network quota.

Equally, do not make assumptions about the data rate available to a mobile device. Think about your use of large resources such as images and video. Some users will have the capacity to quickly download such content, but many won't, and a low-bandwidth option is always welcome in my experience.

You should also be prepared to deal with the network being unavailable. I used to commute by train, and the network would drop out whenever I went into a tunnel. A well-written web application expects connectivity issues, reports them to the user, and recovers elegantly when the network becomes available again. Sadly, most applications are not well-written.

Avoiding Unrealistic Simulation and Testing

The wide variation in mobile devices means you have to test thoroughly. Working with actual mobile devices during the early stages of development can be frustrating. The network requests are routed via the cell network, which requires the development machines to be publically available. There are developer modes for some mobile devices, but they have their own drawbacks.

In short, you want a simulated environment in which to start your development, something that gives you the ability to build and test rapidly and conveniently and to do so without having to expose your development environments to the outside world. Fortunately, there are emulators that provide the facilities you require. I'll describe some of the available options later in this chapter, but they fall into two categories.

The first category of emulator is where the actual mobile browser has been ported to another platform. Everything about the browser is as close to the real thing as possible. The second category relies on the fact that most browsers use a common rendering engine for mobile and desktop machines. So, for example, if you want to get a rough idea of how the iPhone browser will handle a document, you can use the Apple Safari browser because it shares common roots. The emulator is little more than a visual wrapper and a screen size constraint around the desktop rendering engine.

Both approaches can be very useful, and they are worth exploring. I use them often in the early stages of mobile product development. But once I have the basic functionality in place, I start including testing on real devices, and as the project nears completion, I switch to using only real devices and stop using the emulators altogether.

The reason for this is that the emulators have two main failings. The first is that they are not 100 percent accurate in their emulation. Even the best of emulators don't always present content the way that real devices using the same browser will. The second, and to my mind the most important, failing is that the touch inputs are simulated.

The mouse is used to make a touch-enabled browser work on a nontouch desktop PC, and a mouse just doesn't create the same effect as a finger. Three touch factors are missing in a desktop emulation: *tactility*, *obstruction*, and *inaccuracy*.

The Lack of Tactility

The lack of tactility means that you don't get a good idea about how using the web application will *feel*. Tapping and sliding on a glass display is an odd activity. When the application is properly responsive, the effect is elegant and enjoyable. The result is frustration when the application lags behind the input or misconstrues the touch interaction. The mouse isn't capable of giving you feedback about how well you are dealing with touch.

The Lack of Obstruction

I have already alluded to the issue of obstruction. When you use touch devices, even small ones, your finger and hand cover up part of the screen. You need to take this into account when designing a web application for a touch device. You need to place controls carefully so that the user can still see what's happening while they are touching the screen, and you need to bear in mind that roughly 10 percent of the population is left-handed and so a different part of the screen will be obscured for these users. Only touching the buttons and links with your own hands gives you a true understanding of how easy your web application is to use.

■ **Tip** If you go and do some user observation at the coffee shop, look out for users following a distinctive pattern. They touch the screen and then move their hand completely out of the way for a second, before reaching back in and making another touch gesture. This is often indicative of an application that has located its widgets so that the visual feedback resulting from an action is under the user's hand. The user has to move their hand out of the way to see what happened before moving back in for another gesture, a tiring and frustrating experience.

The Lack of Inaccuracy

The issue of inaccuracy is something I find constantly annoying. With the mouse, the user can be exceptionally accurate hitting a target on the screen. Per-pixel accuracy can be achieved with a modern mouse and a little practice. This is not the case with the human finger, and the most accuracy you can expect is "roughly in the area" of the target. This means you have to select widgets that are easy and create layout that takes inaccuracy into account. You can't get a feel for how easy it is to hit your widgets in the emulator. The mouse is not a good enough proxy. You need to test on a range of different screen sizes and resolutions to understand what your users will face. This information provides essential cues as to the size and density of the widgets on your pages.

A PERSONAL TALE OF INACCURACY

My personal frustration goes back to my commute by train. I live in the UK where the timely arrival of a train is seen as an unobtainable goal. In the summer, I didn't really mind when the train was late. I could linger in the sunshine. I never wanted to linger in the winter, and after a few minutes I would want to check to see just how late the train was going to be, which is possible with an online application.

Imagine the scene. The sun hasn't yet come up, the wind is bitter, and the ground is icy. I am wrapped up warm, but the heat I carried with me from the car is quickly ebbing away. I want to load the application, navigate to the information for my local station, and get an idea of how long I will be waiting (and if it is going to be a while, return to my car and consider driving to the office).

As soon as I take off my gloves, my fingers start to feel cold. After a few minutes, I can't flex my fingers properly and my hands start to shake, which is unfortunate because the widgets I need to hit are *tiny*; they are just regular web links displayed in a small font. I *never* managed to easily navigate to the information I wanted. I would hit the wrong link, be forced to wait for the wrong information to load, and then navigate back to try again. All the while, my ability to hit a widget accurately is getting worse as my hand gets colder. I grew to *hate* mobile web applications that assume pixel accuracy and that application in particular.

Using a Mobile Browser Emulator

Even though they have limitations, mobile browser emulators have a useful role to play. In this section, I'll describe some of the options available and the pros and cons of each.

Using the Android Emulator

The SDK for the Android platform includes an emulator. It provides a faithful representation of what the browser on a real device will do, but it is pretty painful to work with. The problem is that the entire operating system is being emulated, rather than just the browser. The emulator is slow and sometimes unresponsive, even on a capable desktop machine, and it is generally frustrating to use. Figure 26-9 shows the example document displayed in the browser that is included in the SDK, which you can download from `http://developer.android.com/sdk`.

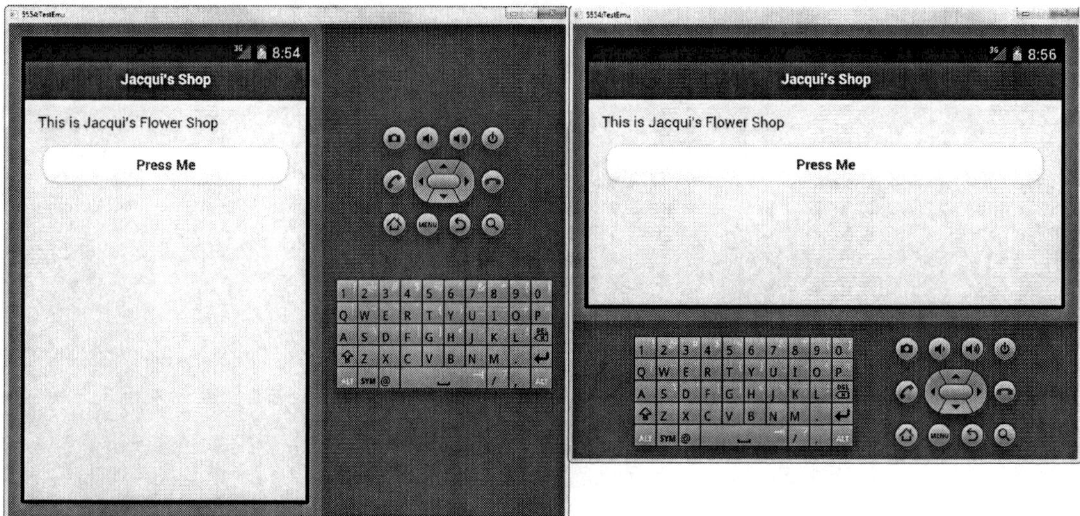

Figure 26-9. Using the Android SDK emulator

Using the iPhone Emulator

Apple includes an emulator for iOS as part of its Xcode development package, which can be downloaded freely from the Mac App Store. Running Xcode requires a Mac, of course, which is why I have never used this package (being a Windows and Linux user).

Using the Opera Mobile Emulator

This is one of the emulators that I use most often, because it allows me to simulate devices with different screen sizes, including tablets and landscape orientations. The Opera Mobile browser is widely used, and the emulator does a reasonable (but not brilliant) job of accurately laying out the content. Some jQuery Mobile features, such as navigation transitions (which I describe in Chapter 27), are not supported. Figure 26-10 shows the Opera Mobile emulator displaying the simple example document.

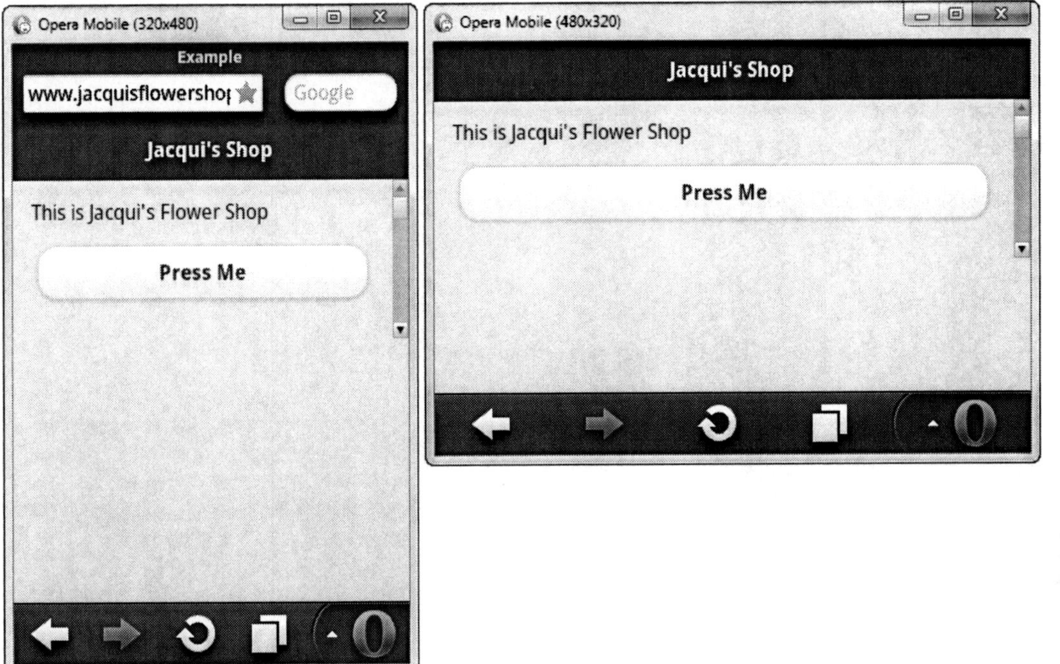

Figure 26-10. Using the Opera Mobile Emulator to display the example document

One nice feature is that you can debug the mobile emulator using the debugger built into the desktop version of Opera. The process for setting this up is a little clunky, but it can be a very helpful feature. The Opera Mobile emulator is available without charge at `www.opera.com/developer/tools/mobile`.

Using the Firefox Mobile Emulator

The Firefox Mobile Emulator is available from `www.mozilla.org/mobile`. It provides a good degree of consistency with the browser running on a real mobile device, but it doesn't have the ability to fix resolutions the way the Opera emulator does or have useful support for landscape orientations. This emulator is available without charge and is supported on a range of different desktop platforms. Figure 26-11 shows the example document displayed in the Firefox Mobile emulator.

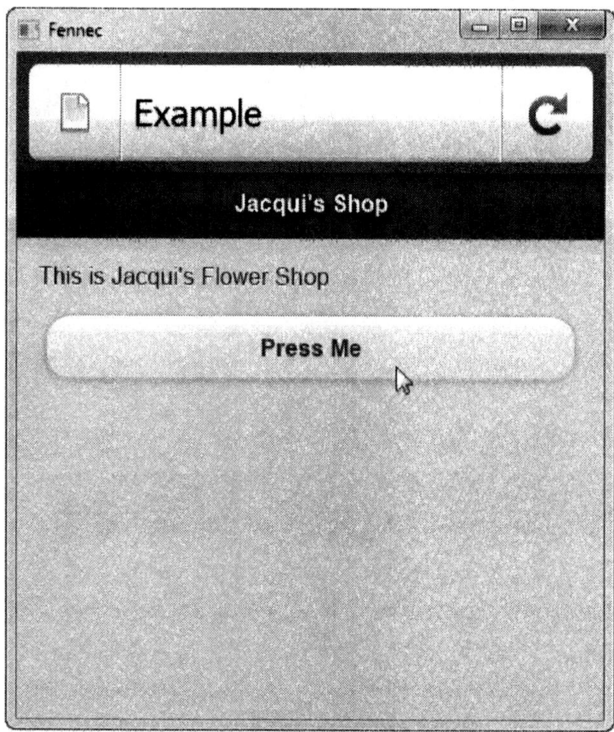

Figure 26-11. Using Firefox Mobile to display the example document

Using Multi-Browser Viewer

The one paid-for package I use is Multi-Browser Viewer (`www.multibrowserviewer.com`). This is a product that includes more than 40 different browsers for compatibility testing, although most of them are not mobile browsers, and it doesn't include the Opera Mobile and Firefox Mobile emulators. It does have simple iPhone and iPad emulators, which use the Apple Safari layout engine, giving a good (but not perfect) idea of how a page will be laid out on these devices. Overall, this is a good product, and I have used it with success on several projects, but it is more of a general testing tool, and its mobile support is really just part of what it does. Figure 26-12 shows the iPhone emulator displaying the example document.

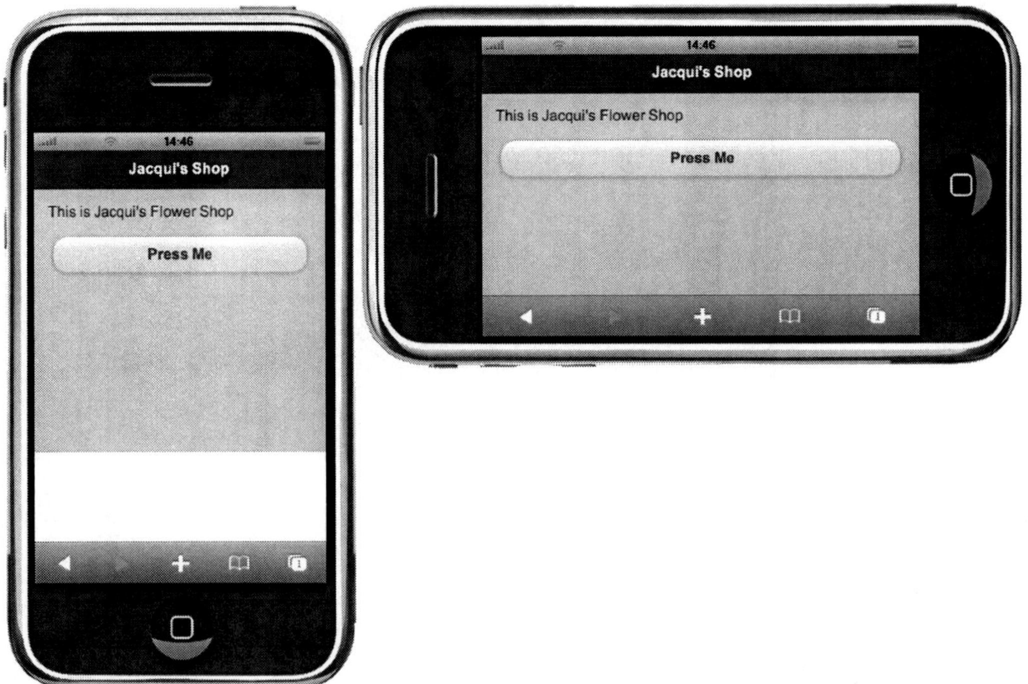

Figure 26-12. Displaying the example document in the Multi-Browser Viewer iPhone emulator

Using the Windows Phone 7 Emulator

The Windows Phone 7 emulator is very well implemented. It is another full-device emulator, but it is a great deal faster than the Android emulator. It is largely consistent with Windows 7 mobile devices and has some nice support for emulating location-based services. It is available as part of the free Visual Studio 2010 Express for Windows Phone package, which is available from `www.microsoft.com/express`. As you might expect from a Microsoft product, it is supported only on Windows. Figure 26-13 shows the Windows Phone 7 emulator displaying the example document.

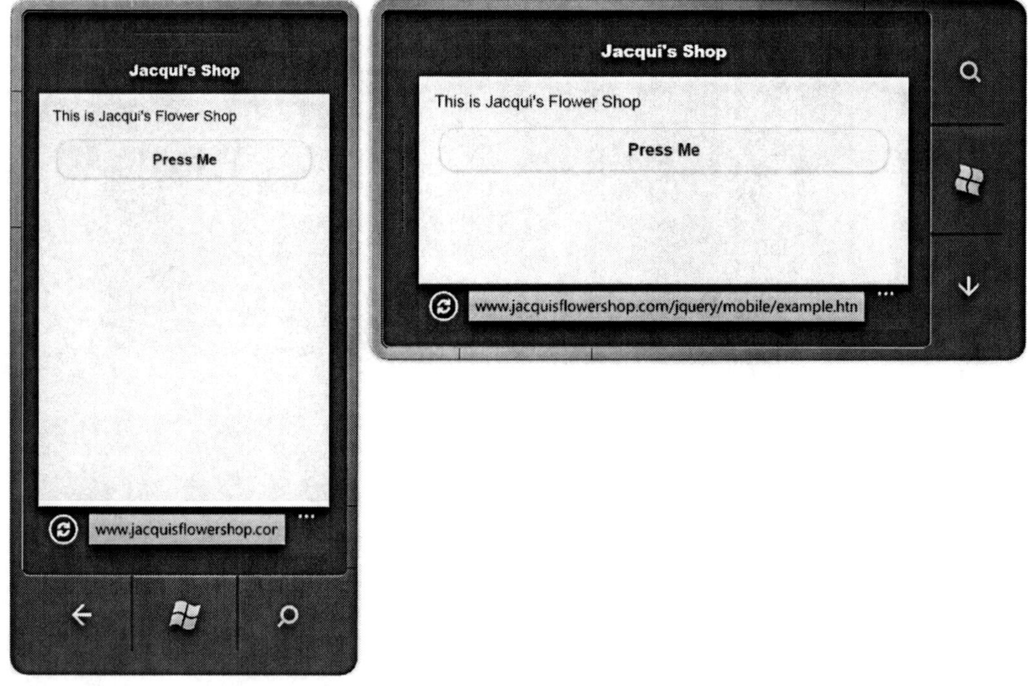

Figure 26-13. The Windows Phone 7 emulator

The download that includes the emulator is more than 500MB, which is not ideal. But the main challenge for this emulator is that the adoption of Windows Phone 7 has been very low. There are Windows 7 Phone devices in the market, but they have not been popular, and as I write this, the future of the platform seems uncertain. I tend to use this emulator when I have encountered an unexpected behavior in my application and I am not sure if it is being caused by the implementation of one of the other emulators.

Using Desktop Browsers

I often use the Google Chrome and Apple Safari desktop browsers as alternatives to the Android SDK and iOS emulators. These are obviously not the same as the mobile versions of the browsers, but they do share common underpinnings and can be useful for quick and dirty testing prior to deploying to real devices. I often use these browsers when I have the major building blocks of an application in place and I am fleshing out the functional areas. The desktop browsers are quicker and more reliable than the mobile browser emulators (and run on platforms that I have), and they have excellent debugging support. I tend to check my progress using an emulator or a real device every now and again to make sure I am on the right track, but for the most part desktop browsers make excellent development tools for the early stages of a mobile project.

Summary

In this chapter, I explained how to obtain jQuery Mobile and add it to an HTML document and set out the basic approach that jQuery Mobile takes for automatically enhancing HTML documents and separating pages from those documents. I described the custom events that jQuery Mobile provides to make it easier to create touch applications, and I set out some basic guidance about how to approach mobile development and testing.

CHAPTER 27

Pages and Navigation

In this chapter, I describe one of the key building blocks for jQuery Mobile applications: *pages*. I touched on pages in Chapter 26, but now I'll go into the detail and show how to define, configure, and navigate between pages. Table 27-1 provides the summary for this chapter.

Table 27-1. *Chapter Summary*

Problem	Solution	Listing
Define a jQuery Mobile page.	Apply the `data-role` attribute to an element with a value of `page`.	1
Add a header or a footer to a page.	Apply the `data-role` attribute to elements using a value of `header` or `footer`.	2, 3
Define multiple pages in a document.	Create several elements whose `data-role` is `page`.	4
Navigate between pages.	Create an a element whose `href` element is the `id` of a page element.	5
Specify a transition effect for an a element.	Apply the `data-transition` attribute.	6
Set a global transition effect.	Assign a value to the `defaultPageTransition` setting.	7
Link to a page in another document.	Specify the URL of the document as the `href` value of an a element.	8, 9
Disable Ajax for a single link.	Set the `data-ajax` attribute to `false`.	10
Disable Ajax globally.	Set the `ajaxEnable` event to `false`.	11
Prefetch a page.	Use the `data-prefetch` attribute.	12, 13
Change the current page.	Use the `changePage` method.	14

Control the direction of the transition effect.	Use the reverse setting for the changePage method.	15
Specify the delay after which the loading dialog is shown.	Use the loadMsgDelay setting.	16
Disable the loading dialog.	Use the showLoadMsg setting.	17
Determine the current page.	Use the activePage property.	18
Load pages in the background.	Use the loadPage method.	19
Respond to page loading.	Use the page loading events.	20
Respond to page transitions.	Use the page transition events.	21

Understanding jQuery Mobile Pages

In Chapter 26, I showed you how you define jQuery Mobile pages within an HTML document using elements with specific roles. To recap, Listing 27-1 shows a simple page.

Listing 27-1. A Simple jQuery Mobile Page in an HTML Document

```
<!DOCTYPE html>
<html>
<head>
    <title>Example</title>
    <meta name="viewport" content="width=device-width, initial-scale=1">
    <link rel="stylesheet" href="jquery.mobile-1.0.css" type="text/css" />
    <script type="text/javascript" src="jquery-1.6.4.js"></script>
    <script type="text/javascript" src="jquery.mobile-1.0.js"></script>
</head>
<body>
    <div data-role="page">
       <div data-role="content">
           This is Jacqui's Flower Shop
       </div>
   </div>
</body>
</html>
```

This is a minimal page, which consists of two key elements, each of which has a data-role attribute. The element whose role is page denotes the region of the HTML content that contains the jQuery Mobile page. As I mentioned in Chapter 26, one of the key characteristics of jQuery Mobile is that the pages that are displayed to the user are not directly related to the HTML elements that contain them.

The other important element has a role of content. This denotes the part of the jQuery Mobile page that contains the page content. A page can contain different sections of which the content is only one, as I'll demonstrate shortly. You can see how the page is displayed in the browser in Figure 27-1.

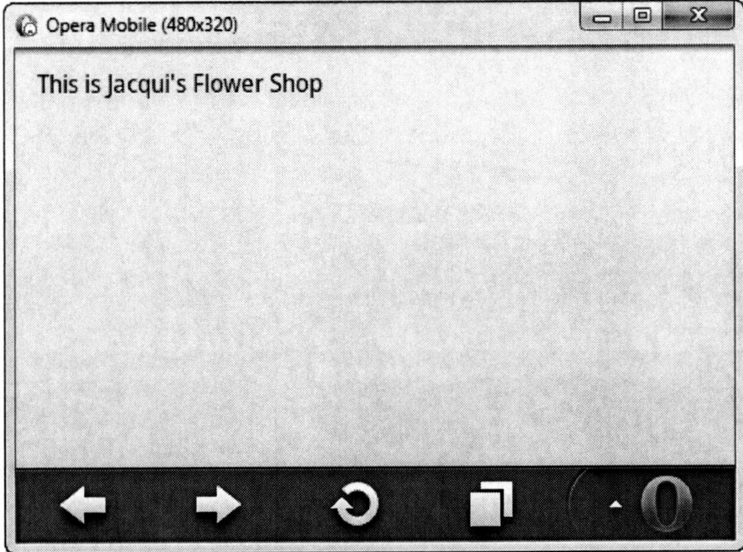

Figure 27-1. Displaying a minimal jQuery Mobile page in the browser

Adding Headers and Footers to a Page

In addition to a content section, a jQuery Mobile page can contain a header and a footer. These are denoted by elements whose `data-role` attributes are set to `header` and `footer`, respectively. Listing 27-2 shows both of these sections added to the example page.

Listing 27-2. Adding a Header and a Footer to the Example Page

```
<!DOCTYPE html>
<html>
<head>
    <title>Example</title>
    <meta name="viewport" content="width=device-width, initial-scale=1">
    <link rel="stylesheet" href="jquery.mobile-1.0.css" type="text/css" />
    <script type="text/javascript" src="jquery-1.6.4.js"></script>
    <script type="text/javascript" src="jquery.mobile-1.0.js"></script>
</head>
<body>
    <div data-role="page">
        <div data-role="header">
           <h1>Jacqui's Shop</h1>
        </div>
        <div data-role="content">
           This is Jacqui's Flower Shop
        </div>
        <div data-role="footer">
           <h1>Home Page</h1>
```

```
        </div>
    </div>
</body>
</html>
```

You can see the effect of these additions in Figure 27-2. The problem with headers and footers is that they can occupy a lot of space on a small screen, as the figure shows.

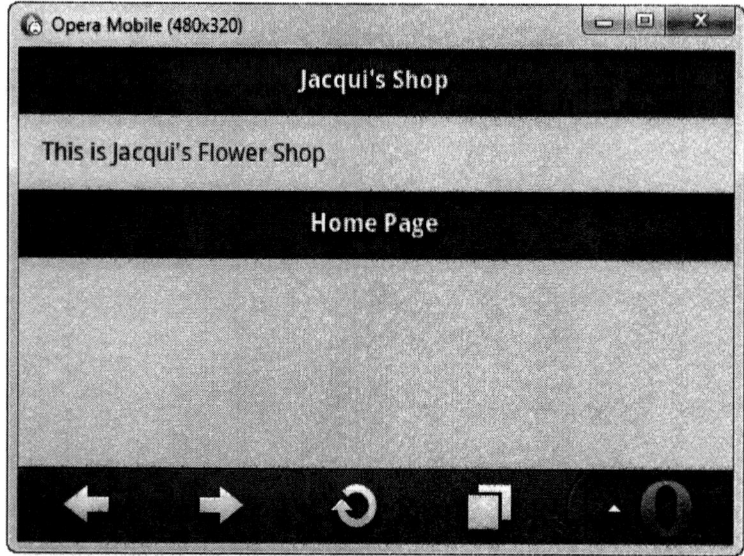

Figure 27-2. Adding a header and footer to the page

You will also notice that the footer is displayed at the end of the content section, rather than at the bottom of the page. You might be tempted to force the position of the footer using CSS, but mobile browsers don't always respond properly to this. Listing 27-3 shows the CSS "fix."

Listing 27-3. Using CSS to Fix the Position of the Footer in the Page

```
<!DOCTYPE html>
<html>
<head>
    <title>Example</title>
    <meta name="viewport" content="width=device-width, initial-scale=1">
    <link rel="stylesheet" href="jquery.mobile-1.0.css" type="text/css" />
    <script type="text/javascript" src="jquery-1.6.4.js"></script>
    <script type="text/javascript" src="jquery.mobile-1.0.js"></script>
    <style type="text/css">
        #footer {position: absolute; bottom: 0}
    </style>
</head>
<body>
    <div data-role="page">
```

```
        <div data-role="header">
            <h1>Jacqui's Shop</h1>
        </div>
        <div data-role="content">
            This is Jacqui's Flower Shop
        </div>
        <div id="footer" data-role="footer">
            <h1>Home Page</h1>
        </div>
    </div>
</body>
</html>
```

The problem is that mobile browsers deal with document height inconsistently. Figure 27-3 shows what you end up with in Opera. The footer is shown as off the page. The first frame of this figure shows the initial page layout, and the second frame shows the footer when I scroll down the page.

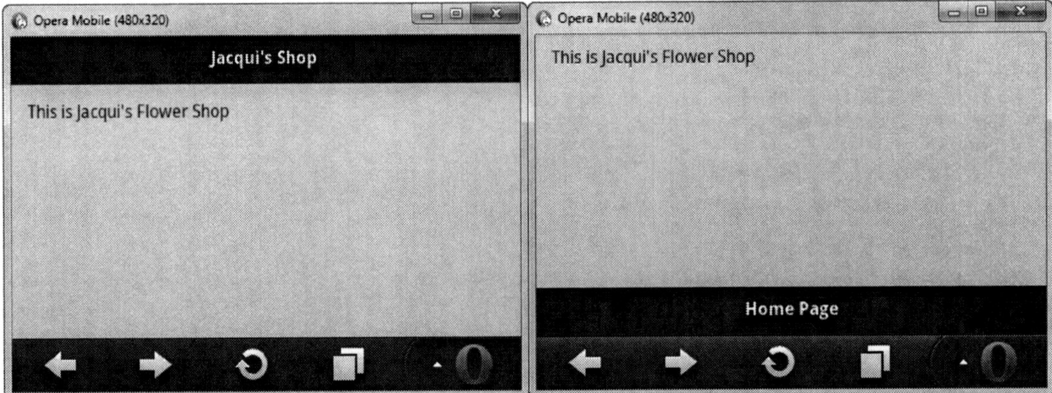

Figure 27-3. Opera Mobile displaying the page footer

You might be tempted to revisit the `meta` element that sets the `viewport` size and try to fix the height. This is an unrewarding task. The support for viewport height in mobile browsers is nonexistent as I write this. It is also a dangerous approach. You can't tell in advance how much of the screen is given over to the browser controls. This means that relying on the device height to set the viewport height doesn't solve the problem, leaving you with the option of setting the height to a set number of pixels. This is impossible to set properly given the variety of screen resolutions available in the smartphone and table markets.

■ **Tip** For these reasons, I tend not to use footers at all. I do use headers, because it adds a degree of consistency between the pages in my jQuery Mobile applications.

Adding Pages to a Document

You can define multiple jQuery Mobile pages in a single document. This can be useful for simple web applications because you can bundle everything you need into a single HTML file. Listing 27-4 shows a multipage document.

Listing 27-4. Defining Multiple jQuery Mobile Pages in an HTML Document

```
<!DOCTYPE html>
<html>
<head>
    <title>Example</title>
    <meta name="viewport" content="width=device-width, initial-scale=1">
    <link rel="stylesheet" href="jquery.mobile-1.0.css" type="text/css" />
    <script type="text/javascript" src="jquery-1.6.4.js"></script>
    <script type="text/javascript" src="jquery.mobile-1.0.js"></script>
</head>
<body>
    <div id="page1" data-role="page">
        <div data-role="header">
           <h1>Jacqui's Shop</h1>
        </div>
        <div data-role="content">
           This is Jacqui's Flower Shop
        </div>
    </div>
    <div id="page2" data-role="page">
        <div data-role="header">
           <h1>Jacqui's Shop</h1>
        </div>
        <div data-role="content">
           This is page 2
        </div>
   </div>
</body>
</html>
```

This example defines two pages in the document. I have used the id attribute to assign each page a unique identifier, and these values form the basis for navigating between pages. To let the user navigate between pages, you add an a element whose href is the id of the target page, as shown in Listing 27-5.

Listing 27-5. Navigating Between Pages

```
<!DOCTYPE html>
<html>
<head>
    <title>Example</title>
    <meta name="viewport" content="width=device-width, initial-scale=1">
    <link rel="stylesheet" href="jquery.mobile-1.0.css" type="text/css" />
    <script type="text/javascript" src="jquery-1.6.4.js"></script>
    <script type="text/javascript" src="jquery.mobile-1.0.js"></script>
</head>
```

```
<body>
    <div id="page1" data-role="page">
        <div data-role="header">
           <h1>Jacqui's Shop</h1>
        </div>
        <div data-role="content">
           This is Jacqui's Flower Shop
           <p><a href="#page2">Go to page 2</a></p>
        </div>
    </div>
    <div id="page2" data-role="page">
        <div data-role="header">
           <h1>Jacqui's Shop</h1>
        </div>
        <div data-role="content">
           This is page 2
           <p><a href="#page1">Go to page 1</a></p>
        </div>
   </div>
</body>
</html>
```

In this example, I have added links between the pages. When a link is clicked, jQuery Mobile takes care of displaying the appropriate page from the document, as demonstrated in Figure 27-4.

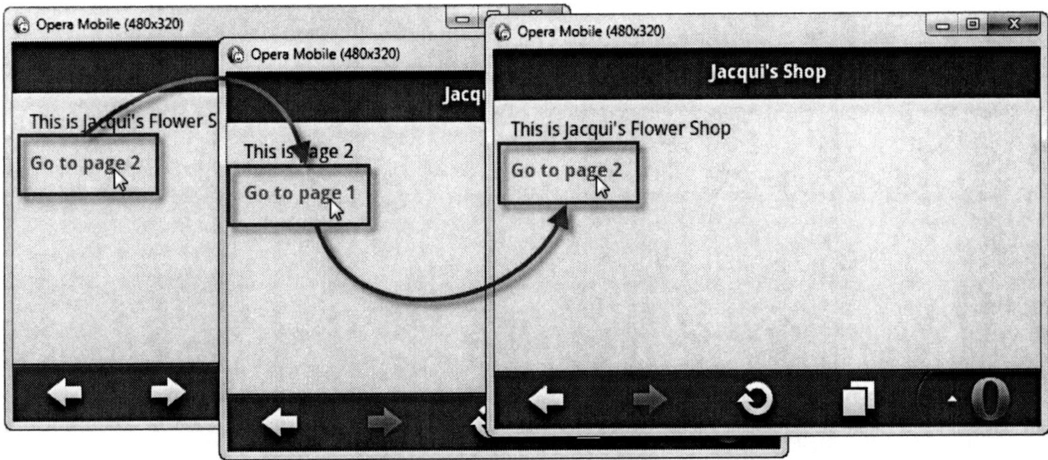

Figure 27-4. Navigating between pages in a document

Configuring Page Transitions

When the user navigates between pages, jQuery Mobile uses an animation effect to transition between one page and the next. The default effect is called `slide`, which has the outgoing page slide to the left while the new page slides in from the right. jQuery Mobile defines six effects, as follows:

- slide
- pop
- slideup
- slidedown
- fade
- flip

As I write this, the flip effect causes problems on Android devices and should be used with caution.

■ **Tip** The mobile browser emulators don't handle transitions very well and generally just ignore them. They work just fine on real mobile devices, however. If you want to see the transition on the desktop, then use either Google Chrome or Apple Safari, both of which handle the effects well.

You can change the way that an individual page transition is animated by using the data-transition attribute on the a element, setting the value to the effect you want. Listing 27-6 provides an example.

■ **Note** I can't easily show you the different animation effects using figures. This example is one that requires experimentation in the browser. You can avoid having to type in the HTML by downloading the source code that accompanies this book and that is freely available from Apress.com.

Listing 27-6. Using the data-transition Attribute

```
<!DOCTYPE html>
<html>
<head>
    <title>Example</title>
    <meta name="viewport" content="width=device-width, initial-scale=1">
    <link rel="stylesheet" href="jquery.mobile-1.0.css" type="text/css" />
    <script type="text/javascript" src="jquery-1.6.4.js"></script>
    <script type="text/javascript" src="jquery.mobile-1.0.js"></script>
</head>
<body>
    <div id="page1" data-role="page">
        <div data-role="header">
           <h1>Jacqui's Shop</h1>
        </div>
        <div data-role="content">
           This is Jacqui's Flower Shop
```

```
            <p><a href="#page2" data-transition="pop">Go to page 2</a></p>
        </div>
    </div>
    <div id="page2" data-role="page">
        <div data-role="header">
           <h1>Jacqui's Shop</h1>
        </div>
        <div data-role="content">
           This is page 2
           <p><a href="#page1">Go to page 1</a></p>
        </div>
   </div>
</body>
</html>
```

When the user clicks the highlighted link, the pop transition is used to display the target page. The pop effect is applied only to that single link. Other links in the page or in other pages in the same document will continue to use the default. Set the data-transition attribute to none if you want to disable the animation effect.

■ **Tip** You can change the direction in which the effect is played by applying the data-direction attribute to the a element with a value of reverse. In the "Changing the Current Page" section, I give an example of reversing the transition direction and explain why it can be useful.

If you want to change the animation effect used for all navigation, then you need to set a global option. jQuery Mobile defines the defaultPageTransition setting, which you can set when the mobileinit event is triggered. Listing 27-7 shows how this is done.

Listing 27-7. Changing the Default Page Transition

```
<!DOCTYPE html>
<html>
<head>
    <title>Example</title>
    <meta name="viewport" content="width=device-width, initial-scale=1">
    <link rel="stylesheet" href="jquery.mobile-1.0.css" type="text/css" />
    <script type="text/javascript" src="jquery-1.6.4.js"></script>
    <script type="text/javascript">
        $(document).bind("mobileinit", function() {
            $.mobile.defaultPageTransition = "fade"
        })
    </script>
    <script type="text/javascript" src="jquery.mobile-1.0.js"></script>
</head>
<body>
    <div id="page1" data-role="page">
        <div data-role="header">
```

```
            <h1>Jacqui's Shop</h1>
        </div>
        <div data-role="content">
            This is Jacqui's Flower Shop
            <p><a href="#page2">Go to page 2</a></p>
        </div>
    </div>
    <div id="page2" data-role="page">
        <div data-role="header">
            <h1>Jacqui's Shop</h1>
        </div>
        <div data-role="content">
            This is page 2
            <p><a href="#page1">Go to page 1</a></p>
        </div>
    </div>
</body>
</html>
```

There is no convenient method for registering a handler function for the mobileinit event, so you have to select the document object and use the bind method. The arguments to this method are the name of the event you want to handle and the handler function to use when the event is triggered.

■ **Caution** The mobileinit event is triggered as soon as the jQuery Mobile script library is loaded, which means you have to register the handler function to change the global jQuery Mobile setting before the jQuery Mobile library is referenced in a script element. You can see how I have done this in the listing. The function will never be executed if the call to the bind method is not defined before the script element that loads the jQuery Mobile code.

To change the value of a global setting, you assign a new value to a property of the $.mobile object. Since I want to change the defaultPageTransition setting, I assign a value to the $.mobile.defaultPageTransition property, like this:

```
$.mobile.defaultPageTransition = "fade"
```

This statement sets the default effect to fade. I can still override this setting with the data-transition attribute, but the default is no longer slide.

Linking to External Pages

You don't have to include all the pages in a single document. You can add links just as you would if using regular HTML. To demonstrate this, I have created a new file called document2.html, the content of which is shown in Listing 27-8.

Listing 27-8. The Content of the document2.html File

```
<!DOCTYPE html>
<html>
<head>
    <title>Document 2</title>
    <meta name="viewport" content="width=device-width, initial-scale=1">
    <link rel="stylesheet" href="jquery.mobile-1.0.css" type="text/css" />
    <script type="text/javascript" src="jquery-1.6.4.js"></script>
    <script type="text/javascript" src="jquery.mobile-1.0.js"></script>
</head>
<body>
    <div id="page1" data-role="page">
        <div data-role="header">
           <h1>Jacqui's Shop</h1>
        </div>
        <div data-role="content">
           This is page 1 in document2.html
           <p><a href="#page2">Go to page 2 in this document</a></p>
           <p><a href="example.html">Return to example.html</a></p>
        </div>
    </div>
    <div id="page2" data-role="page">
        <div data-role="header">
           <h1>Jacqui's Shop</h1>
        </div>
        <div data-role="content">
           This is page 2 in document2.html
           <p><a href="#page1">Go to page 1</a></p>
        </div>
   </div>
</body>
</html>
```

This document contains a pair of jQuery Mobile pages, following the same structure as in the other examples. Linking to pages in other documents is very simple. You just define an a element whose `href` attribute contains the URL of the target document, as shown in Listing 27-9.

Listing 27-9. Navigating to a Page in Another HTML Document

```
<!DOCTYPE html>
<html>
<head>
    <title>Example</title>
    <meta name="viewport" content="width=device-width, initial-scale=1">
    <link rel="stylesheet" href="jquery.mobile-1.0.css" type="text/css" />
    <script type="text/javascript" src="jquery-1.6.4.js"></script>
    <script type="text/javascript" src="jquery.mobile-1.0.js"></script>
</head>
<body>
    <div id="page1" data-role="page">
```

```
            <div data-role="header">
                <h1>Jacqui's Shop</h1>
            </div>
            <div data-role="content">
                This is Jacqui's Flower Shop
                <p><a href="#page2">Go to page 2</a></p>
                <p><a href="document2.html">Go to document2.html</a></p>
            </div>
        </div>
        <div id="page2" data-role="page">
            <div data-role="header">
                <h1>Jacqui's Shop</h1>
            </div>
            <div data-role="content">
                This is page 2
                <p><a href="#page1">Go to page 1</a></p>
            </div>
       </div>
</body>
</html>
```

jQuery Mobile uses Ajax to load the specified document and displays the first page automatically, using a transition effect if one has been specified. You can see the result in Figure 27-5.

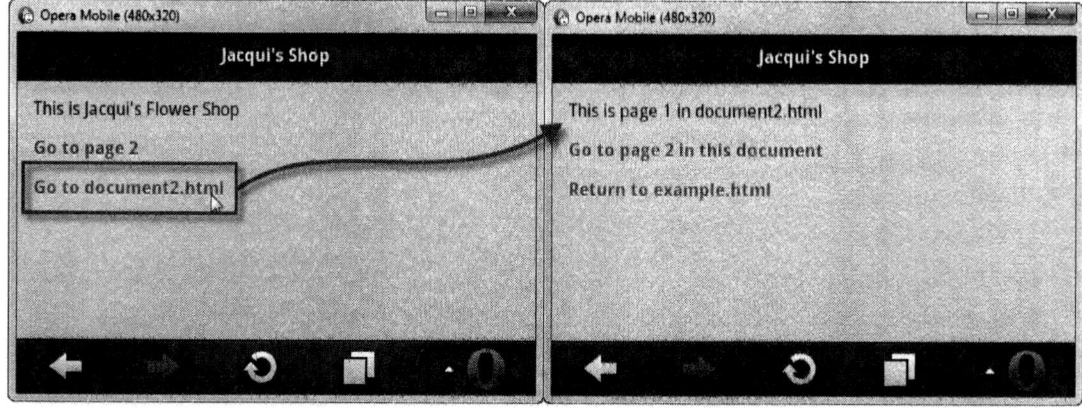

Figure 27-5. Navigating to a page in another document

■ **Tip** jQuery Mobile automatically applies its styles and enhancements to remote documents that are loaded via Ajax. This means you don't have to include the jQuery and jQuery Mobile `script` and `link` elements in files such as the `document2.html` file I used in the example. That said, I recommend you do include those references because it is possible to prevent jQuery Mobile from using Ajax when making such requests, and if this is done, then the automatic processing of content isn't performed.

Dealing with the Ajax/Page ID Issue

It isn't all plain sailing when linking to pages in other documents. There is a conflict between the way that Ajax content is managed and the way that jQuery Mobile pages are defined. Both rely on the value of the `id` attribute of elements. Figure 27-6 shows the problem.

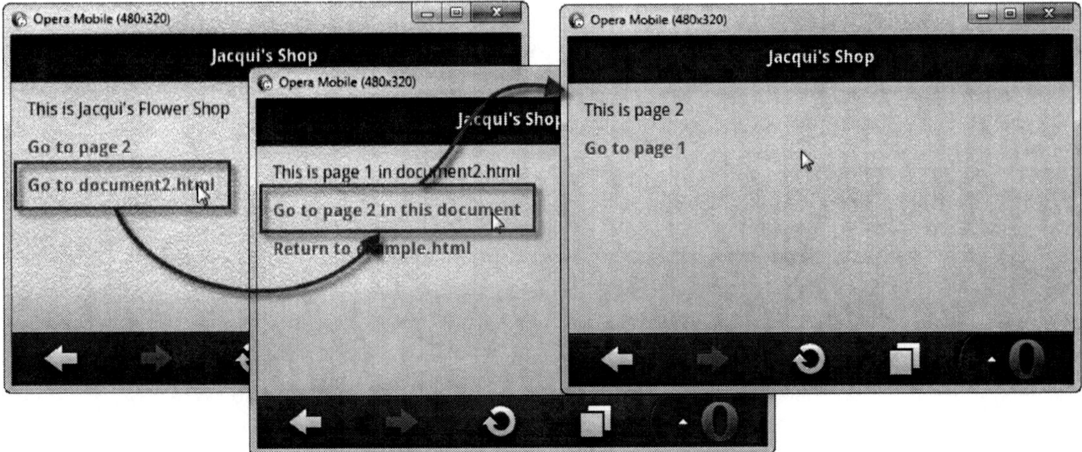

Figure 27-6. The multipage Ajax issue

In this figure, I click the link in `example.html`, which loads `document2.html`. I then click the link that should display the `page2` element in `document2.html`, but what I get is actually the `page2` element in `example.html`, a confusing an unexpected result.

You can address this in two ways. The first, and the one that I use, is to define only one jQuery Mobile page per HTML document. This is also the advice from the jQuery Mobile development team.

The second approach is to disable Ajax when loading multipage documents. This fixes the problem, but it does mean that jQuery Mobile is unable to apply a transition effect when showing the new page. You can disable Ajax for a single a element by setting the `data-ajax` attribute to `false`, as shown in Listing 27-10.

Listing 27-10. Disabling Ajax for a Single Link

```
<!DOCTYPE html>
<html>
<head>
    <title>Example</title>
    <meta name="viewport" content="width=device-width, initial-scale=1">
    <link rel="stylesheet" href="jquery.mobile-1.0.css" type="text/css" />
    <script type="text/javascript" src="jquery-1.6.4.js"></script>
    <script type="text/javascript" src="jquery.mobile-1.0.js"></script>
</head>
<body>
    <div id="page1" data-role="page">
        <div data-role="header">
           <h1>Jacqui's Shop</h1>
        </div>
        <div data-role="content">
           This is Jacqui's Flower Shop
           <p><a href="#page2">Go to page 2</a></p>
           <p><a href="document2.html" data-ajax="false">Go to document2.html</a></p>
        </div>
    </div>
    <div id="page2" data-role="page">
        <div data-role="header">
           <h1>Jacqui's Shop</h1>
        </div>
        <div data-role="content">
           This is page 2
           <p><a href="#page1">Go to page 1</a></p>
        </div>
   </div>
</body>
</html>
```

In this example, I have disabled Ajax for the link that navigates to `document2.html`. As Figure 27-7 shows, this produces the expected navigation sequence.

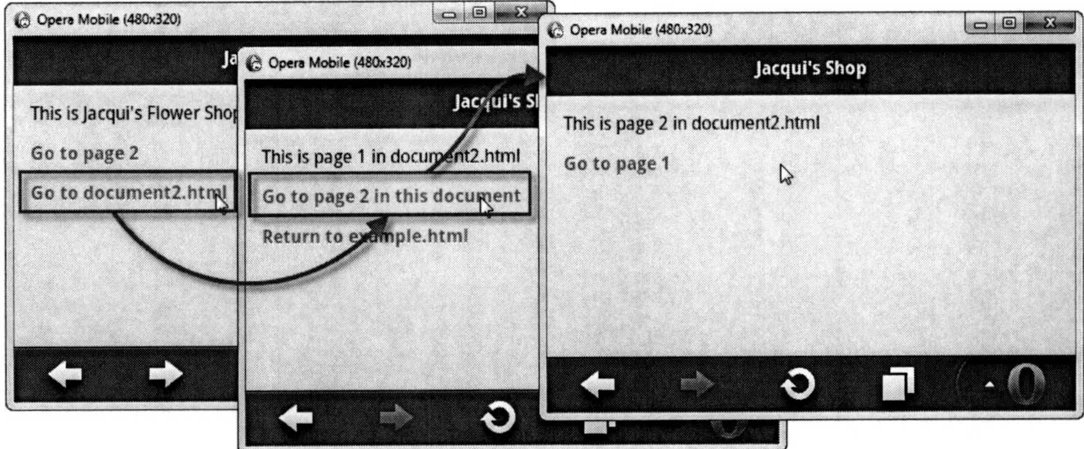

Figure 27-7. Disabling Ajax to avoid an element id conflict

You can turn off Ajax by default using the `ajaxEnabled` global setting, which is demonstrated in Listing 27-11. When this setting is `false`, Ajax will not be used for navigation unless you apply the `data-ajax` attribute to an element with a value of `true`.

Listing 27-11. Using the global Setting to Disable Ajax

```
<!DOCTYPE html>
<html>
<head>
    <title>Example</title>
    <meta name="viewport" content="width=device-width, initial-scale=1">
    <link rel="stylesheet" href="jquery.mobile-1.0.css" type="text/css" />
    <script type="text/javascript" src="jquery-1.6.4.js"></script>
    <script type="text/javascript">
        $(document).bind("mobileinit", function() {
            $.mobile.ajaxEnable = false
        })
    </script>
    <script type="text/javascript" src="jquery.mobile-1.0.js"></script>
</head>
<body>
    <div id="page1" data-role="page">
        <div data-role="header">
           <h1>Jacqui's Shop</h1>
        </div>
        <div data-role="content">
           This is Jacqui's Flower Shop
           <p><a href="#page2">Go to page 2</a></p>
           <p><a href="document2.html">Go to document2.html</a></p>
        </div>
    </div>
```

```
    <div id="page2" data-role="page">
        <div data-role="header">
           <h1>Jacqui's Shop</h1>
        </div>
        <div data-role="content">
           This is page 2
           <p><a href="#page1">Go to page 1</a></p>
        </div>
    </div>
</body>
</html>
```

Prefetching Pages

You can ask jQuery Mobile to prefetch documents so that the pages they contain are immediately available when the user clicks a link. The advantage of this is that you create a more responsive application, but you do so by downloading content that the user may not navigate to. To demonstrate this feature, I created a document called singlepage.html, the content of which is shown in Listing 27-12.

Listing 27-12. The singlepage.html File

```
<!DOCTYPE html>
<html>
<head>
    <title>Single Page</title>
    <meta name="viewport" content="width=device-width, initial-scale=1">
    <link rel="stylesheet" href="jquery.mobile-1.0.css" type="text/css" />
    <script type="text/javascript" src="jquery-1.6.4.js"></script>
    <script type="text/javascript" src="jquery.mobile-1.0.js"></script>
</head>
<body>
    <div id="page1" data-role="page">
        <div data-role="header">
           <h1>Jacqui's Shop</h1>
        </div>
        <div data-role="content">
           This is the only page in this document
           <p><a href="example.html">Return to example.html</a></p>
        </div>
    </div>
</body>
</html>
```

You enable prefetching by applying the data-prefetch attribute to the a element, as shown in Listing 27-13.

DECIDING WHETHER TO PREFETCH CONTENT

The decision about prefetching content is a difficult one. From the point of view of the application, prefetching can be a great idea because it produces immediate responses when the user navigates between pages. This can be particularly important when mobile connections are slow and coverage is spotty. Users don't like waiting, and a connection that keeps dropping out will make your application unusable if the content isn't available.

On the other hand, we run the risk of downloading content in anticipation of navigation actions that the user may not make. This can be unwelcome when mobile data plans charge punitive amounts to download data and have low monthly bandwidth limits. By prefetching content, you are assuming that the user considers your application to be important enough to trade bandwidth (and cost) for performance, something that may well not be the case. The sad fact is that although you may have lived and breathed your project for the last year, it may be nothing more than a mild convenience to your user.

My recommendation is not to prefetch pages. For those users who *do* consider your application important enough, you can give them an option to enable prefetching.

Listing 27-13. Prefetching Content

```
<!DOCTYPE html>
<html>
<head>
    <title>Example</title>
    <meta name="viewport" content="width=device-width, initial-scale=1">
    <link rel="stylesheet" href="jquery.mobile-1.0.css" type="text/css" />
    <script type="text/javascript" src="jquery-1.6.4.js"></script>
    <script type="text/javascript" src="jquery.mobile-1.0.js"></script>
</head>
<body>
    <div id="page1" data-role="page">
        <div data-role="header">
           <h1>Jacqui's Shop</h1>
        </div>
        <div data-role="content">
           This is Jacqui's Flower Shop
           <p><a href="#page2">Go to page 2</a></p>
           <p><a href="singlepage.html" data-prefetch>Go to singlepage.html</a></p>
        </div>
    </div>
    <div id="page2" data-role="page">
        <div data-role="header">
           <h1>Jacqui's Shop</h1>
        </div>
        <div data-role="content">
           This is page 2
           <p><a href="#page1">Go to page 1</a></p>
        </div>
   </div>
```

```
</body>
</html>
```

In this example, I have asked jQuery Mobile to prefetch the target of my URL. When I click the link, jQuery Mobile is able to navigate to the prefetched content, avoiding any delay.

■ **Tip** It can be hard to be sure that features such as prefetching are working when you are developing on a fast, reliable network. I like to check these features by using a debugging HTTP proxy, which shows me the requests that are sent from the browser. If you are a Windows user, then I recommend Fiddler, which is an excellent tool that can be endlessly configured and customized. Fiddler can be downloaded from `www.fiddler2.com`.

Using Scripting to Control jQuery Mobile Pages

You don't always want to rely on the user clicking links to manage page navigation. Fortunately, jQuery Mobile provides you with methods and settings that allow you to control navigation using JavaScript. In the sections that follow, I'll show you how to take advantage of these methods to get fine-grained control over the navigation in a jQuery Mobile web application.

Changing the Current Page

The changePage method allows you to change the page that jQuery Mobile displays. Listing 27-14 shows the basic use of this method, which changes the displayed page based when a button is clicked.

Listing 27-14. Changing the Page That jQuery Mobile Displays

```
<!DOCTYPE html>
<html>
<head>
    <title>Example</title>
    <meta name="viewport" content="width=device-width, initial-scale=1">
    <link rel="stylesheet" href="jquery.mobile-1.0.css" type="text/css" />
    <script type="text/javascript" src="jquery-1.6.4.js"></script>
    <script type="text/javascript">
        $(document).bind("pageinit", function() {
            $('button').bind("tap", function(e) {
                 var target = this.id == "local" ? "#page2" : "document2.html";
                 $.mobile.changePage(target)
            })
        });
    </script>
    <script type="text/javascript" src="jquery.mobile-1.0.js"></script>
</head>
<body>
    <div id="page1" data-role="page">
        <div data-role="header">
           <h1>Jacqui's Shop</h1>
```

```
        </div>
        <div data-role="content">
            <fieldset class="ui-grid-a">
                <div class="ui-block-a"><button id="local">Local</button></div>
                <div class="ui-block-b"><button id="remote">Remote</button></div>
            </fieldset>
        </div>
    </div>
    <div id="page2" data-role="page">
        <div data-role="header">
           <h1>Jacqui's Shop</h1>
        </div>
        <div data-role="content">
           This is page 2
           <p><a href="#page1">Go to page 1</a></p>
        </div>
   </div>
</body>
</html>
```

In this example, I have added two buttons that, when clicked, cause the changePage method to be called. To create this demonstration, I have used some jQuery Mobile features that I explain in later chapters. The event that I listen for using the bind method is tap, which is one of a small set of helpful custom events that jQuery Mobile defines. This event is triggered when the user taps the screen (or clicks the mouse on a nontouch device). I described this event, along with the rest of the jQuery Mobile events in Chapter 26.

The buttons are standard HTML elements that jQuery Mobile automatically converts into button widgets. I describe the options for configuring jQuery Mobile buttons in Chapter 29. Finally, you will notice that I have assigned some elements to the classes ui-grid-a, ui-block-a, and ui-block-b. These are part of the jQuery Mobile support for creating page layouts, which I describe in Chapter 28. Despite using features from future chapters, the result of this example is pretty simple, as Figure 27-8 shows. When the user clicks one of the buttons, the changePage method is called, passing either the id value of a local page or a URL of another document for jQuery Mobile to display. The content is loaded, and the transition effect is displayed, just as when you were using regular links.

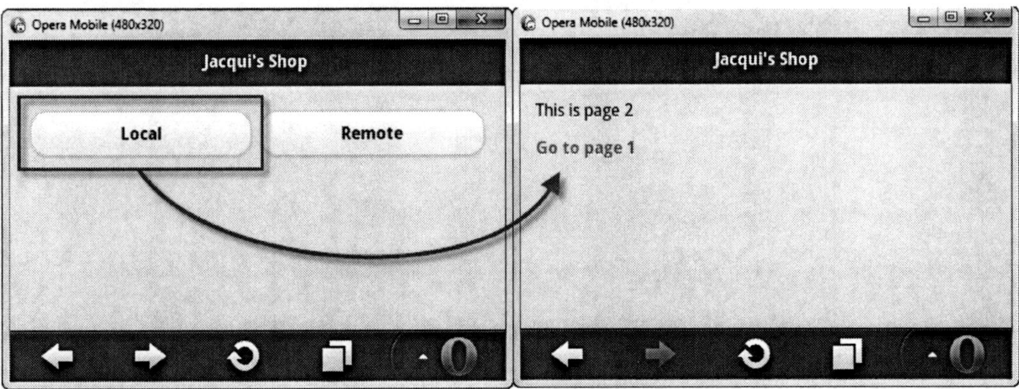

Figure 27-8. Using the changePage method

Now that you have seen the basic use of the changePage method, you can turn to the different configuration options available. To configure the page transition, you pass a settings object as the second argument to the changePage method, specifying values for one or more settings. Table 27-2 describes the settings that are available. Most of these settings are best left with their defaults, but in the sections that follow I show two of the settings that it can be useful to modify more frequently.

Table 27-2. *Settings for the changePage Method*

Setting	Description
`allowSamePageTransition`	When set to `false` (the default), jQuery Mobile will ignore changePage requests where the target page is the current page. A value of `true` allows such requests, although this can cause some problems with the transition animations.
`changeHash`	When `true`, the hash fragment in the URL bar will be updated to the new location (so that the page identifier is included in the URL). The default is `true`.
`data`	Specifies data to be included in the Ajax request used to load a document.
`dataUrl`	Specifies the URL used when updating the browser URL bar. The default is no value, which means the value is taken from the `id` of an internal page or the URL of a remote document.
`loadMsgDelay`	Specifies the number of milliseconds after which the loading dialog will be displayed to the user. The default is `50`.
`reloadPage`	When `true`, jQuery Mobile will reload the contents of a remote document, even if the data is already cached. The default is `false`.
`reverse`	When `true`, the transition effect will be played backward. The default is `false`.
`showLoadMsg`	A value of `true` will show the loading dialog when loading remote documents. The default is `true`.
`transition`	Specifies the transition effect to be used when displaying the new page.
`type`	Specifies the HTTP method used to request a document. The allowed values are `get` and `post`. The default is `get`.

Controlling the Direction of the Transition Effect

The `reverse` setting is the one I use most often. jQuery Mobile will always play transition effects in the same way, which doesn't always make sense when you have presented the user with an action that effectively sends them back to an earlier page or where you are responding to a jQuery Mobile swiperight event. Listing 27-15 shows the problem.

Listing 27-15. Transition Effect Direction Mismatched with Navigation Intent

```
<!DOCTYPE html>
<html>
<head>
    <title>Example</title>
    <meta name="viewport" content="width=device-width, initial-scale=1">
    <link rel="stylesheet" href="jquery.mobile-1.0.css" type="text/css" />
    <script type="text/javascript" src="jquery-1.6.4.js"></script>
    <script type="text/javascript">
        $(document).bind("pageinit", function() {
           $('button').bind("tap", function(e) {
                var target = this.id == "forward" ? "#page2" : "#page1";
                $.mobile.changePage(target, {
                    reverse: (target == "#page1")
                });
           })
        });
    </script>
    <script type="text/javascript" src="jquery.mobile-1.0.js"></script>
</head>
<body>
    <div id="page1" data-role="page">
        <div data-role="header">
           <h1>Jacqui's Shop</h1>
        </div>
        <div data-role="content">
            This is page 1
            <button id="forward">Go to Page 2</button>
        </div>
    </div>
    <div id="page2" data-role="page">
        <div data-role="header">
           <h1>Jacqui's Shop</h1>
        </div>
        <div data-role="content">
            This is page 2
            <button id="back">Back to Page 1</button>
        </div>
   </div>
</body>
</html>
```

There are two pages in this document, each of which contains a button that navigates to the other page. The button on the second page is labeled Back to Page 1. When the button on the second page is clicked, I change the direction of the transition effect by using a reverse value of true. I can't show this effect on a static page, but the effect feels much more natural. There is some subconscious expectation formed about the animation should be played in based on the navigational cue that you are returning to a previous page, rather than progressing to a new one. You will understand exactly what I mean if you view this example in a browser.

Controlling the Load Dialog

jQuery Mobile displays a dialog box when it loads a remote document via Ajax for longer than 50 milliseconds. When using a mobile browser emulator and a fast network, jQuery Mobile is able to load the document so quickly that the dialog box is never shown. But if you use an actual mobile data network or, as I have done, introduce a delay into the request, then the dialog remains on the screen long enough to be seen, as Figure 27-9 illustrates.

Figure 27-9. The jQuery Mobile loading dialog box

You can change the period after which the dialog is displayed by providing a value for the loadMsgDelay setting, as shown in Listing 27-16.

Listing 27-16. Changing the Delay for the Loading Dialog

```
<!DOCTYPE html>
<html>
<head>
    <title>Example</title>
    <meta name="viewport" content="width=device-width, initial-scale=1">
    <link rel="stylesheet" href="jquery.mobile-1.0.css" type="text/css" />
    <script type="text/javascript" src="jquery-1.6.4.js"></script>
    <script type="text/javascript">

        $(document).bind("mobileinit", function() {
            $.mobile.loadingMessage = "Loading Data..."
```

```
        })

        $(document).bind("pageinit", function() {
           $('button').bind("tap", function(e) {
                $.mobile.changePage("document2.html",{
                    loadMsgDelay: 1000
                });
           })
        });
    </script>
    <script type="text/javascript" src="jquery.mobile-1.0.js"></script>
</head>
<body>
    <div id="page1" data-role="page">
        <div data-role="header">
           <h1>Jacqui's Shop</h1>
        </div>
        <div data-role="content">
            <button id="forward">Go</button>
        </div>
    </div>
</body>
</html>
```

In this example, I have specified that jQuery Mobile should wait for one second before displaying the loading dialog to the user.

■ **Tip** You can change the text in the loading dialog by setting a new value for the global `loadingMessage` property, as shown in the example. As with all jQuery Mobile global properties, this should be set in a function executed when the `mobileinit` event is triggered.

You can disable this dialog by specifying `false` for the `showLoadMsg` setting when you call the `changePage` method. This is not something I recommend doing, because providing the user with feedback is always a good thing, but Listing 27-17 shows the setting in use.

Listing 27-17. Disabling the Loading Dialog

```
<!DOCTYPE html>
<html>
<head>
    <title>Example</title>
    <meta name="viewport" content="width=device-width, initial-scale=1">
    <link rel="stylesheet" href="jquery.mobile-1.0.css" type="text/css" />
    <script type="text/javascript" src="jquery-1.6.4.js"></script>
    <script type="text/javascript">
        $(document).bind("pageinit", function() {
           $('button').bind("tap", function(e) {
```

```
                $.mobile.changePage("document2.html",{
                    showLoadMsg: false
                });
            })
        });
    </script>
    <script type="text/javascript" src="jquery.mobile-1.0.js"></script>
</head>
<body>
    <div id="page1" data-role="page">
        <div data-role="header">
           <h1>Jacqui's Shop</h1>
        </div>
        <div data-role="content">
            <button id="forward">Go</button>
        </div>
    </div>
</body>
</html>
```

Determining the Current Page

You can use the `$.mobile.activePage` property to determine the current page that jQuery Mobile is displaying. I have included this property for completeness, but it is not something I find myself using very often. My jQuery Mobile applications tend to consist of small, simple pages that contain very little scripting and a small number of widgets. In my experience, needing to work out where you are is something that arises for more complex applications. There are no hard and fast rules about how complex a mobile web application can be, but if you find yourself in need of this property, then I suggest you take a quick moment to sanity check your approach. You might be trying to do something this is too complex for mobile browsers or (more likely) something that can be handled without using JavaScript. Listing 27-18 shows the use of the `activePage` property.

Listing 27-18. Using the activatePage Property

```
<!DOCTYPE html>
<html>
<head>
    <title>Example</title>
    <meta name="viewport" content="width=device-width, initial-scale=1">
    <link rel="stylesheet" href="jquery.mobile-1.0.css" type="text/css" />
    <script type="text/javascript" src="jquery-1.6.4.js"></script>
    <script type="text/javascript">
        $(document).bind("pageinit", function() {
            $('button').bind("tap", function(e) {
                var nextPages = {
                    page1: "#page2",
                    page2: "#page3",
                    page3: "#page1"
                }
                var currentPageId = $.mobile.activePage.attr("id");
                $.mobile.changePage(nextPages[currentPageId])
```

```
            })
        });
    </script>
    <script type="text/javascript" src="jquery.mobile-1.0.js"></script>
</head>
<body>
    <div id="page1" data-role="page">
        <div data-role="header">
           <h1>Jacqui's Shop</h1>
        </div>
        <div data-role="content">
            This is page 1
            <button id="forward">Go</button>
        </div>
    </div>
    <div id="page2" data-role="page">
        <div data-role="header">
           <h1>Jacqui's Shop</h1>
        </div>
        <div data-role="content">
            This is page 2
            <button id="forward">Go</button>
        </div>
    </div>
    <div id="page3" data-role="page">
        <div data-role="header">
           <h1>Jacqui's Shop</h1>
        </div>
        <div data-role="content">
            This is page 3
            <button id="forward">Go</button>
        </div>
    </div>
</body>
</html>
```

There are three pages in this example, each of which has a button. When the button is clicked, I read the activePage property to get the current page. The activePage property returns a jQuery object that contains the current page, so I use the jQuery attr method to get the value of the id attribute.

My script includes a simple map that tells me what the next page should be for each of the pages in my document, and I use the id value obtained from the activePage property as the argument to the changePage method, ensuring that I progress through my pages in the sequence defined by my map.

Loading Pages in the Background

You can use the loadPage method to load remote documents without displaying them to the user. This is the programmatic equivalent of the prefetching that I demonstrated earlier in the chapter. The loadPage method takes two arguments. The first is the URL of the document to load, and the second is an optional settings object. The loadPage method supports a subset of the settings used by the changePage method: data, reloadPage, and type. Listing 27-19 shows the loadPage method in use.

Listing 27-19. Using the loadPage Method

```
<!DOCTYPE html>
<html>
<head>
    <title>Example</title>
    <meta name="viewport" content="width=device-width, initial-scale=1">
    <link rel="stylesheet" href="jquery.mobile-1.0.css" type="text/css" />
    <script type="text/javascript" src="jquery-1.6.4.js"></script>
    <script type="text/javascript">
        var loadedPages = false;

        $(document).bind("pageinit", function() {
            if (!loadedPages) {
                loadedPages = true;
                var pload = $.mobile.loadPage("document2.html")
                pload.done(function() {
                    $('#gobutton').button("enable").bind("tap", function() {
                        $.mobile.changePage("document2.html")
                    })
                })
            }
        });
    </script>
    <script type="text/javascript" src="jquery.mobile-1.0.js"></script>
</head>
<body>
    <div id="page1" data-role="page">
        <div data-role="header">
           <h1>Jacqui's Shop</h1>
        </div>
        <div data-role="content">
            <button id="gobutton" disabled>Go</button>
        </div>
    </div>
</body>
</html>
```

In this example, I use the loadPage method to preload the document2.html file. The loadPage method returns a deferred object that you can use to receive notification when the page has loaded. I explain deferred objects in Chapter 35, but for now it is enough to know that you can call the done method on the object returned by the loadPage method, specifying a function that will be executed when the Ajax request started by loadPage has completed.

In this example, I use the enable method on the jQuery UI button widget to enable a button in the page and to register a handle for the tap event. When the button is clicked, I call the changePage method to navigate to the prefetched document.

Notice that I have defined a global variable called loadedPages. The pageinit event is triggered whenever jQuery Mobile initializes a page. This means the event is triggered when the document in the example is loaded and again when loadPage loads document2.html via Ajax. I use the loadedPages variable to ensure that I try to preload the content only once. It wouldn't be the end of the world to call loadPage twice (which is what would happen without the loadedPages variable) unless I enabled the reload setting. This would cause the cached copy of the document to be ignored and transfer `document.html` twice. I explain the set of jQuery Mobile page events in the following section.

Using Page Events

jQuery Mobile defines a set of events that you can use to receive notifications about change in pages. These events are described in Table 27-3, and I demonstrate some of the more useful ones in the sections that follow.

***Table 27-3.** jQuery Mobile Page Events*

Event	Description
`pagebeforeload`	Triggered before a page is requested via Ajax
`pageload`	Triggered when a page has been successfully loaded via Ajax
`pageloadfailed`	Triggered when a page has failed to load via Ajax
`pagebeforechange`	Triggered before a page transition is performed
`pagechange`	Triggered after a page transition has been performed
`pagechangefailed`	Triggered when a page change fails (this is usually because the requested document cannot be loaded)
`pagebeforeshow`	Triggered before a page is displayed to the user
`pagebeforehide`	Triggered before a page is removed from the display
`pageshow`	Triggered after a page has been displayed to the user
`pagehide`	Triggered after a page has been hidden from the user
`pageinit`	Triggered when the page has been initialized

Handling the Page Initialization Event

The `pageinit` event is the most useful of the jQuery Mobile page events. It is this event that you respond to when you want to configure your page using a script. I am not going to demonstrate this event again because you have seen it in every example so far, but I will emphasize that using the standard jQuery `$(document).ready()` approach is not reliable when working with jQuery Mobile.

Handling Page Load Events

The `pagebeforeload`, `pageload`, and `pageloadfailed` events can be useful for monitoring Ajax requests made for remote pages, either automatically generated by jQuery Mobile or programmatically via the changePage and loadPage methods. When demonstrating the loadPage method, I used a deferred object to respond when the page had been loaded, but you can achieve the same result using the pageload method (and, of course, the pageloadfailed method when things go wrong). Listing 27-20 shows the loadPage example updated to use the pageload event.

Listing 27-20. Using the pageload Event

```
<!DOCTYPE html>
<html>
<head>
    <title>Example</title>
    <meta name="viewport" content="width=device-width, initial-scale=1">
    <link rel="stylesheet" href="jquery.mobile-1.0.css" type="text/css" />
    <script type="text/javascript" src="jquery-1.6.4.js"></script>
    <script type="text/javascript">

        $(document).bind("pageload", function(event, data) {
            if (data.url == "document2.html") {
                $('#gobutton').button("enable").bind("tap", function() {
                    $.mobile.changePage("document2.html")
                })
            }
        })

        var loadedPages = false;
        $(document).bind("pageinit", function() {
            if (!loadedPages) {
                loadedPages = true;
                $.mobile.loadPage("document2.html")
            }
        });
    </script>
    <script type="text/javascript" src="jquery.mobile-1.0.js"></script>
</head>
<body>
    <div id="page1" data-role="page">
        <div data-role="header">
           <h1>Jacqui's Shop</h1>
        </div>
        <div data-role="content">
            <button id="gobutton" disabled>Go</button>
        </div>
    </div>
</body>
</html>
```

In this example, I have specified a function that will be executed when the pageload event is triggered. jQuery Mobile provides information about the request by passing a data object as the second argument to the function. I use the url property to check that the document that has been loaded is the one I am expecting. The set of properties defined by the data object for the pageload event is described in Table 27-4. You can see from the table that most of the properties correspond to the jQuery Ajax support, which I described in Chapters 14 and 15.

Table 27-4. pageload Data Object Event Properties

Property	Description
url	Returns the URL passed to the loadPage method (this is method is used by jQuery Mobile when it requests pages and by the changePage method).
absUrl	The absolute URL that was requested.
options	The Ajax request options. See Chapters 14 and 15 for details of configuring Ajax
xhr	The jQuery Ajax request object used for the request. See Chapters 14 and 15 for details of this object.
textStatus	The string description of the request status. See Chapters 14 and 15 for details.

Responding to Page Transitions

You can use the page transition events to be notified when the user navigates from one page to another (or when you do this programmatically using the changePage method). These events (pagebeforehide, pagehide, pagebeforeshow and pageshow) are triggered for every page transition, even if the page has been displayed to the user before. Listing 27-21 shows the use of one of these events.

Listing 27-21. Responding to a Page Being Hidden

```
<!DOCTYPE html>
<html>
<head>
    <title>Example</title>
    <meta name="viewport" content="width=device-width, initial-scale=1">
    <link rel="stylesheet" href="jquery.mobile-1.0.css" type="text/css" />
    <script type="text/javascript" src="jquery-1.6.4.js"></script>
    <script type="text/javascript">
        var registeredHandlers = false;
        $(document).bind("pageinit", function() {
            if (!registeredHandlers) {
                registeredHandlers = true;
                $('#page1').bind("pagehide", function(event, data) {
                    $.mobile.changePage($("#page1"))
                })
            }
        });
    </script>
    <script type="text/javascript" src="jquery.mobile-1.0.js"></script>
</head>
<body>
    <div id="page1" data-role="page">
        <div data-role="header">
           <h1>Jacqui's Shop</h1>
```

```
        </div>
        <div data-role="content">
            <a href="document2.html">Go to document2.html</a>
        </div>
    </div>
</body>
</html>
```

In this example, I register a handler function for the pagehide event on the page1 element, by selecting the element I want and calling the bind method. This means I will receive the event only when that selected page is hidden. This is a pretty dumb example, because it simply uses the changePage method to return to page1 whenever the pagehide event is triggered, but it does demonstrate the use of the event. Notice that I am still using a variable to ensure that I register my handler function only once. If I did not do this, then two functions would be registered for the same event on the same element when document2.html page is loaded.

■ **Tip** jQuery Mobile provides additional information about the page transition events by passing a data object as the second argument to the handler function. This object will define a property called either nextPage (for the pagebeforehide and pagehide events) or prevPage (for pagebeforeshow and pageshow). These properties return a jQuery object containing the page element that has just been hidden or shown.

Summary

In this chapter, I described pages, which are one of the key building blocks of jQuery Mobile. The idea of having multiple pages in a single document is something that is unique to jQuery Mobile and that can be helpful for small and simple applications. But for more serious efforts, putting pages in their own document and relying on jQuery Mobile to load them via Ajax is the way to go.

CHAPTER 28

Dialogs, Themes, and Layouts

In this chapter, I describe three useful jQuery Mobile features that are helpful when creating mobile web applications. Each feature is pretty simple, but I will be using them in the chapters that follow, so I wanted you to understand them before I start using them in examples. These features allow you to create dialogs, apply themes to your pages and elements, and lay out elements in multicolumn grids. None of these items is especially exciting on its own, but this is the kind of important plumbing that makes life easier for the mobile web developer. Table 28-1 provides the summary for this chapter.

Table 28-1. *Chapter Summary*

Problem	Solution	Listing
Display a page as a dialog.	Add the `data-rel` attribute to a navigation link with a value of `dialog`.	1
Add a close button to the dialog.	Add a link to the dialog page with a `data-rel` attribute with a value of `back`.	2
Add a button to a dialog that navigates to another page.	Add a link to the dialog page whose `href` attribute is set to the URL of the target page.	3
Manage dialogs programmatically.	Use the `changePage` method to open the dialog and navigate to another page. Use the dialog `close` method to close the dialog.	4
Apply a swatch to a page or an element.	Use the `data-theme` attribute whose value is the swatch that should be used.	5, 6
Lay out elements in a grid.	Use the jQuery Mobile layout CSS classes.	7

Creating Dialogs

One of the nice features of jQuery Mobile pages is that you can use them to easily create dialogs. You do this by applying the data-rel attribute to the a element that navigates to the page, specifying a value of dialog. Listing 28-1 contains an example.

Listing 28-1. Using a Page as a Dialog

```
<!DOCTYPE html>
<html>
<head>
    <title>Example</title>
    <meta name="viewport" content="width=device-width, initial-scale=1">
    <link rel="stylesheet" href="jquery.mobile-1.0.css" type="text/css" />
    <script type="text/javascript" src="jquery-1.6.4.js"></script>
    <script type="text/javascript" src="jquery.mobile-1.0.js"></script>
</head>
<body>
    <div id="page1" data-role="page">
        <div data-role="header">
           <h1>Jacqui's Shop</h1>
        </div>
        <div data-role="content">
            <a href="#page2" data-rel="dialog">Show the dialog</a>
        </div>
    </div>
    <div id="page2" data-role="page">
        <div data-role="header">
           <h1>You clicked the link!</h1>
        </div>
        <div data-role="content">
            This is the content area of the dialog
        </div>
    </div>
</body>
</html>
```

In this example, there are two regular jQuery Mobile pages. The link in the first page is just like the links I was using in the previous chapter, with the exception that I have applied the data-rel attribute and set the value to dialog. When the user clicks the link, jQuery Mobile takes the pages and presents it in the form of a dialog, as Figure 28-1 shows.

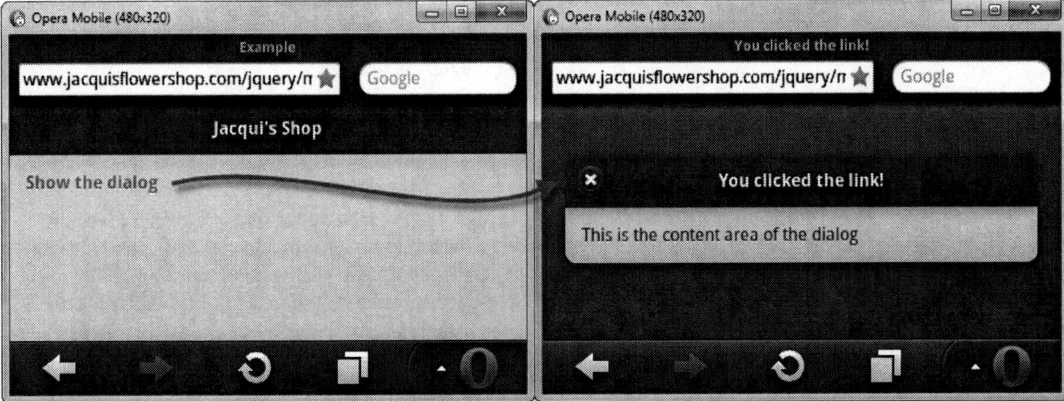

Figure 28-1. Displaying a page as a dialog

The interesting thing about this feature is that you don't have to make any changes to the page at all. Everything is set up in the navigation link, and all without having to write any JavaScript code.

Adding Buttons to the Dialog

In the basic dialog, the user has to click the icon in the top-left corner to close the dialog and return to the previous page. You can add a close button to the dialog by adding a `button` element and using another data attribute, as Listing 28-2 demonstrates.

Listing 28-2. Adding a Close Button to a Dialog

```
<!DOCTYPE html>
<html>
<head>
    <title>Example</title>
    <meta name="viewport" content="width=device-width, initial-scale=1">
    <link rel="stylesheet" href="jquery.mobile-1.0.css" type="text/css" />
    <script type="text/javascript" src="jquery-1.6.4.js"></script>
    <script type="text/javascript" src="jquery.mobile-1.0.js"></script>
</head>
<body>
    <div id="page1" data-role="page">
        <div data-role="header">
           <h1>Jacqui's Shop</h1>
        </div>
        <div data-role="content">
            <a href="#page2" data-rel="dialog">Show the dialog</a>
        </div>
    </div>
    <div id="page2" data-role="page">
        <div data-role="header">
           <h1>You clicked the link!</h1>
        </div>
```

```
        <div data-role="content">
            This is the content area of the dialog
            <a href="#" data-role="button" data-rel="back">Close</a>
        </div>
    </div>
</body>
</html>
```

I have added an a element and applied the data-rel attribute with a value of back. I don't have to specify the target for the link. I just set the href attribute to # and leave jQuery Mobile to figure out what to do. This is a useful because you may want to display a dialog from different pages, and you don't know which of them caused the dialog to be shown. Figure 28-2 shows the effect of adding this element to the dialog.

■ **Tip** You will notice that I have set the data-role attribute on this link to button. This causes jQuery Mobile to create a button widget from the element, which I explain fully in Chapter 29.

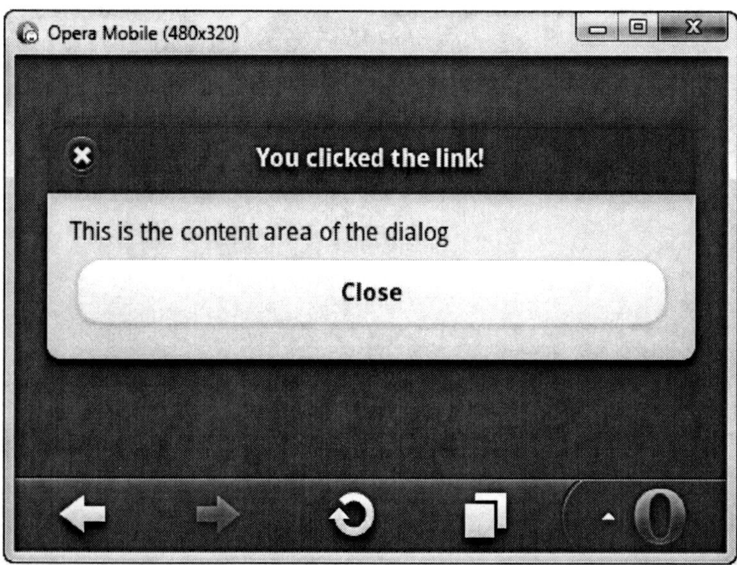

Figure 28-2. Adding a close button to a dialog

Adding Another Button to a Dialog

You have a choice when it comes to adding other buttons to a dialog. If you are offering the user a chance to navigate to another page, then you can simply add an a element and set the href attribute to the page that you want. This is what I have done in Listing 28-3, and I have used the same data-role value as in the previous example so that jQuery Mobile creates a button from the link.

Listing 28-3. Adding a Navigation Link to a Dialog

```
<!DOCTYPE html>
<html>
<head>
    <title>Example</title>
    <meta name="viewport" content="width=device-width, initial-scale=1">
    <link rel="stylesheet" href="jquery.mobile-1.0.css" type="text/css" />
    <script type="text/javascript" src="jquery-1.6.4.js"></script>
    <script type="text/javascript" src="jquery.mobile-1.0.js"></script>
</head>
<body>
    <div id="page1" data-role="page">
        <div data-role="header">
           <h1>Jacqui's Shop</h1>
        </div>
        <div data-role="content">
            <a href="#page2" data-rel="dialog">Show the dialog</a>
        </div>
    </div>
    <div id="page2" data-role="page">
        <div data-role="header">
           <h1>You clicked the link!</h1>
        </div>
        <div data-role="content">
            This is the content area of the dialog
            <a href="#page3" data-role="button">OK</a>
            <a href="#" data-role="button" data-rel="back">Close</a>
        </div>
    </div>
    <div id="page3" data-role="page">
        <div data-role="header">
           <h1>Jacqui's Shop</h1>
        </div>
        <div data-role="content">
            This is page 3. You came here via the dialog.
        </div>
    </div>
</body>
</html>
```

In this example, I have added an a element that takes the user to page3, which I have added to the document. Figure 28-3 shows the navigation from the dialog to the new page.

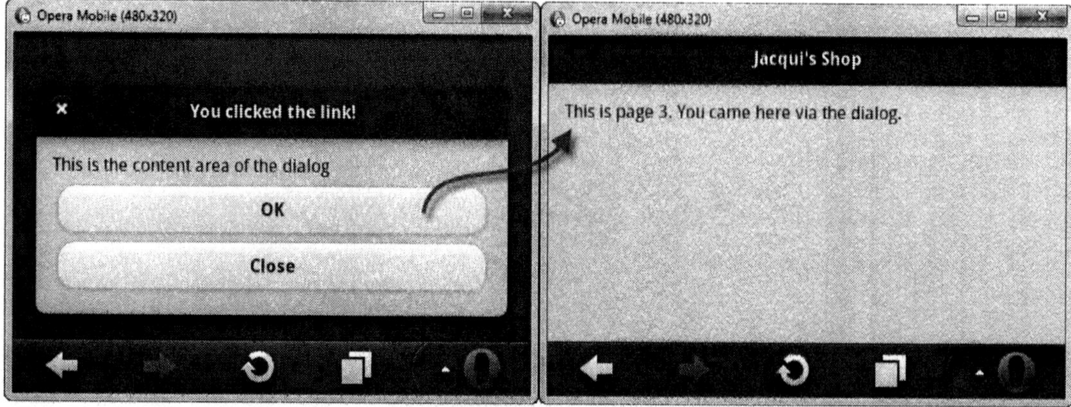

Figure 28-3. Adding a navigation link/button to a dialog

■ **Tip** jQuery Mobile doesn't add the dialog to the browser's history, which means that if you navigate from a dialog to another page, hitting the back button returns to the page shown before the dialog.

Managing Dialogs Programmatically

Although jQuery Mobile tries to minimize the amount of code you have to write, there are times when you want to take more direct control of what is happening. Listing 28-4 shows how you can open and close dialogs programmatically.

Listing 28-4. Opening and Closing a Dialog Programmatically

```
<!DOCTYPE html>
<html>
<head>
    <title>Example</title>
    <meta name="viewport" content="width=device-width, initial-scale=1">
    <link rel="stylesheet" href="jquery.mobile-1.0.css" type="text/css" />
    <script type="text/javascript" src="jquery-1.6.4.js"></script>
    <script type="text/javascript">
        $(document).bind("pageinit", function() {

            $('#openDialog').bind("tap", function() {
                $.mobile.changePage("#page2", {
                    role: "dialog"
                })
            })

            $('#closeDialog').bind("tap", function() {
                $('#page2').dialog("close")
```

```
            })

            $('#okButton').bind("tap", function() {
                $.mobile.changePage("#page3")
            })

        });
    </script>
    <script type="text/javascript" src="jquery.mobile-1.0.js"></script>
</head>
<body>
    <div id="page1" data-role="page">
        <div data-role="header">
           <h1>Jacqui's Shop</h1>
        </div>
        <div data-role="content">
            <button id="openDialog">Show the dialog</button>
        </div>
    </div>
    <div id="page2" data-role="page">
        <div data-role="header">
           <h1>You clicked the link!</h1>
        </div>
        <div data-role="content">
            This is the content area of the dialog
            <button id="okButton">OK</button>
            <button id="closeDialog">Close</button>
        </div>
    </div>
    <div id="page3" data-role="page">
        <div data-role="header">
           <h1>Jacqui's Shop</h1>
        </div>
        <div data-role="content">
            This is page 3. You came here via the dialog.
        </div>
    </div>
</body>
</html>
```

I have replaced the links with button elements in this example because there is no default action for clicking a button outside of a form. I have also added a script element in which I have registered handler functions for the tap event for each button. (I have used separate calls to the bind method because it makes the example easier to explain, but there is no reason why these three functions cannot be combined into a single function, just as I have been doing in earlier parts of the book.)

To open the dialog, you just have to call the changePage method, specifying the URL of the page you want and using a settings object that has a value of dialog for the role property, like this:

```
$.mobile.changePage("#page2", {
    role: "dialog"
})
```

I explained the changePage method in Chapter 27. This is the same method you use when you want to navigate away from the dialog to another page:

```
$.mobile.changePage("#page3")
```

You can see the jQuery UI underpinnings of jQuery Mobile when you close a dialog programmatically:

```
$('#page2').dialog("close")
```

You can learn more about the jQuery UI dialog widget in Chapter 22, although this is the only occasion where the functionality of that widget leaks through into the jQuery Mobile world.

Applying Themes

jQuery Mobile provides support for themes. There is a default theme included in the jQuery Mobile files that you downloaded and installed in Chapter 26, and you can create custom themes using the jQuery Mobile ThemeRoller application, which is a variation on the application of the same name you used for jQuery UI.

■ **Note** As I mentioned in Chapter 26, I won't be creating and using a custom theme in this part of the book. The jQuery Mobile ThemeRoller application is a relatively late addition to jQuery Mobile and, as I write this, has some problems. I expect that these will be resolved by the time that you read this.

A jQuery Mobile theme consists of one or more *swatches*, which is a set of styles that are applied to different kinds of elements. Although I won't be creating a custom theme (see the previous note), you can use the ThemeRoller application to view the default theme. Swatches are identified by a single letter, starting with *A*. The default theme has five swatches, named `A` through `E`. To view the default theme in ThemeRoller, navigate to `http://jquerymobile.com/themeroller`, click the Import link, and paste the contents of the `jquery.mobile-1.0.css` file into the dialog (this is the CSS file that you downloaded and installed in Chapter 26). The ThemeRoller application will process the CSS and display the default swatches, as shown in Figure 28-4.

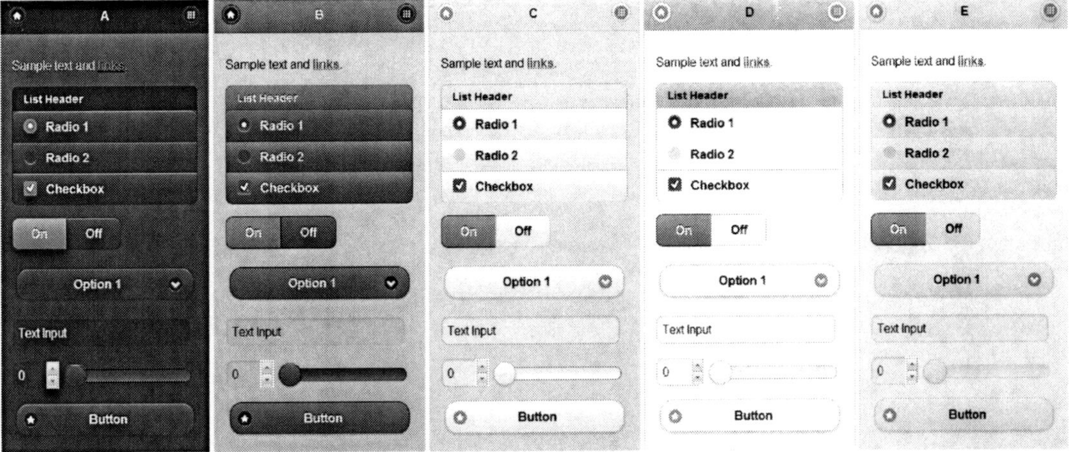

Figure 28-4. The swatches in the default theme

■ **Tip** As I write this, ThemeRoller is unable to properly parse the CSS from the default theme. If you try to modify any of the styles in a swatch, badly formed CSS is generated, and none of the swatches is displayed properly.

You apply a theme to a jQuery Mobile page by using the `data-theme` attribute, setting the value to the name of the swatch you want. Listing 28-5 provides an example.

■ **Tip** There is also a swatch called `active`, which is used to highlight selected buttons. This is applied automatically by jQuery Mobile, but you can use it directly as well. If you do, be sure that you are not confusing the user by creating conflicting active elements.

Listing 28-5. Using the Swatches in a Theme

```
<!DOCTYPE html>
<html>
<head>
    <title>Example</title>
    <meta name="viewport" content="width=device-width, initial-scale=1">
    <link rel="stylesheet" href="jquery.mobile-1.0.css" type="text/css" />
    <script type="text/javascript" src="jquery-1.6.4.js"></script>
    <script type="text/javascript" src="jquery.mobile-1.0.js"></script>
</head>
<body>
```

```
    <div id="page1" data-role="page" data-theme="a">
        <div data-role="header">
           <h1>Jacqui's Shop</h1>
        </div>
        <div data-role="content">
            This is Theme A
            <a href="#page2" data-role="button">Switch Theme</a>
        </div>
    </div>
    <div id="page2" data-role="page" data-theme="b">
        <div data-role="header">
           <h1>Jacqui's Shop</h1>
        </div>
        <div data-role="content">
            This is Theme B
            <a href="#page1" data-role="button">Switch Theme</a>
        </div>
    </div>
</body>
</html>
```

I have applied the data-theme attribute to the page element, which has the effect of applying the specified swatch to all of the child elements within the page. There are two pages in this example so that I can show how the same content is displayed by a pair of contrasting themes—and to make the point that there is no reliable way in jQuery Mobile to change the theme once a page has been through the automatic enhancement process. The data-theme attribute is transformed into a set of CSS classes that are applied to elements during page initialization, and so changing the value of the attribute doesn't do anything to change the classes. You can see the two-page example in Figure 28-5.

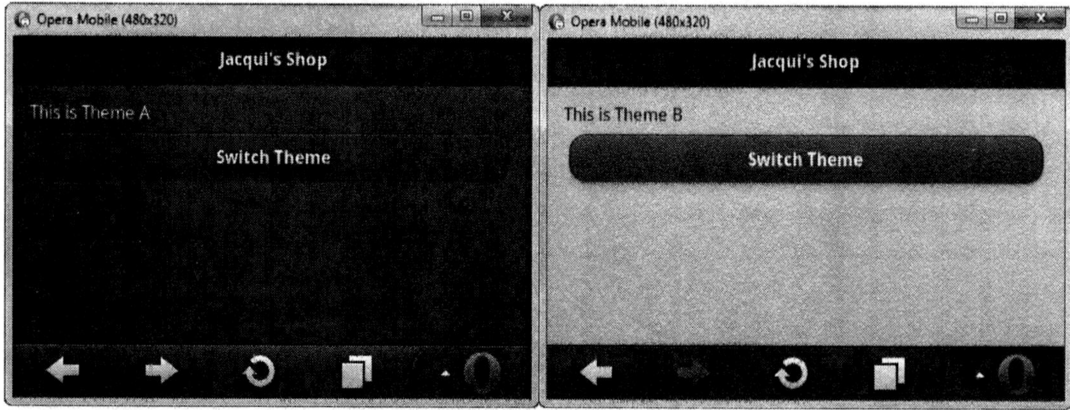

Figure 28-5. Two pages in the same application using different swatches

Applying Swatches to Individual Elements

The previous example shows how you can style entire pages, but you can also apply swatches on a per-element basis, mixing and matching to get a specific effect. Listing 28-6 provides a demonstration.

Listing 28-6. Applying Swatches to Individual Elements

```
<!DOCTYPE html>
<html>
<head>
    <title>Example</title>
    <meta name="viewport" content="width=device-width, initial-scale=1">
    <link rel="stylesheet" href="jquery.mobile-1.0.css" type="text/css" />
    <script type="text/javascript" src="jquery-1.6.4.js"></script>
    <script type="text/javascript" src="jquery.mobile-1.0.js"></script>
</head>
<body>
    <div id="page1" data-role="page" data-theme="a">
        <div data-role="header">
           <h1>Jacqui's Shop</h1>
        </div>
        <div data-role="content">
            <a href="document2.html" data-role="button" data-theme="b">Press Me</a>
            <a href="document2.html" data-role="button" data-theme="c">Press Me</a>
            <a href="document2.html" data-role="button" data-theme="e">Press Me</a>
        </div>
    </div>
</body>
</html>
```

In this example, I have applied the data-theme to the page and to the three button elements, each specifying a different swatch. You can see the effect in Figure 28-6.

Figure 28-6. Applying different swatches to elements in the same page

The jQuery Mobile support for themes is simple and easy to work with. It would be nice if you were able to change the swatches used by elements on the fly, but even with this omission, you can use swatches to tailor the appearance of your mobile applications.

Creating Grid Layouts

jQuery Mobile defines some useful CSS classes that you can use to lay out the contents of your mobile pages in grid form. This is something you could do yourself, but having them built into the library is useful and reduces the amount of custom development is needed, especially for simple mobile applications.

jQuery Mobile defines four grid classes, each of which contains a different number of columns, as summarized by Table 28-2.

Table 28-2. *jQuery Mobile Layout Grid*

CSS Class	Columns
ui-grid-a	2
ui-grid-b	3
ui-grid-c	4
ui-grid-d	5

You apply one of the grid classes to a container element and then apply classes to each of the content items within, starting with ui-block-a, ui-block-b, and so on, for each column. Listing 28-7 shows the use of these classes to create a simple grid.

Listing 28-7. Creating a Grid Using the jQuery Mobile Layout Classes

```
<!DOCTYPE html>
<html>
<head>
    <title>Example</title>
    <meta name="viewport" content="width=device-width, initial-scale=1">
    <link rel="stylesheet" href="jquery.mobile-1.0.css" type="text/css" />
    <script type="text/javascript" src="jquery-1.6.4.js"></script>
    <script type="text/javascript" src="jquery.mobile-1.0.js"></script>
</head>
<body>
    <div id="page1" data-role="page" data-theme="b">
        <div data-role="header">
           <h1>Jacqui's Shop</h1>
        </div>
        <div data-role="content">
            <div class="ui-grid-b">
                <div class="ui-block-a"><button>Press Me</button></div>
                <div class="ui-block-b"><button>Press Me</button></div>
```

```
            <div class="ui-block-c"><button>Press Me</button></div>
        </div>
        <div class="ui-grid-a">
            <div class="ui-block-a"><button>Press Me</button></div>
            <div class="ui-block-b"><button>Press Me</button></div>
        </div>
        <div><button>Press Me</button></div>
    </div>
</div>
</body>
</html>
```

In this example, I have created two grids: one with three columns and one with two columns. Each column contains a button element, and I have added a button outside of the grid to emphasize the default behavior, which is for elements to span the screen. You can see the result in Figure 28-7.

Figure 28-7. Laying out elements in a grid

Summary

In this chapter, I introduced three helpful features of jQuery Mobile: dialogs, swatches, and grid layouts. These are pretty minor features, but I wanted to describe them before I started using them in later chapters. These are simple features, but they help form the structure of most jQuery Mobile applications, so having a thorough understanding of them is important.

CHAPTER 29

Buttons and Collapsible Blocks

In this chapter, I describe two of the jQuery Mobile widgets: *buttons* and *collapsible blocks*. The jQuery Mobile button widget works in a very similar way to the jQuery UI buttons you saw earlier in the book, with the exception that you can create and use simple buttons without using any custom JavaScript code at all. A collapsible block is like a single panel from an accordion; in fact, you can use collapsible blocks on their own or combine several together to form a simple accordion. Table 29-1 provides the summary for this chapter.

Table 29-1. *Chapter Summary*

Problem	Solution	Listing
Create a button widget automatically.	Add a `button` element or an `input` element whose type is `submit`, `reset`, or `button`.	1
Prevent jQuery Mobile from automatically creating button widgets.	Apply the `data-role` attribute with a value of `none`.	2
Create button widgets from other elements.	Apply the `data-role` attribute with a value of `button`.	3
Respond to button events.	Handle the `click` event or one of the jQuery Mobile convenience events.	4
Add an icon to a button widget.	Use the `data-icon` and `data-iconpos` attributes.	5
Prevent button widgets from filling the width of the screen.	Use the `data-inline` attribute.	6
Create a group of buttons.	Use the `data-role` attribute with a value of `controlgroup`. Use the `data-type` attribute to change the orientation.	7, 8

Create a collapsible block.	Apply the data-role attribute with a value of collapsible. Ensure that there is a header element as the first child.	9
Apply a swatch to the content area of a collapsible block.	Use the data-content-theme attribute.	10
Set the initial state of a collapsible block.	Use the data-collapsed attribute.	11
Receive notification when a collapsible block is expanded and collapsed.	Use the expand and collapse events.	12
Expand and collapse a collapsible block programmatically.	Trigger the expand and collapse events.	13
Create an accordion	Use the data-role attribute with a value of collapsible-set value.	14

Using jQuery Mobile Buttons

I already used some button widgets in earlier examples, but now it is time to loop back and explain how they work.

Understanding Automatically Created Buttons

As part of the automatic page-enhancement process, jQuery Mobile creates buttons widgets from button elements or input elements whose type attribute is set to submit, reset, button, or image. You don't have to take any special action for these element types because jQuery Mobile does all the work for you. Listing 29-1 shows a page that contains some of these automatically handled elements.

Listing 29-1. Relying on the automatic creation of button widgets

```
<!DOCTYPE html>
<html>
<head>
    <title>Example</title>
    <meta name="viewport" content="width=device-width, initial-scale=1">
    <link rel="stylesheet" href="jquery.mobile-1.0.css" type="text/css" />
    <script type="text/javascript" src="jquery-1.6.4.js"></script>
    <script type="text/javascript" src="jquery.mobile-1.0.js"></script>
</head>
<body>
    <div id="page1" data-role="page" data-theme="b">
        <div data-role="header">
           <h1>Jacqui's Shop</h1>
        </div>
        <div data-role="content">
            <button>Button</button>
```

```
            <input type="submit" value="Input (Submit)" />
            <input type="reset" value="Input (Reset)" />
            <input type="button" value="Input (Button)" />
        </div>
    </div>
</body>
</html>
```

You can see how a button widget is created for each type of element in Figure 29-1.

Figure 29-1. Button widgets created automatically by jQuery Mobile

Preventing Automatic Button Creation

If you want to stop jQuery Mobile from creating a button widget automatically, apply the data-role attribute to the element with a value of none, as shown in Listing 29-2.

Listing 29-2. Preventing jQuery Mobile from automatically creating a button widget

```
<!DOCTYPE html>
<html>
<head>
    <title>Example</title>
    <meta name="viewport" content="width=device-width, initial-scale=1">
    <link rel="stylesheet" href="jquery.mobile-1.0.css" type="text/css" />
    <script type="text/javascript" src="jquery-1.6.4.js"></script>
    <script type="text/javascript" src="jquery.mobile-1.0.js"></script>
</head>
<body>
    <div id="page1" data-role="page" data-theme="b">
```

```
        <div data-role="header">
           <h1>Jacqui's Shop</h1>
        </div>
        <div data-role="content">
            <button>Button</button>
            <input type="submit" value="Input (Submit)" />
            <input type="reset" value="Input (Reset)" data-role="none" />
            <input type="button" value="Input (Button)" />
        </div>
    </div>
</body>
</html>
```

Configuring jQuery Mobile Buttons

jQuery Mobile defines a number of data attributes you can use to configure buttons and to create buttons from different element types. These attributes are described in Table 29-2.

***Table 29-2.** Data Attributes for Buttons*

Data Attribute	Description
data-corners	When true, buttons are drawn with rounded corners. A value of false means that square corners will be used. The default is true.
data-icon	Specifies an icon to be used in the button.
data-iconpos	Specifies the position of an icon, if one is used.
data-inline	Creates a button that is sized to its contents (rather than filling the screen).
data-shadow	When true, buttons are drawn with a shadow. A value of false means that no shadow will be used. The default is true.

Creating Buttons from Other Elements

jQuery Mobile can also create buttons widgets from other elements. In earlier chapters, you saw me create a button widget from an a element by applying the data-role attribute with a value of button. You can also do this for other types of elements, such as div. Listing 29-3 contains an example.

Listing 29-3. Creating buttons from other elements

```
<!DOCTYPE html>
<html>
<head>
    <title>Example</title>
    <meta name="viewport" content="width=device-width, initial-scale=1">
    <link rel="stylesheet" href="jquery.mobile-1.0.css" type="text/css" />
```

```
    <script type="text/javascript" src="jquery-1.6.4.js"></script>
    <script type="text/javascript" src="jquery.mobile-1.0.js"></script>
</head>
<body>
    <div id="page1" data-role="page" data-theme="b">
        <div data-role="header">
           <h1>Jacqui's Shop</h1>
        </div>
        <div data-role="content">
            <a href="document2.html" data-role="button">A Element</a>
            <div data-role="button">DIV Element</div>
        </div>
    </div>
</body>
</html>
```

You can see how jQuery Mobile deals with the elements in this example in Figure 29-2.

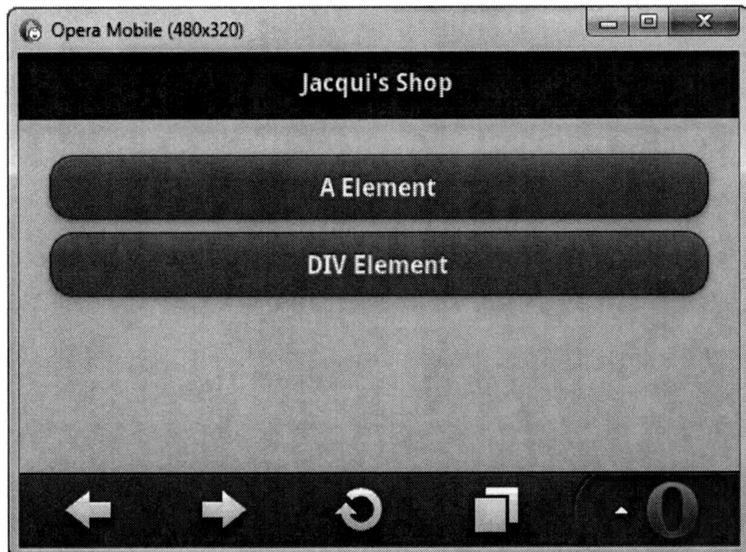

Figure 29-2. Creating button widgets using other elements

Dealing with Button Events

If you create a button from an input element or from an a element, there is a default action that will be performed when the button is clicked. For input elements, the default action is to submit the form that contains the element. (I'll explain more about using forms with jQuery Mobile in Chapter 30.) For a elements, the default action is to navigate to the page specified by the href attribute.

Because of the complexity around touch events that I described in Chapter 26, my advice is to use only the input and a elements when the default actions are useful to you. If you want to create a different effect, use another element to create a button widget and handle the element that suits you best. For me, that's usually the tap event. Listing 29-4 shows how you can handle the events emitted from a button, even when it has been created from a non-button element.

Listing 29-4. Handling events from button widgets

```
<!DOCTYPE html>
<html>
<head>
    <title>Example</title>
    <meta name="viewport" content="width=device-width, initial-scale=1">
    <link rel="stylesheet" href="jquery.mobile-1.0.css" type="text/css" />
    <script type="text/javascript" src="jquery-1.6.4.js"></script>
    <script type="text/javascript">
        $(document).bind("pageinit", function() {
            $('button, #divButton').bind("tap", function() {
                $.mobile.changePage("#page2");
            })
        });
    </script>
    <script type="text/javascript" src="jquery.mobile-1.0.js"></script>
</head>
<body>
    <div id="page1" data-role="page" data-theme="b">
        <div data-role="header">
           <h1>Jacqui's Shop</h1>
        </div>
        <div data-role="content">
            <button>BUTTON Element</button>
            <div id="divButton" data-role="button">DIV Element</div>
        </div>
    </div>
    <div id="page2" data-role="page" data-theme="e">
        <div data-role="header">
           <h1>Jacqui's Shop</h1>
        </div>
        <div data-role="content">
            You pressed a button!
            <a href="#" data-role="button" data-rel="back">OK</a>
        </div>
    </div>
</body>
</html>
```

In this example, I created a page that contains a button element and a div element, both of which will be transformed by jQuery Mobile into button widgets. To respond to the user clicking on these buttons, I use the bind method to handle the tap event, which I described in Chapter 26. When either button is pressed, I use the changePage method to navigate to another page in the same document.

■ **Tip** Notice that I wait for the `pageinit` event to be triggered before I register my handler functions with the `button` and `div` elements. I explained the `pageinit` event in Chapter 26, along with a brief explanation of why you must use it instead of the standard jQuery `ready` event.

Adding Icons to Buttons

jQuery Mobile includes a set of icons that can be used in buttons. These are included in a single image file in the `images` directory you installed in Chapter 26. Table 29-3 shows a list of the icon names and a brief description of each.

***Table 29-3.** Icons Included in jQuery Mobile*

Icon Name	Description
`arrow-l`, `arrow-r`, `arrow-u`, `arrow-d`	Arrows that are facing left, right, up, and down
`check`, `delete`	A check and a cross
`plus`, `minus`	Plus and minus signs
`gear`	A cog
`refresh`, `forward`, `back`, `home`, `search`	Browser style icons to refresh, advance to the next page, return to the previous page, return to the home page, or search
`grid`	A grid of small squares
`star`	A star
`alert`	A caution warning
`info`	A stylized letter i

You apply the icons to a button using the `data-icon` attribute, where the value specifies the name of the icon to use. You can also use the `data-iconpos` attribute to specify where the icon will be located in the button. The default is `left`, but you can also specify `top`, `right`, and `bottom`. If you set `data-iconpos` to `notext`, only the icon is displayed. Listing 29-5 provides an example of using both of these attributes.

Listing 29-5. Adding icons to buttons

```
<!DOCTYPE html>
<html>
<head>
    <title>Example</title>
    <meta name="viewport" content="width=device-width, initial-scale=1">
    <link rel="stylesheet" href="jquery.mobile-1.0.css" type="text/css" />
    <script type="text/javascript" src="jquery-1.6.4.js"></script>
    <script type="text/javascript" src="jquery.mobile-1.0.js"></script>
</head>
<body>
    <div id="page1" data-role="page" data-theme="b">
        <div data-role="header">
           <h1>Jacqui's Shop</h1>
        </div>
        <div data-role="content">
            <div class="ui-grid-b">
                <div class="ui-block-a">
                    <button data-icon="home">Home</button>
                </div>
                <div class="ui-block-b">
                    <button data-icon="home" data-iconpos="top">Home</button>
                </div>
                <div class="ui-block-c">
                    <button data-icon="home" data-iconpos="notext"></button>
                </div>
            </div>
        </div>
    </div>
</body>
</html>
```

In this example, I created three buttons, all of which display the home icon. The first button uses the default icon position, the second button uses the top position, and the last button uses the notext value, which creates an icon-only button. You can see how these buttons appear in Figure 29-3.

Figure 29-3. Creating icon buttons

You can see that each button has a distinctive style. The most striking is the last button, which displays no text. This looks visually appealing, but my experience with this kind of button is that they are hard to hit with a finger and not all users immediately recognize them as a means of navigating elsewhere in the application.

Creating Inline Buttons

By default, jQuery Mobile buttons span the entire width of the screen. You can see an example of the default button width in Figure 29-1. I used the layout grid to create smaller buttons in later examples, but I could have achieved a similar effect using *inline buttons*, which are just big enough to accommodate their content. Listing 29-6 provides an example.

Listing 29-6. Using inline buttons

```
<!DOCTYPE html>
<html>
<head>
    <title>Example</title>
    <meta name="viewport" content="width=device-width, initial-scale=1">
    <link rel="stylesheet" href="jquery.mobile-1.0.css" type="text/css" />
    <script type="text/javascript" src="jquery-1.6.4.js"></script>
    <script type="text/javascript" src="jquery.mobile-1.0.js"></script>
</head>
<body>
    <div id="page1" data-role="page" data-theme="b">
        <div data-role="header">
           <h1>Jacqui's Shop</h1>
```

```
        </div>
        <div data-role="content">
            <div>
                <button data-icon="home" data-inline=true>Home</button>
            </div>
            <div>
                <button data-icon="home">Home</button>
            </div>
        </div>
    </div>
</body>
</html>
```

You create inline buttons by setting the data-inline attribute to true. In the example, there are two buttons, one of which is inline. You can see the effect in Figure 29-4.

Figure 29-4. Using inline buttons

Creating Grouped Buttons

You can create a group of buttons that have no spacing between them by creating a *control group*. You do this by applying the data-role attribute with a value of controlgroup to the parent element for two or more button widgets. Listing 29-7 provides a demonstration.

Listing 29-7. Creating a set of grouped buttons

```
<!DOCTYPE html>
<html>
<head>
    <title>Example</title>
    <meta name="viewport" content="width=device-width, initial-scale=1">
    <link rel="stylesheet" href="jquery.mobile-1.0.css" type="text/css" />
    <script type="text/javascript" src="jquery-1.6.4.js"></script>
    <script type="text/javascript" src="jquery.mobile-1.0.js"></script>
</head>
<body>
    <div id="page1" data-role="page" data-theme="b">
        <div data-role="header">
           <h1>Jacqui's Shop</h1>
        </div>
        <div data-role="content">
            <div data-role="controlgroup">
                <button data-icon="back">Back</button>
                <button data-icon="home">Home</button>
                <button data-icon="next">Next</button>
            </div>
        </div>
    </div>
</body>
</html>
```

In this example, there are three buttons, all of which are children of a `div` element whose `data-role` is control group. You can see the effect in Figure 29-5. Notice how only the top and bottom buttons have rounded corners.

Figure 29-5. A set of buttons displayed in a group

You can change the orientation of the button group by setting the data-type attribute to horizontal, as shown in Listing 29-8.

Listing 29-8. Creating a horizontal button group

```
<!DOCTYPE html>
<html>
<head>
    <title>Example</title>
    <meta name="viewport" content="width=device-width, initial-scale=1">
    <link rel="stylesheet" href="jquery.mobile-1.0.css" type="text/css" />
    <script type="text/javascript" src="jquery-1.6.4.js"></script>
    <script type="text/javascript" src="jquery.mobile-1.0.js"></script>
</head>
<body>
    <div id="page1" data-role="page" data-theme="b">
        <div data-role="header">
           <h1>Jacqui's Shop</h1>
        </div>
        <div data-role="content">
            <div data-role="controlgroup" data-type="horizontal">
                <button data-icon="back">Back</button>
                <button data-icon="home">Home</button>
                <button data-icon="next">Next</button>
            </div>
        </div>
    </div>
</body>
</html>
```

You can see how the browser displays a horizontal button group in Figure 29-6. Once again, notice how the rounded corners are applied only to the outside elements.

Figure 29-6. Creating a horizontal button group

Using Collapsible Content Blocks

jQuery Mobile includes support for creating *collapsible content blocks*, which are sections of content with a header that can be closed so that only the header is available. This is very similar to a single panel of a jQuery UI accordion, which I described in Chapter 19. In fact, you can create a simple accordion by combining multiple collapsible elements together.

Creating a Single Collapsible Block

A collapsible block has a specific structure you need to follow in order to give jQuery Mobile the elements it needs. Listing 29-9 contains an example.

Listing 29-9. Creating a single collapsible block

```
<!DOCTYPE html>
<html>
<head>
    <title>Example</title>
    <meta name="viewport" content="width=device-width, initial-scale=1">
    <link rel="stylesheet" href="jquery.mobile-1.0.css" type="text/css" />
    <script type="text/javascript" src="jquery-1.6.4.js"></script>
    <script type="text/javascript" src="jquery.mobile-1.0.js"></script>
</head>
<body>
    <div id="page1" data-role="page" data-theme="b">
        <div data-role="header">
           <h1>Jacqui's Shop</h1>
```

```
        </div>
        <div data-role="content">
            <div data-role="collapsible">
                <h1>New Delivery Service</h1>
                <p>We are pleased to announce that we are starting a home delivery
                service for your flower needs. We will deliver within a 20 mile radius
                of the store for free and $1/mile thereafter.</p>
            </div>
        </div>
    </div>
</body>
</html>
```

The first thing you have to do is create a div element and apply the data-role attribute with a value of collapsible. This tells jQuery Mobile that you want a collapsible block and that it should look for a header element as the first child of the div. You can use any of the header elements, h1 through h6. I used an h1 element, but jQuery Mobile treats all of the headers equally for this kind of widget. The remaining child elements of the div are used as the content for the collapsible element, creating the effect that is shown in Figure 29-7.

Figure 29-7. Expanding a collapsible block

The block is collapsed when it is first displayed, meaning that the content is hidden and only the header can be seen. As a cue for the user, a plus icon is drawn at the left edge of the header area (which is styled in the same way as a non-inline button). Clicking on the header reveals the content and replaces the icon with a minus sign, indicating that the block can be collapsed again.

Configuring jQuery Mobile Collapsible Content Blocks

jQuery Mobile defines two data attributes you can use to configure collapsible blocks. These attributes are described in Table 29-4.

Table 29-4. Data Attributes for Collapsible Blocks

Data Attribute	Description
data-collapsed	When true, the default value, the block is shown collapsed (that is, only the header is visible to the user). A value of false means that the block is shown expanded.
data-content-theme	Specifies the theme for the content area of the collapsible block.

Setting the Swatch for the Content Area

You can use the data-theme attribute to apply a swatch to the header in the normal way, but you can also apply the data-content-theme attribute to set a swatch for the content area of the collapsible block. This is a useful feature for increasing the contrast between the block's content and the surrounding area, as demonstrated in Listing 29-10.

Listing 29-10. Applying a swatch for the content area

```
<!DOCTYPE html>
<html>
<head>
    <title>Example</title>
    <meta name="viewport" content="width=device-width, initial-scale=1">
    <link rel="stylesheet" href="jquery.mobile-1.0.css" type="text/css" />
    <script type="text/javascript" src="jquery-1.6.4.js"></script>
    <script type="text/javascript" src="jquery.mobile-1.0.js"></script>
</head>
<body>
    <div id="page1" data-role="page" data-theme="b">
        <div data-role="header">
           <h1>Jacqui's Shop</h1>
        </div>
        <div data-role="content">
            <div data-role="collapsible" data-content-theme="e">
                <h1>New Delivery Service</h1>
                <p>We are pleased to announce that we are starting a home delivery
                service for your flower needs. We will deliver within a 20 mile radius
                of the store for free and $1/mile thereafter.</p>
            </div>
        </div>
    </div>
</body>
</html>
```

In this example, I used the data-content-theme attribute to apply swatch E to the content area of the collapsible block. The header has inherited swatch B from the page element. You can see the effect in Figure 29-8.

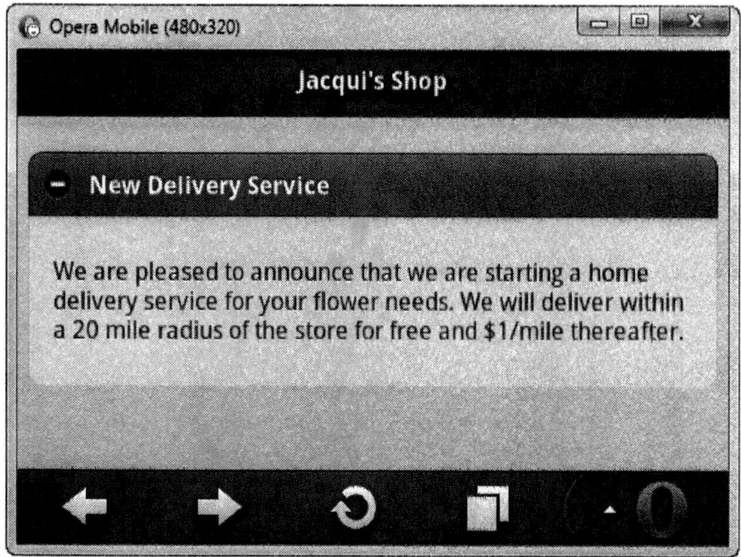

Figure 29-8. Applying a swatch to the content area of a collapsible block

Setting the Initial State

You can use the data-collapsed attribute to control the initial state of the collapsible block. If the value is false, the content elements are displayed. The default value, true, means that only the header is displayed initially. Listing 29-11 contains an example of this attribute in use.

Listing 29-11. Setting the initial state of a collapsible block

```
<!DOCTYPE html>
<html>
<head>
    <title>Example</title>
    <meta name="viewport" content="width=device-width, initial-scale=1">
    <link rel="stylesheet" href="jquery.mobile-1.0.css" type="text/css" />
    <script type="text/javascript" src="jquery-1.6.4.js"></script>
    <script type="text/javascript" src="jquery.mobile-1.0.js"></script>
</head>
<body>
    <div id="page1" data-role="page" data-theme="b">
        <div data-role="header">
           <h1>Jacqui's Shop</h1>
        </div>
        <div data-role="content">
            <div data-role="collapsible" data-collapsed=true data-content-theme="e">
                <h1>New Delivery Service</h1>
                <p>We are pleased to announce that we are starting a home delivery
                service for your flower needs. We will deliver within a 20 mile radius
```

```
                of the store for free and $1/mile thereafter.</p>
            </div>
            <div data-role="collapsible" data-collapsed=false data-content-theme="e">
                <h1>Summer Specials</h1>
                <p>We have a wide range of special summer offers.
                    Ask instore for details</p>
            </div>
        </div>
    </div>
</body>
</html>
```

I defined two collapsible blocks in this example, one of which is expanded initially. You can see the effect in Figure 29-9, which also emphasizes how collapsible blocks can be used to put a lot of information at the disposal of the user in a relatively small amount of screen space.

Figure 29-9. Setting the initial state of a collapsible block

Using Collapsible Block Events

The collapsible block widget supports two events: collapse and expand. As the names suggest, these events are triggered when the block is collapsed and expanded. Listing 29-12 shows how you can use these events.

Listing 29-12. Using the collapse and expand events

```
<!DOCTYPE html>
<html>
<head>
    <title>Example</title>
    <meta name="viewport" content="width=device-width, initial-scale=1">
    <link rel="stylesheet" href="jquery.mobile-1.0.css" type="text/css" />
    <script type="text/javascript" src="jquery-1.6.4.js"></script>
    <script type="text/javascript">
        $(document).bind("pageinit", function() {
            $('#colBlock').bind("collapse expand", function(event) {
                $('#status').text(event.type == "expand" ? "Expanded" : "Collapsed");
            })
        });
    </script>
    <script type="text/javascript" src="jquery.mobile-1.0.js"></script>
</head>
<body>
    <div id="page1" data-role="page" data-theme="b">
        <div data-role="header">
           <h1>Jacqui's Shop</h1>
        </div>
        <div data-role="content">
            The block is <b><span id="status">Expanded</span></b>

            <div id="colBlock" data-role="collapsible" data-content-theme="e"
                    data-collapsed=false>
                <h1>New Delivery Service</h1>
                <p>We are pleased to announce that we are starting a home
                delivery service for your flower needs. We will deliver within a
                20 mile radius of the store for free and $1/mile thereafter.</p>
            </div>
        </div>
    </div>
</body>
</html>
```

In this example, I use the bind method to listen for the expand and collapse events. I do this in a single call to the bind method by listing the events I am interested in, separated by spaces. When one of the events is triggered, I update the content of a span element to reflect the status of the collapsible block. You can see the change in status in Figure 29-10.

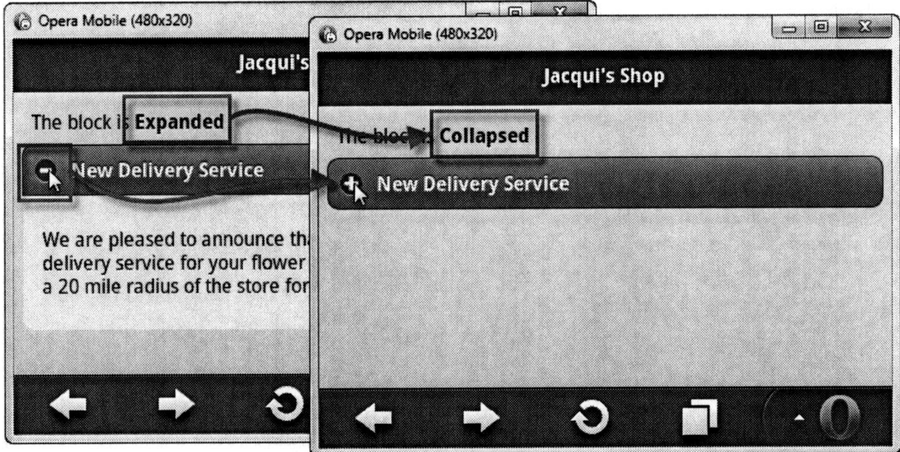

Figure 29-10. Responding to the expand and collapse events

Controlling Collapsible Blocks Programmatically

jQuery Mobile doesn't define methods for programmatically expanding and collapsing collapsible blocks. However, you can explicitly trigger the expand and collapse events, which causes the widget to change its state. You can see how to trigger these events in Listing 29-13.

■ **Caution** This is an undocumented feature and might change in future releases. I found this feature by reading the jQuery Mobile source code, which is a useful way of understanding how jQuery Mobile works.

Listing 29-13. Triggering events to expand and collapse collapsible blocks

```
<!DOCTYPE html>
<html>
<head>
    <title>Example</title>
    <meta name="viewport" content="width=device-width, initial-scale=1">
    <link rel="stylesheet" href="jquery.mobile-1.0.css" type="text/css" />
    <script type="text/javascript" src="jquery-1.6.4.js"></script>
    <script type="text/javascript">
        $(document).bind("pageinit", function() {
            $('button').bind("tap", function() {
                var eventName = this.id == "exButton" ? "expand" : "collapse";
                $('#colBlock').trigger(eventName)
            })
        });
    </script>
```

```
    <script type="text/javascript" src="jquery.mobile-1.0.js"></script>
</head>
<body>
    <div id="page1" data-role="page" data-theme="b">
        <div data-role="header">
           <h1>Jacqui's Shop</h1>
        </div>
        <div data-role="content">
            <div class="ui-grid-a">
                <div class="ui-block-a"><button id="exButton">Expand</button></div>
                <div class="ui-block-b"><button>Collapse</button></div>
            </div>
            <div id="colBlock" data-role="collapsible" data-content-theme="e"
                    data-collapsed=false>
                <h1>New Delivery Service</h1>
                <p>We are pleased to announce that we are starting a home
                delivery service for your flower needs. We will deliver within a
                20 mile radius of the store for free and $1/mile thereafter.</p>
            </div>
        </div>
    </div>
</body>
</html>
```

In this example, I placed two buttons in a grid and used the bind method to listen for the tap event, triggering a function when the user taps either of the buttons. I use the id attribute to work out which button has been tapped and trigger the event that corresponds to the button. To trigger an event, you use jQuery to select the element and then call the trigger method, passing in the name of the event you want—in this case, either expand or collapse. jQuery Mobile configures the collapsible block widget so that it responds to these events, as illustrated by Figure 29-11.

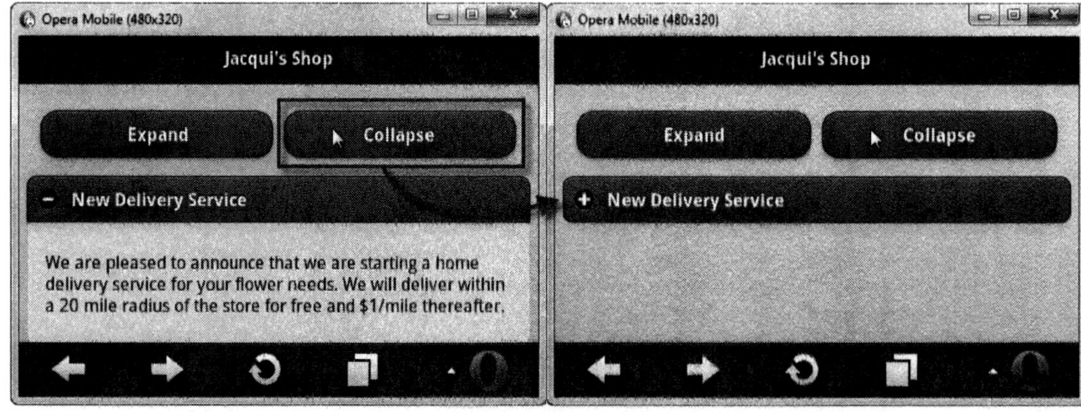

Figure 29-11. Triggering events to expand and collapse a block

Creating jQuery Mobile Accordions

You can create an accordion by wrapping multiple collapsible blocks in a single parent element and applying the data-role attribute to that parent with a value of collapsible-set. You can see how this is done in Listing 29-14.

Listing 29-14. Creating a jQuery Mobile accordion

```
<!DOCTYPE html>
<html>
<head>
    <title>Example</title>
    <meta name="viewport" content="width=device-width, initial-scale=1">
    <link rel="stylesheet" href="jquery.mobile-1.0.css" type="text/css" />
    <script type="text/javascript" src="jquery-1.6.4.js"></script>
    <script type="text/javascript" src="jquery.mobile-1.0.js"></script>
</head>
<body>
    <div id="page1" data-role="page" data-theme="b">
        <div data-role="header">
           <h1>Jacqui's Shop</h1>
        </div>
        <div data-role="content">
            <div data-role="collapsible-set" data-content-theme="e">
                <div data-role="collapsible">
                    <h1>New Delivery Service</h1>
                    <p>We are pleased to announce that we are starting a home
                    delivery service for your flower needs. We will deliver within a
                    20 mile radius of the store for free and $1/mile thereafter.</p>
                </div>
                <div data-role="collapsible" data-collapsed=false>
                    <h1>Summer Specials</h1>
                    <p>We have a wide range of special summer offers.
                        Ask instore for details</p>
                </div>
                <div data-role="collapsible">
                    <h1>Bulk Orders</h1>
                    <p>We offer discounts for large orders. Ask us for prices</p>
                </div>
            </div>
        </div>
    </div>
</body>
</html>
```

In this example, I defined a div element with the collapsible-set value for the data-role attribute, which contains three collapsible blocks.

■ **Tip** Notice that I applied the `data-content-theme` attribute to the outer container. This has the same effect as using the attribute on each individual collapsible block.

The default is for all of the collapsible blocks to be collapsed initially, so I applied the `data-collapsed` attribute to one of the blocks with a value of `false` so that it is expanded when the page is first displayed. When the user clicks on a header, the presently expanded element is collapsed. You can see the effect in Figure 29-12.

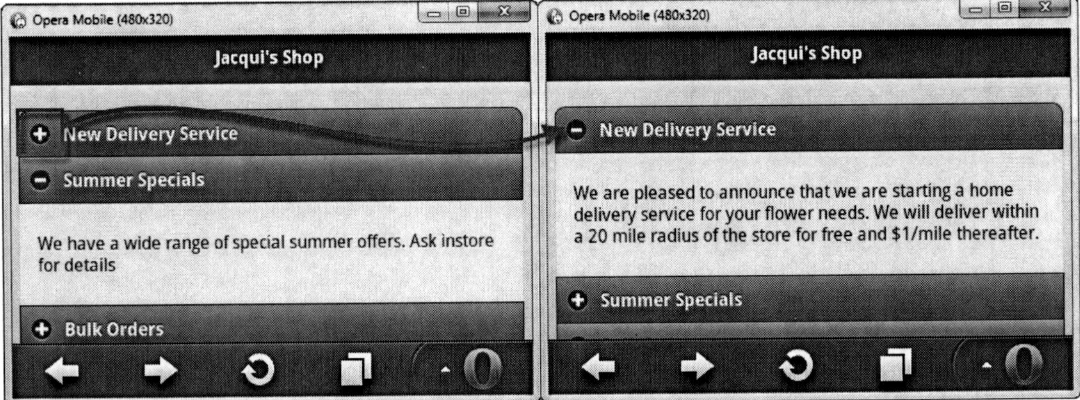

Figure 29-12. Expanding a block in a jQuery Mobile accordion

Summary

In this chapter, I described two of the jQuery Mobile widgets: buttons and collapsible blocks. For the most part, you can use these widgets without any JavaScript code at all, especially if you are using a elements as the basis for the button widgets.

CHAPTER 30

Using jQuery Mobile Forms

Small screens present unique difficulties when presenting a form on a mobile device. There is little enough screen real estate available to start with, and you need to give the user form elements that are easy to manipulate by touch without creating a page that requires endless scrolling to complete. In this chapter, I show you how jQuery Mobile enhances form elements so that they are consistent with other widgets and can be readily used on a touch screen.

jQuery Mobile does a lot of work automatically when the page is loaded. Many form elements are enhanced without your intervention, and Ajax is automatically used when the form is submitted so that jQuery Mobile can smoothly transition to the results returned by the server.

There are, however, some useful configuration options available. One element in particular (the `select` element) requires special attention. You can choose between different widgets to present the element to the user, and you can neatly sidestep some issues with the native implementation of `select` elements.

The jQuery Mobile support for forms is pretty good, but it isn't perfect. In particular, there are some minor layout issues, which means that elements laid out adjacent to one another can have different widths. These are annoying problems, but they do little to undermine the general utility of jQuery Mobile and, given the excitement about jQuery Mobile, I expect these issues to be resolved in a future release.

More broadly, I recommend careful thought when you are creating forms for mobile devices. By their nature, forms are intended to gather input from users, but this can be a tedious process on a small device, especially when it comes to typing. In addition, most mobile devices don't display scrollbars when the user isn't actively scrolling through a page. This means that the user isn't always aware there are form elements just off the immediate display. To create the best possible experience for users, you need to follow some basic guidelines:

- *Require as little typing as you can.* Where possible, use alternative widgets that allow the user to make simple touch selections, such as check boxes or radio buttons. This can reduce the range of inputs that the user can make, but it might have the effect of increasing the number of users who are willing to complete the form.
- *Use navigation between pages to display sections of a form.* This gives users a clear indication of their progress through the form and doesn't require them to speculatively scroll to see if they are missing anything.
- *Eliminate any form elements that are not required.* Mobile forms should be as streamlined as possible, and that can mean accepting less data from mobile users than you get from desktop users.

Table 30-1 provides the summary for this chapter.

Table 30-1. *Chapter Summary*

Problem	Solution	Listing
Display labels alongside form elements	Use a div element whose data-role value is fieldcontain	1
Change the cutoff point for the fieldcontain styles.	Use a CSS media query to change the range of screen widths to which the styles are applied	2
Hide label elements	Use the ui-hidden-accessible and ui-hide-label classes	3, 4
Enhance a select element	Define the element in a page, and jQuery Mobile will apply the basic enhancement automatically	5
Use custom menus for a select element	Set the data-native-menu attribute to false	6
Specify a select placeholder element	Apply the data-placeholder attribute with a value of true to an option element	7
Control a select menu programmatically	Use the open, close, and refresh methods	8
Create a flip switch	Apply the data-role attribute with a value of slider to a select element	9
Create a basic check box	Define a label and an input element whose type is checkbox	10
Apply a label to a check box or group check boxes together	Use the fieldcontain and controlgroup features, along with a legend element to define the label text	11, 12
Create radio buttons	Use the same element structure as used for check boxes	13
Create a range slide	Define an input element whose type is range	14

Understanding Automatically Created Form Elements

jQuery Mobile automatically creates widgets for form elements when the page is processed, just as it creates button widgets automatically (which I described in Chapter 29). Listing 30-1 shows a jQuery Mobile page that contains a `form` element and some form-related child elements.

Listing 30-1. A simple form in a jQuery Mobile page

```
<!DOCTYPE html>
<html>
<head>
    <title>Example</title>
    <meta name="viewport" content="width=device-width, initial-scale=1">
    <link rel="stylesheet" href="jquery.mobile-1.0.css" type="text/css" />
    <script type="text/javascript" src="jquery-1.6.4.js"></script>
    <script type="text/javascript" src="jquery.mobile-1.0.js"></script>
    <style type="text/css">
        #buttonContainer {text-align: center}
    </style>
</head>
<body>
    <div id="page1" data-role="page" data-theme="b">
        <div data-role="header">
           <h1>Jacqui's Shop</h1>
        </div>
        <form method="get">
            <div data-role="fieldcontain">
                <label for="name">Name: </label>
                <input id="name">
            </div>
            <div data-role="fieldcontain">
                <label for="address">Address: </label>
                <textarea id="address"></textarea>
            </div>
            <div id="buttonContainer">
                <input type="submit" data-inline="true" value="Submit"/>
            </div>
        </form>
    </div>
</body>
</html>
```

This is a very simple form, but it lets me set the scene for how jQuery Mobile handles forms overall. There are two form elements: a text `input` and a `textarea`, each of which is paired with a `label` element. You can see the result in Figure 30-1.

Figure 30-1. A simple form displayed by jQuery Mobile

■ **Tip** jQuery Mobile will automatically submit the form when an `input` element whose type is `submit` is included within a form element. The form will be submitted using Ajax by default, but this behavior can be disabled by applying the `data-ajax` attribute with a value of `false` to the `form` element.

Working with Form Labels

In the last example, each form element and its `label` are wrapped in a `div` element. I set the `data-role` of the `div` element to be `fieldcontain`, which tells jQuery Mobile that I want the `label` and the form element displayed in a single line, and you can see the effect in Figure 30-1.

The styles that jQuery Mobile applies to align the label and the form element are used only when the screen is at least 450 pixels wide. Below that width value, the label and the form element are displayed on separate rows, as illustrated by Figure 30-2.

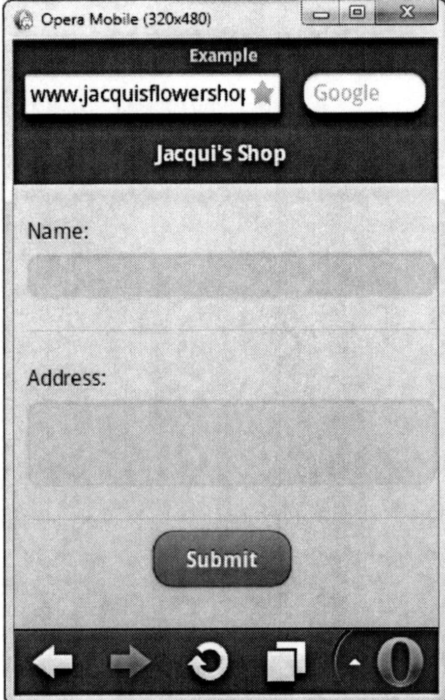

Figure 30-2. Displaying a form in portrait orientation

Changing the fieldcontain Cutoff Point

I don't like the 450-pixel cutoff point. It is arbitrary and doesn't take into account the wide range of mobile device screen sizes and resolutions.

You can easily extend the reach of the `fieldcontain` feature by applying the underlying CSS classes directly to your document and, optionally, use CSS media queries specifying your own rules for when they are applied. Listing 30-2 shows the relevant styles and applies a cutoff point of 100 pixels.

Listing 30-2. Changing the cutoff point for the fieldcontain classes

```
<!DOCTYPE html>
<html>
<head>
    <title>Example</title>
    <meta name="viewport" content="width=device-width, initial-scale=1">
    <link rel="stylesheet" href="jquery.mobile-1.0.css" type="text/css" />
    <script type="text/javascript" src="jquery-1.6.4.js"></script>
    <script type="text/javascript" src="jquery.mobile-1.0.js"></script>
    <style type="text/css">
            #buttonContainer {text-align: center}
```

```
            @media all and (min-width: 100px){
                .ui-field-contain label.ui-input-text  { vertical-align: top;
                    display: inline-block;  width: 20%;  margin: 0 2% 0 0 }
                .ui-field-contain input.ui-input-text,
                .ui-field-contain textarea.ui-input-text,
                .ui-field-contain .ui-input-search { width: 60%; display: inline-block;}
                .ui-field-contain .ui-input-search { width: 50%; }
                .ui-hide-label input.ui-input-text,
                .ui-hide-label textarea.ui-input-text,
                .ui-hide-label .ui-input-search { padding: .4em; width: 97%; }
                .ui-input-search input.ui-input-text { width: 98%;}
            }
    </style>
</head>
<body>
    <div id="page1" data-role="page" data-theme="b">
        <div data-role="header">
           <h1>Jacqui's Shop</h1>
        </div>
        <form method="get">
            <div data-role="fieldcontain">
                <label for="name">Name: </label>
                <input id="name">
            </div>
            <div data-role="fieldcontain">
                <label for="address">Address: </label>
                <textarea id="address"></textarea>
            </div>
            <div id="buttonContainer">
                <input type="submit" data-inline="true" value="Submit"/>
            </div>
        </form>
    </div>
</body>
</html>
```

jQuery Mobile has already applied the classes to the elements in response to the `fieldcontainer` role, which makes it easy for us to change the limit or tweak the CSS.

While I think the 450-pixel limit is arbitrary, I agree that there is a point at which displaying the labels alongside the form elements makes it hard to for the user to activate a form element with a finger and impossible to see all of the contents. Although I have shown a 100-pixel limit in the example, you should test carefully with your target devices and make sure that your application remains usable at the limit you set. Figure 30-3 shows the effect of reducing the limit to below the 320-pixel width of my emulator window.

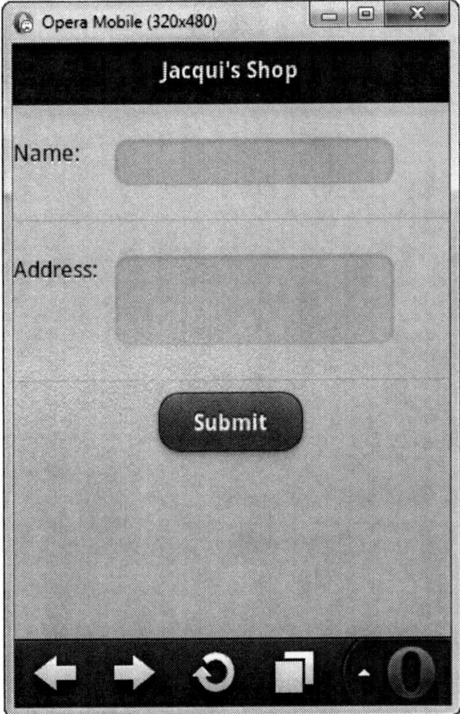

Figure 30-3. Displaying labels alongside form elements on a narrow screen

Hiding Labels

A popular approach is to hide labels when the device is in portrait mode and show them in landscape mode. I am not especially keen on this idea because the labels often provide important context to the user. That said, you can still provide some helpful hints using the HTML5 `placeholder` attribute.

jQuery Mobile provides a CSS class that hides labels in a way that keeps them available for screen readers and other assistive technologies. It does this by leaving the label in the document, but moving it out of site. To hide an individual label, you apply the `ui-hidden-class` to the `label` element. To hide all of the labels in a container element, you can apply the `ui-hide-label` class to the parent element. Listing 30-3 shows the user both attributes along with the `placeholder` attributes to give the user some idea what the form elements are for.

Listing 30-3. Hiding labels for form elements

```
<!DOCTYPE html>
<html>
<head>
    <title>Example</title>
    <meta name="viewport" content="width=device-width, initial-scale=1">
    <link rel="stylesheet" href="jquery.mobile-1.0.css" type="text/css" />
```

```
    <script type="text/javascript" src="jquery-1.6.4.js"></script>
    <script type="text/javascript" src="jquery.mobile-1.0.js"></script>
    <style type="text/css">
            #buttonContainer {text-align: center}
    </style>
</head>
<body>
    <div id="page1" data-role="page" data-theme="b">
        <div data-role="header">
           <h1>Jacqui's Shop</h1>
        </div>
        <form method="get">

            <label for="name" class="ui-hidden-accessible">Name: </label>
            <input id="name" placeholder="Your Name">

            <div data-role="fieldcontain" class="ui-hide-label">
                <label for="address">Address: </label>
                <textarea id="address" placeholder="Your Address"></textarea>
            </div>
            <div id="buttonContainer">
                <input type="submit" data-inline="true" value="Submit"/>
            </div>
        </form>
    </div>
</body>
</html>
```

■ **Tip** Notice that I removed the `fieldcontain` parent element from the first `label` and form element. If you apply the `ui-hidden-accessible` class to a label element that is inside a `fieldcontain` element, the labels isn't visible but the space for it is still preserved in the layout, which limits the size of the form element and offsets it to the right.

You can see the effect of these changes in Figure 30-4.

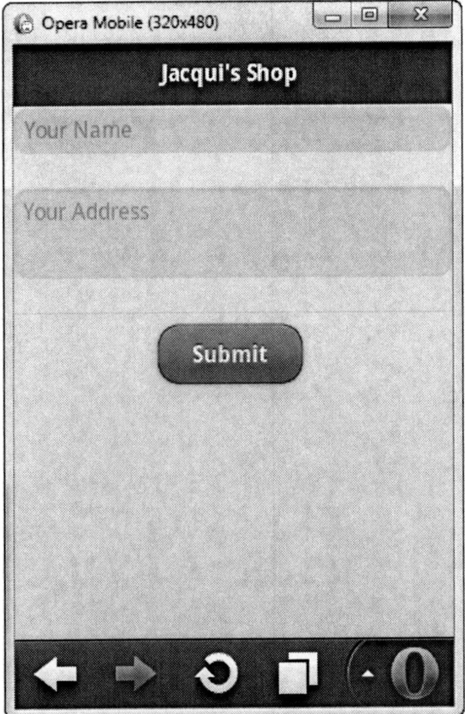

Figure 30-4. Hiding form labels

Hiding the labels is a compromise, and it usually doesn't make sense to hide labels when the device is in landscape mode. You can respond to the `orientationchange` event (which I described in Chapter 26) and selectively add and remove the `ui-hide-label` class, as shown in Listing 30-4. (You need to use `fieldcontrol` `div` elements in this situation to keep the label in line with the form control in landscape mode.

Listing 30-4. Hiding labels selectively

```
<!DOCTYPE html>
<html>
<head>
    <title>Example</title>
    <meta name="viewport" content="width=device-width, initial-scale=1">
    <link rel="stylesheet" href="jquery.mobile-1.0.css" type="text/css" />
    <script type="text/javascript" src="jquery-1.6.4.js"></script>
    <script type="text/javascript">
        $(document).bind("pageinit", function() {
            $(window).bind("orientationchange", function(ev) {
                processOrientation(ev.orientation)
            })
```

```
            processOrientation(jQuery.event.special.orientationchange.orientation())

            function processOrientation(orientation) {
                var elems = $('div[data-role=fieldcontain]');
                if (orientation == "portrait") {
                    elems.addClass("ui-hide-label")
                } else {
                    elems.removeClass("ui-hide-label")
                }
            }
        })
    </script>
    <script type="text/javascript" src="jquery.mobile-1.0.js"></script>
    <style type="text/css">
        #buttonContainer {text-align: center}
    </style>
</head>
<body>
    <div id="page1" data-role="page" data-theme="b">
        <div data-role="header">
           <h1>Jacqui's Shop</h1>
        </div>
        <form method="get">
            <div data-role="fieldcontain" class="ui-hide-label">
                <label for="name">Name: </label>
                <input id="name" placeholder="Your Name">
            </div>
            <div data-role="fieldcontain" class="ui-hide-label">
                <label for="address">Address: </label>
                <textarea id="address" placeholder="Your Address"></textarea>
            </div>
            <div id="buttonContainer">
                <input type="submit" data-inline="true" value="Submit"/>
            </div>
        </form>
    </div>
</body>
</html>
```

The labels are hidden in the portrait mode and displayed in the landscape mode, as Figure 30-5 shows.

Figure 30-5. Selectively hiding form element labels

Using Select Elements

jQuery Mobile provides you with two ways to deal with select elements. The first is to present the element as a button with a down icon, which is the approach that will be used automatically when jQuery Mobile is processing the page and finds a select. Listing 30-5 contains a select element.

Listing 30-5. A page containing a select element

```
<!DOCTYPE html>
<html>
<head>
    <title>Example</title>
    <meta name="viewport" content="width=device-width, initial-scale=1">
    <link rel="stylesheet" href="jquery.mobile-1.0.css" type="text/css" />
    <script type="text/javascript" src="jquery-1.6.4.js"></script>
    <script type="text/javascript" src="jquery.mobile-1.0.js"></script>
    <style type="text/css">
        #buttonContainer {text-align: center}
    </style>
</head>
<body>
    <div id="page1" data-role="page" data-theme="b">
        <div data-role="header">
           <h1>Jacqui's Shop</h1>
        </div>
        <form method="get">
            <div data-role="fieldcontain">
```

```
                <label for="name">Name: </label>
                <input id="name" placeholder="Your Name">
            </div>
            <div data-role="fieldcontain">
                <label for="speed"><span>Speed: </span></label>
                <select id="speed" name="speed">
                    <option value="vfast">Very Fast</option>
                    <option value="fast">Fast</option>
                    <option value="normal" selected>Normal</option>
                    <option value="slow">Slow</option>
                </select>
            </div>
            <div id="buttonContainer">
                <input type="submit" data-inline="true" value="Submit"/>
            </div>
        </form>
    </div>
</body>
</html>
```

You can see how jQuery Mobile enhances select elements in Figure 30-6. I switched to the Windows Phone 7 emulator for this section because the Opera Emulator doesn't display styled select elements properly.

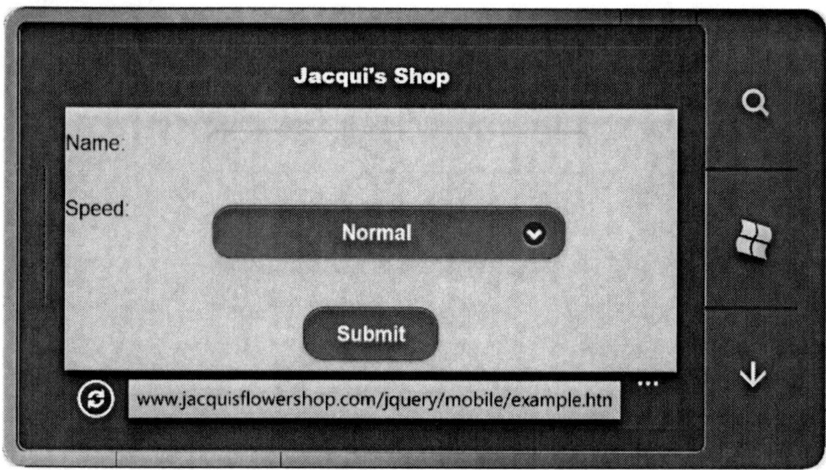

Figure 30-6. A select element that has been enhanced by jQuery Mobile

jQuery Mobile defines some data attributes that can be used to tailor the appearance and behavior of select elements. These attributes are summarized in Table 30-2, and I explain the use of the most important ones in the sections that follow.

Table 30-2. Data Attributes for select Elements

Attribute	Description
`data-icon`	See the corresponding attribute for the button widget in Chapter 29.
`data-iconpos`	See the corresponding attribute for the button widget in Chapter 29.
`data-inline`	See the corresponding attribute for the button widget in Chapter 29.
`data-native-menu`	When `true`, jQuery Mobile relies on the browser's implementation of the `select` menu. When `false`, a custom menu is used. The default is `true`.
`data-overlay-theme`	Specifies the theme for custom select menus.
`data-placeholder`	Explicitly identifies an `option` element as a placeholder.

■ **Tip** Because jQuery Mobile uses button widgets to represent `select` elements, you can group elements together using the same techniques I described in Chapter 29, with the `controlgroup` value for the `data-role` attribute.

Using Custom Selection Menus

Most mobile browsers provide a touch-enabled approach to displaying the options in a `select` element. For example, the Windows Phone 7 browser switches to a new screen that lists the options in a way that makes them easy to select with a finger (as shown in Figure 30-7), while other mobile browsers display a simple popup menu in which the items are displayed large enough to select by touch.

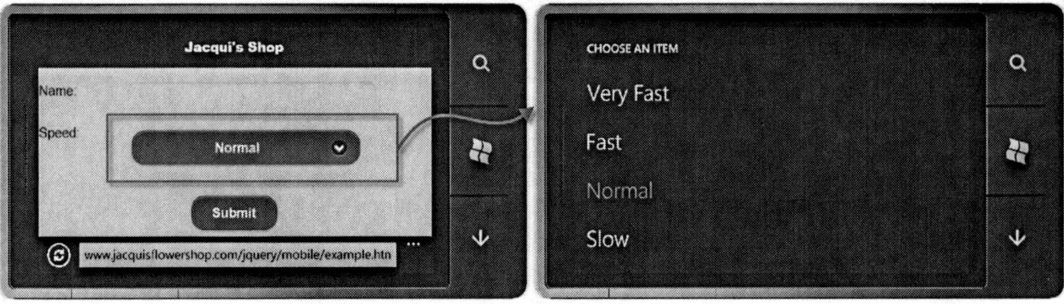

Figure 30-7. A mobile browser dealing with a select element

You can override the native behavior of the browser and have jQuery Mobile create a popup menu that is suitable for touch selection. You do this by applying the data-native-menu attribute to the select element with a value of false, as shown by Listing 30-6.

Listing 30-6. Disabling native select menus

```
...
<div data-role="fieldcontain">
    <label for="speed"><span>Speed: </span></label>
    <select id="speed" name="speed" data-native-menu=false>
        <option value="vfast">Very Fast</option>
        <option value="fast">Fast</option>
        <option value="normal" selected>Normal</option>
        <option value="slow">Slow</option>
    </select>
</div>
...
```

This feature is useful for mobile browsers that don't handle native select elements properly (such as Opera Mobile) and when you want to create an application that has a consistent appearance on both desktop and mobile browsers. When you set the data-native-menu attribute to false, jQuery Mobile removes the select element from the document and replaces it with a button widget that displays a custom menu when it is clicked, as shown in Figure 30-8.

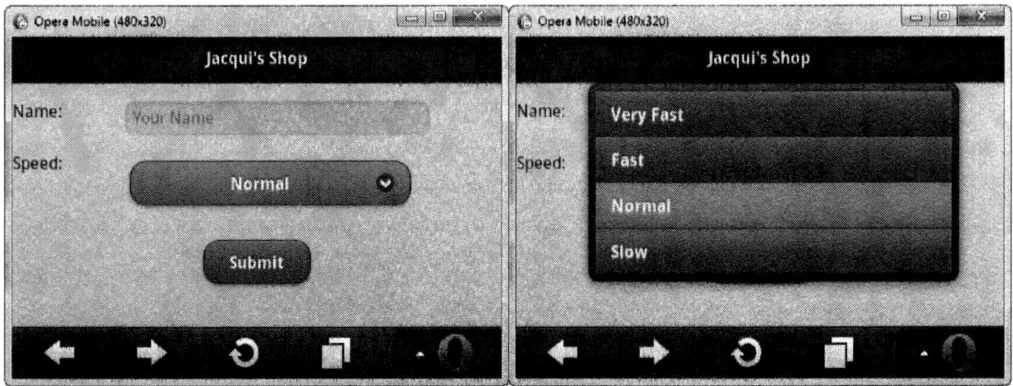

Figure 30-8. Using jQuery Mobile custom menus for a select element

---

■ **Tip** jQuery Mobile uses swatch A for custom select menus by default. You can change this by specifying a different swatch as the value for the data-overlay-theme attribute.

Specifying Placeholder Elements

You can use an option element as the placeholder for a select element by setting the value of the data-placeholder attribute to true. Placeholders are shown when the select element is initially displayed but isn't present in the list of options that the user chooses from. Listing 30-7 shows the use of the data-placeholder attribute.

Listing 30-7. Using the data-placeholder attribute

```
...
<div data-role="fieldcontain">
    <label for="speed"><span>Speed: </span></label>
    <select id="speed" name="speed" data-native-menu=false>
        <option data-placeholder=true value="placeholder">Select a Speed</option>
        <option value="vfast">Very Fast</option>
        <option value="fast">Fast</option>
        <option value="normal">Normal</option>
        <option value="slow">Slow</option>
    </select>
</div>
...
```

You can see the effect in Figure 30-9. I generally like to use placeholders with select menus, but this is an especially useful technique for giving the user context when hiding label elements in portrait layouts.

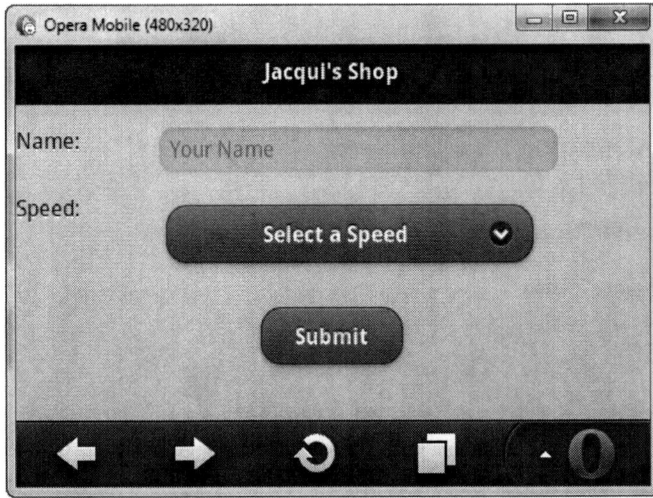

Figure 30-9. Specifying a placeholder element

Controlling Select Menus Programmatically

You can control the select widget menu programmatically using the methods described in Table 30-3. These methods follow the jQuery UI standard of passing a string to the widget method, which is `selectmenu` in this case.

Table 30-3. Methods for select Elements

Method	Description
`selectmenu("open")`	Opens the select menu
`selectmenu("close")`	Closes the select menu
`selectmenu("refresh")`	Refreshes the widget to incorporate changes in the underlying `select` element

Listing 30-8 shows how to use buttons to control the select menu.

Listing 30-8. Controlling the select menu programmatically

```
<!DOCTYPE html>
<html>
<head>
    <title>Example</title>
    <meta name="viewport" content="width=device-width, initial-scale=1">
    <link rel="stylesheet" href="jquery.mobile-1.0.css" type="text/css" />
    <script type="text/javascript" src="jquery-1.6.4.js"></script>
    <script type="text/javascript">
        $(document).bind("pageinit", function() {
            $('button').bind("tap", function() {
                if (this.id == "open") {
                    $('#speed').selectmenu("open")
                } else {
                    $('#speed').selectmenu("close")
                }
            })
        })
    </script>
    <script type="text/javascript" src="jquery.mobile-1.0.js"></script>
    <style type="text/css">
        #buttonContainer {text-align: center}
    </style>
</head>
<body>
    <div id="page1" data-role="page" data-theme="b">
        <div data-role="header">
           <h1>Jacqui's Shop</h1>
        </div>
```

```
        <form method="get">

            <div class="ui-grid-a">
                <div class="ui-block-a">
                    <button id="open">Open Menu</button>
                </div>
                <div class="ui-block-b">
                    <button id="close">Close Menu</button>
                </div>
            </div>

            <select id="speed" name="speed" data-native-menu=false>
                <option data-placeholder=true value="placeholder">Select a Speed</option>
                <option value="vfast">Very Fast</option>
                <option value="fast">Fast</option>
                <option value="normal">Normal</option>
                <option value="slow">Slow</option>
            </select>

            <div id="buttonContainer">
                <input type="submit" data-inline="true" value="Submit"/>
            </div>
        </form>
    </div>
</body>
</html>
```

Creating Flip Switches

If a `select` element contains only two `option` elements, you can elect to create a *flip switch* instead of a regular select widget. You create a flip switch by applying the `data-role` attribute to the `select` element with a value of `slider`, as shown in Listing 30-9.

Listing 30-9. Creating a flip switch

```
<!DOCTYPE html>
<html>
<head>
    <title>Example</title>
    <meta name="viewport" content="width=device-width, initial-scale=1">
    <link rel="stylesheet" href="jquery.mobile-1.0.css" type="text/css" />
    <script type="text/javascript" src="jquery-1.6.4.js"></script>
    <script type="text/javascript" src="jquery.mobile-1.0.js"></script>
    <style type="text/css">
        #buttonContainer {text-align: center}
    </style>
</head>
<body>
    <div id="page1" data-role="page" data-theme="b">
        <div data-role="header">
```

```
            <h1>Jacqui's Shop</h1>
        </div>
        <form method="get">

            <div data-role="fieldcontain">
                <label for="speed"><span>Speed: </span></label>
                <select id="speed" name="speed" data-role="slider">
                    <option value="fast">Fast</option>
                    <option value="slow">Slow</option>
                </select>
            </div>

            <div data-role="fieldcontain">
                <label for="size"><span>Size: </span></label>
                <select id="size" name="size" data-role="slider">
                    <option value="large">Large</option>
                    <option value="small" selected>Small</option>
                </select>
            </div>

            <div id="buttonContainer">
                <input type="submit" data-inline="true" value="Submit"/>
            </div>
        </form>
    </div>
</body>
</html>
```

There are two flip switches in this example. You can see how they are displayed in the browser in Figure 30-10. The user can change the setting either by tapping or clicking on the exposed value or by dragging the slider into position.

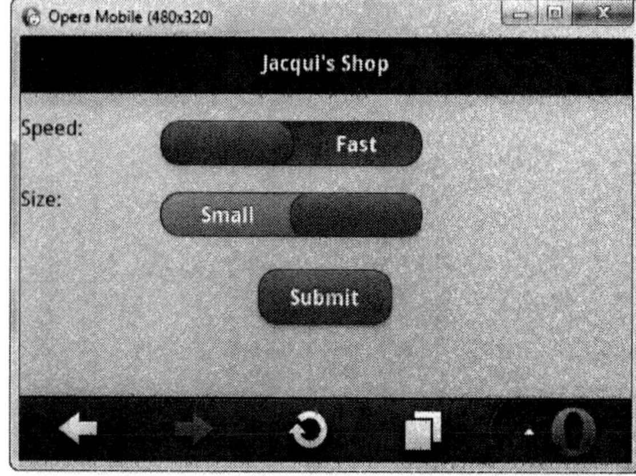

Figure 30-10. Using flip switches

Creating Check Boxes

You can configure the appearance of check boxes in a number of ways. The simplest way is to give jQuery Mobile just an `input` element whose type is `check box`, followed by a `label` element, as shown in Listing 30-10.

Listing 30-10. Creating simple check boxes

```
<!DOCTYPE html>
<html>
<head>
    <title>Example</title>
    <meta name="viewport" content="width=device-width, initial-scale=1">
    <link rel="stylesheet" href="jquery.mobile-1.0.css" type="text/css" />
    <script type="text/javascript" src="jquery-1.6.4.js"></script>
    <script type="text/javascript" src="jquery.mobile-1.0.js"></script>
    <style type="text/css">
        #buttonContainer {text-align: center}
    </style>
</head>
<body>
    <div id="page1" data-role="page" data-theme="b">
        <div data-role="header">
           <h1>Jacqui's Shop</h1>
        </div>
        <form method="get">
            <div data-role="fieldcontain">
                <label for="name">Name: </label>
                <input id="name" placeholder="Your Name">
            </div>

            <input type="checkbox" name="check" id="check"/>
            <label for="check">I agree</label>

            <div id="buttonContainer">
                <input type="submit" data-inline="true" value="Submit"/>
            </div>
        </form>
    </div>
</body>
</html>
```

You can see how this check box is presented in Figure 30-11. I have shown the checked and unchecked state of the check box in the figure.

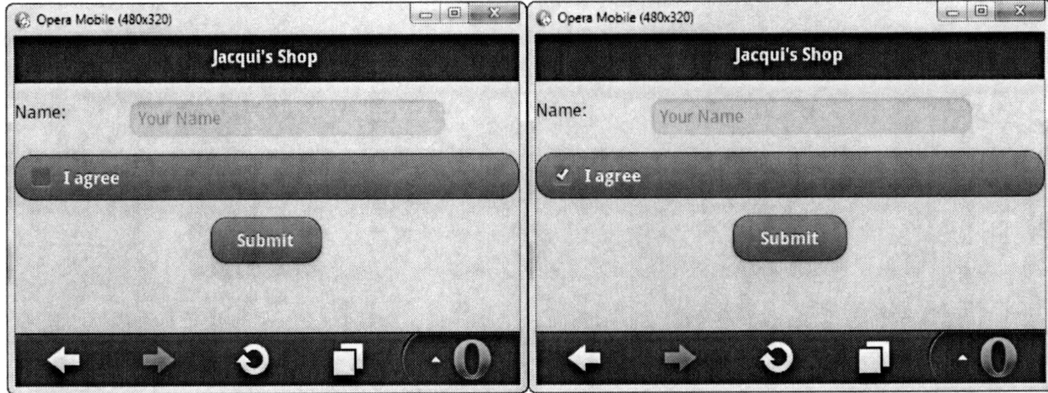

Figure 30-11. A simple jQuery Mobile check box

Applying a Label to a Check Box

By default, check boxes span the entire width of their parent element, which means, in this case, that the check box is the entire width of the screen. You need to use a particular element structure if you want to make the check box fit into the layout so that it matches the text input above it, as shown in Listing 30-11.

Listing 30-11. Changing the layout of a check box

```
<!DOCTYPE html>
<html>
<head>
    <title>Example</title>
    <meta name="viewport" content="width=device-width, initial-scale=1">
    <link rel="stylesheet" href="jquery.mobile-1.0.css" type="text/css" />
    <script type="text/javascript" src="jquery-1.6.4.js"></script>
    <script type="text/javascript" src="jquery.mobile-1.0.js"></script>
    <style type="text/css">
        #buttonContainer {text-align: center}
    </style>
</head>
<body>
    <div id="page1" data-role="page" data-theme="b">
        <div data-role="header">
           <h1>Jacqui's Shop</h1>
        </div>
        <form method="get">
            <div data-role="fieldcontain">
                <label for="name">Name: </label>
                <input id="name" placeholder="Your Name">
            </div>
```

```
            <div data-role="fieldcontain">
                <fieldset data-role="controlgroup">
                    <legend>Terms & Conditions:</legend>
                    <input type="checkbox" name="check" id="check"/>
                    <label for="check">I agree</label>
                </fieldset>
            </div>

            <div id="buttonContainer">
                <input type="submit" data-inline="true" value="Submit"/>
            </div>
        </form>
    </div>
</body>
</html>
```

The outer element should be familiar by now—a div element with the data-role attribute set to fieldcontain. The problem that jQuery Mobile faces is that there is already a label element associated with the input element, so you have to take an alternative path to give jQuery Mobile the information it needs. You do this by adding a fieldset element whose data-role is set to controlgroup and adding a legend element before the input, containing the text you want displayed. You can see the effect in Figure 30-12. The new layout isn't quite perfect, but it is a significant improvement.

Figure 30-12. Changing the layout of a check box

Grouping Check Boxes

You can also use a fieldset element with a data-role of controlgroup to group multiple check boxes together. Listing 30-12 contains a demonstration.

Listing 30-12. Grouping check boxes together

```
<!DOCTYPE html>
<html>
<head>
    <title>Example</title>
    <meta name="viewport" content="width=device-width, initial-scale=1">
    <link rel="stylesheet" href="jquery.mobile-1.0.css" type="text/css" />
    <script type="text/javascript" src="jquery-1.6.4.js"></script>
    <script type="text/javascript" src="jquery.mobile-1.0.js"></script>
    <style type="text/css">
        #buttonContainer {text-align: center}
    </style>
</head>
<body>
    <div id="page1" data-role="page" data-theme="b">
        <div data-role="header">
           <h1>Jacqui's Shop</h1>
        </div>
        <form method="get">
            <div data-role="fieldcontain">
                <label for="name">Name: </label>
                <input id="name" placeholder="Your Name">
            </div>

            <div data-role="fieldcontain">
                <fieldset data-role="controlgroup">
                    <legend>Choose Your Flowers:</legend>
                    <input type="checkbox" name="roses" id="roses"/>
                    <label for="roses">Roses</label>
                    <input type="checkbox" name="orchids" id="orchids"/>
                    <label for="orchids">Orchids</label>
                    <input type="checkbox" name="astors" id="astors"/>
                    <label for="astors">Astors</label>
                </fieldset>
            </div>

            <div data-role="fieldcontain">
                <fieldset data-role="controlgroup" data-type="horizontal">
                    <legend>Font:</legend>
                    <input type="checkbox" name="bold" id="bold"/>
                    <label for="bold"><b>b</b></label>
                    <input type="checkbox" name="italic" id="italic"/>
                    <label for="italic"><em>i</em></label>
                    <input type="checkbox" name="underline" id="underline"/>
                    <label for="underline"><u>u</u></label>
                </fieldset>
            </div>

            <div id="buttonContainer">
```

```
                <input type="submit" data-inline="true" value="Submit"/>
            </div>
        </form>
    </div>
</body>
</html>
```

There are two groups of check boxes in this example. The first set is laid out vertically, which is the default orientation. jQuery Mobile changes the style of the widgets so that there is no space between the individual input elements and only the outer corners of the block are rounded. For the second set, I set the data-type attribute to horizontal, which changes the direction of the layout and causes jQuery Mobile to hide the check box, creating a set of buttons that can be toggled on and off. You can see the result in Figure 30-13.

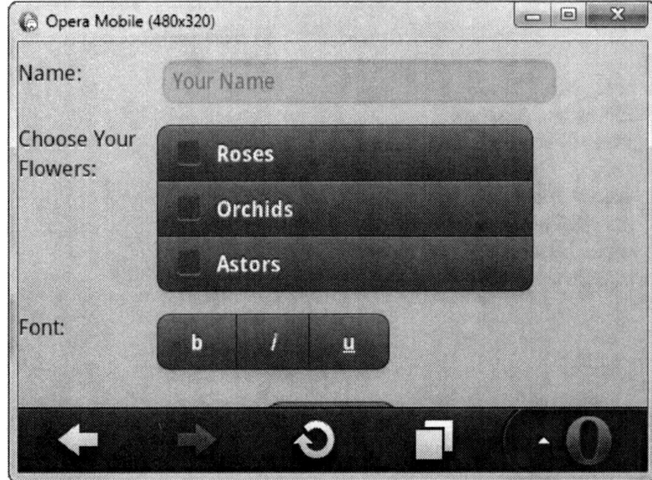

Figure 30-13. Grouping check boxes

Creating Radio Buttons

You format radio buttons in much the same way as you format check boxes. Listing 30-13 contains an example.

Listing 30-13. Creating a group of radio buttons

```
<!DOCTYPE html>
<html>
<head>
    <title>Example</title>
    <meta name="viewport" content="width=device-width, initial-scale=1">
    <link rel="stylesheet" href="jquery.mobile-1.0.css" type="text/css" />
    <script type="text/javascript" src="jquery-1.6.4.js"></script>
    <script type="text/javascript" src="jquery.mobile-1.0.js"></script>
```

```
    <style type="text/css">
        #buttonContainer {text-align: center}
    </style>
</head>
<body>
    <div id="page1" data-role="page" data-theme="b">
        <div data-role="header">
           <h1>Jacqui's Shop</h1>
        </div>
        <form method="get">
            <div data-role="fieldcontain">
                <label for="name">Name: </label>
                <input id="name" placeholder="Your Name">
            </div>

            <div data-role="fieldcontain">
                <fieldset data-role="controlgroup">
                    <legend>Choose Your Flowers:</legend>
                    <input type="radio" name="flowers" id="roses"/>
                    <label for="roses">Roses</label>
                    <input type="radio" name="flowers" id="orchids"/>
                    <label for="orchids">Orchids</label>
                    <input type="radio" name="flowers" id="astors"/>
                    <label for="astors">Astors</label>
                </fieldset>
            </div>

            <div data-role="fieldcontain">
                <fieldset data-role="controlgroup" data-type="horizontal">
                    <legend>Choose Your Flowers:</legend>
                    <input type="radio" name="flowers" id="roses"/>
                    <label for="roses">Roses</label>
                    <input type="radio" name="flowers" id="orchids"/>
                    <label for="orchids">Orchids</label>
                    <input type="radio" name="flowers" id="astors"/>
                    <label for="astors">Astors</label>
                </fieldset>
            </div>

            <div id="buttonContainer">
                <input type="submit" data-inline="true" value="Submit"/>
            </div>
        </form>
    </div>
</body>
</html>
```

Once again, I created horizontal and vertical groups, and you can see how they are displayed in the browser in Figure 30-14.

Figure 30-14. Creating groups of radio buttons

Using Range Sliders

When jQuery Mobile encounters an input element whose type is range, it creates a *range slider*. Listing 30-14 shows the use of this element in a page.

Listing 30-14. Using a range slider

```
<!DOCTYPE html>
<html>
<head>
    <title>Example</title>
    <meta name="viewport" content="width=device-width, initial-scale=1">
    <link rel="stylesheet" href="jquery.mobile-1.0.css" type="text/css" />
    <script type="text/javascript" src="jquery-1.6.4.js"></script>
    <script type="text/javascript" src="jquery.mobile-1.0.js"></script>
    <style type="text/css">
        #buttonContainer {text-align: center}
    </style>
</head>
<body>
    <div id="page1" data-role="page" data-theme="b">
        <div data-role="header">
           <h1>Jacqui's Shop</h1>
        </div>
        <form method="get">

            <div data-role="fieldcontain">
                <label for="name">Name: </label>
                <input id="name" placeholder="Your Name">
            </div>
```

```
            <div data-role="fieldcontain">
                <label for="quant"><span>Quantity: </span></label>
                <input id="quant" type="range" value="5" min="1" max="10" />
            </div>

            <div id="buttonContainer">
                <input type="submit" data-inline="true" value="Submit"/>
            </div>
        </form>
    </div>
</body>
</html>
```

You can see the way that jQuery Mobile enhances this element in Figure 30-15.

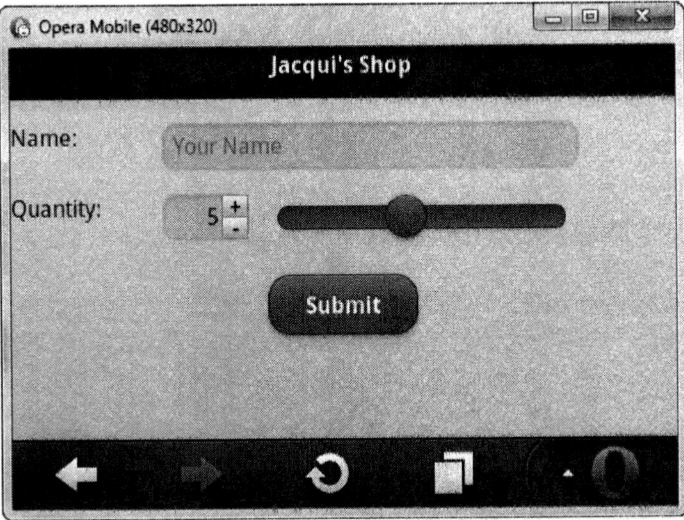

Figure 30-15. Using a range slider

Summary

In this chapter, I showed how jQuery Mobile enhances form elements to make them consistent with the broader touch-enabled style. You don't have to take any special action to submit a form, which is done automatically using Ajax so that jQuery Mobile can smoothly manage the transition to the page returned by the server. You can rely on jQuery Mobile to automatically enhance form elements, but there are some good reasons to apply some additional elements and `data-role` attributes, especially when it comes to dealing with `select` elements. Overall, the way that jQuery Mobile handles forms is reasonably slick and elegant, although there are some minor formatting issues in the way that elements are sized on screen.

CHAPTER 31

jQuery Mobile Lists

In this chapter, I describe the jQuery Mobile list widget. Lists are an important tool in building mobile web applications, and they often provide simple and obvious navigation around the different functional areas of a web application. The beauty of lists is that they are compact, even when the individual list items are large enough to be selected by touch. They are also extremely well understood by users. Simply placing an arrow icon at the right edge of a list item (which jQuery Mobile does by default) makes it clear to most users that selecting the item will cause some kind of selection or navigation to occur. Table 31-1 provides the summary for this chapter.

Table 31-1. *Chapter Summary*

Problem	Solution	Listing
Create a jQuery Mobile navigation list	Define a `ul` or `ol` element that contains one or more `li` elements and has the `data-role` attribute set to `listview`. The contents of the `li` elements should be links.	1
Create read-only or standard HTML lists	Create a read-only list by omitting the links in the `li` elements. Create a standard HTML list by omitting the `data-role` attribute.	2
Create an inset list	Set the `data-inset` attribute to `true`.	3
Create a list whose items are made of two distinct parts	Add a second link to each `li` element.	4
Allow the user to filter the contents of the list	Set the `data-filter` attribute to `true`.	5, 6
Add dividers to a list	Set the `data-role` attribute to `list-divider` on individual `li` elements.	7
Add a count bubble to a list item	Use the `ui-li-count` class.	8

Use different text emphasis	Use the h1-h6 and p elements.	9
Add an aside to a list item	Use the ui-li-aside class.	10

Getting Started with Lists

There are a number of ways you can set up a list using jQuery Mobile. To get started, Listing 31-1 shows a basic list that links to jQuery Mobile pages inside the same document. Each page describes a different flower, and the list provides the user with a mechanism to navigate to these pages.

Listing 31-1. A basic list

```
<!DOCTYPE html>
<html>
<head>
    <title>Example</title>
    <meta name="viewport" content="width=device-width, initial-scale=1">
    <link rel="stylesheet" href="jquery.mobile-1.0.css" type="text/css" />
    <script type="text/javascript" src="jquery-1.6.4.js"></script>
    <script type="text/javascript" src="jquery.mobile-1.0.js"></script>
    <style type="text/css">
        .lcontainer {float: left; text-align: center; padding-top: 10px}
        .productData {float: right; padding: 10px; width: 60%}
    </style>
</head>
<body>
    <div id="page1" data-role="page" data-theme="b">
        <div data-role="header">
           <h1>Jacqui's Shop</h1>
        </div>

        <ul data-role="listview">
            <li><a href="#roses">Roses</a></li>
            <li><a href="#orchids">Orchids</a></li>
            <li><a href="#astors">Astors</a></li>
        </ul>
    </div>

  <div id="roses" data-role="page" data-theme="b">
        <div data-role="header">
           <h1>Roses</h1>
        </div>
        <div>
            <div class="lcontainer">
                <img src="rose.png">
                <div><a href="#" data-rel="back" data-role="button"
```

```
                    data-inline=true data-direction="reverse">Back</a>
                </div>
            </div>
            <div class="productData">
                A rose is a woody perennial within the family Rosaceae.
                They form a group of erect shrubs, and climbing or trailing plants.
                <div><b>Price: $4.99</b></div>
            </div>
        </div>
    </div>

    <div id="orchids" data-role="page" data-theme="b">
        <div data-role="header">
           <h1>Orchids</h1>
        </div>
        <div>
            <div class="lcontainer">
                <img src="orchid.png">
                <div><a href="#" data-rel="back" data-role="button"
                    data-inline=true data-direction="reverse">Back</a>
                </div>
            </div>
            <div class="productData">
                The orchid family is a diverse and widespread family in the order
                Asparagales. It is one of the largest families of flowering plants.
                <div><b>Price: $10.99</b></div>
            </div>
        </div>
    </div>

    <div id="astors" data-role="page" data-theme="b">
        <div data-role="header">
           <h1>Astors</h1>
        </div>
        <div>
            <div class="lcontainer">
                <img src="astor.png">
                <div><a href="#" data-rel="back" data-role="button"
                    data-inline=true data-direction="reverse">Back</a>
                </div>
            </div>
            <div class="productData">
                The name Astor comes from the Ancient Greek word meaning "star",
                referring to the shape of the flower head.
                <div><b>Price: $2.99</b></div>
            </div>
        </div>
    </div>
</body>
</html>
```

Most of this document is given over to the pages that describe the flowers. The actual list is just a few elements, as follows:

```
<ul data-role="listview">
    <li><a href="#roses">Roses</a></li>
    <li><a href="#orchids">Orchids</a></li>
    <li><a href="#astors">Astors</a></li>
</ul>
```

■ **Tip** I used the `ul` element in this example, but jQuery Mobile treats numbered lists (created with the `ol` element) in just the same way.

This is a standard HTML unnumbered list, expressed using the `ul` element, that contains three `li` elements. To create the jQuery Mobile list widget, I set the `data-role` attribute on the `ul` element to `listview`. The basic use for a list widget is to provide navigation and to this end, the content of each `li` element is an `a` element that links to one of the other pages in the document. You can see how the list is displayed in the browser in Figure 31-1.

Figure 31-1. A simple jQuery Mobile list widget

Clicking or tapping the individual list items takes the user to the appropriate page. You can see one of these pages in Figure 31-2. I added a link-based button to each page that takes the user back to the list, using the standard transition (but in reverse).

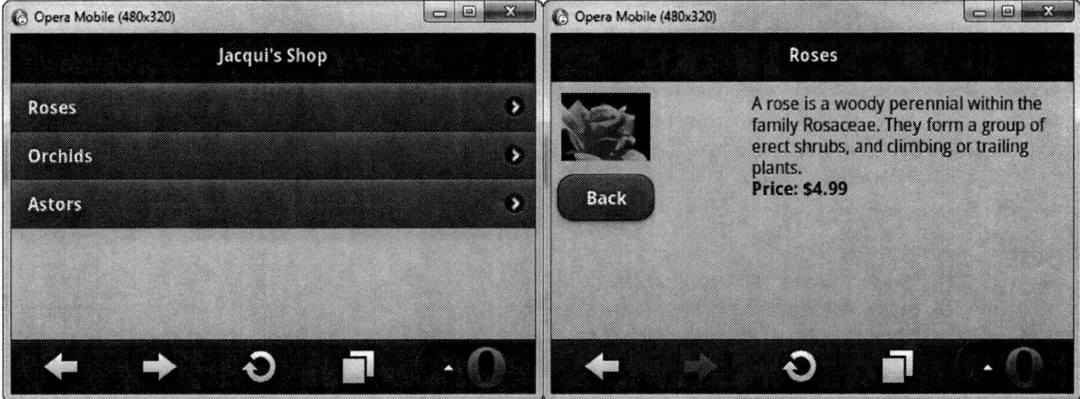

Figure 31-2. Using the list to navigate to another page

Formatting Lists

jQuery Mobile defines a number of data attributes you can use to format lists. These attributes are described in Table 31-2.

***Table 31-2.** Attributes for Formatting Lists*

Attribute	Description
`data-filter`	When `true`, a text box is displayed to the user to filter the contents of the list. The default is `false`.
`data-filter-placeholder`	Specifies a string to use as a placeholder in the text box when `data-filter` is `true`.
`data-filter-theme`	Specifies the swatch to use for the text box when `data-filter` is `true`.
`data-inset`	When `true`, the list is displayed with rounded corners. The default is `false`, which causes squared-off corners to be used.
`data-split-icon`	Specifies an icon to use for split buttons.

Creating Vanilla List Items

I showed list items that contained a elements in the last example because this is the most common use for the list widget. If you omit the links, you create a plain list, also known as a *read-only list.* If you omit the `data-role` attribute from the `ul` or `ol` element, jQuery Mobile doesn't create a widget at all, and you get a standard HTML list. Listing 31-2 shows both techniques.

Listing 31-2. Creating read-only and unformatted lists

```
...
<div id="page1" data-role="page" data-theme="b">
    <div data-role="header">
       <h1>Jacqui's Shop</h1>
    </div>

    <ul>
        <li><a href="#roses">Roses</a></li>
        <li><a href="#orchids">Orchids</a></li>
        <li><a href="#astors">Astors</a></li>
    </ul>

    <ul data-role="listview" data-theme="e">
        <li>Roses</li>
        <li>Orchids</li>
        <li>Astors</li>
    </ul>

</div>
...
```

The first list is the run-of-the-mill HTML list. I included it here because even though I have not created a jQuery Mobile widget, the user can still use these links to navigate to other pages. This is the basic navigation approach I introduced in Chapter 27.

The second list is read-only. When you create a read-only list, jQuery Mobile applies the default content styles from the current swatch, which makes it hard to differentiate between the list and other content in the page. To make the list easier to see, I applied the `data-theme` attribute to the `ul` element, which applies a swatch to all of the list items. You can see both lists in Figure 31-3.

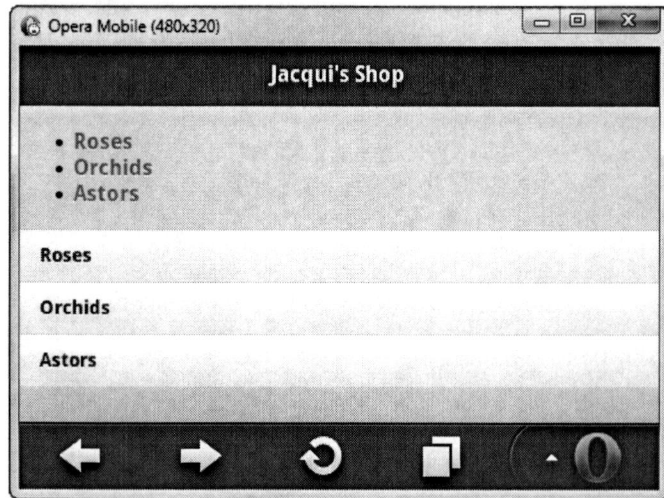

Figure 31-3. A raw HTML list and a read-only list

I recommend being cautious when you consider using read-only lists, especially if you have used other lists to help the user navigate through your application. There isn't enough difference in the appearance of a read-only list, and my user test usually shows the user trying to tap the read-only lists, causing confusion and frustration.

Creating Inset Lists

The default layout for lists is to fill the width of the container element and to have square corners, which doesn't match the style of other jQuery Mobile widgets. To make the style consistent, you can create an inset list, which has rounded corners and can be used in elements that do not touch the edges of the screen. You create an inset list by applying the `data-inset` attribute with a value of `true` to the `ul` or `ol` element, as shown in Listing 31-3.

Listing 31-3. Creating an inset list

```
...
<div id="page1" data-role="page" data-theme="b">
    <div data-role="header">
       <h1>Jacqui's Shop</h1>
    </div>

    <div id="container" style="padding: 20px">
        <ul data-role="listview" data-inset=true>
            <li><a href="#roses">Roses</a></li>
            <li><a href="#orchids">Orchids</a></li>
            <li><a href="#astors">Astors</a></li>
        </ul>
    </div>
</div>
...
```

In this example, I placed the `ul` element inside a `div` element. I used the CSS `padding` setting to inset the list from the edge of the parent element, and I used the `data-inset` attribute to change the style of the list. You can see the result in Figure 31-4.

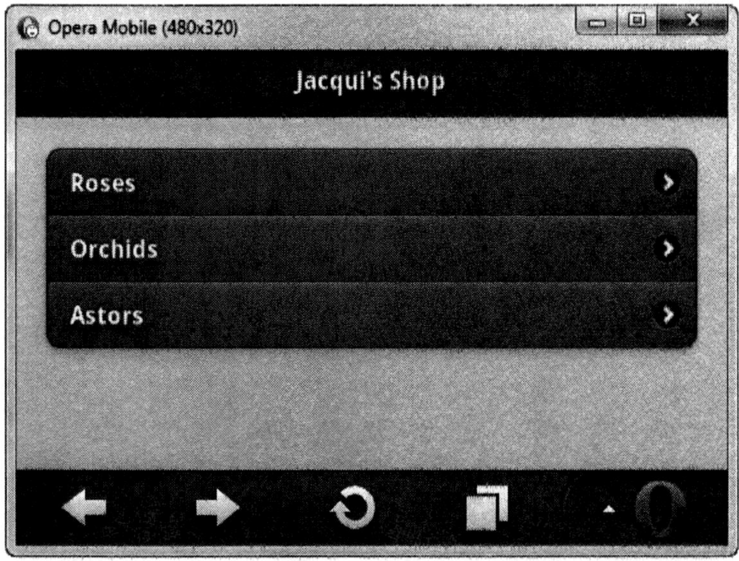

Figure 31-4. Creating an inset list

Creating Split Lists

Split lists are useful when there are two actions that can be performed for each item in the list. The list item is split into two sections, and clicking or tapping on each part of the item leads to a different action. Listing 31-4 shows a split list that allows users to get information about a flower or simply add it to their shopping basket.

Listing 31-4. Using a split list

```
<!DOCTYPE html>
<html>
<head>
    <title>Example</title>
    <meta name="viewport" content="width=device-width, initial-scale=1">
    <link rel="stylesheet" href="jquery.mobile-1.0.css" type="text/css" />
    <script type="text/javascript" src="jquery-1.6.4.js"></script>
    <script type="text/javascript" src="jquery.mobile-1.0.js"></script>
    <style type="text/css">
        .lcontainer {float: left; text-align: center; padding-top: 10px}
        .productData {float: right; padding: 10px; width: 60%}
        .cWrapper {text-align: center; margin: 20px}
    </style>
</head>
<body>
    <div id="page1" data-role="page" data-theme="b">
        <div data-role="header">
```

```
        <h1>Jacqui's Shop</h1>
    </div>

    <div id="container" style="padding: 20px">
        <ul data-role="listview" data-inset=true>
            <li><a href="#basket" class="buy" id="rose">Roses</a>
                <a href="#roses">Roses</a></li>
            <li><a href="#basket" class="buy" id="orchid">Orchids</a>
                <a href="#orchids">Orchids</a>  </li>
            <li><a href="#basket" class="buy" id="astor">Astors</a>
                <a href="#astors">Astors</a>  </li>
        </ul>
    </div>
</div>

<div id="basket" data-role="page" data-theme="b">
    <div data-role="header">
        <h1>Jacqui's Shop</h1>
    </div>
    <div class="cWrapper">
        Basket will go here
    </div>
    <div class="cWrapper">
        <a href="#" data-rel="back" data-role="button" data-inline=true
           data-direction="reverse">Back</a>
    </div>
</div>

<div id="roses" data-role="page" data-theme="b">
    <div data-role="header">
        <h1>Roses</h1>
    </div>
    <div>
        <div class="lcontainer">
            <img src="rose.png">
            <div><a href="#" data-rel="back" data-role="button"
                    data-inline=true data-direction="reverse">Back</a>
            </div>
        </div>
        <div class="productData">
            A rose is a woody perennial within the family Rosaceae.
            They form a group of erect shrubs, and climbing or trailing plants.
            <div><b>Price: $4.99</b></div>
        </div>
    </div>
</div>

<div id="orchids" data-role="page" data-theme="b">
    <div data-role="header">
        <h1>Orchids</h1>
    </div>
```

```
            <div>
                <div class="lcontainer">
                    <img src="orchid.png">
                    <div><a href="#" data-rel="back" data-role="button"
                            data-inline=true data-direction="reverse">Back</a>
                    </div>
                </div>
                <div class="productData">
                    The orchid family is a diverse and widespread family in the order
                    Asparagales. It is one of the largest families of flowering plants.
                    <div><b>Price: $10.99</b></div>
                </div>
            </div>
        </div>

        <div id="astors" data-role="page" data-theme="b">
            <div data-role="header">
               <h1>Astors</h1>
            </div>
            <div>
                <div class="lcontainer">
                    <img src="astor.png">
                    <div><a href="#" data-rel="back" data-role="button"
                            data-inline=true data-direction="reverse">Back</a>
                    </div>
                </div>
                <div class="productData">
                    The name Astor comes from the Ancient Greek word meaning "star",
                    referring to the shape of the flower head.
                    <div><b>Price: $2.99</b></div>
                </div>
            </div>
        </div>
    </body>
    </html>
```

Creating the split list is easy. You just add a second a element to the li elements. I highlighted the split list in the example. jQuery Mobile splits each list item in two and inserts a vertical divider between the parts. Clicking or tapping the left part of the item navigates to the target of the first a element, and clicking or tapping on the right part navigates to the second a element. You can see how the list items are presented in Figure 31-5.

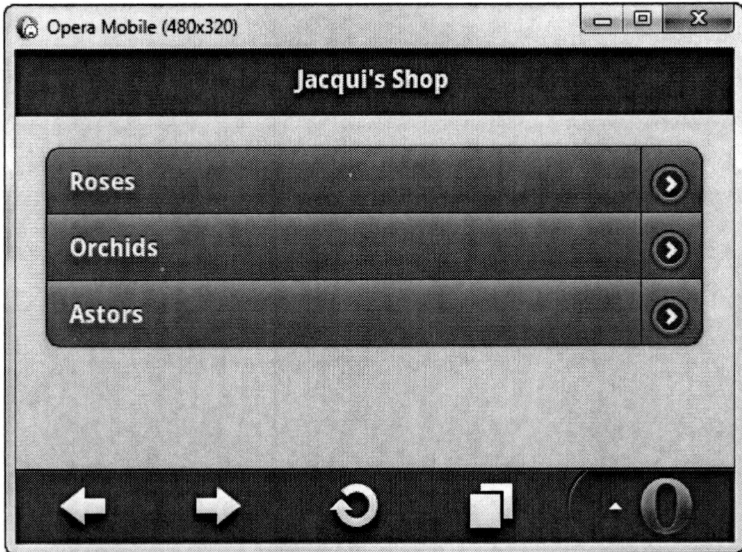

Figure 31-5. Creating split lists

In this example, I set all of the left parts of the list items to point to a new page I added to the document called basket. I'll come back to this example in Chapter 32 and expand on it to put a simple shopping basket in place. For this example, the basket page is simply a placeholder.

■ **Tip** jQuery Mobile uses the arrow icon for the split button by default. You can change this by applying the data-split-icon attribute to the ul or ol element, specifying the name of the icon you want. Chapter 29 contains a list of the available icons.

Filtering Lists

jQuery Mobile provides a mechanism for filtering the content of lists. You enable list filtering by applying the data-filter attribute with a value of true to the ul or ol element, as shown in Listing 31-5.

Listing 31-5. Using list filtering

```
<!DOCTYPE html>
<html>
<head>
    <title>Example</title>
    <meta name="viewport" content="width=device-width, initial-scale=1">
    <link rel="stylesheet" href="jquery.mobile-1.0.css" type="text/css" />
    <script type="text/javascript" src="jquery-1.6.4.js"></script>
```

```
        <script type="text/javascript" src="jquery.mobile-1.0.js"></script>
        <style type="text/css">
            .lcontainer {float: left; text-align: center; padding-top: 10px}
            .productData {float: right; padding: 10px; width: 60%}
        </style>
    </head>
    <body>
        <div id="page1" data-role="page" data-theme="b">
            <div data-role="header">
               <h1>Jacqui's Shop</h1>
            </div>

            <div data-role="content">
                <ul data-role="listview" data-inset=true data-filter=true>
                    <li><a href="#roses">Roses</a></li>
                    <li><a href="#orchids">Orchids</a></li>
                    <li><a href="#astors">Astors</a></li>
                </ul>
            </div>
        </div>

      <div id="roses" data-role="page" data-theme="b">
            <div data-role="header">
               <h1>Roses</h1>
            </div>
            <div>
                <div class="lcontainer">
                    <img src="rose.png">
                    <div><a href="#" data-rel="back" data-role="button"
                           data-inline=true data-direction="reverse">Back</a>
                    </div>
                </div>
                <div class="productData">
                    A rose is a woody perennial within the family Rosaceae.
                    They form a group of erect shrubs, and climbing or trailing plants.
                    <div><b>Price: $4.99</b></div>
                </div>
            </div>
        </div>

       <div id="orchids" data-role="page" data-theme="b">
            <div data-role="header">
               <h1>Orchids</h1>
            </div>
            <div>
                <div class="lcontainer">
                    <img src="orchid.png">
                    <div><a href="#" data-rel="back" data-role="button"
                           data-inline=true data-direction="reverse">Back</a>
                    </div>
                </div>
                <div class="productData">
```

```
                The orchid family is a diverse and widespread family in the order
                Asparagales. It is one of the largest families of flowering plants.
                <div><b>Price: $10.99</b></div>
            </div>
        </div>
    </div>

    <div id="astors" data-role="page" data-theme="b">
        <div data-role="header">
           <h1>Astors</h1>
        </div>
        <div>
            <div class="lcontainer">
                <img src="astor.png">
                <div><a href="#" data-rel="back" data-role="button"
                       data-inline=true data-direction="reverse">Back</a>
                </div>
            </div>
            <div class="productData">
                The name Astor comes from the Ancient Greek word meaning "star",
                referring to the shape of the flower head.
                <div><b>Price: $2.99</b></div>
            </div>
        </div>
    </div>
</body>
</html>
```

As you can see in Figure 31-6, jQuery Mobile adds a search bar above the list. When the user enters characters into the search bar, jQuery Mobile removes all of the items from the list that don't contain that sequence of characters.

■ **Caution** jQuery Mobile doesn't preserve item numbering when filtering a numbered list.

Figure 31-6. Enabling list filtering

■ **Tip** Although you can usually omit the `content` element in a jQuery Mobile page with no ill-effect, this is not the case when using the list filtering feature. Without such an element, the search box size and position are not handled properly.

The ability to filter lists is a great feature, but it isn't always useful on small touch screens. To support character input, most mobile devices show a pop-up touch keyboard when the user activates a text input element such as the search bar. On small devices, the keyboard can occupy so much of the screen that the user can't easily see the results of her filter, as Figure 31-7 shows. This does not mean you should not support list filtering, but it is important to provide other navigation mechanisms if you are targeting devices with small screens.

Figure 31-7. The touch keyboard obscuring a filtered list

Using a Custom Filtering Function

The default filter matches any list item that contains the set of characters the user has entered. These are matched anywhere in the list item text and are case insensitive. You can provide a custom filter function by using a jQuery UI-style method, as shown in Listing 31-6.

Listing 31-6. Using a custom list filter function

```
...
<script type="text/javascript">
    $(document).bind("pageinit", function() {
        $('ul').listview("option", "filterCallback", function(listItem, filter) {
            var pattern = new RegExp("^" + filter, "i");
            return !pattern.test(listItem)
        })
    })
</script>
...
```

The jQuery Mobile list widget is called `listview`, and you set the custom function by calling the `option` method and using the function as the value for the `filterCallback` setting. The arguments to the function are the text from a list item and the filter that the user has entered. The function is called once for each item in the list, and if you return `true`, the item for which the function has been called is hidden. In this example, I use a regular expression to restrict matches to list items that begin with the filter text.

You can see the result in Figure 31-8, where typing the letter R into the filter box matches only the Roses item.

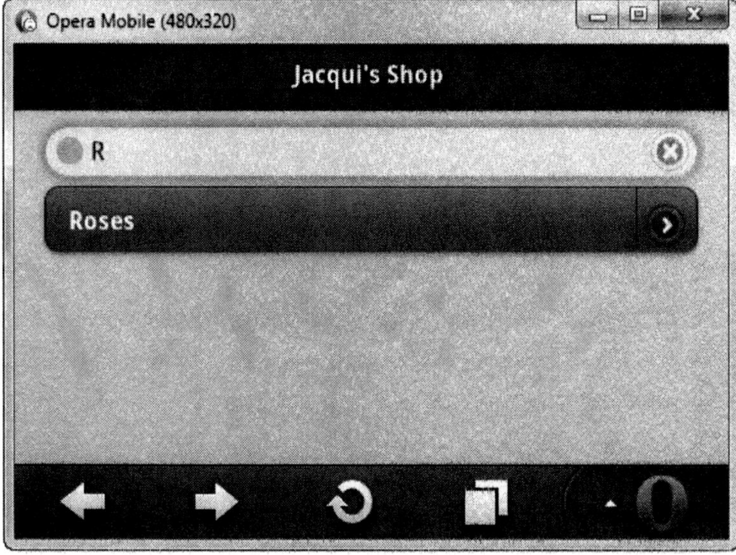

Figure 31-8. Using a custom filter

Formatting List Items

jQuery Mobile defines a number of data attributes you can use to format list items. These attributes are described in Table 31-3.

Table 31-3. *Attributes for Formatting List Items*

Attribute	Description
`data-role`	When set to `list-divider`, the list item acts as a spacer.
`data-icon`	Specifies an icon for a list item, using the same set of values as the same attribute for the button widget. (See Chapter 29 for details.)
`data-theme`	Apply a swatch to the list item.
`data-divider-theme`	Applies a swatch to a list divider (applied to the `ul` or `li` element).

I demonstrate three of these attributes in Listing 31-7. The most interesting is the use of the `data-role` attribute and its `list-divider` value, which creates a static entry in the list that doesn't act as a navigation aid. This is a useful mechanism for adding structure to a list to provide the user with context for the list's content. In the example, I added some additional flowers to the list, sorted the entries alphabetically, and added list dividers for each letter of the alphabet representing the first letter of each entry.

Listing 31-7. Using list dividers

```
...
<div id="page1" data-role="page" data-theme="b">
    <div data-role="header">
       <h1>Jacqui's Shop</h1>
    </div>

    <div data-role="content">
        <ul data-role="listview" data-inset=true data-theme="c"
            data-divider-theme="b">

            <li data-role="list-divider">A</li>
            <li><a href="#astors">Astors</a></li>
            <li data-role="list-divider">C</li>
            <li><a href="document2.html">Carnations</a></li>
            <li data-role="list-divider">D</li>
            <li><a href="document2.html">Daffodils</a></li>
            <li data-role="list-divider">L</li>
            <li><a href="document2.html">Lilies</a></li>
            <li data-role="list-divider">O</li>
            <li><a href="#orchids">Orchids</a></li>
            <li data-role="list-divider">P</li>
            <li><a href="document2.html">Peonies</a></li>
            <li><a href="document2.html">Primulas</a></li>
            <li data-role="list-divider">R</li>
            <li><a href="#roses">Roses</a></li>
            <li data-role="list-divider">S</li>
            <li><a href="document2.html">Snowdrops</a></li>
        </ul>
    </div>
</div>
...
```

You can see the effect that the dividers create in Figure 31-9. I used the `data-theme` attribute to set the swatch for the entire list and the `data-divider-theme` attribute to specify a different swatch just for the dividers.

■ **Tip** You can apply the `data-theme` attribute directly to individual list items if you want a different appearance for just one element.

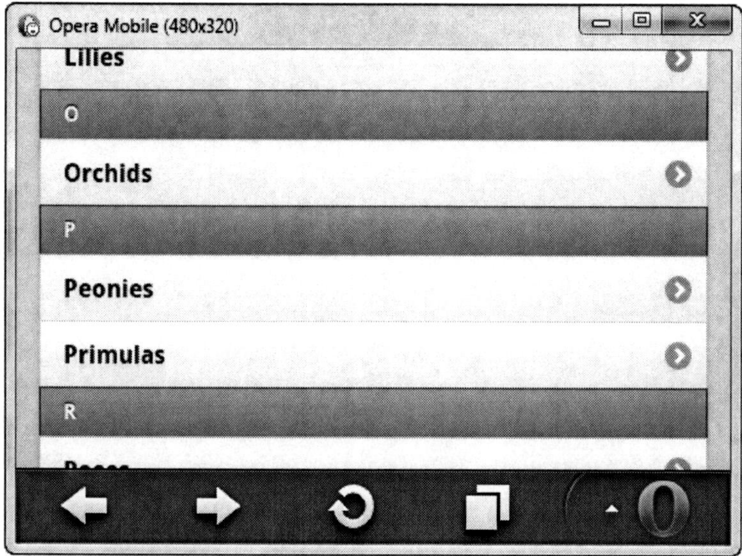

Figure 31-9. Adding dividers to a list

Using Convention-Based Formatting

Some styling options are handled by convention rather than configuration. You already saw an example of this when you looked at split lists. If you add a second a element to the content of an `li` element, jQuery Mobile automatically creates a split list item. You don't have to apply a data attribute to create this effect—it just happens. In this section, I show you three different conventions you can use to format list items: count bubbles, text emphasis, and asides.

Adding Count Bubbles

You can add a small numeric indicator to a list item. These are called *count bubbles*, and they can be useful when list items represent a category of some sort and you want to provide information about how many are available. For example, if your list items represent email folders, you can use count bubbles to indicate how many messages are in each folder. You might also use count bubbles to show how many items are in stock in an e-commerce application.

Although this effect is typically used to present numeric values, you can display any information you like. The meaning of the value needs to be self-evident, because you don't have room to provide an explanation to the user—just the value.

You create a count bubble by adding an additional child element to the contents of an `li` element. This child element must contain the value and be assigned to the `ui-li-count` class. You can see examples of count bubbles defined in Listing 31-8, including one that uses a non-numeric value.

Listing 31-8. Adding count bubbles to list items

```
...
<div id="page1" data-role="page" data-theme="b">
    <div data-role="header">
       <h1>Jacqui's Shop</h1>
    </div>

    <div data-role="content">
      <ul data-role="listview" data-inset=true data-filter=true>
          <li><a href="#roses">Roses<div class="ui-li-count">23</div></a></li>
          <li><div class="ui-li-count">7</div><a href="#orchids">Orchids</a></li>
          <li><a href="#astors">Astors</a><div class="ui-li-count">Pink</div></li>
      </ul>
    </div>

</div>
...
```

Notice that you can position the child element anywhere within the li element. It doesn't have to be the last element (although this is a common convention). You can see how the count bubbles are displayed in Figure 31-10.

Figure 31-10. Using counter bubbles

Adding Text Emphasis

jQuery Mobile will apply different levels of emphasis when you use content that is wrapped in a header element (the h1 through h6 elements) instead of a p element (indicating a paragraph). This allows you to create a list item that contains a headline and some supporting details text, as shown in Listing 31-9.

Listing 31-9. Adding text emphasis

```
...
<div id="page1" data-role="page" data-theme="b">
    <div data-role="header">
       <h1>Jacqui's Shop</h1>
    </div>

    <div data-role="content">
      <ul data-role="listview" data-inset=true data-filter=true>
          <li>
            <a href="#roses"><h1>Roses</h1>
                <p>A rose is a woody perennial within the family Rosaceae.</p>
                <div class="ui-li-count">$4.99</div></a>
          </li>
          <li><div class="ui-li-count">7</div><a href="#orchids">Orchids</a></li>
          <li><a href="#astors">Astors</a><div class="ui-li-count">Pink</div></li>
      </ul>
    </div>
</div>
...
```

In this example, I used the h1 element to denote the name of the product and the p element to denote the detailed information. I included a count bubble, indicating the price of the item. (Prices are ideally suited to count bubbles because the currency symbol provides immediate meaning to the numeric value.) You can see the effect in Figure 31-11.

Figure 31-11. Using text emphasis in a list item

Adding an Aside

An *aside* is an alternative to using count bubbles. To create an aside, you add a child to the li element that contains the information you want to display and that is assigned to the ui-li-aside class. You can see the use of an aside in Listing 31-10.

Listing 31-10. Creating an aside in a list item

```
...
<div id="page1" data-role="page" data-theme="b">
    <div data-role="header">
       <h1>Jacqui's Shop</h1>
    </div>

    <div data-role="content">
      <ul data-role="listview" data-inset=true data-filter=true>
          <li>
            <a href="#roses">
                <h1>Roses</h1>
                <p>A rose is a woody perennial within the family Rosaceae.</p>
                <p class="ui-li-aside">(Pink) <strong>$4.99</strong></p>
            </a></li>
          <li><div class="ui-li-count">7</div><a href="#orchids">Orchids</a></li>
          <li><a href="#astors">Astors</a><div class="ui-li-count">Pink</div></li>
      </ul>
    </div>
</div>
...
```

You can see the style with which an aside is displayed for the Roses item in Figure 31-12.

Figure 31-12. Using an aside

Summary

In this chapter, I described the jQuery Mobile list widget, which can be an essential navigation tool for mobile web applications. I showed you the different kinds of lists you can create, the different styles of list you can present to the user, and the configurations and conventions you can use to manage the content of individual list items.

CHAPTER 32

Refactoring the Mobile Example: Part IV

In prior chapters in this part of the book, I introduced you to jQuery Mobile. In this chapter, I'll build a more complete example that uses the jQuery Mobile functionality. By its nature, jQuery Mobile is a lot simpler than jQuery UI, and there are a lot fewer design choices available. Your development efforts with jQuery Mobile are further constrained by the unique issues that face mobile device development.

Starting with the Basics

In Chapter 31, I showed you an example that used split lists. This example is the starting point for this chapter. We'll use it to build out some additional functionality. Listing 32-1 shows the initial document.

Listing 32-1. The starting point for this chapter

```
<!DOCTYPE html>
<html>
<head>
    <title>Example</title>
    <meta name="viewport" content="width=device-width, initial-scale=1">
    <link rel="stylesheet" href="jquery.mobile-1.0.css" type="text/css" />
    <script type="text/javascript" src="jquery-1.6.4.js"></script>
    <script type="text/javascript" src="jquery.mobile-1.0.js"></script>
    <style type="text/css">
        .lcontainer {float: left; text-align: center; padding-top: 10px}
        .productData {float: right; padding: 10px; width: 60%}
        .cWrapper {text-align: center; margin: 20px}
    </style>
</head>
<body>
    <div id="page1" data-role="page" data-theme="b">
        <div data-role="header">
           <h1>Jacqui's Shop</h1>
        </div>

        <div id="container" style="padding: 20px">
            <ul data-role="listview" data-inset=true>
                <li><a href="#basket" class="buy" id="rose">Roses</a>
                    <a href="#roses">Roses</a></li>
```

```
                <li><a href="#basket" class="buy" id="orchid">Orchids</a>
                    <a href="#orchids">Orchids</a>  </li>
                <li><a href="#basket" class="buy" id="astor">Astors</a>
                    <a href="#astors">Astors</a>  </li>
            </ul>
        </div>
    </div>

    <div id="basket" data-role="page" data-theme="b">
        <div data-role="header">
           <h1>Jacqui's Shop</h1>
        </div>
        <div class="cWrapper">
            Basket will go here
        </div>
        <div class="cWrapper">
            <a href="#" data-rel="back" data-role="button" data-inline=true
               data-direction="reverse">Back</a>
        </div>
    </div>

    <div id="roses" data-role="page" data-theme="b">
        <div data-role="header">
           <h1>Roses</h1>
        </div>
        <div>
            <div class="lcontainer">
                <img src="rose.png">
                <div><a href="#" data-rel="back" data-role="button"
                        data-inline=true data-direction="reverse">Back</a>
                </div>
            </div>
            <div class="productData">
                A rose is a woody perennial within the family Rosaceae.
                They form a group of erect shrubs, and climbing or trailing plants.
                <div><b>Price: $4.99</b></div>
            </div>
        </div>
    </div>

   <div id="orchids" data-role="page" data-theme="b">
        <div data-role="header">
           <h1>Orchids</h1>
        </div>
        <div>
            <div class="lcontainer">
                <img src="orchid.png">
                <div><a href="#" data-rel="back" data-role="button"
                        data-inline=true data-direction="reverse">Back</a>
                </div>
            </div>
            <div class="productData">
```

```
                The orchid family is a diverse and widespread family in the order
                Asparagales. It is one of the largest families of flowering plants.
                <div><b>Price: $10.99</b></div>
            </div>
        </div>
    </div>

    <div id="astors" data-role="page" data-theme="b">
        <div data-role="header">
           <h1>Astors</h1>
        </div>
        <div>
            <div class="lcontainer">
                <img src="astor.png">
                <div><a href="#" data-rel="back" data-role="button"
                       data-inline=true data-direction="reverse">Back</a>
                </div>
            </div>
            <div class="productData">
                The name Astor comes from the Ancient Greek word meaning "star",
                referring to the shape of the flower head.
                <div><b>Price: $2.99</b></div>
            </div>
        </div>
    </div>
</body>
</html>
```

Inserting Products Programmatically

The first thing I'll do is replace the static pages that describe each flower with some that are created dynamically. This change allows me to have a more compact document and to easily add some more flowers for the user to pick from without duplicating HTML elements. I will generate the pages using the data template plugin, which I described in Chapter 12. This plugin works with the core jQuery library, so it fits nicely into a jQuery Mobile application. I created a file called `data.json` that contains the data I need for the flowers. Listing 32-2 shows the contents of `data.json`.

Listing 32-2. The content of the data.json file

```
[{  "name": "astor",
    "label": "Astors",
    "price": "$2.99",
    "text": "The name Astor comes from the Ancient Greek word meaning star..."
},{ "name": "carnation",
    "label": "Carnations",
    "price": "$1.99",
    "text": "Carnations require well-drained, neutral to slightly alkaline soil..."
},{ "name": "daffodil",
    "label": "Daffodils",
    "price": "$1.99",
```

```
        "text": "Daffodil is a common English name, sometimes used for all varieties..."
    },{ "name": "rose",
        "label": "Roses",
        "price": "$4.99",
        "text":  "A rose is a woody perennial within the family Rosaceae. They form a..."
    },{ "name": "orchid",
        "label": "Orchids",
        "price": "$10.99",
        "text": "The orchid family is a diverse and widespread family in the order..."
    }]
```

The data describes five flowers. For each of them, I defined the product name, the label to display to the user, the price per unit, and a text description. I did not show the full text description in the listing, but it is included in the data.json file that is part of the source code download for this book (which you can get without charge from apress.com).

Now that you have the data, you can integrate it into the document. Listing 32-3 shows the changes from static to programmatically generated pages.

Listing 32-3. Adding pages dynamically

```
<!DOCTYPE html>
<html>
<head>
    <title>Example</title>
    <meta name="viewport" content="width=device-width, initial-scale=1">
    <link rel="stylesheet" href="jquery.mobile-1.0.css" type="text/css" />
    <script type="text/javascript" src="jquery-1.6.4.js"></script>
    <script type="text/javascript" src="jquery.tmpl.js"></script>
    <script type="text/javascript">
        $(document).ready(function() {
            $.getJSON("data.json", function(data) {
                $('#flowerTmpl').tmpl(data).appendTo("body");
                $('ul').append($('#liTmpl').tmpl(data)).listview("refresh")
            })
        })
    </script>
    <script type="text/javascript" src="jquery.mobile-1.0.js"></script>
    <style type="text/css">
        .lcontainer {float: left; text-align: center; padding-top: 10px}
        .productData {float: right; padding: 10px; width: 60%}
        .cWrapper {text-align: center}
    </style>
    <script id="flowerTmpl" type="text/x-jquery-tmpl">
       <div id="${name}" data-role="page" data-theme="b">
            <div data-role="header">
               <h1>${label}</h1>
            </div>
            <div>
                <div class="lcontainer">
                    <img src="${name}.png">
                    <div><a href="#" data-rel="back" data-role="button"
```

```
                                data-inline=true data-direction="reverse">Back</a>
                        </div>
                    </div>
                    <div class="productData">
                        ${text}
                        <div><b>Price: ${price}</b></div>
                    </div>
                </div>
            </div>
        </script>
        <script id="liTmpl" type="text/x-jquery-tmpl">
            <li>
                <a href="#basket" class="buy" id="${name}">${label}</a>
                <a href="#${name}">${label}</a>
            </li>
        </script>
</head>
<body>
    <div id="page1" data-role="page" data-theme="b">
        <div data-role="header">
           <h1>Jacqui's Shop</h1>
        </div>
        <div id="container" style="padding: 20px">
            <ul data-role="listview" data-inset=true></ul>
        </div>
    </div>

    <div id="basket" data-role="page" data-theme="b">
        <div data-role="header">
           <h1>Jacqui's Shop</h1>
        </div>
        <div class="cWrapper">
            Basket will go here
        </div>
        <div class="cWrapper">
            <a href="#" data-rel="back" data-role="button" data-inline=true
               data-direction="reverse">Back</a>
        </div>
    </div>
</body>
</html>
```

I removed the per-flower pages and used the data template plugin to generate what I need from the data, which I obtain using the getJSON method (which I described in Chapter 14). The key to this change is the simple custom JavaScript code, as follows:

```
<script type="text/javascript">
    $(document).ready(function() {
        $.getJSON("data.json", function(data) {
            $('#flowerTmpl').tmpl(data).appendTo("body");
            $('ul').append($('#liTmpl').tmpl(data)).listview("refresh")
        })
```

```
    })
</script>
```

I deferred execution of this code until jQuery triggers the ready event, rather than waiting for the jQuery Mobile pageinit event. I want to load my JSON data only once, and the pageinit event is triggered too often to make it a sensible choice. When I obtain the data, I call the tmpl method to add the dynamically generated pages to the body element in the document.

I also use a template to generate the items for the main list of flowers. I tell jQuery Mobile that I have modified the contents of the list, which I do by calling the refresh method on the listview widget, like this:

```
$('ul').append($('#liTmpl').tmpl(data)).listview("refresh")
```

The data templates are pretty simple and use the standard techniques I described in Chapter 12. You can see the result in Figure 32-1—list whose items are generated programmatically and that link to pages that have been added to the document programmatically.

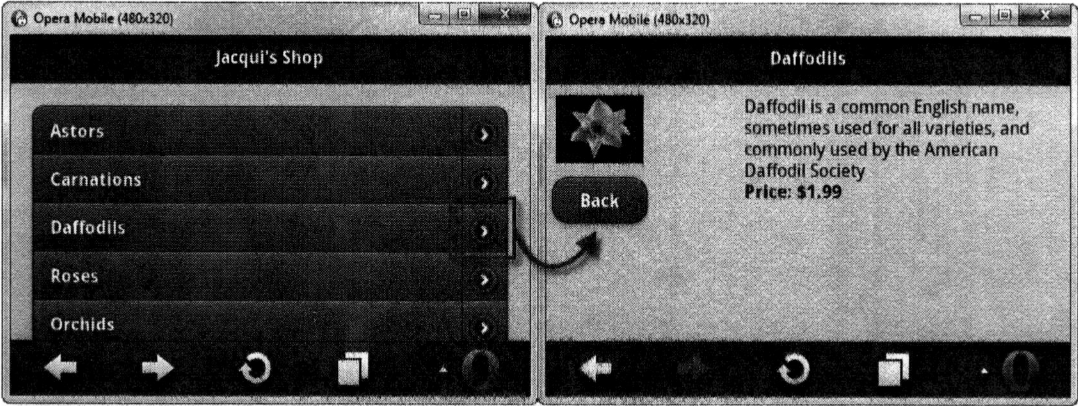

Figure 32-1. Programmatically generated list items and pages

Reusing Pages

I like the data template approach because it shows how jQuery underpins such a wide range of functionality, allowing you to bring together features like templates with an interface toolkit like jQuery Mobile.

That said, you can adopt a more elegant approach for dealing with the per-flower pages. Rather than generate a set of elements for each flower you want to show, you can generate one set of elements and modify them to show the flower that the user has selected. Listing 32-4 shows the changes to the document that make this possible.

■ **Tip** This is an approach that is particularly suited to jQuery Mobile because multiple pages are contained within a single HTML document. As a rule, you want to keep your HTML documents as simple as possible because of the limitations inherent in mobile devices.

Listing 32-4. Reusing a single page for multiple products

```
<!DOCTYPE html>
<html>
<head>
    <title>Example</title>
    <meta name="viewport" content="width=device-width, initial-scale=1">
    <link rel="stylesheet" href="jquery.mobile-1.0.css" type="text/css" />
    <script type="text/javascript" src="jquery-1.6.4.js"></script>
    <script type="text/javascript" src="jquery.tmpl.js"></script>
    <script type="text/javascript">
        $(document).ready(function() {
            $.getJSON("data.json", function(data) {
                $('ul').append($('#liTmpl').tmpl(data)).listview("refresh")
                $("a.productLink").bind("tap", function() {
                    var targetFlower = $(this).attr("data-flower");
                    for (var i = 0; i < data.length; i++) {
                        if (data[i].name == targetFlower) {
                            var page = $('#productPage');
                            page.find("#header").text(data[i].label);
                            page.find("#image").attr("src", data[i].name + ".png");
                            page.find("#description").text(data[i].text);
                            page.find("#price").text(data[i].price);

                            $.mobile.changePage("#productPage");
                            break;
                        }
                    }
                })
            })
        })
    </script>
    <script type="text/javascript" src="jquery.mobile-1.0.js"></script>
    <style type="text/css">
        .lcontainer {float: left; text-align: center; padding-top: 10px}
        .productData {float: right; padding: 10px; width: 60%}
        .cWrapper {text-align: center}
    </style>
    <script id="liTmpl" type="text/x-jquery-tmpl">
        <li>
            <a href="#basket" class="buy" id="${name}">${label}</a>
            <a class="productLink" data-flower="${name}" href="#">${label}</a>
        </li>
    </script>
</head>
<body>
    <div id="page1" data-role="page" data-theme="b">
        <div data-role="header">
           <h1>Jacqui's Shop</h1>
        </div>
        <div id="container" style="padding: 20px">
```

```
            <ul data-role="listview" data-inset=true>

            </ul>
        </div>
    </div>

    <div id="productPage" data-role="page" data-theme="b">
         <div data-role="header">
            <h1 id="header"></h1>
         </div>
         <div>
             <div class="lcontainer">
                 <img id="image" src="">
                 <div><a href="#" data-rel="back" data-role="button"
                        data-inline=true data-direction="reverse">Back</a>
                 </div>
             </div>
             <div class="productData">
                 <span id="description"></span>
                 <div><b>Price: <span id="price"></span></b></div>
             </div>
         </div>
     </div>

    <div id="basket" data-role="page" data-theme="b">
        <div data-role="header">
           <h1>Jacqui's Shop</h1>
        </div>
        <div class="cWrapper">
            Basket will go here
        </div>
        <div class="cWrapper">
            <a href="#" data-rel="back" data-role="button" data-inline=true
               data-direction="reverse">Back</a>
        </div>
    </div>
</body>
</html>
```

I removed one of the data templates from the document and added a new page (whose id is productPage) that I use for each flower. I modified the template used to generate the list items so that there is no target page in the href attribute and to add my own data attribute so that I know which flower any given link relates to. When the data has been retrieved from JSON, the revised script selects all of the per-product links from the list elements I just created using the template and binds to the tap event. When a list item is tapped, I find the appropriate data item and use its properties to configure the productPage page, setting the text and image to display to the user, as follows:

```
<script type="text/javascript">
    $(document).ready(function() {
        $.getJSON("data.json", function(data) {
            $('ul').append($('#liTmpl').tmpl(data)).listview("refresh")
            $("a.productLink").bind("tap", function() {
```

```
                var targetFlower = $(this).attr("data-flower");
                for (var i = 0; i < data.length; i++) {
                    if (data[i].name == targetFlower) {
                        var page = $('#productPage');
                        page.find("#header").text(data[i].label);
                        page.find("#image").attr("src", data[i].name + ".png");
                        page.find("#description").text(data[i].text);
                        page.find("#price").text(data[i].price);

                        $.mobile.changePage("#productPage");
                        break;
                    }
                }
            })
        })
    })
</script>
```

After I configure the page, I use the changePage method to trigger the navigation. There is no change in the appearance of the example, but you have a smaller set of elements for the mobile browser to manage, and it's a nice example of how you can manipulate the page structure of a jQuery Mobile document.

Creating the Shopping Basket

I am using a split list in this example, and the left side of the list item leads to the basket page. In this section, I'll define the elements for the page and add some JavaScript so that there is a simple basket in place. Listing 32-5 shows the changes to the document.

Listing 32-5. Implementing the shopping basket

```
<!DOCTYPE html>
<html>
<head>
    <title>Example</title>
    <meta name="viewport" content="width=device-width, initial-scale=1">
    <link rel="stylesheet" href="jquery.mobile-1.0.css" type="text/css" />
    <script type="text/javascript" src="jquery-1.6.4.js"></script>
    <script type="text/javascript" src="jquery.tmpl.js"></script>
    <script type="text/javascript">
        $(document).ready(function() {
            $.getJSON("data.json", function(data) {
                $('ul').append($('#liTmpl').tmpl(data)).listview("refresh")

                $("a.productLink").bind("tap", function() {
                    var targetFlower = $(this).attr("data-flower");
                    for (var i = 0; i < data.length; i++) {
                        if (data[i].name == targetFlower) {
                            var page = $('#productPage');
                            page.find("#header").text(data[i].label);
                            page.find("#image").attr("src", data[i].name + ".png");
```

```
                        page.find("#description").text(data[i].text);
                        page.find("#price").text(data[i].price);

                        $.mobile.changePage("#productPage");
                        break;
                    }
                }
            })

            $('a.buy').bind("tap", function() {
                var targetFlower = this.id;
                var row = $("#basketTable tbody #" + targetFlower);
                if (row.length > 0) {
                    var countCell = row.find("#count");
                    countCell.text(Number(countCell.text()) + 1);
                } else {
                    for (var i = 0; i < data.length; i++) {
                        if (data[i].name == targetFlower) {
                            $('#trTmpl').tmpl(data[i]).appendTo("#basketTable tbody")
                            break;
                        }
                    }
                }
                calculateTotals();
                $.mobile.changePage("#basket")
            })
        })
    })

    function calculateTotals() {
        var total = 0;
        $('#basketTable tbody').children().each(function(index, elem) {
            var count = Number($(elem).find("#count").text())
            var price = Number($(elem).attr("data-price").slice(1))
            var subtotal = count * price;
            $(elem).find("#subtotal").text("$"+ subtotal.toFixed(2));
            total += subtotal;
        })
        $('#total').text("$" + total.toFixed(2))
    }
</script>
<script type="text/javascript" src="jquery.mobile-1.0.js"></script>
<style type="text/css">
    .lcontainer {float: left; text-align: center; padding-top: 10px}
    .productData {float: right; padding: 10px; width: 60%}
    .cWrapper {text-align: center}
    table {display: inline-block; margin: auto; margin-top: 20px; text-align: left;
        border-collapse: collapse}
    td {min-width: 100px}
    th, td {text-align: right}
    th:nth-child(1), td:nth-child(1) {text-align: left}
```

```
    </style>
    <script id="liTmpl" type="text/x-jquery-tmpl">
        <li>
            <a href="#" class="buy" id="${name}">${label}</a>
            <a class="productLink" data-flower="${name}" href="#">${label}</a>
        </li>
    </script>
    <script id="trTmpl" type="text/x-jquery-tmpl">
        <tr data-price="${price}" id="${name}"><td>${label}</td><td id="count">1</td>
            <td id="subtotal">0</td></tr>
    </script>
</head>
<body>
    <div id="page1" data-role="page" data-theme="b">
        <div data-role="header">
           <h1>Jacqui's Shop</h1>
        </div>
        <div id="container" style="padding: 20px">
            <ul data-role="listview" data-inset=true></ul>
        </div>
    </div>

    <div id="productPage" data-role="page" data-theme="b">
         <div data-role="header">
            <h1 id="header"></h1>
         </div>
         <div>
             <div class="lcontainer">
                 <img id="image" src="">
                 <div><a href="#" data-rel="back" data-role="button"
                        data-inline=true data-direction="reverse">Back</a>
                 </div>
             </div>
             <div class="productData">
                 <span id="description"></span>
                 <div><b>Price: <span id="price"></span></b></div>
             </div>
         </div>
     </div>

    <div id="basket" data-role="page" data-theme="b">
        <div data-role="header">
           <h1>Jacqui's Shop</h1>
        </div>
        <div class="cWrapper">
            <table id="basketTable" border=0>
                <thead>
                    <tr><th>Flower</th><th>Quantity</th><th>Subtotal</th></tr>
                </thead>
                <tbody></tbody>
                <tfoot>
```

```
                    <tr><th colspan=2>Total:</th><td id="total"></td></tr>
                </tfoot>
            </table>
        </div>
        <div class="cWrapper">
            <a href="#" data-rel="back" data-role="button" data-inline=true
               data-direction="reverse">Back</a>
            <button data-inline="true">Checkout</button>
        </div>
    </div>

</body>
</html>
```

I added a table to the basket page, which shows one row for each selected product. Each row shows the name of the product, the quantity, and the subtotal. There is a footer in the table that shows the overall total. I bound to the tap event so that when the user clicks on the left side of the split button, either a new row is added to the table or the quantity is incremented if there is already a row for this product in the table. New rows are generated using another data template, and everything else is handled by reading the contents of elements in the document.

I determine and maintain the entire state of the customer's basket using the DOM itself. I could have created a JavaScript object to model the order and driven the contents of the table from the object, but in a book about jQuery, I like to take every opportunity to work with the document itself. The result is a very simple basket, which is shown in Figure 32-2.

Figure 32-2. The basket page

Adding for Quantity Changes

The basket is functional, but if the user wants two roses, for example, she has to tap the Rose list item, tap the Back button, and then tap the Rose item again. This process is pretty ridiculous, so to make it easier to change the quantity of a product, I added some input elements to the table. You can see the changes in Listing 32-6.

Listing 32-6. Adding range sliders to the basket table

```
<!DOCTYPE html>
<html>
<head>
    <title>Example</title>
    <meta name="viewport" content="width=device-width, initial-scale=1">
    <link rel="stylesheet" href="jquery.mobile-1.0.css" type="text/css" />
    <script type="text/javascript" src="jquery-1.6.4.js"></script>
    <script type="text/javascript" src="jquery.tmpl.js"></script>
    <script type="text/javascript">
        $(document).ready(function() {
            $.getJSON("data.json", function(data) {
                $('ul').append($('#liTmpl').tmpl(data)).listview("refresh")

                $("a.productLink").bind("tap", function() {
                    var targetFlower = $(this).attr("data-flower");
                    for (var i = 0; i < data.length; i++) {
                        if (data[i].name == targetFlower) {
                            var page = $('#productPage');
                            page.find("#header").text(data[i].label);
                            page.find("#image").attr("src", data[i].name + ".png");
                            page.find("#description").text(data[i].text);
                            page.find("#price").text(data[i].price);

                            $.mobile.changePage("#productPage");
                            break;
                        }
                    }
                })

                $('a.buy').bind("tap", function() {
                    var targetFlower = this.id;
                    var row = $("#basketTable tbody #" + targetFlower);
                    if (row.length > 0) {
                        var countCell = row.find("#count input");
                        countCell.val(Number(countCell.val()) + 1);
                    } else {
                        for (var i = 0; i < data.length; i++) {
                            if (data[i].name == targetFlower) {
                                $('#trTmpl').tmpl(data[i]).appendTo("#basketTable tbody")
                                    .find("input").textinput()
```

```
                        break;
                    }
                }
            }
            calculateTotals();
            $.mobile.changePage("#basket")
        })

        $('input').live("change click", function(event) {
            calculateTotals();
        })
    })
})

function calculateTotals() {
    var total = 0;
    $('#basketTable tbody').children().each(function(index, elem) {
        var count = Number($(elem).find("#count input").val())
        var price = Number($(elem).attr("data-price").slice(1))
        var subtotal = count * price;
        $(elem).find("#subtotal").text("$"+ subtotal.toFixed(2));
        total += subtotal;
    })
    $('#total').text("$" + total.toFixed(2))
}

</script>
<script type="text/javascript" src="jquery.mobile-1.0.js"></script>
<style type="text/css">
    .lcontainer {float: left; text-align: center; padding-top: 10px}
    .productData {float: right; padding: 10px; width: 60%}
    .cWrapper {text-align: center}
    table {display: inline-block; margin: auto; margin-top: 20px; text-align: left;
        border-collapse: collapse}
    td {min-width: 100px; padding-bottom: 10px}
    td:nth-child(2) {min-width: 75px; width: 75px}
    th, td {text-align: right}
    th:nth-child(1), td:nth-child(1) {text-align: left}
    input[type=number] {background-color: white}
    tfoot tr {border-top: medium solid black}
    tfoot tr td {padding-top: 10px}
</style>
<script id="liTmpl" type="text/x-jquery-tmpl">
    <li>
        <a href="#" class="buy" id="${name}">${label}</a>
        <a class="productLink" data-flower="${name}" href="#">${label}</a>
    </li>
</script>
<script id="trTmpl" type="text/x-jquery-tmpl">
    <tr data-theme="b" data-price="${price}" id="${name}"><td>${label}</td>
        <td id="count"><input type=number value=1 min=0 max=10></td>
```

```
            <td id="subtotal">0</td>
        </tr>
    </script>
</head>
<body>
    <div id="page1" data-role="page" data-theme="b">
        <div data-role="header">
           <h1>Jacqui's Shop</h1>
        </div>
        <div id="container" style="padding: 20px">
            <ul data-role="listview" data-inset=true></ul>
        </div>
    </div>

    <div id="productPage" data-role="page" data-theme="b">
         <div data-role="header">
            <h1 id="header"></h1>
         </div>
         <div>
             <div class="lcontainer">
                 <img id="image" src="">
                 <div><a href="#" data-rel="back" data-role="button"
                        data-inline=true data-direction="reverse">Back</a>
                 </div>
             </div>
             <div class="productData">
                 <span id="description"></span>
                 <div><b>Price: <span id="price"></span></b></div>
             </div>
         </div>
     </div>

    <div id="basket" data-role="page" data-theme="b">
        <div data-role="header">
           <h1>Jacqui's Shop</h1>
        </div>
        <div class="cWrapper">
            <table id="basketTable" border=0>
                <thead>
                    <tr><th>Flower</th><th>Quantity</th><th>Subtotal</th></tr>
                </thead>
                <tbody></tbody>
                <tfoot>
                    <tr><th colspan=2>Total:</th><td id="total"></td></tr>
                </tfoot>
            </table>
        </div>
        <div class="cWrapper">
            <a href="#" data-rel="back" data-role="button" data-inline=true
               data-direction="reverse">Back</a>
            <button data-inline="true">Checkout</button>
```

```
        </div>
    </div>

</body>
</html>
```

I inserted an input element into the quantity cell in the template, which is used to generate rows for the table. The type of this input element is number, which causes some browsers to insert small up and down buttons alongside the text entry area. These buttons are too small to be useful for touch, but the browser will also filter the characters to discard anything that isn't appropriate for a number. Although it's acceptable for this chapter, this isn't a perfect approach for real projects because floating point numbers are supported, which means that the user can input fractions of products.

I call the textinput method when I add input elements to the document after the pages have been enhanced by jQuery Mobile:

```
$('#trTmpl').tmpl(data[i]).appendTo("#basketTable tbody").find("input").textinput()
```

If I do not add this method call, the browser displays the native input element. Calling the textinput method causes jQuery Mobile to enhance the element, although it doesn't properly assign the swatch. So I defined a style for the input element to set the background color consistently:

```
input[type=number] {background-color: white}
```

I need to calculate the subtotals and totals more frequently now that the user can change the quantity of a product in the basket page. Because I add input elements to the document throughout the life of the application, I use the jQuery live method to handle events. The live method is described in Chapter 9. Here is the event handler code:

```
$('input').live("change click", function(event) {
    calculateTotals();
})
```

I use the live method to associate my handler function with both the change and click events. The browsers that add up and down buttons to numeric input elements trigger the click event when those buttons are pressed, so I need to handle this event in addition to the more expected change event. My handler function simply calls the calculateTotals function when either event is triggered. You can see how the basket looks in Figure 32-3.

Figure 32-3. Adding input elements to the basket page

Adding a Button to the Information Page

The product information describes the flower the user has selected, but it doesn't provide any way for the user to add it to the basket. To round out the basic basket functionality, I added a button to the product page that adds the item to the basket. Listing 32-7 shows the changes to the product page.

Listing 32-7. Adding a button to the product page

```
...
<div id="productPage" data-role="page" data-theme="b">
     <div data-role="header">
        <h1 id="header"></h1>
     </div>
     <div>
         <div class="lcontainer">
             <img id="image" src="">
             <div><a href="#" data-rel="back" data-role="button"
                    data-inline=true data-direction="reverse">Back</a>
             </div>
         </div>
         <div class="productData">
             <span id="description"></span>
             <div>
                <b>Price: <span id="price"></span></b>
                <a href="#" id="buybutton" data-flower="" data-role="button"
                   data-inline=true>Buy</a>
             </div>
```

```
            </div>
        </div>
 </div>
...
```

I defined an a element that jQuery Mobile will transform into a button widget. I added a data attribute (data-flower) so that I can keep track of which flower is being displayed when the user taps the button. To support this button, I made some changes to the script. These changes are shown in Listing 32-8.

Listing 32-8. Adding support for the buy button in the script

```
...
<script type="text/javascript">
    $(document).ready(function() {
        $.getJSON("data.json", function(data) {
            $('ul').append($('#liTmpl').tmpl(data)).listview("refresh")

            $("a.productLink").bind("tap", function() {
                var targetFlower = $(this).attr("data-flower");
                for (var i = 0; i < data.length; i++) {
                    if (data[i].name == targetFlower) {
                        var page = $('#productPage');
                        page.find("#header").text(data[i].label);
                        page.find("#image").attr("src", data[i].name + ".png");
                        page.find("#description").text(data[i].text);
                        page.find("#price").text(data[i].price);
                        page.find("#buybutton").attr("data-flower", data[i].name);

                        $.mobile.changePage("#productPage");
                        break;
                    }
                }
            })

            $('#buybutton').bind("tap", function() {
                addProduct($(this).attr("data-flower"));
            })

            $('a.buy').bind("tap", function() {
                addProduct(this.id);
            })

            function addProduct(targetFlower) {
                var row = $("#basketTable tbody #" + targetFlower);
                if (row.length > 0) {
                    var countCell = row.find("#count input");
                    countCell.val(Number(countCell.val()) + 1);
                } else {
                    for (var i = 0; i < data.length; i++) {
                        if (data[i].name == targetFlower) {
                            $('#trTmpl').tmpl(data[i]).appendTo("#basketTable tbody")
```

```
                                .find("input").textinput()

                            break;
                        }
                    }
                }
                calculateTotals();
                $.mobile.changePage("#basket")
            }

            $('input').live("change click", function(event) {
                calculateTotals();
            })

        })
    })

    function calculateTotals() {
        var total = 0;
        $('#basketTable tbody').children().each(function(index, elem) {
            var count = Number($(elem).find("#count input").val())
            var price = Number($(elem).attr("data-price").slice(1))
            var subtotal = count * price;
            $(elem).find("#subtotal").text("$"+ subtotal.toFixed(2));
            total += subtotal;
        })
        $('#total').text("$" + total.toFixed(2))
    }

</script>
...
```

These changes are pretty straightforward. When the user selects a product from the main list, I set the value of the data-flower attribute on the a element. I register a function to handle the tap event for the button and use the value data-flower to call the addProduct function, which contains code I extracted from another handler function. With these changes, the user can add products to the basket from the main list (by tapping on the left side of the split list item) or from the information page (by tapping the Buy button). Figure 32-4 shows the addition of the Buy button to the page.

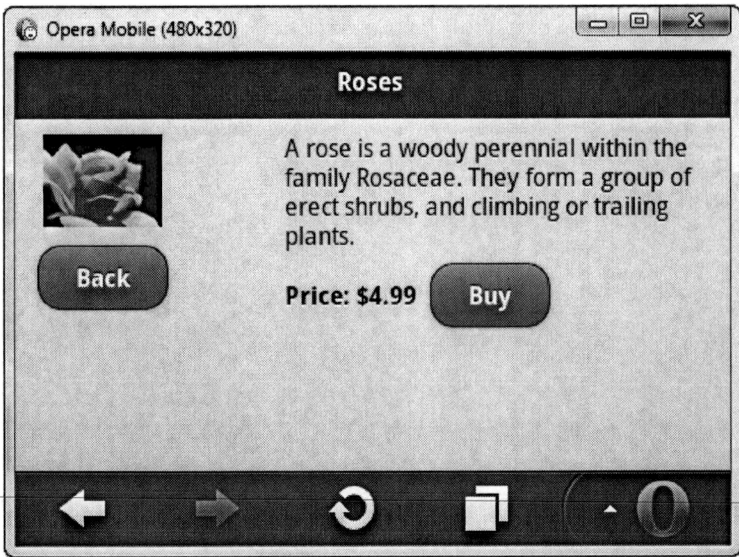

Figure 32-4. Adding a button to the product information page

Implementing the Checkout Process

To round out this example, I'll demonstrate gathering the data from the various jQuery Mobile pages in a form that can be used to make an Ajax request. I will not make the request itself or implement the server. jQuery Mobile uses the core jQuery support for Ajax, which I described in Chapters 14 and 15. Listing 32-9 shows the addition of a page that is shown to the user when the Checkout button is tapped and the handler function that gathers the data.

Listing 32-9. Implementing the checkout process

```
<!DOCTYPE html>
<html>
<head>
    <title>Example</title>
    <meta name="viewport" content="width=device-width, initial-scale=1">
    <link rel="stylesheet" href="jquery.mobile-1.0.css" type="text/css" />
    <script type="text/javascript" src="jquery-1.6.4.js"></script>
    <script type="text/javascript" src="jquery.tmpl.js"></script>
    <script type="text/javascript">

        $(document).ready(function() {
            $.getJSON("data.json", function(data) {
                $('ul').append($('#liTmpl').tmpl(data)).listview("refresh")

                $("a.productLink").bind("tap", function() {
                    var targetFlower = $(this).attr("data-flower");
                    for (var i = 0; i < data.length; i++) {
```

```
            if (data[i].name == targetFlower) {
                var page = $('#productPage');
                page.find("#header").text(data[i].label);
                page.find("#image").attr("src", data[i].name + ".png");
                page.find("#description").text(data[i].text);
                page.find("#price").text(data[i].price);
                page.find("#buybutton").attr("data-flower", data[i].name);

                $.mobile.changePage("#productPage");
                break;
            }
        }
    })

    $('#buybutton').bind("tap", function() {
        addProduct($(this).attr("data-flower"));
    })

    $('a.buy').bind("tap", function() {
        addProduct(this.id);
    })

    function addProduct(targetFlower) {
        var row = $("#basketTable tbody #" + targetFlower);
        if (row.length > 0) {
            var countCell = row.find("#count input");
            countCell.val(Number(countCell.val()) + 1);
        } else {
            for (var i = 0; i < data.length; i++) {
                if (data[i].name == targetFlower) {
                    $('#trTmpl').tmpl(data[i]).appendTo("#basketTable tbody")
                        .find("input").textinput()

                    break;
                }
            }
        }
        calculateTotals();
        $.mobile.changePage("#basket")
    }

    $('input').live("change click", function(event) {
        calculateTotals();
    })

    $('#submit').bind("tap", function() {
        var dataObject = new Object();
        $('#basketTable tbody').children().each(function(index, elem) {
            dataObject[elem.id] = $(elem).find("#count input").val();
        })
        dataObject["name"] = $('#name').val();
        dataObject["wrap"] = $('option:selected').val();
```

```
                    dataObject["shipping"] = $('input:checked').attr("id")

                    console.log("DATA: " + JSON.stringify(dataObject))
                })

            })
        })

        function calculateTotals() {
            var total = 0;
            $('#basketTable tbody').children().each(function(index, elem) {
                var count = Number($(elem).find("#count input").val())
                var price = Number($(elem).attr("data-price").slice(1))
                var subtotal = count * price;
                $(elem).find("#subtotal").text("$"+ subtotal.toFixed(2));
                total += subtotal;
            })
            $('#total').text("$" + total.toFixed(2))
        }

    </script>
    <script type="text/javascript" src="jquery.mobile-1.0.js"></script>
    <style type="text/css">
        .lcontainer {float: left; text-align: center; padding: 10px}
        .productData {float: right; padding: 10px; width: 60%}
        .cWrapper {text-align: center}
        table {display: inline-block; margin: auto; margin-top: 20px; text-align: left;
            border-collapse: collapse}
        td {min-width: 100px; padding-bottom: 10px}
        td:nth-child(2) {min-width: 75px; width: 75px}
        th, td {text-align: right}
        th:nth-child(1), td:nth-child(1) {text-align: left}
        input[type=number] {background-color: white}
        tfoot tr {border-top: medium solid black}
        tfoot tr td {padding-top: 10px}
    </style>
    <script id="liTmpl" type="text/x-jquery-tmpl">
        <li>
            <a href="#" class="buy" id="${name}">${label}</a>
            <a class="productLink" data-flower="${name}" href="#">${label}</a>
        </li>
    </script>
    <script id="trTmpl" type="text/x-jquery-tmpl">
        <tr data-theme="b" data-price="${price}" id="${name}"><td>${label}</td>
            <td id="count"><input type=number value=1 min=0 max=10></td>
            <td id="subtotal">0</td>
        </tr>
    </script>
</head>
<body>
    <div id="page1" data-role="page" data-theme="b">
        <div data-role="header">
```

```
        <h1>Jacqui's Shop</h1>
    </div>
    <div id="container" style="padding: 20px">
        <ul data-role="listview" data-inset=true></ul>
    </div>
</div>

<div id="productPage" data-role="page" data-theme="b">
     <div data-role="header">
        <h1 id="header"></h1>
     </div>
     <div>
         <div class="lcontainer">
             <img id="image" src="">
             <div><a href="#" data-rel="back" data-role="button"
                     data-inline=true data-direction="reverse">Back</a>
             </div>
         </div>
         <div class="productData">
             <span id="description"></span>
             <div>
                <b>Price: <span id="price"></span></b>
                <a href="#" id="buybutton" data-flower="" data-role="button"
                   data-inline=true>Buy</a>
             </div>
         </div>
     </div>
 </div>

<div id="basket" data-role="page" data-theme="b">
    <div data-role="header">
       <h1>Jacqui's Shop</h1>
    </div>
    <div class="cWrapper">
        <table id="basketTable" border=0>
            <thead>
                <tr><th>Flower</th><th>Quantity</th><th>Subtotal</th></tr>
            </thead>
            <tbody></tbody>
            <tfoot>
                <tr><th colspan=2>Total:</th><td id="total"></td></tr>
            </tfoot>
        </table>
    </div>
    <div class="cWrapper">
        <a href="#" data-rel="back" data-role="button" data-inline=true
           data-direction="reverse">Back</a>
        <a href="#checkout" data-role="button" data-inline="true">Checkout</a>
    </div>
</div>

<div id="checkout" data-role="page" data-theme="b">
```

```
        <div data-role="header">
           <h1>Jacqui's Shop</h1>
        </div>
        <div data-role="content">

            <label for="name">Name: </label>
            <input id="name" placeholder="Your Name">

            <label for="wrap"><span>Gift Wrap: </span></label>
            <select id="wrap" name="wrap" data-role="slider">
                <option value="yes" selected>Yes</option>
                <option value="no">No</option>
            </select>

            <fieldset data-role="controlgroup">
                <legend>Shipping:</legend>
                <input type="radio" name="ship" id="overnight" checked />
                <label for="overnight">Overnight</label>
                <input type="radio" name="ship" id="23day"/>
                <label for="23day">2-3 days</label>
                <input type="radio" name="ship" id="710day"/>
                <label for="710day">7-10 days</label>
            </fieldset>

            <div class="cWrapper">
                <a href="#" data-rel="back" data-role="button" data-inline="true"
                   data-direction="reverse">Back</a>
                <a href="#" id="submit" data-role="button"
                   data-inline=true">Submit Order</a>
            </div>

        </div>
    </div>

</body>
</html>
```

The new page is called checkout. I kept this form very simple, prompting the user for a name and providing choices for giftwrapping and the shipping method. You can see how the page appears in Figure 32-5. I have shown the page in the portrait orientation because it allows me to display all of the elements without having to scroll.

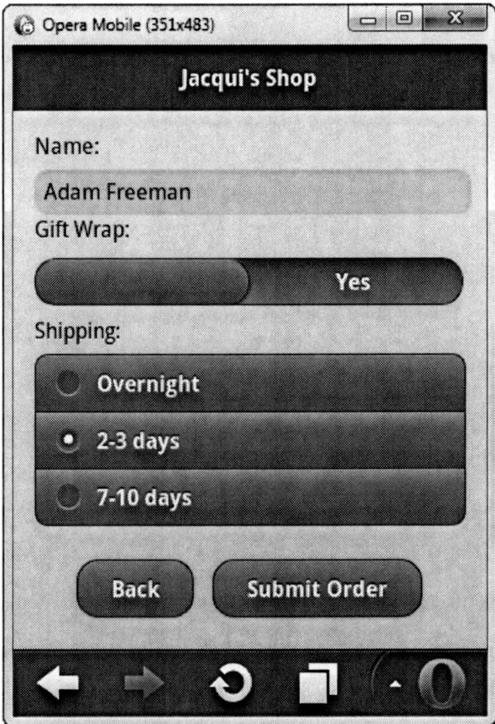

Figure 32-5. The checkout page

When the user taps the `Submit Order` button, I gather the data from the different pages in the HTML document and write the result as a JSON string to the console. The following is an example of such a string:

```
{"carnation":"3","rose":"1","orchid":"1",
    "name":"Adam Freeman","wrap":"yes","shipping":"23day"}
```

Summary

In this chapter, I took some of the core features of jQuery Mobile and combined them to create a simple mobile implementation of the flower shop example. By its very nature, jQuery Mobile is a lot simpler than jQuery UI. The main challenge is to design an approach that gives the user the information he require within the confines of a small screen.

PART 6

Advanced Features

CHAPTER 33

Using the jQuery Utility Methods

jQuery includes a number of utility methods that perform advanced operations on jQuery objects or that supplement the JavaScript language to provide features that are usually present in programming languages. You might never need any of these methods, but they are used internally by jQuery, and making them publicly available means that you can save time and effort when you come across an odd problem that the jQuery team has already solved.

Some of these methods are applied to jQuery objects, and some are called against the main jQuery function, which I have illustrated using the $ notation (described in Chapter 5). Table 33-1 provides the summary for this chapter.

***Table 33-1.** Chapter Summary*

Problem	Solution	Listing
Queue operations for later execution.	Use the general-purpose queues.	1, 2
Filter the contents of an array.	Use the `grep` method.	3, 4
Determine if an array contains a specific object or value.	Use the `inArray` method.	5
Project the contents of an array.	Use the `map` method.	6, 7
Concatenate two arrays.	Use the `merge` method.	8
Remove duplicates from a `jQuery` object, and sort those that remain by the order they appear in the document.	Use the `unique` method.	9
Determine the type of an object.	Use the `isXXX` or `type` method.	10, 11
Prepare the contents of a form for submission.	Use the `serialize` or `serializeArray` method.	12
Parse data into a more useful form.	Use the `parseJSON` or `parseXML` method.	13

Remove the leading and trailing whitespace from a string.	Use the `trim` method.	14
Determine if one element contains another.	Use the `contains` method.	15
Create a proxy for an event handler function.	Use the `proxy` method.	16

Queues Revisited: Using General-Purpose Queues

In Chapter 10, I showed you how you could use the jQuery effects queue to manage a chain of effects to apply to a set of elements. In fact, the effects queue is just one queue and the feature is a general-purpose one you can use more widely. Table 33-2 restates the queue-related methods, tweaked for general-purpose use.

Table 33-2. Queue Methods

Method	Description
`clearQueue(<name>)`	Removes any functions that have not yet been run in the specified queue
`queue(<name>)`	Returns the specified queue of functions to be performed on the elements in the `jQuery` object
`queue(<name>, function)`	Adds a function to the end of the queue
`dequeue(<name>)`	Removes and executes the first item in the queue for the elements in the `jQuery` object
`delay(<time>, <name>)`	Inserts a delay between effects in the specified queue

When you use these methods without specifying a queue name, jQuery defaults to `fx`, which is the queue for visual effects. You can use any other queue name to create a queue of functions.

When applying jQuery queues to general use, you use the `clearQueue` method instead of the `stop` method. Stop has special support for jQuery effects that are not appropriate for broader use. Listing 33-1 provides an example of using a general-purpose queue.

Listing 33-1. Using a queue

```
<!DOCTYPE html>
<html>
<head>
    <title>Example</title>
    <script src="jquery-1.7.js" type="text/javascript"></script>
    <link rel="stylesheet" type="text/css" href="styles.css"/>
    <script type="text/javascript">
```

```
        $(document).ready(function() {

            var elems = $('input');

            elems.queue("gen", function(next) {
                $(this).val(100).css("border", "thin red solid");
                next();
            });

            elems.delay(1000, "gen");

            elems.queue("gen", function(next) {
                $(this).val(0).css("border", "");
                $(this).dequeue("gen");
            });

           $("<button>Process Queue</button>").appendTo("#buttonDiv")
                .click(function(e) {
                    elems.dequeue("gen");
                    e.preventDefault();
                });

        });
    </script>
</head>
<body>
    <h1>Jacqui's Flower Shop</h1>
    <form method="post">
        <div id="oblock">
            <div class="dtable">
                <div id="row1" class="drow">
                    <div class="dcell">
                        <img src="astor.png"/><label for="astor">Astor:</label>
                        <input name="astor" value="0" required />
                    </div>
                    <div class="dcell">
                        <img src="daffodil.png"/><label for="daffodil">Daffodil:</label>
                        <input name="daffodil" value="0" required />
                    </div>
                    <div class="dcell">
                        <img src="rose.png"/><label for="rose">Rose:</label>
                        <input name="rose" value="0" required />
                    </div>
                </div>
                <div id="row2"class="drow">
                    <div class="dcell">
                        <img src="peony.png"/><label for="peony">Peony:</label>
                        <input name="peony" value="0" required />
                    </div>
                    <div class="dcell">
                        <img src="primula.png"/><label for="primula">Primula:</label>
```

```
                        <input name="primula" value="0" required />
                    </div>
                    <div class="dcell">
                        <img src="snowdrop.png"/><label for="snowdrop">Snowdrop:</label>
                        <input name="snowdrop" value="0" required />
                    </div>
                </div>
            </div>
        </div>
        <div id="buttonDiv"><button type="submit">Place Order</button></div>
    </form>
</body>
</html>
```

In this example, I add three functions to a queue called gen that operates on the input elements in the document. First, I use the val method to set all of the input values to 100 and the css method to add a border. Second, I use the delay method to add a 1-second delay to the queue. Finally, I use the val and css methods to reset the input elements to their original state.

I also added a button to the document that calls the dequeue method. Unlike with the effects queue, you are responsible for starting queue processing yourself. You can see the effect in Figure 33-1.

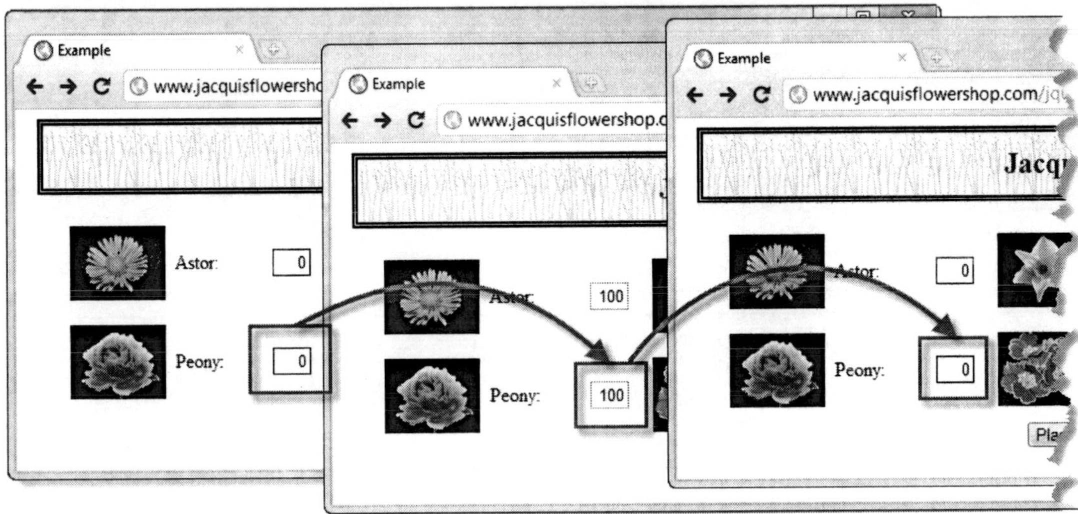

Figure 33-1. Using a general-purpose queue

The functions that you place in the queue work in the same way as for the events queue and, as before, you are responsible for either calling the dequeue method or invoking the function that is passed as an argument. I tend to use the function argument—just because I often forget to specify the queue name when calling the dequeue method, which means that my queue grinds to a halt.

Manually Processing Queue Items

Of course, you don't have to trigger one queued function from another. You can rely on an external trigger to dequeue each item, such as the user pressing the button I added to the document. Listing 33-2 shows how you can do this.

Listing 33-2. Dequeuing functions explicitly

```
...
<script type="text/javascript">
    $(document).ready(function() {

        $('input').queue("gen", function() {
            $(this).val(100).css("border", "thin red solid");
        }).queue("gen", function() {
            $(this).val(0).css("border", "");
        }).queue("gen", function() {
            $(this).css("border", "thin blue solid");
            $('#dequeue').attr("disabled", "disabled");
        });

       $("<button id=dequeue>Dequeue Item</button>").appendTo("#buttonDiv")
            .click(function(e) {
                $('input').dequeue("gen");
                e.preventDefault();
            });
    });
</script>
...
```

In this script, I chained the queue calls together and added a function that sets a border on the selected elements and disables the button element. You must press the button to process each item in the queue—here is no automated chaining. You can see the sequence in Figure 33-2.

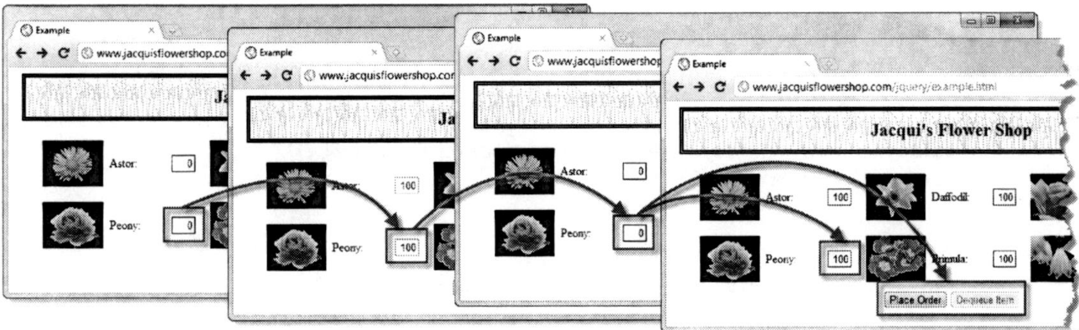

Figure 33-2. Manually processing a queue

Utility Methods for Arrays

jQuery provides a number of useful methods for working with arrays. These methods are described in Table 33-3. For the most part, there are better ways of working with HTMLElement arrays—you can just use the standard jQuery methods for handling and filtering elements. For other kinds of arrays, these methods can be helpful.

Table 33-3. Utility Methods for Working with Arrays

Method	Description
`$.grep(<array>, function)` `$.grep(<array>, function, <invert>)`	Filters the contents of an array based on a function
`$.inArray(<value>, <array>)`	Determines if a particular item is contained in an array
`$.map(<array>, function)` `$.map(<array>, <map>)`	Projects an array or map object using a function
`$.merge(<array>, <array>)`	Appends the contents of the second array to the first
`$.unique(HTMLElement[])`	Sorts an array of HTMLElement objects into document order, and removes any duplicates.

Using the grep Method

The grep method allows you to find all of the elements in an array that are matched by a filter function. Listing 33-3 provides a demonstration of this method.

Listing 33-3. Using the grep method

```
...
<script type="text/javascript">
    $(document).ready(function() {
        var flowerArray = ["astor", "daffodil", "rose", "peony", "primula", "snowdrop"];

        var filteredArray = $.grep(flowerArray, function(elem, index) {
            return elem.indexOf("p") > -1;
        });

        for (var i = 0; i < filteredArray.length; i++) {
            console.log("Filtered element: " + filteredArray[i]);
        }
    });
</script>
...
```

The filter function is passed two arguments. The first is the element in the array, and the second is the array index of that element. This function is called for each item in the array and you return true if you want the current item to be included in the filtered results.

In this example, I use the grep method on an array of strings, filtering out those that don't contain the letter p. I write the contents of the filtered array to the console, producing the following results:

```
Filtered element: peony
Filtered element: primula
Filtered element: snowdrop
```

You can supply an additional argument to the grep method. If this argument is true, the filtering process is inverted and the result contains the elements that the function filtered out. Listing 33-4 shows the effect of this argument.

Listing 33-4. Inverting the selection using the grep method

```
...
<script type="text/javascript">
    $(document).ready(function() {

        var flowerArray = ["astor", "daffodil", "rose", "peony", "primula", "snowdrop"];

        var filteredArray = $.grep(flowerArray, function(elem, index) {
            return elem.indexOf("p") > -1;
        }, true);

        for (var i = 0; i < filteredArray.length; i++) {
            console.log("Filtered element: " + filteredArray[i]);
        }

    });
</script>
...
```

This change produces the following results:

```
Filtered element: astor
Filtered element: daffodil
Filtered element: rose
```

Using the inArray Method

The inArray method lets you establish whether an array contains a specified value. The method returns the index of the item if it is in the array and -1 otherwise. Listing 33-5 demonstrates the inArray method.

Listing 33-5. Using the inArray method

```
...
<script type="text/javascript">
    $(document).ready(function() {
        var flowerArray = ["astor", "daffodil", "rose", "peony", "primula", "snowdrop"];

        console.log("Array contains rose: " + $.inArray("rose", flowerArray));
        console.log("Array contains lily: " + $.inArray("lily", flowerArray));
    });
</script>
...
```

This script checks to see if the array of flowers contains rose and lily. The results are as follows:

```
Array contains rose: 2
Array contains lily: -1
```

Using the map Method

The map method lets you use a function to project the contents of an array or a map object into a new array, using a function to determine how each item is represented in the result. Listing 33-6 shows the use of the map method with an array.

Listing 33-6. Using the map method to project an array

```
...
<script type="text/javascript">
    $(document).ready(function() {
        var flowerArray = ["astor", "daffodil", "rose", "peony", "primula", "snowdrop"];

        var result = $.map(flowerArray, function(elem, index) {
            return index + ": " + elem;
        });

        for (var i = 0; i < result.length; i++) {
            console.log(result[i]);
        }
     });
</script>
...
```

This mapping function is executed for each item in the array and is passed the item and its index in the array as arguments. The result from the function is included in the array returned by the map method. In this script, I transform each item in the array by concatenating the value with its index, producing the following results:

```
0: astor
1: daffodil
2: rose
3: peony
4: primula
5: snowdrop
```

You can use the map method to selectively project an array. There will be no corresponding item in the result if you don't return a value from the function for the item being processed. Listing 33-7 shows how you can selectively project from an array.

Listing 33-7. Selectively mapping an array

```
...
<script type="text/javascript">
    $(document).ready(function() {
        var flowerArray = ["astor", "daffodil", "rose", "peony", "primula", "snowdrop"];

        var result = $.map(flowerArray, function(elem, index) {
            if (elem != "rose") {
                return index + ": " + elem;
            }
        });

        for (var i = 0; i < result.length; i++) {
            console.log(result[i]);
        }
    });
</script>
...
```

Results are generated for all of the array values except rose, which gives rise to the following results:

```
0: astor
1: daffodil
3: peony
4: primula
5: snowdrop
```

Using the merge Method

The merge method concatenates two arrays, as demonstrated in Listing 33-8.

Listing 33-8. Using the merge method

```
...
<script type="text/javascript">
    $(document).ready(function() {
```

```
        var flowerArray = ["astor", "daffodil", "rose", "peony", "primula", "snowdrop"];
        var additionalFlowers = ["carnation", "lily", "orchid"];

        $.merge(flowerArray, additionalFlowers);

        for (var i = 0; i < flowerArray.length; i++) {
            console.log(flowerArray[i]);
        }
    });
</script>
...
```

The items from the second array are appended to the first array, and the array specified by the first argument is modified by the merge process. The script in the example produces the following results:

```
astor
daffodil
rose
peony
primula
snowdrop
carnation
lily
orchid
```

Using the unique Method

The unique method sorts an array of HTMLElement objects into the order in which they appear in the document and removes any duplicate elements. Listing 33-9 shows how you can use this method.

Listing 33-9. Using the unique method

```
...
<script type="text/javascript">
    $(document).ready(function() {

        var selection = $('img[src*=rose], img[src*=primula]').get();
        $.merge(selection, $('img[src*=astor]'));
        $.merge(selection, $('img'));

        $.unique(selection);

        for (var i =0; i < selection.length; i++) {
            console.log("Elem: " + selection[i].src);
        }

    });
</script>
...
```

The sorting process is done in-place, meaning that the array you pass as the argument to the `unique` method is modified. In this example, I created an array of `HTMLElement` objects that contain duplicates and that are not in document order, and then I applied the `unique` method.

Utility Methods for Types

jQuery provides a set of methods that are useful for determining the nature of a JavaScript object. These methods are described in Table 33-4.

***Table 33-4.** Utility Methods for Working with Types*

Method	Description
`$.isArray(Object)`	Returns `true` if the object is an array
`$.isEmptyObject(Object)`	Returns `true` if the object doesn't define any methods or properties
`$.isFunction(Object)`	Returns `true` if the object is a function
`$.isNumeric(Object)`	Returns `true` if the object is a number
`$.isWindow(Object)`	Returns `true` if the object is a `Window`
`$.isXMLDoc(Object)`	Returns `true` if the object is an XML document
`$.type(Object)`	Returns the built-in JavaScript type for the object

Most of these methods are very simple. You pass an object to the method, which returns `true` if the object is of the type that the method detects and `false` otherwise. As a simple demonstration, Listing 33-10 contains an example using the `isFunction` method.

Listing 33-10. Using the isFunction method

```
...
<script type="text/javascript">
    $(document).ready(function() {

        function myFunc() {
            console.log("Hello!");
        }

        console.log("IsFunction: " + $.isFunction(myFunc));
        console.log("IsFunction: " + $.isFunction("hello"));
    });
</script>
...
```

In this example, I use the isFunction method to test two objects. The results are as follows:

```
IsFunction: true
IsFunction: false
```

Using the type Method

The type method is slightly different in that it returns the base JavaScript type of an object. The result will be one of the following strings:

- boolean
- number
- string
- function
- array
- date
- regexp
- object

Listing 33-11 shows the use of the type method.

Listing 33-11. Using the type method

```
...
<script type="text/javascript">
    $(document).ready(function() {

        function myFunc() {
            console.log("Hello!");
        }

        var jq = $('img');
        var elem = document.getElementById("row1");

        console.log("Type: " + $.type(myFunc));
        console.log("Type: " + $.type(jq));
        console.log("Type: " + $.type(elem));
    });
</script>
...
```

In this script, I use the type method on a function, a jQuery object, and an HTMLElement object. The results are as follows:

```
Type: function
Type: object
Type: object
```

Utility Methods for Data

jQuery defines a number of utility methods that can be useful for working with various kinds of data. These methods are described in Table 33-5.

Table 33-5. *Utility Methods for Working with Data*

Method	Description
serialize()	Encodes a set of form elements into a string suitable for submission to a server
serializeArray()	Encodes a set of form elements into an array ready for encoding into JSON
$.parseJSON(<json>)	Creates a JavaScript object from JSON data
$.parseXML(<xml>)	Creates an XMLDocument object from an XML string
$.trim(String)	Removes all whitespace from the beginning and end of a string

Serializing Form Data

The serialize and serializeArray methods are convenient ways to extract the details from a set of form elements in a way that is useful for regular or Ajax form submissions. Listing 33-12 shows both methods in use.

Listing 33-12. Serializing form data

```
...
<script type="text/javascript">
    $(document).ready(function() {

        $("<button>Serialize</button>").appendTo("#buttonDiv").click(function(e) {

            var formArray = $('form').serializeArray();
            console.log("JSON: " + JSON.stringify(formArray))

            var formString = $('form').serialize();
            console.log("String: " + formString)
```

```
            e.preventDefault();
        });

    });
</script>
...
```

In this example, I serialize the form elements in the document using both methods and write the results to the console. The `serializeArray` method returns a JavaScript array that contains one object for each form element in the document. These objects have two properties: the `name` property contains the value of the `name` attribute of the element, and the `value` property contains the element's value. Here is the output from the example document:

```
[{"name":"astor","value":"1"},{"name":"daffodil","value":"0"},
 {"name":"rose","value":"0"},{"name":"peony","value":"0"},
 {"name":"primula","value":"2"},{"name":"snowdrop","value":"0"}]
```

By contrast, the serialize method creates an encoded string, as follows:

```
astor=1&daffodil=0&rose=0&peony=0&primula=2&snowdrop=0
```

Parsing Data

The `parseJSON` and `parseXML` methods are especially useful when dealing with the results of Ajax requests. For most web applications, JSON has taken over as the data format of choice, for the reasons I outlined in Chapter 14. XML is still used, but I find myself using this XML data only when integrating new applications with legacy back-end systems. Listing 33-13 shows the `parseJSON` method in use.

Listing 33-13. Parsing JSON data

```
...
<script type="text/javascript">
    $(document).ready(function() {

        $("<button>Serialize</button>").appendTo("#buttonDiv").click(function(e) {

            var jsonData = '{"name": "Adam Freeman", "city": "London", "country": "UK"}'

            var dataObject = $.parseJSON(jsonData)

            for (var prop in dataObject) {
                console.log("Property: " + prop + " Value: " + dataObject[prop])
            }

            e.preventDefault();
        });

    });
```

```
</script>
...
```

In this example, I define a simple JSON string and use the parseJSON method to convert it into a JavaScript object. I then enumerate the properties in the object and their values to the console, producing the following output:

```
Property: name Value: Adam Freeman
Property: city Value: London
Property: country Value: UK
```

Trimming Strings

The trim method removes all of the whitespace from the start and end of string. This includes spaces, tabs, and newlines. This is a feature that most programming languages support as part of their core handling of character data, but which is missing from JavaScript for some reason. Listing 33-14 shows the trim method in use.

Listing 33-14. Using the trim method

```
...
<script type="text/javascript">
    $(document).ready(function() {

        $("<button>Serialize</button>").appendTo("#buttonDiv").click(function(e) {

            var sourceString = "\n  This string contains whitespace    ";
            console.log(">" + sourceString + "<")

            var resultString = $.trim(sourceString);
            console.log(">" + resultString + "<")

            e.preventDefault();
        });

    });
</script>
...
```

In this example, I use the trim method and write the original and trimmed strings to the console, producing the following results:

```
>
  This string contains whitespace    <
>This string contains whitespace<
```

Other Utility Methods

A number of jQuery methods don't neatly fit into another category, but they can still be very useful. These are described in Table 33-6.

Table 33-6. *Other Utility Methods*

Method	Description
`$.contains(HTMLElement, HTMLElement)`	Returns `true` if the first element contains the second element
`$.proxy(function, <context>)`	Creates a function whose context is always the specified object
`$.now()`	Returns the current time, and is shorthand for `new Date().getTime()`

Checking Element Containment

The `contains` method lets you check to see if one element contains another. Both arguments are expressed as `HTMLElement` objects, and the method returns `true` if the element represented by the first argument contains the element represented by the second argument. Listing 33-15 provides a demonstration of the `contains` method.

Listing 33-15. Using the contains method

```
...
<script type="text/javascript">
    $(document).ready(function() {
        $('img').hover(function(e) {
            var elem = document.getElementById("row1");
            if ($.contains(elem, this)) {
                $(e.target).css("border", e.type == "mouseenter" ?
                                             "thick solid red" : "");
            }
        });
    });
</script>
...
```

In this script, I obtain an `HTMLElement` object using the DOM API and check to see that it contains the element passed to an event handler method. If it does, I set a border for the element that triggered the event.

■ **Tip** This method only works on `HTMLElement` objects. If you want to perform the same check on `jQuery` objects, consider using the `find` method, which I describe in Chapter 6.

Creating a Proxy Function

The `proxy` method allows you to create a function whose `this` variable is always an object that you specify. Listing 33-16 shows how the proxy method can be used.

Listing 33-16. Using the proxy method

```
...
<script type="text/javascript">
    $(document).ready(function() {
        $('img').hover($.proxy(handleMouse, $('img').eq(0)));

        function handleMouse(e) {
            $(this).css("border", e.type == "mouseenter" ? "thick solid red" : "");
        }
    });
</script>
...
```

This example contains a function called `handleMouse` that sets the border on the element represented by the `this` variable in response to mouse events. I used the `proxy` function to create a wrapper around the `handleMouse` function, which ensures that the value of this is always set to the first `img` element in the document. The effect of using the `proxy` method is that regardless of which `img` element triggers the mouse event, the border is always applied to the first `img` element.

■ **Tip** This method is not widely used—not least because only the `this` variable is changed. As a consequence, the `proxy` method has no real effect if you are in the habit of using the `Event.target` property to find out which element triggered the event, for example.

Summary

In this chapter, I described the jQuery utility methods—an eclectic set of helpful functions that can be used to perform advanced operations on jQuery objects or that supplement the JavaScript language features to provide support that programmers commonly need. These are the kinds of methods you are glad exist when you need them, but you can safely forget about them for most web application projects.

CHAPTER 34

The jQuery UI Effects & CSS Framework

In this chapter, I describe two utility features that jQuery UI provides. The first is a set of enhancements to existing jQuery methods so that you can animate colors, changes in element visibility, and the application of CSS classes. The other feature is a set of CSS classes that allow you to apply a jQuery UI theme to the rest of your HTML documents to create a consistent look across all of your web applications. Table 34-1 provides the summary for this chapter.

Table 34-1. *Chapter Summary*

Problem	Solution	Listing
Animate changes in color.	Use the enhanced `animate` method.	1
Animate the application of classes.	Use the enhanced `addClass`, `removeClass`, and `toggleClass` methods and the `switchClass` method.	2, 3
Animate visibility transitions.	Use the enhanced `show`, `hide`, and `toggle` methods.	4
Apply an effect without changing element visibility.	Use the `effect` method.	5
Style an element as a widget.	Use the widget container classes.	6
Apply rounded corners to an element.	Use the corner classes.	7
Apply the styles of a clickable widget to an element.	Use the interaction state classes.	8
Provide the user with cues about the state of an element.	Use the cue classes.	9, 10

Using the jQuery UI Effects

jQuery UI extends some core jQuery methods so that you can animate different transitions for an element. This ranges from color changes to the application of CSS classes. These can be valuable additions to a web application when used carefully, and to supplement these features, jQuery UI also defines some additional animation effects.

Animating Colors

jQuery UI extends the jQuery `animate` method, which I described in Chapter 10, to add support for animating colors. You can animate one of several CSS properties that define an element's colors. Table 34-2 describes the CSS properties that the `animate` method supports.

Table 34-2. *CSS Properties Supported by the jQuery UI animate Method*

Property	Description
`backgroundColor`	Sets the background color of the element

`borderTopColor`
`borderBottomColor`
`borderLeftColor`
`borderRightColor`
	Sets the color for individual sides of the element border

`color`	Sets the text color for the element
`outlineColor`	Sets the color for the outline; used to emphasize the element

To animate colors, you pass a `map` object as the argument to the `animate` method, detailing the properties you want animated and the target values. Listing 34-1 contains an example.

Listing 34-1. Animating colors

```
<!DOCTYPE html>
<html>
<head>
    <title>Example</title>
    <script src="jquery-1.7.js" type="text/javascript"></script>
    <script src="jquery-ui-1.8.16.custom.js" type="text/javascript"></script>
    <link rel="stylesheet" type="text/css" href="styles.css"/>
    <link rel="stylesheet" type="text/css" href="jquery-ui-1.8.16.custom.css"/>
    <style type="text/css">
        #animTarget {
            background-color: white;
            color: black;
            border: medium solid black;
            width: 200px; height: 50px;
            text-align: center;
```

```
            font-size: 25px;
            line-height: 50px;
            display: block;
            margin-bottom: 10px;
        }
    </style>
    <script type="text/javascript">
        $(document).ready(function() {
            $('button').click(function() {
                $('#animTarget').animate({
                    backgroundColor: "black",
                    color: "white"
                })
            })
        });
    </script>
</head>
<body>
    <h1>Jacqui's Flower Shop</h1>

    <div id=animTarget>
        Hello!
    </div>

    <button>Animate Color</button>
</body>
</html>
```

I style the div element in this document so that it has an initial background color of white and a color of black. When the button in the document is clicked, I call the animate method, specifying that these properties be changed to black and white, respectively. The transition from one color to another is done gradually, and both properties are animated simultaneously. You can see the effect in Figure 34-1.

■ **Tip** Notice that I use the standard CSS property names in the style element—background-color, for example. When specifying the same property in the map object, I switched to using camel case—backgroundColor. This allows me to specify the CSS property as a JavaScript object property without having to enclose the term in quotes.

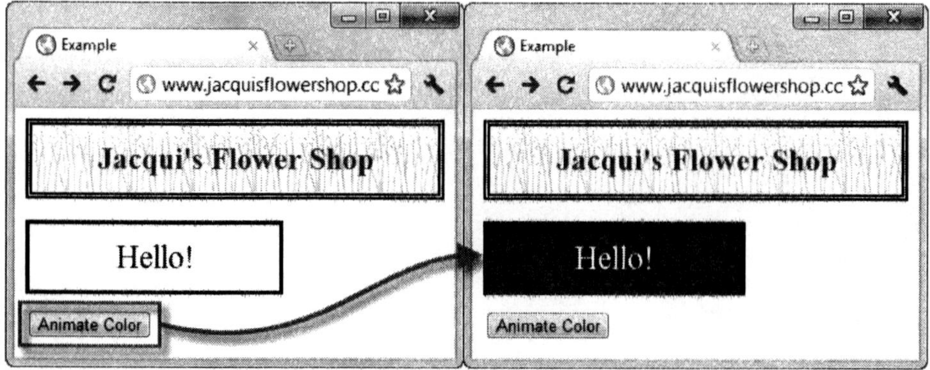

Figure 34-1. Animating colors

In this example, I specified the colors I wanted using the CSS color shorthand values, `black` and `white`. There are shorthand values for a wide range of colors, but the `animate` method also accepts hexadecimal colors (`#FFFFFF`, for example) and RGB function colors, such as `rgb(255, 255, 255)`.

■ **Tip** Aside from the support for the color properties, you use the `animate` method just as I described in Chapter 10.

Animating Classes

jQuery UI provides a convenient way of animating sets of CSS properties using classes. Rather than specify each property, you simply define your properties and values in a class and tell jQuery UI to add the class to one or more elements. jQuery UI will animate the transition from one state to another. Listing 34-2 provides a demonstration.

Listing 34-2. Animating using classes

```
<!DOCTYPE html>
<html>
<head>
    <title>Example</title>
    <script src="jquery-1.7.js" type="text/javascript"></script>
    <script src="jquery-ui-1.8.16.custom.js" type="text/javascript"></script>
    <link rel="stylesheet" type="text/css" href="styles.css"/>
    <link rel="stylesheet" type="text/css" href="jquery-ui-1.8.16.custom.css"/>
    <style type="text/css">
        .elemClass {
            background-color: white;
            color: black;
            border: medium solid black;
```

```
            width: 200px; height: 50px;
            text-align: center;
            font-size: 25px;
            line-height: 50px;
            display: block;
            margin-bottom: 10px;
        }
        .myClass {
            font-size: 40px; background-color: black; color: white;
        }
    </style>
    <script type="text/javascript">
        $(document).ready(function() {

            $('button').click(function() {
                if (this.id == "add") {
                    $('#animTarget').addClass("myClass", "fast")
                } else {
                    $('#animTarget').removeClass("myClass", "fast")
                }
            })
        });
    </script>
</head>
<body>
    <h1>Jacqui's Flower Shop</h1>

    <div id=animTarget class="elemClass">
        Hello!
    </div>

    <button id="add">Add Class</button>
    <button id="remove">Remove Class</button>
</body>
</html>
```

Once again, jQuery UI extends an existing jQuery method to add functionality. In this case, the addClass and removeClass methods have been enhanced. I described the standard versions of these methods in Chapter 8. The jQuery UI versions do exactly the same thing, but you specify a duration as the second argument to the method and jQuery UI animates the transition from one class to the other.

In this example, I defined a class called myClass, and there are buttons in the document that add and remove this class using the duration shorthand of fast. You can see the effect in Figure 34-2.

■ **Tip** The standard CSS style cascading rules apply, which means that the properties in a class will be applied only if the class is the most specific for the target element or elements. In the previous example, I styled the initial state of the element by id, but in this example I use a class so that my modifications have effect. See Chapter 3 for details of CSS style cascading.

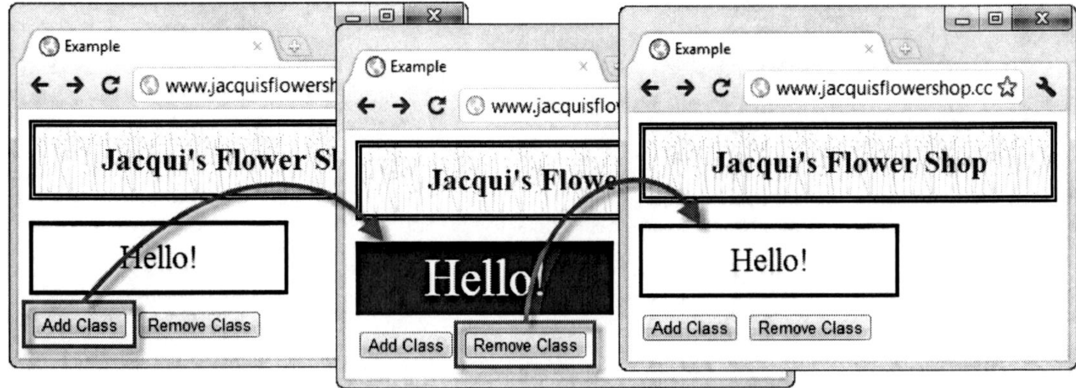

Figure 34-2. Animating elements using classes

■ **Tip** jQuery UI also enhances the `toggleClass` method. This works in the same way as the standard `toggleClass` method I described in Chapter 8, but it takes a duration argument and animates the transition, just as in the `addClass` and `removeClass` example just shown.

Switching Classes

In addition to enhancing some of the standard methods, jQuery UI also defines the `switchClass` method, which removes one class and adds another, animating the transition from one state to the other. Listing 34-3 contains a demonstration.

Listing 34-3. Using the switchClass method

```
<!DOCTYPE html>
<html>
<head>
    <title>Example</title>
    <script src="jquery-1.7.js" type="text/javascript"></script>
    <script src="jquery-ui-1.8.16.custom.js" type="text/javascript"></script>
    <link rel="stylesheet" type="text/css" href="styles.css"/>
    <link rel="stylesheet" type="text/css" href="jquery-ui-1.8.16.custom.css"/>
    <style type="text/css">
        .elemClass {
            border: medium solid black;
            width: 200px; height: 50px;
            text-align: center;
            line-height: 50px;
            display: block;
            margin-bottom: 10px;
        }
```

```
        .classOne {
            font-size: 25px; background-color: white; color: black;
        }
        .classTwo {
            font-size: 40px; background-color: black; color: white;
        }
    </style>
    <script type="text/javascript">
        $(document).ready(function() {

            $('button').click(function() {
                $('#animTarget').switchClass("classOne", "classTwo", "fast")
            })
        });
    </script>
</head>
<body>
    <h1>Jacqui's Flower Shop</h1>

    <div id=animTarget class="elemClass classOne">
        Hello!
    </div>
    <button>Switch Class</button>
</body>
</html>
```

The arguments to the switchClass method are the class that should be removed, the class that should be added, and the duration for the animation. In the example, my two classes define the same properties, but this need not be the case.

Using the jQuery UI Animations

jQuery UI includes a number of animation effects you can apply to elements, much as you did with the core jQuery effects in Chapter 10. My recommendation is to use these effects sparingly. Animations applied carefully can be a genuine enhancement to the user experience, but all too often, they become a source of annoyance and frustration to the user. There are many different animation effects available, including blind, bounce, clip, drop, explode, fade, fold, highlight, puff, pulsate, scale, shake, size, and slide.

■ **Note** In this chapter, I show you how to apply these effects, but I do not get into the details of each individual effect. There is a good summary of the effects and the settings that can be applied to some of them at http://docs.jquery.com/UI/Effects.

Using Effects to Show and Hide Elements

jQuery UI enhances the jQuery UI show, hide, and toggle methods so that you can apply animation effects. I described the original versions of these methods in Chapter 10. To use the enhanced jQuery UI versions of these methods, you simply provide additional arguments specifying the effect you want to use and the duration over which it should be applied. Listing 34-4 shows the use of these enhanced methods.

Listing 34-4. Using the enhanced show, hide, and toggle methods

```
<!DOCTYPE html>
<html>
<head>
    <title>Example</title>
    <script src="jquery-1.7.js" type="text/javascript"></script>
    <script src="jquery-ui-1.8.16.custom.js" type="text/javascript"></script>
    <link rel="stylesheet" type="text/css" href="styles.css"/>
    <link rel="stylesheet" type="text/css" href="jquery-ui-1.8.16.custom.css"/>
    <style type="text/css">
        .elemClass {
            font-size: 25px; background-color: white; color: black;
            border: medium solid black; width: 200px; height: 50px;
            text-align: center; line-height: 50px; display: block; margin-bottom: 10px;
        }
    </style>
    <script type="text/javascript">
        $(document).ready(function() {

            $('button').click(function() {
                switch (this.id) {
                    case "show":
                        $('#animTarget').show("fold", "fast");
                        break;
                    case "hide":
                        $('#animTarget').hide("fold", "fast");
                        break;
                    case "toggle":
                        $('#animTarget').toggle("fold", "fast");
                        break;
                }
            })
        });
    </script>
</head>
<body>
    <h1>Jacqui's Flower Shop</h1>

    <button id="hide">Hide</button>
    <button id="show">Show</button>
    <button id="toggle">Toggle</button>
```

```
    <div id=animTarget class="elemClass">
        Hello!
    </div>
</body>
</html>
```

There are three buttons in this example, and clicking them leads to the `show`, `hide`, or `toggle` method being called. For all three buttons, I specified that the `fold` animation should be applied, using the `fast` duration. These methods work just like their core jQuery counterparts, except that the transition is animated.

Applying Standalone Effects

jQuery UI defines the `effect` method, which allows you to apply an animation to an element without having to show or hide it. When used with the right animation, this can be a useful way of drawing the user's attention to an element in the document. Listing 34-5 contains an example.

Listing 34-5. Using the effect method

```
<!DOCTYPE html>
<html>
<head>
    <title>Example</title>
    <script src="jquery-1.7.js" type="text/javascript"></script>
    <script src="jquery-ui-1.8.16.custom.js" type="text/javascript"></script>
    <link rel="stylesheet" type="text/css" href="styles.css"/>
    <link rel="stylesheet" type="text/css" href="jquery-ui-1.8.16.custom.css"/>
    <style type="text/css">
        .elemClass {
            font-size: 25px; background-color: white; color: black;
            border: medium solid black; width: 200px; height: 50px;
            text-align: center; line-height: 50px; display: block; margin-bottom: 10px;
        }
    </style>
    <script type="text/javascript">
        $(document).ready(function() {

            $('button').click(function() {
                $('#animTarget').effect("pulsate", "fast")
            })
        });
    </script>
</head>
<body>
    <h1>Jacqui's Flower Shop</h1>

    <div id=animTarget class="elemClass">
        Hello!
    </div>
    <button>Effect</button>
```

```
</body>
</html>
```

When the button in this example is clicked, the effect is applied in situ, without any permanent changes to visibility. In this case, I used the `pulsate` effect, which causes the element to pulse on and off.

Using the jQuery UI CSS Framework

jQuery UI manages the appearance of widgets by applying a set of classes to elements that apply some complex CSS styles. Some of these classes are exposed to programmers so that elements that are not part of widgets can be styled in a consistent manner. I used some of these classes in the examples in Part IV of this book.

Using the Widget Container Classes

The three most basic classes in the CSS framework apply the core styles that are used on widgets. These classes are described in Table 34-3.

***Table 34-3.** jQuery UI Widget Container Classes*

Class	Description
`ui-widget`	Applied to overall container elements
`ui-widget-header`	Applied to header container elements
`ui-widget-content`	Applied to the content container element

These classes are applied to *container* elements—that is, elements that contain all of the header and content elements (or, in the case of `ui-widget`, the outermost element you are working with). Listing 34-6 shows how you can apply these classes.

Listing 34-6. Using the jQuery UI widget container classes

```
<!DOCTYPE html>
<html>
<head>
    <title>Example</title>
    <script src="jquery-1.7.js" type="text/javascript"></script>
    <script src="jquery-ui-1.8.16.custom.js" type="text/javascript"></script>
    <link rel="stylesheet" type="text/css" href="styles.css"/>
    <link rel="stylesheet" type="text/css" href="jquery-ui-1.8.16.custom.css"/>
    <style type="text/css">
        body > div {float: left; margin: 10px}
    </style>
</head>
<body>
    <h1>Jacqui's Flower Shop</h1>

    <div>
```

```
        <div>
            Flowers
        </div>
        <div>
            <div class="dcell">
                <img src="peony.png"/><label for="peony">Peony:</label>
                <input name="peony" value="0" />
            </div>
        </div>
    </div>

    <div class="ui-widget">
        <div class="ui-widget-header">
            Flowers
        </div>
        <div class="ui-widget-content">
            <div class="dcell">
                <img src="peony.png"/><label for="peony">Peony:</label>
                <input name="peony" value="0" />
            </div>
        </div>
    </div>
</body>
</html>
```

There are two sets of elements in this example, one of which I applied the container classes to. You can see the effect in Figure 34-3.

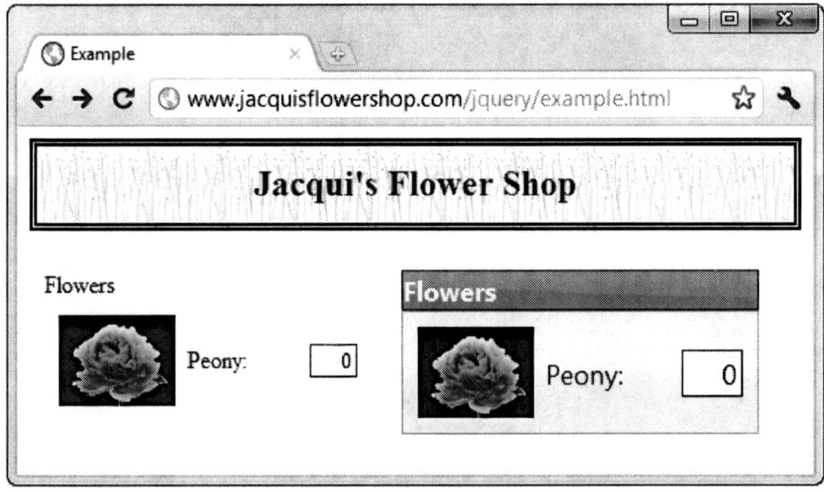

Figure 34-3. Applying the jQuery UI widget container classes

Applying Rounded Corners

The next set of CSS framework classes lets you apply rounded corners to your widget-like elements. Table 34-4 describes the classes in this category.

***Table 34-4.** jQuery UI Widget Rounded Corner Classes*

Class	Description
ui-corner-all	Rounds all of the element's corners
ui-corner-bl	Rounds the bottom-left corner
ui-corner-bottom	Rounds the bottom-left and bottom-right corners
ui-corner-br	Rounds the bottom-right corner
ui-corner-left	Rounds the top-left and bottom-left corners
ui-corner-right	Rounds the top-right and bottom-right corners
ui-corner-tl	Rounds the top-left corner
ui-corner-top	Rounds the top-left and top-right corners
ui-corner-tr	Rounds the top-right corner

These classes take effect only when an element has a background or margin, which means that you can apply them to the `ui-widget-header` and `ui-widget-content` classes, as shown in Listing 34-7.

Listing 34-7. Using the rounded corner classes

```
<!DOCTYPE html>
<html>
<head>
    <title>Example</title>
    <script src="jquery-1.7.js" type="text/javascript"></script>
    <script src="jquery-ui-1.8.16.custom.js" type="text/javascript"></script>
    <link rel="stylesheet" type="text/css" href="styles.css"/>
    <link rel="stylesheet" type="text/css" href="jquery-ui-1.8.16.custom.css"/>
    <style type="text/css">
        body > div {float: left; margin: 10px}
    </style>
</head>
<body>
    <h1>Jacqui's Flower Shop</h1>

    <div>
        <div>
```

```
                Flowers
            </div>
            <div>
                <div class="dcell">
                    <img src="peony.png"/><label for="peony">Peony:</label>
                    <input name="peony" value="0" />
                </div>
            </div>
        </div>

        <div class="ui-widget">
            <div class="ui-widget-header ui-corner-top" style="padding-left: 5px">
                Flowers
            </div>
            <div class="ui-widget-content ui-corner-bottom">
                <div class="dcell">
                    <img src="peony.png"/><label for="peony">Peony:</label>
                    <input name="peony" value="0" />
                </div>
            </div>
        </div>
    </body>
</html>
```

To create an overall effect, I rounded the top corners of the header element and the bottom corners of the content element. You can see the result in Figure 34-4. Notice that I added a little padding to the header element. The rounded corners are applied within the element's content box, which can require some additional space to avoid clipping content.

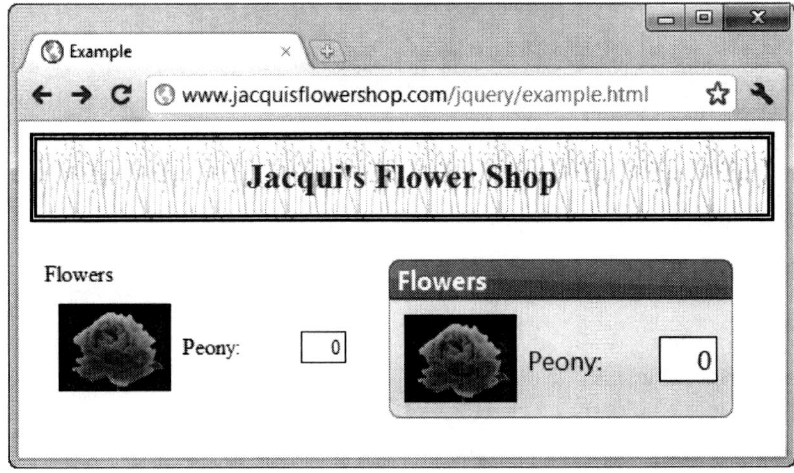

Figure 34-4. Applying rounded corners to elements

Using the Interaction State Classes

You can also apply CSS framework classes to show different interaction states, which allows you to create elements that respond to user interaction in the same way that jQuery UI widgets do. Table 34-5 describes the classes available.

Table 34-5. *jQuery UI Interaction Classes*

Class	Description
ui-state-default	Applies the default style for a clickable widget
ui-state-hover	Applies the style used when the mouse hovers over a clickable widget
ui-state-focus	Applies the style used when a clickable widget has the focus
ui-state-active	Applies the style used when a clickable widget is active.

Listing 34-8 applies these four classes. Notice that I applied padding to an inner span element in each case. The interaction state classes define padding values, and the easiest way to create spacing between the container element and the content is to target an inner element.

Listing 34-8. Applying the interaction state classes

```
<!DOCTYPE html>
<html>
<head>
    <title>Example</title>
    <script src="jquery-1.7.js" type="text/javascript"></script>
    <script src="jquery-ui-1.8.16.custom.js" type="text/javascript"></script>
    <link rel="stylesheet" type="text/css" href="styles.css"/>
    <link rel="stylesheet" type="text/css" href="jquery-ui-1.8.16.custom.css"/>
    <style type="text/css">
        body > div {float: left; margin: 10px}
        span {padding: 10px; display: block}
    </style>
</head>
<body>
    <h1>Jacqui's Flower Shop</h1>

    <div class="ui-widget ui-state-default ui-corner-all">
        <span>Default</span>
    </div>
    <div class="ui-widget ui-state-hover ui-corner-all">
        <span>Hover</span>
    </div>
    <div class="ui-widget ui-state-focus ui-corner-all">
        <span>Focus</span>
    </div>
    <div class="ui-widget ui-state-active ui-corner-all">
```

```
        <span>Active</span>
    </div>
</body>
</html>
```

You can see the effect of each class in Figure 34-5. Some of these states are very similar in the jQuery UI theme that I am using, but you can use ThemeRoller (described in Chapter 17) to create a theme when increased state emphasis is required.

Figure 34-5. The effect of the interaction state classes

Using the Cue Classes

Some CSS framework classes allow you to provide the user with cues about the state of elements in the document. These classes are described in Table 34-6.

***Table 34-6.** jQuery UI Interaction Cue Classes*

Class	Description
`ui-state-highlight`	Highlights an element to draw the user's attention
`ui-state-error`	Emphasizes an element that contains an error message
`ui-state-disabled`	Applies the disabled style to an element (but doesn't actually disable the element itself)

Listing 34-9 shows the use of the highlight and disabled cues.

Listing 34-9. Using the jQuery UI highlight class

```
<!DOCTYPE html>
<html>
<head>
    <title>Example</title>
    <script src="jquery-1.7.js" type="text/javascript"></script>
```

```
    <script src="jquery-ui-1.8.16.custom.js" type="text/javascript"></script>
    <link rel="stylesheet" type="text/css" href="styles.css"/>
    <link rel="stylesheet" type="text/css" href="jquery-ui-1.8.16.custom.css"/>
    <style type="text/css">
        body > div {float: left; margin: 10px}
        span {padding: 10px; display: block}
    </style>
</head>
<body>
    <h1>Jacqui's Flower Shop</h1>
    <div class="ui-widget">
        <div class="ui-widget-header ui-corner-top" style="padding-left: 5px">
            Flowers
        </div>
        <div class="ui-widget-content ui-corner-bottom">
            <div class="dcell">
                <img src="peony.png"/><label for="peony">Peony:</label>
                <input name="peony" value="0" />
            </div>
        </div>
    </div>

    <div class="ui-widget ui-state-highlight ui-corner-all">
        <div class="ui-widget-header ui-corner-top" style="padding-left: 5px">
            Flowers
        </div>
        <div class="ui-widget-content ui-corner-bottom">
            <div class="dcell">
                <img src="peony.png"/><label for="peony">Peony:</label>
                <input name="peony" value="0" />
            </div>
        </div>
    </div>

    <div class="ui-widget ui-state-disabled">
        <div class="ui-widget-header ui-corner-top" style="padding-left: 5px">
            Flowers
        </div>
        <div class="ui-widget-content ui-corner-bottom">
            <div class="dcell">
                <img src="peony.png"/><label for="peony">Peony:</label>
                <input name="peony" value="0" />
            </div>
        </div>
    </div>

</body>
</html>
```

You can see the effect of the classes in Figure 34-6. Notice that I also applied the ui-corner-all style when using the ui-state-highlight class. This class applies a border, which will be shown with square corners by default. If the child elements have rounded corners, you need to round the corners of the highlighted element as well.

Figure 34-6. Applying the highlight cue class

Listing 34-10 shows the use of the error cue.

Listing 34-10. Using the error cue

```
<!DOCTYPE html>
<html>
<head>
    <title>Example</title>
    <script src="jquery-1.7.js" type="text/javascript"></script>
    <script src="jquery-ui-1.8.16.custom.js" type="text/javascript"></script>
    <link rel="stylesheet" type="text/css" href="styles.css"/>
    <link rel="stylesheet" type="text/css" href="jquery-ui-1.8.16.custom.css"/>
    <style type="text/css">
        body > div {float: left; margin: 10px; padding: 20px}
    </style>
</head>
<body>
    <h1>Jacqui's Flower Shop</h1>

    <div class="ui-state-error">
        Oops! Something went wrong.
    </div>
</body>
</html>
```

You can see the effect in Figure 34-7.

Figure 34-7. Using the error cue class

Summary

In this chapter, I described the enhancements that jQuery UI provides for animating transitions for color, visibility, and CSS classes. These are useful features, but they must be used with caution to avoid bombarding the user with distracting and annoying effects. I also described the principle classes of the jQuery UI CSs framework, which allows you to style elements in a way that is consistent with jQuery UI widgets, allowing you to extend the appearance of your jQuery UI theme to the rest of your HTML documents.

CHAPTER 35

Using Deferred Objects

Throughout this book, you have seen examples that relied on *callbacks*. You provide a function that is executed when something occurs. A good example is the way you have been handling events, where you call a method such as `click`, passing in a function as an argument. The code statements in the function are not performed until the user triggers the event. Until that point, your function is dormant.

Deferred objects is the jQuery term for a set of enhancements to the way you use callbacks. When using deferred objects, you can use callbacks in any situation and not just for events. You also gain a lot of options and control over when and how your callback functions are executed. Deferred objects are most often used with background tasks, although this isn't a requirement. In this chapter, I'll start with a reasonably simple example and then build upon it to show the features and some useful patterns for managing deferred objects and background tasks.

I saw *reasonably simply*, because using deferred objects brings you into the work of *asynchronous* or *parallel* programming. Effective parallel programming is a difficult skill to master, and JavaScript makes it more difficult because it lacks some of the advanced features that are present in other languages, such as Java and C#. Most projects don't need to use deferred objects, and if you are new to parallel programming, my recommendation is to skip this chapter until you are working on a project that does. Table 35-1 provides the summary for this chapter.

***Table 35-1.** Chapter Summary*

Problem	Solution	Listing
Use the basic features of a deferred object.	Register a `callback` function using the done method. Call the `resolve` method to trigger the callback.	1
Use a deferred object with a background task.	Use the `setTimeout` function to create a background task and call the `resolve` method when the task is complete.	2–4
Signal a task failure.	Use the `reject` method to trigger the handlers registered using the `fail` method.	5, 6
Register handlers for both deferred object outcomes in a single method call.	Use the `then` method.	7

Specify a function that will be executed irrespective of whether the deferred object is resolved or rejected.	Use the always method.	8
Use multiple callbacks for the same outcome.	Call the registration method multiple times or pass the functions as comma-separated arguments.	9
Create a deferred object whose outcome is determined by the outcome of other deferred objects.	Use the when method.	10
Signal task progress.	Call the notify method, which will trigger callback handlers that have been registered using the progress method.	11, 12
Get information about the state of a deferred object.	Use the state method.	13
Use Ajax Promises.	Treat the response from the jQuery Ajax methods as you would a deferred object.	14

A First Deferred Objects Example

I am going to start by showing you how deferred objects work and then show you how you can use them. Listing 35-1 is a simple example that contains a deferred object.

Listing 35-1. A Simple Deferred Object Example

```
<!DOCTYPE html>
<html>
<head>
    <title>Example</title>
    <script src="jquery-1.7.js" type="text/javascript"></script>
    <script src="jquery-ui-1.8.16.custom.js" type="text/javascript"></script>
    <link rel="stylesheet" type="text/css" href="styles.css"/>
    <link rel="stylesheet" type="text/css" href="jquery-ui-1.8.16.custom.css"/>
    <style type="text/css">
        td {text-align: left; padding: 5px}
        table {width: 200px; border-collapse: collapse; width: 50%; float: left}
        #buttonDiv {width: 15%; text-align: center; margin: 20px; float: left}
    </style>
    <script type="text/javascript">
        $(document).ready(function() {
            var def = $.Deferred();
```

```
            def.done(function() {
                displayMessage("Callback Executed");
            })

            $('button').button().click(function() {
                def.resolve();
            })

            displayMessage("Ready")
        })

        function displayMessage(msg) {
            $('tbody').append("<tr><td>" + msg + "</td></tr>")
        }
    </script>
</head>
<body>
    <h1>Jacqui's Flower Shop</h1>

    <table class="ui-widget" border=1>
        <thead class="ui-widget-header">
            <tr><th>Message</th></tr>
        </thead>
        <tbody class="ui-widget-content">
        </tbody>
    </table>

    <div id="buttonDiv">
        <button>Go</button>
    </div>
</body>
</html>
```

This is a very simple demonstration of how a deferred object works. I will step through it to set the context for the rest of the chapter. First I created a deferred object, which you do by calling the `$.Deferred` method, like so:

```
var def = $.Deferred();
```

The `Deferred` method returns a deferred object. I have assigned this one to the variable called `def`. Deferred objects are all about callbacks, so my next step is to register a function with the deferred object using the done method, like this:

```
def.done(function() {
    displayMessage("Callback Executed");
})
```

When it is executed, the callback function will call the `displayMessage` function, which adds a row to the `table` element in the document.

The final step is to set things up so that I can trigger the callback function, which I do by calling the `resolve` method. Triggering the callback like this is known as *resolving the deferred object*. I want to be able to control when the deferred object is resolved, so I have added a button to the document and use the `click` method to handle an event. The irony here is that I am using one callback mechanism to help describe another. For the purposes of this chapter, I want you to ignore the event system and focus on the fact that the deferred object isn't resolved until the button is clicked. Here is the function that calls resolve and so triggers the callback function you registered with the done method:

```
$('button').button().click(function() {
    def.resolve();
})
```

Until the resolve method is called, the deferred object remains *unresolved*, and your callback function won't be executed. Clicking the button resolves the deferred object, executes the callback, and displays the message in the table, as shown in Figure 35-1.

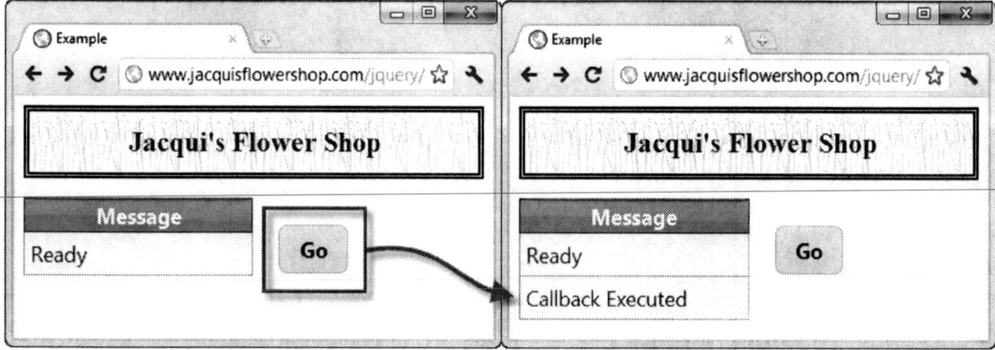

Figure 35-1. Resolving a deferred object

The important thing to understand here is that the deferred object isn't doing anything special. You register a callback function using the done method, and they won't be executed until you call the resolve method. In this example, the deferred object isn't resolved until the button is clicked, at which point the callback function is executed, and a new message is added to the table element.

Understanding Why Deferred Objects Are Useful

Deferred objects are useful when you want to execute functions at the end of some task without having to monitor that task directly, especially when that task is being performed in the background. Listing 35-2 contains a demonstration, which I'll then start to modify to add features.

Listing 35-2. Using Callbacks with a Long-Lived Task

```
...
<script type="text/javascript">
    $(document).ready(function() {
        var def = $.Deferred();

        def.done(function() {
            displayMessage("Callback Executed");
        })

        function performLongTask() {
```

```
            var start = $.now();

            var total = 0;
            for (var i = 0; i < 500000000 ; i++) {
                total += i;
            }
            var elapsedTime = (($.now() - start)/1000).toFixed(1)
            displayMessage("Task Complete. Time: " + elapsedTime + " sec")
            def.resolve();
        }

        $('button').button().click(function() {
            displayMessage("Calling performLongTask()")
            performLongTask()
            displayMessage("performLongTask() Returned")
        })

        displayMessage("Ready")
    })

    function displayMessage(msg) {
        $('tbody').append("<tr><td>" + msg + "</td></tr>")
    }
</script>
...
```

The process in this example is defined by the `performLongTask` function, which adds together a series of numbers. I want something simple that takes a few seconds to complete, and this fits the bill.

■ **Tip** On my system, the `for` loop in the `performLongTask` function takes about 3.5 seconds to complete, but you may need to adjust the upper limit for the loop to get a similar result on your system. Three to four seconds is a good duration for these examples. It's long enough to demonstrate the deferred object features but not so long that you have time to make coffee while waiting for the task to complete.

Clicking the button now calls the `performLongTask` function. That function calls the deferred object's `resolve` method when its work is complete, causing the callback function to be invoked. The `performLongTask` function adds its own message to the `table` element before it calls `resolve`, so you can see the sequence of progression through the script. You can see the results in Figure 35-2.

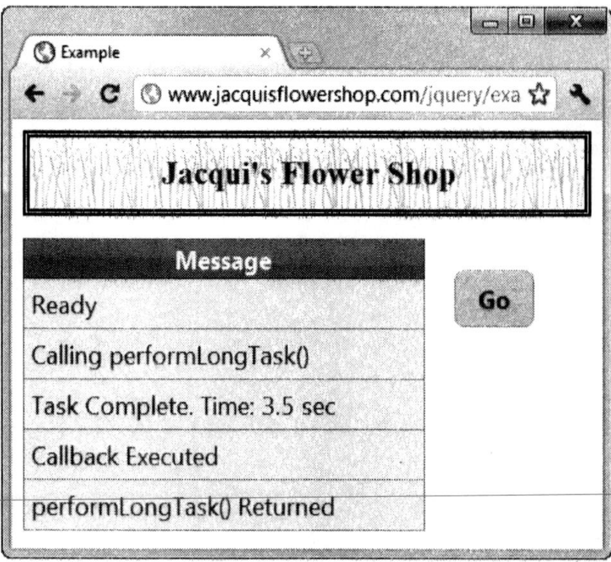

Figure 35-2. Using a deferred object to observe task completion

This is an example of a *synchronous* task. You push the button, and then you have to wait while each function that you call completes. The best indicator that you are working synchronously is the way that the Go button stays in its pressed state while the `performLongTask` function does its work. Definitive proof comes in the sequence of messages displayed in Figure 35-2. The messages from the click event handler come before and after the messages from `performLongTask` and the callback functions.

The major benefit of deferred objects comes when you are working with *asynchronous* tasks, tasks that are being performed in the background. You don't want the user interface to lock up like it did in the previous example, so you start tasks in the background, keep an eye on them, and update the document to give the user information about the progress and result of the work.

The simplest way to start a background task is to use the `setTimeout` function, which means that you are using yet another callback mechanism. This may seem a little odd, but JavaScript lacks the language facilities for managing asynchronous tasks that other languages are designed with, so you have to make do with those features that are available. Listing 35-3 shows the example modified so that the time-consuming part of the `performLongTask` function is done in the background.

Listing 35-3. Performing the Work Asynchronously

```
...
<script type="text/javascript">
    $(document).ready(function() {
        var def = $.Deferred();

        def.done(function() {
            displayMessage("Callback Executed");
        })

        function performLongTask() {
```

```
            setTimeout(function() {
                var start = $.now();

                var total = 0;
                for (var i = 0; i < 500000000 ; i++) {
                    total += i;
                }
                var elapsedTime = (($.now() - start)/1000).toFixed(1)
                displayMessage("Task Complete. Time: " + elapsedTime + " sec")
                def.resolve();
            }, 10);
        }

        $('button').button().click(function() {
            displayMessage("Calling performLongTask()")
            performLongTask()
            displayMessage("performLongTask() Returned")
        })

        displayMessage("Ready")
    })

    function displayMessage(msg) {
        $('tbody').append("<tr><td>" + msg + "</td></tr>")
    }
</script>
...
```

I use the `setTimeout` function to perform the `for` loop in the `performLongTask` function after a delay of 10 milliseconds. You can see the effect this has in Figure 35-3. Notice that the messages from the click handler function appear before those from the `performLongTask` and callback functions. If you run this example yourself, you will notice that the button pops back into its regular state immediately, rather than waiting for the work to complete.

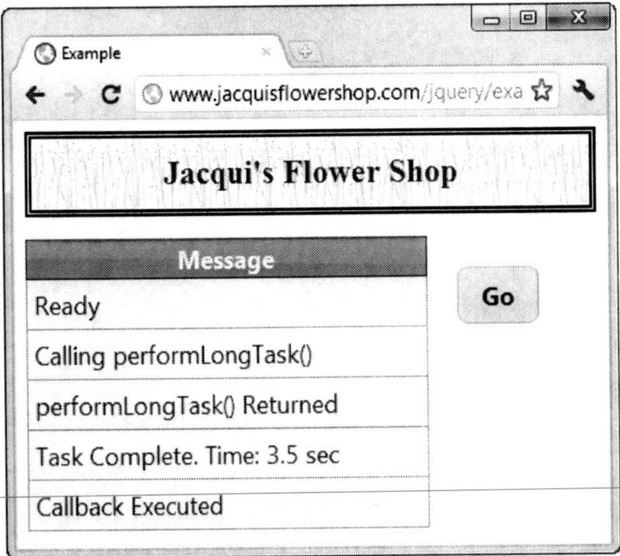

Figure 35-3. Performing the task in the background

Callbacks are particular important when working with background tasks because you don't know when they are complete. You could set up your own signaling system—updating a variable, for example—but you would need to do this for every background task that you perform, which becomes tiresome and error-prone very quickly. Deferred objects allow you to use a standardized mechanism for indicating that tasks have completed, and as I'll demonstrate in later examples, they offer a lot of flexibility in how this is done.

Tidying Up the Example

Before you start digging into the feature of deferred objects, I am going to update the example to use the pattern that I tend to work with in real projects. This is purely personal preference, but I like to split out the workload from the asynchronous wrapper and integrate the production of the deferred object into the function. Listing 35-4 shows the changes.

Listing 35-4. Tidying Up the Example

```
<!DOCTYPE html>
<html>
<head>
    <title>Example</title>
    <script src="jquery-1.7.js" type="text/javascript"></script>
    <script src="jquery-ui-1.8.16.custom.js" type="text/javascript"></script>
    <link rel="stylesheet" type="text/css" href="styles.css"/>
    <link rel="stylesheet" type="text/css" href="jquery-ui-1.8.16.custom.css"/>
    <style type="text/css">
        td {text-align: left; padding: 5px}
        table {width: 200px; border-collapse: collapse; float: left; width: 300px}
```

```
        #buttonDiv {text-align: center; margin: 20px; float: left}
    </style>
    <script type="text/javascript">
        $(document).ready(function() {

            function performLongTaskSync() {
                var start = $.now();

                var total = 0;
                for (var i = 0; i < 500000000 ; i++) {
                    total += i;
                }
                var elapsedTime = (($.now() - start)/1000).toFixed(1)
                displayMessage("Task Complete. Time: " + elapsedTime + " sec")
                return total;
            }

            function performLongTask() {
                return $.Deferred(function(def) {
                    setTimeout(function() {
                        performLongTaskSync();
                        def.resolve();
                    }, 10)
                })
            }

            $('button').button().click(function() {
                if ($(':checked').length > 0) {
                    displayMessage("Calling performLongTask()")
                    var observer = performLongTask();
                    observer.done(function() {
                        displayMessage("Callback Executed");
                    });
                    displayMessage("performLongTask() Returned")
                } else {
                    displayMessage("Calling performLongTaskSync()")
                    performLongTaskSync();
                    displayMessage("performLongTaskSync() Returned")
                }
            })

            $(':checkbox').button();
            displayMessage("Ready")
        })

        function displayMessage(msg) {
            $('tbody').append("<tr><td>" + msg + "</td></tr>")
        }
    </script>
</head>
<body>
    <h1>Jacqui's Flower Shop</h1>
```

```
    <table class="ui-widget" border=1>
        <thead class="ui-widget-header">
            <tr><th>Message</th></tr>
        </thead>
        <tbody class="ui-widget-content">
        </tbody>
    </table>

    <div id="buttonDiv">
        <button>Go</button>
        <input type="checkbox" id="async" checked>
        <label for="async">Async</label>
    </div>
</body>
</html>
```

In this example, I have broken out the workload into a function called performLongTasksync, which is just responsible for performing the calculations. It has no knowledge of background tasks or callback functions. I like to keep the workload separate because it makes testing the code easier during the early stages of development. Here is the synchronous function:

```
function performLongTaskSync() {
    var start = $.now();

    var total = 0;
    for (var i = 0; i < 500000000 ; i++) {
        total += i;
    }
    var elapsedTime = (($.now() - start)/1000).toFixed(1)
    displayMessage("Task Complete. Time: " + elapsedTime + " sec")
    return total;
}
```

I have separated out the code to perform the task asynchronously. This is in the performLongTask function, which is an asynchronous wrapper around the performLongTasksync function and which uses a deferred object to trigger callbacks when the work has completed. Here is the revised performLongTask function:

```
function performLongTask() {
    return $.Deferred(function(def) {
        setTimeout(function() {
            performLongTaskSync();
            def.resolve();
        }, 10)
    })
}
```

If pass a function to the Deferred method, it is executed as soon as the object is created, and the function is passed the new deferred object as a parameter. Using this feature, I can create a simple wrapper function that performs the work asynchronously and triggers the callbacks when the work has finished.

■ **Tip** If you are observant, you will have noticed that there is a chance that calling the `done` method to register a callback function may occur after the task has been completed and the `resolve` method has been called. This may occur for very short tasks, but the callback function will still be called, even if `done` is called after `resolve`.

The other reason that I like to create a wrapper like this is because deferred objects can't be reset once they are resolved or rejected (I explain rejection in a moment). By creating the deferred object inside of the wrapper function, I ensure that I am always using fresh, unresolved deferred objects.

The other change I have made to this example is to add a toggle button that allows the task to be performed synchronously or asynchronously. I will take this feature out of future examples because this is a chapter about asynchronous tasks, but it is a good way to make sure you are comfortable with the difference. You can see the output from both modes in Figure 35-4.

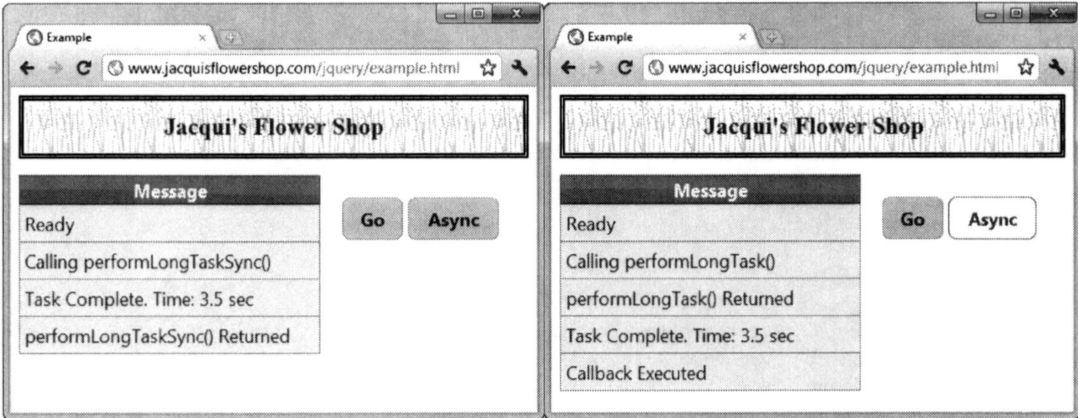

Figure 35-4. Performing the same task synchronously and asynchronously

Using Other Callbacks

Now that you have a basic asynchronous example in place, you can look at some of the useful features that deferred objects. The first is that you can signal different outcomes from your tasks. Table 35-2 describes the methods available for registering callbacks and the methods that are called on the deferred object that trigger them. I have already explained the `done` and `resolve` methods, and I cover the others in the sections that follow.

Table 35-2. Methods for Registering Callbacks

Callback Registration Method	Triggered By
done	resolve
fail	reject
always	resolve or reject

Rejecting a Deferred Object

Not all tasks complete successfully. When they do, you resolve the deferred object by calling the resolve method. But when something goes wrong, you *reject* the deferred object using the reject method. You can register callbacks functions for failed tasks using the fail method. The reject methods triggers callbacks registered with the fail method in the same way that the resolve method triggers callbacks registered with done. Listing 35-5 shows a task that will either resolve or reject its deferred object.

Listing 35-5. Rejecting Deferred Objects

```
<!DOCTYPE html>
<html>
<head>
    <title>Example</title>
    <script src="jquery-1.7.js" type="text/javascript"></script>
    <script src="jquery-ui-1.8.16.custom.js" type="text/javascript"></script>
    <link rel="stylesheet" type="text/css" href="styles.css"/>
    <link rel="stylesheet" type="text/css" href="jquery-ui-1.8.16.custom.css"/>
    <style type="text/css">
        td {text-align: left; padding: 5px}
        table {width: 200px; border-collapse: collapse; float: left; width: 300px}
        #buttonDiv {text-align: center; margin: 20px; float: left}
    </style>
    <script type="text/javascript">
        $(document).ready(function() {

            function performLongTaskSync() {
                var start = $.now();

                var total = 0;
                for (var i = 0; i < 5000000  ; i++) {
                    total += (i + Number((Math.random() + 1).toFixed(0)));
                }
                var elapsedTime = (($.now() - start)/1000).toFixed(1)
                displayMessage("Task Complete. Time: " + elapsedTime + " sec")
                return total;
            }

            function performLongTask() {
```

```
            return $.Deferred(function(def) {
                setTimeout(function() {
                    var total = performLongTaskSync();
                    if (total % 2 == 0) {
                        def.resolve(total);
                    } else {
                        def.reject(total);
                    }
                }, 10)})
        }

        $('button').button().click(function() {
            displayMessage("Calling performLongTask()")
            var observer = performLongTask();
            displayMessage("performLongTask() Returned")
            observer.done(function(total) {
                displayMessage("Done Callback Executed: " + total);
            });
            observer.fail(function(total) {
                displayMessage("Fail Callback Executed: " + total);
            });
        })

        displayMessage("Ready")
    })

    function displayMessage(msg) {
        $('tbody').append("<tr><td>" + msg + "</td></tr>")
    }
  </script>
</head>
<body>
  <h1>Jacqui's Flower Shop</h1>

  <table class="ui-widget" border=1>
      <thead class="ui-widget-header">
          <tr><th>Message</th></tr>
      </thead>
      <tbody class="ui-widget-content">
      </tbody>
  </table>

  <div id="buttonDiv">
      <button>Go</button>
  </div>
</body>
</html>
```

In this example, I have tweaked the task so that a small random number is added to the total in each iteration of the for loop. The asynchronous wrapper function performLongTask checks the total returned by the synchronous function and resolves the deferred object if the total is even. If the total is odd, then the performLongTask function rejects the deferred object, as follows:

```
...
if (total % 2 == 0) {
    def.resolve(total);
} else {
    def.reject(total);
}
...
```

After calling the performLongTask function, my click event handler registers callback functions for both outcomes, using the done and fail methods, as follows:

```
...
var observer = performLongTask();
displayMessage("performLongTask() Returned")
observer.done(function(total) {
    displayMessage("Done Callback Executed: " + total);
});
observer.fail(function(total) {
    displayMessage("Fail Callback Executed: " + total);
});
...
```

Notice that I pass arguments to the resolve and reject methods when I call them. You don't have to pass arguments to these methods, but if you do, the objects you supply will be passed as arguments to the callback functions, which allows you to provide additional context or detail about what has happened. In this example, the status of the task is determined by the calculation total, which I have passed as the argument to both the done and reject methods. You can see the outcome of a resolved and rejected deferred object in Figure 35-5.

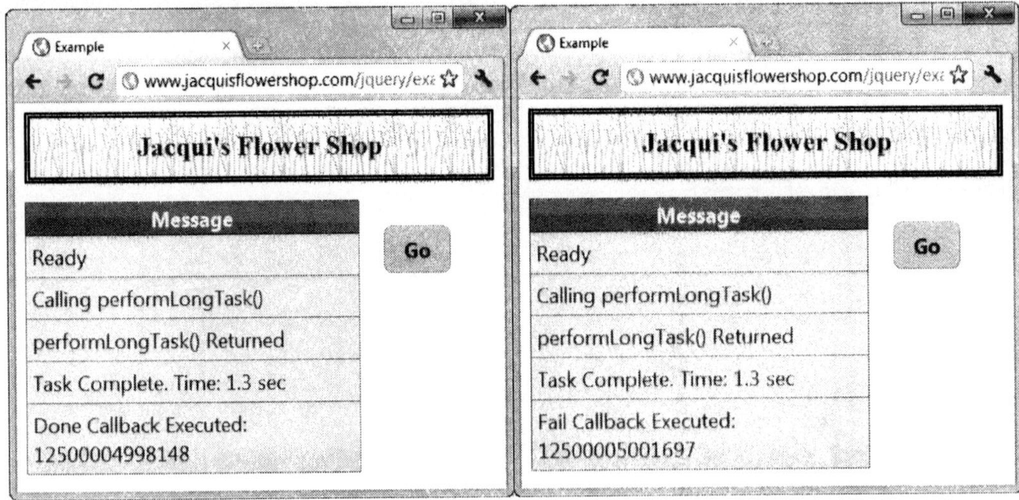

Figure 35-5. A task that can succeed or fail

Chaining Deferred Object Method Calls

The deferred object methods are chainable, meaning that each method returns a deferred object on which you can call other methods. This is something I have been doing with jQuery objects throughout this book. Listing 35-6 shows how the calls to the done and fail methods can be chained together.

Listing 35-6. Chaining Deferred Object Method Calls

```
...
$('button').button().click(function() {
    performLongTask().done(function(total) {
        displayMessage("Done Callback Executed: " + total);
    }).fail(function(total) {
        displayMessage("Fail Callback Executed: " + total);
    });
})
...
```

Covering Both Outcomes

If you have callbacks for each outcome, you can register them in one go using the then method. The first argument is the callback to use if the deferred object is resolved, and the second argument is the callback to use if the deferred object is rejected. Listing 35-7 shows the then method in use.

Listing 35-7. Using the then Method

```
...
$('button').button().click(function() {
    displayMessage("Calling performLongTask()")
    var observer = performLongTask();
    displayMessage("performLongTask() Returned")

    observer.then(
        function(total) {
            displayMessage("Done Callback Executed");
        },
        function(total) {
            displayMessage("Fail Callback Executed");
        }
    );
})
...
```

I tend to use method chaining because I find it produces code where the outcome each function is prepared to deal with more obvious.

Using Outcome-Indifferent Callbacks

There are occasions when you want to execute a callback function irrespective of the outcome of the task. A common pattern is to use the always method to register a function that removes or hides elements that indicate that some background task is being performed and use the done and fail method to display the next steps to the user. Listing 35-8 shows the use of the always method to register a function that behaves the same regardless of the task outcome.

Listing 35-8. Using the always Method to Register an outcome-indifferent Function

```
<!DOCTYPE html>
<html>
<head>
    <title>Example</title>
    <script src="jquery-1.7.js" type="text/javascript"></script>
    <script src="jquery-ui-1.8.16.custom.js" type="text/javascript"></script>
    <link rel="stylesheet" type="text/css" href="styles.css"/>
    <link rel="stylesheet" type="text/css" href="jquery-ui-1.8.16.custom.css"/>
    <style type="text/css">
        td {text-align: left; padding: 5px}
        table {width: 200px; border-collapse: collapse; float: left; width: 300px}
        #buttonDiv {text-align: center; margin: 20px; float: left}
    </style>
    <script type="text/javascript">
        $(document).ready(function() {

            function performLongTaskSync() {
                var start = $.now();

                var total = 0;
                for (var i = 0; i < 5000000  ; i++) {
                    total += (i + Number((Math.random() + 1).toFixed(0)));
                }
                var elapsedTime = (($.now() - start)/1000).toFixed(1)
                displayMessage("Task Complete. Time: " + elapsedTime + " sec")
                return total;
            }

            function performLongTask() {
                return $.Deferred(function(def) {
                    setTimeout(function() {
                        var total = performLongTaskSync();
                        if (total % 2 == 0) {
                            def.resolve(total);
                        } else {
                            def.reject(total);
                        }
                    }, 10)})
            }

            $('button').button().click(function() {
                displayMessage("Calling performLongTask()")
                var observer = performLongTask();
                displayMessage("performLongTask() Returned")

                $('#dialog').dialog("open");
```

```
                observer.always(function() {
                    $('#dialog').dialog("close");
                });

                observer.done(function(total) {
                    displayMessage("Done Callback Executed: " + total);
                });
                observer.fail(function(total) {
                    displayMessage("Fail Callback Executed: " + total);
                });

            })

            $('#dialog').dialog({
                autoOpen: false,
                modal: true

            })

            displayMessage("Ready")
        })

        function displayMessage(msg) {
            $('tbody').append("<tr><td>" + msg + "</td></tr>")
        }
    </script>
</head>
<body>
    <h1>Jacqui's Flower Shop</h1>

    <table class="ui-widget" border=1>
        <thead class="ui-widget-header">
            <tr><th>Message</th></tr>
        </thead>
        <tbody class="ui-widget-content">
        </tbody>
    </table>

    <div id="buttonDiv">
        <button>Go</button>
    </div>

    <div id="dialog">
        Performing Task...
    </div>

</body>
</html>
```

In this example, I have added a jQuery UI modal dialog that is displayed when the task is running. I use the always method to register a function that closes the dialog when the task is complete. This means that I don't have to duplicate the code for tidying up after the task has finished in my functions that handle resolved or rejected deferred objects.

■ **Tip** Callbacks functions are called in the order in which they are registered with the deferred object. In this example, I call the `always` method before calling the `done` or `fail` method, which means that the `outcome-indifferent` function is always called before the functions that handle the resolved or rejected outcomes.

Using Multiple Callbacks

One of the benefits that arise from using deferred objects is that you can partition your code into small functions that handle specific activities. To allow further decomposition of your code, deferred objects provide support for registering multiple callbacks for the same outcome. Listing 35-9 provides a demonstration.

Listing 35-9. Registering Multiple Callback Functions with a Deferred Object

```
...
<script type="text/javascript">
    $(document).ready(function() {

        function performLongTaskSync() {
            var start = $.now();

            var total = 0;
            for (var i = 0; i < 5000000   ; i++) {
                total += (i + Number((Math.random() + 1).toFixed(0)));
            }
            var elapsedTime = (($.now() - start)/1000).toFixed(1)
            displayMessage("Task Complete. Time: " + elapsedTime + " sec")
            return total;
        }

        function performLongTask() {
            return $.Deferred(function(def) {
                setTimeout(function() {
                    var total = performLongTaskSync();
                    if (total % 2 == 0) {
                        def.resolve({
                            total: total
                        });
                    } else {
                        def.reject(total);
                    }
                }, 10)})
        }
```

```
        $('button').button().click(function() {
            displayMessage("Calling performLongTask()")
            var observer = performLongTask();
            displayMessage("performLongTask() Returned")

            $('#dialog').dialog("open");


            observer.done(function(data) {
                data.touched = 1;
                displayMessage("1st Done Callback Executed");
            });

            observer.done(function(data) {
                data.touched++;
                displayMessage("2nd Done Callback Executed");
            }, function(data) {
                data.touched++;
                displayMessage("3rd Done Callback Executed");
            });

            observer.done(function(data) {
                displayMessage("4th Done Callback Executed: " + data.touched);
            });

            observer.fail(function(total) {
                displayMessage("Fail Callback Executed: " + total);
            });

            observer.always(function() {
                displayMessage("Always Callback Executed");
                $('#dialog').dialog("close");
            });


        })

        $('#dialog').dialog({
            autoOpen: false,
            modal: true

        })

        displayMessage("Ready")
    })

    function displayMessage(msg) {
        $('tbody').append("<tr><td>" + msg + "</td></tr>")
    }
</script>
...
```

In this example, I have registered four callback functions using the done method. As the code shows, you can register functions individually or in groups by passing multiple functions, separated by commas, to the registration method. The deferred object ensures that the callback functions are executed in the order in which they were registered.

Notice that I have changed the argument passed to the resolve method in this example, making the result of the calculation a property in a JavaScript object. I did this to demonstrate that callback functions are able to modify the data passed via the deferred object. This can be useful for providing simple communication between handler functions (to declare that some particular action has been taken). You can see the effect of having multiple handlers in Figure 35-6.

Figure 35-6. Using multiple callbacks for the same outcome

■ **Tip** You can specify multiple callbacks for each outcome using the then method by passing arrays of functions as arguments.

Using the Outcomes of Multiple Deferred Objects

You can use the when method to create deferred objects whose outcome is derived from several other deferred objects. This technique is useful when you are relying on the results from several background tasks or when you don't want to start a task until you are sure that a set of other tasks have achieved a specific outcome. Listing 35-10 provides a demonstration.

Listing 35-10. Using the when Method

```
...
$('button').button().click(function() {

    var ob1 = performLongTask()
        .done(function() {
            displayMessage("1st Task <b>Resolved</b>")
        })
        .fail(function() {
            displayMessage("1st Task <b>Failed</b>")
        })

    var ob2 = performLongTask()
        .done(function() {
            displayMessage("2nd Task <b>Resolved</b")
        })
        .fail(function() {
            displayMessage("2nd Task <b>Failed</b>")
        })

    var ob3 = performLongTask()
        .done(function() {
            displayMessage("3rd Task <b>Resolved</b>")
        })
        .fail(function() {
            displayMessage("3rd Task <b>Failed</b>")
        })

    $.when(ob1, ob2, ob3)
        .done(function() {
            displayMessage("Aggregate <b>Resolved</b>")
        })
        .fail(function() {
            displayMessage("Aggregate <b>Failed</b>")
        })
})
...
```

In this example, I have three deferred objects, each of which was created calling the performLongTask function and to which I have attached callback functions using the done and fail methods.

I have passed all three deferred objects to the when method, which returns another deferred object (known as the *aggregate deferred object*). I have attached callback functions to the aggregate using the normal done and fail methods. The outcome of the aggregate is determined by the outcome of the other three deferred objects. If *all* three of the regular deferred objects are resolved, then the aggregate is also resolved, and the done functions will be called. However, if *any* of the regular deferred objects are rejected, then the aggregate is rejected as well, and the fail functions will be called. You can see both outcomes for the aggregate in Figure 35-7.

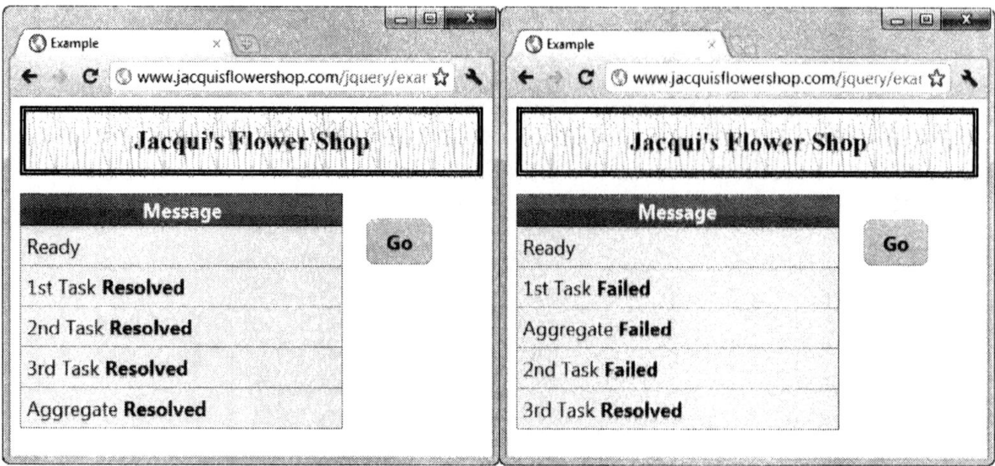

Figure 35-7. Using the when method

■ **Caution** If you look closely at the sequence of messages in the figure, you will spot a timing anomaly. The aggregate deferred object is rejected as soon as any of the underlying objects are rejected; this means the callback functions registered with the `fail` method can be triggered while there are still tasks running. When dealing with a rejected aggregate object, you cannot assume that all of the tasks it depends on are complete.

Providing Progress Information

It is generally a good idea to provide the user with progress information when performing a long-lived task in the background. Deferred objects can be used to pass progress information from the task to callback functions, in much the same way you have been passing information about outcomes. You produce progress information using the `notify` method and register your callback function using the `progress` method. Listing 35-11 contains an example.

Listing 35-11. Producing and Consuming Progress Information via a Deferred Object

```
...
<script type="text/javascript">
    $(document).ready(function() {

        function performLongTaskSync() {
            var total = 0;
            for (var i = 0; i < 5000000  ; i++) {
                total += (i + Number((Math.random() + 1).toFixed(0)));
            }
            return total;
        }
```

```
        function performLongTask() {
            return $.Deferred(function(def) {
                setTimeout(function() {
                    var progressValue = 0;
                    for (var i = 0; i < 4; i++) {
                        performLongTaskSync();
                        progressValue += 25;
                        def.notify(progressValue)
                    }
                    def.resolve();
                }, 10)}
            )
        }

        $('button').button().click(function() {

            performLongTask().progress(function(val) {
                displayMessage("Progress: " + val + "%")
            }).done(function() {
                displayMessage("Task Resolved");
            })
        })

        displayMessage("Ready")
    })

    function displayMessage(msg) {
        $('tbody').append("<tr><td>" + msg + "</td></tr>")
    }
</script>
...
```

In this example, the task is to perform the calculation four times. After each calculation, I call the notify method on the deferred object and pass in my percentage progress (although you can pass any object or value that makes sense for your web application; I am using percentages for simplicity). In the click handler function, I have used the progress method to register a function that will be called in response to a progress update. I use this function to add a message to the table in the document.

This example demonstrates the basic ability to provide progress information, but it doesn't quite work in the way that you might hope. The problem is that the browser doesn't get the change to update the DOM with the new rows until after all four iterations are complete. This is a facet of the way that JavaScript tasks are managed and means that you get all of the progress updates in one go at the end of the task. To address this, you need to add small delays between each stage in the task to give the browser the time it needs to perform updates. Listing 35-12 shows how you can use the setTimeout function to introduce these delays and create a chain of deferred objects. I would usually use a for loop to set up the delays and the deferred objects, but to make this example clearer to read, I have defined all of the steps explicitly.

Listing 35-12. Breaking the Task Down to Allow DOM Changes

```
...
<script type="text/javascript">
    $(document).ready(function() {

        function performLongTaskSync() {
            var total = 0;
            for (var i = 0; i < 5000000  ; i++) {
                total += (i + Number((Math.random() + 1).toFixed(0)));
            }
            return total;
        }

        function performLongTask() {

            function doSingleIteration() {
                return $.Deferred(function(innerDef) {
                        setTimeout(function() {
                        performLongTaskSync();
                        innerDef.resolve();
                    }, 10)
                })
            }

            var def = $.Deferred();

            setTimeout(function() {

                doSingleIteration().done(function() {
                    def.notify(25);
                    doSingleIteration().done(function() {
                        def.notify(50);
                        doSingleIteration().done(function() {
                            def.notify(75);
                            doSingleIteration().done(function() {
                                def.notify(100);
                                def.resolve();
                            })
                        })
                    })
                })
            }, 10);

            return def;
        }
```

```
        $('button').button().click(function() {

            performLongTask().progress(function(val) {
                displayMessage("Progress: " + val + "%")
            }).done(function() {
                displayMessage("Task Resolved");
            })
        })

        displayMessage("Ready")
    })

    function displayMessage(msg) {
        $('tbody').append("<tr><td>" + msg + "</td></tr>")
    }
</script>
...
```

With this change, the progress updates are properly displayed. You can see the updates shown in Figure 35-8.

Figure 35-8. Using a deferred object to provide progress information

Getting Information about a Deferred Object

Deferred objects define the state method, which you can use to establish the state of the object and, by implication, the task that is being performed. The values that the method can return are described in Table 35-3.

Table 35-3. *Values for the state Object*

Value	Description
pending	Neither the resolve nor reject method has been called on the deferred object
resolved	The deferred object has been resolved (using the resolve method)
rejected	The deferred object has been rejected (using the rejected method)

■ **Caution** Be careful when using this method. In particular, you should stop and think if you find yourself polling the status of a deferred object. You may have some design problems in your web application. Polling for status, especially in a while or for loop, can mean that you have effectively made your task synchronous while incurring the overhead and complexity associated with asynchronous tasks.

The only time that I find the state method useful is when I have registered a callback using the always method and I am interested in the outcome of the task. Generally, I use the done and fail methods with separate callbacks functions, but there are times when I have code that is largely, but not quite, the same for both outcomes. Listing 35-13 contains a demonstration of using the state method.

Listing 35-13. Using the state Method

```
<!DOCTYPE html>
<html>
<head>
    <title>Example</title>
    <script src="jquery-1.7.js" type="text/javascript"></script>
    <script src="jquery-ui-1.8.16.custom.js" type="text/javascript"></script>
    <link rel="stylesheet" type="text/css" href="styles.css"/>
    <link rel="stylesheet" type="text/css" href="jquery-ui-1.8.16.custom.css"/>
    <style type="text/css">
        td {text-align: left; padding: 5px}
        table {width: 200px; border-collapse: collapse; float: left; width: 300px}
        #buttonDiv {text-align: center; margin: 20px; float: left}
    </style>
```

```
<script type="text/javascript">
    $(document).ready(function() {

        function performLongTaskSync() {
            var start = $.now();

            var total = 0;
            for (var i = 0; i < 5000000  ; i++) {
                total += (i + Number((Math.random() + 1).toFixed(0)));
            }
            var elapsedTime = (($.now() - start)/1000).toFixed(1)
            displayMessage("Task Complete. Time: " + elapsedTime + " sec")
            return total;
        }

        function performLongTask() {
            return $.Deferred(function(def) {
                setTimeout(function() {
                    var total = performLongTaskSync();
                    if (total % 2 == 0) {
                        def.resolve(total);
                    } else {
                        def.reject(total);
                    }
                }, 10)})
        }

        $('button').button().click(function() {
            displayMessage("Calling performLongTask()")
            var observer = performLongTask();
            displayMessage("performLongTask() Returned")

            $('#dialog').dialog("open");

            observer.always(function() {
                if (observer.state() == "resolved") {
                    $('#dialog').dialog("close");
                } else {
                    $('#dialog').text("Error!")
                }
            });

            observer.done(function(total) {
                displayMessage("Done Callback Executed: " + total);
            });
            observer.fail(function(total) {
                displayMessage("Fail Callback Executed: " + total);
            });

        })

        $('#dialog').dialog({
```

```
                autoOpen: false,
                modal: true

            })

            displayMessage("Ready")
        })

        function displayMessage(msg) {
            $('tbody').append("<tr><td>" + msg + "</td></tr>")
        }
    </script>
</head>
<body>
    <h1>Jacqui's Flower Shop</h1>

    <table class="ui-widget" border=1>
        <thead class="ui-widget-header">
            <tr><th>Message</th></tr>
        </thead>
        <tbody class="ui-widget-content">
        </tbody>
    </table>

    <div id="buttonDiv">
        <button>Go</button>
    </div>

    <div id="dialog">
        Performing Task...
    </div>
</body>
</html>
```

Using Ajax Deferred Objects

Perhaps the most useful aspect of the deferred object functionality is the way it has been incorporated into the jQuery support for Ajax (which I described in Chapters 14 and 15). The `jxXHR` object that you get back from methods such as `ajax` and `getJSON` implement the `Promise` interface, which provides you with a subset of the methods defined by a regular deferred object. A Promise defines the `done`, `fail`, `then`, and `always` methods and can be used with the `when` method. Listing 35-14 shows how you can mix and match Ajax promises with deferred objects.

■ **Tip** You can create your own Promise objects by calling the `promise` method on a deferred object. This can be useful if you are writing a JavaScript library and you only want to allow other programmers to attach callbacks and not to resolve or reject your deferred objects.

Listing 35-14. Using Ajax Promises and Deferred Objects

```
<!DOCTYPE html>
<html>
<head>
    <title>Example</title>
    <script src="jquery-1.7.js" type="text/javascript"></script>
    <script src="jquery-ui-1.8.16.custom.js" type="text/javascript"></script>
    <link rel="stylesheet" type="text/css" href="styles.css"/>
    <link rel="stylesheet" type="text/css" href="jquery-ui-1.8.16.custom.css"/>
    <style type="text/css">
        td {text-align: left; padding: 5px}
        table {width: 200px; border-collapse: collapse; float: left; width: 300px}
        #buttonDiv {text-align: center; margin: 20px; float: left}
    </style>
    <script type="text/javascript">
        $(document).ready(function() {

            function performLongTaskSync() {
                var start = $.now();

                var total = 0;
                for (var i = 0; i < 5000000  ; i++) {
                    total += (i + Number((Math.random() + 1).toFixed(0)));
                }
                var elapsedTime = (($.now() - start)/1000).toFixed(1)
                displayMessage("Task Complete. Time: " + elapsedTime + " sec")
                return total;
            }

            function performLongTask() {
                return $.Deferred(function(def) {
                    setTimeout(function() {
                        performLongTaskSync();
                        def.resolve();
                    }, 10)})
            }

            $('button').button().click(function() {
                displayMessage("Calling performLongTask()")
                var observer = performLongTask().done(function() {
                    displayMessage("Task complete")
                });
                displayMessage("performLongTask() Returned")

                displayMessage("Calling getJSON()")
                var ajaxPromise = $.getJSON("mydata.json").done(function() {
                    displayMessage("Ajax Request Completed")
                });
                displayMessage("getJSON() Returned")
```

```
                $.when(observer, ajaxPromise).done(function() {
                    displayMessage("All Done");
                })
            })
            displayMessage("Ready")
        })

        function displayMessage(msg) {
            $('tbody').append("<tr><td>" + msg + "</td></tr>")
        }
    </script>
</head>
<body>
    <h1>Jacqui's Flower Shop</h1>

    <table class="ui-widget" border=1>
        <thead class="ui-widget-header">
            <tr><th>Message</th></tr>
        </thead>
        <tbody class="ui-widget-content">
        </tbody>
    </table>

    <div id="buttonDiv">
        <button>Go</button>
    </div>
</body>
</html>
```

In this example, I have used the getJSON method and treated the result just as I would a deferred object. I attached a callback function using the done method and use it as an argument to the when method. You can see the output from this example in Figure 35-9.

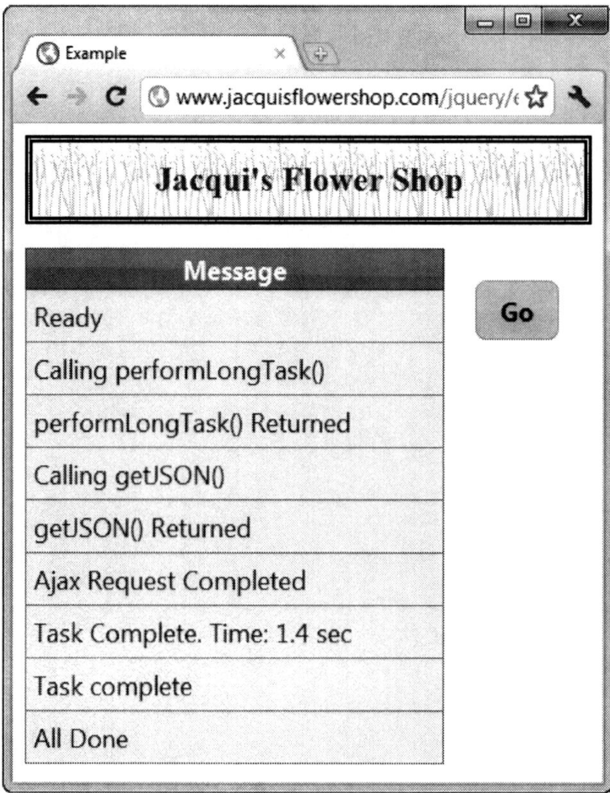

Figure 35-9. Using Ajax promises

Summary

In this chapter, I have demonstrated the jQuery deferred object feature, which lets you signal progress and outcomes of tasks, typically tasks that are being performed in the background. Deferred objects are used within the jQuery support for Ajax, which lets you treat your Ajax requests and your custom background tasks in a consistent manner. Deferred objects are an advanced feature, and most web applications won't need them, but for those projects that do significant background tasks, they can help preserve a response experience for the user.

Index

A

B

C

D

E

F

J

K

L

M

N

O

P, Q

R

S

T

U

V

W, X, Y, Z

CPSIA information can be obtained at www.ICGtesting.com
Printed in the USA
LVOW111015160613

338770LV00006B/218/P